A PEOPLES'S HISTORY OF THE ANTI NAZI LEAGUE

A People's History of the Anti Nazi League
(1977-1981)

Geoff Brown

Bookmarks Publications *b*

A People's History of the Anti Nazi League
By Geoff Brown

Published July 2025

Bookmarks Publications
1 Bloomsbury Street London WC1B 3QE
Phone: 020 7637 1848
email: publications@bookmarks.uk.com

© Bookmarks

Paperback ISBN: 978-1-917020237
           Kindle: 978-1-917020251
           Epub: 978-1-917020268
           Pdf: 978-1-917020275

Design and Production Roger Huddle (Redwords)

Printed by Halstan, Amersham HP6 6HJ

Contents

Introduction |7
1 'Rivers of Blood' | 13
2 The fascists | 23
3 Fighting racism and fascism | 47
4 Grunwick and Lewisham| 81
5 Launching of the Anti Nazi League| 111
6 All power to the imagination | 145
7 A mass movement
   Into the workplace| 177
   Into the movements| 194
   Into schools| 201
   Football fans against the Nazis| 222
   Preparing for an October general election | 228
8 Battles
   Battle of Brick Lane| 235
   'No plugs for NF Thugs'| 249
   Winning Jewish support for the ANL| 259
9 Counting down to the election| 271
10 Taking down the beast| 299
11 Why did the ANL succeed?| 329

Endnotes| 353

Abbreviations/Acronyms| 443

Bibliography| 466

Index | 485

■ Anti Nazi League poster designed by Dave King

Introduction

★On 20 April 1968, leading Tory politician Enoch Powell gave an inflammatory anti-immigration talk at the Conservative Political Centre in Birmingham. It came to be known as his 'Rivers of Blood' speech, and it triggered an explosion of racism and violent attacks on black and Asian communities. Mainstream politics, across the board, quickly shifted to the right with a small fascist party, the National Front, benefitting the most. Over the next decade the National Front grew to a point where they could claim to be Britain's third party, after Labour and the Conservatives. It is the movement against these fascists that forms the core of this book. Dominated by the young, with Asian youth often in the lead, the movement brought together trade unionists, students, school students, members of the women's movement and gays and in a new organisation, the Anti Nazi League (ANL). The ANL, created for the single task of stopping the National Front, greatly strengthened the size and unity of the movement in a mass collective effort. Part of this involved working with musicians, many in reggae and punk bands, and organising hundreds of gigs under the banner of the ANL's sister organisation, Rock Against Racism (RAR). This collaboration led to ANL–RAR carnivals against the Nazis, the biggest of which brought tens of thousands onto the streets.

The anti-fascist movement has a long history. By the mid-1970s there were scores of anti-racist and anti-fascist groups, most locally based, which struggled to coordinate their actions. A new initiative was needed. The first step in creating one was taken by the Socialist Workers Party (SWP), a small revolutionary socialist organisation that succeeded in bringing together people in all parties and organisations active in the working-class movement to establish a united front.

Just eighteen months after its launch, the ANL inflicted a crushing defeat on the fascists when they stood 300 candidates in the general election of 1979. It crushed them again a year later when they briefly revived on the back of mass unemployment created by a global recession made worse by the new Thatcher government. By 1981, at a time of working-class retreat in the face of Thatcher's neoliberal offensive, one part of the political landscape had changed for the better – anti-racism was now a recognised force.

This book aims to show how this came about. The Anti Nazi League rejected the idea that the NF could be stopped by the actions of government, the courts or the police and instead mobilised as many people as possible to stop the fascists wherever they appeared. To do justice to this movement of many tens of thousands, collectively making history, the book is rooted in the context that shaped people's actions. It is a history 'from below', combining both large-scale events and 'countless small actions'[1] and foregrounding what people did, their agency, rather than what they said.

It's impossible to be non-partisan in today's world. As the historian Howard Zinn puts it in his autobiography: 'You can't be neutral on a moving train'.[2] Researching this book has involved many interviews, hours in archives, working through leaflets, bulletins and photos that people have donated.[3] Despite this, keeping the book to a readable length has sometimes required a ruthless selection.[4] As far as possible, materials that have been cut are on the website accompanying this book. Much more could be written. Material which could not be included in the book for lack of space including a chronology, full bibliography and additional images will be published in the accompanying website which can be found at peopleshistoryoftheantinazileague.wordpress.com So far there are only a small number of local histories of the anti-racist anti-fascist movement and the Anti Nazi League.[5] The present author would be happy to share materials, details of potential sources etc. with anyone embarking on such a project. Contact details are on the website.

Race

There is nothing natural about race. It is a social construct.[6] I have used the term 'black' to mean those who are attacked and discriminated against on grounds of their race as perceived by others. There are a number of alternative terms. Ultimately, it is a matter of personal choice how people want to be identified. In the 1960s, 'black' came to be the preferred term of millions who took up the fight against racism. As far as possible I have only used quotes with language that is acceptable today. An exception is those using the word "coloured" which was universal until the rise of the black power movement.

Language concerning disability and mental health

The language used to talk about disability has changed. Words used in the past are now considered disrespectful. As with the language concerning race, as far as possible I have only used language acceptable today. Occasionally I have been unable to avoid using quotes from the time that contain comparisons between political attitudes and mental health that I believe should be avoided today.

Note on the author

Geoff Brown was full-time ANL organiser in Manchester, December 1977 to May 1979.

Endnotes

A longer version of the endnotes, giving additional information and links to web pages is on the book's website, under construction at time of going to print.

Acknowledgements

This book would not have been possible without help from many people to whom I am indebted. They include Kate Alexander, Colin Barker, Ian Birchall, Rick Blackman, Alex Bradley, Colm Bryce, John Charlton, Joseph Choonara, Zak Cochrane, Paul Darlow, Paul Furness, Joanna Gilmore, Donny Gluckstein, Sky Golding, Debbie Golt, Ian Goodyer, Roger Green, Shirin Hirsch, Paul Holborow, Roger Huddle, Charlie Kimber, Bob Light, Dave Lyddon, Mike Luft, Kevin Morgan, Volkhard Mosler, Jim Nichol, Balwinder Rana, Jack Robertson, Camilla Royle, John Rudge, Sabby Sagall, Red Saunders, Mike Simons, Andy Strouthous, Paul Sillett, Mark L Thomas, Bernie Wilcox. I also owe a debt to all those who agreed to be interviewed.

The book could not have been written without the help of Lindsay Cole and Naomi Buckley at the Working Class Movement Library, Darren Treadwell at the Labour History Archive and Study Centre, Paul Darlo at the NUM archive in Barnsley and staff at the Ahmed Iqbal Ullah Race Relations Resource Centre, the Bishopsgate Institute, the British Library, Leeds Discovery Centre, Manchester Central Library, the Modern Records Centre at the University of Warwick, the National Archive and the North West Film Archive.

Above all, I am indebted to Judy Paskell, my life partner, for her work as 'first editor' and her support through the five years of writing this book.

1: 'Rivers of Blood'

★ Just sixteen days after the assassination of Martin Luther King on 4 April 1968, which triggered riots in over a hundred US cities, Enoch Powell, member of the Conservative shadow cabinet, sounded the alarm about immigration at a meeting in Birmingham:

> We must be mad, literally mad, as a nation to be permitting the annual inflow of some 50,000 dependents... It is like watching a nation busily engaged in heaping up its own funeral pyre. So insane are we that we actually permit unmarried persons to immigrate for the purpose of founding a family with spouses and fiancées whom they have never seen.

In his view, the white population:

> found themselves made strangers in their own country. They found their wives unable to obtain hospital beds in childbirth, their children unable to obtain school places, their homes and neighbourhoods changed beyond recognition, their plans and prospects for the future

defeated; at work they found that employers hesitated to apply to the immigrant worker the standards of discipline and competence required of the native-born worker.[1]

His most outrageous claims were put into the mouths of others: 'In 15 or 20 years' time the black man will have the whip hand over the white man.' The future was grim: 'As I look ahead, I am filled with foreboding. Like the Roman, I seem to see the River Tiber foaming with much blood.'[2]

Ted Heath, Conservative Party leader, immediately sacked Powell from the shadow cabinet while tens of thousands wrote to Powell to express their support.[3] Having had little popular support before his Birmingham speech, he was soon challenging Heath in the opinion polls as the best person to lead the Tory party. One poll found 74 percent agreeing with Powell.[4]

There was a dramatic increase in racist violence. In Wolverhampton, where Powell was an MP, a dozen white youths attacked a West Indian family at a christening party shouting 'Powell, Powell' and 'Why don't you go back to your own country?'[5] Author Hanif Kureishi remembers that at school:

> Powell's name soon became one terrifying word – Enoch. As well as being an insult, it began to be used with elation. 'Enoch will deal with you lot', and, 'Enoch will soon be knocking on your door, pal'. 'Knock, knock, it's Enoch', people would say as they passed. Neighbours in the London suburbs began to state with some defiance: 'Our family is with Enoch'.[6]

Their confidence drawn from a tradition of unofficial strikes in the docks industry, with which they were closely connected, six hundred meat porters from Smithfield market in central London marched on Parliament in support of Powell four days after the speech.[7] At a mass meeting in the Royal Group of Docks in London, after the leading shop stewards relied on a Roman Catholic priest to put the case for 'brotherly love' rather than put the arguments in support of immigrants, a thousand dockers voted to strike and march to parliament.[8] Two thousand dockers met at the new Tilbury docks to vote on whether to strike in support of Powell:

Speech after speech, some by shop stewards, backed the strike. One speaker mimicked what he thought was the accent of an Asian worker disembarking from a ship and saying '...tell me what is the way to the social security?'[9]

Terry Barrett, a shop steward active in the union for thirty years, most of them in the Communist Party (CP) and now a member of the International Socialists (IS), told the dockers what they already knew. There were virtually no black or Asian dockers working in the London or Tilbury docks. The employers were determined to destroy jobs by forcing through containerisation with standardised containers, ruthlessly cutting the workforce needed to load and unload ships. He argued the case against racism, against divisions between black and white, that white workers had a common bond with black workers and that the employers had an interest in destroying that bond. Sections of the meeting howled and jeered. Some threw coins. Only five voted against strike action.[10]

Politicians both inside and outside the Tory party knew that Powell's arguments could be used to win votes. In the 1964 general election, which the Tories lost, a local Conservative councillor, Peter Griffiths, won the Birmingham Smethwick seat calling for an end to immigration. When asked about an allegation that children had been organised to chant 'If you want a n****r for a neighbour, vote Labour', Griffiths told *The Times*, 'I would not condemn anyone who said that. I regard it as a manifestation of popular feeling'.[11] In the months before the election, under pressure from the far-right British National Party (BNP), George Pargiter, Labour MP for Southall, an area with a large Indian population, called for a complete ban on immigration to his constituency. Conceding to the opponent's argument backfired. John Bean, the BNP candidate, went on to get 9 percent, at the time the highest vote ever received by an openly racist candidate.[12]

Hostility to immigrants has a long history. As far back as 1901, the British Brothers League, supported by a number of Conservative MPs, opposed immigration, especially of Jewish refugees fleeing pogroms in Tsarist Russia. After the Second World War, Winston Churchill kept a personal file entitled 'Immigration of Coloured Workers to Britain'. As prime minister in the early 1950s, he repeatedly raised 'coloured immigration' in cabinet, proposing that 'Keep England White' should be a Conservative slogan in the 1955 general election.[13] The Birmingham Immigration Control Association, set up in 1961, called for a halt to black and Asian immigration. Despite ongoing labour shortages and emigration consistently higher than immigration, in 1962 the Conservative government yielded to racist pressure and passed the Commonwealth Immigration Act to control the number of immigrants.

When in opposition, the Labour Party had strongly opposed the Immigration Act as racist. Yet, the new 1964 Labour government, haunted by Peter Griffith's success, broke its promise to repeal it. The year before, Harold Wilson had told the House of Commons: 'We do not contest the need for control of immigration into this country... [T]here are loopholes in the Act and we would favour a strengthening of the legal powers... We believe that health checks should become more effective.'[14]

Now in office, Labour's home secretary, Frank Soskice, told MPs: 'The government is firmly convinced that effective control is indispensable'. A few months later he promised to 'secure the repatriation of immigrants who had entered the country illegally'.[15] As Richard Crossman, senior member of the new government, put it:

> Ever since the Smethwick election it has been quite clear that immigration can be the greatest potential vote-loser for the Labour Party if we are seen to be permitting a flood of immigrants to come in and blight the central areas in all our cities.[16]

Labour's determination not to be seen as soft on immigration came to the fore early in 1968. Pursuing its 'Africanisation' policy, the government of the former British colony Kenya suddenly began to push people of Asian descent out of government and business. Within forty-eight hours the Labour government had passed the Commonwealth Immigrants Act restricting the right of entry to people with a British parent or grandparent. It was now clear that the Labour leadership would always prioritise winning elections over tackling racism. Despite its close links with the trade unions, with over ten million members, whose leadership had founded the Labour Party, it rejected the idea that Labour was a working-class party. Overcoming racist divisions would always come second to presenting itself as an all-class party of the 'nation'. It would never take on racism as a weapon of the class enemy. Powell exploited Labour's cowardice, making his 'Rivers of Blood' speech less than two months later.[17]

There was left-wing opposition to racism. Three thousand anti-racists marched to Downing Street to hand in a letter pointing out that the government's attack on the rights of Kenyan Asians 'would give "the green light" to those who discriminate against coloured immigrants'.[18] The senior left Labour MP Fenner Brockway had unsuccessfully introduced a parliamentary bill making racial discrimination illegal nine times before the 1965 Race Relations Act was passed.[19] This only outlawed 'incitement to racial hatred' and 'discrimination on the ground of colour, race or ethnic or national origins' in 'places of public resort' including pubs, restaurants and hotels. It did not cover either housing or the workplace. The West Indian Standing Conference saw it as 'well-meaning but virtually useless'.

One reason for its weakness was that the Trades Union Congress (TUC), together with the employers, the Confederation of British Industry (CBI), had opposed the bill arguing that such legal intervention contradicted the traditions of industrial relations in British workplaces. Claims were made that employers would discriminate in favour of black and Asian workers for fear of breaking the law. In the event it was 'presented as part of a "package deal", which allowed the passing of harsher immigration controls whilst appearing to combat discrimination against those already settled within Britain'.[20] The Labour MP Roy Hattersley put the argument: 'that integration without limitation is impossible; equally, I believe that limitation without integration is indefensible.'[21]

In other words, given that migration was a permanent feature of the modern world, racism would always exist. Integration – adapting to the host culture – was the only way to reduce it. With no acknowledgement that migrants might have a contribution to make to the host country, they were expected to minimise their social and cultural visibility. They were now always exposed to the accusation they failed to integrate.[22]

With a passionate faith in the system, thanking God 'for the gift of capitalism', Powell was the perfect example of an institutional racist.[23] Declaring: 'I have set and always will set my face like flint against making any difference between one citizen of this country and another on grounds of his origin', he had no problem with the profits made from the seizure of millions of Africans set to work on plantations producing tobacco, rice, cotton, sugar cane and indigo and the vital contribution this made to the growth of British capitalism and the establishment of the empire. An ultra imperialist, Powell began his political career determined to hang on to India, the 'jewel in the crown' of the empire and the most valuable colony in the world.[24] Powell never acknowledged the many rebellions that brought first slavery and then the empire to an end. It was only after a revolution in Haiti and slave revolts following it that slavery was abolished in the British empire in the 1830s: Bussa's rebellion in Barbados; the 1823 Demerara rebellion; and the Baptist war in Jamaica, 1831.[25] Britain only left India after it had killed hundreds and arrested over 100,000 in order to suppress the huge 1943 Quit India movement.[26]

As well as racism used to justify slavery and empire, there was anti-Irish racism. Racism remained indispensable to the 'divide and rule' used to control the rapidly growing working class migrants from Ireland and elsewhere that came to work in the boom towns and cities of Britain, France, Germany and the United States. Karl Marx argued this was the key weakness of the English working class:

> And most important of all! Every industrial and commercial centre in England now possesses a working class divided into two hostile camps, English proletarians and Irish proletarians. The ordinary English worker hates the Irish worker as a competitor who lowers his standard of life. In relation to the Irish worker he regards himself as a member of the ruling nation and consequently he becomes a tool of the English aristocrats and capitalists against Ireland, thus strengthening their domination over himself. He cherishes religious, social, and national prejudices against the Irish worker. His attitude towards him is much the same as that of the 'poor whites' to the Negroes in the former

slave states of the USA. The Irishman pays him back with interest in his own money. He sees in the English worker both the accomplice and the stupid tool of the English rulers in Ireland. This antagonism is artificially kept alive and intensified by the press, the pulpit, the comic papers, in short, by all the means at the disposal of the ruling classes.

Marx went on to point out the political importance of this deliberately reinforced conflict: 'This antagonism is the secret of the impotence of the English working class, despite its organisation. It is the secret by which the capitalist class maintains its power. And the latter is quite aware of this.'[27]

Along with racism, workers were encouraged to see themselves as part of a nation that ruled a global empire. This included pushing the idea that the Scots were part of the ruling 'British' nation, with Queen Victoria pretending to have Scottish roots, wearing tartan outfits, spending her summers in Scotland and taking on the title of Empress.[28] This became easier with the decline of Chartism, the world's first working-class political movement, following the defeat of the 1848 revolutions across Europe. As the parliamentary franchise was extended to include male skilled workers and later to all adult males, despite the vast inequalities rooted in brutal exploitation, workers were increasingly persuaded to see themselves as part of the ruling nation.[29]

The reality of the empire, where 'the sun never sets and the blood never dries', was never acknowledged.[30] Instead it was presented as a largely harmonious institution made possible by the self-sacrifice of the empire builders. Rudyard Kipling's poem 'The White Man's Burden' was taught to every schoolchild. Its first verse reads:

Take up the White Man's burden —
Send forth the best ye breed —
Go bind your sons to exile
To serve your captives' need;
To wait in heavy harness
On fluttered folk and wild —
Your new-caught sullen peoples,
Half devil and half child.[31]

Living in a slum area of Salford just before the First World

War, Robert Roberts remembers celebrating Empire Day every year at school:

> Teachers... spelled out patriotism among us with a fervour that with some edged on the religious. Empire Day of course had special significance. We drew union jacks, hung classrooms with flags of the dominions and gazed with pride as they pointed out those massed areas of red on the world map. 'This and this, and this', they said, 'belong to us!' When next King George with his queen came on a state visit we were ready, together with 30,000 other children, to ask in song, and then (in case he didn't know) tell him precisely the 'Meaning of Empire Day'.
>
> ...Each boy wore a rosette of red, white and blue ribbon and each girl wore a blue sash over a white dress. Those without white dresses were allowed to stand at the rear. In happy unison we sang 'Here's a health unto His Majesty', 'Three cheers for the red, white and blue', and:
>
> What's the meaning of the Empire Day?
> Why does the cannon roar?
> Why does the cry 'God save the king!'
> Echo from shore to shore?
> Why does the flag of Britannia float,
> Proudly o'er fort and bay?
> Why do our kinsmen gladly hail
> Our glorious Empire Day?[32]

Empire Day continued till 1958.[33] It was rarely challenged. Eugenics, the 'science of improving [the human] stock' – biological racism – was only fully discredited after the Second World War.[34] There was a professor of eugenics at University College London until 1963. Blackface minstrel shows had white actors, their faces blacked up, playing lazy, simple-minded black characters dressed as dandies. At first this consisted of street performances and music halls, and by the 1960s it was on prime television. The *Black and White Minstrel Show* regularly topped twenty million viewers.[35]

Those seeking their independence from empire were seen as needing time to develop their capabilities before they could manage it. In 1948, shortly after India won its independence, less than ten years before Malaya did, a Tory MP told Parliament: 'I was thinking of the people who for decades and almost centuries have built up Malaya which, before the war, was a peaceful and prosperous area *with the native population well in hand*'. He went on to attack the Labour government for: 'Introducing these manifestations of democracy to immature people, to shed the load which we should have shouldered.'[36]

The early 1960s brought a dramatic change in Powell's racism.[37] The empire all but gone, Powell now saw 'decline, victimhood and enemy occupation'.[38] The challenge was to stop black and Asian immigration. Powell was not alone in his views. Almost twenty years earlier as black and Asian immigration was helping to deal with post-war labour shortages, a senior Home Office official told one of his staff: 'We had hoped that shipping restrictions would have prevented any further influx of West Indians... but I am afraid we must expect small parties from time to time.'[39] Britain's most senior police officer, the Chief Inspector of Police, wrote in 1957 to all chief constables asking:

1. What is the number of coloured people in your area: a) West Indian b) Non West Indian?
2. Is there any definite evidence of large scale crime?
3. Do they mix well with white people?
4. What are the facts of illegitimacy related to West Indians?
5. What is the evidence concerning brothel management and coloured people?
6. What are the conditions under which they live?[40]

Powell's speech brought out existing racism, especially inside the police, who, identifying black youth as the main cause of street crime, made intensive use of the 'Sus law'.[41] This gave them the power to stop and search those whom they suspected were 'likely to commit a crime'.[42] David Michael, the first black police officer to work in Lewisham, an area with a large black population, recalled: 'The police were like an occupying army'.[43] Such a colonial form of control showed how little had changed in post-empire Britain. At a time when young people were looking for much greater freedom in their lives than their parents had enjoyed, reactionary forces also saw opportunities to reassert themselves.

■ National Front march in Leicester 1979

2: The fascists

★ Who benefited from Powell's speech and the upsurge in racism that followed? Having established his reputation as Britain's best known right-wing MP, Powell continued to make anti-immigrant speeches but made no effort to organise his supporters.[1] The party that did this, benefiting from the upsurge, was the newly founded National Front (NF).[2] Robert Taylor, a National Front organiser in Huddersfield, remembered:

> We held a march in Huddersfield in support of what Powell had said, and we signed eight people up as members of the branch that afternoon. Powell's speeches gave our membership and morale a tremendous boost. Before Powell spoke we were getting only cranks and perverts. After his speeches we started to attract, in a secret sort of way, the right-wing members of the Tory organisations.[3]

The National Front was a fascist party. Fascism is a counter-revolutionary mass movement that aims to create a force that can be used in a severe crisis, if need be on the streets, prepared to use whatever violence is necessary to break its opponents. This would open the way to a return to some period of greatness in the past. It has been called 'the most important political novelty of the 20th century'.[4]

Fascist movements have succeeded in taking power in two countries: Italy and Germany. In both cases fascism was born out of the crises of imperialism at the end of the First World War, a time of huge movements of workers and peasants angered by the sacrifices they had made for a war that brought death and enormous misery. From within these upheavals, the fascists recruited a core from those afraid of losing their small businesses, their self-employed status, of slipping down out of the middle class. These were the people who turned in tens of thousands and more to fascism as a force that could save them.

In Italy, fascism became a mass movement after the defeat of a revolutionary movement at the end of 1920, when farm workers seized the estates of big landowners and hundreds of thousands of workers occupied their factories. Seeing that the Italian parliamentary parties were unable to either resolve the crisis or to control the movement, the big landowners and industrialists looked to violence as a means to break the revolutionary movement. The employers' representative, Rotigliano, made this clear, telling union leaders: 'All discussion is useless. The industrialists will not grant any [pay] increase at all. Since the end of the war they've done nothing but drop their pants down. Now we are going to start on you.'[5]

They backed the blackshirted *squadristi*, gangs that ruthlessly attacked working-class organisation in both industrial and agricultural areas, breaking up socialist and trade union meetings, smashing up their print shops and setting labour halls on fire.[6] In October 1922, Mussolini, having gathered his supporters in the capital, which become known as the March on Rome, presented himself and his Blackshirts as a force that could renew Italy. With no regard for democratic procedure, the king appointed him prime minister. His government was now able to control the press and pass laws to increase its powers, while the Blackshirts continued to terrorise both socialists and the newly-formed Communist Party. By 1925, Mussolini was Il Duce, the unchallenged leader of a fascist dictatorship.

In Germany, the Nazis built a movement between 1921

and 1923 in opposition to revolutionary upheavals in the early post-war years. The First World War was brought to an end by a revolution that began in October 1918 when sailors of the German fleet took control of their ships and refused to fight a battle they believed could not stop Germany losing the war. Their mutiny spread quickly among soldiers who abandoned their trenches and marched home carrying their rifles and among factory workers who called mass strikes. The government had no choice but to accept defeat and negotiate a ceasefire. The mutineers and strikers now followed the lead of the Russian workers, peasants and soldiers who just a year or so earlier had organised themselves into councils that were able to take power: a workers, peasants and soldiers' government. In every town, city and military unit in Germany, the people established their own councils.

The new provisional government, established in a secret deal between the generals and the leaders of the Social Democratic Party (SPD), was forced to recognise these councils. Yet, at the same time it organised the most reactionary, nationalist elements of the Imperial Army as a counter-revolutionary force: the Freikorps. This was the force that suppressed an uprising in Berlin in January 1919 – the Spartacist uprising that was a premature attempt by revolutionaries to overthrow the provisional government – and murdered the leaders of the revolutionary left, Rosa Luxemburg and Karl Liebknecht. The following year the Freikorps was used to suppress workers' uprisings in Munich, Bremen, the Ruhr area and other industrial centres of Germany.[7]

The SPD-led government slowly, and often bloodily, defeated the resistance of the workers and soldiers' councils and established a parliamentary democracy known as the Weimar Republic.[8] Some Freikorps members now looked to establishing themselves as a political party. Finally adopting the name National Socialist German Workers Party (NSDAP), shortened to Nazis, they based themselves on the idea that Germany lost the war and its empire after being 'stabbed in the back' from within by the actions of socialists and workers' strikes – behind which, of course, the Nazis saw the hand of a Jewish conspiracy.[9]

The leader of the newly established Nazi Party was the former regular soldier and ultra nationalist Adolf Hitler. In common with many on the far right, he was deeply antisemitic, arguing that Jewish bankers were behind an international conspiracy controlling much of the world's financial system. At the same time he kept the revolutionary movement that had ended the war central to his thinking – reflected in the party's name. Fear of revolution meant that, even though the Nazis failed to establish a significant presence in the organised working-class movement, Hitler never forgot its potential power and the consequent need to appear pro-worker while at the same time aiming to destroy working-class organisation, as Mussolini's *fascisti* had done.[10]

As with all fascism, Hitler's core class base was the middle class, the petty bourgeoisie. Too diverse in social terms, they are incapable of organising themselves as an independent force. In a situation of growing crisis, they are increasingly afraid that they will lose their social position and privileges and be forced down the social ladder. Losing faith in parliamentary democracy with its careerists and their endless scandals, they look for political alternatives. Rejecting working-class organisations – its parties and trade unions – they can be attracted by the fascists' capacity to create a fighting force. For Hitler, this meant bringing supporters onto: 'gigantic mass demonstrations... parades of hundreds of thousands of men, which burned into the small, wretched individual the proud conviction that, paltry worm as he was, he was nevertheless a part of a great dragon.'[11]

In the revolutionary crisis that shook Germany in 1923 and after France sent troops to occupy the Ruhr, Germany's most important industrial centre, Hitler tried to provoke a right-wing seizure of power. Known as the Munich Beer Hall Putsch, his attempt at an armed uprising failed miserably. Recognising that the Weimar republic was now entering a period of stability, Hitler adopted a long-term strategy. He aimed to build both an electoral base and a street movement, the Sturmabteilung (SA), known as the Brownshirts – a paramilitary force that could be used to attack Jews, socialists and trade unionists. The Nazi Party grew modestly, polling only 2.8 percent in the 1928 general election.

All this changed with the global economic crisis triggered by the Wall Street crash in October 1929. Unlike France and Britain, shielded by their captive markets in their colonies, which now included Germany's former colonies, the great depression of the early 1930s hit Germany hard.[12] Unemployment rose to six million, a quarter of the workforce. Promising to tear up the Versailles treaty and begin a massive rearmament programme to get people back to work, the Nazis Party's electoral support, and the SA's presence on the streets, grew rapidly.

The big industrialists, having always believed Weimar's trade unions were too strong and its welfare provisions too generous, urgently needed to restore their profits and competitiveness. The Nazis offered the opportunity to do this as they had the capacity not only to destroy the working-class movement but also to rescue the industrialists, and the big landowners, from any potential revolutionary threat posed by the powerful German Communist Party (KPD). Yet the German ruling class was initially wary of the Nazis, fearing that its radical anti-establishment rhetoric might lead it to attack not just the left and Jews but their power and profits too. Germany's rulers also worried that putting the Nazis into power could provoke German workers into civil war. But by late 1932 at least, having exhausted other non-Nazi authoritarian options and gambling the left could be beaten, Hitler was levered into power by conservative politicians.

With a huge and growing budget deficit, the SPD-led coalition government resigned in early 1930, unwilling to make the cuts demanded by business. Its successor, a coalition led by Heinrich Brüning of the conservative catholic Centre Party, unable to win a majority in parliament, resigned a few months later. This triggered a general election. The working-class vote remained solid; the SPD lost votes to the KPD while remaining the largest party with 24.5 percent. The big winners were the Nazis. Gaining votes from the middle-class centre parties, their share of the vote rose from 2.6 percent to 18.3 percent, a seven-fold increase.[13] The political polarisation between left and right and the refusal of the SPD and KPD to work together resulted in a stalemate in parliament. It was impossible to form a coalition with a parliamentary majority. Under an emergency provision in the republic's constitution, it was the president, the ageing aristocrat Field Marshal Paul von Hindenburg, who decided who should be invited to form a government, which could only rule using emergency decrees. The SPD decided to continue its support for Brüning as the lesser of two evils.

With unemployment continuing to rise and a national banking crisis, including the failure of Germany's second largest bank, the Nazis now presented themselves as the party that could rescue Germany, creating a new 'people's community' purged of what the Nazis saw as 'alien' forces, above all, class-based workers' organisations and Jews. Dressed up in revolutionary, sometimes socialist language, it was a counter-revolutionary mass movement aiming to re-establish Germany as a world power by destroying the working-class movement using whatever violence was necessary. As Hitler put it when on trial after the 1923 Beer Hall putsch, 'If today I stand here as a revolutionary, it is as a revolutionary against the revolution'. This could be seen in daily street battles as the Brownshirts, now recruiting large numbers of unemployed, fought against the left, demonstrating their capacity to take on organised workers.

The ability of the Nazis destroy the working-class movement was made easier by the mutual hostility between the two main working-class parties: the SPD and the KPD. The SPD leadership, determined to protect the status quo, was consistently anti-communist, in deeds as well as words. In 1929, the SPD-controlled police force in Berlin, having banned all public assemblies, responded to a Communist-led May Day march by killing thirty-two demonstrators and arresting around a thousand. For its part, the KPD uncritically followed the ultra-left perspective laid down by Stalin, who was by now in power in Russia, requiring Communist parties to make the revolutionary seizure of power their immediate priority. By working against the working-class seizure of power, the KPD argued, the SPD played a similar role to the Nazis, social democracy and fascism were twins, the SPD were 'social fascists'.

After two years of government without a democratic mandate, a general election in June 1932 saw Nazi support dramatically rise to 37 percent, with the SPD vote falling to 21.5 percent and the KPD rising to 14 percent. A further election in November saw little change. The Nazi vote fell to 33.1 percent, the SPD vote fell a little and the KPD vote rose to 16.9 percent.[14] It remained impossible to form a government with a parliamentary majority.

Two months later, in January 1933, Hitler's long-term strategy succeeded. Asked by Hindenburg to lead a coalition with the second right-wing party, the conservative-nationalist DNVP, he came to power as the constitutionally appointed head of government. Wasting no time, to strengthen his position he used his new powers to call a general election. At the same time, he banned newspapers and public meetings of the left using a fire in the parliament building to justify an emergency decree suspending freedom of speech, the press and association. Thousands of KPD members were arrested.

In the ensuing climate of fear, in the March 1933 elections, the SPD vote dropped to 18.3 percent and the KPD to 12.3 percent. The Nazis received 44 percent. Together with the Nationalists' 8 percent, they had a slim majority, enough for Hitler to pass an Enabling Act giving the government the power to pass laws without parliamentary approval, in effect abolishing parliamentary democracy. Despite this, union leaders were persuaded to support the Nazis' half million strong May Day rally. Yet, the next day trade union offices and funds were seized, trade unions themselves were banned, replaced by the Nazi-controlled German Labour Front. The Nazis now pursued a policy of atomizing individuals. Many social organisations were shut down; those that continued were placed under Nazi control and required to have a majority of Nazi Party members on their executive.

Already in 1932, Leon Trotsky had pointed out what a fascist seizure of power would mean. In his pamphlet *What Next? Vital Questions for the German Proletariat*, he wrote:

> Fascism is not merely a system of reprisals, of brutal force, and of police terror. Fascism is a particular governmental system based on the uprooting of all elements of proletarian democracy within bourgeois society... To this end the physical annihilation of the most revolutionary section of the workers does not suffice. It is also necessary to smash all independent and voluntary organisations, to demolish all the defensive bulwarks of the proletariat, and to uproot whatever has been achieved during three-quarters of a century by social democracy and the trade unions.[15]

Such annihilation made possible enactment of the laws that intensified discrimination against Jews.[16] Disabled people, Roma and gays as well as political opponents were added to the list of those subjected to arrest without trial. Detention in concentration camps became widespread, numbers growing with the outbreak of war in 1939 and further accelerating after the attack on Russia in 1941. Prisoners were increasingly worked to death. Concentration camps became death camps as the decision was made to implement the Final Solution, the genocide of all Jews, Roma, gypsies – the Holocaust.

Oswald Mosley and British fascism

The success of first Italian and then German fascism in taking power inspired fascist parties across Europe. A British fascist party was founded just eight months after Mussolini took power.[17] The first large fascist organisation, the British Union of Fascists (BUF), came out of the economic crisis that began with the Wall Street crash. Its leader, Sir Oswald Mosley, born into a rich, well-connected family, had, aged twenty-three, been elected to parliament as a Conservative in the December 1918 general election. Quickly building a reputation for his skill as an orator, considered by some to be the finest of his generation, he moved to the left, joining the Labour Party in 1924, and was elected as a Labour MP in 1926. A member of Labour's national executive 1927 and minister in the minority Labour government of 1929, he opposed a policy of balancing the budget by cutting welfare payments. Instead, he tried to get the party to adopt Keynesian policies, boosting government spending. Unable to win the argument and disillusioned with the mainstream parties, he played a leading role in the short-lived New Party, which he abandoned after a New Party candidate came a poor third in a parliamentary by-election.[18]

After visiting Italy – where he met Mussolini – and Munich, he moved quickly to set up what became the main fascist organisation in Britain, the British Union of Fascists (BUF), in October 1932. Boosted by the Nazis taking power in Germany a few months later, the BUF took off quickly holding large rallies that made full use of Mosley's oratory skills. Adopting a paramilitary approach with a uniform based on the Italian fascist black shirt, membership grew to over 40,000 in two years. Rich donors helped meet the substantial costs involved. The best-known was Lord Rothermere, owner of the mass circulation *Daily Mail*, which ran front page articles backing the BUF with headlines such as 'Hurrah for the Blackshirts'.[19]

The BUF insisted on strong leadership to defend the increasingly vulnerable empire, weakened by debts incurred in First World War. It called for violent repression when needed, challenging the government's willingness to negotiate with nationalist movements now beginning to demand independence. However, with the captive markets of its colonies keeping Britain's unemployment rate to about half that of Germany, the British establishment had already succeeded in managing the global crisis in 1931. With the National Government, a coalition led by the former Labour prime minister Ramsey McDonald, who had broken from the Labour Party, cutting wages and unemployment benefits, business leaders small and large had no need for a fascist option. When Mosley addressed 10,000 supporters at a rally in London and his stewards – his 'biff boys', as he called them – brutally attacked hecklers, the wave of negative publicity that followed led to most of his rich backers withdrawing their support. BUF membership collapsed from 50,000 to 5,000 and he was forced to sack 300 of his 350 staff.[20]

To rebuild, Moseley turned to antisemitism and adopted the tactic of marching through Jewish communities. He was banned from doing this in Leeds,[21] but a week later he targeted London's East End, home of Britain's largest Jewish community; it was here that the British Brothers' League had campaigned against immigrant Jews fleeing antisemitic pogroms in tsarist Russia before the First World War. On the day, despite police efforts to clear the route of counter-protesters, a mass turnout of over a hundred thousand people stopped the BUF march in what came to be called the Battle of Cable Street.

While this was a major defeat for Mosley, the BUF was not smashed. Mosley continued to build the organisation, which claimed to have helped stop Jewish immigration from Nazi Germany.[22] As international tensions intensified, six weeks before the outbreak of the Second World War, Mosley held a Nazi-style rally of 20,000 calling for peace with Germany.[23]

After it stood a candidate in a by-election in May 1940, the BUF was banned and Mosley and 700 members were interned.[24] On their release shortly before the war ended, small fascist groups began to emerge. They were able to exploit the moment in 1947 when the *Daily Express* published on its front page a photograph of two British sergeants hanging from a tree in British-controlled Palestine, killed by Zionist paramilitaries. Antisemitic violence broke out in towns across Britain. There were riots in Liverpool and Manchester when hundreds came onto the streets: shop windows were smashed and a synagogue and Jewish wedding were attacked. During a riot in nearby Salford, a sergeant major, John Regan, was arrested for public disorder offences after he urged on a crowd of 600 to attack Jewish-owned shops, shouting: 'Hitler was right, exterminate every Jew, every man, woman and child.'[25]

A larger organisation, the Union Movement, was founded in 1948, bringing together a few thousand members including most of the small fascist groups. Mosley became its leader but soon withdrew from active politics as it became clear that outside of the East End it had no serious support. He returned briefly in the aftermath of the Notting Hill race riots but was disappointed with the 8.1 percent he won in Kensington North in the 1959 general election.

The birth of the National Front

The larger fragments of the much-divided fascist movement came together into a single organisation, the National Front (NF), in 1967.[26] It claimed a membership of 2,500, though the active membership was about half that figure and most of them were in middle-class areas in the south and east of England. The exception was London's East End, where there had been an organised fascist presence since before the Second World War.[27] The NF's chairman, A K Chesterton, had been a founder member of the BUF and edited its paper, *The Blackshirt*.[28] A vicious antisemite, he was the leader of the League of Empire Loyalists, a pressure group known for stunts disrupting Conservative Party conferences. Concerned that the new organisation should be 'respectable' and protecting its reputation from the accusation it was fascist, he prioritised recruiting disaffected members of the Conservative Party. One of the smaller fascist groups, the British National Party, had been successful in anti-immigrant campaigning in elections.[29] Struggling with little success to make an impact and win members, the new NF leadership tried to exploit events 'as they hit the front pages of the press'.[30] Public meetings were disrupted, as were showings of the anti-militarist comedy film *How I Won the War*.[31]

A year later, growing for the first time in the wake of Powell's 1968 speech, a group of business supporters offered to contribute to NF campaign costs for the next general election if enough publicity could be generated to justify it, a challenge that was quickly met. As one journalist wrote:

> If success can be measured in acres of newsprint, 1969 was a very good year for the Front. Members of the Front broke up political meetings, notably the Walthamstow by-election meeting addressed by Denis Healey and Arthur Bottomley [two leading Labour politicians]. They stopped films they disapproved of by chanting in cinemas and heckled the sermons of vicars they suspected of leftist ideas.[32]

At the same time they developed a dual strategy. Demonstrations to boost members' confidence and win publicity were combined with standing candidates where there was a prospect of a significant vote. The strategy produced tensions between those committed fascists, accustomed to the use of violence and the 'populists', those more committed to appearing 'respectable', many of whom were recruited from the Tory party.

This did not mean avoiding violence. Chesterton got tickets for the England–South Africa rugby match knowing that anti-apartheid campaigners would be aiming to stop the match using direct action. The NF's November 1969 internal circular explained to members:

> This occasion...will provide us with our most important propaganda opportunity of the winter period. We intend to counteract the fraudulent posturing of the left by turning up in strength and displaying a number of big banners. Through the generosity of Mr Chesterton our tickets for the event will be heavily subsidised and maybe free for some members.[33]

Jim Nichol, one of the anti-apartheid protesters, remembers 'there was one almighty fight with fists flying. There were dozens involved'.[34] Chesterton was nevertheless unhappy with the thug element of the membership: 'If the NF does not become an elite movement it will fail. Ideally we should seek to recruit only the dedicated elite but we do not live in an ideal world and must make the best use of the material at our disposal.'[35]

He particularly wanted to keep out those whose Nazi past would be used against the new organisation. He failed completely with the members of the Greater Britain Movement. This was a split from the openly Nazi National Socialist Movement (NSM), but it was '"the same movement in every respect" as the NSM aside from its leader and name'.[36] They dissolved their organisation and joined the NF as individuals.[37] These included John Tyndall, who became editor of the NF's journal *Spearhead*. He had been jailed for unlawful possession of a gun and ammunition. He was joined by his long-standing collaborator Martin Webster, jailed for assaulting Jomo Kenyatta, the Kenyan president.[38] As NSM activists in the early 1960s both were open in their support for Nazism. Tyndall told a court that he saw Hitler's *Mein Kampf*, 'as his guide'. Webster told the press: 'We are busy building a well-oiled Nazi machine in this country.'[39]

Once in the NF, Tyndall and Webster kept their Nazi beliefs out of sight. Tyndall wrote to an American Nazi:

> I do not believe that a movement with an open Nazi label has a hope of winning national power in Britain or the US. I have, therefore, sought to modify our propaganda, though not, of course, the essence of our ideology... Our propaganda now has to be considerably modified by the Act [the Race Relations Act] which the Jews got through Parliament to stifle free speech... Pure Nazi literature is something that must be used now more as something to circulate privately as a means of training and enlightening the partially converted than as a public selling line... Our strategy is to use the moderate elements, to work behind them as long as is necessary but to effectively control them.[40]

After a sharp factional battle, Tyndall and Webster forced the chair, Chesterton's successor, John O'Brien, and half the

Directorate, the Front's leading committee, to resign.[41] O'Brien, a former Conservative Party member, later described Tyndall's techniques as those of 'the school bully, grown large and grown adult, who has kept his school bully methods'.[42]

The National Front became known for its commitment to 'the compulsory repatriation' of Britain's black and Asian population. It also argued for leaving the Common Market in favour of a 'nationalist' economic programme, as well as the return of capital punishment and compulsory military service.[43]

Behind this facade, it was led by an effective combination of two committed fascists: Tyndall, the leader, and Webster the organiser. They understood that while Tyndall lacked Mosley's skill as a public speaker, they would organise their followers far more effectively than he had. Hitler was their model, not Mosley. Joe Pearce, leader of the Young National Front,[44] remembered how they developed a cadre of 'those that can hate':[45]

> Although the NF's position was always to deny strongly that it was a neo-Nazi party, one could not graduate to the inner-sanctum... within the Party without tacitly accepting Nazi ideology and without secretly regretting the defeat of Hitler and the Third Reich.[46]

Members were trained at weekend camps where they learned about 'the international Jewish conspiracy'. The training included the need to condemn 'class war nonsense', how, instead, the government should unite with trade unionists 'to face the real threat to Britain – the growing monopoly of international economic and political power'.[47] Some were recruited to an 'Honour Guard', organised with military style discipline, marching to a drum beat at the front of NF demonstrations, carrying Union Jacks on spiked poles.

Tyndall and Webster supported the targeted violence used by Mussolini and Hitler. But their NF programme was essentially the same as that of the Nazis, presenting the organisation as a far-right party focused on winning power through the ballot box. Like Hitler's Nazi Party, the NF began with forces too weak to directly target the labour movement it aimed to destroy. Their strategy, modelled on Hitler's, was to win members through organised racism. The Nazis had scapegoated Jews for all society's ills: the

NF added black and Asian people to the scapegoats. Both sought to retrieve lost imperial prestige. Tyndall and Websters' aim was to build 'a well-oiled Nazi machine', including a street presence, modelled on Hitler's Brownshirts, able to attack its enemies.

In full agreement with the methods Mussolini and Hitler used to take power, they refused to acknowledge the consequences of them. They supported the myth of Holocaust denial, circulating the pamphlet *Did Six Million Really Die?*, and refused to recognise that, already by 1938, the Nazi leadership were agreed among themselves that a war of imperial expansion, if need be without allies, was the only way to overcome the shortages of workers and raw materials that were obstructing the rearmament drive. They argued that the Second World War was caused by an 'international Jewish–Communist conspiracy' and that Churchill had been tricked into joining with Stalin to fight Germany rather than allying with Hitler to fight Russia.[48]

Martin Webster, now the NF's national activities director, copied the Nazis' approach: 'the party's rationale was constant movement: movement for its own sake, movement that served as a perpetual confirmation of the party's onward march'.[49] In an article titled 'NF: a movement of action', he wrote: 'Because of the unwillingness of the national press to give fair coverage to the policies of the movement, the party soon realised that it was necessary... to hit the headlines as often as possible by all manner of demonstrations, marches and stunts.'[50]

Webster claimed these activities had evolved using 'a new technique of "nonviolent physical confrontation"'.[51] Targeting a Co-operative conference on racialism was one example, when NF members attempted to gain entry by pretending to be the North London Christian Fellowship. When turned away by stewards, they stood outside with a large Union Jack and banners reading 'Race mixing is treason' and 'Do you want a black grandchild?', reinforcing this message with an eight-car cavalcade with megaphones.[52] Other confrontations included getting members onto coaches from London and the Midlands to confront anti-apartheid demonstrators at the South African rugby match in Cardiff, and breaking up a large meeting at the LSE called to set up a national school students organisation and invading a lecture on 'working class racialism', causing the lecturer, Dipak Nandy, to collapse.[53]

Tyndall supported the commitment to street politics. Echoing *Mein Kampf* on the importance of mass demonstrations, he put the question to party organisers, 'What is it that touches off a chord in the instinct of people to whom we seek to appeal?', answering:

> it may be a marching column; it may be the sound of a drum; it may be a banner or it may just be the impression of the crowd. None of these things contain in themselves one single argument... This is why at certain intervals of the year we concentrate our forces together by transporting members hundreds of miles by coach. We have got to show our strength to the public and to our own people.[54]

Hitler had asserted: 'Mass demonstrations must burn into the little man's soul the proud conviction that though a little worm, he is nevertheless part of a great dragon.'[55] Tyndall had the same view, arguing that 'our great marches, with drums and flags and banners, have a hypnotic effect on the public and immense effect in solidifying the allegiance of our followers, so that their enthusiasm can be sustained'.[56] For Tyndall, unlike any other political party: 'there is a unique quality of enthusiasm in the NF that an appeal to reason alone could not possibly create. We are not ashamed to appeal to people's feelings and utilise those feelings and spurring them on to ever greater efforts.'[57] Rationality was counterproductive:

> It is the single-minded emphasis on intellect for its own sake and its resulting tendency to reduce all vital questions of existence down to a flat, uninspired, pseudo rationale that atrophies the much more potent factors of instinct and will which move great and vigorous races and which ultimately determine history.[58]

While Tyndall argued 'anti immigrant views [are] not at all sufficient to build a movement', racism was the common thread. His book *Six Principles of British Nationalism* supported white rule in South Africa and Rhodesia, calling for South Africa's apartheid system to be adopted in Britain.[59] This, Tyndall claimed, would provide the basis for a new white Commonwealth, enabling Britain to be a world power again. The book also took up the so-called 'conspiracy of international finance', far-right code for the antisemitic myth of Jewish control of international banking.[60] In practice, such principles were a rag bag of extreme right-wing, racist ideas. Inspired by the Nazis, Tyndall shared their lack of originality:

> ideologically speaking...the NSDAP stood for a mixture of ideas and grievances that were far from original and indeed were common to much of the German right; all that was new was the passion and single-mindedness with which the separate ingredients of this ideological mixture were combined on behalf of the struggle against 'the system'.[61]

The most important example was the use of antisemitism to argue it was 'Jewish money power' that explained both capitalist exploitation and Bolshevik communism.[62]

Immigration, racism and the rise of the National Front

Though they denied it when publicly challenged, Tyndall and Webster were hostile to parliamentary democracy. Despite this, elections, especially by-elections, gave the NF an opportunity to build the party's reputation and raise its politics, especially its racism. Webster modelled the NF's electioneering on the Nazis, emphasising the urgency they claimed they saw in the situation

Its first election contest was a parliamentary by-election in Acton, West London, in March 1968. Andrew Fountaine, a rich landowner who had fought for Franco in the Spanish Civil War, was the NF candidate. Fountaine attacked black and Asian people as 'alien immigrants living one third off prostitution, one third off National Assistance and one third off Red gold'. He came fourth with 1,400 votes, 5.6 percent. The 1969 local elections produced more impressive results. In Huddersfield nine candidates averaged 12 percent,[63] leading to plans for an NF northern office in the city.[64]

The NF vote was squeezed by the Conservatives, who won the 1970 general election promising new restrictions on immigration,[65] It was campaigning against immigration that won votes. As a new party, the NF struggled to get its message across. In Leicester, the NF candidate got 2.3 percent. The local Anti-

Immigration Society, standing in a neighbouring constituency, got 5.25 percent.[66]

The Conservatives won the 1970 general election promising new restrictions on immigration. The 1971 Immigration Act introduced the concept of 'patriality' into law, an explicitly racist concept. Admitting only those with British parents or grandparents, overwhelmingly white people who had migrated to Canada, South Africa, Australia and New Zealand, it created a clear racist division between those who qualified and those who didn't.

While publicly declaring for equality, union leaders did little or nothing to oppose the bill or racism in the workplace. When Blackburn gravediggers refused to work at weekends making it impossible for Muslim families to follow the Islamic requirement that burial takes place as soon as possible, they were supported by their union district secretary.[67] The courts were of little assistance. Preston Dockers Labour Club had operated a 'colour bar', only serving white customers, for twenty years. 'A coloured man was awarded £10 damages for having been refused service.'[68]

As always, public attacks on immigration encouraged racist violence. According to Judge Edward Steel speaking in court in Manchester:

> attacks on Pakistanis had become a sport in some areas, particularly in Rochdale. Two men were jailed and a youth sent to borstal after admitting causing grievous bodily harm with intent to Mr Mohammed Ali.[69]

Racism was taken to new levels when in late summer 1972 Uganda's president, General Amin suddenly accused 40,000 Ugandan Asians of 'sabotaging the economy' and ordered their expulsion giving them 90 days to leave.[70] The British government announced they would admit those with a British passport. With the new Immigration Act distinguishing 'patrials' from 'non-patrials', Enoch Powell could respond: 'the so-called British passports do not entitle them to enter Britain'.[71] The NF did not hesitate, getting a hundred supporters to protest outside Downing Street against the government's announcement.[72] The *Daily Mail* and *Daily Express*, with a combined circulation of four million copies a day, seized the moment: the *Daily Mail* ran the headline: 'Asians – the big fear: We can't stop them swamping the ghettos'; the *Daily Express* claimed to 'reveal the astonishing truth: No need to let them in!', and ran a report on several hundred porters from the giant Smithfield meat market, led by Danny Harmston, a meat market supervisor and former bodyguard for Oswald Mosley, marching to the Home Office with 'Enoch is right' placards.[73]

A fortnight later, the *Daily Mirror* ran the headline: 'Asians can stay at a 4-star hotel... free', while the the *London Evening News* accepted an advert paid for by the NF for a protest march to the Conservative and Labour party headquarters.[74] Three hundred members of the NF and British Movement, a smaller Nazi group more focused on street activity, demonstrated at Heathrow airport. 'Dozens...holding banners and shouting "Stop immigration – Enoch is right" and singing "Land of Hope and Glory" were carried by police out of the airport's long distance terminal': ten were arrested.[75] Council meetings discussing the Ugandan Asians were disrupted, the public gallery of Hounslow Town Hall was occupied, and NF members gave out thousands of leaflets at Manchester Airport on a series of Sundays.[76] Far-right demonstrations continued into September. In central London several hundred, led by the Immigration Control Association, chanted 'Enoch Powell for Premier'.[77] In Leicester, where the local paper suggested as many as 15,000 might be on their way, the council declared that its services were 'already stretched to capacity' and placed a notice in the *Uganda Argus* warning those preparing to flee not to come to the city.[78]

The far-right populist Jim Merrick of the British Campaign to Stop Immigration spoke at a protest rally in Leicester. According to *Spearhead*, he had an audience of 2,300 with more than 1,000 on a march that followed.[79] Encouraged by this, the NF promised to stand sixteen candidates in the next council elections.[80] In the following six weeks the NF launched a series of demonstrations: 150 marched in Reading, 600 in Leicester. Strengthening its presence in the north was a national priority and coaches were organised from London and the Midlands to boost a march in Blackburn. Six hundred people heard speeches from Merrick, Tyndall, Webster and a former chair of the local Young Conservatives, John Kingsley Read.

NF recruitment took off. As Webster later put it: 'The

Ugandan Asian invasion sparked our real growth.'[81] A number of the Conservative Party's more right-wing members left to join the NF after an attempt by the Monday Club, a right-wing Conservative Party faction, failed to shift government policy. [82] Two thousand people attended the launch of its 'Halt Immigration Now Campaign' in Central Hall, Westminster.[83] The failure of the campaign led Roy Painter, Haringey businessman and former Tory candidate for the Greater London Council (GLC), and Kingsley Read, both of whom had significant political experience, to join the NF.[84] Monthly recruitment was averaging two hundred.

With the increase in membership, the party expanded its branches. A branch was set up in Bradford. A northern organiser, Walter Barton, was appointed to build a network of NF groups around Manchester – within a year there were groups in Oldham, Stockport, Rochdale and Accrington and proper branches in Bolton, Blackburn and Liverpool. With a general election expected mid-1974, a target was set of fifty candidates, which meant a free party political TV broadcast.

The potential impact of the growth of the NF on elections soon became clear. In a Rochdale parliamentary by-election in October 1972, Jim Merrick, standing as a racist independent, won 9 percent using leaflets headed 'Enoch is right'. The first real election breakthrough for the NF was two months later when it won nearly 9 percent in a by-election in Uxbridge.[85] Then, in the April 1973 council elections in Leicester, the NF got over 10,000 votes, averaging more than 15 percent. Bolstered by these results, Webster made himself NF candidate in a West Bromwich by-election. He organised distribution of 'Send back the coloured immigrants' leaflets, street marches with union jacks, and two mass rallies – one, it was claimed, with 3,000 attending.[86] Webster used the election to push the NF's racist message. Since Pakistan had left the Commonwealth in protest against Britain recognising Bangladesh, Webster demanded that all Pakistanis be removed from the electoral rolls as aliens.[87] With Enoch Powell, MP for a neighbouring constituency, refusing to endorse the Conservative candidate, Webster got 4,789 votes, 16 percent – the first time the NF had saved its deposit in a parliamentary election.[88]

Helped by the West Bromwich vote, the NF vote went up

from 10,000 in the Leicester Country Council elections in April to 18,000 in the June Leicester City elections averaging over 15 percent. A new branch in Nottingham saw one candidate get 22 percent. In Blackburn five candidates averaged nearly 24 percent. The NF was now able to present themselves as a credible alternative to those for whom the government's racist immigration policies did not go far enough.

The political and economic context was now changing. Aiming to boost living standards to help win the next election, the government's 1972 tax cuts triggered an upswing that in less than twelve months saw the economy growing at an unsustainable 10 percent a year. With prices soaring, a wage freeze was imposed. A second shock to living standards followed a year later when members of the Organization of Arab Petroleum Exporting Countries (OAPEC) declared an embargo targeting those countries that supported Israel in the war begun a few days earlier when Egypt and Syria launched a surprise attack on Israel.[89] Across the world petrol station queues grew as the price of oil quadrupled. In Britain, inflation doubled to 16 percent, peaking at 24 percent in 1975. By the end of 1974, with the global economy going into recession, the London stock market had fallen by two thirds from two years earlier, the New York market by half. The post war boom, the "golden thirty years" as they were called in France, was over.[90]

Rising prices and wage controls meant cuts in working class living standards for the first time in forty years. An already weakened government was now challenged by the miners who, despite the best efforts of their right-wing leader Joe Gormley, imposed an overtime ban as winter approached in November 1973. Fearing massive power cuts and widespread chaos, the government took unprecedented action. Emergency legislation forced industry to shut down over Christmas, thereafter only permitted to work three days a week. From January every business was required to work either Monday to Wednesday or Thursday to Saturday. There were growing fears within ruling circles that the government had lost control. Right-wing elements talked of combating industrial anarchy and alternatives to parliamentary democracy. The military coup in Chile overthrowing the left social democrat government of Salvador Allende in September 1973, killing and disappearing thousands was fresh in people's minds. The retired commander of NATO in Northern Europe, General Walker, started to recruit volunteers to his Civil Assistance movement.[91]

The miners held a second ballot getting an 81 percent vote for action which began early in 1974. Within three days of the strike starting Heath called a general election for the end of the month on the question 'Who rules Britain, the elected government or the unions?' Heath lost, albeit narrowly. While the Tories won the largest number of votes, Labour got the largest number of seats – helped by Enoch Powell's call for a Labour vote because of Heath's commitment to joining the Common Market – and formed a minority government.[92]

Labour and the Social Contract

Labour won a small majority in a second election in October. Those in the unions who hoped for the government to back their efforts to defend their living standards were soon disappointed. Wilson was no less determined to defend the status quo than his predecessor. However, unlike Heath, he was in a position to get the trade union leaders to police their members. While earlier wage controls had been enforced by law, always producing a showdown with the unions, it was now the TUC holding down wages. With solid backing from the two most powerful leaders, Hugh Scanlon, president of the AUEW, and Jack Jones, general secretary of the TGWU, both with left-wing reputations, this was now formally agreed. Soon titled the Social Contract, it promised individual and collective rights for workers in exchange for 'voluntary wage restraint' that the TUC would oversee. At the same time there were cuts in health, education and welfare budgets. Unemployment, below 4 percent at the beginning of 1975, more than doubled over the next year and a half, especially among young workers, and black workers were nearly twice as likely to be out of work as white workers.[93] Earnings fell more sharply than they had since the slump of 1921.[94] Many Labour supporters were now disheartened. Rank and file militancy was in crisis as fear of redundancy and traditional loyalty to Labour combined to undermine the willingness to take strike action.[95] Wilson's success meant that ruling class fears that the working-class militancy would have to be suppressed by organising a mass of strike-breakers could be dismissed.[96]

The NF made headway as the Social Contract, backed by the trade union leaders, held down wages, and Labour's working-class supporters grew ever more disillusioned. NF membership was now over 20,000, and the ninety NF candidates in the October 1974 election got a higher average vote than in the general election at the beginning of the year, notably in London, where thirty-six NF candidates stood, ten of whom polled more than 5 percent.[97] The NF also faced little opposition in the media. When parents protested about Richard Edmonds, an NF member, teaching in Brixton in a school with many black pupils, a *Guardian* editorial told readers: 'The National Front is an offensive organisation which panders to racial prejudice and bigotry... [T]he best way of keeping the National Front in its place is to uphold the tolerance to which the present system is committed.'[98]

The NF's election successes produced a leadership challenge by former Conservative Party members: Kingsley Read in Blackburn, Anthony Reed Herbert in Leicester and Roy Painter in Haringey. Determined to replace Tyndall and Webster and rid the party of the accusation that it was led by Nazis, they pushed for a more election-focused strategy rather than the street. This required a more respectable, less authoritarian image with a greater verbal commitment to parliamentary democracy, with the aim of winning those Tories disillusioned with Heath and angered by Powell leaving the Conservative Party. Webster denounced this as populism, a watering down of what he called nationalism. Painter exploited the ambiguity of the term 'nationalism' with an article titled 'Let's make nationalism popular', and, when this approach was rejected, he and the ex-Conservatives directly took on Tyndall, forcing him into his only experience of standing for election in the NF. In a close vote, Tyndall lost and was demoted to deputy chairman with Kingsley Read elected to take his place as chair.

The differences in strategy now clear, an all-out faction fight followed. With the party headquarters nearly paralysed by division, membership and income fell.[99] Campaigning all but ceased. Just sixty candidates stood in the 1975 local elections nationally compared to seventy-three in London alone the previous year. Webster could organise only a few interventions, for example, a hundred members disrupting an anti-EEC meeting, and a group of women members flour-bombing Roy Jenkins, the home secretary, at a meeting in London and heckling him in Chichester cathedral as he promoted the new Race Relations bill.[100] In one incident, a few hundred NF supporters marched through Islington past the Town Hall where the council were refusing to allow the NF to book a room for a meeting.[101] They were outnumbered by anti-fascists two to one, but the massive police presence meant the NF's opponents could do no more than barrack the fascists. *Searchlight*, the newly relaunched anti-fascist magazine, commented: 'Whilst we... are against violence and see no point in fighting with the police, we must respect the handful of youngsters who stood in the path of the march only to be batoned down by the police.'[102]

The 'populists' were more impressive than the Tyndall supporters. On a Friday morning in January 1975, Kingsley Read led nearly a thousand through Manchester city centre to a Race Relations Board hearing, challenged only by a group of anti-NF students hemmed in by police. With his supporters picketing outside, Read told the hearing that he refused to apologise for a letter he had written to white householders in Blackburn urging them not to sell their houses to black people.[103]

As newly elected chairman, Read got the NF Directorate to pass a vote of no confidence in Tyndall. Eventually he managed to get Tyndall and Webster suspended and then expelled, only for the two to get themselves reinstated by the High Court. Read now resigned his membership to set up the National Party, taking a fifth of the membership with him. Inside the NF, Tyndall and Webster re-established control, preparing the ground for a new surge in activity.[104] Though the fascists were now divided into two parties, they presented a threat for which their opponents on the left were far from prepared.

■ Imperial Typewriters strike 1974. Photo: Mirrorpix

3: Fighting racism and fascism

★ Black and Asian resistance

In the 1950s, half the white population of Britain had never met a black person. The legacy of empire meant the idea of white supremacy together with racist abuse, police harassment, employer and landlord discrimination was the norm. 'Colour bars' were everywhere. Landlords included 'No coloureds' in notices advertising properties in newsagents' windows.[1] In the mid-1950s, together with Atvar Singh, Ernie Roberts, a Labour councillor in Coventry and experienced trade unionist, challenged a pub's application for licence renewal because it operated a colour bar. The magistrate dismissed their challenge on the grounds that racial discrimination was lawful.[2]

In many industries in post-war Britain, some white trade unionists insisted on a quota system restricting the number of black and Asian workers, often to a maximum of 5 percent, and there were understandings with management that the principle of 'last in first out' for redundancies would not apply if this meant white workers would lose their jobs before black workers.[3] For seven years up to 1966, Bob Thomas, union secretary for Manchester bus workers, leader of the Labour group in Manchester council, fought against Sikh bus drivers and conductors being allowed to wear the turban as part of their uniform.[4]

Racism didn't go unchallenged. Already in the 1930s, Harold Moody, secretary of the League of Coloured Peoples, was challenging the colour bar. When the matron of the Manchester Royal Infirmary wrote:

> We have never taken coloured nurses for training here... there was a definite rule that nobody of negroid extraction can be considered. If the lady about whom you write has no negro blood perhaps you would kindly let me know, and I will bring your letter to the notice of the Nursing Committee at their next Meeting.[5]

Moody took this up with the hospital governors who replied: 'There is... no rule against the admission of coloured women for training as nurses at the Manchester Royal Infirmary and the board wish it to be understood that each individual application will be considered on its merits.'[6] In a well-publicised case during the war, Learie Constantine, West Indian cricketer and a Ministry of Labour welfare officer, successfully sued the Imperial Hotel in London for refusing a booking he had made.[7] Holborn Trades Council followed the case up with a public meeting calling for an anti-colour bar law.[8]

Who should lead the resistance to racism? The first anti-racist organisations in Britain insisting on black leadership were Pan-African.[9] Focussing on liberating the African colonies of the British and other empires, they also fought racism. In Manchester, for example, Gerald Beard, a Jamaican airman, was arrested by police and charged with murder after a white soldier was stabbed and died. The leading Pan-African Ras Makonnen 'wanted to project the image that the Black man is capable of carrying on his own defence'. He raised the £1,500 needed to fly the black barrister Norman Manley from Jamaica. Manley proved that the police had lied, ensuring Beard was acquitted.[10]

In 1953 Len Johnson, a black Communist Party member and former boxer, was refused a pint of beer in the Old Abbey pub in

Manchester. Together with Wilf Charles, a white scaffolder and secretary of the local CP branch, he reported on the refusal in the *Daily Worker*, got the support of the Lord Mayor, organised a petition and returned two days later with a large number of supporters. The landlord now served Johnson.[11] This success, however, was not followed up with a campaign against the colour bar.[12]

When anti-black riots broke out in Notting Hill, London, in 1958, one group fought back. Believing that:

attack was the best form of defence, [they] made a pre-emptive strike against a local fascist headquarters and a club where white men were known to be planning racist attacks. Some lobbed petrol bombs in the back of each building while others waited in ambush at the front. A number of fascists were put out of action for one night at least.[13]

Organised resistance grew with the institutionalised racism of new laws identifying black people as a problem. The 1962 Commonwealth Immigration Act established quotas, limiting the numbers of immigrants from the 'New Commonwealth', a hypocritical phrase trying to hide the intention to limit the restrictions to countries with a large black population.

The first black-led campaign against racism in Britain was the 1963 bus boycott against the colour bar preventing employment on Bristol buses.[14] Owen Henry, one of four Jamaicans who led the boycott, sat in the back of a bus for a photo that accompanied the press conference announcing the boycott, 'a symbolic defiance of racial segregation, Bristol style'. The boycott ran over four months before Raghbir Singh began work as a bus conductor.[15]

Strikes by black and Asian workers

In the mid-1960s, when black and Asian people constituted just one percent of the population of Britain, it was discrimination in employment that brought the communities together in large numbers. Forced into the hardest, dirtiest and lowest paid jobs, often regardless of their skills and qualifications and typically working night shifts, they found possibilities to resist both the racism they encountered both in the workplace and in the union. The first large strike by black and Asian workers in Britain was at the giant Courtaulds Red Scar Mill near Preston in May 1965. Of its 2,400 production workers, 600 were Asian and 120 West Indian all working on one shift in the key Tyre Cord Spinning department, known for its poor working conditions.

A month earlier, at a rowdy meeting, they jeered when management proposed each worker supervise one-and-a-half machines compared to the current one machine in return for a ten shilling a week bonus – a 50 percent increase in workload for a 3 percent increase in pay. Management's initial response was to suspend the new arrangement, only for it to be suddenly imposed with the support of the Transport and General Workers Union (TGWU) district organiser and four stewards, only one of whom was not white. The workforce immediately started a sit in. After seventeen hours, almost all black and Asian workers walked out, leaving only white workers and supervisors, who, with overtime and speed up, were able to keep production going. Getting only hindrance from the union, the strikers set up a strike committee. Three activists, Michael de Freitas, better known as Michael X, Roy Sawh and Abdullah Patel from the newly established Racial Awareness Action Society (RAAS), came to Preston.[16] Over a fortnight they organised support, framing their arguments in terms of black and Asian workers and white exploiters.[17] The white, Wigan-based, International Socialist Ray Challinor joined the strike committee, organising support and money for the strikers, and helping them with contacts in Manchester. He was warmly received at a mass meeting of 900 strikers and their supporters, getting a standing ovation. At one point as a strike meeting opened with words from the Quran, Challinor was asked to follow with a prayer. 'Our father who art in heaven, lead the strike to victory!', he responded.[18] After three weeks the strikers returned to work defeated but with a 'no victimisation' agreement, having shown that black and Asian workers could organise and fight independently if need be. The management used their victory to go on to impose the same deal on the other, overwhelmingly white, shift.[19]

Seven years later, in 1972, an Asian workers' strike began at Mansfield Hosiery Mills with fifty women and 250 men, spreading to a second factory. After three days, eighty Asian women in a subsidiary factory came out in sympathy. One said:

'The colour bar applies to us all. If our brothers are on strike we have to give them support. They need to feel self-respect, when they are treated like dogs, how can we go in, if our brothers are out.'[20]

Failing to get support from their union, the women marched through the town. They occupied the union offices with chants, demanding that the union support the strike, making it official or else they would not move out. The union were eventually forced to declare the strike official.[21] The Mansfield Hosiery strike saw a fight that had to take on the union officials as much as the employer. The union president claimed: 'We helped the Asians far more than we have helped our own people. This is what stuck in my craw all the time we were trying to get a settlement.'[22] Ernie Roberts attacked this assertion at a conference organised by the strike committee, arguing that the Labour Party, the Trades Union Congress (TUC) and some unions were 'failing to do anything about the problems of racialism'.[23]

The strikers returned after winning pledges of no victimisation, no redundancies and no racial discrimination. But forty-one white trainee knitters were in their place. So, they struck again. They also faced down the National Front when they organised a counter protest chanting: 'Put Britons first.'[24] After nearly two months on strike the workers returned having won a pay rise and the right to apply for higher skilled jobs.

The 1974 Imperial Typewriters strike in Leicester was important for the strength of the Asian strikers, the solidarity of the Asian community and for the NF's efforts to undermine the strike. It began after:

> a mix up... saw an Asian woman wrongly given the pay packet of a white colleague. She and her friends were shocked to see they were getting paid less than whites of the same grade ... When management failed to provide a satisfactory answer, the group spoke to their union representative. Angry at being treated as second class, the group of 39, mostly women, workers walked out on strike.[25]

The TGWU's 'closed shop' agreement requiring all 1,600 workers to be union members had worked well for the employer. The union convenor, Reg Weaver, twenty-two years in office, ten years on the union's national executive, collaborated with management's systematic discrimination against Asian workers, preventing them from becoming shop stewards. Weaver now told the strikers they were 'out of procedure' and declared the strike 'unofficial'. Despite some Asian workers crossing the picket line together with all 500 white workers, there was enormous support for the strike both among the Asian workforce and in the Asian community. Large pickets sustained the action. Production stopped. Asian workers in nearby factories collected money and four workplaces pledged a twenty-four-hour stoppage 'if and when needed'.[26]

The NF, which had several members at Imperial, supported scabs and attacked pickets. An Enoch Powell Support Group was set up inside the factory. Further support for the racists came from the local paper, the *Leicester Mercury,* with a daily circulation of 70,000. Britain's leading business magazine, *The Economist,* described the paper as 'the very reverse of being liberal and helpful, with its almost daily diet of thundering editorials and a letter column which often contains racialist nonsense of the worst kind'.[27] A demonstration starting outside the factory marching through the Asian area of the city was organised with a banner announcing: 'White Workers of Imperial Typewriters'.[28]

By mid-July, 270 Asian workers had been sacked with the convenor's approval. Challenging his role and the full-time officials who supported him, 200 strikers went to TGWU headquarters in London to get support from the general secretary Jack Jones. Jones refused, only willing to promise an inquiry.[29] At their return to work meeting, despite having none of their demands met, only securing a 'no victimisation' agreement, they called for solidarity between black, Asian and white workers and for a union controlled by its members.[30] As the strikers came back into work, proud of having fought for so long, 300 white workers held a meeting. With NF members leading the argument, they rejected the call for unity and voted for a one-day stoppage against the reinstatement of twenty-five strike leaders, taking action the next day.[31] Six months later the damage done by the NF opposing black and white unity became clear. When Imperial Typewriter management announced it was closing all its plants in Britain, the sister factory in Hull occupied in defence of jobs while the Leicester factory closed without a fight.

In all these disputes, black and Asian workers had to battle against the racism of many white trade unionists and their officials, and at Mansfield Hosiery and Imperial Typewriters this was made worse by the presence of the National Front. However, there were also black and Asian-led organisations in the workplace, the strongest were the Indian Workers Associations (IWA).[32] The IWA's leading members, having learned their politics in the highly disciplined Communist Party of India, were strongly committed to organising. Some joined local Communist Party branches, while others saw the CP's membership as weak in both theory and practice. Avtar Jouhl was helped by the local CP in Birmingham to overcome the racism of union branch officers stopping Asian workers from becoming members.[33] Most of the time 'self-help was what we did exactly because we were outside mainstream society'.[34] After Powell's 1968 speech, Avtar Jouhl announced: 'We will not sit back, we will hit back.'[35] In some workplaces, black and Asian workers' confidence in their strength was such that they could be magnanimous in dealing with racists. In Bradford, Asian bus workers supported an NF member's appeal against unfair dismissal after he'd been convicted for his part in smashing windows at the local Community Relations Office. The appeal was successful and the man left the NF.[36]

For many black and Asian people, alongside racism in the workplace, where they lived and where they socialised, the worst experiences of racism they encountered came from the police. Afro-Caribbean youth in particular were regularly stopped by police using the Sus Law to search them claiming they were suspected of committing a criminal act. Growing up in the 1970s in Edgbaston in Birmingham, Benjamin Zephaniah remembers 'being beaten up and chased by the National Front and going to report it at the police station. The police officer went to his jacket and pulled out his National Front card.'[37]

Mounting anger on Bonfire night 1975 in Chapeltown, Leeds led to running street battles with hundreds of black youths throwing stones and setting fire to police vehicles.[38]

Prepared to teach black youth a lesson, the first morning of the 150,000-strong 1976 Notting Hill carnival saw the area 'saturated by uniformed and belligerent policemen'.[39] Darcus

Howe remembers how, after leaving their vans and coaches: 'They stampede in the direction of scuffles. I distinctly hear a police officer say to another beside him, "This is where it starts".'[40]

A six-hour street battle followed with police unable to stop those who fought back. Scores were injured as stone throwing teenagers broke police lines. Inspired by the uprising of black school students in South Africa two months earlier, many chanted 'Soweto, Soweto', the name of the giant black township where the revolt was centred.[41]

It was inevitable that the NF slogan 'If they're black, send them back' would lead to racist attacks. What was the answer to the threats that black communities faced? While every party of the left agreed that fascism should be opposed, there was no agreement on how. Benjamin Zephaniah's reaction to being beaten up by the NF was to learn boxing and kung fu: 'If we did nothing we would be killed on the streets.'[42]

The Labour Party and TUC

The Labour government saw things differently. With hundreds of thousands of members, and hundreds of MPs, it prioritised getting the millions of votes needed to win elections.[43] If keeping promises cost votes, then the promise would have to be sacrificed. Labour in opposition had condemned the 1962 immigration restrictions as racist and promised to repeal them but refused to do so when it won the 1964 election. Its prime concern was to keep the support of voters who backed immigration controls. But such concessions to racism, including the restrictions on immigration in the 1965 and 1968 Acts, opened the door for Powell and the 'numbers game', the idea that only a limited number of immigrants could be 'accommodated'.

Leading figures in the Labour and trade union movement used racism openly. Bill Carron, president of the million-strong Amalgamated Engineering Union (AEU), soon to be made a member of the House of Lords, used his retirement speech to attack immigrants:

> It would be interesting to obtain detailed statistics applying to the grand total that is consumed by educational grants, National Health and subsistence payments that become

immediately obtainable by the ever-growing number of individuals who were not born in the country and who in no way contributed towards setting up a fund into which they so willingly dip their fingers.[44]

William Jarvis, Labour chairman of the West Midlands County Council and trades council president, put the argument even more sharply after the Tories performed well in council elections in Birmingham: 'Black immigrants come and are dependent on the "treacle stick", the social security, for keeping alive. We need to call a halt to immigration to give us time to review the situation and see where we are going wrong.'[45]

Feeling his position as full-time secretary of the Manchester branch of the print union SOGAT was being threatened by the popularity among white rank-and-file colleagues of the black union activist Beresford Edwards, Joe Sheridan collaborated with Edwards's employer to get him sacked. With support of a handful of rank-and-file members of the union, Edwards fought the case through the courts for over three years, winning an award of just under £8,000. He later recounted how the union had spent 'nearly £25,000 at that time to fight me, one stupid little black man. It just shows the hate... and the kind of racist behaviour of even the executives of the so-called people that were supposed to represent you'.[46]

Balwinder Rana remembers that, until he became active politically in 1974:

> I had never really come across a white person who really believed there was racism in this country... A couple of Labour Party activists... said that, if I joined them, I could become the first Asian councillor in the country. But when I talked to them about the racists, they said, 'Don't worry! When they call you names, they don't really mean it.'[47]

The inability of the Labour Party to deal with the fascist threat was rooted in the idea that fascism had been defeated in the Second World War by an all-party coalition government led by a Conservative prime minister, Winston Churchill. The Labour-supporting *Daily Herald* had been opposed to confronting Mosley's supporters at Cable Street in 1936, with an editorial quoting George Lansbury, the East London Labour MP: 'I advise people to keep away from the Fascist demonstration in the East End. That is sound advice by Mr Lansbury.'⁴⁸ Roy Jenkins, Labour home secretary, argued for the same approach towards the National Front:

> In my experience, the technique of the National Front is to operate close to the borders of the law in a provocative way and to hope that those it has provoked will themselves indulge in violence and break the law. I believe that the National Front would be a much less effective organisation if those who are against it would proclaim peacefully, by speech, their detestations of its views and not fall into the trap of behaving on the ground just as the National Front would like.⁴⁹

The Labour Left

Despite the party's right wing controlling every Labour government, the Labour left had thousands of supporters and a thirty-strong Tribune group of MPs with a weekly paper *Tribune*. Many Labour Party members supported local anti-racist campaigns such as Action Against Racism (AAR) in Blackburn, although the local Labour Party branch never affiliated. George Davies recalls how Barbara Castle, the local MP, deliberately avoided committing herself as he unsuccessfully chased her around the Town Hall trying to get her to pay the £5 AAR subscription.⁵⁰ Pia Feig remembers how the Wolverhampton Labour MP Renée Short's silence on racism and the local Labour Party's refusal to make a public stand were key reasons for setting up the Wolverhampton Anti-Racist Committee.⁵¹

The Labour left focused its activities on orderly demonstrations together with public meetings, parliamentary lobbies and letter writing campaigns. Most were opposed to any physical confrontation which could lead to battles with the police. A few disagreed. Inspired by the defence of Madrid following General Franco's coup against the Spanish Republic in 1936, they adopted the slogan 'No Pasaran' (They shall not pass), using it at the Battle of Cable Street that stopped Mosley and his Blackshirts from marching through London's East End.

Communist Party

With over 20,000 members and producing the labour movement's only daily paper, the *Morning Star,* the Communist Party was the largest organisation to the left of the Labour Party and had considerable influence among left officials and activists in the Labour Party and the trade unions. The party had played a decisive role against Mosley after Hitler took power. In 1933 a small CP branch led a large number of National Unemployed Workers Movement (NUWM) members to prevent Mosley establishing the BUF in the Northeast at the Battle of Stockton in County Durham[52] and it was other CP branches that led confrontations in Manchester, Sheffield and elsewhere, and it was CP members who organised the mass heckling that reduced Mosley's 10,000-strong rally in London to a circus.[53]

However, the CP was pulled by orders from Stalin. With Germany rapidly rearming pre-Second World War, Stalin ordered Communist parties to assist with building an alliance with France and Britain. Anti-imperialist solidarity campaigns with those fighting colonialism, such as the support campaign for trade unionists on trial for conspiracy in Meerut, India, were no longer seen as the way forward.[54] The priority now was to build a Popular Front, including not only the Labour Party but also organisations outside the working class movement, to support an alliance with Russia.[55] This meant the Communist Party in the UK acted less and less 'from below' against fascism,[56] and its growing commitment to 'respectability' meant confrontation with the BUF ceased[57] – in July 1939, Mosley was able to speak uninterrupted for two hours to 20,000 supporters in London's Olympia exhibition hall.[58] When the Mosleyites re-emerged after 1945, it was not the Communist Party but the small 43 Group of anti-fascists, mainly Jewish ex-servicemen and some members of the CP, who led the fight.[59]

The party's post-war programme, spelt out in the CP pamphlet *The British Road to Socialism*, placed it in the tradition of fighting for democracy as far back as the 1381 Peasants Revolt and argued for a parliamentary socialist government based on an alliance of Labour and Communist MPs. It saw the same alliance leading the fight against fascism.[60] By the 1970s, the CP leadership, and most of its members, were against direct confrontation with fascists as these could lead to showdowns with the police, associating the left with violence.[61] The solution was to get fascist marches banned.[62]

The CP's commitment to non-confrontation remained unchanged when the NF announced a demonstration in Leicester, in August 1974. Timed to be held in the middle of the Imperial Typewriters strike, the demonstration was to assemble outside the factory and march through Highfields, an area with a high immigrant population. Webster told the press: 'The demonstration will be to show solidarity with the workers at the factory. We want to bring to public attention the tie-up between the extreme left and international capitalism. Everybody else is terrified of the racialist tag but we are not.'[63]

The Inter-Racial Solidarity Campaign (IRSC), led by the Communist Party and supported by the Indian Workers Association, the trades council, union and Labour Party branches, students, churches, Young Muslims and a Sikh temple, called for the march to be banned.[64] The Anti-Fascist Committee, based in the university and working with union and Labour Party branches, called for people to oppose the march, physically if necessary.[65] When it became clear the march would not be banned, the IRSC called for a counter-demonstration, not 'to have a confrontation with the police but to show the solidarity of the opposition to the National Front'.[66] The Anti-Fascist Committee and others were determined, if needs be physically, to stop the march. Writing in *Socialist Worker*, Paul Foot, a leading member of the International Socialists, argued: 'Their marches and their meetings must be stopped ... They cannot be allowed to spread their poison as though it were the bromide of run-of-the-mill party politicians ... THEY SHALL NOT PASS!'[67]

On the day, protected by large numbers of police, the NF had 600 supporters ready to march. With the prospect of thousands on the streets trying to stop the march taking place, the police persuaded the NF to abandon its starting point outside the factory. Despite 'an almost constant barrage of heckling and abuse',[68] the counter-demonstration passed without incident with around 5,000 marching past the factory.[69] It was clear that anti-fascists could successfully confront the fascists with sufficient numbers to stop them from marching wherever they wanted.

There were still CP members drawing on anti-fascist traditions from the early 1930s who identified with this.[70] The week after an NF march in Blackburn, January 1973, the CP dominated Manchester AUEW district committee resolved to: 'Call very quickly a meeting of all Labour and Trade Union Movement and anti-fascist organisations to a meeting to consider Trade Union and Labour Movement activity should the National Front organise similar demonstrations in the Greater Manchester area in the future.'[71]

A week later the union district secretary reported 'a number of organisations at the meeting facilitated by the District Committee' setting up an ad hoc committee, that 'the National Front were going to hold an indoor meeting' in Manchester the following Saturday and that he had written to the organisations involved 'with the suggestion that a mass picket be called'. Five hundred anti-fascists blocked the entrance to the meeting.[72] A fortnight later, a public meeting with speakers from the Labour Party, CP, IS, International Marxist Group (IMG) and the Black Unity and Freedom Party (BUFP) was held in the same hall.[73]

International Socialists[74]

One of the organisations represented at the Leicester anti-NF demonstration, the mass picket of the Manchester NF meeting and the anti-fascist meeting that followed was the International Socialists (IS), a revolutionary socialist group with a few thousand members. The IS argued consistently against relying on the state to ban fascist marches:

Peaceful pickets, pious resolutions, rational arguments alone, will not prevent fascist movements from dominating the street and growing... There is only one way to stop a fascist movement in its tracks. Its adherents have to be driven physically from the streets. Fascist movements disintegrate when they can no longer march and threaten those they hate: there is little else to bind them together.[75]

The IS drew its analysis of the fascist movement and how to stop it from Trotsky's writings on fighting the rise of fascism in Germany between 1930 and 1934.[76] Of all the major industrial powers at the time, Germany was the hardest hit by the economic depression brought on by the 1929 financial crash. Unemployment soared, reaching 6 million by 1932 and the Nazis gained mass support. Almost a lone voice, exiled to Turkey by Stalin, Trotsky argued that the fascist threat needed to be recognised: 'If the Communist Party is the *party of revolutionary hope*, then fascism, as a mass movement, is the *party of counterrevolutionary despair*... Fascism in Germany has become a real danger.'[77] Trotsky insisted that a united front between the Communist Party (KPD) and Social Democrats (SPD) was a matter of urgency. He recognised the fascist threat could only be stopped by building as large a movement as possible within the organised working class. Even with time running out, it could be done. He wrote:

> It is a difficult task to arouse all at once the majority of the German working class for an offensive... But, on the other hand, the organisational solidarity of the German workers, which has almost altogether prevented until now the penetration of fascism into their ranks, opens the very greatest possibilities of defensive struggle. One must bear in mind that the policy of the united front is in general much more effective for the defensive than the offensive.[78]

The united front tactic had been proved in practice. The Bolsheviks, who had led the movement that toppled the tsarist regime in the February 1917 Russian Revolution, used the tactic in August 1917 to unite the working-class movement in defence of the revolution against a counter-revolutionary move by the Russian army. The leader of the coup, General Kornilov, was moving troops towards Petrograd, Russia's capital, in an attempt to oust the Provisional Government, a coalition of socialist parties that had replaced the Tsar. The Bolsheviks were sharply critical of the Government. Only a few weeks earlier it had accused them of being German agents and put many of their leaders, including Trotsky, in jail. But to defend the more progressive government from the reactionary army, they proposed that the socialist parties join in action. Members of all the parties formed the Military Revolutionary Committee to arm the workers, bringing together 40,000 Red Guard. In the event, rail workers managed to misdirect Kornilov's troops and Kornilov's coup collapsed without a shot being fired.

Trotsky recognised that it was this level of unity that was needed to defend the German working class from the fascist threat. With over 100,000 members in 1931, the KPD was well placed to launch such a defence.[79] Instead, the KPD's leadership, as did the leadership of the British CP, followed Stalin, whose focus was national alliances rather than working-class unity. The KPD denounced the SPD leadership as 'social fascist' and destroyed any possibility of a united front.[80] They made matters even worse by downplaying the fascist threat with the catastrophically overconfident slogan 'After Hitler, us'.

The failure to bring together what was at the time the best organised working class in the world into a defensive front of Communists and Social Democrats left the Nazis' route to power unobstructed. Stalin's ultra sectarian policy only changed when the enormity of the defeat became clear. But rather than seeing opposition to fascism as a working-class project, he now sought alliances with France and Britain, the two powers capable of militarily resisting Germany.[81] The new policy, uniting with those ruling classes threatened by Hitler, came to be known as the Popular Front. It meant abandoning the mass mobilisation needed to defeat the fascists to keep more respectable establishment allies on board.

The catastrophic defeat of the German working-class movement was avoidable. The failure to unite the opposition to Hitler left the road open for the Nazis to march to power. Hitler himself acknowledged what could have prevented their rise. At the Nazi Party's 1933 congress he crowed: 'Only one thing could have broken our movement – if the adversary had understood its principle and from the first day had smashed, with the most extreme brutality, the nucleus of our new movement.'[82]

Was it possible to apply the united front tactic to taking on the fascists in the very different circumstances of Britain in the 1970s? A by-election in Newham, May 1974, provided an opportunity for IS members in the docks to organise a united front of dockers 'banded together to put out leaflets attacking the Front and showing them up for what they are – a racialist menace'.[83] The Dockers Against the Nazis campaign was set up as a united front aiming to expose the NF as Nazi. It was launched with a snazzy 3-way fold-over leaflet (to fit more easily through letterboxes).

The front was a picture of Tyndall in Nazi uniform with the headline 'Is This Your Next MP?'. Inside was the straight 'NF is a Nazi Front' fact sheet, playing on the connections between Nazis, the Blitz and the destruction of the East End.[84]

The NF put up a strong candidate, Michael Lobb, a member of the NF Directorate, an ex-Marxist, ex-Labour Party supporter. He claimed there were sixteen NF members at the local Tate & Lyle plant and 300 across Newham, two thirds of them trade unionists. He had run 'a well-managed campaign' against mass redundancies at Tate & Lyle as a result of EEC policy on sugar beet.[85] Reacting with fury to the dockers' leaflet, he got the local paper, the *Newham Recorder*, to support him with a front-page article, headlined 'Nazi smear sparks poll storm', which reported on thousands of leaflets being distributed. The front-page editorial, 'Cowardly attack is pure bigotry', backed Lobb against 'the cowardly attacks and smears on the National Front'.[86]

Disappointed with 11.5 percent of the vote, although beating the Conservative candidate into fourth place, he had a bitter row with Webster, gave up as candidate and resigned from the Directorate.[87] Lobb was not alone in wanting rid of the Nazi tag. Efforts to use the courts to stop hostile election leaflets dragged on without success. Lobb left the NF a few months later after eight million TV viewers saw Tyndall and Webster's Nazi past detailed on the current affairs programme *This Week*.[88]

'No Platform'

With students being an important part of the anti-fascist movement, winning their support and the backing of student unions, was important. The focus nationally was getting the National Union of Students (NUS) to support 'no platform' for fascists, so that no fascist should address a meeting or have any other public platform. After a fiercely argued debate at its 1974 Easter conference, the NUS voted by a small majority to deny 'openly racist and fascist' organisations a platform, stopping them from meeting on campus 'by any means necessary'. The NUS national secretary, Steve Parry, called for mass action, referring to the mass resistance that stopped Oswald Mosley and his British Union of Fascists marching through the Jewish areas of East London and asking: 'Did reasoned argument stop the fascists led by Mosley in the East End?'. He received 'the most sustained ovation of conference'.[89] After many attacks in the press, the NUS executive replied that it would not restrict the activities of the Conservative Party, but, giving Powell as an example, it declared: 'If denying platforms to the apostles of racial hatred was limiting freedom of speech then the NUS pleads guilty'.

The 'No Platform' policy applied only when the violence that lay at the heart of fascism was a clear threat. Powell's speeches, for example, regularly led to attacks on black people. But when students at the London School of Economics prevented the racist psychologist Hans Eysenck from giving a lecture, IS students argued this had been a mistake:

> To debate with Eysenck, to treat him as a genuine scientist, is to indirectly legitimise Powellism. This is not to say that we should go out to break up meetings which he addresses – the real threat lies in organised fascist groups – but rather that we should picket them and organise counter-meetings in order to show up the real nature of his ideas.[90]

Red Lion Square: 15 June 1974

With their confidence boosted by the general and local election results, the NF announced a march and rally in Conway Hall, Red Lion Square, central London.[91] It was certain to be confronted as it was now clear that no NF march would go unchallenged. In the absence of any national anti-fascist organisation or united front initiative, it was the anti-colonial organisation Liberation that gave a lead.[92] It had played a prominent role opposing the 1962 Commonwealth Immigration Bill. Its best-known member, Fenner Brockway, now Lord Brockway, annually submitted a private members bill in parliament to make race discrimination illegal.[93] Liberation had recently published *Danger – Racialists at Work*, an anti-NF pamphlet by Tony Gilbert, a CP activist.[94] The pamphlet concluded: 'The task of preventing present day Fascists from becoming a force in some factories, on the streets or at the polls lies in the hands of the working class – only they can do it.'[95]

Liberation met with the police and agreed to a rally on the north side of the square and a small meeting in a room next to the NF's meeting room in Conway Hall that they had booked. This would avoid any contact with the NF, who were to meet on the south side of the square. On the day, five hundred NF supporters marched to Red Lion Square where they were halted by the police, who were fully prepared with both mounted police and the paramilitary Special Patrol Group (SPG).[96] The SPG was established in 1965 to 'respond to large-scale disorder, emergency or disorder at any location in the city'. Initially created to assist local police forces, it became a 'fire brigade' force brought in to occupy 'trouble spots' and to police strikes and demonstrations.[97]

Anti-fascists, numbering 1,500, were directed by the police to the north side of Red Lion Square. When those determined to confront the NF approached the hall they were stopped by police, some on horseback.[98] Without warning, members of the SPG aggressively tried to force them back, 'cutting through the demonstrators like a knife through butter'.[99] The police violently attacked the anti-fascists who were barracking the NF, aggressively pursuing those who tried to get away and making more than fifty arrests.[100] In the chaos, one of the marchers, Kevin Gately, a student from Warwick University, was killed by a blow to the head from a police truncheon.

Shocked by Kevin Gately's death, 500 Warwick students marched silently in Coventry behind the banner 'Kevin Gately was killed opposing racism and fascism', and the next day, the NUS led 8,000 on a silent demonstration in London.[101] The IS argued that it was not enough to mourn Kevin Gately's death, it was necessary to say why he died and how such murders can be prevented. The IS placards on the demonstration featured a photo of Gately's body being dragged away by the police, stated 'Murdered by the police' and called for the SPG to be disbanded. Hostile to anyone carrying placards, the NUS executive insisted the IS contingent march separately at the back of the demonstration. But the position taken by IS triggered a visit to their London office by Commander Habershon, head of Scotland Yard's bomb squad (later the anti-terrorist squad), who cautioned the editor and publisher of their paper *Socialist Worker* for possible criminal libel, arguing that the poster implied the police officer pictured was the actual killer. They were told that the paper must produce evidence of the killing or 'shut up'. Jim Nichol, the IS national secretary, and Paul Foot, the editor, pointed out that any evidence would only be given to an independent inquiry, not one where the police investigated the police.[102]

The official public inquiry into Kevin Gately's death headed by Lord Justice Scarman met in the autumn. The NUS presented a report, written by the Warwick University Students Union, detailing how Kevin Gately died as 'a direct result of a police attack using batons and horses against an exposed line of demonstrators who had their arms linked together'.[103] While recognising that the Race Relations Act was ineffective and needed 'radical amendment', Scarman's report whitewashed the role of the police and blamed the demonstrators for the violence and Kevin Gately's death.[104] Tony Gilbert wrote a pamphlet, *Only One Died*, detailing much of the evidence given to the Scarman Inquiry. He blamed the Trotskyist International Marxist Group (IMG) for making it easy for the media to blame the left for Kevin Gately's death. The IMG had intended to form a picket to prevent the NF holding their meeting and 'dar[ing] the police to remove them'. This, argues Gilbert, allowed the police lawyers to hold the IMG 'responsible for every incident that followed'.[105] Clearly those anti-fascists who were determined to stop the fascists needed to be better organised when faced by large numbers of police prepared to use extreme force. There could be no doubting the police's determination to ensure the NF's freedom of speech.[106]

'Best conservative prime minister Britain could get'

With unemployment nearing 1.5 million, young people in particular wondered what the future held for them as the post-war commitment to full employment was abandoned. Prices rising, 16 percent in 1976, meant working class living standards fell for the first time in forty years. Health, education and welfare budgets were being cut with public spending set to fall by nearly 10 percent. Britain's leading business magazine, *The Economist*, called James Callaghan, the Labour prime minister, 'the best conservative prime minister Britain could get'.[107] He owed this tribute to Labour's austerity programme, the so-called Social Contract that limited pay rises to well below inflation and, most importantly, ensured the agreement of the union leadership to support these measures.[108] Callaghan's experience as a national trade union official – he was the only cabinet member with such a background – was invaluable in getting this backing.[109]

The TUC was now key to making sure that real wages fell, and so too the number of strikes and workers involved. Committed to supporting the Labour government, union leaders' support for strike breaking undermined the shop floor militancy that had defeated the previous Heath government: 1974 saw 13 million strike days, 1975 had 8 million, but by 1976 it had dropped to 3 million. A key role was played by Hugh Scanlon and Jack Jones, the two best known left-wing trade union leaders. Both called on workers to cross picket lines in strikes that threatened to breach the Social Contract's pay limits.[110] The end of the post-war boom, the attacks on working class living standards and the failure to successfully resist these attacks demoralised many rank-and-file militants. At the same time, it created huge opportunities for fascists.

Its internal faction fight over, the NF's potential as an electoral threat became clear.[111] Labour Party officials listed twenty-one parliamentary seats that could be lost to the Tories with Labour voters switching to the NF.[112] Nearly half of the NF's 160 candidates in May 1976 had got 10 percent or more of the vote.[113] The Rotherham by-election in June 1976 showed the danger even where the NF had no branch. In less than two months, using letters in the local paper, public meetings, a poster campaign and a thousand-strong demonstration, they got 6 percent of the vote, a total of 1,700 votes, just 500 behind the Liberals.[114] In a council by-election in Deptford, East London, the Labour candidate won 43 percent of the vote, while the combined total for the NF and its rival National Party was 44 percent.[115]

In a parliamentary by-election in the almost completely safe Labour seat of Thurrock, outer East London, Robert Relf, notorious for placing a sign with 'For Sale – to an English family' outside his house, marched at the front of the NF's demonstration. Arguing the government was too weak to stop the arrival of Asians holding British passports when Uganda decided 'to unload them on Britain'.[116] the NF won 3,255 votes, 6.5 percent.[117] Now regularly beating the Liberals into fourth place in local council by-elections, they did even better a few months later in the Walsall by-election, coming third with over 7 percent, double the Liberal vote – the first time they had so decisively beaten the Liberals. Their presence was constantly reinforced with street sales, fresh graffiti and stickers. They had around 170 branches, including a new one in Rotherham, members in more than a hundred schools and a National Front Students Association.[118] Boosted by Labour's continuing attacks on working-class living standards, Webster now announced the NF would have 318 candidates in the next general election, to give them equal television time with the three big parties.[119]

NF resurgent: Bradford, 'St George's Day' April 1976

With hundreds of new recruits and dozens of new branches, as well as keeping most of the membership from before the split, Tyndall and Webster were confidently focused on making the NF Britain's third largest party.[120] Looking for publicity in the run up to the 1976 May local elections, they followed their usual approach of 'kicking their way into the headlines' with a march and rally in an area with a large black population.[121]

They chose Bradford, a northern textile city in serious economic decline where they had twenty-two candidates covering every ward in the city. The best known was Jim Merrick, who, inspired by Enoch Powell, had set up the Yorkshire Campaign to Stop Immigration, soon renamed as the British Campaign to Stop Immigration'.[122] An able publicist, Merrick had recently got the campaign on national television on the BBC's *Open Door* programme.[123]

NF members in Bradford had a record of attacking Asian workers, assaulting mixed heritage couples, trashing a Labour Party Christmas bazaar and setting the Trades Council's banner on fire. As efforts failed to get the NF's planned Bradford march banned, an 'ad hoc' committee, led by the Trades Council, organised a counter demonstration, plastering the city with posters in Urdu, English, Gujarati and Punjabi.[124]

A thousand NF supporters assembled behind a cluster of Union Jacks. With a loudspeaker van playing 'Land of Hope and Glory', they set off to a rally in a school in Manningham, the main black and Asian area of the city.[125] Brushing aside a handful of anti-fascists, they set off behind a Highland pipe band chanting

'Send them back, send them back'.[126] There were 'heavy mobs at front and rear... in the middle were largely ordinary-looking people – although some of them, with faces contorted with hatred, shouted a lot of abuse about n*****s and red scum'.[127]

At this point political differences on how to oppose the fascists became very clear. As the march led by the Trades Council set off from Manningham towards the city centre, supporters of the newly established Manningham Defence Committee, mainly young and white, committed to nonviolent direct action (NVDA) prepared to sit down and block the NF route to Manningham.[128] A group of around 200, including a contingent from the International Socialists, harried the NF march, trying to stop it. As these two groups came together to block the road, mounted police charged, cavalry-style, to clear a way through.[129] A large group of black teenagers were outside the school pulling police crush barriers onto the road to stop the horses.[130] The NF were now diverted up an alley to get into the school, defended by several hundred police.[131]

Fazal Mehmood was at the front of the Trades Council march as it neared the city centre when people heard what was happening in Manningham. He remembers the march stopped and a man spoke out asking: 'Why are we going on here when the fascists are back there?', at which point half the march made their way back to Manningham.[132] Outside the school, young West Indians and Asians threw anything they could at the police line protecting the NF. IS member Megan Povey remembers 'the rain of bricks and stones and god knows what that flew over our heads and into the Nazis [as] we acted as a physical barrier preventing the police from reaching the defenders of Manningham'.[133] Struggling to assert control, the police charged, clearing the road, only to be forced to take shelter as the crowd threw more stones, breaking the windows of a police car and van which some ran forward to turn over. Roger Keely remembers the 'reckless courage of some of the youth, many of whom were white'.[134] Only after the stone throwing ended could the police escort the NF back to their buses to a chorus of 'Let's go back, who'll drive their buses? Let's go back, who'll sweep their streets? Let's go back, who'll empty their dustbins?'.[135]

The different tactics used to challenge the fascists showed

the growing divide in Asian communities between the older generation whose leadership had largely adapted to the status quo and a younger generation, many born in Britain, frustrated at the passivity of their elders. Tariq Mehmood, a young Asian living in Manningham, saw the fascists:

> as coming to wipe us out, kick us out of our streets … and we weren't going to have it … The big anti-fascist march, led by the leaders of that time, ended in the city centre… Lots of us lived in Manningham, we marched to Manningham … sneaked past police lines because Manningham was ours and we had to protect it.[136]

The very different approach adopted by the Manningham Defence Committee, committed to nonviolent direct action, could nevertheless be effective. When the NF organised a motor cavalcade through the city a few days after their march, the Defence Committee countered with a seventy-strong sit down on a main road, forcing the NF to abandon their plan.[137] It was less successful as a strategy to build the movement when, a month later, the Committee organised a 'Carnival sit-down against the National Front… an act of mass civil disobedience' with half a dozen giant puppets, many of those taking part 'dressed as court jesters, carrying a giant teddy bear', 'a teddy bear's picnic'.[138] Aiming to show it was possible to have 'fun and be positive and be peaceful and not have to wait to respond', they sat down on a main road, after the police stopped them from occupying the city's main square, where 130 offered passive resistance before being picked up and arrested.[139] Despite their willingness to directly challenge the police, they looked to the state to deal with racism and fascism. The giant banner they carried on the march read 'Enforce the Race Relations Act, Ban the National Front'. The Carnival sit-down was not repeated after the courts fined all those arrested £25, more than half the average weekly wage for women, more than a third of the average weekly wage for men.[140]

The counter demonstrations in Bradford did not stop the NF's twenty-two candidates polling well in the May elections.[141] Enoch Powell seized the moment to make a speech highlighting a leaked government report suggesting there was 'a bottomless pool' of immigrants awaiting entry into Britain.[142] When Asian refugees, expelled from Malawi, arrived in Britain, the *Sun* ran the headline: 'Scandal of £600 a week immigrants in luxury hotels' and the *Daily Telegraph* proclaimed: 'Migrants here just for welfare handouts'.[143] There was no let up. The *Daily Express* claimed that Home Secretary Roy Jenkins had ordered immigration officers at Heathrow to admit immigrants with bogus papers.[144] Surrendering to this racism, the government chief whip, Bob Mellish, told the press: 'This nation has done all it should have done. Its record is one of great honour and integrity, but I say "enough is enough".'[145]

Such concessions made it easy for the fascists to win support. Despite needing hundreds of police to protect their pre-election march and meeting, the National Front won over 9,000 votes in Bradford, nearly 11 percent of the vote, and could now claim to be the third party in the city. A quarter of all white voters in Leicester voted NF.[146] In Blackburn, greatly helped by favourable publicity from the local paper, the *Lancashire Evening Telegraph*, Kingsley Read, National Party leader and another NP member, won council seats. A third member was eleven votes short of getting elected.

Roy Jenkins had recently argued in parliament that: 'It is in the interests of the racial minorities themselves to maintain a strict control over immigration'.[147] He had a junior minister in his department, Alex Lyon, sacked because of his soft interpretation of immigration laws.[148] In practice, Jenkins's support for immigration controls meant that black people in Britain were being presented as the problem. The Labour leadership was not only using racism to make workers' pay for the crisis – they were scared that opposing racism would cost them votes. They remembered how Peter Griffiths had used racism to win for the Tories a decade earlier.

By contrast, the IS insisted that the fight against racism required a clear rejection of immigration controls. 'They're welcome here' was the headline on *Socialist Worker*'s front page and a much reprinted leaflet responding to the arrival of Asians from Malawi.[149] It also required an organised challenge to the NF slogan, 'British Jobs for British workers':[150] 'The appeal of the racialist propaganda is... a direct result of the failure of the official leadership to give any lead on the basic problems facing workers.

The demoralisation resulting from this gives the racialists a clear field.'[151]

The racists' arguments had to be met with an organised working-class response that gave a clear alternative to the 'Stop immigration. Start repatriation' argument pushed by Powell and the NF. The Right to Work Campaign (RtWC) was launched in October 1975 'to organise the unemployed [as] part of the trade union movement'.[152] It gave the unemployed a voice, basing itself 'on direct action as well as on propaganda', using the tactics of the rank-and-file trade union movement of the late 1960s and early 1970s, such as flying pickets and workplace occupations. RtWC marchers would invade workplaces threatened by redundancies. It was an IS initiative, based on the supporters of the rank-and-file trade union papers in a number of industries drawing in as many trade unionists as possible, financed through sponsorship by hundreds of trade union branches, shop stewards' committees, trades councils and student unions. Ernie Roberts was the campaign's national treasurer. A rally of over 5,000 in the Albert Hall welcomed the eighty unemployed on the RtWC march from Manchester to London.[153]

Nowhere did the racists have a higher profile than in Blackburn, where Kingsley Read, the National Party leader, was given regular air time by local BBC radio 'to come out with the most vicious racism... very rarely challenged by the presenter'.[154] The NP also drew strength from the *Lancashire Evening Telegraph*'s hostility to immigrants and the Labour council's surrender to Kingsley Read's campaign against a new mosque. Racism was now respectable.[155] When the National Party held a demonstration celebrating their success, bystanders clapped and cheered as marchers shouted, 'We are the English' and 'If they're black, send them back'. Counter demonstrators, organised by the newly established Action Against Racism (AAR) campaign, faced missiles and screams of abuse.[156] Alan Gibbons remembers: An old lady came up and swung her handbag, trying to hit me, saying "You leave our boys alone". We felt shaken. I remember turning to a friend and saying "This feels like a small town in Germany in 1928".'[157]

Southall

As 'sudden waves of racial tension... swept Britain' in May 1976, two students, Dinesh Choudhri from India and Ribhi Alhadidi from Jordan, were fatally stabbed by white youths while making their way to an East London restaurant.[158] A fortnight later, a young engineering student, Gurdip Singh Chaggar, was murdered by two white teenagers in Southall, West London. Sick of racist and police violence and of their elders' passivity towards it, Southall's young Asians came out en masse. Some demanded 'Blood for blood', attacking white passers-by and stoning cars. When police made arrests among those leaving a meeting in the giant Dominion cinema, a centre of the local South Asian community, hundreds marched without hesitation to the police station and sat down. Surrounded by a sea of protesters, the police got community leaders to pressure those arrested to come out of the police station with the promise that they wouldn't be charged. It was a lie. For Balraj Purewal, the moment this was exposed was 'the moment the Southall Youth Movement (SYM) was formed'.[159]

The elders still dominated the community. When a week later, 6,000 marched in Southall together with church leaders, the elders put themselves at the front, their banners and placards declaring 'Let sanity prevail', 'Cooperation not conflict' and 'Heal the wounds'.[160] Young Asians marched at the back, together with hundreds of white trade unionists and socialists, their slogans, 'Adolf Powell is a murderer', 'We mourn in peace for how long?', 'We will beat up racialist thugs', 'End immigration controls' and 'We are here to stay'.[161] Rallying in a car park, 2,500 heard twenty-two-year-old Harpal Singh Gill ask: 'Where is the leadership? Let's take control. Let's prove something.'[162]

Self-defence was the priority for the SYM. Rejecting the IWA's call for more police patrols, the SYM organised their own, accompanying people to and from school and work, especially for night shifts. The elders' close relationship with the local Labour Party, helping to get the vote out at election time, led to the SYM's demand 'No politics!'.[163] But there was no agreed set of demands and direct action was the method, for example, demonstrating in front of cinemas, forcing them to reduce their prices.[164] A committee was elected with reps in colleges and workplaces with regular meetings in a squatted building.[165] On a march against racism through central London in early July called by Southall IWA, the SYM insisted on taking the lead. A week later, 10,000 marched to Downing Street. When two SYM members were arrested 'for chasing racists on the pavements'; a mass sit-down in Piccadilly Circus forced the police to free them immediately.[166]

Responding to the rise in racism, the fascist provocations and, above all, the murders, the anti-racist movement was growing across Britain. Robert Relf provoked a demonstration when he declared a hunger strike while in jail for refusing to remove the racist 'For sale' sign outside his house.[167] A counter demonstration quickly assembled in nearby Handsworth, a working-class area with the largest black population in Birmingham. Doubling in size to 2,000 on its way to the prison, the marchers were met by lines of police protecting the NF. Bricks and stones flew when mounted police charged with their batons and tried to kettle the marchers.[168] Relf's notice had been taken from his house in Leamington Spa and brought to Southall, providing the opportunity for 750 to march on a joint demonstration in Southall of IS and Asian youth to where Gurdip Singh Chaggar was killed and to set the notice on fire.[169]

Going on the offensive

Suddenly there was a new inspiration for all anti-racists as black youth took to the streets 5,000 miles away in apartheid South Africa. Thousands of black school students in the Soweto township near Johannesburg rose against the apartheid government's decision to impose Afrikaans – the language of the dominant white minority – as the language of instruction. Between ten and twenty thousand students were marching to a rally when the police opened fire. Twenty-three died. Over the next three days at least 176 were killed. The uprising had an electrifying effect. For Rehad Desai, son of South African exiles, at school in London, 'Soweto made a massive impression on me. I decided I've got to do something'.[170] Ramila Patel, at college in Bolton, remembers: 'We in the AYO [Asian Youth Organistion] spoke about how South African youth were organised, so why couldn't we follow too?'.[171]

In Gravesend, Balwinder Rana was working with friends to get people together to confront NF paper sellers who the police insisted had a right to sell papers. July and August 1976 saw six Saturdays of running battles, the police always defending the NF. On the sixth Saturday, the NF attacked the president of the Gurdwara, the leader of the Sikh community, pushing him through a plate glass window as he walked along the street. The news he was badly injured: 'Spread like wildfire. We called everyone to the town centre... There were about six hundred of us facing forty NF... In the ensuing battle many NF were injured as they ran for their lives.'[172]

In Bolton, after weekly confrontations between *Socialist Worker* sellers and the NF, 200 anti-fascists, including Bolton AYO members, mobilised to stop the twenty fascists selling their papers. A hundred police defended the fascists as a special snatch squad charged into the anti-fascist crowd, making selective arrests.[173] Local AYO activist Pravin Parmar told *Socialist Worker*:

> The AYO means there's solidarity across the whole black community for the first time. Before there were rows between Indians and Pakistanis, Hindus and Muslims. Now we've got everyone together. There's solidarity among all of us. The AYO here has over 1,000 members. And it's wider than that. When the police arrested five AYO members and two members of the International Socialists, we had a joint demonstration outside the police station. Three or four hundred whites and blacks shouting together. They released everyone there and then instead of holding them overnight.[174]

For the older generation, challenging the fascists meant letters, lobbying and meetings, some small and some large. In Hackney, for example, 250 attended the first meeting of the local Community Relations Council.[175] For the young, it was on the streets. Jaswant Hunjan, member of the SYM, recalls that this was not new. There had always been self-defence: 'We formed a gang. We went skinhead bashing. Stood round corners with bottles and bricks'.[176] In Blackburn, young Asians had already organised themselves as 'The Warriors', fighting inside and outside schools.[177] The NP march and counter demonstration in

Blackburn 'led to the creation of the Asian Youth Organisation'.[178] It was not 'vigilante groups... Just getting together... to ensure the black workers coming home from the two-to-ten shift were not attacked'.[179] A leading member, Mohammed Ali Dassu explained:

> We were frustrated with the attitudes of our elders, of the local right wing Indian Workers Association and all the rest. We thought the time was right to start organising ourselves and start working within the community and the unions. The election of two NP members [to the council] made the issue urgent. We weren't prepared to go into Action Against Racism around slogans of peace and 'One Race, The Human Race'. When the International Socialists challenged these slogans inside AAR they were thrown out. We wanted to make a stand so we formed the Asian Youth Organisation. The elders were very hostile and some of our members were beaten.[180]

Against the background of ongoing violence against the Asian community, when the NP marched again in Blackburn, they were outnumbered by 4,000 counter-marchers organised by Action Against Racism.[181] This was despite the local paper's 'Keep Away' banner headline a few days before, an appeal by Tory, Labour, Liberal and Ratepayer party chiefs to boycott the demonstration and pouring rain on the day.[182] The march ended with an indoor rally, speeches, street theatre and the Spinners folk group, and from where IS members and others including many Asian youth went on to lay siege to the NP rally.[183] Responding to the growing threat from the NF and NP, 1976 saw Asian youth in Southall, Brick Lane, Gravesend, Bolton and Blackburn emerge as an active, organised force, working with those elements of the left willing to confront the fascists, strengthening the solidarity within their communities.[184]

Working for the Wandsworth Community Relations Council, Labour Party candidate for the GLC, Greg Dyke's experience was very different: 'It struck me that the Labour Party hadn't even begun to discuss these issues.'[185] He wrote an article, 'Race: Can Labour make up the ground it lost by dodging the issue?', for *Tribune*, arguing:

> The danger is that the programme planned by the Labour Party starting today is too little, too late. It is ironic that it has taken the electoral success of racist parties to persuade the Labour Party at last to meet the issue of race head on. After more than a decade of compromise on the issue justified for electoral reasons, the party has ended up in the very situation it had sought to avoid.
>
> The success of the racist parties this spring and summer is easy to see. There has been an awareness within the Labour Party for many years that race is perhaps the only issue which could mobilise significant sections of the working-class Labour vote against the party. Even before the experience at Smethwick in the 1964 general election, race, as an election issue, was seen as a potential vote-loser for Labour.
>
> Labour's reaction to this situation, both within the party and the trade unions, has been to play down the whole issue. There has been no real attempt to educate Labour supporters about who are the immigrants, why they came, what difficulties they met or what contribution they have made to our society.
>
> Instead the party and the unions, with a few exceptions, have been content to sit quietly while a mass of stories and myths critical of immigrants have been allowed to perpetuate. It is only now, with the National Front becoming a real electoral threat that the party has been forced into action.
>
> The task now facing the Labour Party is enormous for, after more than a decade, the myths are widespread and deeply trenched. Anyone who has been canvassing, particularly in a multiracial area, will know the extent to which many of the stories about immigrants are believed.[186]

Three weeks later, Dyke wrote a second article pointing to the weakness of the campaign proposed by the Labour leadership:

> Both in the speakers' notes and in the pamphlet (price 10p) there is a phrase which is intended to reassure people that immigration controls are operating: 'Free entry to Britain is confined to holders of United Kingdom passports who are ALSO patrials,' says the pamphlet... The speakers' notes... say so little. It is difficult to imagine anyone who would

dare to speak at any meeting more political than a women's institute if their knowledge of race were restricted to the contents of these notes.[187]

The TUC General Council decided to join with the Labour Party campaign against racism and called a national demonstration in November 1976.[188] Circulating a report, 'The Facts of Racial Disadvantage', it urged unions to get their branches to campaign with local constituency Labour Parties.[189] The press release was clear about how cautious the campaign would be:

> Much needs to be done to eliminate the discrimination and disadvantage facing ethnic minorities and for their part the [TUC] General Council are advising affiliated unions about steps they should take to strengthen trade union organisation among immigrant and black workers and unity between work people.[190]

It went on to attack the National Front and its attempts to blame unemployment on black and Asian workers. For its part, the Labour Party, recognising that there had to be an end to 'the ostrich tactics on racism by the official labour movement', began their campaign with a party political broadcast that opened with a shot of Oswald Mosley in the East End in 1936 and NF activists marching in Bradford.[191] While showing some progress had been made, the campaign was 'half hearted' with the speakers' notes produced for the campaign making it clear that Labour would not repeal any immigration legislation.[192] Two months later, around 10,000 marched against racism from Hyde Park to Trafalgar Square on a joint TUC and Labour Party demonstration, a sharp contrast to the 80,000 who marched four days earlier on the TUC demonstration against government cuts.[193]

Anti-racism 'from below': strengths and weaknesses

Trying to fill the vacuum left by the official movement's failure to respond adequately, by the end of 1976 there were as many as 200 anti-racist and anti-fascist committees.[194] People from every organisation on the left were involved. In Tower Hamlets, together with others, the schoolteacher Chris Searle, well known for a successful strike by his pupils after he was sacked for publishing their poems, set up the Movement Against Racism and Fascism. In Tooting, South London, the local IS branch set up the Balham and Tooting Campaign Against Racism, organising street patrols in response to the rise in violence targeting the Asian and Afro Caribbean community.[195] Thirty Liberal Parties asked *Searchlight* to put them in touch with local anti-racist groups.[196] While collectively they organised thousands of anti-racists and anti-fascists, their wide variety of names reflected how widely they differed. Some had been set up by Communist Party members, which though in crisis and losing members, had a presence on many local committees.

The weakness of the anti-racist, anti-fascist movement had been brought out clearly a week after Gurdip Singh Chaggar was murdered. As thousands demonstrated in Southall, 800 National Party supporters were able to march unhindered in Newham, East London, chanting: 'If they're black, send them back, if they're white, they're all right'. At their rally, Kingsley Read described the murder of Gurdip Singh Chaggar 'as terribly unfortunate. One down, a million to go'.[197] Some marchers now broke away to attack a nearby demonstration against cuts and unemployment organised by the local West Ham Trades Council, throwing missiles and setting fire to a banner. Bob Light remembers it as a humiliating experience for the Trades Council and its supporters.[198]

The variety of different groups within the movement made co-ordination complicated.[199] Looking for political allies such as the Liberals and ministers in the church, the *Morning Star* rejected any form of physical confrontation with the fascists: 'To answer the appearance of fascism with impulsive, unthought out, little supported, but understandable, reaction leading to impromptu violence or physical confrontation has proved counterproductive.'[200]

The Popular Front approach of the CP was no guarantee of acceptability. A 4,000-strong counter demonstration in Rotherham organised by the CP-dominated local engineering union kept well away from the NF route, finishing with speeches by a Sheffield Labour MP, a local clergyman and an immigrant community leader. This was not enough for *Tribune*, the weekly paper of the parliamentary Labour left, which told its readers: 'Rotherham deserves better than to see a bloody clash of rival factions in its town centre on Saturday... Sheffield shop stewards could best assist the fight against racism in this instance by helping Labour to humiliate the National Front at the polls.'[201]

Other local committees took the position summed up in the slogan used in Cable Street in October 1936, 'They shall not pass', supporting physical force against the fascists. A few, such as Women against Racism and Fascism (WARF) and Christians Against Racism and Fascism (CARAF) were national organisations with a number of local branches. Many groups based themselves on the trade union movement, getting support from local union branches and trades councils. In some areas, such as Doncaster, it was the trades council that founded the anti-racist committee. The bigger groups, such as All Lewisham Campaign Against Racism and Fascism (ALCARAF) and the Inter-Racial Solidarity Campaign (IRSC), founded back in 1969 in Leicester, had a large number of affiliates, including local trade union branches.

Local activity had an impact. Huddersfield Trades Council had been active against the NF from the early 1970s, where the number of local candidates fell from thirteen (out of fifteen) in 1970 to five in 1973 and one in 1975. The movement was much helped by the relaunch of the monthly *Searchlight* magazine in early 1975. Edited by Maurice Ludmer, a freelance journalist and president of Birmingham Trades Council, it reported on 'what the extreme Right and racists are doing in this country and, to a lesser degree, abroad'. With help from *Searchlight*, regional organisations in the Northwest and Midlands were set up.[202] In May 1977, twenty-three London-based groups, including the London Gay Activist Alliance, joined the Anti-Racist Anti-Fascist Coordinating Committee (ARAFACC) and adopted the bulletin produced by Kingston Campaign Against Racism and Fascism as their bi-monthly paper.[203]

There were successful initiatives showing unity against racism. One example was the sixty London dock shop stewards and rank-and-file dockers who signed a Dockers Against Racism open letter 'express[ing] our disgust at the racialist campaign now being carried out by the national press and television against Asian immigrants', and 'to make sure that the fascist National Front does not grow in Britain in the 1970s as the Nazis did in Germany in the 1930s'.[204]

■ Below: Picket at Grunwick. Bottom, Clifton Rise, Lewisham, 13 August 1977.

4: Grunwick and Lewisham

Grunwick

★August 1976, a spontaneous walkout: first two then six, finally 140 workers came out on strike at the non-union Grunwick photo processing plant in North London. Mainly East African Asian women with no knowledge or experience of trade unions, they struck against low pay, stressful working conditions, bullying, victimisation and the constant humiliation of having to ask permission to go to the toilet. One of the first to walk out, Mrs Jayaben Desai, challenged her manager when he compared her fellow workers and her to 'chattering monkeys':

> What you are running here is not a factory, it is a zoo. But in a zoo, there are many types of animals. Some are monkeys, who dance on your fingertips. Others are lions, who can bite your head off. We are the lions, Mr. Manager.[1]

Picketing the workplace, they soon won support from local trade unionists. Jack Dromey, secretary of the local Brent Trades Council, arranged a meeting at the Trades Hall where they elected a strike committee and joined a trade union. The employer's offer of reinstatement without union recognition was rejected by the strikers after which they were all sacked. Visiting local workplaces to get backing, organising several local marches and public meetings, sending letters asking for support and delegations of strikers on tours of the country, the growing solidarity showed, as never before, working class anti-racism was becoming a force in its own right.[2] Working in a nearby rail depot, Roger Cox remembered how:

> As a group of women, overwhelmingly Asian, fighting for what most trade unionists already had, it was very hard for people, even if they were quite racist, to say 'I'm not doing that'. It began to eat into and undermine the generalised racism so it was a turning point, quite fundamental... It made anti-racism respectable because it now operated around the real active struggle of those women.[3]

Through the winter and spring picketing continued despite brutal policing and 'constant intimidation by NF members'.[4] Among the first groups to back the strike were the nearby Cricklewood post workers who refused to handle Grunwick's post.[5] Understanding union leaders' tendency to put union finances first, the far-right National Association for Freedom (NAFF), supporters of apartheid and the white regime in Rhodesia, threatened to take the post workers' union to court. The union executive responded by ordering its members to handle Grunwick's mail. When the Cricklewood post workers carried on refusing to sort mail, the union disciplined and eventually fined them. Meanwhile post office managers in Cricklewood helped NAFF volunteers take dozens of bags of undelivered mail to post in hundreds of local post boxes.

The strike now became headline news.[6] Strikers were invited to meetings across Britain, local activists set up support committees, the TUC general secretary, Len Murray, met the strikers and gave his backing. In May, three Labour ministers joined the picket line. Sir Keith Joseph, Tory shadow minister, suggested that 'Grunwick could be all our tomorrows – we do not choose our battle grounds'.[7] For the TUC and the ministers, keen as they were to be seen as 'doing something', the priority was the

Social Contract, holding down wages and making cuts. Support 'from above' was conditional on the strikers staying within the law.

The strike committee called for a week of mass pickets and thousands responded. Many travelled overnight on coaches from as far as Glasgow. In Preston, the SWP 'used to have a party at a comrade's house and then all tip on a bus in the very early hours, 2 o'clock. It was a real mix of people, dockers, firefighters, lots of engineers'.[8] The first day of a week's mass picketing, Monday 13 June, was organised by women activists.[9] Determined to crush any attempt to organise mass picketing, police kicked and punched the women who gathered, dragging some by the hair, Jayaben Desai among them, throwing them into police vans. By the end of the day more than eighty women pickets had been arrested. As their numbers grew, the pickets adopted the slogan 'The workers united will never be defeated', taken from, 'El pueblo unido jamás será vencido', the anthem of the Chilean resistance against the Pinochet regime.[10]

As the support for the Grunwick strikers grew across the country, a further mass picket was called for 11 July. As around 20,000 joined the picket, the thousands of police, a sixth of the Metropolitan force trying to keep the plant open, melted away.[11] Mickey O'Farrell was one of the pickets:

> Going down to Grunwicks was the first real political thing I did in my life... Up until then [it] had revolved around my peer group in Hatfield and being part of the hooligan culture around Manchester United. In fact I'd just come out of jail for some pointless brawl outside a pub... The whole experience was overwhelming. All these thousands of working class people. Miners from Yorkshire and Kent, dockers from Merseyside and Glasgow, print workers, postal workers, builders from here and there and everywhere. With their wonderfully evocative banners. What really impressed me was the amazing level of militancy. I'd been used to the football terraces where a few dozen people would normally be able to push around crowds numbering hundreds and even thousands. Now I was seeing working class people openly challenging hundreds of police for control of the

streets and sometimes getting the better of them and all in support of a small group of Asian women... I ended up getting arrested for obstruction. When the scab bus came there was a big surge through the police lines and I was one of those pulled in.[12]

Bob Stoker, leading trade union activist in Huddersfield remembers:

There were two issues in which the Trades Council was deeply involved. One was support for the Grunwick workers. There were quite a few coaches that went down to Grunwick. They had collections. Also there was the deportation of Josephine Thomas... The Trades Council organised a petition against the deportation of that West Indian woman.[13]

Despite going down to defeat after nearly two years on strike, betrayed by a union bureaucracy putting their own interests ahead of those they represented, the Grunwick mass pickets showed how the ideas of a massive number of workers changed as they fought together with Asian women workers. Satnam Virdee argues:

The dispute at Grunwick helped crystallise how – in the space of less than a decade – parts of the organised working class had undergone a dramatic, organic transformation in their political consciousness. From being attached to a narrow understanding of class that nested neatly within dominant conceptions of race and nation, key groups of workers had moved towards a more inclusive language of class that could now also encompass racialised minority workers. Key to facilitating this political transformation were socialist activists. A process of Asian, black and white working class formation was taking place – uneven, contradictory, but most definitely present amid the organic crisis of British capitalism in the 1970s.[14]

Above all, Grunwick showed the potential for united action against racism.

Operation PNH

If the Grunwick dispute revealed a growing anti-racist movement, it also exposed the racism of the police. A further example of this racism was highlighted in Lewisham, between 5.30 am and 6 am on Monday 30 May 1977. Two hundred police armed with dogs and sledgehammers broke down front doors and made over sixty arrests, overwhelmingly of young black men. Among the police, the action was known as Operation 39/PNH, Police N****r Hunt.[15] Sixteen-year-old Christopher Foster was frogmarched into the road in his underclothes. At the police station: 'Cathy Cullis, a young white girl... was stripped to her underwear in a cell. Two police come into the cell and joke about the 'disease' she has caught from living with black people.'[16]

Twenty-one people were charged with 'conspiracy with persons unknown to rob persons unknown in the Greater London area'. This charge had already been used by police to cover the role they had played at the 1976 Notting Hill Carnival by charging eighteen black youths, 'the Islington 18', with conspiracy.[17] For black communities, police harassment was almost always a bigger threat than fascist violence. In Lewisham, 'if you'd arrested five blacks, you could wear a special tie that showed the ace, king, queen, jack, ten of spades. The police used to go to court with the tie, wearing it at trials. They had a feeling of immunity'.[18]

The Lewisham 21 Defence Committee was set up to support those charged. It quickly drew a response from the police, who saw its leaflets as libellous and referred them to the Director of Public Prosecutions.[19] Three more were arrested at a street meeting called by *Flame*, the black workers' paper produced by the Socialist Workers Party (SWP), the new name of the International Socialists.[20] Now the Lewisham 24 Defence Committee, it organised twenty supporters outside a black youth centre in New Cross being visited by Prince Charles, with a banner saying 'Defend Lewisham 24. Who will the police mug next?'[21]

A demonstration to build the campaign in early July was attacked by a large group of NF members who poured out of a local pub, throwing bottles, 'rotten fruit and bags of caustic soda at marchers'.[22] 'Shoppers rushed for cover as racialists stormed down New Cross Road.'[23] There were over fifty arrests, the great majority of NF members.[24] The heavy NF street presence was part of the NF's strategy of 'kicking its way into the headlines', made easier by the selective use of police statistics linking mugging to black youth which was promoted by Powell and others and widely publicised in the press.[25] Determined to provoke their opponents, they claimed that '80 percent of muggers are black, 85 percent of their victims are white' and used the 'Your last chance...' poster produced earlier to announce and promote a national 'march against muggers' in Lewisham on 13 August.[26]

Sheila Amrouche, a Socialist Workers Party member in Lewisham, recalls how in the weeks leading up to the NF march:

> Every Saturday was 'brown trousers' Saturday. We had to build up to 20 or 30 people to have the confidence to do a *Socialist Worker* paper sale in Lewisham. You'd see a whole phalanx of National Front on the other side of the road, all male, all big, jacketed, helmets, baseball bats and they were coming for you... We got to the stage where we asked 'Can we carry on doing this?' Comrades promised to come, we took it on faith. We couldn't rely on the Trades Council's anti-fascist committee to do it, we needed the SWP's organisation.[27]

Local NF organiser Richard Edmonds promised 'its biggest ever rally... Everybody will know that the Front is marching'.[28] Webster told a press conference: 'We intend to destroy race relations here.'[29] Relying on police protection from any confrontation, the NF's plan was to assemble in New Cross, which had a large black population, and march through the centre of Lewisham to Catford, which they claimed was one of their strongholds.[30]

The NF had reasons for their growing confidence. In January, Enoch Powell had made a speech talking of the danger of a civil war between black and white people. Rather than damning his speech, Maureen Colquhoun, leading member of the left-wing Tribune group of Labour MPs, argued the Labour Party should listen to Powell:

> I regret the dissent his statement has caused. I am rapidly concluding that Mr. Powell, whom I had always believed to be a racialist before I went into the House of Commons, is not

one. Although he does overstate his case, there is a case to be considered. We have stacked up the most appalling problems for Black and White people living in our overcrowded communities… All my life I have worked for a multi-racial society but I am now living in one and my attitude has shifted. I think this is a problem the Government has got to deal with and not pretend it isn't there.[31]

The Stechford by-election in Birmingham, March 1977, a big victory for the Tories, saw the NF getting over 8 percent, again beating the Liberals into fourth place.[32] *National Front News* quoted the *Daily Telegraph*: 'There was an alarming 9% swing from Labour to the National Front… This is a trend with an air of permanence about it… However the major parties may dislike or hate it, the National Front is clearly becoming a force to be reckoned with.'[33]

Sheila McGregor, the then SWP organiser, remembers that the NF's violence during the Stechford by-election, where the SWP was standing the well-known journalist Paul Foot as a candidate, was so bad that a minimum of six people were needed on *Socialist Worker* street sales to prevent assaults.[34] The NF pushed the Liberals into fourth place and announced they would stand ninety-one out of a possible ninety-two candidates in the May 1977 Greater London elections – compared to just six candidates in 1973. More successful in deprived inner-city areas than the prosperous suburbs, they beat their own target of 100,000 votes, winning 119,000, and overtook the Liberals in over a third of seats.[35] Nationally, the local elections were a disaster for the Labour Party. They lost 900 seats and lost control of Greater London.

Bouyed by the NF's successes, Webster failed to recognise changes on the ground. Anti-fascism was also making progress. The press was not attacking refugees and immigrants as violently as it had a year earlier. Having previously called the NF 'right wing', a couple of national papers now labelled it 'fascist'.[36] Local papers such as the *East Ender* were taking a harder position. As one of its staff, Aidan White, put it at the time: 'the policy of the paper is, essentially, to not report the National Front and, where we do report the National Front, is to report upon them critically.'[37]

Wood Green: 23 April 1977

One change that the NF leadership was aware of was the fall in the numbers they could mobilise. Little more than a thousand supporters came to their first big demonstration of the year, timed for the run up to the May local elections. They chose Wood Green in Haringey, north London, a multi-cultural inner-city suburb with a long-standing Jewish and Irish population and post-war migrants from the Caribbean, Cyprus, India and Pakistan.[38]

When the NF announced their plan to march on 23 April, an ad hoc alliance, the April 23 Committee, was established, supported by twenty-five political and anti-racist organisations.[39] The police rejected a call from the local Community Relations Council for the march to be banned, so the committee began organising a counter-demonstration. Differences between those in the Committee emerged on whether to confront the fascists, though those in favour had some success arguing their case. There was a consensus that numbers were the key, not clever tactics, and planning meetings worked to get as many people out as possible. John Robson, unemployed at the time, remembers 'spending weeks... delivering leaflets and posters. We visited hundreds of Greek and Turkish establishments and work-places to drum up support.'[40]

For many this was the moment to put the strategy of direct opposition, 'They shall not pass', into practice. People, mainly, if not all, men, bought and tested smoke flares. Others, mainly women, sorted flour, rotten eggs and tomatoes into bags for throwing at the fascists.[41] Around 3,000 anti-racists gathered for a Rally Against Racism in a small park, Ducketts Common. Among them, 'delegations from Haringey Labour Party, trade unionists, the Indian Workers Associations, local West Indians, members of Rock against Racism and the Socialist Workers Party'.[42] Lucy Whitman remembers going 'in punky attire, festooned with badges, hair stood up on end', together with 'loads from the Afro Caribbean community of all ages, lots of punks, trade unionists and the traditional left'.[43] Over forty Labour councillors plus a handful of Tories, who had been unsuccessful in getting the march banned, held a large banner, 'Haringey Councillors Against Racism'.[44]

The rally included speakers from churches and the Communist Party. A larger group stood a short distance away preparing to move against the fascists. One Labour councillor, and trade union official, Jeremy Corbyn, walked between the groups.[45]

A hundred yards away at the far end of the common the NF gathered accompanied by a thousand police with horses and dogs.[46] Wearing red roses to celebrate St George's Day, the fascists were celebrating their 17.5 percent vote a week earlier in a council by-election in Waltham Forest, once again beating the Liberals. Drums beating, with banners from branches across the country, they marched off behind the 'honour guard' with its Union Jacks. At the front a loudspeaker van called on people to vote for their National Front candidate.

Mary Littlefield remembers being very nervous as she walked along the dense line of police who were defending the fascists. She was gripping a heavy Sainsbury carrier bag, as was another comrade on the opposite side of the march. As planned, people came up, reached into the bag and fished out a handy-sized bag of flour, which, along with eggs similarly distributed, they chucked over the police line. 'We succeeded in making them look a right mess and I've never felt so relieved at clutching an empty carrier bag.'[47] David Bennie recollects: 'Red smoke bombs filled the air. Everything that could be thrown was thrown. Police horses appeared on the pavement. If shoppers got in the way, that was their hard luck... I picked up a policeman's helmet and used it as my first missile of the day.'[48]

The police soon regained control, moving behind the march to shield it from counter-demonstrators. Julie Davies, a student watching the demonstration as it moved on, was shocked by the protection the police gave to the worst racism she had ever heard in her life.[49] Despite heckling, scuffles and arrests, 'shrugging off the sporadic stones and endless insults on their four mile hike', the NF marched to Enfield, rallying behind a police cordon.[50] Two observers, allowed into the meeting, soon left having been kicked and punched and called 'commies'.[51]

The local press coverage was excellent. The front page of the local *Hornsey Journal* ran the headline: 'Forty years on, the evil march of fascism fouls our streets'. Its editorial backed Jeremy Corbyn, asking why the police had allowed such a provocative march. An op-ed piece headed 'The lesson to be learnt' argued: 'We must do more than realise the dangers of the fascist parties. The time has come for action – and the role of the police illustrates vividly where the authorities are going wrong.' It concluded: 'Let us learn a lesson from the past. We could be five years away from factional strife. We don't believe it is an exaggeration to warn that further inaction will be leading us towards the totalitarian state.'[52]

By contrast, the national press coverage was low key: '50 held at Front rally' (*Observer*), 'The thin blue line' (*Daily Mail*), '"Army" of police checks protesters' (*Guardian*).[53] The *Guardian* report noted that 'The most important success for the left was that its new anti-fascist broad coalition had succeeded in uniting Labour parties, revolutionary left and immigrant groups against the NF'.[54] Despite disagreements on tactics, a degree of unity in opposing the NF had been achieved. It was, however, not enough. While this was the best organised attempt to stop the NF so far, they were still able to march. Jerry Fitzpatrick had helped prepare the counter demonstration. From an Irish background, he had seen the physical resistance in Derry in 1969:

> We wanted to organise in the same way. We had a keen eye on confronting the NF. We bought flares from a boat yard. I thought they would add a sense of colour and cover and make an effective public spectacle. We sought a non-violent context. But we were willing to sharpen the demonstration to confront the Nazis.[55]

For all the care and effort put into the preparation, not everything went as planned. John Lockwood remembers how:

> From nowhere a group of 14-year old black lads appeared, grabbed shoes [from a large tub outside a shoe shop] and hurled them into the middle of the Nazis... the fashion that year was for clogs... Mayhem ensued... Afterwards we realised that if we could increase the audacity of the challenge and substantially increase our numbers then the next conflict would physically stop the Nazis as the Communist Party had led people at Cable Street.[56]

Fitzpatrick drew two lessons for next time: 'First, we needed logistics, more supporters in the area, more street planning, a better sense of what the police tactics would be. Second, there had to be an intense effort in organising among the local community, in this case the black youth living in Brixton and Lewisham.'[57]

Lewisham: preparing for confrontation

After getting a total of 119,000 votes in the London local elections in May, often beating the Liberals into fourth place, the success of the Wood Green mobilisation against them did little to blunt the NF's confidence as they prepared to march in Lewisham. A meeting of 600 people, called by the Lewisham 24 Defence Committee, voted for 'a united mobilisation to stop the Nazis' and called for 'black people, socialists and trade unionists to assemble at 1 p.m. on August 13 at Clifton Rise, New Cross, so that They shall not pass.'[58] Schools were leafleted and Irish community halls and pubs were visited, including making announcements at dances. Fitzpatrick recalls:

> We created an atmosphere especially among black youth. People came in to collect leaflets and posters. You got a sense of people organising things themselves. There was one incident, a small trivial thing really. About three weeks before the demo, the police were chasing a black youth, and he ran into our building. They grabbed him and me too, accusing me of providing him with a false alibi. In court, we provided him with the solicitor. He didn't get off but it was a light sentence and in the days after I had a strong sense that the barriers had come down. The word went round that we would support black youth against police harassment.[59]

Lewisham Trades Council founded the All Lewisham Campaign Against Racism and Fascism (ALCARAF) in early 1977. It included 'representatives from the mainstream political parties, radical-left groups, churches, trade unions, the local council, black organisations and women's groups'.[60] It joined similar groups, such as Women Against Racism and Fascism (WARF) and the neighbouring Southwark Campaign Against Racism and Fascism (SCARF), many of which had worked together preparing the Wood Green counter-demonstration. A few weeks later twenty-three organisations set up the All London

Anti-Racist Anti-Fascist Coordinating Committee (ARAFCC).[61]

The politics of each group reflected the organisations that set them up. In Lewisham, the Communist Party, active in ALCARAF from the beginning, saw the group as a type of Popular Front. This meant seeking to work with as many respectable figures as possible, no matter what their relationship to the working-class movement. The prospect of a confrontation on the streets created a major divide. 'At [ALCARAF's] first meeting it was proposed that the word "fascism" should be removed from the title in case it put people off'.[62] ALCARAF discussed its response to the NF in Lewisham in sometimes fiercely argued debates:[63]

> Believing that there was no possibility of persuading people to confront the Nazis, the Communist Party proposed organising some kind of music event on the other side of the borough: music, poetry, cultural events and prayers. At this, a vicar leapt to his feet to say 'Oh, for goodness sakes, what's the point of that?'[64]

Despite the reticence of the CP, as the largest organisation on the left and Mike Power, a leading CP member, as the chair of ALCARAF, the CP could not be ignored by those trying to build a united front – Power had been a leading member of the Young Communist League (YCL) and had written the pamphlet, *The Fascist Threat*.[65] As Jerry Fitzpatrick saw it: 'If we were seen simply as boot-boys then we would fail. We had to convince the Communist Party, the Labour Party, the trade unions to join with us and broaden our support.'[66] This was certain to be difficult; when the SWP approached the Communist Party proposing joint meetings to discuss how best to support strikes breaking the limits set by the Social Contract, Bert Ramelson, the Communist Party's national industrial organiser responded: 'In our view, and indeed in our experience, your activity and propaganda is divisive and disruptive, making more difficult the development of united mass struggle.'[67]

Despite this, serious discussion was still possible. John Lockwood, one of two SWP delegates to ALCARAF, remembers arguing how, in the context of the racist murders including Gurdip Singh Chaggar the previous year and Kingsley Read's response 'One down, a million to go':

There was no absolute and inalienable right to free speech. Rather people have the right to walk the streets unmolested. The argument was eminently winnable and we pitched ourselves into it, unsuccessfully with the Communist Party... The final outcome was that there would be a gathering in Ladywell Fields in the morning forming into a demonstration, a 'March for Peace', to proceed halfway to the Nazis' assembly point and then disperse. We settled for that because we thought if we mass leafleted the demonstration in the morning, calling on people to stand with the black community, we could persuade people to go on from the morning demonstration to go to Clifton Rise [the NF assembly point]. We were successful in this.[68]

Calling themselves the August 13th Ad Hoc Organising Committee, those supporting this position met to decide how to proceed. They welcomed ALCARAF's decision urging 'full support be given to that march and call[ing] on everyone to stay on to occupy Clifton Rise to prevent the Nazis occupying there'.[69] The NF was due to assemble near Clifton Rise for the march starting mid-afternoon. ALCARAF's march drew wide support. Nationally, anti-racist, anti-fascist and feminist groups organised, backed by the new newspaper *CARF* (Campaign Against Racism and Fascism).[70]

The SWP held briefing meetings for its London branches. Andy Strouthous remembers a meeting at someone's house in Lewisham, looking at maps, arguing 'we had to be very disciplined with stewards in front to stop people from charging too early... not making the mistake of going for the honour guard first [but] going for the soft underbelly and then sweeping up the honour guard'.

The National Front yielded nothing. Having met with the Lewisham police to discuss plans, Webster announced: 'The Reds have had it all their own way and the only way you can fight Communism is to confront it. We believe that the multiracial society is wrong, evil and we want to destroy it.'[71] An 'Emergency Extra' on the NF's July Bulletin told members:

It is essential that we march in Lewisham to let the Reds,

their Mugger friends and above all the Multi-Racialist Authorities know that the NF will never back down in defence of the White British people.
MASS MOBILISATION by all units & nationwide essential. Organise coaches now.
Promote activity via bulletin and meetings, Mobilise! Mobilise![72]

One reason for the willingness of people to join the demonstration to confront the fascists was that ALCARAF's march route into the centre of Lewisham and then on towards Clifton Rise had been agreed with the police. But McNee, the head of the Metropolitan Police, then declared the agreement void and imposed a new circular route. The *Times* pointed out that this 'kept it out of Deptford, an area with a large black population, where the National Front march was allowed to go'.[73] Lewisham Council had refused the NF permission to use a local hall on the day of the march, the Amenities Committee chair declaring: 'The NF is a racialist organisation, and the hall belongs to the community which is multi-racial.'[74] Having voted for the NF march be banned, the council sent its resolution to Merlyn Rees, the home secretary, for his decision. Failing to get a positive response, the council sought a High Court order requiring Rees, as his public duty, to issue a ban. McNee, having already said he was following the advice of Lord Justice Scarman after Red Lion Square, told the court he was 'satisfied that the police are able to maintain control of the situation and prevent any serious disorder occurring'.[75]

For McNee a ban 'would not only defer to mob rule but encourage it'.[76] Rejecting calls from MPs, bishops and the TUC to ban the march and insisting he could handle the challenge, Rees mobilised 4,000 officers, a quarter of the Metropolitan police. The *Times* reported that, as well as helmets, 200 large transparent shields, never previously used in mainland Britain, were being held in reserve and 'hospitals in the area have been told to prepare for many injured people. Lewisham Council has moved old and disabled people away from potential trouble spots, and public buildings, shops and public houses on the route have been closed or boarded up'.[77]

Webster could be confident he would have all the police

support he needed. McNee was clearly determined not to be humiliated as he had been at Grunwick a month earlier. He could have rerouted the NF march, as happened in Leicester two years earlier when the National Front was prevented from going anywhere near the main Asian communities. Instead, he made his preparations knowing a significant proportion of the local black community would be on the streets opposing the National Front. It is difficult to avoid the conclusion that McNee was preparing for a riot, wanting to teach a lesson to those who challenged his control of the streets. Andy Strouthous remembers:

> There were four of us from the leadership, and a group of young black comrades who'd joined the SWP recently. We spent the evening touring round Lewisham. We met people on the estates, black kids, gangs and their leaders.[78] ...A lot of them were very suspicious. We didn't look like street fighters.[79] Nevertheless, when asked 'to bring your people down here tomorrow, we need your help' the response came 'Trust us man, we're bringing a big number'.[80]

It was a national mobilisation. David Glanz remembers:

> working on a Salford council holiday playscheme... sharing a big shed with the permanent park workers. One of them was in the NF and in the run-up to Lewisham he'd goad me about how the NF was going to win the day in London. I'd arrive at work and find that he'd put up NF posters, etc, in the shed to try to freak me out.[81]

Legal and medical support was organised. The Lewisham 24 campaign headquarters, based in an empty shop near Clifton Rise, was emptied of materials needed for the day ahead of an expected police raid, which came on the morning of 13 August. Word spread. Harold Wilson, a skinny 13-year-old whose mother grounded him on the day, remembers how 'the atmosphere in Deptford was one of rage. The black kids were incensed that the NF should ever dare to march through Clifton Rise. Outside the classroom the discussion was what to bring: bricks, wood, chains, nunchucks.'[82] Leila Hassan remembers:

> In those days there wasn't social media, there was a lot of

phone calls. It was all word of mouth. You just got to hear about things. And so we knew, the fascists were coming. In terms of how it was mobilised, it was word of mouth. It just spread. It was very interconnected, the black community of the time. We thought we were on the move.[83]

Some came from a distance. Michael Crowley, a 17-year-old anti-fascist lived on an estate near Watford, where he pulled down NF posters and was chased for doing so. He argued with his parents to let him go and they threatened to throw him out when he told them he was going to Lewisham.[84]

The Battle of Lewisham

The day began at 3am with two bricks thrown through Mike Power's bedroom window, one brick narrowly missing him and his wife. The ALCARAF rallied in Ladywell Fields to hear speakers including the Mayor of Lewisham, the Bishop of Southwark, Gokal Chand, the local IWA secretary, and Martin Savitt from the Board of Deputies of British Jews. In steady rain, 5,000 set off, led by a lorry 'with the Steel and Skin playing'.[85] The protest included: 'Young Liberals, Lewisham Councillors, Young Socialists, Communists and Young Communists, and the Campaign for Homosexual Equality... banners from GEC Elliot's factory, the Electrical Trades Union, Christian Aid, the Indian Workers Association and many more.'[86] The WARF contingent chanted: 'The women united will never be defeated' and 'The women's army is marching'. 'Many gay men took their lead from the women's group which was well stewarded, highly disciplined and sang the best songs throughout the march and demonstration.'[87]

The police stopped the ALCARAF march over a mile from Clifton Rise. When the mayor's request for the march to be permitted to proceed was refused, he called on the marchers to disperse. For many, the police block on their march while 'allowing the National Front to go down the High Street, which the local community saw as a total affront [showed] the police were taking sides'.[88]

Knowing that people were already at Clifton Rise, at least 1,500 now made their way to join the 5,000 who had been gathering since before midday. They had brought flares, rotten fruit and much else.[89] Two hundred joined the Bishop of Southwark for a service against racism and for peace at St Stephens Church on Lewisham High Street where a banner declared 'Justice, love and peace'.[90]

Suzy Harding, an unemployed school leaver from Chiswick in West London remembers:

> Lewisham was my first political demonstration... Four of us travelled across from Chiswick... all punks off the local estate... We made our way to the anti-racist rally, where a big crowd of people were listening to speeches. I really didn't know what to expect but I remember being surprised at the number of black people in the crowd. I suppose I'd fallen for all the media lies about these things being dominated by white, middle-class do-gooders.[91]

Michael Crowley remembers that: 'I'd never been around so many black people before, in a crowd like that. I'd never been to south London before, I didn't know black people at all at that time, I was only 17. It was one of the ways in which the day changed me.'[92]

At Clifton Rise 'the talk was of Cable Street, blocking the route... There was a mood, everyone knew this was historic stuff.'[93] Some had already come a distance.[94] At midday, twenty police kicked their way into the Lewisham 24 Defence Committee campaign HQ, arresting seven lawyers, medical aides and others.[95] Facing the police from mid-morning at Clifton Rise, was:

> a ram-packed contingent of South London Afro-Caribbeans [who] cordially but expertly blocked off the police's first attempt to open a way for the NF procession. On a traffic bollard a Trinidadian giant [Darcus Howe] with a hand megaphone was thoughtfully advising the crowd, rather as a cricket captain might place his field and, in the lulls, making speeches.[96]

There was considerable local support. Julia Poynter remembers 'locals opening their windows to see what was going on, then coming to join us, outraged that the NF were in their area'.[97] Giving evidence to the Undercover Policing Inquiry, Madeleine (pseudonym) recalled:

everybody was kind of kettled at some point… a kind of a crushing situation… People were trying to get away from the crush… There was a wall of police at one end. Behind us, lots of housing… all the windows were open, there was lots of loud music pumping out, there were people hanging out of windows, standing on walls. And it was absolutely solid, solid with people.[98]

David Widgery describes:

An Afro-Caribbean woman who had been watching from the top floor of her home hoisted her hi-fi speaker onto her windowsill. It was playing Bob Marley, *Get Up, stand up*…[99] Almost directly opposite a Cypriot woman replied with a clenched-fist salute from the first floor of her boarded-up kebab and chips shop. Two minutes later an officer with a megaphone read an order to disperse. No one did. Seconds later the police cavalry cantered into sight and sheared through the front row of protesters.[100]

Jenny Bourne remembers:

Maybe because we [WARF] had the largest contingent, maybe because we were well stewarded and therefore our troops were biddable, maybe it was just bad luck. But the WARF group was asked to sit down in New Cross Road blocking the way from Clifton Rise where the NF were assembling. That's what we did. The police tried to get through on foot, to clear a path for the fascists. They could not. So they sent in mounted police, who from horseback, with long batons drawn, rained down blows on head after head – scattering us, beating us as they went, drawing blood and creating mayhem.[101]

One woman remembers 'bricks thrown with excessive enthusiasm at police and fascists going over their heads and hitting other demonstrators'. The brick she threw knocked a policeman's helmet off just at the moment when a gap appeared in the crowd, when she could easily have been arrested.[102] Alan Gibbons remembers: 'At one point a horse nearly pushed us through the window of a Boots the Chemist. The glass was bowing dangerously.

An old age pensioner shoved her fingers up the horse's nose and it backed off. "I fought the Blackshirts", she said proudly.'[103]

Despite this violence, the police had been unable to get the NF march from their assembly point on Achilles Street, little more than 100 yards away, onto the main road. They now opened a route via a small street further down for the 500 National Front marchers. Having been told by Webster as they assembled, inside a protective envelope of police, to maintain discipline, talk to no one and only chant 'National Front, National Front', they now set off behind a large column of police walking at a fast pace four abreast. At the front, the 'colour party' carried a host of Union Jacks on metal tipped wooden spears with a large banner proclaiming 'Stop the muggers: 80 percent of the muggers are black, 85 percent of the victims are white'.[104] As they came round the corner onto Clifton Rise, they looked in horror at the thousands filling the space in front of them chanting 'The National Front is a Nazi Front' and 'The workers united will never be defeated'. Kept going by the police, the 'honour guard' and 'colour party' carrying Union Jacks were able to pass before, at a signal, a raised umbrella, 'a determined SW contingent... drove a wedge into the NF march',[105] and with them, 'black people and trade unionists, old and young, 14-year-olds and veterans of Cable Street, Rastafarians and Millwall supporters, Labour Party members and revolutionary socialists – all joined in'.[106]

> The crowd of antifascists exploded. Sticks, smoke bombs, rocks, bottles were thrown over the heads of the Nazis... Now huddled onto the opposite pavement into bedraggled groups... At least two separate points, anti-fascists rushed across the road to break into the Nazi ranks.[107]
> One young man, perhaps 16 years old, rushed into the Front ranks and grabbed a flagpole from one of them, broke it in half and held the pieces up while the crowd cheered. Others hurled dustbins and fence stakes into the Front column from close range...[108] The protesters then burnt captured NF banners.[109]

Michael Crowley, who had joined the SWP a few weeks before, remembers a man was knocked unconscious during the mounted police charge:

He lay face down on the street outside a house. A woman came out of her front door and threw a bucket of water on him but he didn't move. Someone went through his pockets to look for ID and found an SWP membership card and then called through a megaphone 'any SWP members here?' I came forward and was told to stay with him until an ambulance came. I thought, I've only just joined, what have I let myself in for here? Fortunately, two St John Ambulance guys came along soon.

In his novel *Stories we could tell*, Tony Parsons relates his memories of the battle through a fictional character, student and squatter Leon Peck:

What he [Leon] remembered most was the physical sensation of the riot, the way he experienced it in his blood and bones. His legs turning to water with terror as the air filled with missiles and the police spurred their horses into the crowd, his heart pumping at the sight of the loathing on the faces of the marchers, and the raging anger he felt at the sight of these bigots parading their racist views through a neighbourhood where almost everyone was black. He had never felt so scared in his life. And yet there was never a place where he was so glad to be.[110]

Unable to clear a way for the NF to continue to the centre of Lewisham, police diverted them, flanked by police three deep on either side, through deserted streets, using roadblocks to stop those trying to follow.[111] At a brief rally in a small car park, Webster told the crowd: 'What we've got in this country today is crime on the increase, immorality on the increase, illegitimacy, sodomy, abortion, obscenity everywhere', finishing with three cheers for the police. Tyndall then concluded with support for the police, promising: 'When we get in, the police are not going to go unarmed into these affrays. We will give the police all the necessary equipment, we'll give them the money they deserve, we'll give them the backing they deserve, and we'll give them the authority to sort the Red mob out.'[112]

By the time the rally had finished and the police escorted the fascists to their coaches, the smell of flares slowly dispersing, Clifton Rise was covered with shoes, bottles, dustbin, garden fencing and much else.[113] Not knowing where the fascists were, 'thousands of anti-fascists were already swarming through the streets to stop the Nazis getting to one of their main objectives, Lewisham High Street'.[114] Balwinder Rana remembers:

> We came to the centre of Lewisham and for a time took it over, even directing the traffic. Then the police came into the side streets. There was a real battle, jumping over garden fences looking for anything we could fight back with... also from the windows upstairs people throwing cauliflowers, even buckets of water. That battle took quite a while.[115]

John Sorrell remembers police cowering under dustbin lids and Richard Bundy recalls 'police horses chasing you down the street and you're running into people's gardens and they're following you into the gardens'.[116] Now able to use tactics they had been trained in, the police were 'systematically breaking up the demonstrators with cordons and a horse charge'.[117] They brought out the riot shields, making baton and cavalry charges with Special Patrol Group vehicles driving into the crowd at speed, all the while making numerous arrests. People soon learnt to deal with the SPG vans:

> Bricks poured through their windows and put at least one out of action... A group of demonstrators besieged a police station and broke its windows... Several thousand demonstrators had been marching down the road peacefully chanting 'We stopped the Front' and 'The Workers United will never be defeated' to applause from groups of local people gathered at the ends of their roads. They were clearly about to disperse. Police vans tore into this march from behind, breaking it up, and then chasing black youngsters, running them down at 40 mph. Police jumped from their vans, using batons and hit people at random, arresting anyone.[118]
> The use of the shields was equally aggressive. The pregnant wife of a prominent black boxer was battoned to the ground in one of the rushes. And the police accompanied their charges with a roared battle cry.[119]

The cells of the besieged police station contained those arrested at noon in the Lewisham 24 campaign HQ. Lodged with a few others in one cell:

> We were a total mix from the ultra-respectable to street kids and the solidarity was glorious. Such food, drink and tobacco as we had on us was shared and we were let out late afternoon. We knew even while inside that we had won as we heard the rain of bottles, bricks etc, breaking the glass in the cop shop and some shards even got on the floor of our cell.[120]

The first half dozen to be arrested were in a squat being used as an organising centre very near Clifton Rise. John Dennis, a student at the Royal College of Art, had brought a video camera to film the demo from the top of the building. As the police broke in (despite being told they would be let in), the video was kept running. All six were discharged when the video was produced showing there was no case to answer.[121] Keith Dobie, a socialist building worker, was one of those arrested and held in a police compound. A policeman asked: 'What lot are you with?' 'Haringey National Front branch', he replied. 'In that case you'd better jump over the wall and get away.'[122]

Despite over two hundred arrests, it was not all one way.[123] At one point two lines of policemen carrying riot shields came out of Lewisham Police Station to see around two thousand demonstrators advancing on them. They retreated back into the station.[124]

As Dave Widgery later put it: 'The mood was justly euphoric. Not only because of the sense of achievement – they didn't pass, not with any dignity anyway, and the police completely lost the absolute control McNee had boasted about but also because, at last, we were all in it together.'[125] For David Glanz, going home afterwards was not the end of the matter. He remembers:

> ...pleading with comrades to escort me to work on Monday morning... I was convinced I was going to be beaten up in retribution by the NF member. They said No... I steeled myself to go to work and found... that the NF member couldn't bring himself to look me in the eye. He was so demoralised by the experience of Lewisham that his confidence was smashed and his faith in the NF broken. A month or two after the play scheme ended, I bumped into

another of the park workers and he told me my nemesis had quit the NF.[126]

He was not alone. Joe Pearce, soon to be editor of *Bulldog*, the NF youth paper, contended: 'In the future, the older, respectable NF supporters… would stay away and fade away. In their place a younger, aggressive organisation of young thugs would rise to become self-styled storm troopers of the New Order.'[127]

The media onslaught

It is hard to exaggerate the media's condemnation of the anti-fascists and their solid support for the police, who quickly released a press statement:

> Two lawful marches took place, and, as those who have watched today's newsreels will have seen, a determined extreme element made an orchestrated and violent attempt to prevent one of those lawful marches taking place. Violence escalated and turned on police themselves when normal methods of crowd control frustrated the efforts of the counter-demonstrators to prevent the National Front march.[128]

Thus the *Daily Mail*'s front page was filled with a large photo of a policeman holding a large knife and a studded club next to a headline asking: 'After the Battle of Lewisham, a question of vital importance: Who will defend him?'. The piece continued:

> A carving knife, honed to razor sharpness. A metal pipe, with wickedly lacerating studs. These exhibits, held grimly aloft by a London bobby, come from the murderous weaponry deployed against the police on Bloody Saturday. Truly they are the regalia of hate. Hate for the police, for authority, for law and order and liberties enshrined within that order. Here was no honest, spontaneous anger by decent people against a racist parade. This was a contrived assault, with acid and knife and brick and bludgeon on the police: an evil and premeditated attempt to scar authority, slash liberty and engender panic and fear in an already troubled community. Gashed, bruised and bleeding. Britain's police held the front line for freedom. They have not seen rougher nor more

ominous action since the Thirties. In defending the right of the repellent National Front to march through the racially sensitive areas of Lewisham and Deptford they presented themselves as the prime target for the Red stormtroopers of the Left. But it wasn't bags of flour and placards and jeers they had to face this time. It was blinding ammonia and caustic soda.[129]

With a headline 'Look left, look right... at these arrogant thugs destroying our freedom', Lord Hailsham, a prominent Tory shadow cabinet member, wrote how, on his right the National Front was 'a thoroughly detestable organisation'. On his left 'are the members of the still nastier Socialist Workers Party and their allies and friends'. The article continued: 'It is quite certain that if the police had not acted as they did last Saturday, the riot at Lewisham would have left several dead and permanently injured on the streets.'[130]

Having defended the NF's right to march, 'nor can native-born Englishmen properly be denied the right to march through a part of their capital city merely because it is settled by immigrants', the *Daily Telegraph* argued: 'those who brazenly and publicly incited and organised the violence should not go unpunished. The law of conspiracy exists precisely for such purposes.'[131] For Bob Chamberlain, West Midlands organiser of the Labour Party, the SWP 'are just red fascists. They besmirch the good name of democratic Socialism'.[132] The *Guardian* published a cartoon of a fascist crawling out of a sewer with a police officer pressing down on a manhole cover to keep him down, just as a man holding a placard saying 'Stop fascism now!' comes up to jump with both boots onto the police officer. The cartoon is titled 'A helping boot'.[133]

If the *Times* front page headline 'Bishop accuses the police over Lewisham clashes' went against the stream, the editorial followed the rest of the national press: 'The blame for Saturday's violence must be laid squarely on the Socialist Workers Party, whose members and adherents, some of them armed with vicious weapons, came prepared to fight.' It then challenged McNee:

The Commissioner must also have realised that the

extreme left would not rely purely on non-violent methods. It cannot be said, therefore, that the police were taken by surprise. The presence of some 4,000 or more policemen is proof of that. Yet when the predicted outburst of violence occurred, they could not effectively cope with it. Mr McNee, the Metropolitan Commissioner, has a duty to explain why the reality turned out so different to his own publicly stated expectations.[134]

McNee's inability to account for his failure reflected a general failure of police intelligence. They had a dozen undercover police at work on the day, many working as activists in the SWP and other organisations.[135] There was no lack of information. There was an inability to understand how people would react, underestimating their target. John Deason remembers how, when the police attacked the Right to Work marchers as they got to London, they thought: 'all you had to do was to nab the guy with the megaphone and shut him up and then it'll be quiet. It had completely the opposite effect. It backfired.'[136]

Already on the Sunday morning politics show on TV, there was 'some Labour frontbencher denouncing the International Socialists, although by then we were called the SWP, as being the same as National Socialists and the same as the fascists.'[137]

Tom Jackson, the post office workers union leader, echoed this: 'There is little to choose between the Socialist Workers Party and the National Front... both are political boot boys.',[138] as did Sue Slipman, NUS president and CP executive member, at the NUS Conference in September. Monday's *Guardian* ran a story headlined: 'The real losers in Saturday's battle of Lewisham', ignoring the many local people among those who assembled against the NF at Clifton Rise:

> The inhabitants of this battleground represented by the sad and angry Lewisham councillors were, of course, the total losers. The streets of Lewisham had been given over to riot – mostly by people from outside the borough – and for an area which has attempted a number of radical responses to the race question the events on Saturday were heart-breaking.[139]

Its editorial, 'A day that mocked democracy', joined the attack on the anti-fascists, declaring: 'the only victors in the violent political game played out in the streets of Lewisham on Saturday were the extremists of Right and Left'.[140] It argued that the left's rhetoric was 'almost interchangeable' with that of the fascists. Labelling the anti-fascists 'the rentacrowd left', it accused them of provoking the police so that the police appeared to be defending the NF. Responding in a 'Letter to the editor', Duncan Hallas, SWP national chair, pointed out that the NF had used the same tactic as the British Union of Fascists at the Battle of Cable Street: 'As you must surely know, the object of National Front marches in areas with substantial black populations is exactly the same as the object of Sir Oswald Mosley's BUF marches through the Jewish areas of the East End in the thirties – intimidation of their intended victims.'[141] He challenged the editorial's assertion that 'Each side uses rhetoric that is almost interchangeable':

> Indeed! Who on the Left demands, 'If they are black, send them back?'. With splendid impartiality you condemn those who systematically stir up race hatred and those who systematically oppose racism, those who seek to intimidate and terrorise and those who try to stop the intimidation.[142]

Quoting the Met's assistant commissioner, David Helm, the senior police officer in command on the day in Lewisham, who had assured Hallas on the Wednesday before the Saturday 'that that police would certainly protect the NF', he showed that the *Guardian* had falsely accused the counter-demonstrators of provoking the police.

Reactions on the left

The Communist Party insisted that the battle of Lewisham could not be placed in the tradition of Cable Street. How could a mobilisation of under 10,000 compare with the 100,000 who stopped Mosley marching in the East End? As they saw it, prioritising the preparation for violence would never mobilise such numbers. The Communist Party paper, the *Morning Star*, argued: 'The tactics adopted by ultra-left groups in the struggle are misguided. Pitched battles with the police may give vent to people's frustrations but it's not the way to build a mass anti-racist campaign and isolate the Front.'[143]

The day before the march, the *Morning Star* accused the SWP of preparing itself 'for the definitive game of cowboys and Indians'.[144] Monday's *Morning Star* argued: 'It is in the development of this political, mass struggle, not the staging of ritual confrontations and street fights between the police and handfuls of protesters, that the way will be found to finish with the National Front and it's like.'[145] Syd Bidwell, MP for Southall and a former member of the International Socialists before being expelled for supporting immigration controls, wrote in the Labour Party Annual Report:

> I have no time for hooligans (the NF)... and for those crackpot adventurers who have yet to take their part in responsibility in the real Labour movement. We cannot counter them by a strategy of trying to out-thug the thugs of the National Front, because we have the strength to do it otherwise.[146]

Ten days later, Dave Cook, Communist Party national organiser, wrote a more carefully measured article. He rejected the SWP's claim to have followed the tradition of Cable Street as dangerous nonsense. The campaign to stop Mosley had been prepared on a much larger scale. A hundred thousand signatures had been collected calling on the home secretary to ban the fascist march. 'The line of historical continuity... runs through the approach argued for by the Communists in ALCARAF.' Acknowledging the courage and determination of those who fought the NF, he argued: 'the physical confrontation... gave the capitalist press the chance to present that day as being a violent struggle between two sets of "extremists"'. This made it easier for the press to ignore 'the broad united anti-fascist movement'. There was also 'the problem with street fighting... that only street fighters are likely to apply... mak[ing] it more difficult to achieve the mobilisation of the labour movement'. This was playing into the hands of the fascists, whose demonstrations aimed at provoking this response. It also increased the risk that all demonstrations, including those of the left, would be banned.[147]

Some Communist Party members challenged their party by going to Clifton Rise. Mick Woods remembers that Phil Piratin, active against Mosley in the East End, elected MP in 1945, in good part thanks to the reputation he had built taking on the Mosleyites, 'spoke and really whipped up the crowd'.[148] A small number of Communist Party members such as Jack Dash, the former dockers leader, spoke in pre congress meetings in favour of working with the SWP.[149]

Cook's fears that the left would find itself isolated after Lewisham was not the experience of those that took part. With the headline 'We Stopped the Nazis...and we'll do it again!', *Socialist Worker* had record sales the week after Lewisham.[150] At the top of the great staircase at the entrance to Brixton Tube Station, Danny Phillips sold more than sixty papers in an hour.[151] Richard Buckwell 'was working at the [SWP] centre... The number of letters coming in was amazing'.[152] On the second or third day after Lewisham, Paul Holborow remembers: 'there was a call from some East London newsprint suppliers. I remember I went to see them in Stratford and they said if you get a broad campaign going we will pay for all the newsprint that you can use between now and the general election.'[153]

Anna Raeburn, editor of the Problem page in *Woman* magazine, spoke in favour of what the SWP had done on Radio London: 'I was inspired by Lewisham. I am extremely proud that the left in this country finally said "Sod it. We'll fight." I saw it as a real step forward... I had a friend there who said it was fantastic... a lot of young people black and white who simply said "No more".'[154]

Michael Crowley remembers: 'The anti racists at Lewisham were very working class, mostly local, and not fazed about fighting the police or the NF. It wasn't a protest, it was a street battle.' For Wayne Minter:

> Lewisham was the real tipping point. After, there was such a burgeoning sense of power and liberation in the anti-racist and anti-fascist movement. It's horrible to talk about the glorification of violence as actually achieving anything, but the fact was that people had actually gone out there and defied the Front and the police and the establishment and said "We're not having it." The soundtrack to Lewisham was Rock against Racism.[155]

Lewisham was a turning point for the poet and activist

Linton Kwesi Johnson: 'What persuaded me to discard my cynicism about their [RAR's] motives was the Lewisham Riot in August 1977; that made me sit up and pay attention to what they were doing.'[156] For Jerry Fitzpatrick:

> Lewisham was our Cable Street, we had in mind the slogan from 1936. 'They shall not Pass'. It was our generation's attempt to stop fascism. It was rugged, scrappy. It was a real success. The NF had been stopped, and their ability to march through black areas had been completely smashed.[157]

■ Poster designed by David King linking NF with the swastika

5: Launching the Anti Nazi League

Where now?

★ 'We stopped the Nazis...and we'll do it again'. *Socialist Worker*'s headline the week after Lewisham was defiant but more was needed.¹ Lewisham was a turning point, but it was not decisive. It showed the courage and determination of the anti-fascists, but it did not stop the NF.² The NF boasted about the three hundred candidates it was putting up in the general election, giving them the same TV time as the main parties as well as free distribution of millions of leaflets. *Spearhead* had recently described the NF as 'a force which now no power on earth can stop'.³ Webster wasted no time before he made his next move. Monday's newspapers reported his announcement that the NF's next march would be outside London.⁴ Their growing confidence included an increasing level of violence. Jack Robertson, a member of the SWP Central Committee, remembers that 'It got worse with attacks all over the country on black people and comrades, including women comrades, attacks on elderly Asian women, murders, shit through the letterbox, people kicked in the head. Half the central committee had security wire on their homes.'[5]

The stronger the NF presence, the worse the violence – nowhere more than in the East End.[6] The SWP's main office was in the area, across the road from an NF stronghold which people coming to the office were advised to take care to avoid. In Leeds, 'there was this real sense of fear. The NF were vicious and running riot. Razor blades under stickers, graffiti. We would be selling *Socialist Worker*, they would come and sell their papers. There were fights all the time.'[7]

The support for the Grunwick strike had shown the number of organised anti-racists, many of them active where they worked and in their unions. Across Britain there were over a hundred anti-racist and anti-fascist groups, most of them in areas where the NF were preparing to stand candidates. Some were large and well-organised, some were short-lived. Their politics ranged from those opposed to physical confrontation, including pacifists, to those who saw being prepared to do so as essential.[8] They included: 'political parties, trades unionists, tenants' associations, faith groups, community associations, Community Relations Councils, local authority nominees and, even on occasion, the police themselves'.[9]

In a few areas these groups proved strong enough to seriously undermine the NF's election results. North Staffordshire Campaign Against Racism and Fascism (NorSCARF), founded in late 1976, had an early success with mass leafleting against the NF in the May 1977 local elections.[10] The Leamington Anti Racist Anti Fascist Committee (LARAFC), set up in 'response to the shock number of votes for a British Movement candidate in a local council by-election', met every Friday in a pub, 'creche facilities provided'.[11] However, the record of coordinating activity between groups was weak.[12] When the fascists announced a march, local knowledge was essential. Did this mean that it had to be the local group who took charge on the day? What if, as at Red Lion Square, June 1974, there was no local group? The twenty-six London-based committees which came together after Wood Green to set up the All London Anti-Racist Anti-Fascist Co-ordinating Committee (ARAFCC) failed to make an impact in the preparations for 13 August in Lewisham.[13] While often the involvement of union branches and trades councils visibly strengthened local successes, as a strategy, locally-based groups were not enough.

Lewisham showed the need for an organising centre capable of giving a lead. The question was whether the anti-racist and anti-fascist movement could unite to stop the fascists. The NF would continue trying to march through black communities but Lewisham-type counter-demonstrations would not stop the NF's preparations for the general election. To do this required much larger forces than those at Lewisham. It also required leadership. Defeating the NF at the ballot box was a definite and limited objective. The political forces supporting it did not have to compromise their political independence. One indication that such an initiative could work was the Right to Work Campaign's success in winning a wide range of affiliations within the working-class movement.[14]

There were many examples of short-lived anti-fascist united front initiatives bringing together the left. The hundreds of trade unionists who stopped a meeting of the British Campaign to Stop Immigration and the NF, the 1973 Battle of Manchester, is a good example.[15] There had been many pickets of NF meetings, some of which, such as of the picketing of the NF election meeting in Shoreditch Comprehensive, involved careful political organising.[16] Two Dockers against Racism open letters, both with sixty signatories, many of them shop stewards, were initiated by the IS branch in the London docks. The first was produced shortly after the NF candidate Lobb had polled 11.5 percent in the Newham South by-election in May 1974, the second in the summer of 1976 after the murder of Gurinder Singh Chaddar.[17]

Though the situation called for a national initiative, it was difficult to see how it could be pulled off successfully. The CP had already dismissed a call for joint action, a united front, before Lewisham.[18] Martin Walker, author of a then newly published book on the NF, argued:

There were three lessons from the violent summer.
(1) A march by the NF guaranteed a violent counter demonstration. (2) The old ideological divisions still made it almost impossible for the far left and moderate anti-fascists to compose their differences in a disciplined common front. (3) This division was complicated by the increasing anti-NF

role taken by young blacks and Asians who are often the most militant of all.[19]

Despite Walker's justified scepticism, a united front to stop the NF was the only way to win the support needed.[20] However, despite the media hostility, the SWP and its few thousand members had gained credibility as a significant force. It was not unrealistic to propose a united front to the rest of the left. A general election was now expected in a year's time. Given the consensus in parliamentary circles that Labour would lose twice as many votes to the NF as the Tories would, there was strength in the argument that Labour had much to gain from a campaign persuading voters the NF was not a legitimate party.[21]

For Jim Nichol, the organisation's 'strong, active anti-racist, anti Nazi tradition going back to the beginning of the 1960s', meant there was no alternative to trying to work out what this broader alliance might be.[22] Important as Trotsky's analysis of fascism and the united front was, it did not answer the question of how a united front could be created to stop the new threat. Nichol was clear that 'the numbers involved in taking on the Nazis was growing. Concern at the growth of the NF was much wider than the usual left, Labour and trade unions. That concern encompassed a wide range of people including a few odd Tories.'[23]

However, the fact remained that the left was divided on how to stop the fascists. It included those committed to Gandhian nonviolent direct action, those willing to use physical force, although groups wanting to confront the fascists.[24] There were also those willing to demonstrate against the fascists but only so long as there was no danger of a confrontation. This would lead to police intervention, they argued, as at Red Lion Square and Lewisham, with the left being portrayed as irresponsible and violent.[25]

As the SWP national secretary, Nichol spent much time visiting local branches, at one time driving 61,000 miles in nineteen months. He remembers wrestling with the question of how to take on this threat:

> I knew what was going on with the anti-racist, anti-fascist groups, the 'coordinating' groups, not always connected with us. Sometimes more than one in a particular area... The

idea of a national coordinating committee was around but a coordinating committee with good people was not going to stop the Nazis as a national organisation. It had to go outside of that, 'go higher'.[26]

The new initiative had to include both identifying the fascists as Nazis – that they came from the same tradition that led to the Holocaust – and mobilising the largest possible number in opposition to the fascists in whatever way was necessary. The SWP position of opposition to all immigration controls could not have been included as a demand of the united front itself as this would have restricted the numbers prepared to be involved. However, establishing a united front focused on opposing the Nazis did not restrict the SWP's own anti-racist campaigning in any way.[27]

Did the SWP have the necessary resources? The membership certainly had confidence and the capacity to take the initiative. It helped having a printshop that could quickly meet the needs of a national campaign for well-designed printed materials in large quantities. It was reasonable to see the SWP as meeting the requirement of a 'rough equivalence' of the forces taking part that was necessary in order to make its approach to people in the Labour Party credible.

The name of the organisation was important. The first name Nichol came up with, 'League Against Nazism and Racism', was too broad. It would have meant opposing immigration controls as they are racist in that they inevitably lead to discrimination in favour of some ethnic groups and against others. Such a position would have excluded too many shop stewards and others. Was the way forward a narrower anti-Nazi focus? 'Then "Anti Nazi League" popped into my head'.[28] Would Nichol's comrades agree? The SWP National Committee was a formidable body with a number of shop stewards very aware of their responsibilities when it came to making new SWP initiatives succeed. They were often sceptical of the Central Committee, scrutinising its proposals carefully. Nichol knew the National Committee would not necessarily accept the idea. It 'could well get a lukewarm reception unless the ground was prepared properly'.[29] He tested the idea by approaching, as the SWP national secretary, several prominent people:

Their response to the narrow purpose of the proposal, to stop the NF nazis, was good. I remember particularly Douglas Tilbe, a big wig in the World Council of Churches.[30] He had a reputation as a decent man, an OBE [and JP]. Tassaduq Ahmed, a political refugee from East Pakistan, was an author and publisher, well informed about the Bangladeshi community in East London. He was very positive 'though he was concerned about the number of factions that existed within the black communities'.[31] Mary Holland was a prominent journalist on the *Observer*. She was sceptical from the outset and asked 'You're not putting me up as a front for the SWP are you?' I replied I was telling her the truth. For the first time in a generation, the Nazis were a real threat. They had to be stopped. We could all come together for the first time. It was an attractive proposition. She agreed.[32] Next was Michael Seifert, a hardline CP member, solicitor to the ANC. He thought it was a fantastic idea but said that the CP would do its utmost to kill the idea because of the SWP connection. Michael had a mischievous smile and said that he would not tell the CP that he had been approached.[33]

The next task was to find someone in the SWP who would act as its leading comrade in the ANL. It needed to be someone who looked respectable. The SWP East London organiser, Paul Holborow, was an obvious choice. He had been a member since the late 1960s when, as a student at Dundee university, he had been active in the anti-apartheid Stop the Seventy Tour campaign against the South African Springboks, getting on to the pitch at Murrayfield.[34] Working full time as an organiser for the International Socialists in Wolverhampton in the early 70s, Holborow remembers selling *Socialist Worker* to workers on the line in large factories accompanied by senior union stewards.[35] Some comrades In East London were at first unconvinced that having been educated in private schools, he would succeed. He soon won them over with his skill and courage, particularly in confrontations with local fascists.[36] After taking the time to ask comrades about whether to take the job on, Holborow agreed to do it.[37] Nichol remembers that:

Throughout all of this, the only person I discussed the matter with was Cliff. Cliff was always tolerant of my wild ideas and encouraged most, including this one. The proposal was put to the Central Committee... There was no great discussion – the view was 'suck it and see'. It went through on the nod.[38]

Holborow approached Peter Hain, the best known anti-racist activist in Britain, committed to nonviolent direct action and with an unparalleled record of success in applying it. He had been a leading figure and press officer in the Stop the Seventy Tour campaign, which had successfully forced the cancellation of the all-white South African cricket team's English tour in 1970. A past president of the Young Liberals, he was now in the Labour Party, working as a researcher for the Union of Post Office Workers (UPW), where Holborow went to meet him to drive together to Hain's home.[39] In the twenty minutes of the journey, Holborow went through the founding statement and Hain agreed to be press officer.[40] For all Hain's differences with the SWP, he agreed on the urgent need to confront the NF and on the inadequacy of existing anti-racist and anti-fascist organisations. He explains his position in his autobiography:

> Despite good intentions to oppose the NF, trade union and Labour Party activity had no impact because it was organised in a way that never touched the problem. Similarly, existing left-wing anti-racist groups were having no real impact on the ground where it mattered.
> In the ANL we had a simple philosophy. The problem had to be tackled with real urgency. What mattered was unity in action against the National Front, not endless theorising or repetitive meetings to discuss what might be deemed a more coherent, left-wing or anti-racist approach. An imaginative, radical, new strategy was required, even if that meant appearing to muscle in on territory claimed by more established anti-racist organisations (as some alleged at the beginning had happened with Stop the Seventy Tour). Nothing was working and a new approach was imperative. Not for the first time, I found myself in the 'getting on with it' camp.[41]

Holborow approached Ernie Roberts, for twenty years

assistant general secretary of the main engineering union, the Amalgamated Union of Engineering Workers (AUEW). Joining the Communist Party at a young age, he was expelled for refusing to support the CP's opposition on strikes after Russia became an ally of Britain in 1941. A toolmaker by trade, repeatedly victimised for his shop floor organising, he was one of three representatives who negotiated the Coventry Toolroom Agreement in 1941. For over thirty years this was 'a barometer for all workers in the engineering industry in their demand for parity of earnings'.[42] Now a Labour Party member, he had been nominated candidate for the Hackney North seat in the coming general election. Having been the Right to Work Campaign's treasurer and an active anti-racist for many years, he now agreed to be the ANL national treasurer, a clear signal that the ANL was rooted in the working-class movement.[43]

What was the principled basis on which the united front was formed? The National Front were receiving protection from the state on the basis that they were a legitimate political party. Victory in The Battle of Cable Street was won by mobilising so many people that the police could not clear a way for Mosley to march. The united front had to be for unity in action. For Peter Hain this meant applying the same tactic of non-violent direct action used in the Stop the Seventies Tour campaign against matches with white only teams from South Africa. He was 'interested in practical and effective action, not sectarianism or the niceties of left-wing theology which often amounted to little more than posturing.'[44]

Holborow remembers:

> We [the SWP] didn't want to draw a line between people who wanted to physically confront the Nazis and people who wanted to propagandise against them. The formulation in our founding statement had to be very carefully worded. Wherever the Nazis attempted to organise, they must be countered.[45]

The aim was to avoid unreasonably narrowing down the appeal to those already committed to physical confrontation by keeping the question open, recognising that many would only see the necessity of being willing to stand with others in a confrontation when it became a real-life question. Holborow recalls:

> We were worried – in retrospect unduly – by the question of confrontation with the Nazis on the streets. The statement doesn't mention confrontation. Early October 1977, at the Labour Party Conference, Ernie Roberts got over thirty MPs, with nearly twenty senior union officials to sign. This galvanised me. We were used to other united front campaigns such as the Right to Work campaign. This went much faster.[46]

The prospect of an NF breakthrough at the coming general election, expected in autumn 1978, made clear the urgent need to bring people together. 'The momentum Lewisham gave to everything else was extraordinary.'[47] For the first time, anti-fascism was front page news. This was the moment to overcome the fragmented, ill-coordinated nature of the existing movement, bringing together those prepared to fight and thereby creating an organisation more powerful than its opponent. It had to be a national organisation and more than a co-ordinating body.

Anti Nazi League Founding Statement

The National Front are emerging as a growing force in British politics. In the local elections in London they received over 119,000 votes. In some recent by-elections they have pushed the Liberal Party into fourth place. They intend to stand over 318 candidates in the next General Election.

For the first time since Mosley in the thirties, there is the worrying prospect of a Nazi party gaining significant support in Britain. The leaders, philosophy and origins of the National Front and similar organisations follow on directly from the Nazis in Germany. Like Hitler with the Jews, the British Nazis seek to make scapegoats of black people. They exploit the real problems of unemployment, bad housing, cuts in education and in social and welfare services. Physical assaults on black people are increasing at a disturbing rate. If their evil propaganda takes root we will be facing an alarming development in Britain, which affects every one of us.

In these months before the General Election the Nazis will seize every opportunity to spread their propaganda. During the Election itself, National Front candidates will be entitled to equal TV and radio time to the major parties. The British electorate will be exposed to Nazi propaganda on an unprecedented scale.

This must not go unopposed. Ordinary voters must be made aware of the threat that lies behind the National Front. In every town, in every factory, in every school, on every housing estate, wherever the Nazis attempt to organise they must be countered. Millions of leaflets and posters will have to be distributed. To have the necessary impact, this demands a campaign on a national and massive scale.

■ That is why we the undersigned believe that an Anti-Nazi League has to be built urgently to unite all those who oppose the growth of the Nazis in Britain, irrespective of other political differences

■ The League's objectives will be to organise on the widest possible scale against the propaganda and activities of the Nazis in Britain today.

■ We believe that many people – in the professions and in trade unions – are already aware of the danger. The experience of Hitler's Germany shows that the Nazis will not go away of their own accord.

■ We, the undersigned, appeal for the widest possible support for our efforts to alert the people of this country to the growing menace of the New Nazis.[48]

The media were giving the NF more coverage than ever before. August 1977 saw twice as many column inches about the NF in the national press as had been printed in the previous two years. The *Times* gave Tyndall a lengthy and respectful interview on 30 August. Three months later the BBC's *Tonight* programme interviewed Martin Webster.[49] Some leading members of the NF such as Terry Verity, member of the directorate and holder of the National Front gold medal 'for devoted service', resigned from the organisation. For Verity, Lewisham 'was just a provocative attempt to stir up trouble'. However, the resignations made little impact.[50]

Hyde

Determined not to appear weak after its failure to march through Lewisham, Webster wasted no time before announcing the NF's next demonstration with a call 'to defend British free speech from Red terrorism'. This time it would be through Hyde, a declining mill town near Manchester with a significant Asian population.[51] Manchester had been an important base of the BUF in the 1930s – it was Mosley's home city – and the NF had some support, albeit 'a thuggish, lumpen-ish lot'.[52] But Manchester had a strong anti-fascist tradition and Mosley had never been able to march or hold meetings unchallenged. There was significant support for challenging the NF within the trade unions. The secretary of the North West TUC, Colin Barnett, a hard-working regional official for the fast-growing National Union of Public Employees, NUPE, with a long standing record as an anti-racist, issued a call for the NF march to be banned, making it clear that if the march went ahead, there would be thousands of trade unionists in Hyde opposing it. Manchester Trades Council organised a telegram to Callaghan with 130 names of 'Councillors, Churchmen, footballers etc'.[53]

The new chief constable of Greater Manchester, James Anderton, solidly supported the NF's right to march. Anderton was seen as a 'copper's copper', doing nothing to challenge the deep-rooted racism, sexism and homophobia within the Greater Manchester Police. Equally important, he did not want to be humiliated as McNee had been at Lewisham.

However, with a new motorway bypass being built just yards from the centre of the town, as well as the narrow streets characteristic of old mill towns, there was only one possible route for a march. This had to cross a river, a canal and go under a railway line. Geoff Brown remembers walking round the area with Steve Jefferys of the SWP central committee to see how difficult it would be to secure a route for the NF to march. Anderton came to the same conclusion. Asked to meet the Home Secretary, he produced a map showing:

> the route that the Front proposed to take from the station to the Town Hall, a route whose dangers were clearly shown by photographs of the area. There was no question of the Front

being allowed to take the route they had originally proposed: it was unnecessarily long and it passed numerous arsenals of missiles on building sites etc.[54]

Anderton had no choice. He described his application to the local Tameside council to ban the march as the hardest decision of his life. He met Webster and the two agreed that Webster would symbolically march by himself through Hyde while the NF could march in Levenshulme, south Manchester on condition the route was kept secret. Anderton's plan was described as 'the most sophisticated public order operation in Britain up to that date'.[55]

On his lone march, Webster, carrying a placard reading 'Defend British Free Speech from Red Terrorism', was accompanied by an astonishing 1,000 police. He was accompanied, however, by a lone counter-marcher, Ramila Patel, a member of Bolton SWP and Bolton Asian Youth Organisation, who walked in front of Webster until a police officer grabbed her placard and broke it in half.[56] Most anti-fascists gathered in Stockport, thought to be the most likely place the fascists would meet. The news that the NF would march in Levenshulme, an area with a substantial Asian population, arrived too late for all but a few to challenge the march. Alan Gibbons, one of those who did get to Levenshulme, remembers overhearing a police officer remarking to a colleague as the NF honour guard with its Union Jacks came into sight, 'Here come our boys'[57]

That the NF's march had been 'organised not so much by the National Front as by the police',[58] including the absurdity of Webster's lone march amidst a sea of police, did not stop Webster gaining support in much of the press. The *Times* columnist Bernard Levin found that Webster had displayed considerable courage, his protest absolutely justified as 'the totalitarian left' must not be allowed to 'decide who is permitted to use the streets for political purposes'. The £250,000 spent protecting his right to free speech was a price that had to be paid.[59] However, Anderton's success in preventing a second Lewisham came with a political price as the local Tameside Trades Council set up an Anderton Must Go campaign as part of a larger effort to take on the fascist activity in the area. This was detailed in an SWP leaflet written after the NF's Levenshulme march:

- Asian homes have been attacked and families harassed.
- Shops, buildings, roofs and the local station have been daubed with slogans such as: 'Clearance Sale: P*** slaves half price'.
- An anti-Nazi poster provoked a knife attack.
- The local high school has been leafletted by the NF.
- After the Labour Party broadcast, burning rags were shoved through the letter-box of the local Labour Party Secretary.
- Asian cars have been stoned and the tutor of a newly formed English language class for Asians had his tyres slashed.
- An Irish travel agency has been vandalised and had NF slogans written over it.
- British Movement and NF leaflets have been distributed in the area.
- Stickers against Blacks and the IRA are appearing.[60]

In areas around the country, local people mobilised against the fascists. In Birmingham, where hostility towards the police was arguably even stronger than it was in the Manchester area, an NF by-election meeting in the Ladywood constituency, held three days after Lewisham, needed protection from police with riot shields. Five hundred then marched to the nearby Handsworth police station, the scene of a number of anti-police protests in recent years, which needed four rows of police to protect it.[61]

In Sheffield, the extreme violence of the small and short-lived British National Party produced a united left response several hundred strong that succeeded in occupying the fascists' city centre assembly point, causing them call off their planned rally.[62] A very different response to an SWP call for a counter-picket of an NF meeting in the small town of Hemel Hempstead showed the need to have a national initiative that could unite the movement. The local Liberal candidate denounced the SWP as 'fascist and racist' and the local anti-racist committee condemned 'confrontation' tactics, only backing the picket when the Trades Council voted unanimously to support it. However, when about eighty people, including 'the local Labour MP, members of the Labour Party, the Communist Party, a vicar, SWP, plus a few others', gathered a short distance from the NF meeting, the march was 'led by the vicar and Communist Party... to the hall singing "We Shall Overcome"...and having got there...turned around and marched away, singing the same song.'[63]

Launching the ANL

Ernie Roberts's success in getting over thirty Labour MPs to sign the ANL's founding statement was an indication of the potential. Roberts chaired a meeting in the palace of Westminster that set up a steering committee of five: three Labour MPs, Martin Flannery, Neil Kinnock and Audrey Wise, plus Maurice Ludmer, editor of *Searchlight* and Labour Party member, and Nigel Harris, a leading member of the SWP. A fourth Labour MP, Joe Ashton, joined a few days later. The meeting confirmed Holborow as secretary, Hain as press officer and Roberts as treasurer.[64] The steering committee had to ensure that the officers, the day-to-day leadership, successfully handled what would often be difficult tactical decisions.

Two days later, Kinnock chaired the first ANL press conference in the House of Commons. He argued it was no longer true that the National Front would go away if they were ignored: 'The popular belief that their support would dwindle is not true and the silence of democrats can only help it. We have to give up our silence.'[65] Peter Hain stressed it was a broad-based group anxious to attract people from all sides of the political spectrum as well as from other fields: 'We hope to extinguish their potential. I don't think banning them is the whole answer. Hitler was banned. Our major aim is to make the public aware of their credentials.'[66] Kinnock explained that what many people 'are in favour of is educating the public mind and propagandising against the danger of Nazism. That's why our organisation exists'.[67] The new ANL posters, designed by David King, art editor of the *Sunday Times*, an outstanding graphic designer of his generation, made an immediate impact. The red arrow on a yellow background, used by anti-Nazis in Germany in the early 1930s, gave a sense of taking on the fascists. King had previously designed the five-pointed star logo of Rock Against Racism.[68] He drew inspiration from the agit-prop graphics of the Russian Revolution and the fight against the Nazis in the 1930s, using montage techniques pioneered by the visual artist and German Communist Party member John Heartfield. The posters went everywhere including the window of a retired cleric in the cloisters of Canterbury cathedral.[69]

Roberts emphasised the importance of unions and stressed that:

> Where anti-racist and anti-fascist committees already exist, we would want to work alongside them... Where such committees do not yet exist, we would like to assist in bringing people together who want to be involved in the campaign against the Nazis. Whatever organisational form, our most important task is to convince local people to work with us against the Nazis.[70]

By-election in Bournemouth

The ANL's first test came just a fortnight later at a by-election in the safe Conservative seat of Bournemouth East. The NF candidate, a retired captain in the King's African Rifles, told the press he had 'never been a Fascist or a Nazi' and 'there was no intention to use force' in his party's policy of repatriating black people, including those born in Britain.[71] Kinnock told the local paper that the Anti Nazi League intended to hand out 'anti-Front leaflets to every householder in Bournemouth'.[72] Holborow spoke to the president of the Bournemouth College of Art students' union, who agreed to organise a meeting in the canteen at which a large number supported the ANL.[73] Many joined the pickets chanting outside the National Front's heavily stewarded election rally, where a hundred people heard Tyndall tell them: 'These islands are for the British people, no other... not for browns, blacks or yellows'.[74]

The constituency was leafletted with a leaflet crafted by David King. It was drafted to avoid prosecution, making no mention of the NF candidate's name while identifying the ANL as publisher with a full postal address.[75] 'We were entering a "mini mass" operation as opposed to something more restricted in numbers as the IS/SWP had done previously.'[76] With the national news dominated by the firefighters' all-out strike, the election campaign failed to hit the headlines and turnout fell by over a third.[77] The Tory vote rose to 52 percent, the anti-immigrant New Britain Party got 4.6 percent, the NF 3.0 percent. It was a good 'first outing' for the ANL. Bringing together as many people as possible to carry out mass leafleting targeting the NF with well-produced leaflets was now established as the core activity of the ANL.[78]

Getting a national profile

By-elections were few in number. The key to success was activity on the ground, countering any possibility of a fascist initiative, large or small. Local groups still had to make their own plans. There was not, and could not be, a centralised direction of more than a limited number of nationally organised initiatives.[79]

What was possible was to seize opportunities that kept the ANL in the public eye. A week after the ANL launch, Hubert Meyer, a former high ranking Nazi Waffen SS officer, came to London for a press conference promoting his memoirs. While outside the hotel there were banners with 'Keep Out Nazi Thugs', inside Paul Holborow held up the 'Never Again, Stop the Nazi NF' ANL poster, shouting: 'It's scandalous that we allow these people to enter the country to the affront of everyone.' This made the lead story on the TV *News at Ten* that night.[80]

A second opportunity came with Kingsley Read appearing in court. Eighteen months after his notorious speech talking of "n*****s, w*gs and c**ns", and referring to the racist murder of Gurdip Singh Chaggar with the words 'One down, a million to go', he was charged with incitement to racial hatred. With an Anti Nazi League picket outside, the judge, Neil McKinnon, told the court: 'In this England of ours, at the moment, we are allowed to have our own views still, thank goodness.' He then acquitted Read and wished him well. From the public gallery, Holborow shouted: 'Judge McKinnon, your remarks have led to the acquittal of John Kingsley Read. It is an affront to the black people in this country.' As half a dozen police and court staff moved to carry him out of the court, he continued: 'There is no justice for black people in this country. It makes Nazis respectable. It is outrageous and disgraceful.'[81] Covered in detail by the *Evening Standard* and the *Daily Mirror*, ignored by the *Guardian*, Holborow's protest was followed by a call by black lawyers to boycott Judge McKinnon's court and sixty Labour MPs signed a Commons motion calling for him to be sacked. Someone painted 'Black is beautiful' in large letters on Read's house in Blackburn.[82]

McKinnon was not an isolated figure among judges. Judge Basil Gerrard told NF supporter Duncan Jeffrey, jailed for six months and fined £200 for his part in the attack on the National Council for Civil Liberties meeting in UMIST: 'If you want to be a fascist that's all right by us but you cannot break the criminal law.'[83]

Sponsors

While it was clear from the start that the ANL 'welcomed the support of well-known and established figures, it has always recognised that its real strength lay at the grassroots'.[84] The aim of collecting sponsors was to build public support when much of the Labour Party establishment was unwilling to commit themselves and the NF grabbed headlines with little high-profile opposition. Greg Dyke remembers: 'The politicians were never going to grapple with the question of race as it was a potential vote loser. One way this could be dealt with was by getting popular cultural figures to stand up against it. This was the role the sponsors played when the Anti Nazi League was formed.'[85]

Sabby Sagall, a lecturer at North London Polytechnic, many years active as an SWP member, remembers it was 'quite by chance' he started writing letters, eventually working on it 'almost full time', sending several hundred letters to potential sponsors.[86] Everyone who responded received a reply and those who signed up were kept informed with newsletters.[87] The first printed version of the founding statement had eighty names, almost half of them MPs and members of the House of Lords. The final version had as many as could be fitted on a single sheet, over 250.[88] They included well-known actors, musicians, boxers, football managers, journalists, writers, poets, comedians, film and theatre directors.[89] Manchester and Leeds had their own versions. Southampton's had eighty names including two local Labour MPs, trade unionists and representatives of local Asian organisations. By March 1978, thirteen national unions were sponsors as well as two TUC regional councils together with scores of trades councils, union branches and joint shop stewards' committees.[90]

Sagall became friendly with Miriam Karlin, one of television's best-known actors and one of the first to sign.[91] Wearing an ANL badge when interviewed in her dressing room in a Birmingham theatre, she explained:

> The real reason I am desperately involved with the fight against them [the NF] is this. My family, which is Jewish, suffered from the last upsurge of fascism. My mother came to England originally from Holland. All her family were murdered in Auschwitz. It's as plain and simple as that. My father was a barrister, an expert on industrial law. When I was a small child, about three or four, he would take me up to Hampstead Heath, where Mosley used to rally his supporters. My father would heckle them. I remember one of those louts and this will stay with me to my dying day shouting at my father, 'Shut up you dirty Jew'. In spite of all I know about the gas chambers in Germany, and everything I've learned since, it's those words that stay with me. That's what I know black people go through all the time in this country.[92]

Karlin was one of a number of actors from a working-class Jewish anti-fascist tradition who sponsored the League. They included Warren Mitchell and Alfie Bass, both well-known TV sitcom stars, and the songwriter-composer Lionel Bart. With a large circle of friends and fellow union activists, Karlin worked with Sagall, writing to ask people to sponsor. Many others also signed up sponsors. Joe Ashton MP signed up two of the best-known figures in football, Brian Clough, manager of Nottingham Forest, and Jack Charlton, member of the winning England 1966 World Cup team and Sheffield Wednesday manager. In Leicester, Chris Lymn signed up Stuart Sims, a member of the England Under-21s and Leicester City football teams by walking round to his house and asking him.[93] Sponsors included a wide range of political views. George Melly, the singer and critic, pointed out how party membership was not mentioned: 'the signatories are not drawn from this or that party... I think this is most valuable as it indicates opposition to the fascist philosophy right across the political board, from moderate right to extreme left'.[94]

Glenda Jackson and Margaret Drabble accepted, despite being unhappy with the name.[95] Some gave their support but not their name. Some declined, arguing they were already over-committed as sponsors.[96] Esther Rantzen wrote that she could not sign as that would mean 'the BBC could not then use me as chairman or interviewer in a confrontation with, for example, the National Front'.[97] Recently appointed captain of the England cricket team, Mike Brearley replied: 'I am afraid that I am not willing to have my name added to your list of sponsors, as you will appreciate I have to be most careful of being associated with any kind of organisation, despite my own personal views. Sincerely yours, Mike Brearley.'[98]

Local initiatives followed. In Manchester, Dave Watson, the Manchester City player, and Pat Crerand, recently assistant coach at Manchester United, signed. Given a list of academics to ask, Colin Barker got all but one to agree. Bob Greaves, anchor person for the Manchester-based regional TV news, *Granada Reports*, joined along with most of his colleagues, including Jane Cousins and Tony Wilson. There were those who refused. Greaves asked Violet Carson, known to millions as Ena Sharple, star of Granada's *Coronation Street*. A solid Conservative, she responded: 'How dare you ask me such a question?'[99]

Nigel Harris contacted the leading labour historian Edward Thompson. Thompson rejected the request at the time, arguing the ANL was no more than an SWP front. He soon changed his mind and signed up. A few years later, now a leading figure in the campaign against US nuclear missiles based in Britain, he rang Harris to apologise 'for having been so snooty about building mass movements when he [Harris] had approached him'.[100]

Difficult to ignore, well-known sponsors were important in the media battle. The respected senior journalist James Cameron put a straightforward plug in his weekly *Guardian* column attacking the NF:

> The other day, a developing counter-action was launched in the House of Commons, a movement called the Anti-Nazi League, which is sponsored by a fair mob of MPS and Trades Unionists, as well as the customary ballast of writers and actors and artists and so on. This is seriously and overtly against the NF. If you want to know more about it, contact the organisation at 12 Little Newport Street, London, WC2.[101]

Nor could the press ignore peak time television. *Destiny*, David Edgar's play about the rise of the National Front in a town in the Midlands, had been a critical success as a stage play two years earlier.[102] At the end of January 1978, the BBC showed a TV version in the prestigious *Play for Today* slot. The *Daily Mail* called it 'extraordinary', 'a brilliantly documented drama'.[103] The ANL followed up the broadcast with a quarter page advert in the *Guardian* the next day, with an emergency appeal that raised £3,000 from over 900 letters.[104] Edgar was a leading member of a group of left-wing playwrights who had worked in street theatre through the 1970s, often using an agitprop approach, for example with capitalists wearing outsized top hats and fascists strutting in jackboots. Edgar argued that 'this ignored the fact that fascism can attract people who would, initially, run a mile from a swastika... The process from discontent and frustration expressed as mild racism to full-blown nazism is often as imperceptible as it is inexhaustible'. The play tried to be 'as authentic as possible in the belief that an understanding of how fascism works is in the central part of stopping it'.[105]

Joe Ashton had made an all-out attack on the National Front in a Labour Party political broadcast showing viewers:

> racist graffiti in decaying parts of London, scenes of football violence, Mussolini, and Hitler reviewing jackbooted stormtroopers, and a group of survivors from what looked like a concentration camp, while the Front was denounced as racist, 'out to smash democracy' and practising the 'repulsive fascist tradition' of the politics of hatred and fear.[106]

Recruiting Brian Clough and Jack Charlton as sponsors got the ANL onto the front page of the *Daily Mirror*, daily circulation 3.5 million.[107] Clough was characteristically direct, describing the NF as 'scum – the scum of the earth. If you step in something dirty, you don't just say "How nasty!" You wipe away every trace of that dirt. We must fight the Front menace in every way we possibly can'.[108]

As media coverage grew, cynics looked for where the ANL was vulnerable. Pendennis, the *Observer's* anonymous gossip columnist asked whether 'any of the 300 or so famous sponsors of the newly formed Anti-Nazi League know exactly what they're going to do about streets demonstrations?'

Pendennis went on to suggest that after the demonstration, 'this glittering array may have to consider the matter seriously... Is Frankie Vaughan... likely to find himself beneath a banner across the street from the National Front?' The article concluded 'Peter Hain, the league's press officer, says they have no firm policy on confrontation'.[109] The falsity of Pendennis's patronising suggestion is revealed by the hundreds of sponsors who paid a minimum of £5 and, with just a handful of exceptions, stayed solidly in support.[110] Sagall remembers:

> A large number [of comedians, actors, musicians and others] volunteered to do a concert for us at Wembley, two or three thousand people at an evening of jokes to fund the campaign... They were loyal. Asked if they'd like to do this, they'd go, 'Yeah. All right'. It was partly because at that time the climate had become so toxic.[111]

Sagall wrote to senior figures in the Jewish community. The issue of Zionism came up almost immediately. Greville Janner, Labour MP and vice president of the Board of Deputies of British Jews, declined to commit himself, referring the request to Martin Savitt, chair of the Board of Deputies defence committee. He added:

> Several sources have told me that in fact your organisation does not only deal with anti-Nazi publicity and efforts, but that it is also anti-Zionist orientated... Perhaps you would let me know what the position is in that regard and whether platforms provided by you have in fact been used for anti-Zionist or anti-Israel speeches or statements.[112]

The Board of Deputies was convinced that the anti-Zionism of Peter Hain and the SWP meant they had to reject the ANL and support their own anti-NF initiative. Many Jews rejected this position. The social psychologist Henri Tajfel asked Sagall for its position on Zionism and, finding it 'satisfactory', agreed to be a sponsor.[113]

United fronts have to be built at every level. In the Manchester area it was rooted in an understanding between the SWP and Colin Barnett, the secretary of the North West TUC, also the

NUPE regional secretary. Geoff Brown remembers Barnett was:

> ambitious, he wanted to be an MP. The CP deferred to him. He was a workaholic, a Methodist lay preacher. We [the SWP] were the unruly element. Yet he also recognised that you couldn't have an effective force without us. In return for his cooperation, he insisted on regular meetings with us.[114]

This meant that the North West TUC gave full support to the ANL.[115] Winning over existing anti-fascist organisations was also essential. Much of this relied on trust. The decision of Maurice Ludmer, editor of *Searchlight,* to support the ANL was important.[116] Mike Luft remembers sitting with Graham Atkinson and Martin Bobker, all three of them active for years as anti-fascists in Manchester, waiting for Colin Barker, leading SWP member in the city who had invited them to talk about supporting this new organisation. 'Who is this guy?' asked Bobker sceptically. In the event, all three became active in the ANL, Bobker as its treasurer and Luft as its chair.

There were those who wanted to avoid being seen to take sides. Tony Benn's initial reaction to being told his parliamentary constituency had affiliated to the ANL, was to say 'You must not put people into the position of being for or against'.[117]

To help local ANL groups deal with the media and produce their own leaflets and bulletins, two briefing documents were produced. The first, written by Maurice Ludmer, 'The National Front and the Jews', looked at the NF's attitude to Jewish people.[118] This was quickly followed by 'Documentation on the politics of the National Front', covering the ideas of the NF with quotes from speeches, articles and interviews, mainly by the three full time leaders, Tyndall, Webster and Verrall.[119] It demonstrated the close parallels with the Nazis programme in the Weimar years in Germany between the two world wars, the importance of conspiracy theories, the emphasis on the use of force, its views on race, women, young people, trade unions, the left, democracy and welfare.[120]

Launch meetings

The ANL took off as if people had been waiting for it.[121] The challenge was to bring the local anti-racist and labour movement forces and as many new recruits as possible together to create the largest possible organised presence wherever the fascists might appear. A typical launch meeting had trade unionists, black and Asian activists and representatives of local anti-racist, anti-fascist committees on the platform. Whenever possible, they would be joined by a member of the steering committee. While often much of the initial preparation was done by SWP members – booking speakers, hiring a hall, printing and distributing leaflets, flyposting, contacting the press, arranging security – the enthusiasm with which the ANL was welcomed meant that there were always volunteers from other organisations and none to ensure the new branch was a united front. This required an openness to the ideas and initiatives of all. Many initiatives came from people at their first meeting wanting to get more involved. School Students Against the Nazis started when school students at the Reading ANL launch meeting argued that they were the key to taking on the NF in schools. Encouraged by the rest of the meeting, they produced their own newsletter, *SKAN* (Schools Kids Against the Nazis), which quickly became the paper of SKAN groups around the country.[122]

The founding statement called for a gigantic leafleting and postering campaign. How to make this happen on the ground was left open. A national newsletter included a short, hastily drafted note on local branches, sketching out what would be essential activities: 'Their job will be to 1) raise money locally, 2) ensure wide support from the Labour Movement, 3) organise individual supporters of the ANL, 4) ensure that the leaflets are distributed and that other initiatives are taken up locally'. The last sentence made a key point: 'It is also important to ensure that at all times the ANTI NAZI LEAGUE works closely with any local anti-fascist committees. Our aim should be to help, complement and expand their work.'[123]

ANL branches organised themselves as they chose. This generally differed little from how anti-racist, anti-fascist groups functioned. Some launch meetings were organised jointly with local ARAF groups as in Lambeth with ALARM (All Lambeth

Action Against Racism).[124] A secretary, sometimes called a convenor, was chosen by members. Many groups elected a chair, some had a committee. The larger ones would usually have a treasurer. Money was important. Leaflets and badges had to be paid for in advance. All positions would be subject to periodic election. Some groups produced newsletters, often including brief reports of decisions made at the most recent meeting. Hardly any produced minutes and even fewer had a constitution. People were encouraged to join the ANL, paying £1 and getting a membership card that quoted the 1946 poem by the anti-Nazi priest Pastor Niemoeller:

First they came for the Communists

And I did not speak out

Because I was not a Communist

Then they came for the Socialists

And I did not speak out

Because I was not a Socialist

Then they came for the trade unionists

And I did not speak out

Because I was not a trade unionist

Then they came for the Jews

And I did not speak out

Because I was not a Jew

Then they came for me

And there was no one left

To speak out for me

There was no prescribed format for launch meetings. The local Women's Voice group performed a play as part of the Glasgow launch meeting.[125] The Bristol launch was led off by the MP Joe Ashton showing the anti-NF party political broadcast he had produced. Platform dominated meetings weren't always needed. With the help of the annual Thames Film Festival, the South East London ANL founding meeting showed a documentary, *The California Reich: The true and terrifying story of the rebirth of the Nazi Party in America.*[126]

Neil McAllister in Preston remembers difficulties with the CP on setting up the local ANL:

> For a number of weeks we met together on a Sunday afternoon. The Communist Party was the dominant coherent left force and they and other people were saying we have to have a committee for the Anti Nazi League and we got to have these people on it. It was all about structure and nothing about how we engage people outside ourselves. So it came to the third or fourth Sunday and the SWP members just drove around all day on Sunday and signed up a hundred people to the Anti Nazi League – and then said 'This is the Anti Nazi League'.[127]

SWP members in Cardiff visited every organisation on the left suggesting a jointly organised launch. Insisting it would only be an SWP front, they all said no. In the event, with six days' notice, two hundred came to the launch meeting, so many that the seats had to be removed so everyone could get in. At the end, the chair, Billy Williams, a well-known union militant and SWP member, asked for nominations for a committee. Having received fourteen nominations, Billy proposed a committee of fourteen which included representatives from Plaid Cymru, Labour Party, Communist Party and the SWP. The desire for unity in the room was such that he had no difficulty overcoming the objections from those who wanted to debate Cardiff ANL's constitution.[128]

Launch meetings could be very large. Five hundred came to the Brighton launch. In Acton, 250, including thirty school students, heard Mrs Jayaben Desai, still leading the Grunwick strike in its seventeenth month, speak about the NF harassment of pickets and the many offensive and threatening phone calls she had received from them.[129] The Swansea meeting was sponsored by the local Trades Council, the Fire Brigades Union (FBU), the local hospital workers and civil servants' union branches and the university students' union.[130]

The 180 strong launch meeting in Pontefract, West Yorkshire, with Arthur Scargill, president of the Yorkshire National Union of Miners (NUM), speaking was the first of a number in mining communities.[131] Clear and forthright in his support for the ANL, Scargill was frequently invited to speak at ANL meetings.[132] The

Yorkshire NUM, with 60,000 members, was already affiliated to the ANL.[133] Having received reports that NUM members were involved with the NF – one was a candidate for Rotherham Council in the May elections – the Yorkshire NUM council voted that NUM members should refuse to work with anyone in the NF, 'sending them to Coventry'. Scargill told the press they 'would support any pit branch who votes not to work with a Front member'.[134]

Two dozen printworkers working nights sent apologies for non-attendance to the 130 strong first meeting in Ipswich. This decided to send two coaches to an ANL carnival that had been planned and to ask the Council to remove all Nazi slogans from the walls of the town, failing which the League would organise a public clean up. Students at the meeting agreed to set up a SKAN group.[135] In Manchester, where support was well established in the local trade union movement, a Festival for Equality was organised together with the NCCL and the North West Committee Against Racism to be held in the city's premier venue, the Free Trade Hall, with a line up including Peggy Seeger and Ewan MacColl. Voting to affiliate to the ANL, Leicester Trades Council also decided to organise a picket of NF paper sellers and to help pay the fines of those arrested at a previous picket.[136] There were also victories to enjoy as with the 'Celebration Drink-In' at the King's Arms, Colindale, north west London, after the pub's brewery decided to ban the NF from meeting there.[137]

Running the ANL

Joan Rudder worked in the office full time. She remembers:

The phones were always red hot. There was a creative buzz about the place. We realised how it was growing so quickly as we'd have people write in wanting to join. I'd have to look at a map and think 'Where might there be a group that I can send this to?'... There was far too much mail for one person. I set the volunteers on opening the mail.[138]

Peter Hain fielded press enquiries, helped by Paul Holborow when he wasn't 'on the road, doing meetings'.[139] The seemingly endless round of leafleting, flyposting and putting up stickers, all professionally produced, had to be supplied. Mike Barton remembers how his life in the tiny office was dominated by sending out packages of leaflets and posters supplied by the SWP printshop,[140] which was was big enough to quickly meet the ANL's needs. Peak demand by the ANL in busy weeks, such as before carnivals and elections, was the equivalent to a day's print shop production. Holborow remembers the MP Joe Ashton 'coming to the office to check us out. After half an hour of watching what went on, he was convinced the ANL was a serious runner.'[141]

Early tests

Helped by a Tory council willing to hire its town hall and Chief Constable James Anderton's determination to guarantee the NF's right to free speech, Webster went back to Hyde for the NF's next high profile event – a public meeting in the town hall in late January 1978. Colin Barnett's call for the Public Order Act to be invoked was again dismissed. With 2,000 police mobilised, a thousand anti-fascists were kept at a distance. Their coaches were stopped and searched while the NF's coaches had a police escort. Following instructions from their union's regional secretary, Colin Barnett, the caretakers refused to open the hall, forcing senior staff to do this.

Two weeks later, another NF meeting took place in Greater Manchester, this time in Bolton town hall. With the leading local Tory insisting that the decision to allow the meeting to take place was taken 'in defence of the fundamental political principle of free speech', the NF application went through council procedures 'on the nod'. Lawrence Cunliffe, the Labour deputy group leader, immediately resigned in protest at the Labour group's failure to raise any objection.[142] Opposition grew as tens of thousands of trades council and Anti Nazi League leaflets circulated in factories, schools, pubs and housing estates. Much of the leafleting was done by Asian Youth Organisation members, arguing that Asians should support the picket. Some head teachers held special assemblies to discourage pupils from attending. The night before the picket the local paper gave enormous coverage to local Asian leaders saying: 'The most they can do to us is to smash our windows and cause physical damage... Most of our members don't know about Friday's NF meeting. We just don't care.'[143] By contrast, the Salford University Students Union put together a

'Week Against Racism', supporting an anti-NF paint out, street meeting, demo and RAR gig in south Manchester the previous Saturday, film shows during the week, and a mobilising meeting Friday lunchtime to help fill a coach for Bolton at 5.30.[144]

That morning in Bolton, pickets on the snow-covered steps of the Town Hall were out from 8am carrying a fifteen-foot banner, 'No Nazis in our Town Hall'. An Asian Youth Organisation (AYO) car with loudspeakers toured Asian areas publicising the march and picket. Despite heavy policing of these areas with roadblocks and spot searches, 700 followed the AYO banner marching into the city centre. The Amalgamated Union of Engineering Workers district committee and the local student unions both organised marches of over 350 demonstrators. One hundred and fifty Nazis got into the Town Hall protected by 2,000 police including twenty on horseback. Fourteen-year-old Marcus Smith managed to get into the meeting to be 'appalled by the rubbish the speakers on the platform were talking about and the amount of thugs inside the building stopping any left wing from entering'.[145] After nineteen arrests, including several Asian youths, a defence campaign was quickly established. For all the repeated frustration as once again the NF and police collaborated, the ANL was now on the way in a number of areas to being established on the ground, bringing together trade unionists, students and local anti-racist organisations.

The ANL in Dewsbury, West Yorkshire were quick off the mark organising a march and meeting in protest against Tory controlled Kirklees council's refusal to ban the NF from public buildings. With 'firm support from local Asian people', local councillor Tom Megahy, leader of the Labour group, agreed to sponsor the League together 'with many other local trade unionists', and 700 marched including 250 young Asians.[146]

A week later several thousand joined a demonstration called by Birmingham Trades Council protesting a Young National Front launch rally in Digbeth Hall. The *Times* reported the counter-demonstration was largely peaceful except for a few minutes when black and white youths broke away smashing paving stones to hurl at 'a line of police crouched behind riot shields'. [147]

NF organising inside working-class organisations was not limited to trade unions and workplaces. *Socialist Worker* reported how:

> Labour Party members found some unpleasant characters frequenting Arnold Labour Club in the north of Nottingham recently. Some 20 members of the Arnold Labour Party were found to be handing out National Front leaflets and wearing NF badges. Things came to a head with a punch-up between members of the Labour Party and the Nazis. Three of the Nazis have since been expelled... Last week the club was leafletted by the Anti Nazi League, we are preparing mass leafleting and a demonstration in the area.[148]

A by-election was called early in February in Ilford North, an area where ten percent of the population were Jewish. Their heartland in East London a few miles away, the NF announced a march in the constituency five days before the poll, making a major confrontation that would test the ANL's united front look certain. Notwithstanding his claimed commitment to freedom of speech and assembly, McNee took no chances. He immediately used the 1936 Public Order Act to secure a ban on all political demonstrations in London for two months – the first such ban for fifteen years. The NF responded by announcing a 'mass canvass' and an indoor rally.[149]

Could the NF be effectively challenged? The ANL did not publicly oppose the ban. Instead, putting the argument that Peter Hain gave at the launch, it argued that the NF would not be stopped by bans but by mobilising as many people as possible to challenge them whenever they appeared in public.[150] Bans had always been used more often against the left than the right. Holborow later gave the example of the ban on the Leeds Trades Council's May Day march, which 'was banned on the pretext that the National Front were also marching the same weekend. The position should be that we get to mobilise such a huge movement against the National Front marching that they decide it is better for them not to march.'[151]

The challenge for the ANL was to provide a focus for activity that did not give McNee any pretext to attack those opposing the NF. If there was going to be a confrontation, it was going to be with the police not the NF. It would be more like Red Lion Square than Lewisham. The ANL decision was therefore to hold its own mass canvass 'to see that the lies and distortions of the Front's thugs and bully boys do not go unanswered'. A leaflet with 'Instructions to everybody taking part in Anti Nazi League activities' was given out.[152] The police presence on the day was massive: 6,000 officers, 100 police horses, the Special Patrol Group and four large marquees with a capacity of hundreds to accommodate those arrested. While the NF's 'mass canvass' involved 150 members distributing a low key leaflet that didn't mention immigration, the ANL mobilised 2,500, with groups of twenty to thirty leafleting thousands of homes.

Many found it a frustrating day. Mike Barton remembers the difficult job of being an ANL steward with some wanting to have 'another Lewisham'. Peter Hain remembers being impressed by the discipline shown by the ANL's supporters, not least when the police broke an agreement to allow a picket 150 yards from the NF's indoor rally. Late in the afternoon the NF bussed in 1,000 supporters under police protection, afterwards presenting the rally as a big success.[153] Labour lost the seat with a 10 percent swing to the Tories, while the Liberal vote collapsed. Standing for the first time in the constituency, the NF polled just under 5 percent, a result that will have left some of their members disappointed. The ANL managed the challenge, its momentum unbroken. Holborow argued afterwards:

> The ban was imposed because of the growing strength of the anti-fascists... [The ANL response was] getting people out to take the argument against the Front into people's homes and work. That is what the League is about. This was the Anti Nazi League's first major operation and is just a foretaste of the sort of campaign we will have to mount when the local elections come up in May.[154]

Writing in the *Jewish Chronicle*, Philip Kleinman agreed with Peter Hain giving 'the credit for the failure of the Front's mass canvass to intimidate Ilford's Jews and Asians not to any action on the part of the police but to the counteraction of the Anti-Nazi League. More power to it, I say'.[155]

Further evidence of the ANL's strength came with the decision of the Communist Party, the largest left organisation outside the Labour Party, to overcome its hostility to the SWP and support the ANL.[156] Having printed two positive reports in the *Morning Star* on the ANL – a front page photo of the ANL protest against Judge McKinnon outside the Old Bailey and a report on the launch of the ANL's campaign in the Ilford by-election – it now decided to support the League.[157] Gordon McLennan, the party's general secretary, Mick McGahey, vice president of the NUM, and Vishnu Sharma, IWA, both CP executive members, became sponsors. Bill Dunn, the CP industrial organiser, joined the steering committee. Its Political Committee's Weekly Newsletter reassured members that backing the ANL did not mean abandoning the CP's commitment to the many local anti-racist and anti-fascist committees they were working in and, in some cases, leading:

> We support this organisation [the ANL], as Gordon McLennan's report to the March Executive Committee made clear. Gordon and Mick McGahey are national sponsors. We need to be clear that the ANL came into existence as a propaganda and campaigning organisation against the National Front, and it is for this task that we support it.

However:

> It is not an appropriate body to carry out the detailed systematic work against racism ...for which broad anti-racist committees are the most appropriate, and are already in existence in many cities. Obviously whether to support the setting up of a local ANL alongside a broad Anti-Racism Committee is a tactical question...[158]

Having joined the ANL steering committee, Bill Dunn wrote in the *Morning Star* encouraging people to get involved. He acknowledged that many CP members were unhappy about joining an organisation initiated by the SWP: 'Sometimes it is felt that there is... an attempt to use the Anti Nazi League as a particular form of campaign organisation as the sectarian vehicle for a particular group at the expense of established organisations'. He nevertheless called for 'maximum unity at all levels', insisting that 'Maximum consultation and activity, working with, and not replacing, other organisations locally or nationally is our aim'.[159]

This did not come easily to those accustomed to seeking

control of organisations they were involved in. The CP had long been the major force in the Glasgow labour movement, accustomed to their lead being followed. Despite the enthusiasm of the 250 at the Glasgow launch meeting, clearly a success, some CP members argued a Glasgow ANL branch was unnecessary. The Scottish TUC had been in the front line to stop Kingsley Read's meeting, the Trades Council had worked with the Indian Workers Association leafleting against the NF and the Scottish Immigrant Labour Council (SILC) had a solid record of anti-racist activity. However, the CP was not monolithic. Many of its members were proud of its tradition of anti-fascism, particularly in Scotland, which went back to the Spanish civil war.[160] Bob Cooney, former political commissar of the British Battalion of the International Brigade in Spain, lifelong member of the Communist Party and hitherto hostile to Trotskyists, would soon be speaking to a hundred people at the ANL launch in Aberdeen.[161]

The Communist Party's roots in local labour movements made it easier to get support from union branches and shop stewards' committees. In Bristol this led to the Trades Council affiliating with five of its delegates now joining the Bristol ANL committee. Geoff Brown remembers approaching Stan Cole, chair of the Manchester AUEW district committee and long-standing member of the Communist Party, to get the committee's support. Sitting in a nearby pub after the committee meeting, Cole called the other committee members, sitting with their pints, and reconvened the meeting, which promptly agreed.[162] In North Wales it was the district secretary of the Communist Party, Manny Cohen, who called for setting up a local branch after a boy distributed copies of the NF leaflet 'How to spot a Red Teacher' in a local comprehensive.[163] There were also cases where the initiative came from Labour Party members. After NF members were reported parading the streets in Nazi-style uniform and recruiting in schools in Sevenoaks in Kent, the local Labour Party organised a meeting which decided to form an ANL branch. The ANL branch in Rugby was initiated by the local Labour MP, Bill Price.[164]

By the end of March the momentum on the ground made it possible to talk of take-off. Despite the decision of the national executive of the National Union of Students (NUS) not to support affiliation, Peter Hain was given a standing ovation by delegates at its Easter conference, who then took thousands of leaflets with them as they left.[165] The same weekend the ANL held the largest fringe meeting at the National Union of Teachers's annual conference, with two hundred listening to Kamlesh Gandhi, chair of the Grunwick Strike Committee, Tariq Ali and Paul Holborow.[166]

Even though Holborow was an SWP member and the ANL's initial sponsors included 'advocates of the politics of confrontation' like Paul Foot and Tariq Ali, the *Guardian* now acknowledged that 'somehow, suddenly, the League has become the campaign which came in from the cold'. Quoting Holborow, 'Suddenly we are on the verge of building a mass movement', it noted the ANL's 'growing strength and respectability' with membership 'well over 6,000', 'over 500,000 brutally direct leaflets distributed already this year', sponsors including 'normally non-political types' and 'a stroke of genius' in signing up 'a gaggle of top footballers'.[167] Launch meetings were now frequent, sometimes with large numbers of platform speakers. The ANL's March newsletter reported: 'Over 30,000 supporters' cards have been distributed, 25,000 badges have been sold, 3/4 million leaflets, 65,000 posters and 200,000 stickers have also been sent out.'[168]

The united front had been established.[169] The task now was to make it happen on a huge scale. An anti-racist, anti-fascist presence was still to be established in thousands of workplaces, schools, colleges, union branches, trades councils. Many local organisations still had to be actively involved. National sponsors were no substitute for active members. It was an intensely political affair. Sectarian arguments could be found in many places.[170] Winning a relationship of trust with local anti-racist and anti-fascist committees could only be achieved by working together. Nothing made the problem clearer than the two demonstrations in Lewisham. Could the ANL be big enough to decisively defeat its opponent? Would its roots in the working-class movement be strong enough? With an election expected in less than a year, there had to be a move to a higher gear.

Hundreds of thousands of leaflets needed thousands of leafleters. Every local group needed to recruit members. In Leamington, forty supporters of LARAFC and the ANL signed a letter to the local press calling for united action 'to counteract the flood of race hate propaganda which will reach millions of homes' in the forthcoming election.[171] Where work had been done signing up ANL members, volunteers were not hard to find. Manchester Polytechnic students volunteered in numbers for the May 1978 elections.[172] Mass leafleting worked. After 14,000 households in Watford and South Oxhey were leafletted before the May 1978 council election, the NF vote in Watford fell to an average 3.1 percent. In the Vicarage ward the NF polled only fifty-two votes compared to 395 in 1976. The NF vote in South Oxhey also fell despite intensive NF activity in the estate pubs and in flyposting the shopping area.[173]

The challenge was to sustain the most active elements of the ANL. Launch meetings with representative platforms were necessary for the united front to work but, as Colin McGregor pointed out:

> Nothing is more calculated to piss off the young blacks and punks who are moving with us than a load of boring old farts telling us all how they fought against fascism in the Spanish Civil War and that everything must go through the proper channels. We have to find ways to make it possible for the young enthusiasts to challenge and defeat the old guard, whilst at the same time using the old guard's support to mobilise the rank and file in the workplaces.[174]

Solving this problem required using imagination.

6: All power to the imagination! Be a realist. Demand the impossible! Carnival Against the Nazis

★Young people were always the most active element. Travelling round the country in 1977 visiting SWP branches as the national secretary, Jim Nichol saw the energy young comrades were putting into organising gigs that were part of the Rock Against Racism initiative launched a year earlier. Having organised solidarity concerts and rallies for strikers, he had seen how they could boost a campaign.[1] The 40,000 attending the 1971 fundraising Concert for Bangladesh with the Beatles and Ravi Shankar showed how big an open-air concert in support of a campaign could be. Nichol's idea was an anti-racist, anti-fascist demonstration, built on a national scale, marching to the middle of the NF's strongest base to a Rock Against Racism gig.[2] It had to have a reggae band. Bob Marley's single and album *Exodus* was one of the big hits of 1977. Its lyrics included...

...Jah come to break down-pression,
Rule equality,
Wipe away transgression,

Set the captives free.
Exodus, all right, all right!
Movement of jah people! oh, yeah!
Exodus, movement of jah people!
Oh, now, now, now, now!...

Nichol remembers thinking that 'if the ANL was new territory for the SWP leadership, a demonstration and rock festival was going to be much more so... Rock Against Racism was vibrant. With the people involved, it had a bigger base than the SWP... The reports of the gigs were striking'.[3] But so far RAR had only organised one concert with over a thousand people. Could its organisers, Red Saunders and Roger Huddle deliver?

Saunders had been a mod in his early teenage years, into black music: 'I was just a working photographer and then the art got to me – typography, Rodchenko posters, Mayakovsky poetry.' Saunders remembers:

> CAST, the Cartoon Archetypical Slogan Theatre, was my 'road to Damascus' experience. I was a young photographic apprentice. A friend at work suggested we go to the Peanuts Club, upstairs in a pub in the East End.[4] It started with somebody announcing a show coming on. We all moved back a bit. Suddenly, four people appeared in front of me in jeans with white faces. It was very early CAST. They proceeded to play 'John D. Muggins is dead', why he died in the Vietnam War. Twenty extremely violent, extremely physical and extremely loud minutes and they were gone. Up to then I hadn't been political. It completely blew my mind, my first ever inkling of what imperialism was. Afterwards I chatted to the actors. They invited me to the Working Men's College in Camden where they met. A couple of weeks later I went along and joined.[5]

CAST was founded in 1965 after splitting from the Unity Theatre run by the Communist Party:

> At Unity they ran an old tyme Music Hall... and we actually got to learn and love the old songs, but realised that the nostalgia was crap, people would come and sing *The Black Leg Miner*... it was really quite good... but it was either folk,

which was the Communist Party tradition, or it was old tyme Music Hall! And they weren't the things that turned CAST on, who were, by nature, rock and roll people.[6]

CAST was 'for a long time the only avowedly socialist theatre company of the sixties'.[7] It covered issues such as racism, anti-apartheid and war.[8] In its second show, *Mr Oligarchy's Circus,* where 'capitalism was a circus, the ruling class was a circus master and the Labour Party was its bedfellow... playing at colleges to the radical students' movement in 1968, Red was very strong as Mr Oligarchy'.[9] Saunders remembers:

> We got heavily involved with the Vietnam Solidarity Campaign, VSC... We started to perform for organisations like the International Socialists, IS, and VSC. You started to hear debates and then came Rodchenko, Popova. Visuality is my thing. The biggest thing that hit me was Eisenstein.[10]

Red and others left to set up Kartoon Klowns in 1972, a time when:

> Young, radical theatre-makers threw themselves eagerly into the struggle, producing plays which trumpeted their solidarity with the insurgent dockers, shipyard workers, railmen and miners, rising to a crescendo in early 1974, when the second of two great miners' strikes brought the Heath government to its knees.[11]

The connection worked both ways. Shop stewards from the Royal Group of Docks used to come to rehearsals. Rehearsals were important. Standards were high. As with CAST, 'the act was very tight, not lazy/sloppy like a lot of other acts'.[12]

Roger Huddle was an apprentice printer, training as a compositor and becoming very interested in design when he joined the International Socialists in 1966, at the time a group of just 200 members. He started in the IS print shop in 1971. Five 'exciting and turbulent years' later, he was a typographer and graphic designer, 'a graphic propagandist, fantastically influenced by the avant-garde in the Russian revolution... I think that is what brought Red and me together... Both of us remember the famous photo of Jefferson Airplane coming into a football stadium doing a gig with Vietnam flags flying dressed up as

American soldiers with peace signs'.[13] Always a big music fan, Huddle ran a disco, 'Night Train'.

The two met at a conference in Coventry in the summer of 1976.[14] Saunders explains how they met and where the idea for Rock Against Racism came from:

> Roger was involved with the Right to Work Campaign. We met up to consider the possibility of doing a one-off concert for the Right to Work march, from London to the TUC in Brighton, September 1976.[15] We were both really concerned by the rise of racism and the disillusionment with the Labour government. We had a long chat and agreed we should do a concert called Rock against Racism, a one-off thing. We discussed and discussed it and didn't think any more of it. We came to the conclusion that, if it was to be done, it had to be done properly and there wasn't time, so I DJ-ed on the march one evening with Night Train.[16]

Founding Rock Against Racism

It was rock musician Eric Clapton's racist outburst at the Birmingham Odeon, August 1976 that finally led to RAR. Coming on stage drunk, Clapton asked 2,000 fans:

> Do we have any foreigners in the audience tonight? If so, please put up your hands. So where are you? Well, wherever you all are, I think you should all just leave. Not just leave the hall, leave our country. I don't want you here, in the room or in my country. Listen to me, man! I think we should send them all back. Stop Britain from becoming a black colony. Get the foreigners out. Get the w*gs out. Get the c**ns out. Keep Britain white... The black w*gs and c**ns and Arabs and fucking Jamaicans don't belong.[17]

This was a serious shock. Clapton was not an isolated figure. The same month David Bowie told *Playboy* magazine:

> I think Britain could benefit from a fascist leader. After all, fascism is really nationalism... I believe very strongly in fascism, people have always responded with greater efficiency under a regimental leadership... Adolf Hitler was

one of the first rock stars... You've got to have an extreme right front come up and sweep everything off its feet and tidy everything up.[18]

Saunders drafted a letter of protest against Clapton's racist rant during a Kartoon Klowns rehearsal of a new play *Yes, but – Socialism or Barbarism*. Everyone signed it. Saunders phoned Roger Huddle to add his name: 'We sent it to all the music press – like *Black Echoes*, *New Musical Express*, *Melody Maker*, *Sounds* – and the socialist press – including the *Morning Star* and *Socialist Worker*.'[19]

> When I read about Eric Clapton's Birmingham concert when he urged support for Enoch Powell, I nearly puked. What's going on, Eric? You've got a touch of brain damage. So you're going to stand for MP and you think we're being colonised by black people. Come on...you've been taking too much of that Daily Express stuff, you know you can't handle it. Own up. Half your music is black. You're rock music's biggest colonist. You're a good musician but where would you be without the blues and R&B? You've got to fight the racist poison, otherwise you degenerate into the sewer with the rats and all the money men who ripped off rock culture with their cheque books and plastic crap. Rock was and still can be a real progressive culture, not a package mail-order stick-on nightmare of mediocre garbage. We want to organise a rank-and-file movement against the racist poison in rock music – we urge support – all those interested please write to:
> ROCK AGAINST RACISM,
> Box M, 8 Cotton Gardens, London E2 8DN

Jack Robertson, who worked in the SWP print shop, remembers Huddle storming into the office to read the letter he and Saunders had written. A week later Huddle was fizzing with excitement at the overwhelming response there had been.[20] Within a few weeks four or five hundred people had written in.[21] It was these people that created RAR. They demanded action. From the beginning RAR was a truly grass roots campaign. Chris Ayton remembers: 'I was already an anti-Nazi and wanted to do something. So, when I saw the letter, I was playing in a band. Everyone was in a band. If you were that age, if you were a punk, you were in a band. So I just responded.'[22]

Paul Furness found the letter was 'like an overdue breath of fresh air and I knew that something was going to happen'.[23] Saunders later commented: 'Don't ever think writing letters is a waste of time. Rock Against Racism wouldn't have happened without that.'[24]

Saunders remembers 'As soon as the responses to the letter started coming in, I went "we need a logo" before thinking about a magazine or a manifesto'.[25] He asked a friend, the designer and art editor of the *Sunday Times* magazine, David King, whom he'd worked for as a freelance photographer. King came up with a star. King was a socialist, actively supporting campaigns such as the Anti-Apartheid Movement against the apartheid regime in South Africa. As a student he had been influenced by the filmmaker Eisenstein and the use of montage and dramatic framing. He 'couldn't bear to see so much amateurishly designed print material being pushed out by these small political groups. He wanted to demonstrate that through well thought out and effectively designed material, their messages would stand a far better chance of getting through'.[26]

David King's star derived from the five-pointed red star sewn onto the caps of Red Army Russian soldiers: the five points seen by some as symbolising the five continents. King gave the star a different character by slightly bending the sides outwards, giving it a softer look and using a range of often contrasting colours. John Hall, a serious music fan living in Manchester, remembers that wearing a RAR badge was not like wearing a charity sticker, which was common at the time:

> When you'd see somebody with a badge on, you'd instantly have that rapport and get talking to them. I used to occasionally have people come up to me, 'What have you got there?' and 'What's all that about?' You always felt a bit of fear wearing it. You put it on, you think 'What's going to happen tonight?'... There were sometimes gangs, more in the early, middle '70s, the skinhead phenomenon... That badge definitely gave encouragement and confidence to people and that thing of 'We're not alone'.[27]

Red remembers that '*Socialist Worker* offered a whole page

in the paper and we worked it out to give the history: our letter, the response and the manifesto of the Rock Against Racism Ad hoc Committee'.[28] The manifesto explained RAR's 'Why?', 'What for?' and 'How?'. It rooted Clapton and Bowie's racism in the drive to make money.

> **Musicians...fans...we need you**
>
> So Bowie discovers Hitler and Clapton urges support for Powell. 'Superstars' open their mouths and out comes fascist and racist garbage. Pathetic cover-ups do not alter the fact that they give credence to the ideas of the sewer and make heroes of the rats.
>
> RAR was formed as a gut reaction by socialists and music fans to the unbelievable hypocrisy of musicians who made their money out of black music and then turn against black people. Rock music, reggae, soul, rock 'n' roll, funk, jazz is with us every day. Day and night, on the radio, the TV, the pub, the disco, the cafe. It's always there, the music of the black and white urban working class.
>
> But music is not sacred, it's just like everything else in this society – a product of its environment and money rules, not music. And superstars mean superprofits.
>
> Today's environment is a crisis one. So isolated guitar 'gods' and their record company executives care little for the world of the unemployed school leaver or the black kid getting beaten up in the police station. It's all down to market exploitation (product-wise) and whining about tax problems in the Bahamas. In the first place rock music, black and white, came from the experience of living under the system. For us it must be part of the struggle to change the system. As part of that battle Rock Against Racism exists to fight racism in and out of Rock music.
>
> Roger Huddle & Red Saunders, RAR Ad-hoc Committee [29]

The page quoted twenty fans and musicians who had written in supporting RAR and volunteering to get involved. Saunders later described RAR as the most bottom-up organisation ever, 'so bottom up it had no top'. Nevertheless, it had a phone, a desk, PO box and access to the SWP printshop. When RAR got a phone call from someone asking to be put in touch with their local organisation, Saunders would check the name of the town and tell the caller that *they* were the organisation in the town. They would be sent a box of badges and told how to produce banners.[30] When they asked for financial support to put on gigs, they were told: 'All we have here is a rubber band and two paper clips'. The badges with David King's star were an immediate success, selling thousands, quickly becoming RAR's main source of income. 'At the same time kids were writing to say they'd been making their own t-shirts, knitting them up even – talk about the self-activity of the class'.[31]

Local counter cultures were important for this. There were more than a hundred radical bookshops where young people could find out what was going on, pick up leaflets, buy badges, books, pamphlets, newspapers and fanzines.[32] Jill Catlow remembers the Amamus bookshop in Blackburn which had:

> ...a huge range of publications: revolutionary socialist, anarchist, books on women's liberation, gay rights, ecology and also anti-racist materials. It had *Peace News, International Times,* the *Catonsville Roadrunner, Black Dwarf, Oz...* There was a room upstairs where they held meetings, for example opposing the Vietnam war. The women's group organised pregnancy testing. People came to hang out, especially at weekends.[33]

ANL and RAR also fed into local initiatives. It was always a two-way process. In Telford the fanzine *Guttersnipe* was:

> ...inspired by the activities of the Anti-Nazi League and RAR. Barney Mokgatle, one of the students involved in the Soweto uprising in South Africa... visited Telford a few weeks prior to the launch of *Guttersnipe*. The meeting that Mokgatle spoke at was cited by *Guttersnipe* as 'The kick-off for the ANL in Telford' and seems also to have served as a catalyst for the fanzine.[34]

In London, there were weekly meetings, now called 'RAR Central' in Red's studio. Open to all, they were properly run, discussing strategy, how to involve people with gigs and conferences and going to the pub afterwards.

RAR came out of the work of revolutionary socialists in

music, art, theatre, design, members of the 1968 generation, radicalised by the May events in France, rejecting the hippy culture, some finding roots in the revolutionary Constructivism of Lissitzky, Tatlin and Rodchenko, others inspired by the anarchic Situationists. Saunders spanned both: a revolutionary socialist who, while rejecting Leninism, described himself as a fellow traveller of the SWP, recognising that many of the early members of RAR were SWP members.[35] He called for 'All Power to the Imagination', the May '68 slogan in France, where first students occupied their universities then workers occupied their factories and ten million workers went on strike. Mayakovsky's revolutionary poetry connected with the moment:

> What's the point of toiling in factories, getting dirt all over your face and on your days off looking at others' luxuries with sleep filling your blank eyes?
>
> Enough of the same old rubbish. Wipe clean your hearts.
>
> The streets are our brushes. The squares are our palettes...
>
> Out into the streets, you Futurists, poets and bangers of drums![36]

Roger and Red were not alone in their commitment to art and design as integral to revolutionary politics. One of the first SWP members to get involved with RAR, writer, historian and doctor, David Widgery later wrote how 'in 1975, on the initiative of Roland Muldoon... we set up an informal committee to co-ordinate agit-prop work'.[37] The IS Agit-prop Committee organised film showings from Glasgow to Southampton, Widgery took Cinema Action's film *Miners* round the Yorkshire coalfield. Two hundred attended the first IS Agit-prop conference in Manchester, in September 1975, with sessions on organising theatre, photography, cartooning, 'song-swopping for socialist minstrels' and 'a blistering attack on that appalling left-wing institution "The Social"', parties organised to raise money.[38] This was followed by small groups making silk screen posters, banners, talks on audio cassettes and slide shows with accompanying audio tapes on Chile and Portugal. CAST toured with *Sam the Man* on the hopes and disappointments of the Labour left, North West Spanner showed *Winding up* on the decline and fall of the cotton industry, and 7:84's play looked at the rise of multinationals such as ITT and the need to fight them.[39]

Huddle points out that their work in graphics, photography, agit-prop theatre, music and revolutionary politics meant 'we went for the idea of RAR gigs immediately, coupled with visual images influenced by all the best in our tradition – the Constructivists of the 1917 Russian Revolution, the photomontages of John Heartfield, Dadaism, Pop Art and the anti-Vietnam War Movement in the US'.

It was time to make something happen. 'We decided we'd better put on a gig... At that time pub rock was a big thing. First gig we did was with Carol Grimes. She was pub rock.'[40] RAR began as a soul funk retrospective, determined to avoid the money-dominated mainstream.[41] For Roger Huddle is was important to 'do gigs in East London where the NF were. So we booked The Princess Alice pub'.[42]

> We'd organised things before so we weren't frightened. We got some socialists from the dockers union to do security. I remember putting up the banner on stage. The banners came from the other side of our '60s background – Agitation. We loved artists from Alexander Rodchenko to Andy Warhol.[43]

Young activist Steve Cedar 'hand printed the posters on a stencilling machine in his living room, as everything was in those days, from demos to public meetings'.[44] On the night he kept his eye on the cash box with the takings from the 200 who came. Others took on responsibility for the security. Bob Light remembers how local SWP members:

> ...women and men were placed on all four corners of the junction which the Alice stood on to warn us if the Nazi hordes were coming, and we had a reception committee waiting for them at the top of the stairs. Just in case that proved inadequate, we had six pick axe handles in a cricket bag and several cans of pepper spray that I had bought at a motorway service station in France... In the event, the Nazis bottled it (...they usually did) but for me the evening developed a rhythm that would become all-too-familiar

in the RAR days. You could summarise our evening under the headings, Apprehension, Tension and Frustration. The Apprehension was driven by fear – the fear that the Nazis would come streaming up the stairs, fear that I would get seriously hurt, fear that I would let my fear get the better of me. But as the minutes and hours passed that turned to Tension – we knew we had to keep our guard, we knew we had to keep everyone on their toes, we knew we couldn't afford to drink, we knew we couldn't relax, we knew we couldn't enjoy the gig. Then, as the gig inside was turning into a glorious celebration of anti-racist fun, courtesy of Carol Grimes and her band, came frustration. Frustration that we had not been able to enjoy the evening and even more frustration that we had not been able to give the Nazis the fucking good hiding they certainly would have got.[45]

The second London gig a month later in December 1976 was at the Royal College of Art. It was not the bastion of privilege it sounds like. Its students had recently occupied for a month fighting cuts in education. Two activists, John Dennis and Wayne Minter, joined the SWP where they heard about RAR.[46] Carol Grimes played, joined by Matumbi and Limousine. 'From then our idea [was] to mix styles and try to have a black band with a white one'.[47] Red remembers:

> It quickly became our thing to mix up the bands. We had to have black bands on stage... But putting the black and white bands together broke down the fear. One of the most wonderful gigs we did was at Hackney Town Hall. We had the reggae band The Cimarons on with the punk act Generation X. Everyone jammed together at the end. It became a blueprint.[48]

Punk

The same month, Johnny Rotten, front man of the Sex Pistols, goaded by the presenter of a popular TV programme to be controversial, captured the headlines using the word 'shit' and other obscenities. Punk, with its anarchic, 'fuck everything' attitude, had arrived.[49] Punks were instantly recognisable with their 'do-it-yourself' dress featuring bin bags, chains, safety pins, their hair every possible colour, often with Mohican hairstyles. Only needing to learn basic chords, using cheap electric guitars, punk bands started up quickly in large numbers, their music and lyrics wild and aggressive, their fans jumping up and down 'pogo-ing', as it was called, in time with the music, ritually spitting at the band members.[50] Roger remembers how 'we knew there was an underground, young, nihilistic, [that] we weren't in touch with. We were older. Our experience taught us that this was a real shift. No future, the Labour government has let us down. If we didn't orient on that, we would miss the audience'.[51]

Punk bands adopted names that shocked while trying to be witty and hard to fathom. Some wore 'anarchist symbols, images of Karl Marx and inverted crosses', others, including Siouxsie Sioux and Sid Vicious, wore swastikas as the ultimate shock symbol with many following their example.[52] Neil McAllister remembers a punk band in Bolton called The Hangmen who used to sing 'I wanna smash a hippie' and 'Come back Hitler, all is forgiven'.[53] Johnny Rotten took the opposite view of the fascists: 'I despise them. No one should have the right to tell them they can't live here because of the colour of their skin or their religion or whatever the size of their nose. How could anyone vote for something so ridiculously inhumane?'[54]

Bands could be well received in unexpected places. Chris Ayton remembers the Silver Jubilee celebrations in July 1977:

> There were all these street parties which wanted a band to play. So we hired a little lorry, got on the back, drove up to any street we knew was having a party, parked and started playing, sang a few songs then went to the next one, doing it as anti monarchy. The people there didn't care, it was all part of the fun. Lots of contradictions with all the Union Jacks over the tables in the street. People were quite happy, they weren't pro-queen.[55]

There was also a deliberate use of ambiguity as with The Clash's song 'White Riot', released March 1977. Quite the opposite of what it appeared to many who hadn't listened to the words, it had been inspired by the courage of the black youth who stood up to the police at the 1976 Notting Hill carnival.[56]

...Black man gotta lotta problems
But they don't mind throwing a brick
White people go to school
Where they teach you how to be thick...

...All the power's in the hands
Of people rich enough to buy it
While we walk the street
Too chicken to even try it...[57]

RAR's success owed much to having the same DIY attitude as punk together with a common hatred of commercialism and hierarchy: 'RAR's fight is amongst the youth whose lifestyle is rebellious... Punk is not just the music. It was visual, it revolutionised graphics, it's anti-authority, anarchistic and loud. It has a lot to give Rock Against Racism and RAR has a lot to give it.'[58]

At the same time, there was tension. Saunders described those who failed to recognise the power of music as 'humourless Trots', 'the pint of bitter and pullover brigade', whose indifference to art and music had to be challenged.[59] Widgery attacked the greyness of the left, its failure to use the imagination:

> Go to the average left-wing meeting – a speaker who may be good, but followed by a generally lifeless question-and-answer session and a list of exhortations from the chair. Yet the struggle for socialism is the struggle to tap the immense creative, imaginative ability of working people, the enthusiasm that is crushed by class society.[60]

Kate Alexander puts a different view:

> Although there were occasional tensions, [RAR] was always backed by the [SWP] Central Committee, and branches, to varying degrees, mobilised for RAR events and sometimes organised RAR gigs. The 'tensions' and the 'varying degrees' were inevitable and proper – there were, after all, other priorities as well, and these varied from one locality to another.[61]

Roger was a part-time DJ at fundraising events. At a benefit helping set up a gay switchboard called Icebreaker, he and Red met Tom Robinson, Britain's first openly gay musician to get into the top ten of the music charts.[62] Already involved with the Gay Liberation Front for a number of years, Robinson became a regular at the meetings.[63] After a gig in Scarborough at the beginning of September, young Leeds activist Paul Furness wrote:

> I've just been to see the Tom Robinson Band and, by Christ, ever felt proud? He just stopped short of advertising *Socialist Worker*! Wot a bleedin' great band – a bloody great political band. See 'em! He's someone who ain't scared of fascists. He asks you which side you're on: before the concert the audience might not have known, after it they did – a total stranger joined the SWP![64]

By the end of October, the Tom Robinson Band reached No 5 in the UK Singles Chart with their first single '2-4-6-8 Motorway'. He played it live on the BBC's *Top of the Pops* – typical audience of 15 million – wearing a pink triangle badge and with a Rock Against Racism sticker on his guitar. Robinson remembers: 'The Met were harassing gay men in Earls Court and black youth in Brixton under the Sus laws and opposing them was all part of the same struggle. Once you looked at where rock came from the proposition of Rock Against Racism... was blindingly obvious.'[65]

Such high-profile commitment was hard work. Young student John Baine, later to become known as Attila the Stockbroker, remembers following the Tom Robinson Band 'round South East England for a while. My mates and I would turn up at their gigs, get rat-arsed, pogo furiously and shout "The National Front is a Nazi Front! Smash the National Front!" over and over again, which really pissed Tom off'.[66]

Temporary Hoarding

The main music papers had a combined circulation of over 400,000. From early on RAR got backing from Neil Spencer at *New Musical Express*, Vivian Goldman, features editor at *Sounds*, and the late-night BBC Radio 1 presenter John Peel. David Seymour, who was active in an art college in Devon recalls: 'Our source of information was the music press – NME and *Melody Maker* – and getting involved was a simple matter of calling RAR and getting sent a box of badges.'[67]

The left-wing monthly *The Leveller* introduced its readers to 'the first music-based political campaign, Rock Against Racism, the IS-backed campaign to attack racist popular culture and bring revolution into rock'.[68]

Red saw the importance of a print publication:

> It was very important that we pitched our propaganda with a very high visual language... We wanted to produce some form of newspaper/magazine that held the group together and made noise. We came up with the idea of *Temporary Hoarding*. This would carry posters, news from RAR groups and a gig guide so that supporters could do their own gigs.[69] Now, as the punk rock movement grew, all these fanzines appeared. I'd seen the most famous one called *Sniffin' Glue*. We mixed that with Chinese wall posters that I knew about. These were newspapers designed to be pasted on a wall. They were a temporary hoarding, just intended to last for a bit. So that's what we based our magazine on and why we called it *Temporary Hoarding*. And quite often we literally designed it as a poster so you could paste it on a wall. We wanted lots of visual images. The left is too wordy sometimes.[70]

The first issue was put together by Roger Huddle, Andy Darke, Red Saunders and David Widgery in the art room of the SWP print shop in Hackney and launched on May Day 1977 at the Roundhouse in Chalk Farm, London. With 1,500 people and a mood sharpened by the Battle of Wood Green a week earlier, it was RAR's first big gig. Red describes how 'We had huge fuck-off banners made of the brightest psychedelic material with our slogan "Love Music, Hate Racism" stencilled in big letters, all hand made to a high standard. The whole of the Roundhouse was covered'.[71] 'At the end of the night history was made with the reggae band Aswad jamming with Carol [Grimes] and about 20 other musicians.'[72] The money raised was given to the Right to Work Campaign and the Islington 18 Defence Committee.

Temporary Hoarding's front page announced:

TEMPORARY HOARDING

ROCK AGAINST RACISM
20p.

We want rebel music, street music. Music that breaks down people's fear of one another. Crisis music. Now music. Music that knows who the real enemy is.

Rock against racism.

**LOVE MUSIC
HATE RACISM**

■ TH Number 1: the fact that RAR appeared in *TempoRARy* was noticed after the design was complete, but before printing. A lucky accident

> We want rebel music, street music.
> Music that breaks down people's fear of one another.
> Crisis music.
> Now music.
> Music that knows who the real enemy is.
> Rock against racism.
> LOVE MUSIC, HATE RACISM

Dave Widgery wrote a passionate, vivid and closely argued piece, 'What is racism?'.[73] A page on 'Guidelines for RAR gig organisers' spelt out the essentials that had to be got right, checking the venue, the PA, sorting out the bands, the pickets, the posters, the money, decorating the hall, and the security – 'try and get your own local heavies'. The graphic designer Ruth Gregory and photographer Syd Shelton, both working at the SWP print shop, became involved from issue 2.[74] The carnival issue, no.3, opened up to an A1-sized montage which could be put up as a wall poster.

RAR kept being 'bottom-up'. Tom Robinson notes how 'The most refreshing thing about RAR in those early days was its grassroots nature – the way unknown reggae and punk bands could be found sharing stages at small venues'.[75] Paul Furness, already a veteran of clashes with the NF in Leeds, organised the first RAR gig outside London: 'It was in a prefab, some sort of social club used by trade unions, that backed onto Leeds Poly... There was a hard core of us – myself, Linda, Barry, Dave and a few others from the SWP – who set up the Leeds RAR Club... We deliberately made the gigs feel political.'[76]

With *Temporary Hoarding* coming out every few months, RAR now kept in touch with its supporters. Bob Humm, who worked on the magazine, remembers selling out of it at gigs and people enthusiastically waiting for the next issue.[77] With 'a strong centre focused on achieving concrete ends providing propaganda, encouragement and help for anybody willing to have a go', local RAR groups sprang up from Brighton to Edinburgh.[78] John Baine, a nineteen-year-old student at Kent university, 'was learning fast, one of a group selling *Temporary Hoarding*, badges, stickers', organising 'sporadic' RAR format events that were nevertheless 'incredibly successful'.[79]

Kate Webb, who ran the RAR office, reflects on the audience for RAR:

> We'd all squeeze into RAR's tiny office, sackfuls of mail strewn around the floor. From the letters flooding in it was evident that there was a nation of kids out there, bored out of their minds, and horrified by the spectre of the National Front marching on their high streets. They described living in nowhere towns and suburbs that closed down at seven o'clock, while they ached for a wider, more glamorous world which they tried to discover by listening to John Peel late into the night or reading James Baldwin under the covers by torchlight.
>
> RAR became a network before we knew what a network was. We told these kids: here are the addresses of other music fans in your area. Set up a RAR group, design a poster, put on a gig, write your own fanzine, and challenge the local National Front. We told them anyone could do it and wrote step-by-step Gig Guides showing them how. And in *Temporary Hoarding*, the Mekons published an article explaining how to build your own PA system, while the Au Pairs described how they recorded their first single by borrowing their mum and dad's holiday money. The explosion of punk and reggae meant that there were bands all over the country hungry for gigs. And there was massive energy and frustration everywhere you turned, which RAR tapped into and transformed into action.[80]

At the Hackney Town Hall gig in August: 'The mood was euphoric, ending with the singers of the two bands [Cimarons and Generation X] clasping upraised hands while the crowd chanted "Black and White Unite". Afterwards you could smell change on the East London breeze, the taste of the world upside down.'[81]

Derek Merrill, a Southall teacher, remembers suggesting that the brothers of one of his school students in West London might play for RAR. Their band, Misty in Roots, performed in the first Ealing RAR gig in July 1977 and the second a few months later, both sold-out events. Ealing RAR concentrated on local bands and sound systems. Where necessary they went to the audience when the audience couldn't come to them, as with a school in nearby Southall because Asian girls couldn't attend otherwise.[82]

In Newcastle, after the local SWP organiser got a heavy metal band to play, the landlord of the venue pulled the plug only to change his mind when it was explained to him what would happen if he didn't. The *Newcastle Chronicle* wouldn't take the advert for the gig at first but changed their mind and put it in for free after a picket was organised.[83] The gig was a wild success with punks joining afterwards in flyposting Right to Work campaign posters on a Tory MP's office windows.[84]

In Manchester, Bernie Wilcox, a young draughtsman living in Partington, an overspill council housing estate on the edge of Manchester, got together with the musician Dick Witts, to promote RAR putting on gigs, if possible in working-class venues like Partington Community Centre. In Birmingham a RAR club held gigs at the Digbeth Civic Hall, the Communist Party's Star Club and other venues. Volunteers designed, produced and flyposted the posters.

A march in 1977 from Liverpool to the TUC congress in Blackpool had hundreds marching, almost all young, often school leavers. Most signed up outside the social security office where they made their weekly visit to claim unemployment benefit. It was a small step to organise RAR gigs on the march, important given the racist ideas of many of those taking part.

Live punk rock,
presented by Rock Against Racism and
The Right to Work,
all proceeds to Chloride occupation.
North East London Poly,

25 June 1977.[85]

The energy of punk could be overwhelming. Asked to organise gigs in Kirkby, Wigan and Blackpool for the march to the TUC Congress in September 1977, Manchester RAR booked Wigan Casino for the Saturday night only for 2,000 punks to turn up

Photograph: Richard Arridge

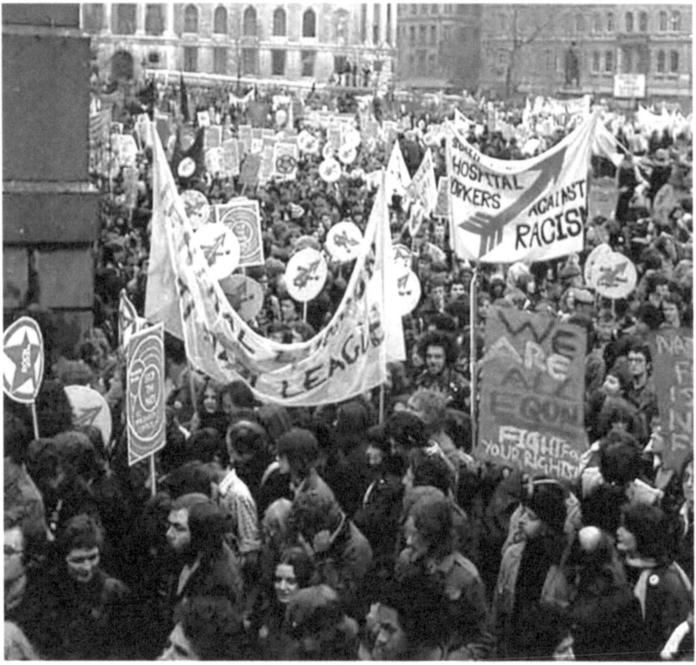

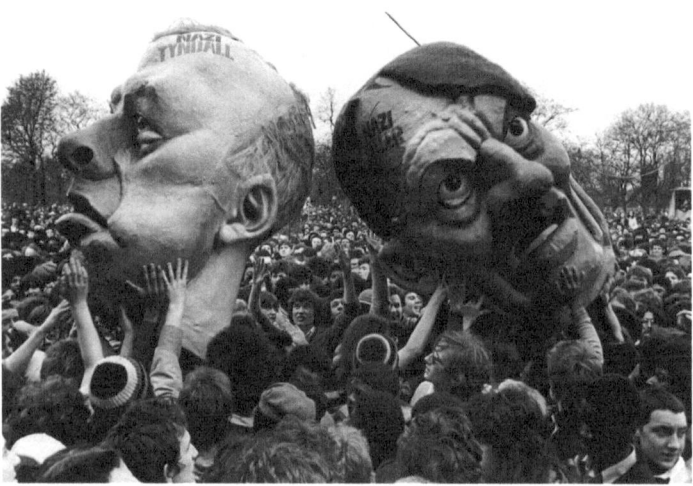

■ Saturday 30 April 1978 march to Victoria Park forms in Trafalgar Square

■ Fluck & Law's heads of Tyndall and Hitler passed across the Carnival audiance

having heard a rumour that the Sex Pistols were playing.[86]

Victoria Park Carnival

The growth and vibrancy of RAR, the Right to Work Campaign's ability to organise marches with large numbers of young people, the anti-racism in workplaces shown by the Grunwick mass pickets and, above all, Lewisham and the take-off of the ANL meant Jim Nichol had little difficulty getting the SWP Central Committee to support the idea of holding a rally in Trafalgar Square followed by a march with banners and placards to Victoria Park for a carnival.[87] But, as with the launch of the ANL, convincing the National Committee was much tougher. It meant persuading leading comrades who played important roles in their workplaces where they would have to win people to support the idea. Nichol focused on Peter Bain, a worker intellectual who worked at Chrysler in Glasgow where he had helped build a factory branch. A big fan of pop music and part of a branch that had organised people to travel 400 miles overnight to the Grunwick picket line, Bain agreed immediately and seconded the proposal at the National Committee. Nichol believes that without this support the Carnival wouldn't have happened.[88]

Jerry Fitzpatrick remembers the preparation for the Victoria Park Carnival:

> We started planning the Carnival... at least three months beforehand. I sat down with Roger Huddle. I remember booking the event through the GLC [Greater London Council]. The form said that if you had more than ten thousand people you needed portaloos, and all that. So I booked a mini festival, for ten thousand, not more. I knew we had no money. I wasn't expecting more than twenty thousand, tops. We made a deal to book the PA. Myself and Roger Huddle went to Covent Garden. Roger knew his sound systems and I knew how to hustle. We paid three thousand there and then, four thousand on the day. Paul [Holborow] drew the money out. I had to sew it into the lining of my leather jacket, so it wouldn't get pinched...
> Red and Roger booked the bands. Tom Robinson and Steel Pulse. Tom Robinson got X-Ray Spex. Two weeks before the

Carnival, we started trying to book the Clash. There was a meeting with the band. Red, Roger, Syd Shelton and Kate Webb were absolutely brilliant. Mick Jones [Clash guitarist] flicking ash into their hair, as manager Bernie Rhodes said 'Why should we bother?' Finally Joe Strummer spoke, and said, 'Fuck it, we'll show them, we'll fucking show them'. That was just 10 days beforehand. But it was the Clash that did it. The word went round the back streets of London. (No mobiles at that time). The Clash were huge.[89]

Gered Mankowitz, photographer working with the Rolling Stones, remembers being part of a growing movement and helping to 'organise equipment for the carnival, calling contacts and encouraging them to support us… I don't think it was difficult as the movement had become such a force that people seemed very happy to help!'[90] Some help came from unexpected quarters. Taking up Red's suggestion, Tom Robinson asked for and got 10,000 whistles from the chief executive of his record company, EMI.[91]

RAR 'put itself on the line' in early March, testing its capacity to hold a gig in an area where the NF was strong, with an event in Barking, five miles from Victoria Park, following the RAR format of reggae and punk with Misty and Sham 69. Sham 69's previous London gigs had ended in near riot. *Socialist Worker* reported: 'Skinheads, NF and BM terrorising the audience… High tension all night. Racists isolated by RAR supporters. Sham played their hearts out. Misty with fantastic energy lifted the music. Solidarity dance. Jimmy Pursey from Sham sang "The Israelites" with Misty in the end. RAR survived. Live music will not be stopped.'[92]

Leaflets and posters for the Carnival were distributed. The Communist Party sent 'publicity material… to all Districts'.[93] Always aiming to establish a united front at every level, the carnival was a joint initiative. The publicity made it clear that it was organised by 'the Anti Nazi League and Rock against Racism in association with Hackney Community Relations Council, Hackney Campaign against Racism, Tower Hamlets Movement against Racism and Fascism'. *Socialist Worker* began advertising it a month before, with big adverts and a double page spread that reminded people 'don't forget your dancing shoes'.[94]

The same week, the front page of *Sounds* showed how

many rock musicians could be deported if the National Front controlled immigration. Inside a long feature put together by Vivien Goldman was headlined: 'It can't happen here or can it?'. Over eight pages it detailed the arguments against immigration controls, why the Race Relations Act was so ineffective, why the swastika should never be used as a means to shock people. One page was filled with quotes from musicians attacking the NF. It also challenged Thatcher's claim in a TV interview two months earlier that 'people are really rather afraid that this country might be rather swamped by people with a different culture', asking 'When were you last swamped by a one to thirty minority?'. The last half page was an interview with RAR. The downside, by far the biggest article, was an interview with Martin Webster who, as usual, used the opportunity to present himself as reasonable, arguing for the compulsory deportation of black people.[95]

Meanwhile, the NF sent letter bombs to a paint sprayer in the giant Ford factory in Dagenham, ten miles from Hackney.[96] In response, the ANL collected signatures on a 'Ford Workers Against the Nazis' solidarity statement and got the shop stewards committee to affiliate.[97] They went on to collect money for a coach to the carnival for colleagues.[98] In Wales, the West Glamorgan Fire Brigades union distributed leaflets to every fire station.[99] At the Gardner diesel engine factory in Eccles with 2,500 workers, after a sharp debate about the National Front, the shop stewards committee voted for the committee's members themselves to leaflet the workforce. The move did much to introduce political questions as legitimate issues for the committee's agenda, putting the right-wing on the defensive. A number of stewards resigned following the vote, mostly to be replaced by more active reps willing to take up political matters.[100] The newly established 'Spurs Against the Nazis' leafleted a home game, calling on fans to join them at the carnival under their own banner.[101]

The rally and Carnival was timed for the run up to the May local elections when campaigning against the NF would be at its peak. One example was Leamington where the NF were exploiting the fact that Robert Relf, notorious for erecting the sign 'For sale – to an English family only' sign on his house, had decided to join them. The day before the carnival, 1,000 marched against the NF in Leamington. *Socialist Worker* reported that it was 'a huge success with a large number of Asian and West Indian marchers and a large number of school kids under the SKAN banner'.[102] In Stoke, 'after the local anti-fascist group North Staffs CARF (NorSCARF), the Labour Party, Liberal Party and SWP put out thousands of Anti Nazi League leaflets', the NF vote was cut from 'over two hundred a couple of years back to a derisory TWENTY TWO'.[103]

Boosted by local activity, the coverage in the music press and support shown at the teachers' union (NUT) conference, coach bookings took off. On the day, Reading sent seven coaches, Leicester sent five, thirty came from the Northeast, from Nottingham twenty-five, Bristol twenty-five, Manchester 42. Geoff Brown remembers booking the last coach at 10 pm the night before.[104] The Aberdeen coach did a round trip of over a thousand miles. Ilford Skins and SKAN organised a coach for school students.[105] John Edmondson, about to do his A levels in Huddersfield, remembers his 'trendy English teacher Mr Simpson hired a coach'.[106] Two buses were filled by the SKAN activists at a Finchley school, north London.[107] *Time Out* reported one inner London school had an official school party, organised by the deputy headmaster.[108]

Having wondered whether the 20,000 attendance predicted by the ANL was possible, the mood on the Leeds coaches improved as they stopped at a service station to find the car park 'crammed with coaches going to the Carnival'. Back on the motorway 'it seemed that all the world was going to the Carnival with...coaches behind and in front of us as far as the eye could see. In London, many buses... could get no nearer Trafalgar Square than Westminster, so we held an impromptu procession up Whitehall'.[109] Already before dawn punks had gathered noisily in Trafalgar Square. By midday it was awash with colour.[110] When Colin Poole arrived with work colleagues from a Tottenham factory with a mostly young and black workforce who 'talked about racism and played a lot of reggae... we were just blown away... The noise, the colour, the mix of people was just incredible'.[111] Ramila Patel had never seen such a sea of yellow lollipops and banners. Eighteen-year-old Marian Peacock, on her first ever demonstration, remembers 'being surrounded by people with lollipops and banners... The huge number gave very little sense of the violence of the fascists'.[112] The only fascists were the three monstrous papier mâché heads of Tyndall, Webster and Hitler carried on the back of a truck.[113] Bands tuning up on the backs of wagons together with the whistles donated by EMI, helped to realise the claim that: 'RAR's unannounced ambition was to turn the event into the biggest piece of revolutionary street theatre London had ever seen, a tenth anniversary tribute to the Paris events of May 1968.'[114]

Eight platform speakers each got five minutes.[115] Unrecognised by most of the crowd, Audrey Wise MP was cheered when she said: 'It's rubbish to blame people because of race. We've got to look at the problems and start solving them.'[116] Ian Mikardo, leading Labour-left MP, put the ANL position: 'There are too many people in the Labour movement who believe if you leave it [fascism], it will go away. There is only one way to fight it – head on'. The best reception went to Tom Robinson: 'The message of this Carnival, not only to the loonies of the National Front but all bigots everywhere, is hands off our people: black, white, together, tonight and forever.'[117]

Fifty thousand people joined the march from Trafalgar Square to Victoria Park. It was 'so dense that we filled the whole road and both pavements'.[118] Pia Feig, one of 400 from Wolverhampton, remembers a contingent of older Sikh men in traditional dress shuffling along together with hordes of young black guys trying to get us to move on.[119] Pip Smith with 'Gay and here to stay' in large letters on his back, selling RAR badges, counted 400 in the gay contingent.[120] The front of the march reached Victoria Park before the tail had left Trafalgar Square.[121] Andy Makin, a young SWP comrade, marched the five miles to the park listening to the band Gang of Four playing on the back of a lorry: 'Going through the East End... people [were] waving out the windows or coming out to join in' Red Saunders remembers as the march reached the East End, it passed:

> the Blade Bone... a well-known National Front pub. Inside the fascists were all getting tanked up and then coming outside... shouting, 'Sieg Heil, Sieg Heil, red scum'. The march is coming and the march is coming and the march is coming, and it's ten minutes and it's twenty minutes: 'Si-eg H-eil'; and it's thirty minutes and they're really weary:

'S-i-eg... H-e-il...'; and it's forty minutes and the march is still coming. And then finally there's this group from Gay Liberation holding up a placard: 'Queer Jew-boy socialist seeks a better world' and waving it at the fascists, and they went back into the pub, overwhelmed.[122]

In the park, 'scaffolders from Donegal put up the stage the night before. We were expecting trouble'.[123] The mixing desk and the stage had to be protected overnight at all costs. Those 'on duty' all dressed smartly in case the police started to ask questions.[124] Kevin Corr was one of those who:

> had to give our lives for the mixer. About a dozen or 15 of us stayed hidden. We were all tooled up. We were there all night... Another group were under the stage. Everyone was hypersensitive so if there was the slightest noise... A car only had to backfire at 4 in the morning or a loud voice coming from somewhere. As it got light we thought 'They'd left it a bit late if they're going to do it now'. Then gradually, as the hours went by, we got the message that Trafalgar Square was packed and people were leaving to make their way down to Victoria Park. By that time an off-licence was open and we got stacks of beer. It took quite a while for people to get to the park. By the time they arrived we were absolutely pissed, a mixture of joy and relief.[125]

It had rained a lot during the week. The grass was sodden. The forecast was more rain.[126] Gurinder Chadha was too scared to go to Trafalgar Square and came early to the park.[127] Thinking that no one was coming, she walked towards the gate and heard:

> this bizarre sound, a kind of high-pitched buzz that was growing louder and louder: what was it? Should I run away from it? But then I heard music and chanting... I found an old box to stand on. When I looked down the street, what I saw changed my life forever. From that moment I became the political filmmaker I am today, hundreds and hundreds of people marching, side-by-side in the display of exuberance, defiance and most importantly, victory. I couldn't believe my eyes, these were white, English people –

many with long hair like the rockers I could never relate to – marching, chanting to help *me* and my family find our place in our adopted homeland.[128]

David Rosenberg, member of the Jewish Socialist Group, remembers it as the first anti-racist demonstration that 'especially in the park... was a black and white demonstration'.[129] For Dave Gilchrist, a young punk, it was like 'a wonderful militant circus when it turned up. People dressed in all kinds of outfits, punks, skinheads, dreads... When the Clash came on the place kinda exploded. It was punk nirvana'.[130] The security fence soon collapsed and people started fainting – first aiders pulling them out as the crowd nearly overwhelmed the stage.

Huge yellow bins stood at the entrances collecting money. Leading student activist Andy Strouthous remembers, 'we sold thousands of ANL badges at Victoria park. Sadly I missed the Clash as I was guarding the badge money in a tent'. £12,000 was collected, almost all in coins, hardly any notes.[131]

With a PA system that could have worked for 20,000 trying to cater for 80,000, the sound was often poor. Nor was everyone happy with the lineup. Some of the crowd booed and threw bottles when Patrik Fitzgerald played acoustic guitar. Saunders, wearing a Kartoon Klowns cape, roared 'This ain't no fucking Woodstock. This is the carnival against the fucking Nazis'. Steel Pulse sang 'Ku Klux Klan' wearing Ku Klux Klan outfits.[132] The Clash got the biggest cheer and had to have the plug pulled on them to get them to stop and let Tom Robinson play.[133]

As the giant heads of Tyndall, Webster and Hitler were carried through the crowd, the gig finished with a jam session bringing musicians from the bands together chanting 'Black, White. Together, Tonight''.[134] Jimmy Pursey, lead singer of Sham 69, showed courage as he challenged the racism of many of his skinhead followers. He shouted with his hands apart, 'Everyone told you we were going to be like this'. Then bringing his hands together, he shouted 'But we went like this'.

Gurinder Chadha remembers:

The whole of the park was jumping up and down to The Clash. It was an incredibly emotional moment because, for the first time, I felt surrounded by people on my side. That was when I thought that something had changed in Britain forever... Before RAR, there was no sense that it wasn't OK to be racist. But with RAR, we got to see that there were others willing to speak out against racism and talk about a different kind of Britain.[135]

Buzz Rodwell was 'standing near the back of the huge crowd, near the gates, when a bunch of Nazis came in, carrying baseball bats and the like. They took one look at the numbers, turned and disappeared'.[136]

Hassan Mahamdallie, a school student at the time, saw:

> towards the end of the day a team of helpers started going round with buckets collecting for the ANL/RAR and selling the punk fanzine, *Temporary Hoarding*. I looked beside, around and behind me at the mostly white faces, and something clicked. I realised for the first time that there were lots of white people who hated racism and were prepared to fight it. Maybe Powell and NF skins weren't an inevitable part of life and could be fought and perhaps driven back or even overcome? It sounds naive now as I recount it, but some kind of negative psychological burden was lifted that day in Vicky Park. It was an utter, complete revelation and changed my life forever.[137]

Musician and activist Billy Bragg was:

> standing under a banner that said 'Gays Against the Nazis' and when Tom sang 'Sing if you're glad to be gay', all these blokes around us started kissing each other on the lips. I'd never seen an out gay man before. My immediate thought was 'What are they doing here? This is about black people'. And literally in the course of that afternoon I came to realise that actually the fascists were against anybody who was in any way different and just liking black music and being a punk rocker was sufficiently different for the National Front to be the enemy. I realised this was how my generation were going to define themselves, in opposition to discrimination of all kinds. This was our Vietnam, our 'Ban the Bomb'. It had a very powerful catalytic effect on me.[138]

John Lockwood, in prison on the day of the Carnival having been arrested at Lewisham, remembers:

> one of the worst and the best days of my life. That day we were locked down all weekend… Two Nazi screws (who had threatened to kill me) were on rota and shouting filthy racist abuse through my cell door… but as the day developed and reports came through on the radio, other cons (most of whom were somewhat racist themselves if truth be known) began to shout abuse at the Nazis and bang on the pipes to show support for the demonstration. With every hourly report the numbers doubled until sometime in the afternoon a hundred thousand was reported and the whole prison rang out in a deafening crescendo. It was as if the spirit of hope on the streets in triumph over hatred had reached into every part of society… even into the depths of despair in the dungeons of their state. The Nazi screws never troubled me again. The events of the day saved my life… I sometimes think, perhaps even literally.[139]

For the young Bolton activist Prav Parmar, getting there was a struggle, 'Every penny counted. You made your butties on the coach and drank water at the service stations. But the atmosphere down there was colossal, fantastic'. Coming back to Bolton: 'you want to do something. We have to do something. And the best thing was all the skinheads were coming on board. Mods and rockers were coming on board and were totally different. They were chasing you before, calling you also. Now and especially all these new bands, new wave bands were coming through.'[140]

Having given the carnival less than a column inch two weeks before, *New Musical Express* now put it on the front page followed by two pages of photos and a full-page article.[141]

Student activist Colin Byrne remembers the day as 'the first time that you felt you were part of a mass populist movement… It wasn't full of depressing-looking lefties and donkey jackets. It was fun… Rock Against Racism was reaching out to people who didn't see themselves as political'.[142] Sharon Spike, a young punk who wrote for *Temporary Hoarding*, remembers:

> What was amazing was all the different people enjoying it, skinheads, punks, teds, Rastas, some old hippies, greasers,

disco-kids and loads of middle-aged people and all. There were quite a few dogs. There was such a big turn-out that people at the back felt it hard to hear what the bands on stage were singing. But it didn't matter too much because it was all so interesting just to walk around. It is very hard to describe what it felt like. Not Love and Peace and all that rubbish. It was more than music. Feeling all together. Not being scared of one another. Making you feel strong in a good way.[143]

For Paul Furness, an activist from Leeds, it was 'Unbelievable... confirmation we were right'.[144] The Communist Party's Political Committee report agreed:

> The Anti-Nazi League carnival was the biggest, most inspiring and politically important demonstration for some years... It demonstrated the strength of anti-racist and anti-fascist feeling in Britain and the readiness of large numbers to unite and fight this menace. Thousands of those taking part in the demonstration were participating in political action for the first time in their lives. This is particularly true of many of the young people. Indeed, perhaps the most significant feature of the demonstration was the large volume of support it received from the youth, and notably from working class youth.[145]

Eighty thousand people at a Carnival in Victoria Park, East London could not be ignored. The police were 'astonished' by the size of the event. ITV's *News at Ten* ran it as its first item. Tariq Ali declared 'Hats Off to the SWP'.[146] The historian Raphael Samuel described the march as 'the most working-class demonstration I have been on, one of the very few of my adult lifetime to have sensibly changed the climate of public opinion'.[147] It deserves to be called historic. Lewisham and the Victoria Park Carnival were the two big moments. Lewisham set things moving, the Carnival was the turning point. 'The combination of the ANL and RAR worked brilliantly to mobilise tens of thousands.'[148] The day changed people. It showed that anti-racism was a force. It raised the question asked by many as they went home, talking to friends about what they could do, how they could turn inspiration into action where they lived, worked and studied. However, not everybody was there. The Bangladeshi youth of Brick Lane in the East End were absent: 'They ought to be in the front line of the movement against racialism as were the Jews in the 1930s.'[149] There was more to do.[150]

7: A mass movement: May 1978 to September 1978

★ Into the workplace

Writing in *Socialist Worker* after the Victoria Park Carnival, Tony Cliff pointed out that it was overwhelmingly made up of young workers, school leavers and school pupils with a smattering of middle-class elements.[1] He concluded: 'The fact that the Nazi NF infiltrates factories, hospitals, post offices, schools, and that racism, passive or even active, is widespread, means that the fight against Nazism and racism is bound to go on, and not lose its vigour.'[2]

Growing economic insecurity and falling real wages had created a favourable political climate for NF members in the workplace. Their members in British Leyland in Birmingham, Tate & Lyle's plant in Silvertown and Imperial Typewriters in Leicester had shown they could intervene in unionised workplaces if they seized the right moment.[3] Even where shop floor union organisation was strong, putting right-wing arguments could build a base among those voting against strike action or wanting to cross picket lines.[4]

The fascist record of organising workers showed that despite their pro-worker propaganda, in practice they supported the employer. It had been different in Italy before the war where the violence of the *squadristi* made the fascists' pro-employer and landlord politics clear. In Germany, the organised strength of the German workers' movement had defeated the Nazis' attempts to build a base in workplaces. The National Socialist Workplace Cell Organisation (NSBO)[5] failed to recruit shop floor workers or to win their support.[6] In Britain, some ex-Labour Party members who followed Mosley into the BUF established the Fascist Union of British Workers (FUBW), setting up clubs for unemployed youth and intervening in strikes. They helped a tenant who had been evicted by bailiffs get his furniture back into his house.[7] However, for all the BUF leadership rhetoric about revolution, as soon as it became clear the FUBW was supporting workers against employers and landlords, Mosley shut it down.[8]

Anti-fascists had no illusions in the threat the BUF posed to trade unionists after the Nazis shut down the German trade unions in May 1933. But in Britain trade union delegations were a large part of the hundred thousand who opposed the 3,000 Blackshirts when, protected by 6,000 police, they rallied in Hyde Park in September 1934.[9]

Fascist efforts to establish a presence in unions and workplaces revived after Powell's 1968 attack on immigration. Danny Harmston was one of the founders of the Trade Union Anti-Immigration Movement (TRUAIM) in 1970.[10] Its achievements were modest, helping NF members get elected onto the Rover car factory's stewards committee in Solihull and Luton trades council. There was also Bill Roberts, union convener in a Bolton engineering factory, well known as an NF member who successfully overcame opposition to being re-elected as convener.[11]

However, the strength of organised workers repeatedly humiliating and finally bringing down the Heath government in 1974 led to the NF adopting a populist stance. Having first criticised the Tories' 1971 Industrial Relations Act as too weak – they called for detention without trial of any union leader who sought to sabotage efforts to get industry going – they did a U-turn in the run up to the 1974 miners' strike, now opposing the Act and backing the miners. A year later, boosted by their intervention in the Imperial Typewriter strike and inspired by the Ulster Workers Council's crushing defeat of the Labour government's plans for 'power sharing' with the Catholic minority in Northern Ireland, they set up the National Front Trade Union Association, NFTUA.[12] Tyndall argued that a future NF government should not use repression as this could repress 'much that is legitimate union activity'. The alternative was 'to win the battle in advance by winning control of the trade union movement by the normal democratic process'. Consequently, 'the intention of the National Front is to do what the Tories have not done and cannot do, fight the Left on its own ground in the unions'.[13]

Tyndall could point to the example of the strong NF presence in two large north London postal sorting offices, particularly in the North London Divisional Post Office in Upper Street, Islington, known as 'the NDO'.[14] This base was built by exploiting the demoralisation that followed the defeat of the six-week all-out national postal workers strike in 1971. By the late 1970s, with an estimated twenty-five active members and a hundred sympathisers, they dominated the 1,500 strong union branch.[15] Mark Dolan, just starting in the NDO on the sorting office floor, member of the Labour Party Young Socialists and ANL supporter, along with many of his black, Turkish, Greek and Asian school friends, remembers being completely shocked:

> The first Friday I was there... I saw this guy walking round collecting money... As he approached, he was wearing a union jack badge with NF in the middle and he came up to me and said, 'Money for the National Front'. I did a bit of a double take and I went, 'You fucking what?'. People around me went pretty quiet, particularly a couple of the black guys, they kind of put their heads down. Anyway, I just said, 'I ain't giving you any fucking money'. There was a bit of altercation and he said 'Look, you need to keep your head down or, you know, things are gonna happen'... it was really strange, a really strange atmosphere. They did that every Friday for a while.[16]

Their collection raised £100 a week.[17] Some of this was used to pay the £150 deposits for about ten NF candidates in the 1979 general election.[18] A number of NF members in the NDO also stood in the May 1979 local elections.[19] One union rep at the NDO told an Islington ANL meeting:

> I'm fed up of going to union conferences, saying I'm from Upper Street and being told 'Oh, the Nazi lot'... In the canteen we don't just ignore the little cells of the National Front, we get in among them and argue. When you argue with them, you find that a lot of them haven't got a clue about politics anyway. One of them, J R Smith, just goes red in the face and screams if you try to argue with him. That's what their politics is all about. Of the 50 candidates standing for the National Front, 16 of them are known to me as members of the UPW [Union of Post Office Workers]. But even the candidates are not all convinced of what they're doing. When I argued with two of the candidates standing in Clerkenwell ward, they ended up asking 'Is there some way we can withdraw our names?' Unfortunately, it was too late by then.[20]

The widespread racism among prison officers helped the NF to establish themselves in a number of prisons including Dartmoor, Wandsworth, Pentonville and Manchester Strangeways.[21] Manchester's Strangeways prison had an estimated ninety members among warders.[22] The NF also had 'a 'cell' of sixteen members in Tate & Lyle's plant in Newham, where Michael Lobb, the NF candidate who got 11.5 percent in the Newham by-election, ran a 'well-managed campaign against the possible mass redundancy at Tate & Lyle's, where sugar workers face an uncertain future as a result of Common Market Policy on beet'.[23]

Longbridge
The NF boasted they had seventy members at the Longbridge car plant in Birmingham. Their main strength flowed from the company's racist employment policy. 'The dirtiest, hardest, lowest paid jobs were often done by West Indians with a few Asians working in the foundries' while 'the better paid, "direct labour", working on the track as well as craftsmen, tended to be white... [and] the management, with one exception, were all white'.[24] Against this, the organised presence of Communist Party

and Labour Party shop stewards meant that the NF was unable to operate openly. Any stewards that they may have had 'tended to keep very quiet. They were a kind of secret force. They didn't circulate a bulletin, just stickers and graffiti. it was impossible to know if they were there in any numbers. They emerged when opportunities presented themselves'.[25] Longbridge's huge mass meetings, for example, gave them the chance to bring banners with slogans attacking proposals being put to vote by the stewards committee.

Such moments could come without warning. The two bombs planted by the IRA in pubs in Birmingham on the evening of 21 November 1974 stunned the entire city. Anyone who was Irish became suspect. Many experienced violence, both verbal and physical.[26] As thousands of workers started work the following morning, no one, either from the left or from the right, had been able to organise their response. Frank Henderson, member of the International Socialists and a senior steward in Longbridge, went to work to find that the tracks had stopped:

> No one was working... Everybody was going round asking what had happened. During the course of the day all sorts of vile anti-Irish things came out... A head of steam was building for a demonstration – a real pogrom – against anyone Irish. I spent all morning going round arguing against this with everybody I could find. I knew a march had been planned around the plant with a demonstration outside... the top administration block. Everybody was baying against the Irish. 'Kick all the Irish bastards out', 'We ain't working with these Irish sods', 'Sack 'em all, they're killers'. We found out during the course of the morning that one of the kids caught in the explosion, who had both his legs blown off, worked in our place... everyone was inflamed.

Henderson spoke at a stewards meeting representing about 2,500 workers:

> People were raging mad... It was a lynch mob sort of atmosphere. I thought, I've got to do it. I've got to put the blame for this on British imperialism and call for the withdrawal of British troops but I was scared stiff. 'If I kept

my mouth shut', I thought, 'after a week or so, it will all fade out and people will have forgotten it'. In the end I got up and argued against the witch hunting, against any pogrom. I said that the people responsible for the bombing were the people responsible for all the trouble in Northern Ireland and that was the British imperialists and the only way the problems of Ireland could be solved was by destroying the influence of British imperialism on the future of Ireland and that meant the withdrawal of British troops from Ireland'. I sat down shivering. ringing wet with sweat and expecting a real onslaught. Instead what I'd said was more or less dismissed as 'Well, that's Frank on again'.

The meeting finished with an agreement to go on the march. I don't think I would have had the nerve under normal circumstances to get up and argue the way I did in a meeting of that sort if I hadn't been a member of the IS. That is the advantage of being in a party. It gives you a bit of backbone when things are tough. I think, without being a member of the International Socialists, what I would have done was sit there, keep my thoughts to myself and let the whole thing wash away. But I noticed, possibly as a result of what I'd said, that a lot of the banners saying 'Sack all the Irish bastards', 'Kill the Irish bastards', and slogans like that were chucked on the floor and people were walking over them. From the end where I'd spoken, people were carrying banners saying, 'Bring our boys home'.[27]

NF members' deliberately low profile made them hard to get rid of. One NF member, Ivor Morgan, was provoked by a long-established steward, Dave Halliday, to the point where he couldn't stop himself giving a Hitler salute. Two hundred workers went on strike, staying out until the management removed him:[28]

> What we used to try to get to was a situation where the NF members would publicly have to rip up their membership card and announce they were quitting the Front. That was the gold-plated result we were looking for and it happened on a good number of occasions. Quite a few had to do that to avoid the pressure coming down on them and risk losing their jobs.[29]

In Manchester Town Hall, the ANL and RAR worked together to get rid of an NF member, Anthony Jones. John Hall remembered how:

> we started our own kind of Anti Nazi League within the Environmental Health Department. [Jones] was an environmental health officer in houses in multiple occupation... So we had a series of events including a 'Jig against Jones' that drew attention to the fact that he was a racist working with minority groups and then he was moved... and suddenly disappeared. That was seen as a massive victory.[30]

Having organised groups in workplaces made it easier to respond quickly to events. After *World In Action*'s documentary about the NF, 'The Nazi Party', was shown on TV: '150 League badges were sold in the South Works, Longbridge. Shop steward Ken King said workers from all races and all age groups in the factory were buying them.'[31]

The ANL carnival in Victoria Park created new possibilities for workplace activists.[32] Shop stewards at the giant Ford Dagenham factory in East London followed up their support for the carnival with selling badges: 'in 48 hours on one shift we sold 500 ANL "Stop the NF Nazis" badges... On my assembly line practically every West Indian, African and Asian, and many white workers – particularly young white workers – proudly and defiantly wear ANL badges.'[33]

The Longbridge ANL branch was founded by shop stewards on the way back from the carnival. They had a tradition that they would stop at a favourite pub in the Cotswolds when returning from demonstrations in London.[34] Recognising 'the cooperation we already had when it came to the Nazis', the new branch's officers included Communist Party, Labour Party and SWP members with 'most of the rest of the coach... signed up on the last leg of the journey'. Back at work, the new branch produced its own stickers and badges, systematically removing NF stickers and graffiti in the toilets and elsewhere.[35]

Encouraged by the eleven Manchester Polytechnic Students Union coaches that went to the carnival, Colin Barker organised a meeting of staff, 'with over 175 people and a collection of £76'.[36]

Eighty people joined the ANL, their names, departments and union listed on a leaflet, headed 'Anti Nazi League Manchester Polytechnic Ad Hoc Committee', inviting other staff to join.

The message of the carnival was that racism and fascism had to be confronted where people lived, worked, studied, where they listened to live music, where they watched football:

> We deliberately played down formal organisation. The phrase used was 'Lots of activity and few meetings'... Lots of different left groups had difficulty in coping with this... [U]sed to long meetings, they thought that nothing could be sorted in an hour... I remember one meeting in early '78... Everything was discussed, and we reached the end of the agenda... A whole bunch of people couldn't believe the meeting... could be done that fast.[37]

For many the carnival was the first political action they had been involved in. The following week at the Star Centre College of Further Education for disabled students in Cheltenham, over a third of the student body came to the first meeting of the ANL in the college. Despite some staff being hostile, all but two voted to set up a group. Star Centre College student Uduaci Okon told *Socialist Worker*: 'It's great to know for once that we can prove to society that we're not just vegetables and that things aren't just going over our heads. Being disabled doesn't give you much choice but to oppose the NF.'[38]

The boost to rank and file confidence that came from repeatedly defeating the Heath government shifted the balance of power in workplaces making political campaigning easier. Getting rid of Nazis in the workplace also connected with trade union traditions such as how to treat strike breakers. The union convenor in one Stockport engineering factory dealt with an NF member by throwing the NF member's tools over the gate. Bullying supervisors were often referred to as 'little Hitlers'. When one of these turned out to be a genuine fascist, trade union action could deal with them. Sixty electricians on the London Underground refused to take orders from their foreman, an NF organiser. When they were 'taken off the clock', their pay suspended, they went on strike only resuming work when management agreed to the inquiry they were demanding.[39] It was a Grunwick striker addressing 800 overwhelmingly white workers at a canteen meeting in Seddon Atkinson lorry factory in Preston that persuaded one worker to leave the NF. He said 'If that little Asian guy can get up in front of 800 of us and tell us what we should be doing, I want some of that'.[40] Ashley Saltman, secretary of the joint shop stewards committee at the large Molins factory in Deptford, got thirty-six stewards to sign a leaflet for circulating locally setting up South East London Trade Unionists Against the Nazis. The leaflet highlighted the Nazis' destruction of free trade unions after they came to power.

Some fascists were smarter. Eddie Morrison, leader of the fascist splinter group, the British National Party (BNP), successfully exploited the climate of racism, presenting himself to work colleagues as a reasonable, moderate individual, not pushing his politics, going to the pub with them at lunchtime.[41] When the management gave him twenty-four hours to resign after the union committee in the office had gone to them without involving the members, Morrison organised a petition that enabled him to stay on. He then got himself a union card from head office and 'at a union meeting both defended his right to call himself a racialist and moved a left-sounding motion on pay. The meeting resolved that if the branch committee should circulate material, he was entitled to have BNP material circulated with it'. It was only when a Right to Work campaign leaflet went in detailing a public attack on a well-known socialist causing serious injury, that Morrison, losing his cool, reacted aggressively and a few days later resigned.[42]

Union support for the ANL grew rapidly in the early months of 1978. By mid-April sponsors included: '30 AUEW branches and districts, 25 trades councils, 11 NUM areas and lodges, 50 local Labour parties and six to ten branches from each of a number of unions: TGWU, Civil and Public Services Association (CPSA), Technical, Administrative and Supervisory Section (TASS), NUJ, NUT, NUPE.[43]

Encouraging as this was, the challenge was to eliminate the NF's shop floor presence and having just thirteen shop stewards' committees sponsoring the League, large as some of these workplaces were, showed there was still a long way to go. Things got ever more difficult as the Social Contract saw union officials actively suppressing attempts to organise pay strikes.

Rail

In early 1977, the National Front Railwaymen Association (NFRA) was launched. Based around a group of National Front members in Watford and north London, it circulated leaflets in toilets and mess rooms when there was no one there.[44] These included anonymous letters attacking the the branch secretary of the rail drivers' union ASLEF at one depot.[45] Ray Buckton, ASLEF general secretary, called on union members to have nothing to do with the 'disgusting screed' the NFRA was circulating so that its attempts to organise would be 'doomed to a complete and speedy failure'.[46] Along with NUPE, ASLEF was one of the first union sponsors of the ANL.[47] Buckton spoke from the ANL Carnival platform in Trafalgar Square.[48] The national executive of the National Union of Railwaymen, NUR, the largest rail union, discussed whether to expel NF members, resolving to warn them that 'From now on any member "publicly engaged" in Front activities could be expelled'.[49]

But in the face of hostile press reaction, for example in the *Daily Express*, it was decided not to expel NF members from the union. The NUPE conference in May, 300 of whose delegates signed up as ANL sponsors, made the same decision resolving that local branches could discipline NF members trying to use the union to push racist ideas.[50] This seems to have helped deal with Ken Brack, National Front member and NUPE branch chair in a Sheffield hospital who was careful to '[keep] his politics to himself at work'. The AUEW in Sheffield took a stronger position: NF membership was incompatible with holding a position in the union.[51]

The NUR's position was strengthened, at least on paper, with a unanimous vote at its July 1978 conference condemning the National Front's activities, 'pledging the NUR's wholehearted opposition to all forms of racism' including affiliation to the ANL.[52] ASLEF's annual conference took a similarly hard position.[53] However, as John Rose's pamphlet, *Solidarity Forever: 100 years of Kings Cross ASLEF*, points out, more needed to be done:

> There was still an undercurrent of racism which they [the fascists] could tap into and they were still a threat in some

areas where they could come and beat you up... they could try to stitch you up to management They could spread rumours... So they were still a danger.

At the grassroots workers from all the unions were concerned about these divisions and the Railway Worker group offered an alternative where we could all work together to defend jobs, conditions and wages. At King's Cross we always had informal joint meetings and always had people from NUR, ASLEF and the Transport and Salaried Staff Association (TSSA) meeting together.[54] It wouldn't be through the formal union branch structure, it would just be a rank and file meeting and we were very aware that similar meetings were being held at British Rail and London Transport depots and stations across the country.

So we tried to connect all of these groups through the rank and file grouping we called 'Railway Worker'. As well as addressing all the issues in the industry we also campaigned against the National Front Railwaymen's Association. We were pointing out to people that they were trying to divide us whereas 'Railway Worker' was trying to unite. The development of Rail against the Nazis as part of the growing Anti-Nazi League was in some ways a natural progression of something that already started as a rank and file movement.

At King's Cross station:

> first, signatures on an ANL petition were collected... Then ASLEF members began wearing anti-nazi badges and putting up stickers all over the station. A meeting was called and 40 people turned up. A Kings Cross ANL committee was set up. One of its tasks was to organise a group of rail workers to go to Brick Lane in East London and prevent National Front members selling their poisonous rag and intimidating the Asian community there. Kings Cross then took the initiative in setting up a national organisation – Rail Against the Nazis.[55]

Workers on London Underground now refused to take out trains that had National Front stickers on them.[56] Other train staff taking the same stand triggered a number of cancellations after which the management prioritised cleaning fascist graffiti

off trains.[57] Dave Welsh remembers:
> The union was beginning to get the idea of not just passing resolutions... We produced badges. I would sell them in depots and stations. I had a bag of them I carried. As a guard I would have a minute on the station platform to ask someone 'Have you seen this?' and sell them one for 25p. We leafletted depots. We knew there were pockets of National Front supporters... it was rare to have a confrontation with them though there were some big arguments in mess rooms.[58]

Getting union branches to be active could be a struggle. One London Underground worker, wanting to challenge the NF presence at work, frustrated that there were never more than a handful of members at union meetings, decided to 'put up a poster saying that at the next meeting we would affiliate to the Anti-Nazi League. About 50 people came, and there was a big row, but we affiliated. After that the branch never looked back'.[59] Steve Forey recalls:

> These badges proliferated around King's Cross. It was really good because it connected you to people you didn't know. In the depot of 500 drivers, I knew them all but there were probably another 500, maybe 600 guards and another 500 station staff so you couldn't know everybody. But once you saw someone wearing one of those badges, suddenly you hit it off and black workers in particular realised there were more anti-racists than racists around.[60]

Paul Salveson, a member of the Communist Party and NUR branch secretary in Blackburn, initiated the northwest Rail Against the Nazis group, producing its own leaflet, selling badges across the region. He remembers: 'the party line from the CP was cautious engagement with the ANL because of the distrust of the SWP. On the railways, perhaps because there were so few of us both in the CP and the SWP, we got along fine, a positive partnership.'[61] Steve Forey argues: 'Rail Against the Nazis was a fantastic brand. We made a great Rail Against the Nazis banner with a High Speed Train rushing towards a fascist on the tracks with the ubiquitous arrow pointing out his imminent demise.'[62]

Hospitals
Already in 1975, Bill Tizard, Hammersmith hospital shop steward, called on readers of the *West London Hospital Worker*[63] rank-and-file bulletin to protest outside the NF's annual conference in Chelsea Town Hall October 1975. For Anne Robertson, a leading 'Hospital Worker' activist based at the large North Manchester General Hospital, the NF's electoral ambitions meant:

> the campaign had to be as big and wide as possible, getting people involved and pushing people on anti-fascism. There were regular meetings in the hospital's nurses' home with speakers on 'What is fascism?' and also controversial questions like 'Are immigration controls racist?' One of the biggest meetings was with Jim Allen, the playwright. A local celebrity, he wrote the script for the four part television drama 'Days of Hope' about the 1926 General Strike which had recently been broadcast.[64]
> There were literally hundreds of us. We didn't just sell badges. They became members, paid a pound and they got a card. From there, we built in other workplaces such as Wilson's Brewery where Jim Allen's brother, John, was the convener. Once we knew about the Northern Carnival, we had an 'open house', day in and day out, where people would come to the nurses' home and paint banners and make placards. So, we had the 'syringe' banner painted on hospital bed sheets.[65]

It was a hospital bed sheet that NUPE Stockport hospitals branch used for the banner at the Northern Carnival rally with the slogan 'The blood of all races nourishes the NHS'.

Civil servants
With political enthusiasm at an all-time high following civil servants' first ever national strike on pay in early 1973, the unions at the British Museum organised a protest against Portugal's fascist dictator, Marcello Caetano. A hundred staff walked out, picketing the gates as Caetano, on a state visit to celebrate Portugal's 600-year-old alliance with Britain, swept in with a cavalcade of cars and police motorcyclists.[66]

Organised by rank-and-file activists in *Redder Tape*, which included members of the CP as well as the SWP, 200 civil servants met in London to set up Civil Servants against the Nazis (CSAN). Fifty-five met to set up Glasgow CSAN.[67] In little over a month, 7,000 CSAN badges were sold. Many more were sent out from the Tooting Job Centre where Mike Healy, secretary of a large CPSA branch, became, in effect, the national CSAN secretary. Thanks to the 'blind eye' of his manager and support from colleagues, he set up an 'office', a large store of boxes of leaflets, stickers and badges in a corner somewhere, taking phone calls and posting materials.[68] Another measure of the support for the ANL was the twenty staff who walked into Holloway Unemployment Benefit Office, all wearing Anti Nazi League badges and fully expecting to be suspended from work: 'The staff were welcomed by a picket of over 30... CPSA NEC members, benefit claimants, Anti Nazi League supporters and other anti racists. The staff refused to remove their badges and were not suspended. The management backed down.'[69]

Rank-and-file strength was such that senior management right up to the top, including the Secretary of State for Employment, Albert Booth, decided the issue be resolved by negotiation without using the disciplinary procedure. They now struggled to reach a settlement of the question, eventually deciding that badges saying 'Anti Nazi League' were acceptable under the civil service regulations while 'Stop the NF Nazis' was not. The former was not 'party political', the latter was.[70]

Council workers
Council Workers Against the Nazis (CWAN) was launched in the same way as the ANL itself with a founding statement and thirty signatories together with nine local government union branches and a shop stewards committee. Jim Allen spoke at the Manchester CWAN meeting the week before the May 1978 elections. Campaigns often combined 'outside' and 'inside'. Ten thousand leaflets were given out in Cardiff demanding the librarian John McLellan, British Movement member and one of their 'Leader Guard', be 'removed from direct dealings with the public'. Eighty ANL supporters picketed the central library.[71] School caretakers would often refuse to unlock schools for NF

meetings. In Bedfordshire school caretakers, NUPE members, announced a strike if a planned NF election meeting went ahead with the local union recommending that a caretaker offering to help at the meeting should have his membership card withdrawn.[72]

Miners Against the Nazis
Advertising their presence through the local press, the National Front had around thirty members in the Yorkshire coalfield with a hard core of about a dozen, the largest group in the Silverwood pit near Rotherham.[73] The first ANL meeting organised by NUM members was in Pontefract, March 1978. One hundred and eighty heard Scargill and Holborow speak, the NUM affiliating nationally a few weeks later.[74] After Silverwood NUM member Tony Cooper stood as NF candidate in the May local elections, speaking alongside East London activist Aloke Biswas in the Silverwood Miners Welfare, Scargill called for Miners Against the Nazis groups at every pit:

> I am asked, am I prepared to accept the National Front among us? I know that if I worked at a factory or a pit where there was a member of the National Front then I wouldn't work with him, I wouldn't speak to him. I would treat him as though he was infected by the plague.
> We will never stop the National Front by pacifism. If they're marching then we should be marching and we should tell the authorities that if they want to defend law and order then they should stop the merchants of hatred.[75]

Young miner Ian Mitchell remembers helping establish the ANL in Silverwood. It took off with stickers:

> It seemed you couldn't find hardly anybody without an Anti Nazi League sticker. As miners we used to get a sticker to show you supported something. So you'd have some people with loads of stickers on their helmet amongst all the grime and dirt. Anti Nazi League stickers were hugely popular... I was a sticker dealer. People used to come to me asking 'Have you got any of those stickers Ian?' Working in our job, you wore a helmet for a reason. They used to get scratched, they

A mass movement **191**

got covered in dirt. If you worked on the face you needed a new sticker every week… I remember at the pit bottom when you were waiting for the cage, on your shift there were two or three hundred people all queuing up, and they were being passed back and slapped onto helmets. Now you imagine if you're Cooper [the NF member]. All this anti-fascist propaganda everywhere you go.[76]

Stickers could be used in many situations. In July, Durham cathedral was full of miners and their families at the Durham miners' gala's annual service at which new banners are blessed by the bishop. With banners held high and brass bands playing, as the congregation left the cathedral to march through the city, Jim Nichol saw that all the miners were wearing Miners Against the Nazis stickers.

To get rid of two active NF members, Tony Cooper, the NF candidate for Wakefield, and his brother, rank-and-file NUM activists Steve Hammill and Pete Beevers put a motion to the NUM branch to expel them from the union. There was a clause in the Yorkshire NUM rule book, dating back to the 1930s that membership of the union and of a fascist organisation were incompatible. The branch decided that taking their NUM membership off them was effectively a decision to sack the pair and voted the proposal down. Arguing there was 'more than one way to skin a cat', there was now a campaign 'sending them to Coventry'.[77] Where possible people gave Cooper a hard time. One of the office staff responsible for allocating staff to where they were needed was able to allocate Cooper to those sections most likely to turn their backs on him. Eventually Cooper left:[78]

Yorkshire NUM funded Mike Clapham as secretary of Miners against the Nazis, based in its offices in Barnsley, sorting out a free coach for members to go to the Manchester carnival in July and four more for the London 'Carnival 2' in September.[79] Working with the ANL national office, he organised the Miners against the Nazis national conference, with 200 people coming with every coal field in Britain represented in Sheffield, February 1979.[80]

Not every union affiliated to the ANL. Equity's national

council decided not to, saying 'it firmly believed that racial discrimination could best be fought by unionists within their Industries and unions and not by confrontations with racist minority movements in the streets'.[81] Where unions did commit to support – thirteen national unions did so – the issue was always turning these decisions into action.[82] Holborow argued: 'It was not enough to get support from sympathetic and politically aware convenors etc., as such support often only went through branches via a resolution "on the nod". What was needed was something that really got to people.'[83]

Bus workers against the Nazis
With the growing shortage of labour in the post war boom, local councils running bus services took on black and Asian workers and made much use of overtime. The union leadership consistently failed to campaign seriously for improvements in pay and conditions. With many local authorities under Labour control and the union officials frequently active in the local Labour Party, there was often collaboration when it came to dealing with any rank-and-file militants challenging their control. Whenever overtime was cut, racists would blame black and Asian colleagues for doing too much and call for a limit on the number of black and Asian workers. There were a number of strikes where employers failed to do this.

John McLintock, a bus worker in Old Kilpatrick, near Glasgow, was one of three out of 120 union members that voted no to a one-day strike against the employment of Pakistani bus conductors. The vote came after the meeting was addressed by Alec Grant, president of Glasgow Trades Council, who failed to oppose either the strike or racism. McLintock argued it was the failure to abolish overtime that led to 'the scrambles and fights BETWEEN workers which can cause anything from blacklegging to colour prejudice'.[84] Sikh bus workers had to fight many times for the right to wear the turban at work. In Manchester the council agreed after much campaigning over seven years.[85]

Unity against racism was shown by bus workers in Merton garage in London who took strike action three days after the death of Ron Jones, a black bus conductor killed at work by two passengers.[86] All London buses stopped on the day of his funeral with several thousand bus workers attending. Jack Jones, the union general secretary, spoke, 'the disgrace of discrimination and racialism clearly acts against all that is meant by trade unionism. It is surely right, therefore, that all good trade unionists should set their face against those who attempt to stir up trouble by trying to set worker against worker. Disunity and division can only develop if the racialists succeed'.[87]

Unlike Jones, most TGWU officials did not organise against racism. It was the 'Bus workers against the Nazis' group in Stamford Hill, Tottenham, Chalk Farm and Holloway garages, who led the refusal to take out buses with racist graffiti and shop stewards who advised members not to stop in Bruce Grove in Tottenham because of the threat from NF paper sellers.[88] Similarly, it was the Indian Workers Association (IWA) which got the ball rolling that led to a one day strike to protest the racist violence against black and Asian bus workers and police racism in Coventry.[89] The TGWU branch at the Birchfield garage in Manchester affiliated to the ANL after an arson attack on the home of one of its members, Sher Afgan, led to one of his children being hospitalised. Mass leafleting in the nearby Longsight market followed, demanding the police take action.[90] In High Wycombe, school students, many Asian, were the driving force in organising an ANL march. This was a protest against the attack on the bus worker Roger Prouse after a parcel bomb, addressed to him, was sent to the bus garage where he worked. It arrived a few days after he had spoken the previous week at a RAR rally.[91] He had earlier put a motion to his union branch that the chairman and election agent of the local NF branch, who worked at the garage, should be expelled from the union.[92]

Into the movements

Many people are active in more than part of the working-class movement. Ideas and arguments that start in one often spread into others. Arguments about direct action, parliament, and how to fight racism and fascism are found in all of them.

Women Against the Nazis

The National Front threat to women was taken directly from

Hitler's conviction that 'for the German woman her world is her husband, her family, her children, and her home'.[93] *Spearhead* argued that women needed a society 'that respected and cherished the feminine role as principally one of wife, mother and homemaker ...there are few greater symptoms of national decadence than the contemporary derision of maternity and domesticity'.[94] Grunwick saw women challenge these myths as they faced both police violence and mass arrest on the picket line. At Lewisham Women against Racism and Fascism (WARF) blocked New Cross Road with such strength that the police failed to shift them and were forced to reroute the start of the NF's march.[95]

Despite the many women involved in WARF and over a hundred other anti-racist anti-fascist groups – roughly a quarter of Leeds 600 ANL members were women – media reports created a public image of Wood Green and Lewisham as overwhelmingly male, of 'man on man' violence.[96] It was not just the media. Sexism on the left was widespread. Dave Lyddon remembers someone saying before a confrontation, 'The women shouldn't go'.[97] Women were outnumbered two to one among Britain's twelve million trade unionists. Ninety percent of the 1,100 delegates to the annual TUC congress were men. Women had to fight 'every inch of the way' to get TUC backing for the 40,000 strong October 1979 demonstration defending abortion rights.[98]

Often the question was how to challenge both the fascists and the sexism of many anti-fascists. When women challenged the sexist lyrics sung by the Fabulous Poodles at a Brighton RAR gig, the band refused to discuss the issue, telling women who objected they could leave.[99] Having failed to disconnect the band's equipment and knock over the microphones, seven women wrote to *Temporary Hoarding*. RAR responded with an apology, agreeing that 'it is not enough to make a stand against one form of repression – the exploitation of [black people] – if they are going to contribute to another – the degradation of women'. It introduced a protocol for RAR organisers requiring them to check out bands in advance.[100] Under the name Lucy Toothpaste, Lucy Whitman went further launching Rock Against Sexism, getting bands to back RAS and producing *Drastic Measures*, a four-page magazine. Its first issue's main article 'love sex, hate sexism' described how the sexism of rock music reflected the sexism and homophobia of society as a whole. It concluded, 'Rock Against Sexism hopes to break into this vicious circle by attempting to change the current image of women in rock, encouraging women musicians to play, and giving women a chance to express our own point of view'.[101]

The women's movement was, however, in crisis, as was the left as a whole. In Britain the success of the Social Contract holding down working-class living standards, including the 'social wage', undermined the confidence of all movements. The women's movement now found itself increasingly divided between those rejecting the working class movement as a form of male domination, for whom men were the enemy, and those determined to fight on as part of the working class movement.[102] Nearly a hundred women came to the workshop run by the North London WARF on racism and fascism at the Socialist Feminist conference in Manchester, January 1978.[103] However, an acrimonious debate at the last national women's liberation conference, April 1978, further deepened the division in the women's movement'.[104]

Anna Keane argued that Women Against the Nazis had to be different from other ANL groups:

> It's much more difficult than with other groups [against the Nazis] because you have to put forward more radical politics. You can't just say to women 'You must stand up against the Front because they want to keep you in the home'. You have to explain rather more than that.[105]

This meant 'do[ing] it the opposite way from the ANL. They start out with big public meetings and then try to build the local activities'. Women Against the Nazis (WAN) was built from the ground up, 'In WAN, where there is someone wanting to do something locally, we say "Go ahead", produce the literature for them and build from there… Our plan starts out with leafleting on estates, followed up by small meetings… based on just one street, in a small community centre or someone's home. Most of the women we make contact with will not have much experience of big public political meetings and would be rather put off by the idea, but really do want to do something'.[106]

By May, 100,000 copies of the WAN leaflet, 'Our kids are healthy... don't let them catch the racist bug!', had been sent out.[107] By the end of the summer 10,000 copies of the 5 pence *Women Against the Nazis* pamphlet had been sold.[108] Peggy Eagle helped set up a WAN group on her estate in London, leafleting all 200 houses, going door to door to ask if people wanted a babysitter; 'We had the meeting in the community hall, and we asked Miriam Karlin to speak. Seven women came, which we were really pleased with. They were ordinary housewives, the women who we have to involve in WAN.'[109] About thirty women attended a Coventry *Women's Voice* meeting to discuss opposing the NF's racist and fascist ideas going on to sell the *Women Against the Nazis* pamphlet around Hillfields flats. Leeds WARF, with twenty-five activists, affiliated to the ANL. One activity led by these women was painting out racist graffiti. As part of the Women Against the Nazis 'Paint out' Day, South Hackney and Shoreditch Anti-Nazi League was launched with a paint out starting from one of Hackney's Sunday morning markets: 'It was a mini carnival. We had a float with reggae music. We leafletted, sold badges, used a megaphone to address all the people around, collected signatures on a petition in support of our action, and our numbers just grew and grew.'[110]

Gays Against Nazis
Like the women's movement, the gay movement saw the fascist threat. The NF followed the politics of the Nazis who persecuted gay men, requiring them to wear a pink triangle in public, sending many thousands to concentration camps. Just as women had to be forced back into the home to be mother and wife, so men had to be aggressive and virile – and heterosexual. No deviation could be tolerated: 'The National Front believes in making Britain a land for decent people to live in – not homosexuals, drug-addicts and degenerates'.[111]

These views were widespread. The fight against them was transformed by the gay liberation movement that came out of the radicalisation of the late 1960s. Its best-known organisation, the Gay Liberation Front (GLF), was set up in New York shortly after the 1969 Stonewall riots resisting police harassment in New York.[112] Huey Newton, leading member of the Black Panthers, acknowledged the gay liberation movement, 'We must relate to the homosexual movement because it's a real thing'.[113] The GLF quickly found supporters in Britain with hundreds attending its weekly meetings in London. A movement, not an organisation, it went into decline towards the end of 1972 as arguments about how to make 'revolution as personal liberation' undermined collective action.[114]

The political downturn that came with the 1974 economic crash and the Wilson and Callaghan government's move to the right led to increasing attacks on gays. Strongly backed by the right-wing press, Mary Whitehouse, a devout Christian and opponent of sex education in schools, took out a private prosecution for blasphemy against *Gay News*.[115] The Gay News Defence Committee raised over £25,000 to cover legal costs, including appeals going as far as the House of Lords. All these were lost, though the nine-month suspended prison sentence given to the editor, Denis Lemon, was dropped. The February 1978 demonstration in support of *Gay News*, 5,000 strong, the largest ever gay march in Britain, boosted confidence and within weeks, a new organisation, the Gay Activists Alliance (GAA) was launched, with a dozen local groups across the country. It was the GAA who gave out thousands of copies of their leaflet, 'Gays against fascism – The face of HATE. Is this the future you want?'[116]

There was a long history of 'queer bashing', physical attacks on gays. Gays were victimised at work, not infrequently by Labour councils.[117] In 1968, homosexuality was still classified as a mental disease in the official Diagnostic and Statistical Manual of Mental Disorders.[118] Police harassment was a constant threat. The number of arrests of gay men trebled after the 1967 Sexual Offences Act which decriminalised private homosexual acts between men aged over twenty-one but at the same time imposed heavier penalties on street offences.[119] Manchester's chief constable, James Anderton, a committed Christian, used an 1882 law to veto 'licentious dancing' and ordered a raid on a gay sauna.[120] The National Front also played their part in this repression of gays, mounting frequent violent attacks. NF members broke up a meeting on gay sex education in Crawley. A group of up to twenty smashed up the Royal Vauxhall Tavern, a well-known gay bar in London. In Leeds they repeatedly attacked the Leeds Gay Centre and also the Fenton Hotel, hospitalising a number of people, one of whom lost an eye.[121]

A 'Gays Against Fascism' placard was on the first Gay Pride march in London in 1972. Lesbians and gay men were at the Wood Green demonstration where *Gay News* reported, 'Gays were out in strength'. The same was true on the Grunwick picket line.[122] At Clifton Rise, Lewisham, as Andy Strouthous, stewarding a contingent ready for the big push through the police, called on people to 'Stick together': 'Rex, tall and languid, with his hand behind his head, said "Stick together, darling, we fuck together".'[123]

In early 1978, Tom Robinson wore a pink triangle on *Top of the Pops* and Denis Lemon, editor of *Gay News*, sponsored the ANL.[124] Andy McKechnie made a rousing speech at an Anti Nazi League meeting in Glasgow, attended by seventeen gay people. With banners and homemade placards, the gay contingent on the Victoria Park carnival numbered around 400.[125] Pip Smith came with leaflets and badges and 'Gay and Here to stay' in large letters on his back. In his article for *Gay News*, he described:

> Several young heavy-looking skinheads approach[ing]: 'You got any of them there badges,' pointing to the Gays Against Fascism one that I'm wearing... Pink triangles pinned to leather jackets, they eventually move off contented... The GAA contingent reassembles behind the Women Against Racism and Fascism and the women from Lesbian Line. We begin the march down the Strand... The march quickens. So many gay friends and faces all round me chanting, singing, chatting, some of them veterans of the old GLF days, others new to gay demos... 'If you hate the National Front clap your hands... If you want Gay Liberation clap your hands'.[126]

Eddie Prevost was part of the security on the stage in Victoria Park:

> There was a rumour the Front were going to attack the stage, so we had to stay there. We had no idea how many were coming on the march. When they came, it was just unbelievable. I was next to the sound system. We had to stay there to keep people out. I was with John Lindsay. He

had been a sergeant in the South African army. He was gay. When Tom Robinson sang 'Glad to be gay', he was crying. It was an emotional day.[127]

There was homophobia on the left to be challenged. On the Lewisham demonstration in the morning, a speaker: 'attacked the police for being "queer". This fact spread very rapidly among the gay people on the march, and would certainly have gone much further... if the presence of gay support for the march had not been acknowledged by SWP speakers at the rally.'[128] Iain Ferguson remembers Tom Robinson on the September 1978 Right to Work march:

> One evening, round the campfire, as soon as Tom stood up to sing, a lot of the Glasgow kids started to make homophobic mutterings. Tom's response to this was to begin with saying 'Some of you know that I am gay. I know that some of you might feel uncomfortable with that. And if you do, there's really only one thing I want to say... and that's this'. Tom made an 'up yours' gesture, holding his upper right arm with his left hand, defiantly raising his right fist. The whole place burst into laughter and the evening ended with the 50 punks singing 'Glad to be gay'.[129]

Gay News ran an article 'Carnivals: All summer long': 'A SUMMER of demonstrations against extreme Right-wing political groups brought more homosexuals out in support than ever before following the attacks earlier this year on... the Vauxhall Tavern in South London and the Fenton Hotel in Leeds.'[130] The demonstrations culminated in the massive Anti Nazi League Carnival in Brixton:

> Arriving in Brixton the marchers had a special welcome from local gays who had slung their enormous banner of greetings across the street. And from an adjacent windowsill they received an ever so Gracious and Regal Wave (rehearsed to perfection) from one of the community's leading Queens. Earlier this summer, gays in Manchester and Edinburgh were out in force at similar events. In Edinburgh they even organised a float for their carnival, and gay liberation groups

were in evidence too in Manchester bringing together Gay Lib supporters, Campaign for Homosexual Equality [CHE] members and students from Gaysoc.[131]

Just as RAR had responded with Rock Against Sexism when the issue was raised, it also challenged homophobia. *Temporary Hoarding* included persecuting gay people in its portrait of a Britain ruled by the NF: 'If we're gay we're locked away...sexual orthodoxy, patriotic ditties on the radio, mashed potato for tea'.[132]

In Leeds: 'when Gay Pride came around, we went to the market for tons of pink cloth and made "Gays Against Nazis" banners to hang on the walls of the club, which we also listed as a gay venue in *Gay News*.'[133] Bob Cant remembers:

One of the most important advances for gay politics in this period came from outside the movement itself with the establishment of the Anti-Nazi League (ANL)... [and] Rock Against Racism (RAR). Their success was such that people felt confident enough individually to identify themselves as supporters of the ANL even when they were away from the demonstrations and the gigs. Anti-Nazi badges could be seen everywhere. Prominent among these were the Gays Against the Nazis badges. Not only was the culture of ANL and RAR anti-racist and anti-Fascist, it was also welcoming of lesbians and gay men. The music of the gay singer and ANL activist, Tom Robinson, played an important part in generating that atmosphere. When he sang anti-Fascist songs everyone joined in; when he sang 'Glad to be Gay' everyone joined in. Being gay in that atmosphere was much less isolated than being gay anywhere else on the Left had been and many lesbians and gay men came out and became politically active through this whole experience. In that period, it was possible to be openly gay, to be politically active and to have a good time. A period to be cherished.[134]

Into schools
Anti-racism in schools
A hundred teachers from across Britain launched the first national initiative against institutional racism in schools. The

Teachers Against Racism teach-in in London, November 1972, was opened by Gus John, black author and activist: 'When schools even now emphasise that they do not regard the colour of children anymore and that children to them, are "Just kids", that school is in fact taking a racist position by denying the colour of children and the characteristics and culture that go with that colour.'[135]

John went on to 'discuss the various aspects of the destruction of the black or brown child's self image, self confidence, and educational prospects which takes place in the British school system as it is at present'. Bernard Coard, author of *How the West Indian Child is Made Educationally Sub-Normal in the British School System*, then spoke spelling out the many ways 'the racialist education system manifests itself', his last instance being: 'not just in the contempt for parents, their culture, language, history and heritage, but in the pitting of children against their parents, teaching them to be contemptuous of their parents and their background.'[136]

In this context, Coard argued 'the way the system operates is a combination of conscious racism and unconscious racism', concluding:

> You must see teachers both as conscious agents in some cases, as well as pawns in a much wider number of cases. But you should be just as much ashamed of being a pawn as of being an overt racist. You should be ashamed of being a lackey, as of being a bigot. What matters is that once you know what your role is, you do something about it right away.[137]

The widespread failure to challenge racism in schools gave a huge opening to the fascists, one which the Labour government did not try to close. Roy Jenkins, Labour's Home Secretary, was clear that the NF should not be confronted because of the danger of being provoked and consequently behaving like them.[138] A black student from Hackney, east London, who was interviewed in a Thames TV piece about SKAN pointed out that anti-racism was weakened by the refusal to confront the fascists. In her experience:

what's going on in school now, all the racism, is because most fights which happen in school are caused by racism. It's not just jealousy or hate or something which crops up between them. It's mostly racism… and the headmistress constantly keeps on saying 'Let's be one big happy family' and it's really depressing.[139]

A white student in the same interview added: 'Teachers in our school don't talk about the National Front. They think it's going to go away if you don't talk about it. It's silly because it won't go away. It's going to be there. It's going to grow if you don't talk about it.'[140]

Teaching at a school in Balham, south London, Greg Dyke remembers that the general consensus among colleagues who were 'by and large, liberal, was: "Don't talk about race. We don't talk about race". They knew that the white kids, by and large, came from disproportionately quite hostile families. Institutions didn't take these things on at that time for that reason. And that's why the Labour Party didn't take it on.'[141] Despite this, a substantial number of teachers were willing to speak up. Kevin Corr remembers:

> At one point, before the ANL was established, we got 1,000 teachers to sign a petition against racism to send to the local paper, the *Newham Recorder*. The editor, Tom Duncan, refused to print it. He found some pretext such as whether all the signatures were genuine. He didn't want to antagonise the readership of the paper. We used to call it the Nuremberg Recorder.[142]

One measure of the seriousness with which many teachers saw the need to challenge racism was the astonishing 2,500 who attended the All London Teachers Against Racism and Fascism (ALTARF) meeting in March 1978.[143]

NF in schools
In 1974 Richard Edmonds was teaching in a school in Brixton that had many black pupils. Two school governors called for his resignation after he was seen with a National Front placard on the NF march in Leicester. Edmonds's employer, the Inner London

Education Authority (ILEA), refused to act. A *Guardian* editorial argued that on the available evidence, 'there is no case for disciplinary action': 'To discipline the teacher if his only offence has been to join the National Front would be to start down the road to which NF politics naturally lead – totalitarianism... The best way of keeping the NF in its place is to uphold the tolerance to which the present system is committed'.[144] In contrast, the *Rank and File Teacher* paper called for people to identify NF members: 'Wherever they raise their ugly head and weed them out, wherever they are, like the vermin they undoubtedly resemble'.[145]

Within a month of the decision not to act, Edmonds had filed his parliamentary nomination papers as NF candidate for nearby Deptford for the October 1974 general election. He got 4.5 percent of the vote. It took over a year to get him out of the school and key to getting him to leave was the many teachers at Tulse Hill who 'sent him to Coventry'.[146]

After 'How to spot a Red Teacher' leaflets appeared in Holloway School, north London, the headteacher, George Spinoza, worked with the NUT rep, Shaun Doherty, to produce an anti-racist statement.[147] A surviving draft proposes the confiscation of National Front literature and challenging racist language. This would involve explaining the reasons to pupils, providing well-resourced anti-racist education in school and running a campaign to get these policies adopted as widely as possible.[148] Drawing much publicity, which Doherty remembers as being almost uniformly favourable, the nearby Quintin Kynaston school soon adopted the same policy.[149]

While it was hard work in schools overcoming liberal attitudes against actively challenging racism, it was similar in what was generally recognised as the more progressive of the two large teaching unions, the National Union of Teachers (NUT). Plans to sell *SKAN* magazine outside schools in Birmingham and recruit teachers to Teachers Against the Nazis were opposed by John Bowdler, NUT West Midland executive member, insisting that 'Schools should not become "political battlegrounds"'. Bowdler reflected the layer of headteachers who had dominated the NUT for many years.[150] He got support from a Conservative councillor who, responding to concerns that the Young National Front rally in Birmingham the previous week would have strengthened its support in schools, reported that 'letters had already been sent to teachers advising that youngsters should not become associated with extremist groups and recommending that no political pamphlets should be circulated in schools'. He added: 'We have a long tradition of toleration within our schools and I hope it will continue. We have no evidence that the National Front is making any considerable inroads into any school'.[151]

Against this, Simon Fuller, organising secretary for Teachers Against Nazis, argued:

> teachers have a general duty to counter racialist and Nazi propaganda, and present it to pupils as being unacceptable. We should point out the dangers of the creed just as we would point out the dangers of a serious drug, such as heroin. Otherwise we are doing an injustice to pupils and parents.[152]

A more aggressive 'top-down' approach was taken by the education committee in Wolverhampton, which threatened both school students and teachers with disciplinary action if they were found to be spreading NF propaganda.[153] At the same time, however, employers could take a hard line against those opposing the NF. Hillingdon Council in northwest London decided David Potter, SWP member and secretary of the local NUT branch, having allowed fourth-year students of government and politics to read an Anti Nazi League leaflet, was 'unsuitable for employment'.[154]

It was very different in Pimlico Comprehensive School in central London where the policy at the school had been to avoid discussing 'race' matters. Students chanting 'National Front' assaulted an Asian teacher after which, while the head responded by suspending two pupils, the school NUT branch resolved to do everything possible to keep racist literature out of the school at the same time as distributing ANL leaflets and sponsoring the ALCARAF meeting.[155]

Not every NUT branch took such a determined position. On the contrary, Nick Grant remembers seconding a motion to affiliate to the ANL at a large meeting of the Ealing NUT: the secretary, a member of the Communist Party, shouted at him 'You are exactly the kind of people who lost us the Spanish Civil

War'. The motion was defeated, though this decision was later reversed.[156] The Barking NUT Association decided to support headteachers in reporting any sign of NF leaflets and to set up a branch of the National Association for Multi-Racial Education.[157] The NUT at Daneford School in Bethnal Green agreed 'to sponsor and make a (voluntary) financial contribution towards the Anti Nazi League'.[158] As we have already seen, the ANL held the largest fringe meeting at the NUT's 1978 conference but did not get the national union to affiliate.

Working in a comprehensive school in a largely skilled working-class part of Bristol in the 1970s, one teacher became aware that the National Front were organising in the area:

> Kids and – from what they said – some of their family members were joining it or felt sympathy with it. Some of the students were walking around wearing black shirts and black trousers and Confederate flag badges. Kids were starting arguments in class, wanting to ban all immigration, and coming out with all the usual racist arguments about immigrants taking 'our' jobs and 'our' houses and 'our' country. I wanted to encourage classroom discussion but it could get deeply unpleasant as more children were being drawn into expressing support for nakedly fascistic policies, like rounding up all immigrants and forcibly 'repatriating' them, or wanting to 'lock up all the communists'. They said they hated blacks, Pakistanis, the Irish, the Scots and some of them said they admired Martin Webster and John Tyndall. Sometimes *Spearhead* was distributed outside the school gates. It felt as if this area of Bristol was becoming a hotbed of the National Front. I felt it was threatening my control of some of my classes – I felt some of these kids were being revved up to behave like this, and against 'communist teachers'.

When the NF held an election meeting in the shcool, there was a huge turnout for a counter-protest.

> Before it started, during the day, RE classes throughout the school had made posters for interracial harmony which were pinned up on the walls of the school hall. There was a counter demonstration outside, which I wanted to go on, but

I felt I couldn't because I knew that the NF would be likely to start violent confrontations and I thought my job would be on the line if I got arrested.

In some personal anguish I stayed at home but gathered afterwards that some other teachers went along to observe what happened. The press were there, and it was reported that a few parents or members of the public got up in the meeting and tried to argue with the fascists. They were assaulted and brutally thrown out in an imitation of the tactics of Mosley at the Blackshirt rally at Olympia in the 1930s. So, it was a dreadful occasion. There was quite a well-supported and noisy counter-demonstration against the NF outside the school.

At some point after the election rally, one of the kids passed me a copy of *Spearhead* that had come into the school and was being passed around. I took it to the head and said 'Read this, these are the ideas that were being promoted at that election rally.' He took the copy and then he came to see me afterwards and said, 'This is disgusting. I didn't realise'. But he had let a big cat out of the bag.

Not long afterwards... the Anti-Nazi League was formed. One of the great, wonderful things the ANL did was to publish leaflets for use outside and inside schools. These were incredibly effective. One afternoon children started bringing in this leaflet which ANL members had handed out outside the school at lunchtime. The next class I had after lunch, a lot of the kids came in holding copies. They were gobsmacked by this leaflet. It showed a picture of bodies piled up in a concentration camp when it was liberated in 1945, and the slogan 'Never again!', with quotes from John Tyndall and Martin Webster about how they admired the Nazis and what they wanted to do to immigrants. It was very hard hitting and many of the children who read it expressed shock and surprise. For example, one boy in my tutor group had previously started saying he supported the NF and hated all foreigners. I'd pointed out to him that his family had been Travellers and that under the Nazis they would have been sent to concentration camps, but he just said, 'Oh, that's all in the past'. Students like him weren't thinking about the realities of what they were saying. Those leaflets made him think, and his attitude changed. The concentration camp pictures were horrifying, and the quotations from Tyndall and Webster in the leaflet proved that leading figures in the National Front were violent anti-Semites and racists who supported what the Nazis had done to Jews and wanted to treat other groups in a similar way. This was news to many of the children, but it was news they needed to hear.

The ANL leafletting had this tremendous, immediate effect. The students read the leaflets, we talked about them, they took them home. I think some of them talked about them with their mums and dads. From that time onwards it got easier at school and the National Front started to lose popularity. It was a gradual, slow process, but being an NF member wasn't cool anymore and for some of the kids being an anti-Nazi was definitely cool. The ANL started to organise demonstrations in Bristol against NF mobilisations – Bristol had a very active Bristol Anti Nazi League. The NF would turn out in force, carrying their massive union jacks with big spikes on the top... but now there were also bigger counter-demonstrations. I remember seeing more school kids on them and a lot of young football supporters – especially from Bristol City, but some from [Bristol] Rovers as well – turning out for the Anti-Nazi League and massively strengthening our numbers. And bit by bit the tide was turned and the NF were weakened.

So it was a very big effect that the Anti-Nazi League had and a huge relief, both at work and outside. This sense of relief was like a physical thing, like a sense of an illness or sickness that was lifting as people gathered to oppose this foul thing that had become so popular and so prevalent. However, it became clear, and is still to this day, that there are parts of Bristol where, when fascists have mobilised, they have been able to get some electoral support. We've also had some horrible racist attacks in Bristol.[159]

SKAN: School Students Against the Nazis[160]
Encouraged by the sharp rise of youth unemployment and

boosted by the May 1977 GLC election results, at the start of the new school year the NF launched *Bulldog: Paper of the Young National Front*. A thousand copies of the first two issues were distributed free in schools in Barking. By the third issue, a further thousand in east London schools.[161] Its sixteen-year-old editor, Joe Pearce, called on readers to 'distribute *Bulldog* in your school and upset the Red teachers. You can upset the teachers and help the NF at the same time. All youth should take part in Operation NF – Spread the racialist word, distribute *Bulldog*... and help the Front keep Britain white'.[162] How to 'Help the Front keep Britain white' was spelt out: 'The National Front is growing stronger and stronger every day. In fact, we are so strong that nothing can stop us from taking power. Our time will come, and when it does the blacks are going back home to their own countries.'[163]

The Young National Front (YNF) was launched with a demonstration. The target was the Inner London Education Authority (ILEA) film studios where a TV drama *Somebody's Daughter*, about a pregnant seventeen-year-old white girl and the father, her Caribbean boyfriend, was being made.[164] Seeking further publicity, the NF held a press conference announcing that a quarter of a million 'How to Spot a Red Teacher' leaflets were ready for distribution.[165] Headlined 'Keep Communism out of the Classroom', it detailed arguments to use against 'Red teachers':

> Ask the Red teachers why they support Black Nationalism but oppose White Nationalism. Tell them that there have been more civil and religious wars than wars caused by nationalism. Tell them World Government would be a tyranny like George Orwell's 1984. Above all, tell them you are proud to be British.[166]

The leaflet was backed up with a pamphlet, 'How to combat Red Teachers', calling on pupils 'to fight falsehood with truth', to stop Marxists who 'have heavily infiltrated schools and universities' from 'ceaselessly using their positions to indoctrinate their classes with their poisonous philosophies'.[167] NF members with school age children took action. Derek Day, a leading NF activist in the East End, withdrew his daughter from Haggerston School because it had black pupils.[168] An NF member in Sheffield campaigned to stop primary school children being re-allocated to a secondary school with more black pupils.[169] A further NF pamphlet, 'Education for National Survival', called for parents to have the right to vote to get rid of hard-core Marxist teachers and for providing 'immigrant children with separate education facilities from British children until they, along with their parents, can be repatriated'.[170]

Local leafleting also got press coverage. The *Derbyshire Times* told readers: 'The National Front swooped on Matlock this week to drum up recruits for its youth movement'.[171] The Glasgow-based *Sunday Mail* reported: 'The National Front have infiltrated Scots classrooms. About 50 pupils in Edinburgh and Glasgow have joined and are distributing leaflets among their classmates.'[172] Every increase in NF activity was accompanied by an increase in racist attacks. Tower Hamlets Movement Against Racism and Fascism reported: 'a campaign of racial terror had been unleashed in schools' with Asian pupils being let out of school fifteen minutes early to avoid attacks. Some teachers accompanied groups of pupils back to where they lived.[173]

The YNF exploited the political establishment's failure to give a lead against racism in schools. There was no lack of awareness of the problem. A confidential paper circulated in Whitehall on the need for political education in schools to 'help provide children with the "intellectual weapons" to resist "anti-democratic movements"'.[174] The TUC urged the Secretary of State for Education, Shirley Williams, to advise local authorities to ban National Front speakers and materials from schools.[175] The National Union of Teachers announced it was referring *Bulldog* to the Director of Public Prosecutions.[176] The Commission for Racial Equality called a meeting to find 'a common strategy to combat National Front activities'.[177]

Both the National Union of Teachers and the National Association of Headteachers advised its members to confiscate racist literature handed out to children as they go to school. In Wolverhampton school children were warned they could be expelled if caught handing out NF literature.[178] The day after the NF leafleted Spurley Hey High School in Manchester the headteacher held a special assembly 'to tell pupils not to be provoked. Everyone in my school will be treated in exactly the same way whatever their race or religion'.[179] School students' hostility to teachers' telling them what to think may in some cases have helped rather than hindered the NF to build a presence in schools.

The response had to come 'from below'. Weyman Bennett grew up in the East End in a Jehovah's Witness family. He recalls:

> It was a very political area. There were lots of gas workers and dockers in the area. The Communist Party had a presence and there were also a few families which included Holocaust survivors... a number of people in the local Jehovah's Witnesses congregation were Holocaust survivors.[180] And there were people who remembered and had been active in the Battle of Cable Street in 1936. So there was a 'collective memory' about Nazism and what it meant.[181]

When the NF started selling *Bulldog* outside his school:

> there was a group of us in school who were determined to stop them. We'd see these lads on the NF marches, or selling their paper in the town – but we knew they had to come back to school. So there'd be these Nazi skinheads and then us – punks and soul boys[182] – who were determined to get them out of the school. There would be fights in school and sometimes in lessons... And that then spilled out to the surrounding area. There were often running battles down Stratford High Street as we tried to clear them off the street... The police response was often really slow so sometimes these battles would last for a couple of hours. But eventually we physically removed the NF from the school and stopped them selling their rag.[183]

Sometimes the response appeared to be spontaneous. When a group led by Nick Griffin, one of the YNF's main organisers,[184] tried to leaflet Chantry School in Ipswich with 'How to spot a Red Teacher', they were chased away by 200 students. They fared no better at nearby Copleston High School, where one NF leafleter was taken away by ambulance with Griffin complaining he had been pulled from his car, punched and kicked.[185]

The fightback often had its origins in institutional racism. David Kersey remembers there was a lot of racism in his comprehensive school in Sheffield:

Some of the African Caribbean school students including a couple of lads in my class started to fight back... I remember they were constantly treated as though they were the source of all problems in the classroom by the teacher, but they were not just apologising, they were fighting back. They were getting in the face of people who got in their face and they weren't going to take shit off people.

Two were both already identifying as Rasta... they were demanding to be allowed to wear the tam, the Rasta hat. School uniform was the first big issue I got involved in... I think they got suspended for walking into the classroom with the hat having been told not to.

The National Front leafleted schools in Sheffield and the black school students in my school said that you've got to take sides. You're either on our side or you are on theirs. Obviously if we were on their side we'd have a big problem with them... It was a very tense period. I was in a school where there was a lot of tension anyway and a lot of the white school students took the side of the people fighting back against racism.[186]

In Barking, where Joe Pearce had started *Bulldog*, a group of RAR supporters responded with a handout titled 'Bullshit', arguing 'NF=No Fun, No Freedom, No future'.[187] The National Union of School Students (NUSS) took on *Bulldog*, leafleting two Islington schools.[188] When YNF member Kevin Randall, sixth former at the Latymer School in Enfield, north London, spoke in an ultra-reasonable tone of voice at the launch of 'How to spot a Red Teacher', he was described by Webster as the 'voice of white British youth'.[189] In Latymer School, however, he was isolated:

> 400 turned up at an anti-racist meeting at the school, nearly the whole of the 4th, 5th and 6th form. The feeling of the meeting was that they didn't want to be lectured to about the evils of racism by vicars. They wanted action against the NF. A speaker from the Anti Nazi League got a warm reception.[190]

Not only warmly received, the ANL was actively supported:

■ Hackney Downs school walkout 1978

> 150 or so of the students wear anti-racist badges and 100 wear Anti-Nazi league badges. It was the League's leafleting of our school which brought the issue to a head and led the head to allow a meeting against racism.
> Quite a few of us think we should go further, convincing the younger kids and leafleting the public at large. The older teachers want to keep publicity away from school gates but you can't keep the kids out of politics. When the Front have got kids of 14 we have to start young as well. If we're allowed to get married or work at 16, we also have a right to be involved in politics. I think we should be out arguing at the May local elections, even if we can't vote.[191]

When the NF tried to meet at the local girls' high school in Walthamstow, 400 people, mainly school students, turned out for a picket at just two days' notice after the head had tried to keep it quiet:

> Slogans went up all over the school reading 'Stop NF Nazis'.

A mass movement

Teachers were furious at not having been told about the meeting. That afternoon some kids ran off leaflets, 'Stop The NF from meeting at our school. Be there'.
Straight after school a group leafletted all the schools in the area. On the Thursday afternoon, 40 of the 4th years had gone and sat in the playground and refused to move for two lessons until the headmistress was forced to answer the questions they fired at her. The sixth formers wrote to the headmistress expressing their disgust at the NF using the school.
At the meeting that night the teachers turned up and bravely went into the meeting where they were threatened by NF bully boys while outside school kids chanted all evening 'Get that scum out of our school', 'The school kids united will never be defeated', 'We are black. We are white. We are fucking dynamite!'[192]

Polly Wilson, already involved with RAR, was at the school:

> Our school was multicultural and we felt it was a right smack in the face... It didn't take much to get a lot of people there because if you were black or had black mates you knew or had already had encounters with the NF... A lot of friendships were made and a lot of us became politicised that evening. It still gives me goosebumps when I think of the feeling of unity.[193]

The undercover police squad, the Special Demonstration Squad, later reported on Walthamstow SKAN as:

> very successful. Set up initially by [Redacted[194]] and now almost entirely run by [Redacted] the group can, with short notice, get large numbers of school students onto the streets, should the need arise (for example, to heckle an impromptu National Front meeting). The group started about a year ago when the National Front held a public meeting at [Redacted] school in Walthamstow. At that time an Anti-NF picket of about 200 persons was organised; following the inevitable confrontation with police, 18 arrests were made and of these all but one were black. This gave good impetus to the formation of SKAN as a youth anti-Nazi group and it

has since been adopted and promoted nationally. Indeed, it is largely through these student activities that the ANL in Waltham Forest has been able to earn any success.[195]

Young people dominated the opposition to the National Front in High Wycombe with 200 marching round the town centre to promote a RAR gig. A week later they marched again.[196] Two hundred and fifty came to the gig, which saw the band Crisis jumping off the stage to join the audience in chasing off fascists who were trying to break up the gig.[197]

A small group of school students calling themselves Reading Schools Against Nazis responded to NF leafleting their schools with their own leaflets. They called a meeting after these were banned by headteachers and some members threatened with expulsion. Press publicity helped get twenty-five school students to come, most of whom joined after a discussion that included opposition to school uniforms and corporal punishment.[198]

Encouraged by the support they got at the Reading ANL launch meeting, they put together *SKAN* on a kitchen table, the first edition of *SKAN* chimed with the experience of school students everywhere that 'Most teachers and school authorities have stood by and done nothing while the Nazi scum have appeared in our schools'.[199] Identifying RAR as a sister organisation, *SKAN* 1 told readers: 'Music and our generation go together. RAR and SKAN fight the Nazis together'. It went on 'You can organise RAR gigs... all you do is ring SKAN or RAR and we'll help if you want us to'.[200]

The 3,000 copies of *SKAN* 1 went quickly and 5,000 more were printed. The production of *SKAN* 2 moved to London, focusing on the Victoria Park Carnival at the end of April with an article by Andie Page, one of the Reading school students, asking Tom Robinson at the pre-Carnival press conference: 'What do you think about keeping politics out of our schools?' Robinson replied 'Where one guy says "Hey man, I'm not interested in politics", another guy replies, "No man, but politics is interested in you"'.[201]

Letters from school students, many as young as fourteen, poured into the ANL office, asking for information, membership, leaflets and badges. Some wanted to set up a SKAN group in school.[202] Five sixteen-year-old school students from Crewe wrote that they were: 'hoping to set up an anti Nazi organisation to crush the NF into the ground and out of existence. We are not violent people but something must be done against the NF'.[203] Julia Stockton wrote, 'Dear Sir, I wish to apply for a membership, if such a thing exists, to the Anti-Nazi League'. She went on to explain that 'as a person with many coloured friends,' she was 'deeply opposed to the National Front'.[204] Some had already been to RAR gigs, many were hoping to get to the carnival. J Flowers expressed a common view saying: 'Most of the propaganda for the Anti-Nazi League came because the Tom Robinson Band, Steel Pulse, the Clash, X-Ray Spex etc have come out in support of it and this has been noticed by people who read the music press.'[205] One included a poem, another came from a serving soldier, telling the ANL to stop writing to his son, an instruction that was ignored. Many wrote about racism, one wrote about 'playground chanting of "NF"'. Among a number of letters from young Jews, one read 'I hate Nazis because they killed Jews and they killed a lot of mum's family and she spent all her childhood running away from the Nazis'.[206]

Badges were sold, large and small. Where the wearing of badges was banned, 'a lot of kids wear them inside their lapels which made them even more popular'.[207] School students in Oldham and Stockport were caned for wearing them.[208]

Inspired by the Soweto uprising, Rehad Desai started his political activity producing a duplicated fanzine at school in Finchley, north London and got people talking, the immediate challenge was to take on the headteacher's ban on political badges in a school.[209] With almost half the students from immigrant families, the issue was: 'The right to dignity, racial dignity. We weren't going to stand by and watch black students in our school being intimidated by the prospect of the fascists coming to our school. That's what they promised. And that's why we set up School Kids Against the Nazis.'[210]

Two coaches were booked to leave from Finchley for the Victoria Park Carnival. With a small charge to help cover costs, they filled quickly. 'We made a massive banner, "Finchley School Kids against Nazis". I think we had about 150 people behind our banner, probably one of the largest contingents'.[211] Brian Capeloff had been at a Hackney primary school where he remembers

National Front stickers starting to appear in large numbers in the mid-1970s. A couple of boys at his secondary school, Hackney Downs, wanted to do something: 'We started to hear about "School Kids against the Nazis". It was Laurence who was the main person who kickstarted us... he organised us handing out leaflets, got badges and helped coordinate a march on Hackney Downs.'[212]

As Laurence explained to a Thames TV journalist, 'After the carnival we started up SKAN, School Kids Against the Nazis. We're opposed to the idea of the National Front and we want to sort of stop it at the beginning in schools'. And stop it not only in schools; it was members of the Chelmsford SKAN group who organised the first Chelmsford ANL meeting with forty people.[213] The carnival showed SKAN was a national organisation with banners from Tyneside to Southampton. It had grown without publicity. Its only national coverage was the lively, factual, mostly supportive article 'S.K.A.N. ROOLS OK' in *New Musical Express*, circulation over 200,000, by the journalist Tony Parsons.[214]

Working in the ANL office Joan Rudder remembers SKAN as the ANL youth section, 'a great group of kids, totally anarchic'. Helen Blair in Glasgow found this when she and Henry Maitles:

> decided we wanted to help set up a SKAN group in Hamilton on the outskirts of Glasgow. We didn't think through the fact that we were teachers, not pupils. We knew a couple of school students who were interested. With them, we called a committee meeting, early in September, to see if we could get a few more to talk about the carnival that was coming up. The venue was the café in the British Home Stores. Expecting two or three, we picked a small quiet table. We hadn't leafleted for the meeting; we didn't advertise it. We were astonished when around 25 school students from several schools turned up, including from my school. One of the girls, the daughter of one of my school's senior teachers, turned up at the café dressed in plastic. They knew about the carnival coming up. They took over the whole café, didn't order anything and spooked the management who called the police. We had to lead the group down to a park and hold the meeting under a bridge.[215]

This anarchic energy was given a lead by more organised groups in some schools. Desai remembers 'we had mates in other schools. We were reaching out to three or four other schools.' However:

> the only SKAN branch was in my school discussing what we're going to do: leaflets, mobilising, signing people up to the coaches and for the counter demonstrations. There was also quite strong Jewish participation. They tended to be a bit more serious. So they'd be signing up for the counter demonstrations [when] we'd go to East London, Brick Lane, and other places... It was tremendously brave. We'd turn up at a counter demonstration. Our average age was probably about 15 or 16, because we've got a few students 19 or 20 with us, and we go down there to tackle these hardline Nazis.[216]

SKAN 2 reported Sheffield SKAN was meeting weekly, getting leaflets and badges into twenty schools and the local ice rink, scrubbing off racist slogans and posters and 'selling tickets like mad' for its first RAR gig.

SKAN only got widespread national coverage when four ANL sponsors, including the talk show host Michael Parkinson and the comedian Dave Allen, decided to leave the ANL, giving their reason as the use of the word 'fuck' eight times in the most recent issue of SKAN magazine.[217] A report in the *Sunday Times* quoted Brian Clough, arguably the best known of more than 200 sponsors: 'I dissociate myself from that article and I dissociate myself from the Anti-Nazi League. This is the very type of thing I'm opposed to. They have used my name and position. I believe the people who are running it are as bad as the National Front if they urge that kind of thing.'[218]

The next day, however, the *Guardian* reported the *Sunday Times* article had caused confusion. Clough denied the report.[219] For its part, the ANL steering committee wrote immediately to every sponsor pointing out that:

> It is 8 words out of a total of some 4,000 of a 16-page issue of SKAN which have given offence. Inevitably mistakes and indiscretions are made and the ANL steering committee –

without stifling important initiative or enthusiasm – will have to take a firmer hand in the future. In no way would we, however, accept the right of the *Sun* newspaper to pontificate about SKAN's 'offensive language' in an editorial placed next to a picture of two nude women.[220]

Joan Rudder helped the SKAN writers draft a letter of apology. She remembers that they really didn't want to do this. Their view was that there was only one four letter word they were worried about and that was 'Nazi' but agreed to the steering committee's request:

> It was quite a mild thing but it made clear that they hadn't intended to offend anybody, but they didn't retract anything they'd said... One of the responses was a fantastic letter from Spike Milligan, full of effing and blinding... a fantastic response to the situation which was really quite ludicrous and he saw it as ludicrous... A lot of people recognised it as just youth. From that point on, Paul [Holborow] had to vet things that were published by the youngsters which we hadn't up to that point, they'd had free reign, which was part of the way things developed. It was such a big thing, you couldn't actually control it.[221]

An unapologetic Mike Pearse, SKAN press officer, pointed out that, while SKAN had eight swear words, 'the latest edition of *New Musical Express*, for example, contains 34 and *Sounds* 70 such words', adding 'If SKAN is to have any impact at all it must talk to schoolkids in their own language. The language of the playground and the football terraces'.[222] Arthur Scargill wrote to Brian Clough urging him to stay with the ANL and join him speaking at an ANL meeting.[223] Clough replied: 'it would be my privilege if, as you say, we could share a platform under the banner of the Anti-Nazi League'.[224]

The 200 High Wycombe school students marching behind a RAR banner were one example of how school students organised themselves, adopting whatever organisation could be adapted to meet their immediate needs. Growing confidence led to new demands. Anarchic as their meetings often were, SKAN groups were political, from the beginning, challenging school rules, uniforms and corporal punishment. Organising leafleting, badge selling, RAR gigs, the dynamic of SKAN was to go beyond the politics of anti-fascism. The Reading school students got involved with the NUSS.[225] Some joined revolutionary left groups such as the Socialist Worker Youth Movement, better known by its acronym SWYM. A SWYM placard at the counter NF protest at the ILEA studio carried the slogan:

Punks and Teds, Natty Dreads,

Smash the Front, + Join the Reds.[226]

The SWP replaced SWYM with Red Rebel.[227] About sixty came to a Rebel weekend in London. For Scotty, a punk Right to Work marcher from Glasgow: 'the best talk was Red Saunders on "Sex, Drugs & Rock & Roll". Also we really liked the talk on fighting the National Front and the Right to Work Film was very good.'[228]

Nigel Flanagan

I was a teenager in an inner city school in Leeds in 1977-1978. I don't think I would have really got interested in politics if it hadn't been for the Anti Nazi League and that push back against the National Front.

My family were not particularly political. Ordinary working class people, 'Vote Labour, join a union', that's kind of the end of it really. But the school I went to was quite a tough school in a lot of ways. It was right on the edge of an estate in Leeds called the Burmantoft Estate, which back in 1977 was covered in NF graffiti and all kinds of slogans and stuff and had that reputation around the school as being a National Front area. And it was a bit of a joke amongst all my friends that my initials, NF, were getting spray painted all around the estate and everything. So that's how I first noticed it really because people said, 'Oh, it's you!'

I think it is true to say when I reflect back at the time I had quite a bad set of racist ideas and racist assumptions. I was really more into playing football, listening to music and hanging out with my mates than I was into any kind of politics. But what happened was that the National Front kind of laid claim to our school. I think because they felt it was in the middle of the estate that it was their school. And there were a few kids in the school, I remember two in particular, a year above me in school, were really into the National Front, wearing the badges, giving out the leaflets. One day they turned up outside the school with other fascists and they were leafleting the school, and that leaflet, that was the first thing I ever saw, 'How to spot a Red Teacher'. And because I was really keen on football, I played a lot of football, and some of the lads in our school team were black, West Indian. Chapeltown was adjacent to where our estate was. There was no problem between me and them. We all got on all right, playing football and all the rest of it. But you had all the stuff, I could remember all the stuff about Ugandan Asians coming in, and then you used to see the National Front, they used to have a leaflet of an older guy being mugged by somebody who was obviously meant to look African or West Indian. So all that was around.

When the NF started leafleting the school, I and a few other kids went to see the teacher and said, 'What's all this about? What's going on?' And some of the teachers in the school were very union active. The NUT rep at the time was our art teacher.... He used to spend a bit of time talking to us about it. And he kind of introduced us to the idea that these people were unacceptable, were to be resisted and then, coincidentally, the Anti Nazi League did turn up outside our school at the same time as the National Front in an effort to counter leaflet, if you like, and talk to kids going in and out of school and it was just through talking to them, I got an Anti Nazi League badge off them. I wore it in the school. A couple of teachers tried to tell me to take it off. I wouldn't take it off but it never got pushed any further and, looking back, I think that was probably down to the teachers' union with the reps there saying, 'No, no, that's important. Some of the kids wear this stuff'.

And I did get pushed around quite a bit, particularly by these two older lads because I was wearing a badge. I was no leader, I was a 16 year old, loved football and all that kind of stuff. But I started wearing the badge. And then I noticed that other kids were wearing a badge and there was no meeting, there was no discussion, there was no sort of organisation, other than that the ANL turned up outside the school to make sure the kids – that included me – got a little bit of an idea of something else. And then the big event for us was a Rock against Racism gig in the middle of Leeds, and we went along to that, again just wanting to be supportive and wanting to be part of something, and it was just fantastic... I remember it was a place called Hyde Park in Leeds and we... and I went with a sort of girlfriend at the time who went to a different school. And we just kept bumping into people from her school that were all wearing the ANL badge.

Then a really significant fellow, one of my best mates near where we lived went to a different school from me, and his teacher... Colin Burgon,[229] he organised my mate Steve and all his mates, 'Get down there to the ANL concert, go on this ANL march'. I used to go along with them because they were getting organised by Colin.

And, from then on, I never looked back in terms of my politics, because he taught me the value of doing things on the ground. I used to think politics was watching Jim Callaghan and Margaret Thatcher or whatever it was, obviously so boring. But this was like real stuff. It really, really enthused me. And that started me on a journey into trade union politics and activism. This always stayed with me and it's meant I have always had the Anti Nazi League really close to my heart.[230]

Football Fans Against the Nazis, 1977–78

Violence at football matches both on the terraces and outside the grounds was increasing through the 1960s and 1970s. Newspapers attacked those fighting as 'animals', to which one response from fans was the chant 'We hate humans'.[231] The hatred was mutual. While attacking the violence, the press ignored the relentless 'in your face' racism that often accompanied it. The black footballer Brendan Batson, playing for West Bromwich Albion, remembers: 'We'd get off the coach at away matches and the National Front would be right there in your face. In those days, we didn't have security and we'd have to run the gauntlet.

We'd get to the players' entrance and there'd be spit on my jacket or Cyrille [Regis]'s shirt.'[232]

They received hate mail at home and, on at least one occasion, a petrol bomb.[233] There was the chant 'Pull the trigger, shoot the n.......' when Laurie Cunningham touched the ball.[234] None of this abuse was ever mentioned in the local or national media nor was it ever taken up by the FA.[235]

The NF was quick to exploit the racism: 'NF activists became a common sight outside stadiums on a Saturday afternoon, particularly in London and the northern cities, handing out their poisonous pamphlets and literature'.[236] A 1977 BBC Panorama documentary on Millwall football club, located in the middle of London's increasingly desolate and abandoned dock area, talked to young fans. Accepting the NF's racism, unsure if they wanted to be members, they told the interviewer, 'what the NF offers is the opportunity for a good ruck'. Picking up on the possible gains to be made, Martin Webster told *Panorama*:

> We will recruit patriotic pro-British youngsters... We are very glad to recruit youngsters who are of a robust disposition and who are willing and able to defend our legal activities from communist assault... I think there's a lot you can do with a soccer hooligan. I think that people resort to mindless violence and vandalism because they have not been given by society a point and a meaning to their lives.

He continued with a rewording of the Hitler quote: 'Mass demonstrations must burn into the little man's soul the proud conviction that, though a little worm, he is nevertheless part of a great dragon'. Webster's version was:

> People do like to identify, they do like to associate themselves with something which is big and glorious and noble, which they, the little individual, can associate themselves with and feel proud that they somehow belong. And we feel that the very, very fanatical adulation by supporters with their particular club is a sort of sublimated patriotism.

The BBC responded: 'So it's a case of Millwall today and National Front tomorrow', Webster replied: 'We hope so'.[237]

Joe Ashton, MP and lifelong supporter of Sheffield Wednesday, was one of the first to sign the ANL founding statement.[238] Two months later he wrote and narrated a Labour Party political broadcast savagely attacking the NF, telling viewers: 'They [the NF] are the people who are out to smash democracy in this country'. Ashton pointed to football fans as potential NF supporters, naming Tottenham, Chelsea, Millwall and Arsenal as targeted clubs. When sharply attacked in the press for doing interviews for the broadcast without telling interviewees what he was doing this for, he responded saying that the broadcast only repeated what *Panorama* had shown. This was a teenage soccer fan explaining that: 'the only reason any football supporter wants to join them is they say, "Well, come and join the National Front and you have a good punch-up every Sunday morning after Saturday afternoon".'[239] Ashton was right. There were Leeds fans who travelled with the NF to the march in Levenshulme in October 1977 assured of a fight with the anti-fascists. Prevented from this by the heavy police protection, they began a fight with NF supporters.[240]

The ANL's first front-page article in the national press was the *Daily Mirror* report announcing that Jackie Charlton, Sheffield Wednesday's manager, and Brian Clough, manager at Nottingham Forest, were now ANL sponsors.[241] Clough had already made an impact. He:

> was completely non-racist and was fantastic, not least because of the club's initials, NF. He introduced Viv Anderson as captain and he became the first black player to get into the England team. Anderson used to get barracked with banana chants. Clough walked out onto the pitch and addressed the fans 'I will not have racism in my club. I'm not standing for it'.[242]

A black fan, whose attendance at matches depended on his army postings, remembers: 'Mixing with some hard core fans, including away matches where we used to sneak into home ends for 'entertainment'. A good few of us were Black and all respected because we were usually at the front so I reckon any NF at NFFC wouldn't have lasted long.'[243]

Important as Clough and Charlton's support was, the only force that could challenge the fans chanting 'National Front! National

Front!' and 'Tyn-dall! Tyn-dall!' were the fans themselves.[244]

Although well known for its Jewish supporters, Tottenham Hotspur had had an NF presence for a couple of years. Mel Norris, lifelong Spurs supporter, remembers:

> 'Spurs against the Nazis' was the first ANL group of football fans. John Deason was the driving force... We contacted Garth Crooks and said we would like to make a start against racism on the terraces, we wanted to get a leaflet out.[245] He said 'Okay, come and see me'. He arranged for us to meet Steve Perryman, captain of Spurs at the time, and a player, John Duncan, who was the players' union rep. We had a conflab with them. We explained we wanted to give a leaflet out and have their signatures on it. Steve Perryman was reluctant and some of the other players were a bit cagey. A crowd of about 20 of us gave the 10,000 leaflets out around the Spurs ground. We got a bit of a bumpy ride in some areas, in others it was okay.[246]

Richard Buckwell remembers Spurs Against the Nazis starting cautiously with leaflets for the Victoria Park Carnival:

> The first time we leafleted the High Street in Tottenham and only then did we try outside the Spurs ground. None of us had done anything like this before, and most people were nervous about what might happen. The first time we showed up, there was a group of NF leafleting outside the ground as well, and there were a lot more of them than there were of us. We had these old Jewish men walk up to us, and say 'You're doing a really good job lads', and then walk off. It was all worrying and then we saw a crowd running towards us and we got more worried! That was until we saw it was a crowd of about fifty black and white teenagers, quite young. They ran right past us, charged into the NF lot, and kicked them off their pitch. After that, it was fine.[247]

The success of the leafleting for the carnival led to Spurs Against the Nazis leaflets being given out at the last two games of the season plus a badge, with the aim of getting a Spurs supporters contingent to march from Trafalgar Square on the day of the carnival. A meeting to launch the group got sixty people, some of them young fans from outside the ground.[248]

Having football managers sign as sponsors helped launch groups organised by fans.[249] When, mid-March, Hounslow Anti Nazi League organised a big meeting of 200, one of the meeting sponsors was Brentford Football Club, thanks to the support of Brentford manager Bill Dodgin and club chair Dan Tana, both individual ANL sponsors. Brentford Supporters Against the Nazis began a couple of weeks later with a leaflet telling fans: 'Brentford United can never be defeated. Up Brentford, down racialism'. The chair of the supporters' club argued that football and politics should not be linked and accused the ANL of misleading fans. ANL supporters responded with a leaflet headed 'Stand up against mindless fans'. It pointed to the need to: 'do something about the little group of fans who chant at every black player who plays against Brentford: "If they're black, send them back. Join the National Front," and other obscenities'.[250]

Over a dozen groups of fans supporting the ANL were set up.[251] At Leeds where, 'NF paper-sellers appeared regularly from the mid-1970s', Leeds Supporters Against the Nazis brought together 100 fans.[252] At Leyton Orient in London, Steve Cedar remembers how:

> Because of its Jewish tradition, and the early introduction of young black players, there was very little open racism from the Orient fans... but visiting fans would always have a group of racists on the lookout for the vulnerable, the wolves and vultures looking for prey. They nearly found it on that day against Bristol Rovers. Despite selling a lot of badges and stickers and distributing leaflets, I was the only one of our group to enter to watch the game: everyone else hated football, and Orient were not exactly an attraction. A group of Bristol Rovers racists were waiting for me [inside the ground] at the top of the stairs. I sought refuge from the state, glueing myself to a policeman for the whole game.[253]

Sheila Amrouche, a young SWP member, remembers: 'The enemy was not always as we thought'. Selling *Socialist Worker* the week after the Battle of Lewisham, going from pub to pub in Lewisham where the sellers were: 'very welcome, we saw these guys coming down the road with Union Jack's and we thought

"We're going to be pasted, all three of us". "Don't worry, love", they said, "We're Millwall".'[254]

Support came in many forms. A lifelong West Ham fan, Doug Beesley remembers deciding:

> to leaflet West Ham with anti-racist leaflets especially as I had two black friends who had played for West Ham and I knew Clyde Best as well.[255] A group came around the corner, not kids, late 20s, early 30s. They said 'We're the Dagenham Axe Clan'. Nowadays you would fall about laughing. They kicked one of the students. It looked like there was going to be a face off and I think we would have probably come out worse, there was less of us. We had women doing the leafleting as well. Round the corner came a [black] guy called Cass Pennant who is famous in East London. He was a bit of a West Ham hooligan, the Inter City firm at West Ham. He came up to me and said, 'What's all going on here, eh?' I said, 'We're just handing out this leaflet and these guys have objected to it'. So he snatched the leaflet and read it and turned round and said to them, 'The only colour in West Ham is claret and blue'. Suddenly these guys started to disappear. It's a recurring theme in my life that people don't have to be political to oppose them. People just oppose them because they know it's decency.[256]

Some club managements were supportive, like Brentford. Nottingham Forest offered the ANL space in the match programme. By contrast, the Tottenham management took a 'Keep politics out of sport – or else' position. They sent a writ claiming breach of copyright, particularly for using the club's 'cockerel' logo. 'We wrote back a letter saying, in effect "Sue us". We heard nothing, even though we continued to hand out leaflets with their cockerel logo'.[257] Leyton Orient management also threatened legal action unless all Orient Against the Nazis leaflets were destroyed, demanding 'substantial' damages for misuse of the club's name.[258]

In Norwich, Canaries Against the Nazis ridiculed the NF's leaflet inviting supporters to join them in 'Football, marches, booze ups, holidays, demos, discos and much more':

The Nazi attempt to gain support from Carrow Road is nothing less than pathetic. Sport without blacks would rob this country of some of its finest athletes, Whites only in football is an even bigger joke. Do Ardiles and Villa count as white or coloured? That is the sort of question that would count if the NF ever run the country.[259]

In Bristol, Tom Archer, journalist and SWP member, reacted to pro-NF chanting at matches with *The East Ender*, a fanzine with the headline: 'Are we really a bunch of racists?', arguing 'The NF are just using racist lies to get themselves power'. Expecting a 'thumping' when they handed out the fanzines, 'they only got a few hostile comments – and a lot of support too'.[260]

For all the racism and violence outside and inside grounds, there was never an automatic bias of young fans towards the fascists. Football Fans Against the Nazis showed the ANL's ability to connect with young people, not least thanks to its sponsors. Dave Cook, national organiser of the Communist Party, pointed out 'Banners like "Swansea City against the Nazis" showed the significance of ANL sponsorship by Brian Clough and Terry Venables'.[261] As Richard Buckwell put it:

> It wasn't just about football. The Anti Nazi League had a massive impact on youth culture at the time. Our slogan was 'NF= No Fun'. It was all based around that. Often initiated by non-football fans, many seasoned fans did support the [Football Fans Against the Nazis] groups, especially youngsters. At the grounds where fans against the Nazis organised, such as Spurs, it seriously dented the NF.[262]

Preparing for an October general election

The NF had a record 900 candidates in the May 1978 local elections. *NF News* tried to give a positive report but apart from 10 percent in Wolverhampton and a handful of encouraging results where an NF candidate was standing for the first time, many were disappointing.[263] What *NF News* didn't tell its readers was that mass leafleting against them had had an impact, especially in Bradford and Leeds, also in Preston and East London.[264] The

ANL 'having originally planned to print 200,000 leaflets, this rose to 800,000'.[265] It also strengthened the ANL. In mobilising large numbers of members and supporters, mass leafleting established a public presence going door-to-door, sometimes taking precautions against possible attacks by NF supporters, sometimes talking with people as they took a leaflet.[266]

In Preston, where 40,000 leaflets were delivered house to house, the NF's fifteen candidates averaged less than 4 percent, down from over 8 percent from three fascist candidates two years earlier.[267] In Leeds, after tens of thousands of leaflets, 2,000 posters and 4,000 badges were distributed, the eighteen NF candidates averaged 2 percent, half the vote of their ten candidates two years earlier. In Bradford the NF vote fell to just over a quarter of the 1976 figure. The 600 NF candidates in Greater London saw their average vote fall by two fifths.[268] While the NF's hopes of a breakthrough were weakened, the results were uneven. In areas like South Hackney they continued to get 25 percent of the vote.[269]

Encouraging as this was, the urgency and scale of a general election expected in October 1978 was a huge challenge. There were nine million households in the 300 constituencies with NF candidates. The NF could be expected to campaign seriously in a hundred of these, including thirty-eight marginal seats that 'could influence the result of a general election'.[270] The ANL had five million leaflets printed in preparation for the election. The response that emerged came overwhelmingly 'from below'. Many local ANL launch meetings had over a hundred people. Within days of the Carnival, 360 people came to meetings in north London setting up three new branches. Oxford set up a branch with a meeting of 450, Bath had a hundred, Swansea seventy.[271] Two hundred came to the second meeting of Brighton ANL, which was forced to meet outside after the NF, thrown out of the hall, left behind a bottle leaking fumes.[272] A RAR gig in Newport with 200 led to forty at a founding ANL meeting. Getting local trade union support became easier with Communist Party members involved. The launch in Irlam, Greater Manchester, listed sponsorship by the local trades council, three union district committees, a union branch, a joint shop stewards committee and Lancashire NUM, all with a significant CP presence.[273]

By mid-June, Greater Manchester had sixteen local groups with six anti-fascist and CARF groups affiliated. All its universities had both staff and student groups as did bus workers, council workers and teachers, two hospitals, a college, an engineering factory and the Albert pub. There were also two SKAN groups and Manchester RAR. Affiliations included fourteen union branches, two trades councils, four shop steward committees, the district Confederation of Shipbuilding and Engineering Unions (CSEU) covering tens of thousands of engineering workers across Greater Manchester, two constituency Labour Parties (CLPs), Tameside Community Relations Council, Rochdale Human Rights Campaign, the Grass Roots Bookshop and the post-punk band, The Fall.[274] Margaret Smith remembers 'Albert Against the Nazis' was set up by:

> a group of young comrades who met almost daily in the pub. There were SWP meetings in the room upstairs. The group had a youthful confidence. Politics was not a separate part of their lives. We spent a lot of time together. It was important socially and emotionally. There were a lot of relationships within the group, including shared houses…. The landlord of the Albert, Gerry, was Irish, very friendly. It may have helped that we drank a lot of beer. He never had a problem serving women beer in pint glasses. The pub had a strong Irish contingent.[275]

The fascists had long used graffiti to establish their presence in an area. Anti-fascists responded by painting them out or 'adapting them'[276]. 'NF' could become 'No Fun' and 'BM' 'BoredoM'.[277] Leicester had a group dedicated to painting out racist graffiti.[278] Jim Barlow remembers giving out an SWP leaflet to staff in the Dundee bus garage's canteen about their colleague, Ian Bunce, the local NF candidate. The message was reinforced by 'Nazis live here' and 'Fuehrer Bunce is a Nazi' painted in two-foot-high letters on the walls of his home facing a busy bus route. The next day Bunce announced he was standing down.[279] One paint out team in Manchester approached a Communist Party steward in a small factory where the union provided the ladder needed to get to the graffiti: 'Several workers took badges. They all supported what we were doing. It was that kind of atmosphere'.[280] 'On the Sunday afternoon of the paint out [in Manchester], several dozen people came and the cleaning materials were provided by Granada Reports.'[281]

Many anti-fascist and anti-racist groups affiliated to the ANL while keeping their names and identities. Telephone trees, built up by anti-fascist committees to mobilise members to physically confront the NF wherever they appeared, now expanded.[282] The CARF newspaper continued to be published monthly. Paul Holborow's call to 'Let a hundred flowers bloom' reflected the division between labour and the ANL national office. National initiatives like conferences, producing circulars to keep branches in touch, providing a central point of contact and sending out press releases kept the staff plus volunteers fully occupied. The hundreds of branches and groups could not be organised from above. They had to organise themselves.[283]

By mid-May, Leeds ANL had recruited over 600 members, taken a thousand people to the ANL Carnival and distributed over 100,000 leaflets. All ANL branches were self-financing. Leeds spent £3,000 in its first six months, was £800 in debt and about to launch an appeal for £5,000.[284] Local branches set their own rules. Most were unwritten; East Kent had a detailed constitution with provision for an AGM, a committee meeting monthly, two monthly general meetings, and paid subscriptions.[285] Living in a shared house in south Manchester one group made a 'Scarsdale Road Against racism' banner for the Northern Carnival against the Nazis, July 1978.[286] National membership cost £1, though many people saw wearing the badge as evidence of membership.[287]

Fundraising was key to organising. Coaches to demos and carnivals were expensive and money had to be raised to help pay the fines for those convicted after demonstrations. Legal costs were often covered by *pro bono* work by sympathetic lawyers.[288] Even if there was already access to a typewriter, leaflets required money for paper, ink and stencils. In most areas meetings were very open. Some, particularly public meetings, needed to be stewarded. Northwest Hackney ANL's first meeting was 'invaded by an organised gang of twenty-five who arrived waving Anti-Nazi League membership cards'.[289]

Most groups had aims relating to an area, an industry or

a workplace, or campaign: 'launched at the Hunt Saboteurs Association AGM as part of a general motion abhorring the National Front', Vegetarians against the Nazis (VAN) aimed to bring the threat posed by the NF and BM 'to the attention of our fellow workers in the animal welfare movement'. Helped by press and TV coverage, by early 1979 VAN had a national membership and 4,000 badges had been sold. Its launch meeting included Fenner Brockway, Arthur Latham MP, novelist Brigid Brophy and the poet and lesbian activist Maureen Duffy.

Once groups were established, the day-to-day leadership varied greatly. Chris Lymn remembers in Leicester:

> SWP members carried most of the load. We... established a loose knit organisational form in which a membership card was exchanged for £1 and any individual lawful activity against fascists was offered support... This mix of individual reaction and the more structured collective activity had its strengths and flaws but most importantly, nothing attempted by the NF went unopposed in this area. The eye-catching ANL 'arrow' became increasingly prominent.[290]

By contrast, North Manchester ANL was led by older Labour Party members, some active against Mosley in the 1930s, working with the well-established North Manchester Campaign Against Racism (NORMANCAR).

There was already a tradition of quick responses to a fascist presence. Leicester activist Chris Lymn remembers the importance of a good telephone network.[291] Richard Dunn recalls before the ANL was formed rushing to join half a dozen SWP comrades in High Wycombe shopping centre, one bringing a placard 'No Nazis in Wycombe' to confront eight NFers selling *NF News*. They chanted against the NF, their numbers growing as they were joined by fifty or more kids, black and white, until the NF gave up and left, escorted by the police.[292]

Carnivals

Exhilarated by the experience, some had left the Victoria Park Carnival asking, 'Why don't we do this?'[293] The answer was simple; making it happen was not. For a start it involved securing a suitable venue, and organising and financing a stage and sound equipment.[294] For many the biggest problem was the 'fight for space', overcoming the hostility of many local councils and gig venue owners.[295] Coventry council first agreed to a carnival in a suitable park, then withdrew the offer, proposing a park six miles from the centre. Rejecting the 'offer', a Carnival Procession Against the Nazis was organised in the autumn with a Carnival Against Racism in the spring.[296] On the morning of the Southall Carnival Against Racism, Ealing council sent a 'previously unseen seven page document... detailing all the conditions and terms that had to be signed and agreed in advance' such as the number of fire extinguishers required. A local fire equipment shop promptly closed at lunch and brought the number needed. Many councils refused to cooperate. York's Rock Against Racism concert only went ahead after overcoming police opposition. Many gigs and at least one carnival didn't happen because of councils refusing permission.[297]

Some large events were already in preparation. In Manchester the ANL worked with the North West Committee Against Racialism to organise 'A Festival for Racial Equality', in the Free Trade Hall, the city's largest indoor venue with Peggy Seeger and Ewan MacColl, John Cooper Clark, Exodus and others.[298] In London, a fortnight later 11 June 1978, 2,000 were at the biggest ANL sponsor-led initiative, an 'Evening of Music and Comedy' in the Wembley Arena.[299] A thousand people came to the Folk Against Racism concert, the line up including Martin Carthy and John Martyn, two of the best known folk singers in Britain.[300]

The summer saw a surge of carnivals. All of them had thousands taking part. Manchester's was the largest with 15,000 marching and 25,000 at the concert in Moss Side.[301] Edinburgh had 8,000, Cardiff had 5,000 as did Southampton. The annual free festival in Bristol changed its name to Rock Against Racism/Free Community Festival.[302] It was now clear that the movement had the numbers and strength needed to defeat whatever campaign the NF mounted up to and including the general election, whenever it was announced.

■ Anti Nazi League in London 1978

8: Battles

★ The battle of Brick Lane

People's confidence in taking on the NF grew with the growth of RAR and the ANL. Nowhere was this more critical than in the Bangladeshi community living in Spitalfields, a few minutes' walk from the territory the NF saw as theirs.

Bangladeshis had been arriving in Tower Hamlets in large numbers from the early 1970s, when the struggle for independence, won in 1971, cost at least half a million deaths and millions fleeing their homes. The struggle had created a resilience in the community of over 10,000 centred on the Spitalfields area.[1] Having left socially conservative farming communities, where women were largely confined to the family home, few spoke English. Their first battle, getting a place to live, led to many joining London's 30,000 squatters with the help of other squatters.[2] In February 1976, working with the *Race Today* collective, 'seventy heads of Bengali families' set up the Bengali Housing Action Group (BHAG).[3] BHAG organised a squat in the Pelham building in Whitechapel with forty-one families moving in the next three months into 'BHAG's fortress'.[4] Also, the same year 300 Bengalis marched with BHAG to Bethnal Green Town Hall where they 'urged the GLC and Tower Hamlets Council to stop all eviction notices until there had been alternative offers and to rehouse the residents in the E1 [Spitalfields] area'.[5]

The community experienced racist violence from the beginning. Even magistrates recognised that 'Paki bashing' was commonplace.[6] In April 1970, Tosir Ali, a Pakistani restaurant worker was stabbed to death a few yards from his home in nearby Bow.[7] Most men of the community worked in small, non-union garment factories, some in restaurants and as office cleaners. Women often worked from home, sometimes as sewing machinists.[8] For security, people walked to work in groups, using taxis at night.[9] Rafique Ullah remembers having arrived in England aged fourteen being so excited to be going to school only to be set on and attacked the moment he got to the school gates with no one coming to help him.[10]

Spitalfields was a mile from the NF heartland of Hoxton. Some estates were known as 'no-go' areas for Asians, who would apply to transfer to other properties or 'sometimes in desperation... leave their council flats to squat nearer the main centres of Bangladeshi settlement... in Tower Hamlets'.[11] The racist violence they faced was relentless. Spitting, punching and stone throwing were everyday experiences. *Blood on the streets*, a lengthy pamphlet published by the local trades councils, records over a hundred major racist attacks between January 1976 and August 1978.[12] Besides low wages, unemployment at 15 percent was almost three times the national rate.[13] Many Asian families found themselves living under siege in their flats, more than one family was physically prevented by racists from moving in.[14]

The GLC openly acknowledged that 'non-white applicants were disproportionately allocated to the oldest and most unpopular types of accommodation' and that 'GLC allocations are maintaining and even reinforcing the pattern of immigrant disadvantage which is so characteristic a feature of the private housing market'.[15] In neighbouring Newham, the council deliberately prioritised the length of residence in the area in applications for council housing over factors such as needs in order to keep black families on the waiting list. Housing officials were encouraged to discriminate, giving properties to families with English or Scottish sounding names, not always successfully as in the case of the McIntosh family, who turned out to be black. People saw joining the Labour Party as a way to get a better place to live.[16] Tower Hamlets council had an almost exclusively white workforce. When Ghosh Ray, the GLC's first Bengali-speaking housing officer started the job, he found he was being 'mainly used for "policing" activities, translating at the evictions of Bengali families'.[17]

Already in 1968, following Powell's 'Rivers of Blood' speech, the IWA groups in the Midlands organised self-defence committees, declaring 'we will not sit back, we will hit back'.[18] The Black Unity and Freedom Party set up classes in Stepney in 1971 to teach Pakistanis self-defence.[19] In the summer of 1976, as 2,500 marched in Southall protesting the murder of Gurdip Singh Chaggar, a big meeting filled the Naz cinema on Brick Lane in the middle of Spitalfields. It was organised by the main community organisation, the Bangladesh Welfare Association, together with the *Race Today* Collective and others.[20] The slogan 'Self-defence is no offence' was raised and Darcus Howe, the Trinidad-born editor of *Race Today*: 'prowled the platform, snarling lucid defiance, superbly sending up the worthies on the stage and insisting, with every pore of his being, that the black communities, Asian and Afro-Caribbean, must set their own agendas, command their own organisations and to their own selves be true.'[21]

As the cinema emptied, around 2,000 gathered to march to the local police station.[22] It was an anti-climax after the meeting. 'The worthies on stage', whom Howe criticised, elders of the Bangladesh Welfare Association, were still in charge. They were so factionalised that their building had been ordered to be locked by the courts. Howe's call was taken up by twenty young Bangladeshis, mostly teenagers working in garment factories. They set up the Bangladesh Youth Front (BYF), meeting regularly after work. Challenging the deeply conservative approach of the leading members of the older generation, they took up housing issues, racist attacks and police harassment.[23] While they opposed revenge attacks, like many other young Bangladeshis they went to judo and karate classes.[24]

As the attacks continued, the police response was that 'a number of the victims… were themselves arrested for threatening behaviour or for carrying offensive weapons'.[25] Anti-racists organised in local trade unions and trades councils, often with a strong Communist Party presence. More than 3,000 anti-racists marched in October 1977 through East End areas where the NF was strong to a multicultural festival in Victoria Park, Hackney.[26] Racist graffiti was removed and painted over, even on the wall of Bethnal Green police station. Five members of the Campaign Against Racist Slogans were found not guilty of defacing a railway bridge after painting over NF slogans.

At the centre of their base in East London, the NF booked Shoreditch Comprehensive School for a pre-election meeting. The students were a mix of white, Afro Caribbean and Bangladeshi from the Brick Lane area. Anna Paczuska, an SWP teacher, remembers:

> The school population was divided. The Afro Caribbean kids used to take on the Bengali kids. At one point we walked with the kids back to Brick Lane as a group. They couldn't go singly. They would go straight home and sew jeans in the evenings. The money would go back to Bangladesh… We used to get quite a lot of racist graffiti around the school and the staff sometimes stayed behind and painted it out. We would ask the council to paint it out over the weekend so it was clean when we came back on Monday morning.[27]

One of the school governors was an NF member and when there was a riot between white and Afro Caribbean boys in the science lab, the NF approached the school management with a deal saying that, if they stopped taking black children from Dalston, the NF would try to see there was an end to the rioting.[28] The school said no. With only a few days' notice of the NF election meeting, the staff met and decided to do a leaflet, organise a picket and to write to parents at home. Paczuska remembers working with CP members, a woman who had been imprisoned in South Africa and an Irish Republican. Together with students they made placards and mounted a wall display in the main hall: 'Nearly 500 people, teachers, pupils, dinner ladies and parents, turned out to picket the meeting. The school had to be protected by two lines of police and horses. That showed the kids whose side the police were on.'[29]

When an ad hoc committee tried to place an advert in the *Hackney Gazette* supporting the picket, it was refused. Journalists on the paper came out on strike against the paper's acceptance of an advertisement for the NF meeting itself, saying 'We don't want the *Hackney Gazette* to be used in any way by a party whose main platform is racial hatred'.[30] Journalist Juliet Alexander remembers: 'It was an immediate decision to go out on strike. I was doing the front-page lead article that day. I put it in my bag and walked out. We were out for three days, and picked up a hell of a lot of signatures supporting our action.'[31]

The East End had been Mosley's most important target in the 1930s. Old Mosleyites were still selling their paper on Brick Lane in the early 1970s. The National Party and National Front's combined vote in the 1976 local by-election in Deptford, just four miles away, was 44 percent. On May Day 1978, the day after the Victoria Park Carnival against the Nazis, as around 6,000 trade unionists marched on the official labour movement event, a thousand NF members and supporters paraded from central London to Hoxton, one of the areas in East London where they were strongest.[32] The local elections three days later were, however, a massive disappointment. The forty-one NF candidates in Tower Hamlets saw their combined vote fall 40 percent to 3,300.

That evening, twenty-five-year-old Altab Ali, a member of the Tailor and Garment Workers Union, was stabbed in the neck, dying in the street near Brick Lane on his way home from the garment factory where he worked as a machinist. The news spread across the Bangladeshi community 'with electrifying speed'.[33] Parents told their children, 'Don't go out! Don't go out!'[34] The following day in the quickly unlocked Bangladesh Welfare Association building, twenty members of the Bangladeshi Youth Front met with a smaller number of community elders. Rafiq Ullah remembers:

> that people couldn't take the racist abuse any longer. It had to be faced. It had to be challenged. We had to defend ourselves... The young people became so angry... It felt like a

war. The meeting decided to have a demonstration with the coffin of Altab Ali... We took responsibility for leafleting and postering... phoning people in other cities.[35]

Organising the demonstration brought together 'all the major groups in the Asian community, Tower Hamlets Movement against Racism and Fascism, the Trades Council and the rapidly growing forces of the Anti Nazi League'.[36] On Sunday 14 May over 7,000, mostly Bangladeshis, marched in pouring rain behind the symbolic coffin, chanting the slogans 'Law and order for whom?', 'Black and white unite and fight', 'Who killed Altab Ali? Racism! Racism!', 'Here to stay, here to fight', 'Self-defence is no offence'; they were also carried on a banner.[37] Across London hundreds of Asian shops, cafés and restaurants closed.[38] The march rallied in Hyde Park then went on to Downing Street with a letter for the prime minister demanding justice for Altab Ali, an end to racist violence and equal rights for all.[39]

The news now broke that the Greater London Council (GLC), the body managing social housing in London, was thinking of setting aside certain blocks of flats for Bengalis, using a list given by the Bengali Housing Action Group of estates which it considered safe. In response a 500 strong meeting in Spitalfields rejected this, pointing out that such blocks would inevitably be seen as 'ghettos'.[40]

The next day, Sunday 11 June, applying the NF's view of the GLC's 'ghetto' announcement and Powell's speech, 150 white youths in a concerted attack coming from three sides, rampaged down Brick Lane. Shouting 'Kill the black bastards', they smashed windows and attacked shopkeepers.[41] The police had ignored calls for help, afterwards insisting it was not politically organised, 'There is no evidence to connect this with the National Front'.[42]

Joining with the new Bengali Youth Movement against Racialism and others, the ANL called a demonstration the following Sunday, 18 June. It was a measure of the ANL's strength that it was able to go on the offensive so decisively.[43] Several thousand marched through Brick Lane demanding an end to the racist intimidation.[44] Criticising the police for handling the NF with kid gloves, Aloke Biswas, a local Bengali militant and member of the SWP, argued, 'The police will not rid us of fascist gangs. We must do that ourselves. Self-defence is no offence'.[45] The police record was one of consistent bias on the side of the NF. In any confrontation, more anti-fascists were arrested than fascists. Anti-fascists would be checked for concealed weapons while fascists walked freely. Members of the BYF were now:

> directly involved in confronting the NF thugs, patrolling around the streets of Brick Lane and Spitalfields. The older generation sometimes opposed the younger generation for taking matters into their own hands; they preferred to live quietly, even suffering in silence, keeping their heads down believing that they would soon return to Bangladesh, as they never saw the UK as their home.[46]

A week after the Brick Lane march against racist violence, two miles away in Hackney, fifty-year-old Ishaque Ali was attacked and killed by a group of white youths. Aloke Biswas wrote in the following week's *Socialist Worker*, 'When I came to this country there was Paki-bashing. But it was never more than abuse. We could almost treat it as a joke. Then about two years ago it changed. The attacks became vicious. They meant to kill'.[47] An emergency meeting of trade unionists, ethnic minority organisations, political and anti-racist groups – twenty-six in all – set up the Hackney and Tower Hamlets Defence Committee, organising a silent march of 500 people with black flags through Hackney a few days later.[48] Nine days after Ishaque Ali's murder, thirty white men in cars attacked sixty Asian workers leaving a local bottling plant with bricks, bottles and stones. The police arrived after the press.[49]

The killings were clearly connected with the NF, who were determined to mount a counter-offensive against the rising movement trying to break them. The Defence Committee called a demonstration on Brick Lane insisting people had the right to give out leaflets at the top of Brick Lane, which the police had unilaterally designated as the NF's patch for selling *NF News*.[50] The Defence Committee called people to support a 'Rally against Racist Violence' on Sunday 16 July and the following day 'A Black Solidarity Day Strike against Racism'. The numbers boosted by *World in Action*'s 'The Nazi Party' broadcast two weeks earlier, on the day 'thousands of anti-fascists – from the local Bengali community, the Anti Nazi League, the Hackney and Tower Hamlets Defence Committee, and others from around London – occupied Brick Lane'.[51] It was the start of 'a deliberate defiance campaign by the Asian community and the antiracist forces'. Speaker after speaker called for support for Monday's strike. Chanting 'Sunday after Sunday', people vowed to return. Despite a dozen arrests for threatening behaviour, assault on the police and obstruction, for the first time the NF were prevented from selling papers.[52]

The next day, Monday 17 July, Black Solidarity Day, was the turning point. 'More of a stay away than a strike, a mixture of defence, respect and defiance', it was the first ever industrial action in Britain against racist violence.[53] It showed 'not despair and resignation but anger and organised revolt'.[54] Eight thousand black and Asian workers in factories, shops, restaurants throughout East London, including hundreds from the night shift at Fords Dagenham, went on strike.[55] Home Secretary Merlyn Rees's contribution was to hold a meeting with the Bangladeshi High Commissioner.[56] Meanwhile:

> Hundreds of youngsters from Robert Montefiore, Tower Hamlets, Clapton and other schools, stayed away from their classes or walked out of school. That evening a huge march of the strikers was making its way down Bethnal Green Road. A group of white hooligans in a car provoked the demonstrators. The police seized two Bengalee youths and a white marcher who was trying to help them. The youths in the car were not stopped, but allowed to go free by the police. The marchers saw in this one incident the classic pattern repeating itself. Racist provocation; angry response; police arrest victims; racist thugs go free. The march moved on to Bethnal Green Police Station.[57]

Dave Widgery was one of the three thousand who sat down for over an hour, blocking the main road outside the station 'in an improvised street party, singing, shouting and speech-making in the sunshine, until the police released their prisoners'.[58] As people saw this concrete proof of their collective strength, enormous cheers erupted with the three being carried shoulder-high.[59]

The day was a key victory in the battle of Brick Lane, 'a defining moment for the Bangladeshi community in Britain'.[60] Martin Luther King wrote of a similar moment, the 1956 bus boycott in Montgomery, Alabama, triggered by Rosa Parks' refusal to move to the back of the bus: 'Our non-violent protest in Montgomery is important because it is demonstrating to the Negro, North and South, that many of the stereotypes he has held about himself and other Negroes are not valid.... In Montgomery we walk in a new way. We hold our heads in a new way.'[61]

Aloke Biswas argued for union organisation as the way forward. For Biswas, the July 17 strike showed:

> the whole area... bubbling with enthusiasm and determination to continue the struggle. I don't believe our victory was due only to the racists' attacks. What I saw that weekend was a whole community expressing itself against injustice, privilege and oppression. The struggle poses a threat to the old Bengali leadership. The majority of the people who went out to fight the Nazi NF come from the garment industries. They work long hours in bad conditions for lousy wages. The clothing industry is making great profits out of the labour of these workers. The time has come for the workers to organise themselves into the National Union of Tailor and Garment Workers around these demands:
>
> • Better working conditions. The sweat shops must go.
>
> • More pay and better rates for piece work and forty-hour week.
>
> If the garment workers fail in their fight for basic trade union rights, they will not be able to defend their community from the racists and fascists. From now on we go on the marches as workers.[62]

The battle of Brick Lane was far from over. Brick Lane activist Azad Konor remembers how, unable to get an agreement with the police who continued to insist that the top of Brick Lane was available to any group on a 'first-come, first-served' basis:

> We decided to take matters into our own hands, the Bangladesh Youth Front and the SWP members used to

go to the top of Brick Lane and corner of Bethnal Green Road every Saturday evening and we slept on the footpath to ensure we got the stall before the NF members. Our community leader Ahmed Fokriuddin and his wife Aminur Nassa used to bring us food and drink. We slept overnight with banners and posters with slogans such as 'Black and white unite and fight' and 'Self-defence is no offence'.[63]

No matter in what numbers or how early they arrived, even with massive police protection, the NF supporters, unable to march down Brick Lane, could only vent their frustration until around noon they left.[64] Steve Cedar remembers:

I used to shit myself on the Sunday morning before going down to Brick Lane. But you couldn't show it because you had to show people that the Nazis were cowards and we weren't, that we were right and they were wrong. I've memories of feeling the nerves. Very often my voice, my mouth, was my biggest weapon, because I was always able to take the piss out of the Nazis and humiliate them, and shout out loud, having a trained opera voice as a kid, useful for football and politics, but not opera.[65]

All the while, the racism of the police and judiciary was evident. Two days after Black Solidarity Day, Joginder, Valrinder, Mohinder and Sukhrinder Virk, four Sikh brothers from Newham, were sentenced at the Old Bailey to a total of twelve years after being found guilty of attacking a group of five white youths who had abused and then attacked them. People compared the sentences with how the alleged murderers of Ishaque Ali were released on bail.[66]

In response, Asian organisations collected 10,000 signatures.[67] The Indian Workers Association in Southall, the Standing Conference of Pakistani Organisations, and the Federation of Bangladeshi Organisations all declared their solidarity with the Bangladeshi community's resistance in Tower Hamlets.[68] 'Once again it was seen that the victims of an attack were the ones arrested, and the "offence" of self-defence, the crime that was punished.'[69] In the past they had opposed self-defence and vigilante groups against racist attacks despite the total failure of the 'supposed forces of law and order'. Now they followed up Black Solidarity Day with a meeting in the IWA Southall office on 29 July:

> where other prominent Asian groups and leading members of the Asian communities are to be invited to consider proposals for joint action. Also invited are the Anti Nazi League, The Board of Deputies of British Jews, the editors of ethnic minority newspapers and sections of the Radical Press.[70]

This meeting was unprecedented in bringing together the main IWA groups in Britain, all established by communist cadres trained in India.[71] As Naranjan Singh Noor, president of the IWA (GB) (Marxist) put it: 'The unity of the whole working class, black and white, is the greatest vigilante group that is possible'.[72] Holborow told *Socialist Worker*:

> August 20 is a major date for the anti racist movement. Brick Lane is where the Nazis are making their greatest push. Saturday's conference showed that increasing numbers in the Asian and West Indian communities see the national importance of what is happening in Brick Lane. They know that what the Nazis do in Brick Lane today, they will be doing in Wolverhampton, Bradford and Leeds tomorrow. We in the Anti Nazi League are determined to see that the black people in this country do not stand alone. After the racist murders have disappeared from the headlines, WE remember them. The stakes are very high. We have to throw our full weight behind the demonstration on August 20. We have to make sure the Nazis are kept off Brick Lane every week. If you can push the Nazis out of the East End of London after their local election humiliations, they can be made a spent force in British politics. All out on August 20.[73]

A stream of senior figures visited Brick Lane. David Lane, chairman of the Commission for Racial Equality, promised a major investigation into the situation. The High Commissioner for Bangladesh 'wondered what the British Government would do if British expatriates in another country were the victims of a similar storm of racist savagery to that which his people were suffering'.[74] Len Murray, TUC general secretary, and Bill Keys, chair of the TUC Equal Rights Committee, visited and later issued a joint statement promising that the TUC would 'do all in our power to support those who are working for peace, tolerance and fairness'.[75] Arthur Latham MP, chair of the Greater London Labour Party, spoke in the House of Commons calling for the Home Secretary to visit Brick Lane and for an official inquiry. There was no inquiry and the Home Secretary stayed away.

Having successfully occupied the top of Brick Lane for several Sundays, 4,000 marched with the Tower Hamlets Defence Committee and the Anti Nazi League from Brick Lane to Hoxton, where it was 'greeted with cheers by many local people'.[76] There were signs that the larger battle was being won. The Defence Committee reported: 'Far fewer racist attacks have taken place in Brick Lane over the last few months which the local people attribute not to the increased police pressure but to the active defence which is being carried out by black people and anti-racists.'[77] The trades council reported that:

> September began with a whole blossoming of cultural events by the Bengalee community in the East End to celebrate the end of Ramadan, and the new confidence of the community in their own strength and identity. Perhaps the most significant event was the [local] Carnival Against Racism organised in St Mary's churchyard, where Altab Ali had been murdered; a multiracial festival that would have been inconceivable at the beginning of the summer.[78]

A second ANL-RAR Carnival was organised for Brockwell Park, Brixton. It was timed for just before the general election and after a summer of carnivals and over a hundred RAR gigs. This second major carnival had far more organised support than the carnival at Victoria Park. The IWA (GB) (Marxist) sent coaches, as did Yorkshire NUM.[79] Lambeth council donated £1,000 towards the costs.[80] Every train that British Rail had available on the day was booked by ANL branches to bring people from cities across the country.[81] This time the PA was powerful enough to do justice to the performers. Bill Keys, Patrick Kodikara, Arthur Scargill and Tony Benn spoke at the opening rally in Hyde Park.[82] An estimated 60,000 then marched five miles crossing the Thames to Brockwell Park in southeast London accompanied by bands on flat-back lorries. Their banners included Vegetarians Against Nazis, Spurs

Against Nazis, Gays Against Nazis, Sunderland Against Nazis, Bracknell Against Nazis, Skateboarders Against Nazis, Corby Against Nazis and Grans and Kids Against Nazis, together with significantly more trade union banners than the Victoria Park Carnival.[83] As they neared the park they went under a large 'Brixton Gays welcome anti-fascists' banner hung across the road, next to a drag queen with gown and tiara, waving to all. A hundred thousand listened to Stiff Little Fingers, Misty and Elvis Costello on the main stage with other musicians playing in tents around the park.[84] A key moment was when Jimmy Pursey, who, with his band Sham 69, had many fans among young NF supporters and having earlier pulled out because of death threats, came on stage. His voice full of emotion, he told the crowd how 'this little kid had said to me, "You're not doing it because all your fans are NF"... But I'm here. Nobody's going to tell me what I should not do. I'm here because I support Rock Against Racism'.[85]

A week before the carnival, news broke that the NF's new headquarters were not, as had previously been reported, in Tottenham, north London but in Shoreditch in the East End, ten minutes' walk from Brick Lane.[86] The NF announced that they would march to Excalibur House, their new headquarters, to celebrate its opening on the day of the carnival, going on to deny that they would march through Brick Lane.[87] Paul Holborow seriously considered cancelling the carnival and getting people to confront the Nazis in Brick Lane. The SWP's Tony Cliff persuaded him this was wrong, arguing that the NF could not be allowed to dictate the ANL's strategy, 'from the point of view of the broader support of the ANL, who would attend a carnival but not a physical confrontation'.[88]

Most ANL supporters agreed that the NF's manoeuvre should not sabotage the carnival. Understandably, members of the Hackney and Tower Hamlets Defence Committee argued it was more important to defend Brick Lane.[89] The ANL announced it would ensure that 2,000 supporters would protect Brick Lane.[90] On the day, with 8,000 police mobilised, between 1,500 and 2,000 National Front supporters, many young skinheads, surrounded by police, marched from the Embankment near Charing Cross to their new headquarters. With Webster and Tyndall speaking from the back of a truck, they rallied in a nearby side street, surrounded by hundreds of police.[91] A slightly larger number of anti-fascists stood protecting Brick Lane, waiting for reinforcements from the carnival. Neil McAllister remembers the plan was 'we would get everybody to London... then we would divert a small but significant number of our members and militant anti-fascists to go to Brick Lane'.[92] In practice, this proved to be too late.

The ANL stewards in Brick Lane organised people to move towards the NF rally. Halfway there, at Shoreditch High Street, they were attacked by the Special Patrol Group (SPG) who made thirty-five arrests, blocking any further movement.[93] At first, in Brockwell Park, the crowd had been told that Brick Lane was safe. As it became clear that this was not the case, an appeal was made for volunteers to go immediately to Brick Lane. Two thousand set off from the park only to arrive in time for some of them, together with others leaving Brick Lane, to be ambushed by NF supporters on the underground.[94]

The following day, the *Morning Star* quoted Kodikara attacking the ANL for leaving Brick Lane vulnerable.[95] Graham Kennedy, a member of Newham Young Communist League, rejected this accusation. He defended the carnival organisers, pointing out that the dominant force in Brick Lane was the police.[96] The following week Tony Cliff argued that while it was absolutely right for the carnival to go ahead to preserve the unity of the ANL, there had been a serious organisational failure to ensure enough people were persuaded to go to Brick Lane in time to confront the NF.[97] Holborow then backed up this approach writing as ANL secretary to *Socialist Worker*:

> NO EXCUSES, NO EVASIONS. The fact that there was not a substantial influx from the Carnival to Brick Lane was a major failing. Rightly anti-racists in Brick Lane and the Bengali community felt abandoned. It happened because on the day our organisation in Hyde Park quite simply collapsed under the sheer weight of numbers.[98]

Leading a united front against fascism that involves tens of thousands and includes many political forces, means many decisions have to be made based on incomplete and sometimes contradictory information.

'No plugs for NF thugs'

Publicity was a priority for Webster. The NF had to keep 'kicking its way into the headlines'.[99] In the early days, disrupting public meetings was their most frequently used tactic, averaging twice a week in the late 1960s. Care was taken to avoid arrests that might upset business backers whose money was to help fund the expected 1970 general election campaign. These backers had made it clear that there had to be enough publicity to justify funding thirty candidates, but some were unhappy with the widely reported flour bomb attack on the former Labour secretary of state, Arthur Bottomley, during the 1969 Walthamstow by-election.[100]

Jim Merrick adopted a more sophisticated approach. TV was now more important than newspapers as people's main source of news. Merrick approached the BBC to use *Open Door*, its regular half hour slot for minority community interests wanting to make their own programme.[101] It should have been rejected out of hand. Merrick was an NF candidate and political parties were excluded from using the programme; even more so a party that boasted about its racism. Also, Carleton Greene, its director-general, had insisted about the BBC's commitment to impartiality: 'We are not impartial about everything. There are, for instance, two very important exceptions. We are not impartial about crime... nor are we impartial about race hatred.'[102]

The emptiness of this commitment became clear when Merrick was allowed to produce a programme linking immigrants to gambling, drugs, disease and anti-social behaviour with himself as presenter and including an interview with an NF member.[103] It was an NF party political broadcast in all but name. Merrick even used the publicity for the programme to make a direct attack on the BBC's claim to be politically neutral: 'This programme is dedicated to the silent majority who until now, because of a sinister veil of censorship, have never had the opportunity to give their views to the British public. The freedom of speech should be granted to all.'[104]

Charles Curran, Greene's successor as director-general, weakened Carleton Greene's position, insisting that the BBC 'must not single out any party or ideology for special treatment on the basis of a value judgement'.[105] Justifying this shift, BBC Chairman Sir Michael Swann attacked those who wished to 'suppress' the NF's propaganda, describing the NF's views as 'legitimate', proclaiming that 'freedom of speech must be indivisible'.[106] This fitted perfectly with Webster's position as shown by the slogan 'Defend British Free Speech from Red Terrorism' on the placard he carried on his much publicised march through Hyde in October 1977, accompanied by 1,000 police.[107]

The BBC did not take criticism well. The Campaign Against Racism in the Media (CARM) made an *Open door* documentary: 'It ain't half racist, Mum', showing the BBC's bias when reporting on immigration and uncritical coverage of Kingsley Read that received around 600 letters of support. The BBC's response was to make the programme unavailable for showing to local groups'.[108]

The BBC's line on racism, formally opposed but practically never challenging it – as we have seen, sports journalists 'accepted an almost laissez-faire attitude to the abuse of black players' – was similar to that of most newspapers.[109] Much of the local press, with over a hundred dailies, circulation six million, and over 1,300 weeklies, circulation 8.5 million, had always supported an overwhelmingly 'white' image of the area they covered.[110] The local black population was largely invisible except when the news was about crime. As far back as 1870, Marx noted how the press sustained such images of minorities, labelling Irish immigrants as outsiders and worse.[111] The day after Powell's 'Rivers of Blood' speech, the *Wolverhampton Express and Star*: 'Simply reprinted Powell's words on the front page with a call for readers to write in to the paper to show either support or opposition.'[112]

Reports such as the May 1976 *Daily Express* story headlined 'Asian influx will swamp us' were often followed by violent, sometimes deadly, attacks on Asians. There were also many sins of omission such as the 7,000-strong demonstration after the murder of Altab Ali all but ignored by the mainstream press.[113]

The NF could also take comfort from the media's overwhelmingly hostile treatment of anti-fascists at Lewisham.[114] It is hard to exaggerate how the mindset of many journalists in their views of the left, especially the SWP, was so fixed they could justly be called 'the press pack'. Sheila McGregor remembers: 'being interviewed by the BBC after the riot that took place during the final days of the Ladywood by-election, four days after Lewisham. I told the interviewer, "We don't take weapons". He became apoplectic. He was full of the idea of "Red fascists" [that had dominated the media since Saturday]. The interview had to be stopped and restarted.'[115]

While the *Manchester Evening News* rejected open hostility to anti-fascism, it could still ignore it. It took an editorial decision five days before the July 1978 Manchester carnival not to report the event. Only the noise made by the 'rehearsal' and the disruption to traffic caused by the march, were reported. The latter nevertheless included an excellent photo of the march rather than the traffic jam, probably inserted by an editor sympathetic to the ANL.[116]

The NF also exploited the media's need for material. Joe Pearce, editor of the NF's *Bulldog*, was able to get onto BBC Radio 1's pop current affairs programme as 'an ordinary teenager', giving his views on rock.[117] He told listeners that 'a mate of his... saw a "Rock Against Communism" gig at the Conway Hall and told him White Boss were 'a great band'. He went on to talk about 'Moscow control of the music biz, blood-curdling accounts of physical assaults by swarthy aliens, and how the Race Relations Act was about state repression'.[118] Later, a programme researcher admitted that they already knew who Pearce was – he had organised the Conway Hall gig. They had already used him 'as an "authentic youth" to talk about the Vietnam boat people'.[119]

Despite such failures, there were some papers that took a stand against the NF. Paul Furness remembers the importance of the mass circulation *News of the World* putting Tyndall's criminal record on the front page.[120] For millions of people the first time they heard of the ANL was when the *Daily Mirror* front page carried the news that Brian Clough and Jackie Charlton were joining as sponsors.[121] Some attacks on the NF were unexpected, such as the fashion magazine *Harpers & Queen* and the deeply conservative *Reader's Digest*, whose article ended with the former Conservative MP and Lord Chancellor, Quintin Hogg, Lord Hailsham, putting the right-wing parliamentarian argument against the NF: 'A thoroughly detestable organisation.

Their policies could not be carried out without dictatorship and bloodshed. Perhaps the nastiest of all their characteristics is that they proclaim their odious and divisive policies under the shadow of massed Union Jacks, the very symbols of national unity and pride.'[122]

A small number of local newspapers adopted anti-racist and anti-fascist editorial policies, shaping the media debate in their area. In practice this meant working within the NUJ Code of Conduct requiring: 'A journalist shall not originate material which encourages discrimination on grounds of race, colour, creed, gender or sexual orientation.' The NUJ had guidelines for journalists on race and reporting racist organisations.[123] These were supported by an agreement with the print union, the National Graphical Association (NGA), covering these issues and included recognition of 'the right of members to withhold their labour on grounds of conscience because employers are providing a platform for racist propaganda'. Thus, on local election day May 1977, the *South East London Mercury* front page had an editorial attacking the NF and NP with a further article inside attacking racism and calling on readers not to vote for racist parties. Following a complaint to the Press Council, the editor, Roger Norman, defended his stand, explaining:

> that his paper's policy was to improve and consolidate good relations between the races through news and comment columns... The only real method of countering racist propaganda was through the local press and so... he decided to go for a Page One article on the election morning... '[It] did not set out to be fair. It expressed the opinions and fears of my staff, leading members of the community, and, judging by the number of letters the paper received, the fears of many ordinary people living in the area.'[124]

Under the heading 'Biased and proud of it', a *Bradford Telegraph and Argus* editorial told readers: 'We are biased against ignorance, intolerance and bigotry; biased against crude forms of jingoism which place nationalism above humanity. We are biased against claims of racial supremacy which point the way to division, exploitation and hatred.'[125] Aidan White, a journalist working for *The East Ender*, put the position of that paper:

We're a local paper. We have to reflect what's going on in our area in the interests of the people who live and work in that area. The National Front has a political policy which is geared towards creating rancour and division and hatred within the community. So therefore the policy of the paper is, essentially, is not to report the National Front and, where we do report the National Front, is to report upon them critically. It is true that we are not neutral. We're biassed... in favour of this community... What we do is geared towards improving it, not towards dividing it or wrecking it.

Now for a local newspaper, where you've got a high immigrant population, you've got a whole set of social problems, is it a reasonable thing to give publicity... to a group of people who are purely interested in putting the whole of the responsibility... on... its immigrant population, but those people must not only take responsibility for it but will be forcibly repatriated?[126]

There were also journalists identifying with the growing anti-racist and anti-fascist movement. In March 1975 six NUJ members stopped working when *Camden Journal* and *Hornsey Journal* management refused to remove a paid advertisement for a National Front rally in Islington.[127] When the NF barred Charles Lauder, a black journalist, from its meeting, the Leeds NUJ branch voted to 'instruct its 350-plus members not to enter National Front meetings in future'.[128] A meeting of sixty, mainly NUJ members, launched the Campaign Against Racism in the Media (CARM) in July 1976.[129] Balwinder Rana, member of IS and Kent Workers Against Racism, spoke at a well-attended CARM meeting a few months later.[130] CARM helped organise a protest outside the *Tottenham Weekly Herald* office in North London.

The week after the April 1977 anti-NF demonstration in Wood Green, journalists and photographers on the *Hackney Gazette* in East London struck for three days, refusing to work on an edition carrying an advert for the National Front.[131] Management would often threaten those who challenged the NF's 'right to free speech'. Local BBC radio phone-ins were a great opportunity for the National Front. Not having a tape delay system, comments

Battles **253**

could be made without interference. When NUJ members at Radio Leicester decided they would refuse to work on a phone-in with a local NF leader, BBC management supported the NF, telling NUJ members that this could lead to their suspension and possible dismissal.[132] On the day, while the trades council picket stood outside, other anti-racists tried unsuccessfully to jam the phone-in.[133]

BBC staff did not have the same 'right to free speech'. BBC Radio Bristol reporter, Julian Dunne, was censured by management for carrying a placard on an anti-racist demo with the slogan 'Decent people detest racism'.[134] Similarly, Ken Burgess, the sports editor of the *Islington Gazette, Hornsey Journal and Camden Journal*, was warned that his attacks on the NF were too provocative. One of his articles had warned football fans 'Don't be conned by Nazis!'. He had also reported Arsenal's Jewish supporters' decision to join the Anti Nazi League. His report was watered down, and he was threatened with the sack.[135]

Threats could also come from work colleagues. Despite their paper's record of taking a principled position against the NF, three staff resigned from the *East Ender* after being subjected to months of intimidation by a racist colleague after he came into the office having been drinking with NF members to tell them that the three colleagues' names had been given to several NF thugs.[136] The ANL position was that the NF: 'should not be allowed to have broadcasts. The question of people's freedom is not absolute and it is a question of balance. You either get freedom for Nazis to propagate their ideas, or the freedom of black people to go about their lives free from fear and harassment.'[137]

The task was straightforward: 'The media has to stop treating men like Martin Webster as though they were respectable, they must identify them as a racist and white supremacist party. The NUJ Code of Practice insists that members do nothing that assists racism. "We have to commit the media to this".[138]

The ANL's case to exclude the NF from using television as a platform was put most powerfully by David Edgar in 'The National Front: The Case for No Television Platform'.[139] Edgar pointed to how the BBC's acceptance of Enoch Powell's calls for 'repatriation' was such that it no longer saw opposition to greater restrictions on immigration as feasible, even though this had been official Labour Party policy until 1964. The BBC's coverage of the Brixton by-election had inaccurately called all black people 'immigrants', a local white worker was presented as reasonable in rejecting a job transfer from London to Scotland while a black youth was seen as unreasonable in being unhappy to work for less than £60 a week.

Edgar's main focus was on the need to reject the free speech argument. There had always been legal limits to free speech:

> Some of these laws, like the Libel, Copyright and indeed the Race Relations Acts, we may approve of. Others, like the Obscene Publications Act, the Official Secrets Act and the Blasphemy Law, we may be less sure about. But the fact remains that no country in the world allows people complete licence to say anything, however dangerous and anti-social and offensive it may be.[140]

Together with legal censorship there was also economic censorship: 'In the age of the printing press and the electronic media, freedom of speech is a matter of access.' Editors decide what voices are heard. Edgar quoted the Tory MP Julian Critchley claiming that the left-wing producer Tony Garnett's *Law and Order* TV drama, showing corruption in the British police and legal system, had offended millions and that Garnett's proper place was 'fringe theatre'. Given the unaccountability of broadcasting producers, 'rank-and-file broadcasters, and indeed the general public, have the right to intervene in this process, and express their views through the channels available to them'.[141]

In the absence of this, the abuse of the right to free speech by the NF led to increased physical violence against the black and Asian people. Despite its view that black and Asian people were in themselves a threat which could only be dealt with by 'repatriation', the NF was able to present itself on television as a party entitled to participate fully in the democratic process. Edgar detailed how, when interviewed on the BBC by the well-known journalist Ludovic Kennedy, Webster succeeded both in passing off his Nazi record as 'youthful indiscretion' and in lying about the NF's record of Holocaust denial.[142]

Television had a massive influence. The *World in Action* 'The Nazi Party' documentary, broadcast July 1978, was watched by millions. Its impact was such that Webster called meetings to try to deal with demoralised members.[143] Despite Granada TV's refusal to make copies available, ANL branches put on showings with some areas toured by the Bookmarks 'book bus', which also toured with a photo exhibition using the *Camerawork* photos of Lewisham.[144] David Edgar's play *Destiny*, shown on BBC1 January 1978, had a significant impact, as shown by the 900 letters and £3,000 in donations sent in after the ANL advert in the *Guardian* the following day.[145]

With the 'Nazi' label increasingly widespread, the NF struggled to find the means to counterattack. There were still opportunities such as letters to the local press. *Spearhead* explained that:

> Such letters need not directly advertise the fact that the writer is a NF member – indeed, depending on the game being played in any particular letter, the very opposite impression might usefully be given. NF members who have gained publicity as NF activists should adopt a *nom de plume*... Our phantom letter-writers must work overtime to put to the test that 'nice and respectable' multi-racialism! On this theme letters should come from individuals who do not betray any party political leanings.[146]

The NF's opponents also wrote to the local press. Encountering the National Front as a teenager, Doug Beesley's way of opposing them was to write to 'the *Newham Recorder* and to the *Stratford Express*. I got some friends to sign some of these letters. I sent five letters in all. Both the *Newham Recorder* and the *Stratford Express* printed all the letters. That was my first idea about racism'.[147]

Eccles ANL sustained its presence in the *Eccles Journal,* responding to every letter supporting the NF as did Leamington Anti Racist Anti Fascist Committee. Unity Against Racialism, the Leicester anti-racist organisation, collected hundreds of signatures and sufficient funds to pay for a full page in the local daily paper, the *Leicester Mercury*, on the Saturday before the May 1977 elections.[148] This seemed to have a dramatic impact on the paper as it made a U-turn in its line the day before the election declaring: 'To give the National Front the chance of power to implement its cruel policies would be rejection of humanity.'[149] When *Cosmopolitan* magazine published an interview with a woman member of the NF, ANL supporters picketed their office with leaflets, getting three people to join the ANL.[150] The Brighton and Hove Anti-fascist Committee organised a seventy-five-strong march to the *Brighton Evening Argus* in protest against its pro-NF bias.[151] Merseyside ANL picketed Liverpool Radio City when Tyndall was invited, though was unable to stop him telling listeners that 'black immigrants were to blame for Liverpool's inner city problems and the NF intended to do something about them'.[152] Twenty protestors in Leeds occupied the BBC offices to protest against both a fifteen-minute interview with Tyndall on the BBC *Look North* programme and giving twenty minutes of free publicity to Kingsley Read in a programme about Blackburn.[153]

There was also the work persuading ANL sponsors to refuse invitations to debate with NF members on radio and TV. The issue was discussed at an early steering committee meeting which agreed that ANL sponsors should be approached individually. There were precedents for this. Roy Hattersley, standing as Labour candidate for Sparkbrook, Birmingham in October 1974, was one of a number of Labour MPs who refused to take part in a BBC TV programme because the National Front candidate was speaking.[154]

Printers and Media Workers Against the Nazis
The launch of Printers and Media Workers Against the Nazis in June 1978 was backed by the NUJ executive, Alan Sapper, general secretary of ACTT, the film technician's union, Bill Keys, general secretary of SOGAT, and Owen O'Brien, general secretary of the printing union NATSOPA. In a 'crowded meeting' Denis MacShane, NUJ president, saw the launch as 'an exciting moment of co-operation between unions that too often keep a firm distance'.[155] It quickly got support – the printworkers SOGAT voting to back it and affiliate to the ANL at the conference.[156] A breakthrough came when the TV freelance branch shop of ACTT, organising workers in ITV, 'unanimously passed a motion instructing its 800 members not to work on NF Party political broadcasts during the next election'.[157] This was accompanied by

the BBC staff union, the Association of Broadcasting and Allied Staffs (ABS), passing 'a motion pledging support to individuals who refuse to handle NF material on grounds of conscience'.[158]

The starting point of the campaign was that there was no legal requirement for the BBC and ITV to provide party political broadcast time, even though it was custom and practice. Fifty campaign supporters were at the BBC headquarters as a letter was delivered to the Director-General of the BBC.[159] It was always clear, however, that the argument had to be backed by industrial action if necessary.

The threat of action to stop the NF broadcasts brought the ANL under fire as never before. Suddenly the establishment woke up to the fact that the ANL was challenging their control of the media. The *Times*, *Sunday Times*, *Daily Telegraph*, the *Mirror*, *Sun* and *Guardian* all attacked the campaign.[160] Under the headline 'Peter Hain and the forces of darkness', the *Sunday Times* columnist Hugo Young told readers: 'The Hyde Park carnival is a rally against racism, yes. But it is also a forerunner of the forces of darkness'.[161] The *Times*'s well-known columnist Bernard Levin wrote two articles, the first attacking the NUJ's code of conduct, the second condemning the ANL's attack on free speech.[162] The *Daily Telegraph* followed its editorial with an article quoting the *Law Society Gazette* accusing ACTT members of threatening to take the law into their own hands.[163] James Cameron, an early sponsor of the ANL, founder member of CND and *Guardian* columnist, while unwilling to speak in favour of party political broadcasts, dismissed Hain's arguments rejecting the NF's right to freedom of speech.[164] By way of balance, David Edgar got a right of reply in the *Sunday Times*. The *Times* refused to do this, only publishing a letter from Hain and Holborow.[165]

In the event, eight days before polling day, the NF got a single five-minute broadcast. As the broadcast went out, there were pickets outside the BBC headquarters and BBC TV centres in nine other cities.[166] Though the campaign had failed to stop airtime for the NF, the BBC and ITV limited the NF to the same provision it got in the 1974 election.[167]

Winning Jewish support for the ANL

The NF usually substituted 'Zionist' for 'Jew' or 'Jewish' in its propaganda. Under the headline 'Labour hysterical as "Smash the NF" campaign flops', *National Front News* told its readers that:

> 1977 was the year in which the Zionist movement determined to 'smash the National Front once and for all'. Their campaign – co-ordinated by the Zionist 'Board of Deputies of British Jews' – mobilised the Labour government, Labour's ideological cousins in Marxist revolutionary groups, neo-Marxist factions within the church, and last, but not least, the mass media. All these are either heavily infiltrated by Zionist personnel and/or are beholden to Zionist financial patronage.[168]

The NF's ill-concealed antisemitism was not only propaganda. There was verbal and physical abuse in the street, cemeteries desecrated, tombstones vandalised, a pig's head left on one, arson attacks on synagogues, synagogues painted with swastikas and slogans, 'Yids get out', 'Six million was not enough'.[169] NF members threw eggs at members attending a Yom Kippur service at the Loughton synagogue in Essex.[170] Young Jews in Leeds joined patrols organised by the local Association of Jewish Ex-Servicemen and Women (AJEX), especially of buildings and cemeteries which had been vandalised.[171] Having heard that synagogues were going to be attacked on the fortieth anniversary of Kristallnacht, 9 November 1978, Clive Gilbert, member of Prestwich ANL, and two others were protecting the isolated Hillock synagogue when suddenly they were attacked by Nazis. They saw off the fascists but Gilbert got a bloody nose.[172]

Jews were deeply divided on how to oppose the fascists. The dominant organisation, well established politically, was the Board of Deputies of British Jews, mainly composed of representatives from synagogues and Jewish establishment organisations. The Board had always been opposed to any physical confrontation with the NF, arguing 'The way to defeat the National Front is at the ballot box'.[173] While arguing that wherever possible the media should avoid publicising antisemitic attacks, as its Defence Committee monitored fascist activity closely, the Board insisted that it alone had the authority to organise Jews against the NF.[174]

When the Jewish Socialist Group leafleted against the NF in the October 1974 general election, they were condemned as a 'danger to the community'. At the same time the Board began 'quietly producing anti-NF literature which was made available to other groups for distribution', mainly leaflets used by local Labour Parties and others campaigning against NF candidates. [175] In the October 1974 general election, 'over a quarter of a million of the Board's "Hatemonger" leaflets were distributed by the main political parties in some 56 constituencies'.[176] In the 1976 local elections in Leicester, over 50,000 leaflets were delivered in areas where the Front had previously polled well. Leicester AJEX helped get support for a full-page advertisement in the *Leicester Mercury*, on the day before the election, 'signed and paid for by hundreds of people'.[177]

At the same time, there was a strong tradition challenging the Board's insistence that it alone should organise Jews against the fascist threat. Among the older generation there were opponents of Mosley who had been active alongside people from other communities before and after the war, many of whom were or had been members of the Communist Party. Some like Martin Bobker and Aubrey Lewis, both active anti-fascists in Manchester for many years, helped set up the local ANL.[178] The ANL founding statement included well known Jewish actors such as Miriam Karlin, Warren Mitchell and Alfie Bass, soon joined by the singer Frankie Vaughan. Karlin spoke at many ANL meetings, large and small, making it clear that she was both a 'totally committed Zionist' and an ANL supporter.[179]

Such support did not prevent a stream of attacks on the ANL. Within days of the ANL launch, the Jewish MP Maurice Orbach, having been one of the League's first sponsors, resigned from the ANL, citing Peter Hain's support for the Palestinians and anti-Zionism.[180] The Leeds Jewish Representative Council denounced both Hain's anti-Zionism and the local ANL secretary's membership of the SWP.[181] When Henry Grunwald and Jerry Lewis, two younger members of the Board of Deputies argued for co-operation with the League, Martin Savitt, chairman of the Board's Defence Committee, replied that the ANL had broken an agreement with the Board not to ask synagogues and other Jewish organisations to join and make donations.[182] The Board of Deputies accused the ANL's mass canvass in Ilford of raising the NF's profile.[183]

If the criticisms came thick and fast, so did the replies. Peter Lazenby, Leeds ANL chair and press officer, related how the SWP member who chaired some of the early Leeds ANL's meetings had insisted that anti-Zionist views 'would not be discussed and did not form part of the brief of the Anti Nazi League'.[184] Responding to the Board's call for Jews to stay at home, criticising the ANL's mass canvass in Ilford, Holborow wrote to the *Jewish Chronicle* quoting a woman in Ilford who had lost seventy relatives in the Holocaust, whose husband was guarding the local synagogue and who was 'not going to kow-tow to these NF people'.[185] Two Jewish students argued that Jews should not isolate themselves, noting that: 'At the recent NUS conference – a conglomeration of widely diverse political viewpoints – the decision to affiliate to the Anti-Nazi League was well-nigh unanimous. On this issue, students have realised that political differences should be put aside in favour of a united stand against fascism.'[186] In contrast, they argued that the Board's attitude showed: 'patent arrogance on the part of a pontificating monolith locked away in an ivory tower.'[187]

A second letter from Holborow challenged the Board's inactivity during the Ilford by-election. Rejecting the claim that increased publicity was the basis of the NF's increased vote, it contended that it was the worsening social and economic situation that had led to results like the NF and NP's combined 44 percent vote in Deptford, beating Labour, and that: 'Failure to mount peaceful counter-demonstrations against provocative Nazi marches into immigrant areas is therefore to encourage them increasingly to intimidate ethnic minority groups.'[188]

The 1978 Victoria Park Carnival Against the Nazis raised the question of organising against the fascists separately or with others with a new intensity. David Rosenberg remembers getting to the carnival:

> with other Jews... but not without a fight. Our 'leaders', the Board of Deputies, had pulled out all the stops to try to prevent Jews from supporting the biggest anti-fascist mobilisation in Britain since the 1930s... When the ANL held a public meeting in the Jewish heartland of Golders Green,

and with Jewish speakers on the platform, it was forced to hold it in a Unitarian church because the Board had told synagogues not to let their premises to the ANL...

Like the East End Jews of the 1930s before them, lots of suburbanised young Jews... ignored the Board. When we arrived in Trafalgar Square on that day, some of the first people we encountered were other Jewish youths from left-Zionist groups – Mapam and Habonim – who knew exactly why they were there.

That day was a crucial step on a political journey for many people. Some of those young Zionists will have pondered on the contradiction of a Zionist movement that told them that you can only escape from antisemitism, not fight it, while they marched within a huge multi-racial crowd, that was optimistic that it could defeat racism and fascism and build a truly equal multi-cultural society, as they chanted: 'Here to stay, here to fight!'[189]

There was another powerful argument for attending. Len Rolnick, who ran the Communist cell in the 43 Group after the Second World War, came to the carnival having decided: 'It must be the duty of every man and woman who is alive at the expense of the millions who perished to show their support by attending'.[190] At the Manchester communal council meeting after the carnival, the newly elected youth delegate Tania Beale: 'suggested that not enough Jewish youth attended the recent Anti-Nazi League carnival in London. It would have been a credit for more Jewish youth to have been there.'[191]

The ANL reinforced the importance of countering the NF's antisemitism with a briefing document, 'The National Front and the Jews', which showed how the NF used antisemitism and made clear how: 'The National Front leadership is, in the strictly technical sense, Nazi. That is to say, they derive their primary inspiration from the record of the German National Socialist Workers Party (the Nazis) and the writings of its preeminent leader, Adolf Hitler.'[192]

The document detailed how the NF leadership satisfied NF supporters' pride in Britain's victory over Germany in the Second World War, while at the same time openly supporting Nazism. Using the antisemitic myth of Jewish domination of international finance, the NF argued Churchill was manipulated into declaring war on Germany, Britain's 'natural ally', and then persuaded to ally with Jewish-dominated Russia, the source of the 'myth' of the gas chambers and the Holocaust.[193]

An opposing view of the NF threat came from the *Jewish Chronicle* columnist, Ben Azai. Acknowledging that the carnival, 'Sunday's "anti-Nazi", rally was an impressive affair, he accused 'the ultra-Left, as represented by the Socialist Workers' Party and similar groups' of:

> inflating the NF as a bogey out of all proportion to its actual or potential size, and shrieking 'Nazis' at the tops of their voices. They represent, in my mind, an evil every bit as dangerous as the one they claim to be fighting, and the fact that they are against racism does not, in itself, atone for the fact that they are also against freedom, against tolerance and against truth.[194]

Azai's view was not that of the Chief Rabbi who put out a statement just before the May local elections: 'In view of the large number of National Front candidates contesting the Borough Council elections on May 4, the Chief Rabbi asks all ministers to urge congregants to go to the polling booths and exercise their voting rights.'

The NF's poor election results were analysed in detail in the *Jewish Chronicle*. Martin Savitt, who saw the NF as a threat to be taken seriously, argued at the deputies' monthly meeting that the 'massive leafleting campaign has awakened the public to the dangers of the hate-mongering dictatorship. I feel the Defence Committee's policy has been vindicated'.[195] On the other hand, echoing Azai, the *Jewish Chronicle* editorial reviewing the election results, asked whether 'we should continue to help them [the NF] in this [their campaign against black people and Jews] by overexposing their activities through high-powered counter campaigns, which can only result in their continuing to enjoy the kind of publicity they are otherwise unlikely to receive'.

Azai's view was challenged at a northern regional conference of Board deputies. Henry Guterman, secretary of the Manchester Representative Council and chair of the North West Committee against Racialism, warned the Board of Deputies 'not to act as it had done in the 1930s when, he alleged, it had urged people not to fight Mosley and the fascists'. He went on to tell Dr Gewirtz, executive director of the Board of Deputies Defence Committee, to be 'very careful' in his attacks on the Anti-Nazi League: 'Our young people find they can work with the ANL, and with a lot of bad publicity, many young Jews will be alienated.'[196]

In a third letter to the *Chronicle* from the ANL, Paul Holborow and Miriam Karlin also challenged Dr Gewirtz. While acknowledging that the Board of Deputies had 'for many years… worked to combat the extreme Right,' they continued: 'But rarely has it or any other anti-racialist body been able to reach an audience beyond that already "politicised". By contrast, the Victoria Park carnival of April 30 (some 80,000 strong) showed that the League has gone well beyond that audience.'

They concluded: 'Think again, Dr Gewirtz. If pressure on the Board is what he seeks to avoid, he really must not make speeches of the kind reported, since it can only enormously increase that pressure.'[197] In reply, Gewirtz, recognised 'the idealism of those individuals and organisations that have chosen to affiliate with the Anti-Nazi League' but took issue with 'the handful of adherents of the extremist Socialist Workers' Party and their allies who plan, manage and direct the overall programme of the ANL'. The Board saw the need '[t]o unify the various forces opposed to racism and fascism' and consequently: 'took the initiative to bring into being the Joint Committee Against Racialism, which includes the Labour, Conservative and Liberal Parties, as well as the Trades Union Congress, the British Council of Churches, the National Union of Students, the ethnic minorities themselves, and other reputable national organisations'. In contrast, he claimed, 'we have the Anti Nazi League's announcement last week that it intends to fight the Tories in the forthcoming Parliamentary elections'.[198]

The debate among Jews about what attitude to take towards the ANL continued as the Brockwell Park Carnival and the expected general election neared. Under 'Forthcoming events' the *Chronicle* advertised:

SUNDAY, SEPTEMBER 17
Anglo-Jewish Attitudes to the Anti-Nazi League. Come
and hear speakers from AJEX, Liberal and Progressive
Synagogue, Poale Zion and Young Mapam debate this
subject at Young Mapam. 37 Broadhurst Gardens. London
N.W.6. (behind Finchley Road tube) at 8.00 p.m. Admission
50p.[199]

And a week later, a call to join the march to Brockwell Park:

Jews Against the Nazis – Join the Anti-Nazi League march
and carnival, which is starting in Hyde Park today. We
must show the National Front that the Jews of England are
standing firm against today's Nazis. Meet 11.00 a.m. outside
the Odeon, Marble Arch, Edgware Road.[200]

The *Jewish Chronicle* now commissioned Dr Geoffrey Alderman 'to take a close look at the Anti-Nazi League and its activities'. In a major article, Alderman gave a detailed account of the ANL concluding that the NF threat was real and that: 'Co-operation between the Board and the ANL would cause consternation and dismay at National Front headquarters. And that can do us all nothing but good.'[201]

Among Board members, Martin Savitt was quick to insist that Alderman had 'completely misread the current situation'. Other members took a softer line. Eric Moonman MP suggested the Jewish community should try to influence the policies of the ANL. Lawrie Nerva suggested that 'If the ANL works against the NF then it is not for the Board to pick at the political persuasions of some members of the ANL'.

Alderman's article triggered 'a large number of letters' with the *Chronicle* printing a dozen carefully chosen to present a balance for and against supporting the ANL.[202] Much of the support for the ANL came from younger Jews, including young Zionists, and also those who remembered how, before the war, Jews were together with others as part of a united movement against Mosley.

Dr Gewirtz's reply summarised the Board's arguments and pointed out that the Board of Deputies had been active against the NF on a national scale several years before the ANL was founded. It failed to deliver a decisive blow.[203] By the end of

October, the *Jewish Chronicle* was clear that: 'Public debate and the correspondence columns of this newspaper suggest that no issue in recent years has so divided Jewish public opinion as the argument for and against supporting the Anti-Nazi League campaign against the National Front'. It concluded:

> What patently is needed is some form of cooperative endeavour in which the Board, without ceding its independent status, or appearing to give support to Israel's enemies, could loosely co-operate with the ANL in those areas of anti-racialist endeavour where the Board can satisfy itself that there is no political gain to the Socialist Workers' Party or other anti-Zionist forces... With strict guidelines, there are surely areas in which their [the ANL and Board of Deputies] different strengths could be co-ordinated for the general good. There must be some in both organisations who are willing to give it a try.[204]

Other voices were now speaking up. Maurice Ludmer, *Searchlight* editor, always careful not to engage with the different views among anti-fascists over the Israel–Palestine question, wrote: 'In the face of mounting attacks against the Jewish community, both ideologically and physically, we have the amazing sight of the Jewish Board of Deputies launching an attack on the Anti-Nazi League with all the fervour of Kamikaze pilots.'[205]

A hint of peace

Under the headline 'Hint of peace with the ANL', the *Jewish Chronicle* quoted Lord Fisher, president of the Board, at one of its monthly meetings:

> We were delighted when others – including the Churches, political parties, trades unions and the media – followed the example we set and when new bodies, including the Anti-Nazi League, were set up. We bless the efforts of all who fight those who wish to drag Britain back into the Dark Ages. We proclaim that the struggle against the evil creed of racialism is, like peace, indivisible. To say this – and to mean it – does not suggest that we must necessarily agree with all the

methods employed by other groups, or that we can close our eyes to the role of certain individuals who, while they fight racialism in Britain, describe Israel as a racialist State and Jews (or Zionists, the terms are interchangeable) as racists... [W]e seek to co-operate with others who fight the same fight, given the proper guarantees and assurances that we are duty bound to seek and are entitled to have. We do not wish to dissipate our energies and limited resources on internecine warfare, and we shall seek to reach a reasonable understanding with the enemies of our enemies whom we hope one day to be able to count among our friends.[206]

Fisher followed this with a meeting with Ernie Roberts and Neil Kinnock from the ANL steering committee. The atmosphere was 'cordial' and it was agreed to meet again.[207] In contrast, the atmosphere at the Union of Jewish Students (UJS) annual conference a week later saw 'some of the noisiest exchanges seen for years' as for an hour the conference debated whether to renew affiliation to SCAN (Student Campaign Against the Nazis). However, after an hour's debate the resolution was passed:

That while SCAN may contain groups which are sectarian and anti-Zionist, only through membership of SCAN can the UJS contain these groups and influence SCAN's policy; that ethnic and cultural minorities should be encouraged to join SCAN in order to ensure that the methods used by SCAN to combat racism and fascism are integrated with the methods used by UJS and are not offensive to the principles of UJS.[208]

Richard Friend, a Jewish member of School Kids Against the Nazis, was critical of the Board, writing to the *Chronicle* to point out its failure 'to distribute [its leaflets] on a large scale, or convert the teenagers from the National Front'.[209] The Board of Deputies line was confirmed by Hayim Pinner, secretary general of the Board, who explained that the Board, 'while disagreeing with the ANL, wanted to find a way of avoiding confrontation between the various elements fighting the National Front'.[210] Efforts to find those ways took place at the Board's offices in January with Paul Holborow and Ernie Roberts meeting Lord Fisher. Afterwards Fisher reported:

that no close working association or affiliation was possible, but the name-calling slanging match had to stop. Both sides agreed that our primary objective is to avoid mutual recrimination and public squabbling... It should be recognised that the sole purpose of the exercise is to destroy the National Front, and therefore nothing should be done which indirectly helps build up the National Front.[211]

The Board had not changed its position at all. It still insisted that there had to be recognition that the Jewish community was the responsibility of the Board. There should be no public criticism of the Board and no approaches should be made by the ANL to Jewish groups – including synagogues – for funds. The ANL was not to be used as a vehicle for anti-Zionist propaganda, spoken or written. The distribution of literature of this kind should be banned at League meetings. Confrontations on the streets should cease.

The Board declared its opposition to the 'pull the plug' campaign. They also criticised the ANL's 'magazine for school children', *SKAN*, as 'obscene and militant' and recommended that it should be 'cleaned up'. Lord Fisher told deputies that the steering committee of the ANL would 'consider these demands and we have been promised a reply after their own meeting at the end of this month'.[212] The ANL's reply found:

> the discussion between our two organisations was very useful and should in due course lead to a more harmonious and understanding relationship. We also wanted to reiterate that the ANL was formed for the purpose of combating the influence of the National Front... It is therefore not appropriate for the League to take positions on other political questions, such as Israel and Zionism, or indeed many other issues about which sincere and strong opinions are held. It does, however, go without saying that the ANL is unequivocally opposed to all forms of anti-Semitism.[213]

Fisher responded, pointing out that anti-Zionism 'is often used as a cloak for antisemitism. Therefore, the ANL should not be used as a vehicle for the dissemination of anti-Zionist propaganda, and the distribution of anti-Zionist literature should be banned at ANL meetings'. He added that the ANL should make clear its 'abhorrence of the anti-Jewish activities – under whatever guise – in the universities... neither can it condone the participation in such activities by those holding official positions in the ANL'. He concluded: 'The Board and the League have agreed to keep in touch on an "informal friendly basis, exchanging information and ideas and resolving differences in a sensible fashion".'[214]

At the April AJEX conference a few weeks later, in the run up to the NF march in Leicester, Martin Savitt continued to describe the Anti Nazi League as a front for the Socialist Workers' Party, urging Jews 'to steer clear of the NF march and leave the situation to the Chief Constable'. By contrast, when winding up the conference as the Board's president, Fisher avoided these criticisms, telling delegates the NF was 'better established' in Britain than Hitler and his party were in Germany in 1923'.[215] Without yielding its position an inch, the Board now tacitly accepted that it had lost the argument with many young Jews and a significant number of the older generation. Its attacks on the ANL and its Jewish supporters ceased. This left Jews, including both Zionists and non-Zionists, free to work with non-Jews against the fascists. The ANL had succeeded in maintaining the united front. The task now was to make final preparations for the general election.

■ Southall demonstration against NF meeting, April 1979. Photo Virginia Turbett

9: Counting down to the election

★ Campaign conference

Six months after it was launched, with five months to go to the expected general election, the ANL's first conference was called for early July 1978.¹ The total of 800 delegates showed impressive growth. As the Communist Party told its members: 'The ANL is continuing to develop as a central factor in the fight against fascism'.² Two hundred delegates were sent by union bodies sponsoring the ANL, around 500 came from an estimated 250 ANL branches, together with those representing anti-racist committees. Leeds sent delegates from engineering, garment worker and council worker union branches, the All Leeds Campaign Against Racism, the local branch of Women Against Racism and Fascism, the Campaign Against Racism and Fascism and the Gay Liberation Front as well as local ANL branches.³

With a membership estimated at 30,000, the ANL was now a serious force. Interviewed in the *Morning Star* together with Bill Dunn, Holborow argued 'It has given the entire movement a new lease of life... Before the ANL we used to react to events. Now we are taking the offensive'.⁴

Could the conference do justice to these achievements? Or would it be dominated by arguments about the ANL's constitution?[5] Calling it a 'campaign conference' would not stop it being a talking shop. The danger was clear to Sid Harraway, the CP convenor of Ford Dagenham, who pointed to the weakness of much debate at trade union conferences: 'We have to turn paper resolutions into mass activity on the streets.'[6] For *Socialist Worker* it had to be 'a conference of activists, of builders not a gathering dominated by the worthy representatives of the non involved or by those who want to split hairs rather than create a mass movement'.[7]

How to deal with the many disagreements amongst those delegated to attend? Delegates had to understand that many differences were irrelevant to the task in hand. When Red Saunders told the conference, 'Frankly, I don't give a shit what your line on Kronstadt is. Love music and hate racism', the delegates responded with applause and laughter.[8] It was also necessary to show that the ANL could deal with differences, starting with the most important, the question of immigration controls. The Labour Party had given up opposing them when it came into government in 1964, swiftly strengthening them in February 1968 to stop the arrival of Kenyan Asians.[9] The Communist Party called for the labour movement to support their campaign against 'racist immigration laws', without success since no convincing case was made for how non-racist immigration controls could work.[10] The SWP defended its opposition to all immigration controls while at the same time ensuring the ANL would be sustained as a united front. A caucus of SWP members met before the conference to draft a motion. This opposed all immigration laws and also made it clear that it was 'in no way binding on supporters or sponsoring organisations of the ANL'. To the surprise of many, it was passed by a large majority.[11]

The ANL leadership was coming under scrutiny as never before. Brick Lane was headline news.[12] Webster and Tyndall's reaction to the NF's poor results in the local elections was to push harder to capture headlines and bolster their authority within the NF, which led to more confrontation and more violence. This included an arson attack on the ANL office in Soho, setting fire to the Albany Empire in Deptford, venue of many south London

RAR gigs, and a parcel bomb sent to the Peace News bookshop.

Inevitably, there were arguments within the organisation. Each attack required an organised response that could draw in as many people as possible.[13] Responses could be challenged by affiliated anti-racist anti-fascist groups. When, after his son Karl was shot at in Lewisham, David Foster, a local black activist, approached others to jointly organise a demonstration in protest, South East London ANL supported the call. Two affiliated groups, ALCARAF and SCARF, opposed it.[14] ALCARAF's secretary argued that the SWP was 'manipulating the ANL'. The ANL's national steering committee was asked to intervene. Audrey Wise MP agreed to investigate the allegation. Bill Dunn explained: 'All we can do is encourage our people to take maximum steps to bridge any gaps that have occurred'.[15] None of the groups involved that were rooted in the working-class movement left the ANL. It was different when it came to those who were not. The Federation of Conservative Students, having affiliated to the ANL in May, disaffiliated less than four months later, claiming without evidence that Peter Hain had said the ANL would be campaigning against the Conservative Party in the election.[16] Their chair also showed their ignorance, presumably wilful, of the ANL when they added: 'The league is also saying that the Front should not be allowed to advertise their policies during the election, and we feel that goes against the free speech principle'.[17] A low key 'semi-withdrawal', only publicised in the local press, was made by the Liberal MP for Colne Valley in West Yorkshire, Richard Wainwright. After an argument with Leeds ANL, he declared himself no longer willing to work with the ANL nationally, only with the Huddersfield and Oldham branches.[18]

The rank-and-file revolt

The political temperature was rising across the country. Callaghan's acceptance of the Treasury mandarins' belief in keeping the sterling exchange rate high had done little to reduce inflation. His answer – to continue year after year with the Social Contract – had produced the sharpest cut in real wages anyone could remember, down 10 percent in just eighteen months. Four years of public spending cuts had led to dozens of hospitals and schools being closed. Despite this, inflation was still over

10 percent.[19] Yet, facing little or no organised opposition from Labour MPs and party members, he was confident he could get away with imposing a 5 percent ceiling on pay increases in the fourth year of the Social Contract. It was bound to cause shop floor anger. Nevertheless, with the fall in the number of unofficial strikes pointing to a sharp decline in rank-and-file confidence, Callaghan believed he could rely on union officials to hold the line.[20]

With a small pre-election boom helping Labour to close the gap with the Tories in the opinion polls, Callaghan was expected to call the election in October 1978. The alternative was to hang on to power as long as possible with a small and uncertain majority in parliament. Early September, using an old music hall song to pile on the political charm, Callaghan told the TUC at its annual conference the last thing they had expected to hear: he had decided to put the election off.[21]

Callaghan's calculated risk turned out to be a mistake of historic proportions. Two weeks after his speech, 2,500 workers at the Ford Halewood plant in Merseyside walked off the job demanding a 15 percent rise. Most of the remaining 50,000 workforce came out on strike the next day bringing Ford plants to a halt across the country. The strike was front page news for nine weeks before mass meetings were offered and the full 15 percent was accepted.[22]

Just as the Ford strike was ending, 30,000 firefighters went on strike over pay, the first and only national strike action against the Social Contract. The government declared a state of emergency bringing in the army as strike-breakers. The strike ended after nine weeks, with a settlement that did not breach the 5 percent limit. Despite this defeat, many workers looked to the Ford deal as a clear sign that the pay limit could be breached. Within ten days of the end of the Ford strike, 8,500 oil tanker drivers were threatening to stop work in pursuit of a 25 percent rise. After a secret government plan to use troops to break the strike was abandoned, the oil companies agreed to pay 17 percent within hours of the strike starting.[23]

The press would later describe the strike movement as the 'winter of discontent'.[24] It was better understood as 'four years of mass discontent finally boiling over', showing that, despite the demoralisation caused by the Social Contract, workplace union organisation was still powerful.[25] Lorry drivers began unofficial strike action early in January picketing docks and oil refineries. They blockaded Hull's two main roads so effectively that the press called it 'siege city'. Meeting every day, the union dispensation committee required employers to queue for their turn 'to have the group of stewards determine if the movement of their supplies was essential'.[26] By the end of the month, the employers agreed a 22 percent pay rise. On 22 January, one and a half million public sector workers struck against low pay with further action by public sector workers including NHS ancillaries, gravediggers and refuse collectors. The Finchley SKAN group backed the caretakers' strike: 'Half the 1000 students came out. We put pickets on and the dinner ladies refused to cross. We marched to other schools in the area and pulled three of them out.'[27]

Having been just ahead of the Tories in the polls in October, by March 1979 Labour was trailing by around 10 percent.[28] Astonishing as it may appear given the class warfare Thatcher launched against unionised workers when she became prime minister, the Tories could now use strikes against Labour in the forthcoming election.

NF under pressure

Hating the working-class democracy that the shop floor revolt relied on, NF members found it impossible to act effectively in the workplace. Almost always forced to operate under cover, they could do no more than try to organise those opposed to taking action.[29] Tyndall and Webster were under growing pressure with 'secret caucuses of disgruntled NF members' attacking their leadership.[30] The best they could do nationally was to get members to Whitehall for Remembrance Sunday, a long-standing fixture in the NF's calendar. Two thousand five hundred marched past the Cenotaph in Whitehall, protected by a mass of police, challenged by several hundred Anti Nazi League supporters, twenty-eight of whom were arrested.[31] One way of strengthening members' support was to step up the antisemitism with a sizable new pamphlet, *Lifting the Lid off the Anti Nazi League*. This claimed to be an 'exposé' of the ANL, showing how it was part of 'the international Jewish conspiracy', subsidised by 'Russian-Jewish city bankers'.[32]

Though well attended with 1,500 present, including 170 parliamentary candidates, the NF conference in January 1979 was held in secret.[33] Hiring venues was increasingly difficult. Hackney Council received a 20,000 signature petition calling on it to prevent the NF from using the warehouse it had bought from being used for 'offices, meetings, recreational pursuits, storage and printing', as Tyndall had told the conference.[34] While many councils now had a policy of refusing to let rooms to the NF, some relief came from councils now under Conservative control.[35] In Hillingdon, north west London, protesters had to be cleared from the public gallery by police as the 1973 Labour ban on the NF booking council venues was reversed.[36]

As older NF members prepared for the general election, newer, younger members increasingly focused on violence. As before, Asian and black communities were the main target, in particular those living near the new NF headquarters in Hackney.[37] Michael Ferreira, an eighteen-year-old mechanic, was the fourth victim of racist murder in the East End in eight months.[38] Meeting after his murder, 200 people, mainly black, founded the Black People's Defence Organisation and organised a march. There were weekly confrontations between NF members and anti-fascists on Brick Lane and Chapel Market in Islington.[39] NF members attacked a Yom Kippur service at a synagogue in Essex.[40] An assault by 150 NF members on Sinn Fein's Bloody Sunday commemoration marchers in London saw forty-one arrests, all but two were NF members.[41] ANL steering committee members had excrement and razor blades through their letter boxes.[42] 'The Eleventh Hour Brigade', a secret organisation many of whose members were also in the NF, carried out arson attacks.[43] Fake ANL leaflets appeared with the headline 'The Union Jack is a Nazi Flag. It must be banned', and the claim that Paul Holborow had concealed his Jewish roots, his real name being 'Holborowicz'.[44]

There were no shortcuts to stopping the violence, which was mostly carried out by youngsters. Few of these young people were organised fascists. In their *Socialist Worker* article, 'Build in the back streets' in East London, Newham ANL argued that the 350 ANL members and another 1,000 members in affiliated anti-fascist organisations in the area had to create a network, street by street, 'to draw disillusioned white kids towards us'.[45] A start was made with a petition calling on Hackney Council to shut down Excalibur House, the new NF headquarters. This building, strongly defended with 24-hour security, was the organising centre of the violence. Across the East End, ANL members collected signatures, with more than 500 signatures collected in a single session in Hoxton market. Over three months, the total number of signatures rose to 20,000.[46] Two hundred and fifty ANL supporters demanded the council take action as they demonstrated outside Hackney Town Hall at the end of January.[47]

As preparations for an October election were put aside, ANL branches now focussed on local activities.[48] Following the example of 'Spurs Against the Nazis', football fans got together in over a dozen clubs to challenge the NF presence at matches, giving out leaflets and selling badges. Greater Manchester ANL organised protests to the Tameside council, a weekly picket and a monthly mass occupation of the pitch to stop the NF's all white youth football team, the Lillywhites, playing in the Tameside Sunday League. Nottingham ANL organised a Day of Action, leafleting and petitioning against the local Nazi HQ.[49] Yarmouth Trades Council campaigned against the Tory controlled council's decision to let the NF hold its annual conference in the town.[50] Camden ANL in north London got people to picket a local butchers where an NF member had been threatening black customers and ANL badge wearers.[51] Glasgow reinforced the united front with a public meeting with James Milne, Scottish TUC general secretary, Maggie Osborne, secretary of the Scottish Immigrant Labour Council, and Paul Holborow on the platform.[52] The same was true in Oxford with an ANL meeting in the Oxford Union with Tariq Ali and Phil Piratin, the former CP member of parliament whose book, *Our Flag Stays Red*, about fighting the Mosleyites in the 1930s, had just been republished.[53]

An NF member in a hospital presented ANL supporters with the task of isolating him. Ken Brack was chair of the NUPE branch at Middlewood Psychiatric Hospital in Sheffield where he kept quiet about his NF membership. The ANL group in the hospital responded by selling badges, producing a bulletin, raising money to get people to the Victoria Park Carnival and discussing with fellow workers the attitude adopted by the German Nazis to people with a learning disability.[54] Rail Against the Nazis had an anti-fascist film evening, showing the Czech classic *Closely Observed Trains* and *World in Action*'s 'The Nazi Party'.[55]

Local activity was anti-racist as much as it was anti-fascist. Hounslow had a 'Festival against Racialism' in September, and 1,500 came to Bradford's Multi-racial Festival, organised by the ANL and the Community Relations Council.[56] When Coventry's Tory council refused to make a city centre park available, over 800 joined a Carnival Procession Against the Nazis composed of 'punk rock followers and students... supported by the trades council, Labour and Communist Parties, SWP and IMG, plus the Indian Workers' Association'.[57] At the same time an anti-racist carnival was planned in Coventry for summer 1979, selling 15,000 raffle tickets to pay for it.[58] Ealing Town Hall was picketed in protest against the Tory council decision to ban carnivals in Ealing.[59] The Birmingham Action Committee Against Racism in Clubs campaigned against the colour bar operated by the Pollyanna nightclub, with pickets every Saturday demanding: 'Pollyanna must back down or close down'. One week they organised an anti-racist gig followed by a torch-lit march to the club.[60] An Anti-Racist Week, organised by students at the South Bank Polytechnic, along with meetings, films and an open forum, included an ANL benefit disco, a RAR gig and CAST's anti-NF play *What happens next?*[61] In a demonstration called by the local ANL and the All Lambeth Anti Racist Movement, 200 marched through Brixton against the Sus laws and harassment by the SPG, who had sealed off a street and searched every home.[62] As it became clear that the open hostility of the Board of Deputies towards the ANL was now at an end, nearly 200 came to an ANL launch meeting in Golders Green in north London, an area with a large Jewish population.[63]

The strength of the ANL's workplace and union groups was shown in the ANL's national trade union conference with over 500 delegates including twenty-nine national union executives. Held at the TUC's headquarters, Congress House, it was chaired by Bill Keys, chair of the TUC's Equal Rights Committee. Keys insisted that the police could 'do more to prosecute racists under existing law', arguing 'that if the government believed this law to be inadequate it must quickly change it'.[64] For most delegates, however, the priority was activity in the workplace, wherever possible building ANL workplace branches.[65]

This priority was demonstrated in practice by the strength of ANL activity at the local level. Dave Cook, CP national organiser, commented approvingly on how different the ANL was from other campaign organisations the CP had been involved in. Whereas in Anti-Apartheid, the campaign against apartheid in Sought Africe, where the national organisation worked to ensure control of local branches, the ANL was not 'a directing centre for the anti racist forces'. The steering committee should keep 'its loose and informal relation to the organisation as a whole.'.[66] In fact, the steering committee *did* take a formal role, meeting monthly to ensure the ANL remained focused on the task of breaking the NF as an electoral force, as set out in the founding statement. As Peter Hain explained: 'We constitute an extraordinarily wide coalition of political forces, ranging right across the ideological spectrum, and this requires a delicate balancing role by the ANL leadership'. Given that 'the wider movement beneath the ANL steering Committee is independent: there is no central command structure', the leadership had to make it clear to local groups that 'it is imperative to retain a wide involvement and to avoid sectarianism at all costs'.[67]

Confident that the ANL would deal with the NF, *Searchlight* now looked to the future, calling for 'a unified national movement that will challenge and expose entrenched and institutionalised racism with the same tenacity and widespread appeal that the ANL and other organisations have brought to the campaign against resurgent fascism in Britain'.[68]

This left unanswered the question of whether such a national movement could be organised on the same basis as the ANL. *Searchlight* had reported how, in contrast to the ANL's successful conference, the two-day ARAFCC conference held a few weeks earlier with 350 delegates had failed to launch a national antifascist and anti-racist organisation, with the ARAFCC disbanding a few months later.[69] At the time, *Searchlight* blamed 'certain women, Gay and Left groups' who 'sought continuously to confuse issues and saw the question of 'sexism' as one of the dominant themes of the conference'. This led to a number of trade unionists and black and Asian delegates leaving the conference early.[70] One delegate, John Thackara, criticised those who saw the conference as an opportunity to present their politics, 'present[ing] full revolutionary positions'. This did not build the movement.[71]

Desperate to hold a march as the general election approached, Webster seized the chance offered by the jailing of Robert Relf, the self-confessed Nazi in Winchester prison on hunger strike against his fifteen-month sentence for contempt of court.[72] The ANL committed to confront the NF, the local chief constable mobilised 2,500 police and got an order under the Public Order Act preventing the NF from marching to the prison while, at the same time, banning the ANL from the city centre. In freezing rain, 800 NF supporters marched for twenty minutes in the city centre where they were met by ANL supporters throwing eggs, tomatoes and smoke bombs.[73] Meanwhile 2,000 ANL demonstrators were able to march to the prison chanting 'Let Relf rot'.[74] *Socialist Worker*'s editorial commented: 'Many of those who had travelled long distances and yet did not glimpse the Front found it a frustrating day'.[75] However, the huge police numbers meant there was no alternative to accepting that 'tactics on the day have to be determined by the relation of forces, although kicking the Nazis wherever possible remains our firm commitment'.[76]

RAR's national profile had been built through its carnivals. Its strength rested on the groups of RAR supporters 'in over fifty towns putting on small scale gigs run by a mixture of culture-conscious lefties and punk and rasta kids'.[77] Manchester, Liverpool, Leeds and Sheffield all had weekly club nights.[78] Now, after 'a deliberate decision at RAR's second national conference to scale down from the open-air carnivals of 1978 and get back to the roots', Militant Entertainment, a national tour, was organised: 'RAR was growing at a pace that no one predicted... We tried many different ways to consolidate that enthusiasm into a coherent organisation. In the end the most outrageous and wildly ambitious project galvanised groups across the country and established RAR as a national campaign able to organise a major event independently of the ANL.'[79]

The plan was 'a tour that would include as many of the RAR groups as possible providing the local support bands. We [RAR central] secured the headline bands, national publicity, logistics and funding. We managed to get over 20 well-known bands to commit to the project'.[80]

The Manchester gig showed the grass roots strength of RAR when all the 'names' cancelled. Debbie Golt and Maggie Ross Turner organised a completely 'bottom up' event and a packed house.[81] The final gig had 5,000 at the 'Ally Pally', Alexandra Palace in North London, Easter Sunday, 14 April 1979. Fourteen bands played over six hours on a stage with a thirty-foot rhino, the emblem of the tour, under a giant banner 'Here is your alien culture'.[82]

A week later, the election now called, advertisements in the music press told readers: 'Don't just rock against racism... Vote against it. Vote Labour'. Red Saunders responded:

> Don't just what? We've just 'rhino-ed' around the country, arguing and playing our unmistakeable anti-racist message and it's left us seven grand in debt... Ok, it seems like most of us will be putting our shaky little crosses in Labour's box on May 4th. Rock Against Thatcher – we mean it! But no illusions. We're looking forward to seeing Labour start to really Rock Against Racism: ending the racist immigration laws, abolishing Sus, etc.[83]

Election called

Struggling for months to keep a parliamentary majority, the government lost a vote of no confidence at the end of March 1979, forcing Callaghan to call an election for early May. A dull five-week campaign followed.[84] Thatcher lacked the confidence to take on Callaghan in a TV debate.[85] She targeted the government's record on employment, inflation, the unions and strikes, all of which were more important to voters than immigration, according to the polls which showed the Tory lead narrowing throughout the campaign. Determined to outflank the Tories, Webster began the NF's election efforts announcing: 'We're going to be fighting a very, very heavy racist campaign.'[86] In practice, the work done by the NUJ and the ANL meant that journalists were now being much more careful about reporting on the NF. Despite the NF contesting 300 seats, the BBC and ITV decided the NF should have one five-minute party-political broadcast, the same as in 1974.[87]

The NF used the free postal mailing available to all candidates only in its 150 'Class 1' campaigns. 'Class 2' were merely 'skeleton campaigns... to add credibility to candidates in other areas by adding to the total'.[88]

Mass leafleting, postering and mobilising to stop NF public events was always going to be the ANL's biggest challenge, particularly with many Labour and Communist Party ANL supporters committed to supporting their own party's campaigns.[89] Greater Manchester ANL branches leafleted every constituency with NF candidates.[90] They also picketed both TV stations in Manchester on 26 April, organised a coach for the Southall demonstration on the 28th, an ANL public meeting in Middleton on the 29th, and a coach from Manchester to the picket of the NF election meeting in Rochdale on the 30th.[91] ANL branches in south London collected signatures and sponsorship from 150 trade unionists for a half page advert headed 'Danger – Nazis at Work' in the *South London Press*, published on 1 May, two days before the election. In Leicester the NF lost ground with the local paper now clearly against them.[92]

Across the country, an often young turnout almost always challenged any appearance by the NF, who were now completely dependent on police protection. A thousand police protected the NF election meeting in Bradford.[93] Another thousand protected fifteen people and Scotland's only NF candidate from a 600 strong picket in Glasgow.[94] A thousand police in West Bromwich were only able to protect Tyndall's meeting for eleven minutes from 500 demonstrators, seventeen of whom were arrested.[95] In Crawley, five hundred anti-fascists stopped the NF candidate, protected by 300 police, from saying a single word at his open air rally. Council workers helped by refusing to wire up amplification equipment when they found out that the Front had booked the space.[96] In Gravesend the NF candidate called off a motorcade when he saw the 150 gathered to stop it. In Canterbury, '500 plus students came down from the university... There was a real determined hardcore that this meeting wasn't going to go ahead'.[97] 'A huge number of us [were] tightly packed outside the meeting in Canterbury. The National Front couldn't get out of or into the meeting.'[98] One thousand picketed a private meeting with Tyndall in Merseyside.[99] Three hundred stopped a secret

NF conference in Gloucester.[100] Ipswich NF cancelled their election meeting when its time and place became public.[101] After the Devon chief constable, John Alderson, decided that a public meeting meant the public were free to enter, 100 ANL supporters filled the NF's venue in Plymouth, forcing Tyndall to leave without speaking.[102] Brent council cancelled the NF's booking on the grounds that the NF did not admit the public; the decision was upheld by the High Court.[103]

Leicester

Needing a national mobilisation in the run up to election day, Webster decided on a St George's Day march in Leicester, still one of the NF's strongholds with four candidates for parliament and forty-eight in the local elections.[104] Seven thousand people had voted for the NF in the three Leicester seats in October 1974. There was no difficulty in setting it up. The chief constable was determined to ensure the NF could march, later saying: 'We have fought wars for freedom and the National Front were exercising one of those freedoms.'[105] He also took care to learn from Lewisham, assembling 5,000 police from twenty-one forces, a helicopter, riot shields, dogs and the SPG. A double line of police on all sides protected the NF's 600 marchers as they assembled.[106] For the ANL, the march was a challenge. As Peter Hain wrote: 'This deliberately provocative demonstration in an area with a large Asian population represents the Front's biggest push since they marched at Lewisham in August 1977.'[107]

The NF had to be opposed; the question was how. The city was full of police roadblocks and diversions, coaches to the counter-demonstration were stopped and searched. The police were clearly determined to make physical confrontation impossible. Leicester ANL had a good relationship with the city's anti-racist and anti-fascist organisations. Together with the trades council, the Leicester Inter-Racial Solidarity Campaign (IRSC) and the Indian Workers Association (IWA), it issued a leaflet calling on people to assemble together.[108] The Leicester Council for Community Relations (LCCR) went to court to get the march banned and when this failed, called a march that was away from the NF. A thousand IRSC supporters joined the LCCR on its march.[109] Around 4,000 now moved towards the NF's march.

The ANL told its supporters to go in small groups to the city centre to block the NF route to the school where it would hold its meeting.[110] The NF had marched for about 200 yards when they and their police escort came under attack. Hidden behind an advertising billboard, a group organised by the SWP showered them 'with explosive yacht flares and brickbats'.[111]

The police now abandoned the planned route through the city centre, taking the NF through side streets on a ten-minute march to the school where Tyndall spoke, describing the LCCR chair as 'a hook-nosed dwarf'.[112] Those marching through side streets to the school were 'challenged and beaten back by police in full riot gear', driving vans into groups of marchers and using 'wedges' to break groups up.[113] 'Using riot shields, batons and dogs the police systematically broke up the demonstration.'[114] People regrouped on the university campus near to the school where the NF were meeting protected by a mass of police.[115] Here they were attacked even more viciously by police using riot shields and dogs. By the end of the day eighty-seven anti-fascists had been arrested.[116]

Ned Newitt of the IRSC called the anti-fascists' success in stopping the NF marching through the city centre 'a pyrrhic victory'.[117] It was more than that. Leicester was the last of the NF's national mobilisations of any size. The NF could only come to Leicester under massive police protection. At the final rally in the park where anti-fascists had assembled at noon, Steve Cedar was asked to speak from the back of a truck as one of the few who got through the police lines. He told people, 'the way we stop them is numbers'.[118]

Southall

Numbers were again of crucial importance two days later in Southall in what became the largest confrontation the ANL was involved in and, as was Leicester, one of the biggest tests of the united front. For the Asian community of Southall, one of the largest in Britain, the NF booking a room for an election meeting in Southall Town Hall was shocking news, a deliberate provocation of a community that had neither forgotten the murder of Gurdip Singh Chaggar nor had any illusions in the police.[119] Even though Beatrice Howard, the Conservative leader of Ealing Council, dismissed the booking as 'routine administrative matter', the provocation was clear.[120] Southall's town hall is a small building, the room booked for the meeting had less than sixty seats.[121]

With two representatives from each local organisation, and others from all over west London representing trade unions and religious, women's and cultural groups, eighty people came to a meeting called by Southall IWA.[122] It was agreed to have a petition calling on the council to cancel the booking, with a march on Sunday to Ealing Town Hall to present it. If that was unsuccessful, all shops would close from midday on Monday and workers would be asked to strike at the same time and join a massive sit-down outside the town hall starting at 5:30 pm.[123] A five-member coordinating committee was agreed including the Southall ANL representative, Balwinder Rana, who was appointed chief steward.

On Wednesday 18 April, representatives of the coordinating committee met with the home secretary, Merlyn Rees, as he visited Ealing as part of Labour's election campaign. Rees insisted he possessed no powers to ban an election meeting. Holborow, Tariq Ali and Balwinder Rana, went to Scotland Yard where they met Commander Helm, in charge of the police operation in Southall. Rana remembers him saying: 'If you want your people to stay safe then you should tell them to stay at home'.[124] The chief superintendent of Southall police requested a meeting with community leaders including protest organisers such as Vishnu Sharma. Rana remembers: 'When I came in, they were sitting there with their hands clasped. It looked like they were praying.' The superintendent made a speech warning that left wingers wanted to destroy the town: 'Next week evil is coming'. Rana responded that 'he only knew "one kind of evil, the racism of the National Front". Then Vishnu Sharma jumped up and supported what I said. Then all the others began to nod their heads in agreement'.[125]

The police began to establish their presence in the area on Friday.[126] On Sunday, as 5,000 assembled in the Dominion Centre car park to march to the Ealing Town Hall, they encountered a mass of police, some on horseback. Despite protests against their unnecessary presence, they insisted on accompanying the marchers. When Rana, the chief steward, asked the police officer in charge why so many police, he was told that they were there to protect the marchers, but Rana had insisted that they were quite capable of protecting themselves.

But the real purpose of masses of police soon became clear. As people marched past the police station, police arrested a black fourteen-year-old boy for some petty offence, dragging him into the police station. Leading the demonstration from the top of a small truck, Rana called a halt and, together with Vishnu Sharma, went inside the police station to get the youth released. After first threatening to arrest both Sharma and Rana, the police released the boy, the march resuming with the boy on the top of the truck for everyone to see. Police harassment continued all the way with twenty more arrests until the march reached Ealing Town Hall, which was surrounded by hundreds of police and a line of police horses in front of them. The petition with 5,000 signatures was presented to the council. A stewards' meeting was organised in the evening. A senior steward was appointed for each of the four roads leading to the town hall where the mass sit-down would take place and other stewards were appointed or were to be appointed on the day. Provision was made for loudspeakers, legal support, doctors, nurses, a first aid post and an ambulance.

The next day police began to arrive at 9 am. Their coaches and vans lined the main road while masses of police patrolled the streets. At noon, shops and banks all closed and were boarded up. People began to arrive, including strikers from London Airport and the Ford Langley factory. Members of the Southall Youth Movement (SYM) went to get the 'ok' from the police community liaison officer, Inspector Gosse, that they could stand in front of the town hall. When they returned police turned them away saying 'Who the fuck's Gosse?' and then proceeded to make the first arrests as they forced the youth to move on.[127] As hundreds gathered with the banner of the Southall Youth Movement, tempers rose with a few minor skirmishes. When Rana approached the police officer in charge, saying to him, 'I am the chief steward and I will talk to the youth', the response was 'Fuck off'. Despite heavy rain and the efforts of stewards, a bus with young racists abusing passengers was attacked, walls were knocked down, the bricks used as missiles. Mounted police and police with riot shields now moved in, beating back the youth who retreated into side streets.[128]

By 3 pm, the centre of Southall was occupied by 3,500 police, lined up row upon row, some with riot shields. All four main roads were blocked about a quarter of a mile from the town hall. It was now impossible for people to reach the centre of Southall. Groups of demonstrators gathered at the roadblocks where they were repeatedly charged by police with truncheons. When the IWA tried to get people to sit down at one of the roadblocks, many were truncheoned and arrested. Later when protestors tried to break through the police lines, the police responded by driving vans into crowds, squads jumping out to make arrests. Mounted police wielding 30-inch (75 cm) batons charged into the crowds followed by police on foot who beat youngsters, dragged them out and threw them into police coaches.

By 5.30 about 2,000 people, many of them ANL supporters, had gathered near the Peoples Unite art centre, five minutes from the town hall.[129] By 6.30 some had lost patience and decided to walk into the three deep police lines stopping them from approaching the town hall. A few flares were thrown at the police lines. Suddenly, the police lines opened and dozens of mounted police charged the protesters, using their long truncheons to hit people on their heads as they fled into the nearby park and church yard and the nearby People Unite centre. Men and women, young and old, all got the same treatment. Rana remembers climbing over someone's garage to escape.

Full of racist and sexist abuse, the SPG now forced their way into the People Unite Centre, took control of all three floors and ordered everyone to leave. As people tried to get out, they were truncheoned by police lining the stairs. Most were hit on their heads, some badly injured including Clarence Baker, one of the senior stewards and manager of the Misty in Roots reggae group, who was hospitalised for months, some of it in a coma. Before leaving, the police destroyed all the music equipment worth £10,000, smashed toilets and ripped out water pipes and phone wires. Joan Rudder remembers:

> I had my head split open by a truncheon. I was in the Peoples Unite Centre where people were taken because the police weren't allowing them through to the St. Johns ambulance. There were people really badly injured. Eventually we realised we had to get out because the police

- Top: Southall demonstration for Blair's funeral
- Above: Anti Nazi League members picket New Scotland Yard
- Left: Blair Peach

were about to storm it. Police wielding truncheons formed two ranks, on either side of the door. There was no other way out, you had to run between those ranks. It was terrifying. Everyone – those injured and not – were beaten. The instinctive thing – you don't think about it – is to lower your head. There's a part of my head where the hair doesn't grow where I had six stitches.

People took us *en masse* to hospital. The reaction there was not good, because the staff had dealt with injured coppers. They thought we were just rioters. They didn't understand what was going on, the sheer hell out there.[130]

At 7 pm, less than fifty NF members, mostly heavies, all from outside the area, were escorted into the town hall. A member of the Southall Community Relations Council, described as 'hostile' by an NF steward, was turned away by the police. Only a handful of members of the public were admitted:[131] 'In the meeting one of the speakers told the audience that when the NF came to power they would demolish Southall and construct a beautiful English hamlet'.[132]

A large number of demonstrators were on Ealing Broadway, held back by three or four lines of police. Close enough to the town hall to see the police bringing the NF into the meeting, they roared with anger, pushing at the police lines. When it was clear they could not break through, the noise subsided and the mood changed. People started to make their way home. Suddenly a petrol bomb was thrown. There was a big flash, a police coach reversed into the crowd to avoid the flames, and the police lines parted. First came the mounted police, quickly followed by vans.[133] Among those leaving was Blair Peach, a special needs teacher heavily involved in Teachers Against the Nazis, president of the East London Teachers Association and an SWP member. As he walked with friends up a small side road off the Broadway, two SPG vans, driving at speed, abruptly stopped. Parminder Atwal saw what happened:

> I was in my garden when two police vans came and about twenty policemen got out. The police were carrying shields and black truncheons. They tried to break up the line of

people and came running down the road pulling people, pulling them by the hair and hitting them with their sticks. This boy was standing on the corner next to the wall when everybody came running past. He (Mr Peach) got tangled up in it and was knocked over. Then, when he was lying on the ground, the police came rushing past him as they chased these other blokes down the road.

As the police rushed past him, one of them hit him on the head with the stick. I was in my garden and I saw this quite clearly. When they all rushed past, he was left sitting against the wall. He tried to get up; but he was shivering and looked very strange. He couldn't stand. Then the police came back and told him: 'Move! Come on move!' They were very rough with him and I was shocked because it was clear he was seriously hurt. His tongue seemed stuck in the top of his mouth and his eyes were rolled up to the top of his head. But they started pushing him and told him to move; and he managed to get to his feet. He staggered across the road and came to where I was in the garden. I tried to sit him down. He was in a very bad state and he couldn't speak. Then he just dropped down. I got a glass of water for him, but he couldn't hold it and it dropped out of his hand.[134]

The Atwal family took him into their home from where an ambulance took him to hospital. He died a few hours later.

The next day, with 700 arrested, 342 charged, dozens badly injured and Blair Peach murdered by the SPG, the whole of Southall was in a state of shock.[135] Two hundred met in the Dominion cinema. Outraged by the press's uncritical acceptance of Metropolitan Police Commissioner McNee's lie that the police had been subjected to an unprovoked attack, members of the IWA, SWP, ANL, Asian youth and elders, agreed to set up a defence campaign, hold a demonstration on Saturday, organise a strike on the day of Blair Peach's funeral and call for an independent inquiry.[136]

On the Thursday before the planned demonstration, Commander Helm spoke of how 'a strong police presence' would be needed in similar situations in future. As the names of those arrested, overwhelmingly from Southall, became public, the police lie that the trouble was caused by 'outsiders' was exposed. It was McNee who decided that the police should use violence against the people of Southall and, in so doing, make Blair Peach a martyr. It was also clear that Ealing council could have followed Brent council in refusing to let the NF have a room because, in restricting who could attend, it was not a public meeting as specified in election law.[137] Leicester and Southall were both victories for the police. Overall, they succeeded in ensuring the NF marched and had their meetings but only using substantial force. But the ANL came through the double test of Leicester and Southall without loss of support and able to claim it had succeeded in preventing the NF from appearing in public without massive police protection.

Election day: 3 May 1979

Though the Labour election campaign had seen the Conservative lead in the opinion polls fall, the result saw a 5.2 percent swing from Labour to the Conservatives, the biggest swing in a general election since Labour won in 1945. Thatcher now had a majority of forty-three. The recent strike wave had broken the Social Contract, but it failed to fully restore working-class confidence and solidarity, the support for not crossing picket lines that had brought down Heath.

The NF's 303 candidates averaged just over 1.25 percent. Their total vote was 190,063, with thirty-four candidates getting 1,000 or more votes. In October 1974 their ninety candidates got 113,843 votes. Of these fifty-six won 1,000 votes or more.[138] In Bolton, Bradford, Bury, Huddersfield, Manchester, Rotherham, Sheffield, Tameside and Warwick and Leamington, previously areas of substantial NF activity, they put up no candidates at all.[139] They failed to be 'Britain's third party' anywhere, losing to the Liberals in all 299 seats where both parties stood.

Thatcher's reference on *World in Action* in January 1978 to people's fears of being 'rather swamped by people with a different culture' boosted her poll ratings.[140] However, in the run-up to the general election, the opinion polls showed that people prioritised unemployment, the cost of living and strikers before immigration.[141] The Conservative election advertising, its posters and newspaper adverts followed this line.[142] Thatcher spoke about immigration only once in the campaign, responding to a question on a radio phone-in two weeks before polling day. She told listeners she 'stood *absolutely* by her remarks last year that some Britons felt swamped by immigration'.[143] Apart from standing firm on her 'swamping' speech, there is no evidence that Thatcher 'played the race card' in the 1979 general election.

As the *Sunday Times* pointed out, some of Thatcher's statements were the same as the National Front's.[144] The NF benefitted from being able to tell people to vote for the 'original' rather than the 'copy'.[145] Undoubtedly the Tories benefited from the collapse in the NF vote, without making it part of their campaign. The collapse was down to the success of RAR and the ANL sticking the Nazi label on the NF so effectively that the great majority of voters knew that they could not be treated like any other party. As Ian Goodyer put it: 'there is... a danger in believing that politics is all top down, that Thatcher just pulled the rug from under the racists' feet, but the truth is that by 1979 Rock Against Racism and the ANL had thoroughly discredited the National Front.'[146]

Paul Gilroy has argued that in getting the message across that the NF were Nazis, the ANL was appealing to those who saw the Second World War as a struggle against fascism.[147] This is simply wrong. It does not appear in any ANL publication. ANL leaflets focussed on the consequences of Nazism, in particular the Holocaust.[148] The argument that opposition to the NF was patriotic was used by right-wing politicians opposed to the ANL such as Quintin Hogg.[149]

The aftermath

For the ANL, the immediate tasks were to support those arrested in Southall, Leicester and West Bromwich and to back the calls for the SPG to be disbanded and for a public inquiry into what happened in Southall. These were huge challenges given the numbers being charged and the government's determination to strengthen the police and 'the rule of law'.

All this was made much harder by the media's immediate acceptance of the police version of events. The manufactured reports sent on the day via ticker tape by the police press office, were accepted without question by most of the press. The

Sun reported that demonstrators had besieged the hospital, 'screaming abuse at officers in the casualty department'. However, hospital staff reported seeing no demonstrators. The *Daily Mail* told readers that 'Police noted... the high proportion of addresses from outside the Southall area given by those detained'. In fact, only two of over 300 arrested lived outside the area.[150] McNee stated that: 'The disturbances were unprovoked acts of violence against police and property by groups of people determined to create an atmosphere of tension and hostility... Police have no part to play in the political arena but have a bounden duty to see that the laws of the land pertaining to free speech are enforced.'[151]

In Southall, people were outraged that the NF meeting, composed overwhelmingly of NF members from outside Southall, was presented as 'democracy' but, if people travelled to Southall to support the demonstration against the NF, that was 'a threat to democracy'. Ealing Council also praised the police. After a motion was passed commending the police for their 'courage and patience... thirty protestors were thrown out of the public gallery for jeering and hissing while the vote was taken'.[152] Within two days of the arrests and the murder of Peach, Callaghan told Rees he wanted the reports about Southall and Blair Peach off the front pages as soon as possible.[153] The official Labour view that the police were the only body that could legitimately use force and that the chief police officer's operational independence had to be respected at all times was now questioned by many potential Labour voters.

The Southall Defence Committee march in protest at the events, headed by the Southall Youth Movement with their banner remembering both Blair Peach and Gurdip Singh Chaddar, grew steadily as it progressed silently through Southall, with 10,000, mainly local Asians, at the final rally.[154] By now the Southall Defence Committee had taken statements from most of those arrested and set up a defence fund to raise money for their legal costs. Together with the ANL it called for the SPG to be disbanded and a public inquiry.[155] With Merlyn Rees already having rejected the call for a public enquiry into the death of Blair Peach, the SWP argued that the defence campaign must prioritise political activity and reject any illusions that the police could be brought under democratic control.[156] As five years earlier in Red

Lion Square, the demonstrations in Leicester, Southall and West Bromwich all showed the police's determination to teach those who counter-demonstrated a lesson. Chief Constable Alderson in Devon was the isolated exception, deciding that NF stewards would not control who could attend their public meeting in Plymouth. Elsewhere, McNee and chief constables had jointly planned NF marches with Webster and allowed NF stewards to select who attended election meetings.

The mass arrests generated huge solidarity as people demonstrated at Blair Peach's funeral a few days later, outside the inquest and over many months as cases came to courts. At least £75,000 was needed to represent those arrested. £300 was quickly collected at Ford Langley for the Blair Peach Memorial Fund, supporting Blair's dependents and funding anti-racist work.[157] Workers at Sunblest bakery in Southall collected over £800 for the defence campaign and the Blair Peach Fund.[158] NUPE London Divisional Council donated £300 to the Southall Defence Fund, writing to branches asking for donations to raise this to £1,000 and a request to the union NEC for it to donate £1,000.[159]

Two packed out Southall Kids are Innocent concerts raised £5,000 at the Rainbow in July.[160] 'Pete Townshend stole the show... show[ing] you don't have to be a boring old fart who votes Tory to be a superstar.'[161] Together with other groups, RAR raised money for the Defence Fund from a small entry charge at weekly gigs upstairs at Southall's Dominion Cinema.[162] RAR organised 'mini tours' with twenty 'Dance and Defend' gigs for 'Leicester – Southall – West Bromwich'. 'Who Killed Blair Peach? A Political Answer', a four-hour event, was staged at the Royal Court Theatre with witnesses from Southall taking part. A reggae band, theatre groups, teachers, militants, residents of Southall, writers and poets expressed their anger in words and music at the murder of Blair Peach and the behaviour of the SPG. The evening ended with the cast and audience chanting 'SPG are murderers' as they carried a fifteen-foot effigy of McNee outside, where it was set on fire and the chant changed to '*Who* killed Blair Peach? *You* killed Blair Peach' when police attempted unsuccessfully to disperse them.[163]

Of the 342 Southall demonstrators summoned to court, the

police charged 23 percent with assaulting a police officer, 28 percent with obstruction, 26 percent with threatening behaviour and 15 percent with possessing an offensive weapon. Other charges included actual bodily harm, grievous bodily harm, malicious wounding, criminal damage, abusive language. Most defendants had to travel twenty miles to Barnet magistrates court, making it 'difficult for the Southall community to show its solidarity with the defendants'.[164] The Barnet magistrates had 'a history of harsh treatment of black defendants and militants'. The conviction rate was over 80 percent, compared to a national average of 52 percent for similar cases.[165]

Defendants found they were presumed guilty unless they could establish their innocence. One young person was found guilty of threatening behaviour and carrying an offensive weapon, holding a stick in his right bandaged hand. Seven eyewitnesses, including a lawyer, a doctor and a paramedic, all insisted that he was being treated at that precise time. Nevertheless, the magistrate fined him £100.[166] By December fourteen had been given prison sentences. With four members of Peoples Unite up before Barnet magistrates and Clarence Baker facing trial the following day, the Southall Defence Committee and Peoples Unite called a picket of Barnet magistrates' court.[167] Saturday 19 January was named Southall Saturday, aiming to raise £10,000 for the defence fund.

The next day several hundred marched from Euston station to picket Pentonville prison.[168] In late September, the Southall Defence Committee had an *Open Door* slot on BBC2. The film *Southall on Trial* brought hundreds of letters in response.[169] There was little difference in the treatment of the eighty-seven who were arrested in Leicester the day before Southall. Most were charged with 'threatening behaviour', the Leicester magistrates imposing heavy fines ranging from £250 to £750. Their defence costs totalled £20,000. Four demonstrators were jailed, including Martin Hughes, a miner from Edlington Main pit, Doncaster, sentenced to four months.[170] A protest demonstration of 200 in Leicester on 21 July was backed by Yorkshire area NUM.[171]

The cover up

Blair Peach's partner, Celia Stubbs, was interviewed by Deputy Assistant Commissioner Powis and Commander Cass, head of the Criminal Investigations Bureau on the night of the killing. Both said to her they were treating their inquiries as a murder investigation.[172] However, the next day Merlyn Rees rejected the call for a public inquiry. The urgency expected of a murder investigation now vanished, with the police seeking to delay matters as much as possible. The funeral had to be postponed after the police asked the coroner not to release the body. No officer was suspended from duty. There was no identity parade for almost three months.[173] When the pathologist's report was released by the ANL, claiming that Peach was probably not killed by a police truncheon but by a lead-filled cosh or pipe, the London evening papers tried to give the impression that Peach wasn't killed by a policeman.[174] The TV news highlighted that he wasn't killed with a police truncheon. The truth began to emerge on Thursday morning with the *Daily Mirror* having 'Riot cop in death quiz' as its front-page headline, reporting on the member of the SPG held for questioning and that SPG lockers had been searched at Barnes and Leytonstone police stations. The late edition of the *Evening News* announced: 'Riot death: Cosh found – detained PC's locker searched'. The following Tuesday, the *Daily Mirror* told its readers that the killer may well have been identified by laboratory tests on truncheons carried by members of the SPG.[175] At the first hearing of the inquest on 24 May, the police asked for a further three months to continue their inquiries.[176] The decision not to hold a public inquiry, in contrast to what happened after the police killed Kevin Gately in Red Lion Square, is a clear example of government bias in favour of the police. Even when the police kill demonstrators, the ruling class can be relied on to defend them.[177]

On the day of the funeral, 4,000 came to the Dominion Cinema to pay their respects.[178] The coffin was carried through East London, along Brick Lane to the graveside accompanied by thousands of mourners and thirteen national trade union banners. Hundreds stood in silence on the pavement as the march passed. A bus stopped, the crew stepping down and standing to attention. Ken Gill spoke on behalf of the General Council of the TUC, condemning the role of the Special Patrol Group, 'They should be disbanded immediately'. The SWP's leading member, Tony Cliff, gave the last tribute: 'It is no use building monuments of brass and of stone... let us mourn, but let us organise and mobilise'. As the coffin was lowered, those gathered sang the Internationale.

10: Taking down the beast

★ Thatcher

Within ten days of the murder of Blair Peach, Thatcher had become prime minister. A swing to the Conservatives of over 8 percent gave her a majority of forty-three. The election campaign had been uneventful. Thatcher lacked the confidence to take on Callaghan face to face. The Tories had some success with a poster using the slogan 'Labour isn't working' and an image of a giant queue of unemployed pasted on billboards around the country.[1] The Tory campaign focused on unemployment, inflation, unions and strikes. There was almost no mention of immigration by either party;[2] Callaghan was closer to Thatcher politically than either of them wanted to acknowledge.

Once in office, Thatcher got down to business. Her aim was a decisive shift in the balance of class power. By the autumn it was clear that she would use unemployment, cuts in real wages and welfare, anti-union laws and racism to break resistance. The unions had to be defeated. She was not alone. Internationally there was a determination by ruling elites that the growing confidence of organised workers going back to the 1960s had to be broken.³ The *Sun* warned its readers what to expect from the Thatcher government: 'You cannot wield the axe without shedding blood. Councils will be badly hit... hospitals and schools will have to undergo serious cuts... thousands of workers will become redundant.'⁴

Thatcher was an anti-Communist, supporting a new nuclear arms race. For her Russia was 'the enemy without' and unionised workers were 'the enemy within'.⁵ Following what had been drawn up as a secret plan by a senior Tory MP, Nicholas Ridley, the Ridley Plan, she adopted a step by step approach to break union resistance, looking to the police to protect strike breakers and lorry drivers willing to cross picket lines.⁶ 'Strong, efficient police forces with high morale' were an essential part of her plan.⁷ She started with what she saw as a soft target, the steelworkers. Their large union had a right-wing leadership hostile to all rank-and-file activism and had not had a strike since 1926. Despite this, the steelworkers fought for three months before they were defeated. Thatcher's first anti-union law was passed in the summer of 1980. This included making flying pickets unlawful, limiting unfair dismissal and maternity rights and requiring an 80 percent 'Yes' vote to have a closed shop.⁸

At the core of Thatcher's convictions was her unquestioning faith in the capitalist market; the so-called 'free market' was the only way forward. Abandoning the commitment to full employment made by all governments since 1945, she argued that freeing the labour market of restrictions imposed by trade unions would create jobs.⁹ Her counter-inflation strategy was based on the theory that inflation was caused by an excessive supply of money. This had to be brought under control by raising interest rates. This early use of neo-liberalism, known as monetarism, had already been applied by the Pinochet government in Chile after it took power in 1973 through a bloody coup, leading to thousands of deaths and disappearances and savage cuts in working-class living standards.¹⁰ Applying monetarism in Britain, pushing up interest rates, meant a sharp rise in the value of the pound. Exports were more expensive and imports cheaper leading to factories closing in unprecedented numbers. Unemployment doubled to three million over the next two years with young workers hit hardest.¹¹

There was much organised resistance. Across the country, campaigners fought to defend jobs and services in factories, hospitals and schools. But such campaigning became harder with the torrent of job losses. Night after night, TV news reported on new workplace closures. The slogan 'No return to the Thirties' no longer made sense as unemployment approached the same level as in 1936. There were occupations to resist mass redundancies but only one – 2,500 workers occupying the Gardner's diesel factory in Salford – succeeded, saving 500 jobs.[12] When an announcement of twenty-four pit closures triggered a walk out by 24,000 South Wales miners and a possible national miners' strike, the government, not yet ready to take on the miners, did an immediate U-turn and dropped the proposal.[13] It took Thatcher six years and a year-long strike to defeat the miners and complete the Ridley Plan.

Under greater pressure than at any time since the 1930s, the left struggled to find a way forward. Blaming Labour's election defeat on the Social Contract, many Labour Party members fought to move the party to the left. Their efforts focused on campaigning for Tony Benn as the party's deputy leader.[14] The Communist Party was increasingly divided between those remaining loyal to Moscow's leadership, concentrating on work in the unions, and those openly critical of Russia and its satellites, moving away from the party's historic commitment to the working-class movement. Inside the SWP there was a sharp debate on whether it was possible to continue building the rank-and-file movement or whether the movement was now in retreat, a serious downturn in class confidence.[15]

Racism in Britain had largely moved on from the discredited idea of biological superiority. Racism was increasingly now presented as an issue of supposedly incompatible 'cultural' differences with the claim that '[Black people] have a culture and a way of life that is *different*'.[16] When justifying the war with Argentina to recover the Falkland Islands in 1982, her line was, 'We must recover those islands... for the people on them are British and British stock', it was 'British culture' not 'biological purity' that was threatened.[17] The Tories' British Nationality Bill used the racist concept of 'patriality' to restrict the right to enter Britain to those born in Britain, their children and grandchildren, an overwhelmingly white group. The entitlement of everyone born in Britain to British citizenship would be removed.[18]

The humiliation of the NF in the general election meant that many now asked if it was time to wind up the ANL. The overwhelming majority of almost 300 delegates to the ANL's post-election conference agreed with Peter Hain that it would be a waste to lose the momentum created by the ANL.[19] With a consensus that dominated the conference, it declared: 'The confidence of the anti-racist movement is immeasurably greater as a result in part of what the ANL has done. No longer do anti-racists feel weak and isolated. There is a strength of purpose and sense of direction that did not exist before.'[20]

One measure of the ANL's success was the support it had won among black and Asian workers. It had helped overcome long standing divisions between the Indian Workers Associations getting their joint support for the march in Brick Lane on 20 August, for the September carnival and for joining the ANL.[21] At the conference, Avtar Jouhl, general secretary of the Indian Workers Association, and Vishnu Sharma, president of Southall IWA, were both elected to the fifteen-member steering committee.[22]

Tribune reported: 'The central theme of the conference was an extension of the ANL's work beyond that of combating the National Front to include a general assault on institutionalised racialism as a whole'.[23] The conference resolved to:

> open a broader campaign against racism. This will include campaigns against harassment by immigration officials, by police and courts, and against discrimination in housing, jobs, welfare and education... and working with the major ethnic minority organisations and the Joint Council for the Welfare of Immigrants to challenge the Tories' proposals to change the immigration laws and to pass a new British Nationality Act.[24]

The lesson of Lewisham was that before the foundation of the ANL the anti-fascist anti-racist groups had been unable to act as a single force when the fascists came onto the streets. For the ANL to sustain this capacity, it had 'to maintain its structure intact and be in a position to respond should the need arise'.[25] This had always been a challenge for an essentially reactive organisation such as the ANL. It was even more the case when many, if not most, ANL activists were committed as socialists and trade unionists to countering the Thatcher anti-union offensive. While some branches continued to meet, many kept in touch only when there was fascist activity.[26] The national organiser, Peter Alexander (now Kate Alexander), reported to the national conference in March 1981:

> This was a period of decline in activity and organisation, which affected almost every aspect of the League's work. This decline reflected the fortunes of the Nazis, particularly the National Front, who became demoralised and divided following their electoral demise. Nevertheless, even in this period, there were a number of important mobilisations, particularly those connected with the Blair Peach cover-up and Southall Defence, the Campaign against Racist Laws, and counter-demonstrations against the NF.[27]

The ANL's success continued to strengthen local activity. Harrow had a Multiracial Carnival against the Nazis in September. Leamington held an impressive trade union day school on 'Racism in the Workplace'.[28] The campaign to close the NF's HQ in Hackney succeeded, albeit taking almost two years to win.[29] A number of local groups supported anti-deportation campaigns. Many groups were now supporting the Southall and Leicester defendants and challenging the Blair Peach cover-up.[30] At the ANL conference, it was Vishnu Sharma, speaking about the campaign in defence of the Southall defendants being victimised by the courts, and Amanda Leon, calling for Blair Peach's murderers to be put on trial, who got the warmest response from conference delegates.[31]

The Campaign Against Racist Laws (CARL)

The ANL conference decision to campaign against racism led directly to launching the Campaign Against Racist Laws at a conference convened by the leading Indian Workers Associations (IWAs).[32] The government's new anti-immigrant legislation, the sentences handed out by the courts to the Southall defendants and the ongoing harassment by the police all showed that state racism continued to oppress black people on a massive scale.

CARL's role was to give a lead in the counter-attack. Targeting proposed new immigration regulations and the Nationality Bill, it adopted the same united front approach as the ANL, gathering as wide a range of sponsors as possible. This included all the major ethnic minority organisations, the TUC Race Relations Advisory Committee, the London Labour Party, the Liberal Party, thirty-three MPs and anti-racist campaign organisations.[33] More than 10,000, mainly Asian workers, were on its first demonstration a month later on 25 October 1979. The largest numbers were mobilised by the Indian Workers Associations.[34]

The strengthened confidence of anti-racists fed into the growing number of campaigns defending families divided by existing immigration law. In Oldham, the campaign in support of Abdul Azad organised pickets outside the youth detention centre where he was held for three months.[35] All night vigils and a march of 600 supported Nasira Begum, who was threatened with deportation after her husband deserted her.[36] Anwar Ditta started campaigning to reunite with her children, whom the Home Office refused to allow to join her in Britain, after she went to a public meeting in south Manchester campaigning against the deportation of Nasira Begum and Nasreen Akhtar.[37] Petitioning, speaking at nearly 400 public meetings and demonstrating – one march in Rochdale had 1,000 people – her campaign grew to the point where Granada TV's *World in Action* programme agreed to arrange blood tests for Anwar and her children, an examination that she had always offered to undertake. All three campaigns were successful. In Anwar Ditta's case, the Home Office reversed its decision the day after the broadcast that showed the results proving the children were hers.[38]

In Southall, together with the Indian Youth Association, the ANL turned out to confront police racism. They picketed police stations to protest against a physical attack by the police on a sick fifty-four-year-old Asian, Mohammed Sarwar, who had called the police after continuous harassment by young fascists.[39] Twenty ANL members occupied the surgery of the far-right MP Harvey Proctor, who called for 'black repatriation', forcing him to find an alternative venue.[40]

The 300 who attended the CARL conference in January 1981 included representatives of every large black and Asian organisation.[41] Preparing for the April demonstration against the Nationality Bill was the central focus. CARL meetings were organised in Bradford, Leamington, Southall, Waltham Forest with a rally in the Africa Centre in central London and a demonstration called by Leeds 'Scrap the Act' campaign.[42] In Glasgow, the IWA and ANL jointly organised a coach. Across the country IWAs played the key role.[43] Ten thousands marched in London accompanied by the six-piece punk band Alien Kulture playing on the back of a lorry. Avtar Jouhl noted 'more than one hundred black community banners on the march but few from the official labour movement'.[44]

Justice for Blair Peach

Five days before the inquest into Blair Peach's death reopened in October 1979, the Special Branch reported 'at 6pm outside Woolwich Police Station... some thirty persons attended a picket in aid of the Blair Peach Memorial... it was peaceful'.[45] It was one of fifty pickets organised by the ANL and the Friends of Blair Peach in a 'Nationwide Evening of Action'.[46] In Blackburn, the young Anti Nazi League secretary Azeem Khan said: 'Police stations all over the country are being picketed today to remind the police and the public that we are still aware of the death of Blair Peach'.[47] There were 'dozens of flaming torches' outside Stoke Newington police station.[48] The huge banner outside Sheffield police station included a portrait of Inspector Murray, seen by many ANL supporters as Blair Peach's killer.

Three thousand marched the day before the inquest restarted. They carried posters naming the six suspected Special Patrol Group members. Outside Scotland Yard, they responded to the question 'Who killed Blair Peach?' by chanting 'Murray, White, Lake, Freestone, Scottow, Richardson'.[49] The Home Office now asked the police to investigate possible legal action against the Friends of Blair Peach, the poster's publishers. The Director of Public Prosecutions also considered a possible contempt of court action against the *Sunday Times* for publishing the names of the six.[50] *Socialist Worker* demanded the report by Commander Cass into the killing of Blair Peach, the result of over 30,000 hours of police time, be made public: 'It must be in the hands of the jury at the inquest into Blair's murder.'[51]

In early April 1980, reacting against police harassment, black youth in the St Paul's area of Bristol fought back. Black and white rioters forced the police to retreat for several hours while shops were looted and buildings burnt down.[52] On 23 April, the anniversary of Blair Peach's death, Bristol ANL members:

> gathered around a home-made coffin painted black... At first there were embarrassingly few... But as the march proceeded through St Pauls, led by the coffin and the band X-Certs on the back of a lorry, numbers of supporters – black and white – steadily grew. By the time it reached Bridewell Police Station there were some 500 people... The police... closed the doors but were besieged within. Before the march moved off to Castle Park for speeches, the coffin was used as a battering ram against the Bridewell's doors. A defiant chant of 'No arrests' went up, and there were none.[53]

Pickets outside the resumed Blair Peach inquest demanded 'a full public enquiry into the death of Blair Peach and events in Southall' and 'the disbanding of the Special Patrol Group'.[54] While the inquest offered the opportunity to present evidence in public, the bulk of the evidence was still only available to the police and to the coroner. It was over a year after the killing before the jury decided it was Death by Misadventure, an absurd verdict, reached only after the coroner had told them: 'You have to decide if a policeman in that situation believed that Blair Peach was one of the rioters. If he did, even if he was mistaken, he's still protected by law.'[55]

NF in crisis

The 1979 election disaster had left the NF much weakened. For their October conference, they booked a hall costing £6,000 for a thousand delegates and hundreds of supporters. Less than 400 attended, protected from an ANL and trades council demonstration and picket by 1,500 police with a sea patrol boat.[56] As the Thatcher government began to show its teeth over immigration, some NF members left to join the Tories. This included both of the NF's parliamentary candidates for Preston. Lez Scott recalls 'the Burnley NF organiser rang one of us up to say he had left, "Please don't bother me any more"'.[57]

One ex-NF member told *Socialist Worker*: 'The growth of the ANL was demoralising the NF... The ANL was often discussed. Many members no longer wanted to turn up on demos. The ANL was turning activists into non-activists. The NF were bitterly disappointed with the election results.'[58]

Many NF members called for Webster to be sacked for failure to deliver promised action and abusive behaviour.[59] NF vice chairman Andrew Fountaine suspended Webster only to be overruled by Tyndall, who used his position as chairman to suspend Fountaine and reinstate Webster.[60] Fountaine's suspension was soon followed by his expulsion along with other leading members. Setting up his own grouping, he complained bitterly that Tyndall and Webster's leadership was an insurmountable barrier to progress. In a twenty-page confidential document, he asked: 'How is it possible for the Anti-Nazi League to be successful?... to brand us all as some kind of fascist cum neo-nazi party?', and went on to argue:

> The answer is simple. Two members of the Party, Martin Webster and John Tyndall... are singled out, not for their preeminence in the practice of today's politics, but because of their antics and tomfooleries in the days before they joined the National Front... So they're stuck with it and we're stuck with them unless the Party is prepared to face the reality and do something about it.[61]

A vicious leadership contest between Tyndall and Fountaine now followed, fought with a flood of internal documents and a court injunction brought against Tyndall, who blamed the 'unfavourable publicity' created by the Anti Nazi League as a main reason for the NF's demise.[62]

Tyndall won with a much-reduced vote. The paid-up NF membership was now little more than 6,000.[63] Reed Herbert left to found the British Democratic Party together with most of the Leicester membership, the NF's largest branch outside London. Fontaine left to found the National Front Constitutional Movement, claiming a membership of 2,000.[64] With the NF facing two competitors, Tyndall resigned as chairman arguing he could not lead properly without being given 'effective laws'. Maurice Ludmer wrote in *Socialist Worker*:

The campaign by the Anti Nazi League to make the public aware that the NF is nazi has had a devastating effect on their morale. Tyndall's opponents have acknowledged this in print. Tyndall's reputation for being the past master at the art of surviving the many 'Nights of the Long Knives' that have beset the fascists since the early '60s is now seriously at stake as the pressure grows.[65]

Tyndall now asked local branches for support, making a break a few months later to found a third competitor, the New National Front.[66] Leading the now much smaller and weaker National Front, Webster looked to the despair created by mass unemployment, youth unemployment eventually tripling to 22.3 percent, as the way forward. Even with the Nazi label, the twin track approach was still possible, albeit with electoral work taking second place. The immediate priority for the NF was to continue kicking its way into the headlines. When Thatcher agreed to accept refugees from Vietnam rescued by a British freighter just weeks after the election, Webster seized the moment. With leaflets headlined 'What now of Mrs Thatcher's no more "swamping"?', he got 800 on an NF march attacking Vietnamese refugees.[67] While always lower than four years earlier, some NF council candidates had a higher vote in 1980 than in 1979.[68]

Already after the poor election results of May 1978, the NF leadership was under pressure to be more openly fascist and violent or lose members to the fast-growing British Movement (BM). Founded in 1968 by Colin Jordan, it was an organisation undeterred by the 'Nazi' label with a uniform, a leader guard and paramilitary training camps that included sessions about Nazism. It was best known for attacks on black people, Jews and left-wing activists.[69] It had recruited a large number of young unemployed, mainly skinheads. By June 1980 it claimed around 3,000 members. Glennis, an ANL member and Leeds United supporter, counted twenty BM members and sympathisers where she lived in York: 'You take your life in your hands wearing an ANL badge round Elland Road [Leeds United football ground]... The youth here is divided into groups of skinheads, skinheads and skinheads':[70]

They focused on schools, football matches and gigs. While equipped with leaflets, badges and newspapers, the promise of violence was the key to recruitment.[71] A group of twenty at a gig could pull others with them to seize the stage and wreck the event.[72] Sham 69 was unable to get a venue to play live after a BM-led gang invaded the stage, July 1979.[73] In Manchester, John Hall remembered:

> my most frightening gig was… the Specials at the Apollo [November 1979]… We were on rows 4 or 5 and just surrounding us were these skinheads sieg-heiling throughout the gig and as soon as a black woman walked on they were throwing bananas at her, sieg-heiling and hitting people. The bouncers just couldn't control it… fights were everywhere.[74]

The BM's mobilisations were often organised at short notice by word of mouth, quickly going out of control. In Woolwich, 100 BM skinheads carrying 'knives, wood with nails driven in, iron bars, chains and pickaxes' laid into a large group of black and Asian youths waiting to get into a late-night film. As most of the queue ran, the BM entered the building pursuing those who had fled inside and trashing the interior.[75]

Competing head on with the BM, Webster prioritised building a street presence, arguing that if:

> it is true that the National Front has no hope of gaining power under conditions that are stable economically, socially and politically, we should not be preoccupied with making ourselves more 'respectable'. We must appreciate that the 'image' that we have been given by the media and which may well lose us some potential support today, will be a positive asset when the streets are beset by riots, when unemployment soars, and when inflation gets even beyond the present degree of minimal control.[76]

Giving up 'respectability' meant accepting organised violence as part of the strategy. Over a third of all the ninety-one racist murders in Britain from 1970 to 1994 took place in 1980–81.[77] Arson attacks included synagogues and community print shops. Meetings were often attacked. Fifty NF members carrying iron bars, bricks and bottles attacked a Manchester meeting on Ireland. Outside Manchester's Strangeways prison, forty NF supporters assaulted pickets supporting the rights of IRA prisoners.[78] In Gravesend in Kent, NF supporters painted graffiti, made threatening phone calls and smashed the Labour Party's office windows.[79] In Oldham, described by one activist as like Southall 'on a smaller but potentially just as nasty scale' where 'Asian workers have been attacked with sticks and iron bars by a large gang of racists, doors have been broken down, mosques bricked, and an Asian household petrol-bombed, the NF march was the last straw'.[80]

When eighty NF supporters marched, ostensibly protesting against the town's two left-wing MPs: 'Mills in Oldham had to shut down because the workers were out to stop the fascists. Two groups of 300 workers, mainly Asian, marched to the rallying point, where they joined a counter demo totalling two thousand.'[81]

'British jobs for British workers' was now a key demand. The NF used it to leaflet Calne, a small town in Wiltshire where a bacon factory had closed, destroying 450 jobs.[82] Members carried the slogan on placards marching through Lewisham and again in Corby, a Midlands steel town facing massive jobs cuts.[83] Marches every few weeks – thirteen between March and October 1980 – were now the means to recruit and retain the mainly young unemployed new members.[84]

Relaunching the ANL

The revival of fascist activity made it 'increasingly clear that our mobilisations were suffering from the lack of a general campaign against the Nazis'.[85] When 1,500 marched in protest two days after Akhtar Ali Baig was fatally stabbed by four skinheads – the fifth racist murder of black and Asian youth in east London in five years – the poor SWP presence on the march triggered a letter from Peter Alexander and Balwinder Rana, both based in Southall, to the SWP Central Committee.[86] The fascists were reviving across the country. This included Wales where they had been weak in the past. The SWP CC agreed that a nationally coordinated response was needed. A relaunch of the ANL with Alexander as national organiser was proposed and agreed at the September Steering Committee meeting in a committee room in

Parliament.[87] Alexander remembers: 'In a sense the decision was taken by the SWP and the Labour Party people who mattered were not opposed to this. Nothing was said, presumably because the SWP had initiated the ANL, but the formality was important because we were not imposing or taking people for granted.'[88]

The NF's call to march for 'British Jobs for British Workers' in West Bromwich in mid-August was a clear test of whether the ANL was 'in a position to respond should the need arise'. An emergency meeting of the local Sandwell CARF (SCARF), Birmingham ANL, the IWA and others agreed on a common plan for a counter-demonstration that would be supported nationally by the ANL.[89] Acknowledging that the ANL 'had experienced a lull' and that 'this demo must change that', a national ANL circular called on branches to order leaflets, book transport and hold local 'August 17 mobilising meetings'.[90]

With 150,000 leaflets in English, 10,000 in Punjabi, 10,000 in Urdu and 25,000 posters, ANL supporters leafleted factories, dole offices, housing estates, mosques and temples. Twenty-seven leading trade unionists in Birmingham signed a statement calling for support for the counter-demonstration. Avtar Jouhl, IWA (GB) president, wrote in *Socialist Worker*: 'We will be mobilising our members throughout the country behind the call of the ANL.'[91] A RAR gig was organised for the night before, a feeder march was planned from Handsworth to West Bromwich and twenty coaches were booked across the country. However, with the NF no longer credible as a legitimate political party, the West Midlands Chief Constable Philip Knights declined to defend the NF's right to march. For the first time since the Ilford by-election, the 1936 Public Order Act was used to get an NF march banned.[92] When Webster responded with notices of marches in Wolverhampton, Walsall, Dudley, Birmingham and Coventry, Knights responded promptly, getting banning orders for all five marches and mobilising 3,000 police.[93]

Meanwhile it was clear that the NF were planning to march in Warwickshire, whose chief constable, Roger Birch, had decided not to apply for a ban despite Webster's cat-and-mouse tactics keeping the location of the march secret as long as possible. Instead, he adopted McNee's 'blanket policing' model, saturating the area with police. The anti-fascists gathered in Leamington, welcomed by members of the local Sikh community who fed them with samosas from their gurdwara kitchen. As the ANL coaches set off, looking for the NF march, they were repeatedly stopped and searched deliberately delaying their arrival in Nuneaton when it became clear this was where the NF were assembling. Just two coaches out of twenty got through the police checkpoints to join the 700 counter demonstrators who tried to stop 250 NF supporters, escorted by 1,500 police.[94] Geoff Brown remembers how the much-delayed Manchester contingent was forced by the police to get off their coach on the outskirts of town: 'Walking towards the centre we got to a roundabout just as two NF coaches were leaving. Seeing our late arrival, NF members bragged through the windows until forced to duck as a hail of missiles covered them in glass fragments.'[95]

The revival of fascist activity and the linked increase in violent, sometimes fatal attacks on black people required a revival of anti-Nazi campaigning, albeit not on the same level as 1977–79. The 17 August 'West Bromwich' mobilisation worked well getting ANL branches up and running.[96] The ANL had to continue ensuring the fascists would never march unopposed, while recognising that 'blanket policing' meant this 'could be a frustrating and inconclusive exercise on many occasions'.[97] It was also necessary to ensure:

> a youth conference to focus the campaign against the nazis in the schools, on the terraces, and in the discos and clubs… [t]he strengthening of branches, the restoration of branches that have ceased to exist, as well as re-establishing a stronger national office with full-time workers, properly funded (through regular affiliations and bankers orders) and capable of producing a regular bulletin… [and] hold a national conference in the New Year.[98]

Concerned that the fascist revival should be taken on, the well-established Leamington ARAFC called a conference asking local groups to 'ensure representatives attend'.[99] With nearly a hundred activists, it was, in *Searchlight*'s view, 'ANL branches, not anti-racist committees, which formed the base of the conference, a reflection of the fact that they are taking on the local anti-racist work'.[100] Alexander mapped out the ANL's future direction: 'New leaflets with greater concentration on schools, with a youth conference in 1981. An international anti-fascist rally in December and an internal newsletter to help spread experiences.'[101]

There was no time to lose. Even if the BM were humiliated in the north in Dewsbury as the police stopped their sixty supporters from marching 'for their own protection', they were now organising their first national demonstration in London near Paddington, a serious test for the ANL.[102] Gary Hardie, National Union of School Students (NUSS) executive member, told *Socialist Worker*: 'By this weekend 50,000 leaflets will have been distributed in the area. Many of those are NUSS leaflets going into schools'.[103] The ANL and Paddington Campaign Against Racism (PCAR) mobilised over 4,000 while, having predicted they would have 2,000, the BM had just 500, only allowed by the police to march for just fifteen minutes. It was a decisive moment in preventing the BM from holding a national event.

Peter Hain did the relaunch press conference in the House of Commons.[104] Nearly one million ANL leaflets had been or would be distributed inside or outside schools and at football grounds and two carnivals were planned for the summer of 1981: Brixton 30 May and Leeds 4 July. In doing this, he explained: 'the main task is to rebuild the machinery'.[105] As he put it in an interview:

> The climate has changed and in a sense become harder, now the shift of gear among the Nazis and racist groups towards more overt and direct violence (although some of it is clandestine) demands a different response... The major priority over the next six months is to try to undermine the attraction that the BM especially has got for alienated kids, working class kids, who really have no prospect of jobs or any sort of future and have swung behind Nazis ideas.[106]

Across Europe, the misery produced by the global recession boosted the fascists' confidence to use violence. In Italy, 'the culmination of the cycle of right-wing terrorism' saw Italian fascists explode a bomb in Bologna's Centrale railway station, killing eighty-five people and wounding over 200.[107] At the end of September a bomb in Munich killed thirteen and injured 200 and, a week later, a bomb attack on a Paris synagogue killed four and wounded nearly fifty. The fascists' links with Europe, particularly 'the increasingly well supported annual festival of the extreme Right at Diksmuide in Belgium', needed an organised response: 'The sense of outrage produced by the recent incidents [should be used] as a weapon against them. As part of this process of internationalizing the issue, the ANL will be holding an *international meeting* in London with representatives of the main European anti-Nazi movements.'[108]

The central message of the international rally was that the state could not be relied on. Anti-fascists had to organise. Speaking to the 800 present, Giovanni Favilli, member of the Bologna city council, pointed to the failure of the Italian authorities to act on warnings of fascist attacks given by judge Mario Amato. Amato was himself gunned down by fascists.[109] Concentration camp survivor Leo Heinemann explained how in the camp: 'We took an oath... to exterminate them root and branch. We must not allow the Nazis to have any part in the streets again'.[110] Tony Benn, now the leading figure of the left in Britain, argued that the fight against the fascists was the property of no particular party: 'There is no hope if we do not stick together... It must be a united struggle to make sure it does not happen again'.[111] The most controversial contribution came from Jean-Pierre Grene from the French Autonomous Federation of Police Unions who took up the question of racism in the police. He attributed it to... 'the "intolerable" lack of emphasis on civil and human rights in the training of police officers and structural racism and the crisis... in other words, state racism... Fascism is public enemy number one... no one must forget the recent past when racism led to the extermination of millions of men and women'.[112]

The need to get the argument about the international threat and the importance of an effective response by the left was shown within weeks of the rally. Just before Christmas, Paul Mercieca, Communist mayor of Vitry, a working-class suburb of Paris, led an attack by fifty men using a bulldozer to smash up a dormitory intended to house 300 immigrants.[113] While there was opposition – a CGT member refused to drive the bulldozer – two weeks later, the general secretary of the French CP, George Marchais, led a march of 5,000 in support of Mercieca.[114]

Mass unemployment, youth, music and football

The key to beating the NF and BM was building a side involving large numbers of young people, particularly skinheads. Black and white youth were both being hammered by mass unemployment. Many were forced onto so-called job creation schemes, often exploited by employers, always on insulting rates of pay. Their frustration opened them to recruitment without knowing what a Nazi was. They could be persuaded to swap sides with football and music providing opportunities that could bring them together. Alexander remembers: 'If football became multiracial (in terms of top players and fans), or the good music was two-tone, or the violence involved black youth alongside white (as did happen in 1981), there was a possibility of "BM kids" ending up on our side.'[115]

It had to be based on activity carried out *by* them, by young people themselves, not *for* them. The battleground was whatever brought young people together, especially music and football. Skinheads, black as well as white, with no particular politics, keen on football and ska, first appeared in the late 1960s, a working-class reaction to 'mod' culture.[116] The skinhead revival ten years later was rooted in the rising unemployment confronting young people. With songs like 'Borstal breakout', Sham 69 was the band that connected best with their ever-tougher lives.[117] While the NF and BM were well placed to recruit skinheads, there was opposition from anti-racist skins, black and white. Sharon Spike, a first-generation skin, was in a group of anti-Nazi skins in Ilford, which was involved with the local Carnival Against Racism. Sixty people responded to the piece she wrote in *Temporary Hoarding*.[118] Skins Against Nazis was soon giving out leaflets and selling badges.[119] Skins turned out in force against the NF election meeting, April 1979 in West Bromwich. Several hundred young unemployed were on the Right to Work march from the steel and mining areas of South Wales via Eton College, Southall, Hackney and Brixton to the Tory party conference in Brighton. Here they joined 'the biggest union demonstration during a Conservative Party conference for many years'.[120]

Jay Williams came to the Youth Against the Nazis conference in a coach full of skinheads from Sheffield. He remembers their pride as skinheads, when: 'We burst through the doors and they just go 'Skinheads! Skinheads!'...the back rows of the conference stand up, chairs in hand. I say "Shush! Cool! They're with me".'[121] Steve, a skinhead from Cardiff, got a huge round of applause from the nearly 300 at the conference when he told them how, 'the British Movement are just using us skins. We're okay for beating up [black people] but they still call us degenerates. That's why I left the BM and joined the Anti Nazis.'[122]

The discussion was about activity, finding ways to talk to young people influenced by the fascists and put forward an alternative: organising around schools, football matches and dole offices. A national day of action leafleting football matches was agreed as was backing for the People's March for Jobs. The People's March brought together forces in the Labour Party, the Communist Party and trade union officials with support from the Right to Work Campaign.[123] Three marches, from Liverpool, Newcastle and Basingstoke crossed England over four weeks in May, coming together in London, where 40,000 joined a Mass Rally Against Unemployment in Trafalgar Square. A fourth march started from Glasgow, where 70,000 had marched against unemployment in February. The marchers crossed central Scotland to Perth. The climax in London was a 'Rock for Jobs' gig in Brockwell Park with Pete Townshend of The Who and poet Linton Kwesi Johnson.[124]

In Sheffield the number of racist attacks was rising, youngsters were joining the BM. 'Sieg heiling' had started at football matches where the BM gathered on Saturdays, selling papers with up to fifty supporters. Together with the NUSS, Sheffield ANL members leafletted schools, went door-to-door with members of the Bengali Citizens Organisation and organised RAR discos. One skinhead supporter of the BM in Sheffield was won over after he joined and became active in the NUSS in his school.[125] It became possible to:

> [Take] on the BM in the town centre... [with a] turn out
> of over 100 supplemented by further numbers of kids,
> especially skins, who appeared from all over the town centre
> to help. Along with a contingent of Asians and groups of
> Rastas, the leafleting became a very graphic demonstration
> of solidarity, repeated... on four subsequent mobilisations
> showing that there are large numbers of kids, particularly

skinheads, who are looking for an identity which is opposed to, but as strong as, the appeal of the Nazis. The response from the leafleting has been... over forty letters received so far, many from teenagers.[126]

A fan of punk, the fascist Eddie Morrison saw the possibilities music offered. In a letter to *Sounds* responding to the 'It can't happen here' feature on the NF, shortly before the April 1978 carnival, he argued: 'Already the signs of a reaction against lefty-domination of the music racket is becoming apparent... punks dragging bands *off* the stage for singing anti-NF songs (F Club, Leeds).'[127]

Morrison pushed the idea of Rock Against Communism with bands sympathetic to the NF including The Dentists. Paul Furness remembers a big event in the F Club in Leeds with lots of punk bands playing: 'We put in a couple of RAR bands. The Dentists were playing. We got people in and, when the Dentists came on, we pulled them off stage. There was a bit of a ruck and then the RAR bands played. The club owner couldn't do anything about us taking things into our own hands.'[128]

Joe Pearce picked up Morrison's idea of copying RAR. Making an ambitious start, Rock Against Communism's first gig was in Conway Hall, a month after Sham 69's concert was broken up. With just three days' notice, RAR got 200 supporters led by the band Charge with a banner announcing: 'We're all your "Alien Kulture"'. The gig could only proceed with the protection provided by two coach loads of police.[129] While there were no further Rock Against Communism gigs, there were bands that supported it, sometimes secretly. Often music fans couldn't decide which side they were on. Music genres could be fought over with the fascists claiming 'Oi!' as their own while others refused to accept this.[130]

ANL supporters turned out in numbers after people leafleting for a Liverpool "Rocking Against Racism" gig were attacked.[131] Sometimes the fightback needed no organising. When supporters of the Front attacked black and white dancers at a rave in Ladbroke Grove, west London, the dancers defended themselves. The black street-poet Benjamin Zephaniah was there and dedicated his poem, 'Call It What Yu Like', to the young punks who fought off the National Front that evening:

> Outside is a shout
> De Punks are about
> A shout
> Nazis out, Nazis out
> O Punk, O Punk, de fight nu long
> Yu battle well.[132]

Sheffield RAR restarted in 1981.[133] It focused not on gigs but on building:

> a base of anti racist support among kids who might otherwise be open to the influence of the Nazis... small regular gigs using a disco as the basic attraction ... playing their sort of music which they can't hear in a commercial disco.[134] As a result they're very sympathetic to our ideas. Out of the series of gigs at the Bow, an unemployed centre, we were getting 40 from an audience of 150 coming down town to oppose the fascists in the city centre on the morning after a Friday night gig. Out of that also came the Skins against the Nazis Group who have... helped to see off NF paper sellers a couple of times. Recently RAR provided the music float for the Sheffield Skinheads march against police harassment with 600 to 700 kids on the march.[135]

With the start of the 1980–81 football season, *Bulldog* celebrated the *Daily Mail*'s article 'The Front invades soccer clubs':

> Mr Stan Baker, stadium manager of Second Division Chelsea, says there is increasing National Front activity at Stamford Bridge... 'It's very unpleasant to see so-called supporters giving Nazi salutes and chanting "Sieg Heil"... Outside the West Ham social club near the ground, 'six burly men' were selling badges and T-shirts and giving out application forms to join WHAM 'West Ham against Marxists'.[136]

Some clubs began to act against them, usually banning all political activity. West Ham announced: 'Anyone seen to be using the area or any other part of the ground for political purposes will be ejected. We will not tolerate having this club's fine reputation being tarnished by political propaganda.'[137]

The change was only slow. The racists were silent when Justin Fashanu was able to select a team of eleven black players in the benefit match for the long-standing Crystal Palace player Cannon.[138] But, having reappeared after their humiliation, the fascists in Leeds had to be challenged again with a further turnout of sixty ANL supporters giving out leaflets at all home games for the rest of the season.[139] Spurs Against the Nazis did mass leafleting three times. Reds Against the Nazis again leafleted Old Trafford supported by Pat Crerand, former Manchester United and Scotland player.[140] A national ANL day of action at twenty-two League football grounds was planned, 21 March 1981.[141] Most matches were covered. At Chelsea where the NF had prepared with a leaflet calling on 'all good racists in London' to come to Chelsea and 'get Hain', there were packs looking for ANL supporters. Some clubs such as Manchester United and Bristol City, were quiet with little or no support for the fascists. Leeds ANL had fifty supporters challenging the organised NF presence. At Millwall, well known for racist activity, the leafleting went well.[142] More needed to be done. A hundred returned for the next West Ham home game to leaflet again as did Reds Against the Nazis.[143] It didn't always go well. Alexander remembers being massively outnumbered when leafleting at Chelsea, 'skinheads by every lamp post leading to the ground... Afterwards I had to take comrades for a whisky to calm some frayed nerves.'[144]

Riots and collective resistance

In January 1981, thirteen young black people were killed in a fire at a party in New Cross. The police first said they were investigating murder, but then switched from investigating a racist firebombing to looking for someone at the party who was responsible. Grief now turned into rage with the cry 'thirteen dead, nothing said'. Over a thousand people met to set up the New Cross Massacre Action Committee calling a Black People's Day of Action. Without a national black organisation with a mass base, transport was organised locally. Six coaches came from Manchester. Taking place on a Monday, it was Britain's largest ever black organised demonstration. Fifteen thousand marched for twelve miles, eight hours, from Deptford through central

London to Hyde Park.[145] Kate Alexander remembers going to at least one of the organising meetings: 'The organisers made it clear they didn't welcome white participation, but for the big march we (black and white SWP members) tacked ourselves on at the back, and that was accepted.'[146] Unable to resist the pressure to act against racist attacks, Whitelaw set up an inquiry.[147] *Socialist Worker* argued this was not out of a concern for the victims but to defend the government and the police.[148] Unashamedly copying Kingsley Read's comment on the murder of Gurdip Singh Chaggar, the NF announced a march passing the site of the fire with '13 down, 2 million to go' posters. One hundred and fifty opponents, mainly ANL supporters, confronted the rally they organised after the march was banned.[149]

The chief constable in Glasgow had secured a month long ban on all marches in early 1980 after a large labour movement counter-demonstration was announced in response to a planned NF 'Smash the IRA' march.[150] With the NF's thug element increasingly prominent, its credibility as a political party increasingly in doubt, Chief Constables made growing use of banning orders.[151] The ban on the NF marching in the New Cross area was extended to cover all of London, allowing only religious and ceremonial marches. When the NF publicised a march in Leeds, Whitelaw banned all marches in Leeds for a month. Webster responded by threatening an unannounced march in one of four towns in Yorkshire, picking the name out of a hat on a Sunday morning.[152] By early April there were nine police bans: Glasgow, London, Wolverhampton, Leicester and five in Yorkshire – Leeds, Sheffield, Doncaster, Rotherham and Barnsley. The bans, however, did not only stop the NF. The first day of the Trans-Pennine CND march from Leeds was made illegal as was the Scottish TUC unemployed march that set off from Glasgow to join the People's March on 2 May.[153]

The March 1981 ANL conference opened with its 150 delegates shocked by the death of Heather Bridget the day before. She was burnt to death in the boot of a stolen car, where she had been incarcerated by an NF supporter, who then jammed the car into the door of the SWP's Birmingham bookshop before setting it and the car on fire.[154] Delegates gave further reports of the growth of fascist and racist violence. Steve Marsh, NUSS Executive, told the conference:

> The BM and NF are recruiting white youth. We have to replace their activity with our own. We have to turn their rebelliousness onto the Tories and the bosses. It's no good simply branding them as nazis any more – we have to provide a positive, exciting alternative... Music is crucial. We have regular discos – now if you say in Sheffield that skinheads are Nazis, you would probably be killed![155]

Hence the backing for the People's March for Jobs: 'If the response of workers to unemployment is weak, the fascists will grow. We can undermine support for the fascists by a successful march with a massive pop concert at the end'.[156] The central argument of the conference was put by Simon Ogden, Sheffield ANL organiser: 'The only way to stop the fascists is by building mass activity to isolate them and confront them in an open way', avoiding 'tit for tat' responses. One example was when twenty NF armed 'with truncheons and an iron bar' invaded an SWP meeting on 'Labour and the Cuts' in Brixton with Holborow speaking – the response was to ensure the meeting took place two weeks later.[157]

Organised resistance continued.[158] Fascists were now confronted wherever they mobilised. Markland Chambers, a young black man, was murdered in Swindon by a Nazi in a fight between black youth and a large number of young whites, many of them skinheads. There were 100 protesters with ANL leaflets outside the police station the following day. A demonstration had been called for a fortnight later, but that was cancelled and not held until two months later , when 300 marched in the town with a banner reading 'Black and White Unite against Racialist Attacks'.[159] When the British Movement announced they would leaflet schools in Cheltenham, the ANL leafleted two of the schools the next morning and chased the BM off when they turned up at a third. A BM demonstration in Oxford 'melted away when over 500 anti-fascists, mostly local and young, marched against them'.[160]

As the May elections approached, in Gravesend, 700 demonstrators, led by the Indian Youth Federation, besieged an NF election meeting in a school attended by many Asian children. Protected by 250 police, a handful of NF members and twenty skinhead supporters took cover from 'bricks, stones and clumps of earth' to get into the building only to abandon the meeting after a few minutes and be helped over a back wall by the police. Eighteen demonstrators were arrested so the demonstration besieged the police station until they were released.[161] In Southall, having failed to get a school for an election meeting after the council refused permission and the caretaker refused to open the building, Webster announced he would hold a meeting in front of the school gates. In less than twelve hours, a committee including the ANL, the Indian Workers Front and the Indian Youth Association mobilised 500 people, many of them school students, forcing Webster to abandon his plan.[162] In the May 1981 local elections, the NF vote in Greater London fell to 21,000, compared to 119,000 four years earlier.[163]

NF marches had now shrunk to a few hundred and were only able to take place with police protection. One thousand seven hundred officers, more than half the South Wales police force, were unable to ensure that Webster's counter-demonstration in Cardiff opposing a Bloody Sunday Commemoration march could go according to plan. The ANL demonstration was able to force the fascists to change their route and hold their rally in the street.

John Carr was on the People's March for Jobs in early May 1981 as it arrived in Coventry on its way from Liverpool to London. Skilled engineering workers in Coventry had been among the highest paid in post-war Britain. Unemployment in the city doubled in 1981. Almost no school leavers found work. John remembers: 'On the outskirts of Coventry, loads of trade unionists with their banners... came to cheer us on... We came to the middle of the main shopping square... It was like the parting of the seas. There were hundreds, even thousands of people there clapping us.'[164]

In April a racist had murdered the young student Satnam Singh Gill in broad daylight in the centre of Coventry. The next day 400 people, members of Asian community groups, the IWA, Labour Party, CP, SWP and ANL, met and set up the Coventry Committee Against Racism. After some argument between young people and the committee, it was agreed to back self-defence groups and to pay any fines. When the BM appeared a couple of weeks later and the police arrested four of those who chased them away, 200 people went straight to the police station demanding their release. Fascists were now trying to stir up a 'race war' with almost daily attacks on Asians. The hall due to accommodate the People's March in Coventry had been firebombed a couple of days before the march arrived.

Three days after the People's March arrived in Coventry, 8,000 marched in protest against the murder of Satnam Singh. Phil Allsop remembers 'join[ing] thousands of others, including large numbers of local Asian youths'.[165] As the marchers reached the city centre, they were confronted by a 'racist street army' of around 200, throwing missiles, giving Nazi salutes and chanting 'Sieg Heil'. John Carr was one of a group on the People's March who joined the demonstration. He remembers how there were:

> Loads of people from various backgrounds. The turnout from the Asian community was amazing with women, young and old, at the forefront... We got to the end of the march and there was a police cordon with horses... behind them were young skinheads, a couple of hundred and more, throwing bricks and stuff at us, and shouting abuse and spitting. The next thing was the police lines opened up and these young skinheads came charging towards us. It was a combination of 'I can't believe the cops have just done that' while naively thinking they were supposed to be here to protect us and here they were letting these idiots, these far right scum, attack a peaceful march.[166]

Three weeks later, Dr Amal Dharry was stabbed in the heart by a seventeen-year-old skinhead. He died after ten days. His young attacker gave himself up admitting he had done it for a £15 bet that he would 'get a Paki that night'. Despite threats, The Specials, the chart-topping two-tone band, held a festival for racial harmony in their hometown's rugby stadium. Recognising that the labour movement had been absent on the demonstration that followed the murder of Satnam Singh, the ANL organised a Labour Movement Day of Action Against Racism, leafleting workplaces, shopping centres and housing estates. Forty thousand 'Will it happen again?' leaflets were given out with all big workplaces covered.

Riots: 'The language of the unheard'[167]

Boosted by Thatcher's support, police attacks on black and Asian communities grew with challenges to their actions rejected out of hand.[168] James Anderton, Manchester's chief constable, went so far as to say in his annual report: 'It is the duty of the state to protect its police.'[169] Three years of police harassment, mostly targeting young black people, prepared the ground for three days of rioting in Brixton in early April. The harassment had escalated with the 1981 officially titled Operation Swamp, with over a hundred plain clothes officers stopping and searching over a thousand people and arresting more than 150. The trigger was young people seeing 'the police put this kid who had been stabbed into a police car... remember[ing] Michael Ferreira who was stabbed... and not taken to the hospital but to the police station where he died from loss of blood'.[170] With local youths using petrol bombs, over 300 people were injured, many of them police, more than 100 vehicles damaged or destroyed and thirty buildings burnt out, with many more damaged, including a number of large supermarkets that were looted.[171]

Three months later in Southall, in the early evening of Friday 3 July, several hundred skinheads, led by Nazis, arrived by coach and cars for a concert at the Hambrough Tavern, well known as a pub used by fascists. Walking to the venue, they shouted racial abuse, smashed shop windows and attacked an Asian woman: 'As [the] news of the invasion spread... several hundred local youths – mostly Asian, but with a fair number of West Indians and some white youths – gathered at the Hambrough... Police arrived to protect the skinheads'.[172]

However, as Balwinder Rana reported, with bricks and petrol bombs and led by the Southall Youth Movement, the youth: 'Pushed the police and the fascists down the road. The whole community joined in the defence. Old men and women were coming out of their homes with stones and bottles in their hands and handing them over to the younger people... and the pub was set on fire.'[173] The next day, around the ashes, several thousand 'gathered chatting about how the fascists and the police had been taught a lesson. It was a lesson as well for the racist pubs in the area'.[174]

As the Hambrough was burning, in Toxteth, Liverpool, a crowd was rescuing Leroy Cooper, a black youth who had been wrongly arrested. A full-scale riot developed the following night, with overturned cars, barricades and petrol bombs. Barricades were built again the third night. By this time 'as many whites as blacks had joined the rioting'.[175] Seizing milk floats and a concrete mixer to drive at the police lines, they made 800 police retreat. Buildings were set on fire including a bank and a businessmen's club. With the police kept out of the area, people used trolleys to loot supermarkets. The police were clear that 'the rioters were mostly white'.[176]

By the fourth night the police were back in control, only for rioting to spread to Moss Side in Manchester for three nights where, on the second night, the local police station was nearly set alight.[177] Further rioting on a smaller scale now spread to dozens of cities and towns.[178] In Bradford, as rumours grew of an NF march, a group of Asian youth, members of the United Black Youth League, made petrol bombs in preparation for a possible attack on the community. Though the petrol bombs were never used, the police charged twelve members of the group with 'conspiracy to make explosives... for unlawful purposes'. After a thirty-one-day trial, arguing that their action was self-defence and therefore no offence, all twelve were acquitted.

Countering the argument that it was subversive elements who caused the riots, the SWP chair, Duncan Hallas, ridiculed the suggestion: 'You ask whether we exploited them [the riots]. So do the police. Law and order is a good way of diverting attention from the real problems of the inner cities. So long as we can, we will continue to organise youth into right-to-work and anti-fascist campaigns.'[179]

While Thatcher refused to acknowledge that institutional racism and unemployment were causes of the uprisings, her government quickly found money to expand the black voluntary sector, support local black businesses and finance regeneration of the inner-city areas.[180] It was a major shift in government strategy towards aiding the expansion of a black middle class.[181]

Leeds had the worst record of fascist violence outside London. Leeds ANL became one of the best organised in the country and held the successful Northern Carnival Against Racism on 4 July

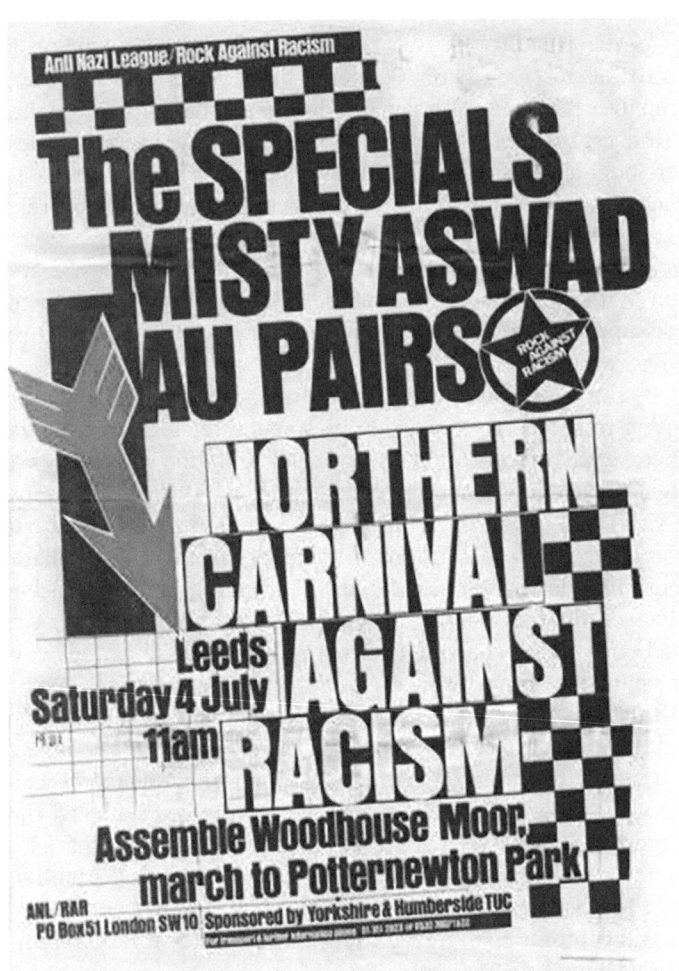

■ Leeds Carnival poster designed by Roger Huddle 1981

1981, the day after Leroy Cooper was rescued from the police and the Hambrough Tavern was set alight. Sponsored by Yorkshire & Humberside TUC, Sheffield Skins Against Nazis helped steward the march to Potternewton Park. Almost 20,000, including hundreds of skins, marched from Woodhouse Moor to the park, where the numbers grew.[182] 'It was like a Zebra crossing, black and white, black and white, as far as you can see.'[183] Alexander remembers:

> So wonderful, so big! The police came and negotiated with us. We had a cadre of young blacks. There was a problem of shops being looted as we marched. We organised an impromptu meeting and put the argument that we should show that this is our march, our day, and show our strength by stopping the looting, keeping the march focused. This was accepted and the looting stopped.[184]

With the Specials, Misty, Aswad and the Au Pairs on stage, Jerry Dammers remembers: 'The vibe out front and backstage was fantastic'.[185] Black and white unity was on stage with the Specials, a two-tone band. Their new release, 'Ghost Town', was heading to No.1 in the charts. Capturing 'the atmosphere of decay' of Thatcher's Britain, it was about to be taken up as 'the soundtrack to the riots'.[186] 'The most mixed Carnival we held' was proof that the corner had been turned.[187] Saunders recalled: 'When you saw 2-Tone, you went 'Job done'... This is what we dreamt of in 1976'.[188] The journalist Paul Wellings remembers the gig as 'the biggest show of unity I've ever seen and when they did "Ghost Town" I remember these black kids at the front losing their pork pie hats in all the carnage. To me Two-Tone was more revolutionary than punk with the way it brought working-class people of all colours together and this gig was the greatest example of that'.[189]

■Unity on march for Northern Carnival July 1978.

11: Why did the ANL succeed?

★ In July 1981, on the eve of the Leeds carnival, ten days of riots began in Liverpool. By the time they ended the NF's claim to lead white youth was damaged beyond repair by the black and white unity shown in taking on the police. As a leading rail trade unionist from Liverpool told a Labour activist conference in July: 'Toxteth saw the first white army in history to have black generals.'[1]

While police racism continued, so did the resistance to it. Only now it was more confident than before. Ten thousand, black and white, mainly young, marched through Liverpool six weeks after the riots demanding the resignation of the Merseyside chief constable.[2] Thrown onto the back foot, Thatcher's government was forced to shift from relying solely on the police and the courts to controlling black working-class youth. A combination of 'stick and carrot' was necessary. Despite cuts in government spending on everything except the military and the police, money for 'the carrot' was found. Often referred to as 'riot money', it paid for projects in deprived inner-city areas. Many of these projects gave jobs to youth activists.³ Balwinder Rana remembers picketing a meeting about funding in Southall set up by Michael Heseltine, Thatcher's Secretary of State for the Environment: 'Some of the leaders of the Southall Youth Movement were following him into the meeting like sheep and we were shouting "bloody traitors"'.⁴

The NF lost its ability to mobilise beyond its small, shrinking Nazi cadre. A national demonstration in support of Joe Pearce, jailed for six months for articles in *Bulldog* 'intended to stir up racial hatred', drew fewer than 400.⁵ Webster was banned from marching at the 1981 West Indian carnival. Only permitted to hold a rally, he was reduced to shouting over the voices of 150 ANL supporters who got through police barriers. He was further humiliated when, having been invited to speak at a high-profile debate in the Cambridge Union, the debate was cancelled because no credible opponent could be found willing to debate with him.

Increasingly, fascist activity meant 'hit and run' violence.⁶ An arson attack on the Khan family in Walthamstow in July 1981 killed Parveen Khan and her three children, with only her husband surviving.⁷ Young Asians set up a Massacre Action Committee and 10,000 ANL leaflets were distributed for a demonstration on the day of the Khans' funerals. This was called off after Home Secretary Whitelaw issued a thirty-day ban on all marches in Walthamstow. Nevertheless, despite a massive police presence on the day of the funeral, hundreds demonstrated, mainly young Asians, their protests continuing till late evening.

Weakened as the NF was, anti-fascist campaigning still required persistence. When students at Harrogate College picketed NF chairman Andrew Brons's lectures demanding he be sacked, he brought in Young NF members to threaten the pickets and attack members of the union executive. It took a year's campaigning, including two 500-strong demonstrations and a college occupation, to force him to keep a low profile in the college.⁸ The Kent university librarian, Dennis Whiting, survived a number of campaigns to get him sacked but was required to work in a 'non-student-facing role'.⁹ But the decline of the NF was clear. A long-standing NF member, who became an anti-fascist, remembers how the NF group he was part of in Manchester slowly became an ever smaller crowd who did no more than drink together in a pub.¹⁰ While the NF was able to keep up a local presence in Brighton during the 1980s,[11] the May 1981 Greater London election reflected their general decline. Their vote fell from 119,000 in 1977 to 21,600 in 1981, although the Conservatives also did badly, their votes falling from 1,197,000 in 1977 to 894,000. In the 1983 general election, the sixty NF candidates averaged 450 votes. Together they attracted just 0.1 percent of the total vote.

The ANL's campaigning from August 1980 to July 1981 weakened the fascists to the point that a national anti-fascist organisation with full time staff was no longer needed. The NF's inability to disrupt the carnival in Leeds, a city that had long been one of their strongholds, showed that local organisation could handle the fascists. The ANL was wound down without any announcement and the office was closed. A mailing list was kept ready for the organisation to be re-established if the fight had to be restarted, but, for now, it had done its job.

Darcus Howe, leading black activist and writer, speaking at the memorial service for David Widgery in 1992, illustrated the impact of the Anti Nazi League. Howe was the father of five children, 'four of which had grown up angry, forever fighting all around them'. The fifth had grown up 'black and at ease'. Howe attributed her space to the Anti Nazi League.[12] Selwyn Brown, Steel Pulse keyboard player, recalls 'how nervous we were when we played our first punk event. That simple act of black artists sharing the same stage as white artists was something that the Punk Rock, Roots Reggae, Two Tone and Rock Against Racism era helped to establish as the norm. Up to that time, this was very much a rarity.'[13]

The work of ANL and RAR strengthened the credibility of black and white unity fighting racism and fascism. The anti-racism of hundreds of thousands changed everyday language. Open racism was now more frequently challenged. 'Racist' became a dirty word with racists often starting their comments with the words 'I'm not a racist but...'. For Hassan Mahamdallie: 'The unifying vision that drove the ANL/RAR has been made real in the grassroots, multifaceted multiculturalism from below that has steadily advanced in recent years, despite the efforts of hostile forces to stunt its development and even reverse it... whatever challenges we presently face, the 1970s still feels a world away.'[14]

The experience changed many lives. Jerry Fitzpatrick, an organiser of the main carnivals, argues:

> It was a political action with passion and vision of its time and place. It was an insurrectionary and revolutionary moment post 1968 if you combine the mass carnivals and the determined resistance to Nazi marches. The turbulence was sometimes visceral as well as intellectual and politically inspiring and for that moment it demonstrated that the left could organise mass action with the potential to change the world.[15]

Unity in action

The ANL and RAR strengthened the anti-racist anti-fascist tradition, developing the ideas and skills of a new generation of activists. How was this done? The combination of the ANL and RAR had been a breakthrough. As Ian Birchall put it in his review of Widgery's *Beating Time*, the first history of the ANL and RAR to be written:

> The ANL did not succeed simply because it had the 'right line' on fighting racism, but rather because of how that line was presented. And that point has a wider relevance for the question of socialist propaganda; as Widgery argues: 'If socialism is transmitted in a deliberately doleful, pre-electronic idiom, if its emotional appeal is to working-class sacrifice and middle-class guilt and if its dominant medium is the ill-printed word and the drab public procession, it will simply bounce off people who have grown up on this side of the sixties watershed and leave barely a dent behind.'[16]

The movement was overwhelmingly made up of young people. Most of those who responded to the letter attacking Clapton's racism were between the ages of twelve and eighteen.[17] The success of RAR and the ANL lay in giving the youth their head. Young people formed the majority of the counter demonstrators at Lewisham and those who marched in protest against fascist killings and attacks. In their thousands, they challenged racist remarks, came to the demonstrations, carried lollipops, wore badges and danced at gigs and carnivals.

Trade unions, dominated by an older generation, moved more slowly. Nevertheless, despite the damage done to rank-and-file confidence by the Social Contract, in many workplaces ANL members strengthened the anti-racist anti-fascist presence using arguments reinforced by badges, leaflets and posters. This forced fascists to keep their heads down, getting management to take action against them. In some larger workplaces, ANL branches were established and though it took a persistent effort, every attempt by NF members to establish an organised presence in the workplace was broken. There were also many successes in getting union organisations at every level to affiliate, to donate money, to publicise ANL and RAR events and get members to take part with their banners. The ANL can take some credit for following through on the spirit of the Grunwick mass pickets, getting the TUC to campaign against racialism in the workplace such that *Searchlight* commented on how the TUC campaign bulletin showed a 'determination to oppose racialism at all levels and in particular within the trade union movement itself'.[18]

The 10,000 women in the ANL made up roughly a quarter of the total membership. In some areas, women's organisations such as WARF were affiliated. Women often played the leading role in teachers, hospital workers and other workplace groups. Nevertheless, their underrepresentation reflected the strength of sexism at the time. At a time when the women's movement was in crisis, Women Against the Nazis focussed on engaging women whose family commitments made taking part in collective action difficult. Rock Against Sexism stood out as an initiative that organised against the widespread, often unchallenged, sexism. Marian Peacock remembers how:

> on the question of male dominance, there was a tendency for men to be keen on their own leadership and an absence of the women's movement's emphasis on collaboration and agreement. My memory is of being pragmatic on the question, responding with a roll of the eyes, taking the piss and going off and doing your own thing anyway.[19]

Small groups of fascists still gathered at some football grounds, trying to exploit the racist abuse that targeted black players on the pitch.[20] Their much-reduced presence was not achieved through violence but through the force of large numbers of well organised opponents. A punk in Southall, Lewis Young, remembers:

> We were supporters of the Young National Front, everyone I knew was a racist, we were all racists, hard core. We engaged in petty intimidation and bullying of Asians and much graffiti work, putting up stickers and such like. But everywhere we went those fucking yellow lollipops appeared and their fucking stickers. Every time we put up an NF sticker, a RAR or ANL one would appear over it, or ours would be scratched off altogether. Those fucking lollipops man, you couldn't get away from them at school. In the end it sort of ground us down, too many black and Asian people against us, the white people who we thought of as traitors at the time, kept putting forward arguments that started to make sense to us. But ultimately, it was the music that did it. If Strummer and Costello and Malcolm [Owen, from The Ruts] were against us and we loved, really loved them, then maybe it was us who was wrong?[21]

Webster acknowledged this. Peter Hain described how when Webster tried, unsuccessfully, to defend himself against a libel case brought by Hain:

> [he] was extremely bitter and remarkably candid. The picture he gave, and he clearly believed it, was that prior to 1977, the NF was unstoppable and he was well on the way to becoming Prime Minister. Then suddenly the ANL was everywhere and knocked hell out of them. It obviously still hurt. He said the sheer presence of the ANL had made it impossible to get NF members onto the streets, had dashed recruitment and cut away at their vote. It wasn't just the physical opposition to the marches; they had lost the propaganda war too.[22]

Activity was key. Pete Jackson remembers: 'The work done by the ANL was crucial in keeping me away from the NF, and them away from me. Their inability to take to the streets without resistance meant they never managed to make contact with youngsters like me.'[23]

Building the united front

The starting point in the fight against the NF had to be recognising the danger it presented. The threat the organisation posed had to be spelt out plainly, it's members exposed as Nazis. Those who would be given the choice of voting for them in the general election expected in autumn 1978 had to know that there was mass opposition to accepting them as a legitimate political party with the same right to free speech as other parties. They had to recognise the 'NF=Nazi' label, even if they did not fully accept it.

This could only be done by mobilising tens of thousands, organising events that engaged hundreds of thousands and getting the arguments across to millions of potential voters. Every appearance by the NF had to be challenged whether in workplaces, in schools and colleges or in the media. Above all, they had to be confronted whenever they tried to march.

The numbers needed to do this could only be brought together as a united front. This involved two elements. It meant grasping the central argument made by Trotsky in his writings on the united front against fascism, summarised in one SWP internal document as: 'Fascism can only be smashed if revolutionaries succeed in drawing reformist influenced workers' organisations into the struggle against it.'[24] Had revolutionaries demanded that being anti-fascist required accepting the general politics of the revolutionary left, the response would have been narrow and isolated – and incapable of defeating the significant fascist force of the NF in the late 1970s.

But Trotsky's writings, invaluable though they were, were written for the situation in Germany between 1931 and 1933; they did not, as Jim Nichol pointed out, 'answer the question how a united front could be created to stop the new threat'.[25] So the second element necessary was to find ways of translating the united front into practice in the context of Britian in the late 1970s. As well as drawing in sections of the trade union movement, the Labour left and later the Communist Party and the Indian Workers' Associations, the ANL also involved being innovative, recruiting a large number of well-known people as sponsors, working with RAR, holding carnivals, organising football fans, letting 'a hundred flowers bloom'.

RAR played an essential role. For musician and RAR activist Mike Hobart, the response to the RAR letter revealed that 'the anti-racist mood in Britain, once mobilised, was stronger than that of the racist filth peddled by the Nazis and sections of the establishment. The organisation it gave birth to tapped into a reservoir of creativity and created an anti-racist wedge'.[26] A school student and RAR fan at the time, Nina Hammill remembers that 'RAR was about much more than just music, it taught me about unity, culture, politics and revolution, and how music is an important part of all those things, and showed me that if enough of us get together, we can stop racists and fascists from spreading their filth'.[27] For John Dennis, full-time RAR organiser between 1978 and 1981: 'RAR had created a confidence in a community and a sense of belonging... Racism became identified with the state, institutional racism in the police, not racism person to person.'[28]

RAR and the ANL became inseparably intertwined. Red Saunders disagreed with 'people like Dave Widgery [who] felt [RAR] didn't need the ANL, but I thought it was important. If there was a carnival, who was leafleting the factory? Who was booking the coaches? Who was getting trade union money? Suddenly we had money and that let us book huge venues. Where were you going to get the £10,000 to book the PA?[29] Jerry Fitzpatrick saw the events of 1978 and 1979, in particular Lewisham and the two carnivals, as:

> a unique coming together of politics, music, Rock and Culture. A political coordinated burst of energy that made a real difference. Of course I'd say that. I was one of the organisers. But it wasn't just me. There was Peter Hain, working in ways that were never acknowledged, winning us allies, breaking it away from the usual supporters. Peter was our most powerful advocate of 'Unity in action'. Remember the Stop the 70s tour. There were the local activists across the country and people like Mike and Joan [in the national office].[30] How many leaflets do they send out, how many hours do they spend stuffing envelopes? There are plenty of individuals who did a huge amount, and it was one of the most successful moments in the history of the political left.[31]

Unity against the fascists was at the heart of the success. As the *Morning Star* put it: 'If Paul Holborow and Bill Dunn [CP industrial organiser] can work together, despite political differences, then so can organisations, groups and people up and down the land. No one except racists – the new nazis – are excluded. The "secret" formula for success is unity.'[32] Jerry Fitzpatrick points out that it 'made a major impact. We mobilised way beyond anything the left had done in years. The NF was neutered, demoralised, in retreat'.[33] It was clear that every attempt by fascists to appear in public would be challenged by a united front to stop them.

But how was this possible? For the ANL it was providing the means for a united response with the speed and skill that made it possible to overcome the sectarianism that dogged the left. The skill lay in identifying the objective – working together to stop the National Front in the forthcoming general election and making it happen on a massive scale. This included convincing three Labour MPs, two union officials, the editor of *Searchlight* and two SWP members to work together. For RAR, 'It was the sixties that made us'.[34] RAR connected the creativity of the revolutionary movement of the 1960s with a generation whose life opportunities were being trashed as the long boom ended.

From the start, with Labour MPs and leading trade unionists the first to sign the Founding Statement, the ANL was rooted in the working-class movement. Its rapidly growing membership, including many unconnected to the movement, led some to argue it was a popular front modelled on those of the 1930s established by Communist parties after Hitler came to power. These popular fronts aimed at winning support from all parties committed to parliamentary democracy, including those parties outside the working-class movement. This gave the non-working class parties the ability to threaten to leave if actions were too militant for their liking. Communist parties dealt with this by restraining their own activities and propaganda to keep the popular front together. In both Spain and France, where strong popular fronts had been established, this had catastrophic consequences and led to a fascist victory.[35] The ANL rejected this approach, instead allowing all parties to keep their political independence, leaving them free to criticise the others on all issues except the objectives of the united front. Thus, although working together with Labour Party members in the ANL, *Socialist Worker* was free to attack the Callaghan government, and consistently did so.

The success of the ANL's collaboration with RAR in organising the Victoria Park Carnival meant the anti-racist anti-fascist movement became a mass movement that hundreds of thousands could identify with. As *Socialist Worker* said of the Carnival: 'A whole new generation of young marchers made Sunday a turning point. The ANL is now a mass movement. After years of small committees against racialism, many of them hog tied by conventional politics or by sectarianism, the ANL has proved that there are masses of people who hate fascism and will march against it.'[36]

ANL and RAR activists were overwhelmingly in their teens or twenties. Today, fifty years later, many still have their ANL badges, a memento of how they became politically active. Their 'learning by doing' was strengthened by working with those who had fought the fascists in the 1930s and again after the Second World War.[37] The strong support of both a large number of left Labour MPs and the Communist Party was significant. The CP's presence in the working-class movement opened many doors, even if its top-down, 'socialism from above' tradition of organising made it slow to get involved.[38]

The anti-fascist collaboration overwhelmed every effort of the fascists to return to the offensive. The NF was decisively defeated in the May 1979 general election. Shortly after, without one dissenting voice, the ANL conference agreed to move on from targeting the NF to taking on state racism and setting up a new national organisation, the Campaign Against Racist Laws – an enormous and ongoing battle which is far from being won.

The ANL and RAR's success made possible the swift relaunch of the national ANL in August 1980 for a second campaign that defeated the NF's capacity to organise on the streets. This was despite many activists being heavily involved in campaigns to defend jobs, living standards, welfare, public services and union rights. The movement led by the ANL and RAR in the 1970s and early 1980s contributed to the strength of anti-racism today.

The SWP and the ANL

Some journalists wanted to show the ANL was being used by the SWP. On the day of the Victoria Park Carnival, the *Sunday Express* told readers:

> many of those marching will be ignorant of a behind-the-scenes bid by the Trotskyist Socialist Workers Party to take over the League. Clear proof of this is contained in a confidential 18 page internal bulletin prepared by the SWP which already has one of its staunchest members, 29-year-old university graduate Paul Holborow, installed as the League's full-time paid secretary.[39]

Interviewed by a journalist, Holborow 'made no bones about his membership of the SWP', telling the interviewer he 'was very happy to be a member'. When the interviewer asked whether the influence of the SWP in the ANL was too strong, Holborow referred to a recent letter to the *Times* from himself and Peter Hain which acknowledged that:

> along with many other individuals of varying affiliations – socialist, liberal and the politically non-aligned – members of the SWP do play a role in the Anti Nazi League. But that does not detract from the broad based, non-sectarian character of the League. Indeed, it enhances it, by bringing together tens of thousands of people who may disagree between themselves on other issues and on tactics, but who are united in their determination to wage an activist campaign against Britain's new Nazis.[40]

Was the SWP trying to recruit out of the ANL? The *Sunday Express*'s accusation that the SWP hoped that it would win new members from its activity in the ANL was correct. In practice, though, it was not a straightforward matter. For many who came to the carnival, it was their first active engagement with politics. Revolutionary ideas were only one part of the rich mix they encountered. Jim Nichol had arranged for Cliff to come to Newcastle to speak at an SWP public meeting the week after the carnival and made sure there was an SWP member on each of the eight coaches with a supply of leaflets for the meeting. He remembers that not one person came to the meeting because of the leaflet.[41]

One reason was that the confidence in working-class self activity had been in retreat since the Labour government had taken over in 1974. The working-class victories over the Heath government had been replaced by a decline in strikes, falling living standards, cuts and rising unemployment. Arguing for revolutionary politics as the way forward had become harder.[42]

In truth, every organisation that supported the ANL hoped to win members. Joe Ashton MP told the Bristol ANL launch meeting that 'the Labour Party anti-Front political broadcast had brought in 3,000 new recruits for the Labour Party, and he was looking for more'.[43] Peter Hain would later say:

> In the end, it was the Labour Party which benefited most from young people joining the ANL, as they went on to join Labour rather than the SWP. Most ANL activists had not been involved in politics before. Through their experience, in the ANL, of anti-racist activity, they were politicised. But contrary to what the SWP no doubt hoped and as the SWP leaders privately admitted, the Labour Party mainly benefitted from recruitment of people whose first experience was ANL.[44]

Writing in the *Daily Mirror* in September, Keith Waterhouse dismissed fears about the SWP's role:

> On the whole, the League has managed to do what no one has done since the heady days of the Aldermaston marches. It has persuaded the young that there ARE some brave new causes left. If it is all a Trot conspiracy, tough luck on the conventional political parties which play it all so safe and down the middle that they have the popular appeal of yesterday's gravy.[45]

There were those who supported the launch of ANL while arguing that a conference was needed to set up a democratic organisation, including the election of a national leadership. John Shiers was one of those who contended:

> We need not just a conference about it, but some kind

of machinery in which the anti-fascist movement can democratically decide its strategy on demonstrations. Where people in SWP can put their views and people like me can put mine, and where people who choose to march under an anti-fascist movement banner would respect the democratic decision on strategy made. The whole issue of what slogans to use and what demands to make (e.g. whether or not to demand that the State ban the NF) can be fully discussed there.[46]

This was never going to be a simple task. *Guardian* journalist and author Martin Walker had argued a year earlier that 'a disciplined common front' of the left was 'almost impossible'.[47] The two day national conference organised by the All London Anti-Racist Anti-Fascist Coordinating Committee (ARAFCC) in June 1978 failed to set up a national anti-racist anti-fascist organisation.[48] By contrast, the ANL conference the following month succeeded in both discussing political differences – the question of immigration controls – and showing how the united front strategy was working successfully.[49] In practice, the growth of the ANL as a mass movement shifted the relationship between competing organisations from debating ideas to testing them in the real world. While there were serious differences, most importantly the question of whether change comes through parliament or through mass mobilisation, unity in action against the National Front grew.[50]

The accusation that the ANL was an SWP front insulted the intelligence of the tens of thousands who were involved. The ANL's supporters included fifty local Labour parties, twenty-five trades councils, thirteen shop steward committees, eleven NUM lodges. Thirty union branches of engineering workers were affiliated to the ANL. There were also affiliated branches organising railway workers, civil servants, textile workers, local government staff, print workers, journalists, TV and radio technicians, post workers, firefighters. Twenty-six union executive committees voted to support the ANL.[51]

Kate Webb, RAR's first full-time paid worker, told *Sounds* 'I don't know how many times we've got to say it but RAR is completely independent. I'm not an SWP member, other people aren't. In fact, most aren't'.[52] In a lengthy *Times* article on the role of the SWP, Peter Hain explained that neither he nor Neil Kinnock were being manipulated by anyone. The article gave an example of how a united front can contain unresolved tensions; at the ANL fringe meeting at the 1978 NUT easter conference, Martin Flannery, MP for Sheffield Hillsborough, although due to speak, 'refused to do so when he found Mr Tariq Ali and members of the SWP on the platform'.[53] Such examples are to be expected. A united front on the scale of the ANL will always require a huge number of decisions about when and how action is taken. Not all will be successfully resolved. They can only be overcome if those taking part work together on the agreed objective, despite the many differences. The SWP's central committee insisted: 'We have to be clear what the Anti Nazi League is. It is not a front for the SWP. It is a united front between us and many other people formed around a political programme that does not go nearly as far as our own'. [54]

Given these comments, it could be asked 'Could a campaign against the NF have succeeded without the SWP?' Such counterfactual questions are by their very nature impossible to answer with any certainty. It is nevertheless reasonable to claim that the SWP played a critical role in the ANL's success. Its insistence on working-class self-organisation, particularly in workplaces, was not only central in its propaganda. The organisation had a track record of putting its ideas into practice, for example, organising rank-and-file groupings and the Right to Work Campaign.[55] Its growth from a few hundred to a few thousand over the previous decade helped it develop a confidence in its revolutionary politics. It had revived a tradition that was all but invisible in a political landscape dominated by Social Democracy – the Labour Party – and, to a declining extent, Stalinism – the Communist Party. It had a cadre that had the capacity to launch the ANL. Kate Alexander argues that this would not have been possible without the SWP's: 'Commitment, discipline and sometimes the courage of its members, [their] eagerness to work alongside other anti-fascists, most importantly members of the Labour Party, and the dexterity and imagination in putting this united front into practice.'[56]

Lucy Whitman was a RAR activist, member of *Temporary*

Hoarding's editorial collective writing as Lucy Toothpaste, and co-founder of Rock Against Sexism. Her description of the SWP's contribution to RAR is worth quoting at length:

> One of the great strengths of RAR was that from the outset it attracted an incredibly talented team of writers, designers, photographers and amateur impresarios, who were united both in their dedication to the anti-racist cause and in their genuine enthusiasm for the music. It would have fallen flat on its face if it was just a bunch of well-meaning lefties who had no interest in the cultural explosion that was going on at the time. However, the roots of some of the founder members in the organised left (primarily the International Socialists, forerunner of the Socialist Workers Party), though scoffed at by some, was advantageous in many ways: there was a bedrock of experience in organising events and demonstrations; there was a network of contacts which made it possible to protect our events from the very real danger of attack by fascist thugs, and to link up eventually with the Anti-Nazi League for the carnivals; there was a knowledge base about the history of political and cultural struggles which informed our whole approach, especially the look, feel and content of our fanzine, *Temporary Hoarding*; and last but not least, there was the use of the SWP print shop in Hackney, without which it would have been a lot more difficult to produce all our wonderful artefacts.[57]

The relationship between the SWP and the ANL was described by the journalist Gavin Weightman: 'Raise the lid on any part of the ANL and you are likely to find an SWP member inside, but it would be wrong to conclude from that that the league is SWP-controlled. The ANL is barely controlled at all, except in the sense that it has been efficient in producing and distributing its propaganda.'[58] As was often explained, the ANL steering committee, meeting in the House of Commons, had twice as many Labour MPs on it as SWP members.

Nor was the SWP an all-seeing, always correct party. The political context of the shift from the growing class confidence of 1974 to its opposite over the years of Labour's Social Contract was only slowly recognised. It was not 'smooth sailing'. Some large SWP districts lost members. In that difficult situation, the success of RAR and the ANL triggered a crisis over the editorial line of the SWP's 'flagship', *Socialist Worker*. The issue was whether to maintain the focus on experienced militants or to have stronger coverage of music and sport, less space allocated to industrial reports, and a design aiming to attract younger readers, the short-lived 'punk paper'.[59]

Not all SWP members understood and accepted the united front and the strategy of mass mobilisation. The understandable tendency to look for shortcuts caused some to lose sight of the essential need to mobilise the largest number possible prepared to confront the fascists. Instead, they formed squads to attack the enemy physically. The SWP's policy:[60]

> has always contained two elements – the widest possible mobilisations against the fascists plus an insistence that these mobilisations cannot be content merely to protest at them but must endeavour to drive them from the streets... However the need for physical measures against the Nazis often gives rise to... the belief that physical measures by small, highly organised secretive groups can smash Nazism. Those who [hold this belief]... tend not to take part in the organisation of mass mobilisations... Instead they concentrate their efforts of forming small squads of comrades which keep apart from the main body of people on demonstrations, beat up isolated Nazis in the side streets and emphasise retaliatory violence against Nazi attacks.
> There is an alternative to squadism. It lies in public mobilisation, public responses to Nazi attacks, on building a base among wider groups of people on the housing estates and in the factories in order to isolate the fascists instead of going underground and isolating ourselves...
> If we can isolate the hard core Nazis from their periphery, then things are much easier for us. If we carry out open propaganda and agitation then people will understand what we are at when we defend ourselves and when we mobilise to keep the Nazis off the streets and may even come to our support. If we rely on squadist retaliation then they will see it all as nothing more than a form of sub-political gang

warfare, and we will be left alone to suffer the worst that the fascists can offer.

Overall, the ANL and RAR and the SWP's role in both 'reminds us that revolutionaries have been capable of mass mobilisation and of affecting the course of events. The collapse of the NF in 1979 was not inevitable.'[61] Peter Hain explained to the Undercover Police Inquiry how: 'The insistence that the ANL was based on the working class movement meant there was a clear political orientation for this to be renewed whenever there was a need to relaunch which it can be argued grew stronger as the generation who were young in 1978 gradually took more and more position within the movement.'[62]

The ANL did not produce large numbers of recruits for the Socialist Workers Party. The main benefit for the SWP was learning to lead, better able to 'punch above its weight'.[63] Julian Goss remembers a national mobilisation by the NF against a Bloody Sunday Commemoration march in Cardiff in 1981:

> We had to organise on two fronts. I think we did it well. By then we had experience that really helped. We were able to take on the fascists first and join the Irish demonstration once the fascists had been defeated. That required real discipline and political understanding. It meant we were leading people. It's one thing not to lose a committee meeting. It is another to be leading hundreds of people on the street.[64]

The ANL and RAR both benefitted from and contributed to anti-apartheid struggle. One reason Jerry Dammers gives for working with RAR was his involvement nine years earlier, aged fifteen, in the campaign against apartheid. Preparing to go on a demonstration against the all-white South African Springboks rugby team, he 'put stickers around the school and managed to recruit a posse of about two others to come on the demonstration'. In turn, his involvement with RAR was an important influence when he wrote his song 'Free Nelson Mandela'. That led to:

> Dali Tambo, the son of the leader of the ANC Oliver Tambo, asking me to organise Artists Against Apartheid in Britain. We held a series of concerts, based to an extent on the

Rock Against Racism model, and that sense of concerts grew into the largest Anti Apartheid demonstration ever held anywhere at the time, the 200,000 strong Clapham Common concert in 1986. That in turn led to the two Wembley Stadium Mandela concerts that were seen by millions of people around the world. I think it is highly likely all that would not have happened in the way it did, if it hadn't been for the inspiration, success, and not to mention the support, of Rock Against Racism. That organisation and Red Saunders, as well as the Anti Nazi League do deserve a share in some of whatever credit may be due for all that stuff happening in Britain.[65]

Just as the ANL benefitted from the collective memory of pre-war anti-fascists, so, when a fascist won a council by-election on the Isle of Dogs in 1993, the memory of the successes in the 1970s made it easier to relaunch the ANL. Julian Goss rang Rhodri Morgan, leader of both the Welsh Assembly and the Welsh Labour Party. Goss told Morgan: "The Anti Nazi League is going to be relaunched and we're going to put an advert in the *Guardian* and we want as many people as possible signing it'. Before I could finish the sentence, he said, 'Put my signature on it". I said, "You haven't seen the statement yet." This was before emails. "Doesn't matter. Put my name on it".[66] In the summer of 2018 Tommy Robinson and thousands of his supporters rampaged through Whitehall, briefly occupying Trafalgar Square. This led John McDonnell, Shadow Chancellor of the Exchequer, to ask whether this was the time for the Anti Nazi League to be re-formed.[67] In response, a letter from leading members of the ANL and RAR argued that it was still relevant to apply: 'the ANL's tactics of mass propaganda, unrelenting opposition to the racists and fascists wherever they organise, and the cultural appeal that ANL/RAR pioneered, with large-scale music and similar events asserting the values of our multiracial and diverse society.'[68]

The carnivals' combination of politics and music was quickly adopted in different contexts. The summer of 1979 saw two Rock Against Repression concerts in Catholic Belfast.[69] The same summer in Germany, 40,000 broke a police ban to march to a Rock Gegen Rechts (Rock Against the Right) concert in

Frankfurt, challenging a rally by the fascist National Democratic Party of Germany.[70] In the US, a Rock Against Racism tour covered a dozen cities.[71]

Lessons learnt and not learnt

Using the ANL experience to apply the united front tactic in opposition to fascist forces in other countries was a much greater challenge. An important example is KEERFA, United Against Racism and the Threat of Fascism, in Greece. Responding to the rise of LAOS, a far right, populist party in the early 2000s, KEERFA was initiated by SEK, the SWP's sister organisation. Supported by many unions and artists such as Mikis Theodorakis, the famous composer, KEERFA was a united front bringing together unions, left-wing parties and migrant, Muslim and LGBT+ communities.[72]

The 2008 financial crash tipped Greece into a deep crisis that the European Union and the IMF insisted could only be resolved through massive cuts in people's living standards. As workers fought back with a series of general strikes, the governing coalition of centre left and centre right parties (that also included LAOS) lost support and were heavily defeated in the 2012 general election. The fascist anti-refugee Golden Dawn took over as the main force on the far right with twenty-one seats in parliament. They now intensified their violence, smashing up shops owned by migrants, burning mosques and killing the Pakistani retail worker Shazad Luqman and the anti-fascist rapper, Pavlos Fyssas. They were protected by the police who carried out mass arrests of immigrants, strip-searching 100,000 and holding 8,000 in a detention centre.

Built from the bottom up, organising counter demonstrations as large as possible to deprive the fascists of public space and undermining their claims to be respectable, KEERFA worked with other anti-fascist coalitions and local groups in order to defeat the Nazis. Local councils were called on to deny halls, squares and other spaces to Golden Dawn. Campaigns were launched in the unions, particularly in schools and hospitals, to make sure that refugees and their children were not excluded. A campaign was launched to stop Golden Dawn appearing on the state-run radio and TV, ERT, the union threatening to strike if the fascists were put on air. KEERFA lawyers played a leading role in getting Golden Dawn's leadership into court to face charges. The activity around the trial was an important part of KEERFA's election campaign, which triumphed with Golden Dawn losing all its seats in the 2019 parliamentary elections. Soon after, Golden Dawn began to split, its headquarters were closed, the website shut down, its leadership imprisoned. After this decisive victory, KEERFA acknowledged the parallels with the struggle against the NF: 'We owe a lot to the Anti Nazi League which provides an example of how to fight the Nazis and we have built on that tradition.'[73]

The contrast with France is significant. Within three years of the National Front's defeat in Britain at the hands of the Anti Nazi League, the French Front National of Jean-Marie Le Pen made its initial breakthrough. In 1983 the FN won control of the council in a small town fifty miles from Paris, Dreux (thanks in part to an electoral alliance with the traditional conservative right). The following year it gained over two million votes in elections to the European Parliament, just under 11 percent of the overall votes.

Formed in 1972 on the initiative of the fascist group *Ordre Nouveau* (New Order), the Front National sought to both pull together the various strands of the French far right and to attract more respectable figures towards it. The aim was that such 'camouflage' would allow it to move out of the political margins and gather significant electoral support. As the leaders of *Ordre Nouveau* put it: 'The success of this policy requires that we should not appear in the eyes of the public to be the main component, even if such is the reality.'[74] Having attracted a wider audience through masking its continued commitment to fascism, the aim would be one of 'transforming them in our own image' – hardening initially softer racist supporters into committed fascists.[75]

Yet the new organisation made little wider impact in its first decade. In 1981 having announced Jean-Marie Le Pen as its candidate for the presidential election, the FN was unable to collect the required number of signatories to take part in the election.[76]

This changed from 1983, thanks in large part to widespread

disillusion with the Socialist-led government of the victor of the presidential race, François Mitterrand. Mitterrand's promised programme of expanding public spending was quickly abandoned with a sharp turn to austerity in 1982 and 1983. Both the parliamentary left – Mitterrand's Socialists and the French Communist Party – and their conservative opposition used attacks on immigrants to compete for support. The impact was to legitimise Le Pen, who now also began to gain access to the mass media.[77]

By the 1986 French parliamentary elections, the FN was able to more than double the size of its electorate to 4.375 million, a result that now gave it thirty-five MPs. In the 1988 presidential election, not only was Le Pen able to gather sufficient signatories to stand but he took fourth place. Over the following decades the Front was able to entrench itself in the French political system, changing its name to Rassemblement National in 2018 under the leadership of Marine Le Pen, Jean-Marie's daughter.

The dominant anti-racist initiative in the 1980s, SOS Racisme, took an approach very different to that of the Anti Nazi League. Led by Harlem Désir, SOS Racisme showed an initial potential to give anti-racism mass appeal. It held a series of huge multicultural music concerts and its famous badge and slogan 'Don't touch my pal' was bought reportedly by a million people. Yet, as the historians Fysh and Wolfreys put it, overall SOS Racisme had 'little effect in countering the rise of the NF'. Why was this?

The initiative to found SOS Racisme had come from Mitterrand's office itself: 'the association [SOS Racisme] owed its meteoric rise to help from the Socialist [Party] establishment, astutely aware of their need to widen their bases of support of Mitterrand's campaign for re-election.'[78] But this came with an insistence on a political direction acceptable to the Socialist Party leadership. Crucially this meant avoiding any campaign directly targeting the Front National, substituting instead a general moral version of anti-racism – a 'vague melting-pot vision of a non-racist society'.

Desir told *Le Monde* that far from targeting the Front when it tried to organise in public, the key was to fix the lifts in rundown housing estates which acted as breeding ground for the Front.

Desir also would suggest that Mitterrand's re-election would bring the growth of the Front 'to a halt'.[79] Instead, once re-elected Mitterrand quickly betrayed his allies in SOS Racisme, declaring that France had now reached a 'threshold of tolerance' for immigration, while his prime minister Edith Cresson boasted that planes would be chartered to deport illegal immigrants.[80] This only boosted Le Pen and the FN further.

Crucially, the French revolutionary left did not attempt to construct an anti-fascist united front as the SWP had with the Anti Nazi League. This could have sought to focus on challenging the FN's legitimacy and confronting it with mass mobilisations when it appeared in public – which by necessity would have had to involve reaching an audience far beyond the revolutionary left. Instead, the initiative was left in the hands of the Socialist Party establishment, which subordinated anti-racism and anti-fascism to its own electoral calculations. The price was heavy – Le Pen and the FN were given the space to root themselves in the French political system and society.[81]

Into the twenty-first century: The beast is not dead

A century ago, the Italian revolutionary Antonio Gramsci wrote: 'The old world is dying… the new world struggles to be born. In this gap, many "monsters" appear.'[82] Today, the climate crisis, pandemics, financial meltdowns and wars herald a new Age of Catastrophe.[83] Racism continues to be indispensable for ruling classes to divide and rule.

The crisis of the liberal centre is once again opening the door to the far right and fascists. Such forces are making gains in country after country on a scale far beyond anything seen since the Second World War, if not yet with the scale of street armies that Hitler and Mussolini came to possess in the interwar decades. Yet all is not lost – far from it, if we act decisively. But we can afford neither complacency nor panic and political paralysis.

Anti-racism is a force as never before. The Black Lives Matter movement that exploded after the murder of George Floyd by a police officer, 25 May 2020, in Minneapolis, saw between 7,500 to 10,000 protests in the US, protests that were 'much more multiracial and much more likely to penetrate into suburban and into rural areas than had previously been the case'.[84] The

New York Times reported a survey suggesting between fifteen and twenty-six million took part in protests in the US by early July 2020 – the largest in American history.[85] On Saturday 6 June, 15,000 marched in Manchester. The next day 10,000 demonstrated in Bristol with the statue of the slave trader Edward Colston being pushed into the city harbour. A week later, the home secretary, Priti Patel, told parliament that 210,000 had protested in demonstrations in Britain in 160 towns and cities over the previous weekend.[86]

Can we mobilise such forces to defeat today's far right and fascist threat? In the fight against the politics of despair, the history of the ANL is a source of hope. Since the destruction of the NF, every attempt by fascists to launch electoral or street-based fascist initiatives has been defeated with the ANL's successor organisations, Unite Against Fascism and Stand Up to Racism, playing a leading role.[87] A tradition has been established rejecting any reliance on the state in favour of mass collective action applied with confidence and imagination. As Lenin put it, people must 'rely on *their* OWN forces, on *their* OWN organization, on *their* OWN unity, and on *their* OWN weapons alone'.[88] We face a double task – to defeat today's fascist threat *and* to defeat the system that opens the door to them. If we are to put the brakes on the locomotive of history taking us over a cliff into unimaginable barbarism, we have to destroy the monsters once and for all. We have to use our power to make a society that realises the principle 'From each according to their ability, to each according to their needs'.[89]

■ Northern Carnival July 1978

Endnotes

Introduction

1   The phrase 'countless small actions' is from the historian Howard Zinn. He argues that: 'The history of social movements often confines itself to the large events, the pivotal moments... Missing from such history are the countless small actions of unknown people that lead up to those great moments. When we understand this, we can see that the tiniest acts of protest in which we engage may become the invisible roots of social change'. Howard Zinn, *You Can't be Neutral on a Moving Train: A Personal History of Our Times* (Beacon, 1994), p.24. Robert Paxton also prioritises deeds over words. See his *The Anatomy of Fascism* (Penguin, 2005), pp.10–15.

2   Zinn, 1994.

3   See interviews and archives in the Bibliography. There are histories of the ANL in cities such as Bristol. I'm keen to help people to write their histories of their own towns and cities. It can be argued that memories are more unreliable than written texts. I would suggest that both are unreliable in their own ways, and it is always a matter of judgment how to use them. See Christopher Hill, *A Nation of Change and Novelty* (Routledge, 1990), ch.2.

4   There is a website accompanying this book that includes additional material.

5   See Colin Thomas, *Facing up to the Fascists: Confronting the National Front in Bristol* (Bristol Radical Pamphleteer, 2019); Tony Greenstein, *The Fight against Fascism in Brighton & the South Coast* (Brighton History Workshop, 2011).

6   Theodore Allen, *The Invention of the White Race: The Origin of Racial Oppression* (Verso, 2021).

'Rivers of Blood'

1   The full text of the speech is available here https://anth1001.wordpress.com/wp-content/uploads/2014/04/enoch-powell_speech.pdf. Powell believed that, even as its colonies won independence, some form of British imperial power remained possible. It was in this paternalist spirit that, as minister of health in 1960, he actively recruited nurses from the Caribbean to work in the NHS.

2   See https://anth1001.wordpress.com/wp-content/uploads/2014/04/enoch-powell_speech.pdf

3   Powell claimed he had received 65,000 letters of support within days with only thirty against. Olivier Esteves found 20 percent of these letters were critical of the speech. See Olivier Esteves, 'Wrathful rememberers: Harnessing the memory of World War II in letters of support to Powell', in Olivier Esteves & Stéphane Porion, eds., *The Lives and Afterlives of Enoch Powell: The Undying Political Animal* (Routledge, 2019).

4   '74 pc back Powell on immigrants', *Daily Telegraph* 7 May 1968. A Gallup Poll between 26 and 29 April asked 'In general, do you agree or disagree with what Mr Powell said in his speech on coloured immigrants?' 74 percent agreed, 15 percent disagreed, 11 percent didn't know.

5   'Coloured family attacked', *Times* 1 May 1968, p.1.

6   Hanif Kureishi, 'Knock knock, it's Enoch', *Guardian* 12 December 2014. See also Hanif Kureishi, *My Beautiful Laundrette & The Rainbow Sign* (Faber, 1986).

7   *Times* 25 April 1968. Danny Harmston, one of London's best-known fascists, a supporter of Oswald Mosley, worked as a supervisor in Smithfield meat market.

8   Ian Birchall remembers that Jack Dash, the leading dock worker militant, member of the Communist party, was 'ill' and didn't turn up. Birchall, private communication 11 December 2023.

9   Jim Nichol, private communication 16 October 2021. 'Social security' was the name of the welfare benefits system in this period.

10 Ian Birchall, *The smallest mass party in the world, Socialist Workers Party, 1951–1979* (Socialists Unlimited, 1981), p.15; Ian Birchall, *Tony Cliff, A Marxist for His Time* (Bookmarks, 2011), p.284–5; Jim Nichol private communication, 16 October 2021. The International Socialists (IS), which became the Socialist Workers Party (SWP) in January 1977, responded to Powell's speech by proposing a single organisation of revolutionary socialists to meet 'The urgent challenge of fascism', Nigel Copsey, *Anti-Fascism in Britain* (Routledge, 2016), p.112; David Widgery, *The Left in Britain 1956–68* (Penguin 1976), pp.411–12. Ian Birchall thinks one of Barrett's leaflets was written by Paul Foot. For a full description of Powell's anti-immigrant politics, see Shirin Hirsch, *In the Shadow of Enoch Powell* (Manchester, 2018). Barrett joined the picket line with his own placard and leaflet headed, 'Strike Against the Employers – not your Fellow Workers'. Some weeks later, 'Terry was at a mass meeting moving an overtime ban only to be heckled by a few racists who shouted that he had scabbed on the strike. The cry went up that he had not. He had been on the picket line armed with his own views', Jim Nichol, private communication 16 October 2021.

11 *Times* 11 March 1964, cited in Paul Foot, *Immigration and Race in British Politics* (Penguin, 1965), p.44.

12 The BNP led by John Bean merged into the National Front in 1967. See Chapter 2.

13 Rick Blackman, *Babylon's Burning* (Bookmarks, 2021), p.82. When visiting Jamaica as prime minister in the 1950s, Churchill made his opposition to immigration clear, saying to his host, the governor of Jamaica, 'We don't want to become a magpie nation, do we?', in Margaret Renn, *Paul Foot: A Life in Politics*, (Verso, 2024), p.292.

14 Martin Walker, 'The National Front', in H. M. Drucker, ed., *Multi-Party Britain* (Macmillan, 1979), p.55.

15 Walker, p.56.

16 Richard Crossman, *The Diaries of a Cabinet Minister*, vol.1 (Cape, 1975), p.149–50.

17 Shortly before the speech, Powell told a journalist 'I deliberately include at least one startling assertion in every speech in order to attract enough attention to give me a power base within the Conservative party', *Sunday Times* 29 December 1968. Quoted in Hirsch, 2018, p.21. The

new Race Relations bill, strengthening the provisions of the 1965 act over housing and employment, was to be debated the following week in parliament, Race Relations bill, *Hansard* 23 April 1968, https://hansard.parliament.uk/commons/1968-04-23/debates/a7bab9b3-9009-4102-aa9c-d5f34f8f1dfc/RaceRelationsBillv

18   *Guardian* 26 February 1968; 'A racialist law for Britain', *Tribune* 1 March 1968. The demonstration was supported by the National Council for Civil Liberties (NCCL), Joint Council for the Welfare of Immigrants (JCWI), Movement for Colonial Freedom (MCF), Campaign Against Racial Discrimination (CARD) and the Society of Friends, the Quakers.

19   Brockway had a long record of opposing racism. See John Newsinger, 'In the middle of the road: Fenner Brockway, the Independent Labour Party and the class struggle', *International Socialism* 179, Summer 2023. I have taken the phrase 'reducing their social and cultural visibility' from Fred Lindop, 2001, 'Racism and the working class: Strikes in support of Enoch Powell in 1968', *Labour History Review* vol.66, no.12.

20   https://thehistoryofparliament.wordpress.com/2017/03/21/parliament-and-the-1965-race-relations-act/

21   *Hansard*, 23 November 1965. Private members' clubs were excluded. In February 1973 the House of Lords rejected a case brought by the Race Relations Board, deciding that the East Ham Conservative Club could legally refuse to admit an Indian as a member as the club was 'simply a collection of private persons and that there was no public element'. Dockers' Labour Club and Institute Limited v. Race Relations Board, https://hansard.parliament.uk/commons/1968-04-23/debates/a7bab9b3-9009-4102-aa9c-d5f34f8f1dfc/RaceRelationsBillv

22   Lindop, 2001, p.80.

23   'Often when I am kneeling down in church, I think to myself how much we should thank God, the Holy Ghost, for the gift of capitalism': Enoch Powell speech to a luncheon of lobby correspondents (c. early 1968), quoted in T E Utley, *Enoch Powell: The Man and his Thinking* (William Kimber, 1968), p.114; Paul Foot, 'Obituary of Enoch Powell', *Socialist Review*, March 1998.

24   'Churchill once contacted the Conservative Party research department where Powell worked, to ask, "Who was that young madman who has been telling me how many divisions I will need to reconquer India?"', Utley p.60, cited in Paul Foot, *The Rise of Enoch Powell* (Penguin, 1969), p.19.

25   The slave trade was abolished in 1808 and slavery in British colonies ended in 1838. The Slavery Abolition Act 1833 targeted plantation slavery, paying generous compensation to the slave owners. Debt bondage was unaffected. See 'What is bonded labour?' *Anti-Slavery International*, https://www.antislavery.org/slavery-today/bonded-labour/

26   A much longer list could be added. For example, the naval mutiny in Bombay, February 1946. See 'Our last war of independence: The Royal Indian Navy Mutiny of 1946', https://indianhistorycollective.com/our-last-war-of-independence-the-royal-indian-navy-mutiny-of-1946/

27   Karl Marx, 'Letter to Meyer and Vogt', April 1870, https://www.marxists.org/archive/marx/works/1870/letters/70_04_09.htm. Marx also argued that slavery in the US had to be destroyed if workers were to make

any progress: 'In the United States of North America, every independent movement of the workers was paralysed so long as slavery disfigured a part of the Republic. Labour cannot emancipate itself in the white skin when in the black it is branded.' Karl Marx, *Capital*, vol.1 (Penguin, 1976), ch.10.

28   Eric Hobsbawm & Terence Ranger, eds., *The Invention of Tradition* (Cambridge University Press, 1983). The Royal Titles Bill, 1876, declared Victoria Empress of India.

29   Satnam Virdee, *Racism, Class and the Racialized Outsider* (Palgrave, 2014), p.40.

30   The quote comes from 'The New World: A Democratic Poem' by the leading Chartist, Ernest Jones, 1851, in Simon Rennie, *The Poetry of Ernest Jones* (Routledge, 2016).

31   https://www.kiplingsociety.co.uk/poem/poems_burden.htm Edward Said put the view that Kipling was not a racist. See Edward Said, *Culture and Imperialism* (Vintage, 1994).

32   Robert Roberts, *The Classic Slum*, (Penguin, 1971), p.142–3.

33   Empire Day, renamed Empire and Commonwealth Day, was held in May every year until 1958.

34   UNESCO published a 'Statement on Race' declaring that there was no scientific basis or justification for racial bias, *New York Times* 18 July 1950.

35   David Harewood on *Blackface*, BBC2 27 July 2023, https://www.radiotimes.com/programme/b-94usof/david-harewood-on-blackface/. The show ran till 1978.

36   Walter Fletcher, Conservative MP for Bury, Lancashire, House of Commons, 8 July 1948, quoted in *Tribune*, 16 July 1948. Italics added by *Tribune*.

37   'Suddenly the florid rhetoric about the "open door" turns to equally florid rhetoric about the desecration of "England's green and pleasant land". In 1950, Powell's "ultimate conception" was that "His Majesty's Dominions throughout the world are in reality a whole", but by 1964, the "natives" had taken control of the Dominions and the "whole" had to be replaced by a narrow nationalism. Citizenship laws, Queen's Titles and all the other ideological cards in the game of British supremacy could be shuffled and discarded at will, and no one shuffled them more cynically than J. Enoch Powell'. Paul Foot, *The Rise of Enoch Powell*, p.42.

38   Hirsch, 2018, p.21.

39   Trevor Phillips & Mike Phillips *Windrush: The Irresistible Rise of Multi-Racial Britain* (HarperCollins, 1998), pp.82–3, https://www.gov.uk/government/publications/the-historical-roots-of-the-windrush-scandal/the-historical-roots-of-the-windrush-scandal-independent-research-report-accessible published by the Home Office, September 2024, found that 'during the period 1950–1981, every single piece of immigration or citizenship legislation was designed at least in part to reduce the number of people with black or brown skin who were permitted to live and work in the UK'.

40   Darcus Howe, 1980, 'From Bobby to Babylon', *Race Today* vol.12, no.1

41   See Larry Bartels, 'The Populist Phantom: Threats to Democracy Start

at the Top', *Foreign Affairs* November/December 2024.

42   The 'Sus law' was the Vagrancy Act, passed in 1824. It declared that 'every suspected person or reputed thief, frequenting... any highway or any place adjacent to a street or highway; with intent to commit an arrestable offence... shall be deemed a rogue and vagabond'. The Vagrancy Act was repealed in August 1981, as recommended by the 1979 Royal Commission on Criminal Procedure.

43   'No quick fix', *Economist* 20 September 2008.

The fascists

1   Powell left the Conservative Party because of his opposition to Edward Heath's decision to join the European Economic Community, forerunner of today's EU. He resigned a few days before the February 1974 general election, going on to call for a vote for Labour. He was elected an Ulster Unionist Party MP in October 1974.

2   There is a striking parallel with Home Secretary Suella Braverman's speech condemning the Palestinian solidarity demonstrations as 'hate marches' followed by Tommy Robinson mobilising a thousand supporters to the Cenotaph. *Socialist Worker* 6 November 2023.

3   Martin Walker, *The National Front* (Fontana, 1977), p.115.

4   Robert O. Paxton, *The Anatomy of Fascism* (Penguin, 2005), p.21.

5   Paolo Spriano, *The Occupation of the Factories* (Pluto Press, 1975), pp.45–6.

6   John Foot, *Blood and Power: The Rise and Fall of Italian Fascism* (Bloomsbury, 2022), pp.54–57. The fascists took their name from *fasces*, the axes bundled with rods that symbolised the power of the Roman Empire.

7   Chris Harman, *The Lost Revolution* (Bookmarks, 1982), pp.96–156, ch.6–8.

8   Weimar was the town to which the provisional government fled during the Spartacist uprising.

9   On the origins of the myth of the 'stab in the back', see Richard J. Evans, *The Hitler Conspiracies* (Allen Lane, 2020), ch.2.

10   Foot, 2022, details the violence of the *squadristi* including murder, torture and arson.

11   *Mein Kampf* (My Struggle), Hitler's autobiographical manifesto, in Anton Kaes et al., *The Weimar Republic Sourcebook* (Univeristy of California Press, 1995), p.131.

12   Germany's most important colonies had been in Africa. They included Namibia and parts of Tanzania, Burundi, Rwanda, Cameroon, Togo and Ghana.

13   The SPD share of the vote fell from 28 percent to 24.5 percent.

14   June 1932: the SPD vote fell to 21.5 percent; the KPD rose to 14 percent. November 1932: the Nazi vote fell to 33.1 percent, the SPD's share fell 1 percent to 20.4, the KPD vote rose to 16.9 percent.

15   Leon Trotsky, *The Struggle against Fascism in Germany* (Pathfinder,

1971).

16   Victor Klemperer, *I Shall Bear Witness* (Weidenfeld & Nicolson, 1998).

17   Thomas Linehan, *British Fascism, 1918–1939: Parties, Ideology and Culture* (Manchester University Press, 2021), p.61.

18   The by-election was in Ashton-under-Lyne, April 1931. According to John Strachey, at the time a leading member of the New Party, it was the New Party's poor performance, 16 percent of the poll, that persuaded him to establish a fascist party in Britain, John Strachey, *The Coming Struggle for Power* (Gollancz, 1932), pp.161–2.

19   *Daily Mail* 15 January 1934 and 22 January 1934.

20   It recovered to around 20,000 by 1939, G. Webber, 1984, 'Patterns of membership and support for the British Union of Fascists', *Journal of Contemporary History*, p.579.

21   *Times* 28 September 1936.

22   'Jewish invasion stemmed', *Action* 26 November 1938.

23   *Manchester Guardian* 17 July 1939.

24   The by-election was in Middleton and Prestwich. The BUF got 1.3 percent. In Manchester one member made six black shirts out of the blackout material all householders were required to put up covering every window (interview with John Maffia, 8 April 2020). The BUF won a few local council seats in East London, getting 25 percent of the vote in one ward.

25   *Manchester Evening News* August 1947.

26   Richard Thurlow, *Fascism in Modern Britain* (Sutton, 2000). 'On the patriotic frontier: A who's who of the fringe Right in British politics', Dennis Barker, *The Observer* 2 June 1972. A number of small fringe organisations, often with overlapping membership, continued to challenge the new organisation.

27   Martin Walker, 'The National Front', in H. M. Drucker ed., *Multi-Party Britain* (Red Globe Press, 1979), p.183.

28   Chesterton was also author of Mosley's official biography, *Oswald Mosley: Portrait of a Leader*.

29   There is no connection with the better known British National Party founded in 1982.

30   Walker, p.195.

31   *Guardian* 25 October 1967. A local presence could be established with graffiti such as 'Keep Britain Great'.

32   Michael Cockerell, 'Inside the National Front', *Listener* 28 December 1972. Healey was Secretary of State for Defence, Bottomley had till recently been Minister of Overseas Development.

33   'Footnotes', *Private Eye* 9 December 1969.

34   Geoff Brown & Christian Hogsbjerg, *Apartheid is Not a Game* (Redwords, 2020), p.58.

35   Walker, p.75.

36   Graham Macklin, *Failed Führers: A History of Britain's Extreme Right* (Routledge, 2020), p.357.

37   Stan Taylor, *The National Front in English Politics* (Macmillan, 1982), p.18.

38   Mike and Heather Luft, interviewed by Geoff Brown November 2018; 'Prison for assault on Mr Kenyatta', *Guardian* 7 August 1964.

39   'Sickened at Britain's "decline" in the world: Tyndall talks of "Mein Kampf"', *Guardian* 12 October 1962.

40   See footnote above.

41   The battle for control cost members. Five years after it was founded, NF membership in July 1972 was below 2,000.

42   John O'Brien, *This Week*, ITV current affairs series, September 1974, quoted in Tom May, '"An ideology red, white and blue in tooth and claw": David Edgar's *Destiny* (1978), part 1' (British Television Drama, 2017), para.10, http://www.britishtelevisiondrama.org.uk/?p=7040

43   John Tyndall, *Beyond Capitalism and Socialism: Industrial Policy for the Modern Age* (National Front, 1975).

44   See Chapter 5 'Launching the Anti Nazi League'.

45   Walker, p.184.

46   Joseph Pearce, *Race with the Devil: My Journey from Racial Hatred to Rational Love* (Saint Benedict Press, 2013), pp.81–2.

47   *Britain First* Jan–Feb 1974, British Library; Nigel Fielding, *The National Front* (Routledge, 1981), p.72.

48   Richard Verrall, appointed editor of *Spearhead* by Tyndall, wrote the pamphlet *Did Six Million Really Die?*. It was published under a pseudonym, Richard Harwood, in 1974.

49   Devlet Peukert, *The Weimar Republic* (Penguin, 1991), p.236.

50   Walker, p.88.

51   *Sunday Times* 30 March 1969. The article continues: 'The object is to remind the Left that the street belongs to everyone, but for the NF to do this safely, it must do it in large numbers.'

52   *Observer* 30 March 1969.

53   *Sunday Times* 5 January 1969. See also Steve Cunningham & Michael Lavalette, *Schools Out!* (Bookmarks, 2016), p.91, endnote 288, also 'Should pupils have a voice?' *Illustrated London News* 1 November 1969. The attempt to set up a national school student organisation, 'Unison', was unsuccessful, *Times* 5 January 1969.

54   Walker, p.137.

55   Hitler, *Mein Kampf*, quoted in C. Cross, *Fascism in Britain* (Barrie & Rockcliffe, 1961), p.98.

56   Walker, p.184.

57   Walker, p.144.

58   John Tyndall, *Six Principles of British Nationalism*, quoted in Walker, p.78.

59   Walker, p.116. Based on the dispossession of its African population,

Rhodesia was created as a British colony in the 1890s. Today's Zimbabwe was called Southern Rhodesia until Northern Rhodesia, today Zambia, won its independence in 1964. A liberation war began in 1965. It was victorious in 1980 defeating the white settler regime and replacing it with black majority rule.

60   Walker, p.80.

61   Peukert, p.236–7. There is a very detailed analysis of Nazi ideology in John Bellamy Foster, 'The New Irrationalism', https://monthlyreview.org/2023/02/01/the-new-irrationalism/. Jim Wolfreys points out how post Second World War, 'the defeat of the pro-Nazi Vichy regime, rapid economic modernisation and decolonisation' French fascists could adapt their ideas because of the absence of any kind of dogma. Jim Wolfreys, 2002, '"The centre cannot hold": Fascism, the left and the crisis of French politics', *International Socialism* series 2, no.95,

62   Antisemitism as a political force had a long history before the Nazis. The openly antisemitic Karl Lueger was elected Mayor of Vienna in 1895. See Carl Schorske, *Fin-de-siecle Vienna: Politics and Culture* (Knopf, 1980), pp.133–146. The anti-Zionist tradition of the left, including many left-wing Jews, has always challenged antisemitism and rejected the equation of Jews with Zionism.

63   The NF fielded candidates in Huddersfield West, Wolverhampton North East, Leicester South-West, Cardiff South-East, Islington North, Ilford South, Southall, Battersea South, and Deptford. The forty-five candidates averaged 8 percent. Walker, pp.90–1.

64   The initial NF membership was heavily concentrated in London and the south of England.

65   The NF manifesto called for Britain to stay out of the Common Market, the scrapping of what it called 'the coloured Commonwealth' to be replaced with 'a white Commonwealth', and for 'extremist troublemakers at universities' to lose their student grants.

66   The NF stood ten candidates: Battersea South, 3.3 percent; Cardiff South East, 1.9 percent; Deptford, 5.5 percent; Enfield West, 3.1 percent; Huddersfield West, 3.5 percent; Ilford South, 0.5 percent; Islington North, 5.6 percent; Leicester South West, 2.3 percent; Southall, 4.4 percent; Wolverhampton North East, 4.7 percent.

67   'Blackburn fascists dig for dirt', *Socialist Worker* 3 May 1975.

68   *Morning Star* 5 May 1972.

69   *Manchester Evening News* 16 January 1971.

70   *Times* 5 August 1972.

71   *Times* 17 August 1972. Powell was addressing the Merridale Ladies' Luncheon in Wolverhampton.

72   *Daily Telegraph* 19 August 1972; Walker, p.103; Macklin, p.367.

73   'Asians – the big fear', *Daily Mail* 25 August 1972; *Daily Express* 25 August 1972.

74   *Daily Mirror* 5 September 1972.

75   *Times* 13 September 1972; Walker, p.136.

76 Michael Cockerell, 'Inside the National Front', *Listener* 28 December 1972. Walker, p.135. The figure given is 20,000. Walker reports that 'four million leaflets were delivered in 1972-3, the bulk of them attacking the Ugandan Asian arrival... Each branch's obligation to purchase 3,000 leaflets a week means a minimum distribution of 5 million in 1974', p.166.

77 *Daily Mail* 11 September 1972.

78 *Uganda Argus* 15 September 1972.

79 Walker, p.136.

80 As previous endnote.

81 As previous endnote.

82 Monday Club rules did not require members to be members of the Conservative Party; Lisa Mason, 'The development of the Monday Club and its contribution to the Conservative Party and the modern British right, 1961 to 1990', (unpublished doctoral thesis, University of Wolverhampton, 2004), p.60.

83 *Sunday Telegraph* 17 September 1972. According to this report, the 500 were members of the International Socialists. Mason, p.57.

84 Walker, p.137.

85 There were two other fascist candidates. Together they got nearly 13 percent.

86 *Times* 21 May 1973. The figure given by Walker is 3,000. None of the national broadsheet papers were reporting on NF activities during the campaign.

87 It was known as East Pakistan until Bangladesh won independence in December 1971.

88 Webster was also helped by there being no Liberal Party candidate, the Liberals often doing well getting anti-government protest votes in parliamentary by-elections. Powell never endorsed the National Front. 'We should not abandon democracy in the hope of finding something better in the gutter', Macklin, p.369, footnote 212.

89 *Times* 9 October 1973.

90 The crash was not out of the blue. From the mid-1960s onwards there were many signs of growing weakness of the boom, in the British economy in particular.

91 'General Walker may recruit three million', *Daily Telegraph* 28 August 1974; 'Obituary: General Sir Walter Walker', *Daily Telegraph* 13 August 2001. In an interview in the *Evening News* in 1974, he raised the possibility that the Army might have to take over in Britain. Soon afterwards, Walker set up Unison, an 'anti-chaos' organisation. The name was changed to Civil Assistance. This aimed to establish a force of 'trustworthy, loyal, level-headed men', able to organise essential services if there was a breakdown in public order. The Conservative cabinet minister, John Davies, is alleged to have thought that this might be the last time his family would be able to celebrate Christmas.

92 Powell left the Conservative Party and returned to parliament in October 1974 as an Ulster Unionist MP.

93 Yaojun Li, 'Racial inequality in employment worsened in recessions' (University of Manchester, 2014), http://blog.policy.manchester.ac.uk/featured/2014/09/racial-inequality-in-employment-worsened-in-recessions/

94 The next comparable cut in living standards came in the 2008 crash, https://www.tuc.org.uk/news/uk-workers-suffering-most-severe-squeeze-real-earnings-victorian-times

95 Labour disputes: total working days lost, Office for National Statistics, https://www.ons.gov.uk/employmentandlabourmarket/peopleinwork/employmentandemployeetypes/timeseries/bbfw/lms

96 The Special Demonstration Squad officer, 'Michael Scott (alias)', giving evidence to the Undercover Policing Inquiry, UCPI, said 'There weren't any right-wing groups who were demonstrating, or causing any problems as far as I can recall, at the time' https://powerbase.info/index.php/Michael_Scott (alias). This ridiculous claim reflects the police priorities at the time which were shaped by the concern that the new Labour government would not be able to tackle the militancy that had toppled the Heath government and had produced the manoeuvrings of General Walker and Colonel Stirling.

97 Walker, pp.174–5.

98 'Politics in the Classroom', *Guardian* 31 August 1974.

99 According to Special Branch infiltrator, 'Peter Collins', the 'nationalists' organised a faction 'National Assembly' within which a separate organisation, the League of St George, was recruiting members. See Special Branch report concerning formation of Legion of St. George comprising of members of National Front, 8 December 1975, https://www.ucpi.org.uk/publications/special-branch-report-concerning-formation-of-legion-of-st-george-comprising-of-members-of-national-front/.

100 This may have been an important moment in persuading Labour councils to stop hiring out meeting rooms to the NF. See 'National Front's tactics', *Guardian* 14 Apr 1975.

101 *Socialist Worker* 22 March 1975; Kevin Corr, private communication 20 January 2021.

102 *Searchlight* September 1975.

103 *Guardian* 25 January 1975; *Red Weekly* 30 January 1975.

104 'Nazi press changes tone', *Searchlight* January 1982. *National Front News* was first published in 1976.

Fighting racism and fascism

1 Ian Birchall notes that discrimination had a class dimension. He remembers a notice that read 'No coloured except embassy', private email 11 December 2023.

2 'Colour bar "to keep trade": Licence Renewed', *Guardian* 5 February 1955. See also 'A menace to us all', Phillip Higgs, Joint Shop Stewards Committee convenor, Rolls-Royce Bristol Engine Division, Coventry, *Labour's Voice* February 1955.

3 John Wrench, 'Unequal Comrades: Trade Unions, Equal Opportunity

and Racism', *Centre for Research in Ethnic Relations* (University of Warwick, 1986), p.8.

https://warwick.ac.uk/fac/soc/crer/research/publications/policy/policyp_no.5.pdf

4   'Uproar as council changes its mind on Sikh busmen', *Guardian* 6 October 1966; Beetham, 1970, *Transport and Turbans: A Comparative Study in Local Politics* (Oxford University Press, 1966), p33–4. Thomas was knighted in 1965. His autobiography makes no mention of this: Robert Thomas, *Sir Bob* (Senior Publications, 1984).

5   League of Coloured Peoples, Annual Report, 1937–8, pp.3–5, quoted in Sonya O. Rose, 'Race, empire and British wartime national identity, 1939–45', *Historical Research* vol.74, no.184, May 2001, p.227.

6   *The Keys*, Official Organ of the League of Coloured Peoples, Jan–Mar 1937.

7   Learie Constantine, *The Colour Bar*, (Stanley Paul, 1954) p.137; *Guardian* 3 September, 4 September, 19 September 1943. See also letter from Harold Moody, *Guardian* 11 September 1943.

8   *Daily Worker* 28 October 1943.

9   International African Friends of Abyssinia (Ethiopia) was founded in 1935. It became the International African Service Bureau (IASB) in 1937.

10   Ras Makonnen, *Pan-Africanism from within* (Disaporic Africa Press, 2016) pp.142–3. Norman Manley became Jamaica's first prime minister.

11   '"Fifty pints of lager, please!": Half a century of British Asian struggles', Balwinder Rana, *International Socialism* 172, Autumn 2021, https://isj.org.uk/british-asian-struggles/

12   'Len Johnson turned out: Colour bar in Manchester pub', *Daily Worker* 1 October 1953; 'Pub Colour bar is removed: Len Johnson wins another fight', *Daily Worker* 3 October 1953; Michael Herbert, *Never Counted Out! The Story of Len Johnson: Manchester's Black Boxing Hero and Communist* (Dropped Aitches Press, 1992), pp.99–100; Shirin Hirsch & Geoff Brown, 'Breaking the "colour bar": Len Johnson, Manchester and anti-racism', *Race & Class*, vol.64, no.3, 2023; Rana, 2021.

13   Peter Fryer, *Staying Power: The History of Black People in Britain* (Pluto, 1984), p.379.

14   The US civil rights movement had started with the year-long bus boycott in Montgomery, Alabama, 1955, triggered by Rosa Parks refusing to sit in the back of a segregated bus.

15   Madge Dresser, *Black and White on the Buses: The Colour Bar Dispute in Bristol* (Bookmarks, 2013).

16   The RAAS was founded after Malcolm X visited London.

17   Rosalind Eleanor Wild, 'Black was the colour of our fight: Black Power in Britain, 1955-1976', (unpublished PhD thesis, Sheffield, 2008), p.110.

18   Colin Barker, interviewed by Geoff Brown April 2017.

19   For a fuller account, see Ian Birchall, 'Ray Challinor and the 1965 Courtauld Strike' (London Socialist Historians Group) https://londonsocialisthistorians.blogspot.com/2011/05/ray-challinor-and-1965-

courtauld-strike.html.

20   Bennie Bunsee, 'Women in struggle: The Mansfield Hosiery strike'. Originally published in *Spare Rib* no.21, 1974, https://libcom.org/article/women-struggle-mansfield-hosiery-strike.

21   As footnote above.

22   Peter Pendergast, National Union of Hosiery and Knitwear Workers (NUHKW) general president quoted in Paul Foot, 'Workers against racism', https://www.marxists.org/archive/foot-paul/1973/xx/racism.html.

23   *Birmingham Post* 4 June 1973, quoted in *Race Today* July 1973.

24   *Socialist Worker* 11 December 2022, https://socialistworker.co.uk/features/confronting-racism-and-exploitation-50-years-since-the-mansfield-hosiery-strike/.

25   The Strike at Imperial Typewriters, *B3 Media*, https://strikeatimperial.net/about/timeline/

26   Ron Ramdin, *The Making of the Black Working Class in Britain* (Verso, 1987), p.271.

27   *Economist* 16 December 1972.

28   Ramdin, p.12.

29   Ramdin, p.280; *Socialist Worker* 20 July 1974.

30   'Asian strikers are back at work', *Guardian* 19 July 1974.

31   *Socialist Worker* 24 July 1974 and 31 July 1974.

32   The IWA, established in Coventry in 1953, was named after Udham Singh, who assassinated General O'Dwyer, lieutenant governor of the Punjab under whose authority hundreds were killed in the Jallianwala Bagh massacre in Amritsar in 1919. Adopting the name Mohamed Singh Azad to show his commitment to Muslim, Sikh and Hindu unity in fighting for Indian freedom, he went on hunger strike for over a month before being found guilty after a one-day trial at the Old Bailey and sentenced to death by hanging. A. Sivanandan, 'From resistance to rebellion: Asian and Afro-Caribbean struggles in Britain', *Race & Class*, vol.23, no.2–3, pp.111–152, 1981.

33   Avtar Jouhl, 'Life-long fighter against racism', *International Socialism* 164, Autumn 2019.

34   Ambalavaner Sivanandan, *Communities of Resistance: Writings on Black Struggles for Socialism* (Verso, 1990), p.65.

35   Shirin Hirsch, *In the Shadow of Enoch Powell* (Manchester University Press, 2018), p.50.

36   *Peace News* 19 May 1978.

37   Zephaniah interview with Vick Hope, 'Songs to live by', BBC podcast, 19 March 2021, https://www.bbc.co.uk/sounds/brand/p09b3h1l. Steve Cedar recalls how Canning Town police station in East London was known as the uniformed branch of the National Front: Steve Cedar, interviewed by Geoff Brown 10 August 2020.

38   'Youths "attacked police" on bonfire night', *Times* 7 November 1975; *Race Today* article reprinted in Chapeltown News, https://harehills111.wordpress.com/wp-content/uploads/2016/12/december-1975.pdf

39   David Widgery, *Beating Time* (Chatto & Windus, 1986), p.61.

40   Darcus Howe, *From Bobby to Babylon: Blacks and the British Police* (Bookmarks, 2020), p.105.

41   Widgery, 1986, p.61. Founded by the black Communist Claudia Jones in the aftermath of the 1958 anti-black race riots, the annual Notting Hill Carnival became Britain's biggest celebration of black culture with around 150,000 taking part in a day of music, dance and masquerade.

42   *Guardian* 29 February 2016.

43   Labour Party had 650,000 members in 1976.

44   Speech to the Amalgamated Engineering Union (AEU) National Committee, April 1967. Trevor Carter, *Shattering Illusions: West Indians in British Politics* (Lawrence & Wishart, 1986), p.79. Soon to be made a member of the House of Lords, Carron's contempt for the rank and file was shown by his description of shop stewards as 'werewolves', see Jules Townshend, 'Communist Party in Decline 1964 to 1970', *International Socialism* 62, September 1973, p.20

45   'What we're up against', *Socialist Worker* 22 May 1976.

46   Roots History Project, vol.2, Berry Edwards, p.61.

47   Rana, 2021.

48   *Daily Herald* 1 October 1936.

49   *Hansard* 24 June 1976. Jenkins was not a racist. Ian Soady remembers Jenkins, MP for Stechford, Birmingham, an inner-city constituency, 'being followed by a black man as he was walking into the Labour Club on Wright Rd. And when Roy walked in, the doorman stopped the black man, and Roy turned round and said, "If he's not coming in, I'm not coming in"', Saltley Stories, unretrievable.

50   George Davies, interviewed by Geoff Brown 11 March 2020.

51   Pia Feig, interviewed by Geoff Brown 29 January 2020.

52   Rosie Serdiville, *The Battle of Stockton: How a Small Town Saw Off Fascists in 1933* (The Historical Association, 2018)

53   'Mosley's circus at Olympia', *Guardian* 8 June 1934. The CP played the same role in Manchester three months later, https://radicalmanchester.wordpress.com/2010/01/07/fascism-and-anti-fascism-in-1930s-manchester/

54   Priyamvada Gopal, *Insurgent Empire: Anticolonial Resistance and British Dissent* (Verso, 2019), pp.245–60.

55   The CP's call to go to Cable Street to resist Mosley's march was a last-minute decision made when it was already clear that there would be mass opposition on the streets. The success of Cable Street was followed a year later with a similar action in south London, in the mainly Irish Catholic area of Bermondsey. 'Disorderly London Scenes: Mosley's Blackshirts', Australian Associated Press, 3 October 1937, https://trove.nla.gov.au/newspaper/article/41819805

56   Joe Jacobs, *Out of the Ghetto: My Youth in the East End, Communism and Fascism, 1913-39* (Janet Simon, 1978), pp.222–58.

57   Martin Walker suggests the left overplays the importance of Cable

Street, Martin Walker, *The National Front* (Fontana, 1977), p.21. He misses the point that Cable Street was the first mass mobilisation of a local community that succeeded in preventing a fascist march. As such it remains a model for anti-fascists.

58   *Manchester Guardian* 17 July 1939; *Times* 17 July 1939.

59   Morris Beckman, *The 43 Group* (Centerprise, 2000); Daniel Sonabend, *We Fight Fascists: The 43 Group and Their Forgotten Battle for Post-War Britain* (Verso, 2019). The name 43 Group refers to the number attending its founding meeting in 1946.

60   The programme came out of discussions between Stalin and Harry Pollitt, CPGB general secretary. Revised four times, the last version of *The British Road to Socialism* was published in 1977. Race was almost completely absent from all versions: Satnam Virdee, *Racism, Class and the Racialized Outsider* (Palgrave, 2016), pp.104–7.

61   'Communist call for united drive, Stem the flood of racist poison', CP national executive meeting report, *Morning Star* 13 July 1976.

62   'Unite to ban the Front', Gordon McLennan, Communist Party general secretary, *Morning Star* 13 August 1977.

63   'National Front plans two even bigger marches', *Guardian* 3 August 1974.

64   The IRSC was set up in 1969 on the initiative of the Young Communist League and Communist Party after NF slogans were painted on a synagogue.

65   Lorna Chessum, *From Immigrants to Ethnic Minority: Making Black Community in Britain* (Routledge, 2000), pp.216–7.

66   *Guardian* 7 August 1974.

67   *Socialist Worker* 10 August 1974.

68   This included a coach of young Asians from Gravesend: Balwinder Rana, private email March 2020.

69   The IRSC's leadership was strongly challenged by the revolutionary left with the International Socialists the largest contingent on the march, 'No major clash at Front march – but trouble may lie ahead', *Guardian* 26 August 1974

70   Michael Crowley, *Comrades Come Rally: Manchester Communists in the 1930s and 1940s* (Bookmarks, 2022).

71   Manchester AEU District Committee minutes, 23 and 30 January 1973.

72   '"Human wall" defeats fascists', *Socialist Worker* 10 February 1973.

73   'Keep the Fascists Out!' Leaflet for public meeting, Manchester, 17 February 1973. Speakers included John Forrester, TASS divisional organiser and Labour NEC, Bernard Panter, CP and AUEW Manchester district secretary, Ron Phillips, Black Unity and Freedom Party, Tariq Ali, IMG, Editor *Red Mole*, Wally Preston, IS and AUEW convenor, Vic Eddisford, CP North West District Secretary, Pete Cockcroft, Greater Manchester Anti-Fascist Committee.

74   For background, see UCPI report on the IS conference 1978 https://

www.ucpi.org.uk/wp-content/uploads/2021/04/UCPI0000013228.pdf

75   'Fists Against Fascists', *International Socialism*, June 1974. This article re-used the title of an earlier piece, 'Fists Against Fascists', *International Socialism* 10, Autumn 1962. Margaret Renn remembers being at a fascist meeting in the late 1960s which started with someone coming up to the speaker and punching him in the face. Ian Birchall remembers disrupting meetings of far-right candidates in the 1966 general election, private email 11 December 2023. See also Colin Sparks, 'Fascism in Britain', *International Socialism* 71, September 1974, https://www.marxists.org/history/etol/newspape/isj/1974/no071/sparks.htm. This concludes: 'The fascists will not go away: they are part and parcel of a rotting and dying capitalism. They are, potentially, our most dangerous enemy. We have to meet them and defeat them both politically and physically'.

76   A double issue of *International Socialism* was devoted to Trotsky's writings: 'Fascism, Stalinism and the United Front, 1930–34' *International Socialism* 38/39, August/September 1969, https://www.marxists.org/history/etol/newspape/isj/1969/no038/intro.htm. Full versions of these writings were published two years later in Leon Trotsky, *The Struggle Against Fascism in Germany* (Pathfinder, 1971), with an introduction by Ernest Mandel.

77   Leon Trotsky, 'The turn in the Communist International and the situation in Germany', 1930, https://www.marxists.org/archive/trotsky/germany/1930/300926.htm. Trotsky, *The struggle against Fascism in Germany*, p59. Emphasis in the original.

78   Leon Trotsky, 1931, *What next? Vital questions for the German proletariat* (January 1931), https://www.marxists.org/archive/trotsky/germany/1932-ger/next03.htm, Trotsky, 1971, p.248.

79   Catherine Epstein, *The Last Revolutionaries: German Communists and Their Century* (Harvard University Press, 2021), p.23 & 39.

80   When right-wing parties initiated a referendum aimed at forcing the SPD government of Prussia out of office following orders from the Comintern, the KPD supported it, calling it the Red Referendum.

81   Already before this point, when Stalin instructed the Comintern first to stop criticising French imperialism then British imperialism, the Trinidadian communist George Padmore resigned his Comintern position. Padmore began to establish a Pan African alternative in 1937, together with CLR James, Ras Makonnen and others, setting up the International African Service Bureau based in London, determined to sustain its black leadership.

82   International Socialists, *National Front: The new Nazis* (International Socialists, 1974), p.9; Daniel Guérin, *Fascism and Big Business* (Monad Press, 1973), p.111. This quote may be slightly paraphrased but is essentially correct. See 'Did Adolf Hitler Say the Nazism Could Have Been Stopped by "Smashing the Nucleus" of the Movement?' https://www.snopes.com/fact-check/adolf-hitler-smashing-the-nucleus/

83   'Dockers' leaflet unmasks the racists', *Socialist Worker* 1 June 1974.

84   Bob Light private email, 7 December 2020. No copy of the leaflet has been found. 'According to Micky Fenn, the Shop Stewards Committee actively mobilised against further outbreaks of racism in the docks, ensuring there was no repetition of a pro-Powell mobilisation. In 1974, Dockers

Against Racism was formed but this post war anti-fascist tradition among dockers still awaits documentation': *Newham: The forging of a Black Community* (Newham Monitoring Project, 1991), p.15.

85   Christopher Hitchens, 'White socialism?', *New Statesman* 31 May 1974.

86   *Newham Recorder* 23 May 1974.

87   Hitchens, 1974; Walker, 1977, p.152. Lobb later stood as a National Party candidate.

88   'The National Front', *This Week* 5 September 1974, https://www.imdb.com/title/tt2214327/?ref_=ttrel_rel_tt. See Gavin Shaffer, 'The vision of a nation: Making multiculturalism on British television, 1960–80'; *North West Anti-Fascist News* October 1974, p.4.

89   'Students decide to disrupt speeches by fascist groups', *Guardian* 5 April 1974; 'NUS vow to smash ultra-right', *Leeds Student*, Friday, 26 April 1974.

90   *Red Agitator Special*, LSE IS, 'No platform for fascists'. See Evan Smith, https://hatfulofhistory.files.wordpress.com/2015/11/red-agitator-lse-is.pdf. Pete Cockcroft remembers how at Manchester Uni, the Tories mounted campaigns to invite National Front speakers to the student's union. 'The politics were obvious – wedge the left as being anti freedom of speech. Our position was that they were violent thugs who should not be invited into our place. I spoke forcefully in a number of these debates and carried the floor every time'. Peter Cockcroft, private email, 23 December 2019.

91   The NF were protesting against the new Labour government's amnesty of immigrants who had been made retrospectively liable to deportation by the 1971 Immigration Act.

92   Liberation was founded as the Movement for Colonial Freedom in 1954 by a large group of Labour left MPs, led by Fenner Brockway, who called for colonial independence against official party policy. It changed its name to Liberation in 1970. Supported by a number of national trade unions and the Communist Party, with about 1,000 individual members, Liberation was a top-heavy organisation with an impressive list of sponsors and little membership organisation outside London. The CP-dominated London area Council was the only local Liberation organisation that had the capacity to mobilise.

93   John Newsinger, 'In the middle of the road: Fenner Brockway, the Independent Labour Party and the class struggle', *International Socialism* 179, 2023, https://isj.org.uk/fenner-brockway-ilp/.

94   Tony Gilbert, *Danger: Racialists at Work* (Liberation, 1974). Gilbert was one of Liberation's leading activists, for many years a CP member and rail worker based at King's Cross. Gilbert had fought with the International Brigades in Spain, as had Jack Jones, who wrote the Foreword for Gilbert's book and got the TGWU to order 1,000 copies.

95   There was a second pamphlet with a foreword by Jack Jones: Brian Nicholson, *Racialism, Fascism and the Trade Unions*, TGWU, Region 1, Docks Group. Nicholson, a TGWU official in the London docks, is most unlikely to have been the author, though it will have helped his career.

It may have been written by Ken Coates after he, Jack Jones and Brian Nicolson met, possibly at an Institute of Workers Control conference. Theoretically ambitious, it draws on Oliver C. Cox, *Caste, Class and Race* (Monthly Review Press, 1948). Cox was a black Trinidadian/American sociologist, one of the first to use a Marxist approach to analyse slavery and racism. Nicholson was one of more than a hundred trade unionists recruited to spy on behalf of MI5. He was known in the docks as 'Special Agent Nicholson': Bob Light, private email, 3 December 2020.

96 Metropolitan Police Operation Order for the demonstration at Red Lion Square, 13 June 1974. https://www.ucpi.org.uk/wp-content/uploads/2023/01/MPS_0748330.pdf; Nigel Copsey and Matthew Worley, 'White Youth: The Far Right, Punk and British youth culture', *JOMEC Journal*, Issue 9, 2016, p.116.

97 M. J. Keene, *Police Journal*, vol.40, Issue 4, April 1967. Unofficial Committee of Enquiry, Southall 23 April 1979, p.170. The SPG's 200 members were trained in unarmed combat, use of riot shields and CS gas, practising 'the wedge' to break up demonstrators into more easily controllable groups and 'snatch squads' to arrest individuals. Its vans were equipped with riot shields, pistols, rifles, sub-machine guns, truncheons and visors.

98 Liberation's London Area Council had booked the room in Conway Hall so that the NF would be 'confronted on their own ground', *Times* 17 June 1974.

99 See Peter Chippendale & Martin Walker, 'Left-wing deliberately started violence', *Guardian* 17 June 1974; Tony Bunyan, 1981, 'The police against the people', *Race & Class,* vol.23, no.2–3, p.166. Bunyan quotes an SPG officer giving evidence to the inquiry chaired by Lord Scarman.

100 *Observer* 23 June 1974. Fifty-four were arrested. For an eye-witness account of the police attack that killed Kevin Gately, see Nick Mullen & Monty Goldman's accounts: Dave Hann, *Physical Resistance* (Zero Resistance, 2013), pp.240–4. Monty Goldman, a CP member, argues that the ultra-left wanted to provoke the police but would never admit to it.

101 See one minute video https://www.youtube.com/watch?v=MM4vXhCJfQA.

102 Jim Nichol, private communication, 8 April 2024. Habershon was well known as the police officer responsible for investigating the Angry Brigade bomb attacks between 1970 and 1972, including one targeting the Home Secretary. As a result, five members were sentenced to ten years in prison. *Socialist Worker,* 29 June 1974, published a detailed statement about Habershon's visit, rejecting his demands and supporting the NCCL's independent inquiry: 'Red Lion Square anti-National Front demonstration', Hull University Archives, Hull History Centre, GB 50 U DCL/638/4. It is worth noting how none of the undercover police officers in the SDS have more than vague memories, see
http://campaignopposingpolicesurveillance.com/2021/05/06/ucpi-daily-report-5-may-2021/, nor have any of the many reports of the demonstration that must have been written appeared.

103 National Union of Students, 1974, *The Myth of Red Lion Square*.

104 The Under Cover Policing Inquiry which began work in July 2015 has

shown the extent of police infiltration of left organisations, strengthening the argument that the police attack on the demonstration was carefully planned.

105 Tony Gilbert, *Only One Died* (Kay Beauchamp, 1975), p.ix.

106 NF–police relations deteriorated in 1978, see Webster, 'Now the police are mobilised against us', *Spearhead* May 1978, and 'The NF and the police', *State Research Bulletin* no.7, August-September 1978, p.126.

107 *Economist* 2 October 1976.

108 The austerity programme was presented as imposed by the International Monetary Fund, which was called in to deal with a sterling crisis. The then Chancellor of the Exchequer, Denis Healey, would later blame government statisticians for giving him the wrong information on which he based the request for IMF assistance. Denis Healey, *The Time of My Life* (Methuen, 2015), p.434.

109 Callaghan was the assistant secretary of the newly formed Inland Revenue Staff Federation 1936–1942.

110 Hugh Scanlon was president of the AUEW, Jack Jones, general secretary of the TGWU, the two largest unions in the TUC. The clearest example of the TUC leadership solidly backing the government was their refusal to support the FBU, the Firefighters' union, in their nine week all out strike from mid November 1977 to January 1978.

111 The National Front made much of the success of Martin Webster's candidacy in the West Bromwich by-election in 1974, the first and only time the National Front retained its deposit of £150, returnable only to those candidates getting over 12.5 percent of votes cast. It needs to be noted that there was no Liberal candidate.

112 Walker, 1977, p.200.

113 Walker, 1977, p.198.

114 'How the National Front organised in Rotherham', *Leveller* November 1976. The official history of Rotherham Trades Council, *No Mean Response: A brief history of Rotherham Trades Union Council, 1891–1991*, mis-records the event: 'A huge counter-demonstration, mustered in co-operation with the Anti-Nazi League, easily affirmed the authority of the democratic, non-racist ideal and Stan [Crowther]'s majority at the ballot box comfortably consigned the shaven-headed storm-troopers to their rightful place in history's rubbish heap'. Crowther was the Labour candidate.

115 'Anti-immigration parties win biggest share of poll', *Times* 2 July 1976; *Sunday Times* 4 July 1976.

116 'National Front have Amin to thank for Thurrock vote', *Daily Telegraph* 17 July 1976.

117 Walker, 1977, p.199.

118 *Spearhead*, NF founding 10th anniversary issue, March 1977.

119 *Times* 2 July 1976.

120 The NF claimed 600 new members in June, 2,000 since the beginning of the year together with forty-one new branches.

121 Webster's often quoted phrase, *Spearhead* 103, March 1977, p.3.

122   The BCSI had got 6,363 votes, 5.1 percent, in Bradford in 1973. Merrick got 28 percent in the 1975 elections. See Stuart Bentley, 'Merrick and the British Campaign to Stop Immigration: populist racism and political influence', *Race & Class*, vol.36, no.3, 1995.

123   The British Campaign to Stop Immigration, BBC, 28 February 1976. Efforts to prevent a repeat broadcast failed.

124   The posters were organised by the Ad Hoc Committee against Fascism secretary Reuben Goldberg, *Yorkshire Post* 26 April 1976.

125   *Searchlight* reported 700 on the NF March. The *Yorkshire Post* reports 1,000.

126   *Yorkshire Post* 26 April 1976. The NF assembled on waste land near Westgate. One of the anti-fascists who attacked the NF here ran off with the keys to the speaker van. The anti-NF march assembled three quarters of a mile away in Salt Street.

127   Roger Ballard, 'Up Against the Front', *New Society* 6 May 1976. A lecturer on race relations, Ballard was interested in the young West Indians and Asians. Quoting a 1970 *New Society* article on race by A. H. Halsey, he wrote: 'When will the blacks revolt? The time of posing such questions has now long passed. Alienated young black people in Britain are increasingly being forced towards Insurrection', Ballard, 1976.

128   NVDA had been widely used in the struggle for Indian independence against the British by Gandhi and his followers in the 1930s and 1940s and in the US civil rights movement by Martin Luther King and others in the 1950s and 1960s. In Britain, the Committee of 100, a breakaway from the Campaign for Nuclear Disarmament used it to organise mass sit-downs in the early 1960s.

129   See Associated Press archive video 24 April 1976, 'Demonstrators clash with police protesting against a National Front march in Bradford', https://www.youtube.com/watch?v=k4Br6V9cAGE. Also, Bradford Anti-National Front demonstrations and May Day parade, Yorkshire Film Archive, https://www.yfanefa.com/record/8924

130   This was the Manningham Defence Committee.

131   Geoff Robinson, *Never Again: The Lessons of 1976*, Bradford Trades Union Council; Ballard, 1976; *Socialist Worker* 1 May 1976; S*earchlight* June 1976. There were rumours that Bradford would become the NF's national headquarters, see Manningham Defence Committee, 1976; Louis Charalambous, 'Obituary: Geoff Robinson', *Guardian*, 23 May 2006.

132   Robinson, *Never Again*; Fazal Mehmood, interviewed by Geoff Brown 16 May 2023.

133   Megan Povey, private email 13 May 2023.

134   Ballard, 1976; 'Witness Seminar: Anti-Fascism in 1970s Huddersfield', *Contemporary British History*, vol.20, no.1, March 2006, pp.119–133.

135   Ballard, 1976; Robinson, *Never Again*; *Red Weekly* 29 April 1976; *Socialist Worker* 1 May 1976. There is also an Associated Press video, NF march in Bradford, https://www.youtube.com/watch?v=k4Br6V9cAGE and a police video https://player.bfi.org.uk/free/film/watch-anti-national-front-demonstrations-bradford-1978-online

136 Anandi Ramamurthy, *Black Star: Britain's Asian Youth Movements* (Pluto Press, 2013), p.25. The black activist magazine *Race Today* pointed out that in Manningham, 'the black community... incensed at the fascist invasion, were concerned with defending their home territory', *Race Today* 1976, quoted in Ramamurthy, 2013, p.24.

137 *Yorkshire Post* 3 May 1976. Many of those arrested dressed up for their court appearances.

138 Jill Catlow, private email 19 June 2021.

139 Manningham Defence Committee, 1976, *Carnival Sit-down against the National Front;* 'Court jesters get the thumbs down from bench', *Guardian* 21 July 1976; *Peace News* 6 August 1976; Howard Clark, 'Non-violent resistance and social defence', in Gail Chester and Andrew Rigby, eds., *Articles of Peace: Celebrating Fifty Years of Peace News* (Prism Press, 1986), pp.58–60.

140 https://api.parliament.uk/historic-hansard/written-answers/1976/oct/28/wages.

141 They averaged 11 percent of the vote.

142 'Immigrants: How Britain is Deceived', Anthony Shrimsley, *Daily Mail* 25 May 1976; 'A bottomless pool?', *Observer* 30 May 1976. He had also made use of a mistake in Home Office statistics: 'The immigrant numbers game', *Times* 6 January 1976.

143 *Sun* 4 May 1976; *Daily Telegraph* 5 May 1976; Benjamin Bland, 'Publish and be damned? Race, crisis, and the press in England during the long, hot summer of 1976', *Immigrants & Minorities*, vol.37, no.3, 2019.

144 'Powell's new shock: Angry immigration officials say "We can't cope with Asians because of Home Office ruling"', *Daily Express* 19 June 1976; 'Jenkins denies "bogus papers" order', *Daily Express* 25 June 1976.

145 *Times* 19 May 1976.

146 This was not an isolated result. In the West Bromwich by-election, the NF got 17 percent of the white vote.

147 Race Relations Bill debate, House of Commons, 4 March 1976.

148 Roy Jenkins's speech debating the new Race Relations bill, *Guardian* 5 March 1976; 'A bottomless pool', *Observer* 30 May 1976.

149 *Socialist Worker* 29 May 1976; 'Race work perspectives', IS Central Committee, September 1976. Tariq Ali, editor of *Red Weekly*, the IMG's paper, publicly applauded the headline. Hundreds of thousands of the leaflets were distributed.

150 '[T]he twin themes of fighting racialism and fighting for the right to work now dominate our immediate perspectives for the next few months... Our prime responsibility...[as] a largely white organisation must be to win white workers to fight racialism'. 'The Anti-racialist Fight and the Right to Work Campaign', IS Central Committee, 24 June 1976, IS post-conference bulletin, p.3, quoted by Ian Goodyer, *Crisis Music: The Cultural Politics of Rock Against Racism* (Manchester University Press, 2009), p.58.

151 John Deason, 'One year of the Right to Work Campaign', *International Socialism* 93, November 1976.

152 John Deason, interviewed by Geoff Brown 23 December 2023.

153   Right to Work Campaign, Interim Report of the March of Unemployed Workers, Manchester–London, 27 February–20 March 1976. The united front tactic could be applied to fight different threats. It needed real forces, and someone had to give a lead. After the National Party's success getting two members elected to Blackburn council in May 1976, much of the support from shop stewards' committees and Labour parties for the Blackburn Right to Work Committee wavered. At a meeting organised by the committee, it was Terence Hill, deputy chair of Whitbread's JSSC, who gave that lead as he 'spoke of his experiences of discrimination as a Catholic. "He understood and witnessed the damage that discrimination causes to any working class fight for jobs"', *Socialist Worker* 22 May 1976.

154   Lez Scott, private email, 13 October 2016. Mr Roy Martin, chairman of the North-West Race Relations Board, 'The Telegraph has a lot to answer for over what has happened in the town', *Searchlight*, June 1976.

155   The National Party, *World in Action*, Granada TV, 1976.

156   *Searchlight* June 1976. Also, Aubrey Lewis's letter to *Tribune* 28 May 1976.

157   Alan Gibbons, phone interview with Geoff Brown, 8 May 2018.

158   Walker, 1977, p.195.

159   Young Rebels: The Story of the Southall Youth Movement, https://www.youtube.com/watch?v=OGWX233kHPg The leading political organisation, the Southall Indian Workers Association, founded by Communist Party of India members who had been hardened in the struggle for independence, had become dominated by business interests such as the owners of local cinemas who profited from extortionate ticket prices for Indian movies they showed. The IS Conference resolution, June 1976, "The Black work and the fight against Racism" acknowledged "We must admit that our comrades have been outflanked on occasions by the militancy of the black sections on anti- NF demonstrations", *IS post-conference bulletin*, June 1976.

160   The *Guardian* counted 5,000, the *Leveller* 7,500.

161   John Rose, 1976, "The Southall Asian Youth Movement", *International Socialism* 91, September 1976, https://www.marxists.org/history/etol/newspape/isj/1976/no091/rose.htm. A further reason was the community leaders prioritising the State of Emergency in India called by prime minister Indira Gandhi - on which they were deeply divided, seeing it as more important than the racism in Southall.

162   We won't be sheep, *Observer*, 13 June 1976.

163   John Rose, 1976.

164   *Youth Rebels: The Story of the Southall Youth Movement* https://www.youtube.com/watch?v=OGWX233kHPg

165   *Socialist Worker* 10 July 1976. *Youth Rebels: The Story of the Southall Youth Movement*. The squat was at 12 Featherstone Road.

166   'Scuffles at London protest march', *Morning Star* 13 July 1976; *Socialist Worker* 10 July 1976

167   *Times* 8 May 1976.

168   *Observer* 16 May; *Times* 17 May; *Red Weekly* 20 May; *Socialist*

Worker 22 May. Twenty-eight were arrested. According to *NF News* August 1976, hundreds of signatures in support of Relf were collected on a petition in two factories in Wolverhampton, GKN Sankey and Guy Motors.

169   Rose, 1976.

170   Rehad Desai, private communication, 28 February 2022.

171   Ramila Patel, private communication, 12 May 2023. Some local Asian youth groups called themselves AYO some AYM.

172   Gravesend, Kent, *Socialist Worker* 21 August 1976; Balwinder Rana, private email, 8 January 2020. The figure of 600 is from police reports.

173   *Socialist Worker* 28 August 1976.

174   *Socialist Worker* 11 September 1976.

175   'Special Branch report on the first public meeting of the Hackney Community Relations Council defended by a picket of left-wing groups, 4 August 1976', https://www.ucpi.org.uk/search-results/?fwp_search=UCPI0000010769 . The report refers to 'impassioned speeches on racialism generally' with trouble occurring only when an NF member intervened during questions and was 'ejected... amid a shower of fists and invective'.

176   *Young Rebels: The Story of the Southall youth movement*, https://www.youtube.com/watch?v=OGWX233kHPg .

177   Jill Catlow, interviewed by Geoff Brown 16 June 2021.

178   'More attacks on Asians as Right gets stronger', *Observer* 20 June 1976.

179   *Spare Rib* November 1976, p.12. There was some ill-thought-out direct action. One group cut the brake cable of a fascist's car parked on a hill. Brian McDonald, interviewed by Geoff Brown 23 March 2021.

180   *Red Weekly* 16 September 1976. Khadim Quereshi, AYO member, was quoted at length in the *Observer*: 'We are fed up with the slave mentality of our so-called community leaders, the guys who sit on the local Community Relations Council. These guys were in the front of the anti racist march without banners, walking quietly like dummies, while we were at the back waving banners, chanting and shouting'. The young demonstrators were joined by the local Communists and other leftist groups. The same article also quoted another young Asian: 'Recently the Communists have been active in the Asian areas, knocking on doors, telling us that the major parties are using us as pawns to win cheap popularity," said Mohammad Dassu, a 25-year-old Malawi Asian, who is a maintenance worker with an engineering firm. "The other day the Communists held an open-air meeting in Altom Street and attracted a crowd of 150 Asians, mostly young. The Communists are the only whites we see in our area who take an open anti-racialist stand"', *Observer* 20 June 1976,

181   The march was to back the NP candidate in a by-election after Frankman was disqualified because of an undeclared suspended prison sentence. A dossier collected by the local Community Relations Council listed over thirty attacks on people and property in ten days. 'The National Party', *World in Action* 22 November 1976.

182   Walker, 1977, p.199; *Socialist Worker* 18 September 1976; *Red*

Weekly 16 September 1976; Action against Racism '[brought] together people from the Indian and Pakistani communities, trade unionists, church leaders, community relations workers and members of the Labour, Liberal and Communist parties', *Searchlight* June 1976.

183   *Searchlight* June 1976. *Red Weekly* estimated the far left comprised about half the march.

184   Ramamurthy, 2013, p.44; Hassan Mahamdallie, 'A history of Muslim workers in Britain', *International Socialism* 113, 2007, https://www.marxists.org/history/etol/newspape/isj2/2007/isj2-113/mahamdallie.html

185   Greg Dyke interviewed by Geoff Brown 1 September 2021.

186   'Race: Can Labour make up the ground it lost by dodging the issue?', *Tribune* 3 September 1976.

187   Gerg Dyke, 'Labour's half hearted campaign on race', *Tribune* 24 September 1976.

188   TUC General Council decision to campaign against racialism in cooperation with Labour Party, letter to affiliates, 7 October 1976.

189   TUC Circular, 'The facts of Racial Disadvantage', PEP report 5 August 1976; NUM Circular, 'Immigration and Race Relations' 13 September 1976.

190   TUC press release July 1976. See Robert Miles & Annie Phizacklea, 'The T.U.C. and Black Workers 1974-76', *British Journal of Industrial Relations*, vol.16, no.2, 1978, p.199. The TUC also set up a new subcommittee, the TUC Equal Rights Committee.

191   Pat Wall, chair of Bradford Trades Council, Action against Racism conference, Blackburn, 18 June 1977. The party political broadcast was on 14 September 1976.

192   Dyke, 1976. Tony Benn chaired the campaign launch but did not mention it in his daily diary. The speakers' notes include reference to 'patriality', the racist term used in immigration law to distinguish those with parents or grandparents born in Britain.

193   *Times* 22 November 1976.

194   See the book website for a list of local anti-racist and anti-fascist groups.

195   Dave Peers interviewed by Geoff Brown 27 March 2023.

196   'Organising the fight back against the ultra-right', *Leveller* November 1976.

197   'East End boy dies after race marches', *Observer* 13 June 1976.

198   Bob Light, in Roger Huddle & Red Saunders eds., *Reminiscences of RAR* (Redwords, 2021), p.156; *Guardian* 14 June 1976. There were 2,000 on the anti-cuts demonstration. When the local Labour MP, Reg Prentice, at a school prize giving a short distance away, was told what was going on, he echoed Roy Jenkins, commenting: 'I cannot see that marches and demonstrations are of any help at all'. Letter from Tony Kelly, *Tribune* 25 June 1976. The day ended with Asian and white youths being questioned at a local police station about the fatal stabbing that afternoon of a white teenager, Christopher Vernon Adamson. The police told the press: 'Any suggestion that this incident was inspired by racial conflict would be purely speculative': 'East End boy dies after race marches', *Observer* 13 June 1976.

199 In March 1979, there were eleven anti-racist groups in Leicester. See website for a list of local anti-racist and anti-fascist groups.

200 *Morning Star* 26 June 1976.

201 *Tribune* 18 June 1976.

202 Hann, p.255.

203 Rick Blackman, *Babylon's Burning* (Bookmarks, 2021), p.137.

204 *Socialist Worker* 19 June 1976.

4: Grunwick and Lewisham

1   Jayaben Desai, 'We are those lions, Mr Manager', *TUC 150 Stories* (TUC, 1978), https://tuc150.tuc.org.uk/stories/jayaben-desai/.

2   Yuri Prasad, 'Here to stay, here to fight: How Asians transformed the British working class', *International Socialism* 153, Winter 2017.

3   'Grunwick changed me', Radio 4, 17 August 2016, https://www.bbc.co.uk/programmes/b07npvfh

4   Jayaben Desa speaking at Acton Anti Nazi League launch meeting, *Socialist Worker* 4 February 1978

5   Working Class Movement Library, https://www.wcml.org.uk/our-collections/protest-politics-and-campaigning-for-change/grunwick/

6   'Strike Fury!', *Daily Mirror* 17 June 1977; 'Grunwick Will Sue Postal Workers', *Financial Times* 17 June 1977.

7   *Times* 21 June 1977.

8   Neil McAllister, interviewed by Geoff Brown 12 February 2018.

9   John Deason suggests that the first mass picket was on Thursday 5 May. The first mass picket was on Thursday 5 May. A large number of trade unionists had come to the Old Bailey where John Deason was on trial, charged with 'intent to cause grievous bodily harm' when the police attacked the Right to Work march a year earlier, *Socialist Worker* 27 March 1976; *Socialist Worker* 14 May 1977. When the 'Not Guilty' verdict was made, it was decided to go the Grunwick picket line rather than the pub. John Deason interviewed by Geoff Brown 23 December 2023.

10   Edith Moody, 'Victor Jara: My Song Has Found a Purpose', *Plough* 14 September 2018,

https://www.plough.com/en/topics/culture/music/victor-jara-my-song-has-found-a-purpose

11   'New Picket Law Hint as 18,000 March', *Financial Times* 12 July 1977; 'Mob violence worse than murder – Mark', *Daily Mail* 13 July 1977. Sir Robert Mark was McNee's predecessor as Metropolitan Police Commissioner. Tyndall's response to the mass pickets at Grunwick: 'Equip the police with water cannon, tear gas and rubber bullets, with full authority to use those implements as the situation required… When we obtain the mandate to govern this country, as one day we will, we will take all measures necessary to restore the rule of law to our streets and places

of work, learning and leisure', *Spearhead* July 1977.

12   Dave Hann, *Physical Resistance: A Hundred Years of Anti-Fascism* (Zero Books, 2013), pp.257–9.

13   Paul Ward, Graham Hellawell, Sally Lloyd, 2006, 'Witness Seminar: Anti-Fascism in 1970s Huddersfield', *Contemporary British History*, vol.20, no.1, p.127.

14   Satnam Virdee, 'Anti-racism and the socialist left, 1968–79', in Evan Smith & Matthew Worley, eds., *Against the Grain: The British Far Left from 1956* (Manchester, 2014), p.135.

15   Tony Bogues, 'Black Youth in Revolt', *International Socialism* series 1, no.102, October 1977.

16   *Socialist Worker* 11 June 1977.

17   Islington 18 Defence Committee, *Under Heavy Manners: Report of the Labour Movement Enquiry into Police Brutality and the Position of Black Youth in Islingto*n, Saturday July 23rd 1977.

18   Danny Phillips, interviewed by Geoff Brown 2 June 2020; Martin Kettle, 'Mcnee makes his mark, Report of the Commissioners of Police of the Metropolis for the Year 1977', *State Research Bulletin* No 7, Aug Sept 1978; David Michael, the first black police officer to work in Lewisham in 1973, commented: 'The police were like an occupying army': 'No quick fix', *Economist* 18 September 2008. The Blackburn police brought a case of 'conspiracy to loiter with intent' against Asian youth. The case was demolished by the barrister after the prosecuting police officer brought in an Asian police officer from Preston as a witness whose ignorance of Blackburn meant he was unable to answer simple questions about where the young Asians accused of conspiracy had been loitering. Brian McDonald, interviewed by Geoff Brown 23 March 2021; Webster 'was invited by the Durham Constabulary to address a course on public order for senior police officers': 'The NF and the police', *State Research Bulletin* No 7, Aug Sept 1978, p.126.

19   *Kentish Mercury* 16 June 1977.

20   The name changed at the beginning of 1977 after a vote at the IS annual conference, November 1976.

21   *Socialist Worker* 11 June 1977; *Kentish Mercury* 16 June 1977. To the intense annoyance of the police, Prince Charles stopped to talk to protestors and invited Kim Gordon to visit him.

22   *South London Press* 5 July 1977.

23   *Kentish Mercury* 5 July 1977.

24   *Guardian* 4 July 1977.

25   'Enoch Powell pinpoints a growing peril: mugging', *Daily Mail* 12 April 1976.

26   *National Front News* December 1976.

27   Sheila Amrouche, contributing to 'Confronting the Nazis: The Battle of Lewisham 1977', Marxism festival 2017, swpTVuk, https://www.youtube.

com/watch?v=fi14X0zEzW0. There were regular clashes between SW sellers and NF sellers, David Renton, *Never Again: Rock Against Racism and the Anti-Nazi League 1976–1982* (Routledge, 2019), pp.74–5.

28   *South London Press* 5 July 1977.

29   'Synd 13 8 77 National Front demonstration in London', AP Archive, https://www.youtube.com/watch?v=hK0aURnC314

30   Ted Parker, 2007, 'Ted Parker remembers the Battle of Lewisham', http://lewisham77.blogspot.com/2007/08/.

31   *Daily Telegraph* 23 January 1977.

32   The by-election was triggered by Home Secretary Roy Jenkins leaving British politics to become president of the European Commission.

33   *Daily Telegraph* 2 April 1977; *National Front News* June 1977.

34   Sheila McGregor, interviewed by Geoff Brown 30 September 2020.

35   The NF beat the Liberals in thirty-two constituencies.

36   Tim Potter, 'Lessons of Lewisham', *International Socialism* series 1, no.101, September 1977; 'Mirror Comment', *Daily Mirror* 14 July 1976.

37   "Anti Nazi League| Rock against Racism | Protest | Demonstration | Thames Television |1978', broadcast 22 February 1979, https://www.youtube.com/watch?v=tvmUVE05XRQ. See Chapter 8.2. 'No plugs for NF thugs'.

38   David Widgery, *Beating Time* (Chatto & Windus, 1986), p.43.

39   See 'Special Branch report on an election campaign aggregate meeting of the South London IMG', p,2, https://www.ucpi.org.uk/publications/special-branch-report-on-an-election-campaign-aggregate-meeting-of-the-south-london-img/. There was also the Enfield Committee for Racial Harmony. See 'Wood Green, April', *CARF* August September 1977, Working Class Movement Library.

40   Keith Flett, 'The Battle of Wood Green 23rd April 1977', *KMFlett's Blog*, 13 August 2017,
https://kmflett.wordpress.com/2017/08/13/the-battle-of-wood-green-23rd-april-1977/, 2017.

41   As previous footnote.

42   *Platform*, The Paper of the London Transport Rank & File Organisation, n.d early 1977, Modern Records Centre, University of Warwick.

43   Lucy Whitman, London against Racism Timeline, https://londonagainstracism.wordpress.com/timeline/ (accessed 27 June 2020).

44   *Hornsey Journal* 29 April 1977. Together it was forty-five. The council had sixty members.

45   Keith Flett, 2019; New information on the Battle of Wood Green, *KMFlett'sBlog* 23rd April 1977, https://kmflett.wordpress.com/2019/04/17/new-information-on-the-battle-of-wood-green-23rd-april-1977/

46   *Times* 25 April 1977.

47   Mary Littlefield interviewed by Geoff Brown 5 August 2020.

48   Kieth Flett, 'New information on the Battle of Wood Green', *KMFlett's Blog* 23rd April 1977, https://kmflett.wordpress.com/2019/04/17/new-information-on-the-battle-of-wood-green-23rd-april-1977/

49   Julie Davies, private notes of Haringey Co-operative Party meeting, 16 June 2021.

50   *Guardian* 25 April 1977.

51   Gavin Weightman, 'Red Roses and drums', *New Society* 27 April 1977. Richard Buckwell remembers being attacked on the way home, interview with Geoff Brown 24 May 2022

52   *Hornsey Journal* 29 April 1977.

53   *Observer* 24 April 1977; *Daily Mail* 25 April 1977; *Guardian* 25 April 1977.

54   *Guardian* 25 April 1977.

55   Widgery, 1986, pp.43–4; Jerry Fitzpatrick, in Roger Huddle & Red Saunders eds, *Reminiscences of RAR* (Redwords, 2016), p.76.

56   John Lockwood, speaking in 'Confronting the Nazis: The Battle of Lewisham 1977', Marxism festival 2017, swpTVuk, https://www.youtube.com/watch?v=fi14X0zEzW0. Richard Buckwell remembers 'loads of Turkish, Greek and black kids throwing shoes', Richard Buckwell, n.d., 'Spurs against the Nazis', p.28, *https://antifascistarchive.net/wp-content/uploads/2012/09/spurs-against-the-nazis.pdf*

57   Jerry Fitzpatrick in Huddle & Saunders, 2016, p.76

58   *Kentish Mercury* 28 July 1977. The meeting was in Lewisham Concert Hall.

59   Fitzpatrick, 2016, p76.

60   Copsey, 2017, p126.

61   CARF August-September 1977; Jenny Bourne, 'Lewisham '77: Success or failure?', *Institute of Race Relations*, 2007, https://irr.org.uk/article/lewisham-77-success-or-failure/

62   John Lockwood, speaking in 'Confronting the Nazis: The Battle of Lewisham 1977', Marxism festival 2017, swpTVuk, https://www.youtube.com/watch?v=fi14X0zEzW0.

63   John Lockwood, as above

64   As above

65   Mike Power, *The Fascist Threat: A Young Communist Review of Fascist and Authoritarian Trends (*Young Communist League, 1974). Mike Power was a member of the Communist Party History Group and author of the pamphlet *The Struggle against Fascism and War in Britain, 1931–1939* (1977).

66   Fitzpatrick, 2016, p77.

67   *Socialist Worker* 9 July 1977, p.13, https://www.marxists.org/history/etol/newspape/sw-gb/1977/535-09-jul-1977.pdf#page=12.90&gsr=0

68   John Lockwood, speaking in 'Confronting the Nazis: The Battle of Lewisham 1977', Marxism festival 2017, swpTVuk, https://www.youtube.com/watch?v=fi14XozEzW0. An SWP leaflet urged people to go to Clifton Rise after the ALCARAF demonstration. There was also a Communist Party leaflet that condemned 'the harassment and provocative march planned by the SWP', attacking 'those who insist on the ritual enactment of vanguardist violence.' Chanie Rosenberg, 1988, 'Labour and the fight against fascism', *International Socialism*, series 2, no.39, pp.76–77. https://www.marxists.org/history/etol/writers/rosenberg/1988/xx/antifascism.html. According to Copsey, it was the CP leaflet that attracted the most attention, Nigel Copsey, *Anti-fascism in Britain* (Macmillan, 2000), p.123.

69   *South London Press* 5 August 1977.

70   Widgery, 1986, p.45. The final call to assemble at Clifton Rise was made by 'the August 13 Organising Committee, supported by Lewisham 21 Defence Committee, SWP, Right to Work Campaign and individual members of the Labour Party and Communist Party', *Socialist Worker* 13 August 1977. ARAFCC called on people to support both the ALCARAF demonstration and to go to Clifton Rise. Unsure whether the ARAFCC stewards would be sufficiently disciplined, the SWP organised its stewards separately. 'Haringey lit the fuse, Lewisham is the explosion', *Socialist Challenge* 4 August 1977, https://www.marxists.org/history/etol/newspape/socialist-challenge/sc-n09-aug-4-1977.pdf#page=8.00. *Socialist Challenge* was the weekly newspaper of the International Marxist Group. Tariq Ali was its best-known member.

71   *South London Press* 5 August 1977.

72   National Front members bulletin July 1977, 'EMERGENCY Extra', *Socialist Worker* 30 July 1977.

73   *Times* 15 August 1977.

74   *Kentish Mercury* 28 July 1977.

75   *Times* 30 July 1977.

76   *South London Press* 12 August 1977; Renton, 2019, p.74.

77   *Times* 13 August 1977.

78   Andy Strouthous quoted in David Renton, *When We Touched the Sky: The Anti-Nazi League 1977–1981* (New Clarion Press, 2006).

79   Andy Strouthous, contributing to 'Confronting the Nazis: The Battle of Lewisham 1977', Marxism festival 2017, swpTVuk, https://www.youtube.com/watch?v=fi14XozEzW0.

80   Andy Strouthous, interviewed by Geoff Brown 1 July 2020.

81   David Glanz, private email, 31 July 2022.

82   Harold Wilson, speaking in 'Confronting the Nazis: The Battle of

Lewisham 1977', Marxism festival 2017, swpTVuk, https://www.youtube.com/watch?v=fi14XozEzW0. Nunchucks are martial arts weapons made popular by the actor Bruce Lee in films such as *Fist of Fury*.

83   David Renton, 'Anti-fascism in the North West, 1976–1982', *North West Labour History Journal* no.27, 2002, p.73.

84   Michael Crowley, interviewed by Geoff Brown 2 October 2019.

85   Widgery notes the indignation they show at a distance from the fascists. Widgery, 1986, pp.45–7. Michael Crowley remembers it being 'very grey. It threatened to rain all day but never did. Lewisham in the seventies was grey in general. The housing was pre-war. Ungentrified. Buildings and brickwork were still smog stained… It was not a part of London that tourists went near'. Michael Crowley, interviewed by Geoff Brown 23 September 2021.

86   *Kentish Mercury* 16 August 1977.

87   *Times* 15 August 1977. The slogans came from the WARF members who had been on the Grunwick picket lines, Bourne, 2007; Nigel Young, 'Crossroads – which way now?', *Gay Left* no.5, Winter 1977.

88   'Madeleine', UCPI Tranche 1 (Phase 2) Evidence Hearings - Day 13 - Transcript p47, https://www.ucpi.org.uk/publications/evidence-hearings-t1-p2-day-13/ .

89   Ted Parker, n.d., gives '3,000–4,000'. The Special Branch report gives a figure of 1,500. According to the Special Branch report, Nick Bradley, Labour Party Young Socialist, called on all those present to attend Clifton Rise later, raising some local enthusiasm in the process, all the others pleading in varying degrees for restraint.' ARAFCC called on its members to be at both demonstrations, Bourne, 2007.

90   *South London Press* 16 August 1977.

91   Hann, 2013, p.268.

92   Michael Crowley, private email, 23 September 2020.

93   Ted Parker, n.d., 'Ted Parker & the Battle of Lewisham', *London Against Racism*, https://londonagainstracism.wordpress.com/films/ted-parker/

94   Hann, 2013, p.267. Though organised by SWP members, this coach was in addition to the call in *Socialist Worker* 13 August 1977 for 'All SWP branches and members in London, Midlands and Home Counties to support'.

95   The following quotes give an idea of how journalists relied on the police for their information: 'The SWP were occupying the derelict shop next to the New Cross House pub. Police broke down a door and evicted the squatters, arresting 7 and taking a quantity of propaganda and banners', *Kentish Mercury* 18 August 1977. 'The first clash came… when police ousted Socialist Workers Party members from the New Cross Road shop they were squatting in, overlooking Clifton Rise', *South London Press* 18 August 1977.

96   Widgery, 1986, pp.46–7.

97   Julia Poynter, Statement to the UCPI, 11 March 2022, UCPI0000034801.pdf p.18, https://photos.google.com/album/ AF1QipPxcGO6o7tLohOpfjwADr_js8mzK4tTd_edGKZz/photo/ AF1QipMLW7EsfLJ6UdhYLOylDbo-fztxOq-ETsSrloa6

98   UCPI Tranche 1 (Phase 2) Evidence Hearings - Day 13 – Transcript, p.48
https://www.ucpi.org.uk/publications/evidence-hearings-t1-p2-day-13/ .

99   Others remember it was Junior Murvin 'Police and Thieves'. John Sorrell remembers Bob Marley.

100   Widgery, 1986, pp.46–7.

101   Bourne, 2007.

102   Name withheld, private conversation, July 2020.

103   Alan Gibbons, Facebook, 13 August 2019.

104   *Guardian* 15 August 1977; *Times* 15 August 1977.

105   Fitzpatrick, 2016, p.81.

106   *Socialist Worker* 20 August 1977, p.7.

107   *Socialist Worker* 20 August 1977.

108   *Kentish Mercury* 18 August 1977.

109   *South London Press* 16 August 1977.

110   Tony Parsons, *Stories We Could Tell* (HarperCollins, 2005), p.11.

111   *South London Press* 16 August 1977; John Sorrell, London against Racism Timeline.

112   *Camerawork 8*, 'Lewisham: What are you taking pictures for?', https://www.fourcornersarchive.org/archive/view/0000009

113   Michael Crowley, private email, 1 October 2020

114   *Socialist Worker* 20 August 1977, p.8

115   Balwinder Rana, contributing to 'Confronting the Nazis: The Battle of Lewisham 1977', Marxism festival 2017, swpTVuk, https://www.youtube.com/watch?v=fi14XozEzWo.

116   John Sorrell, *London Against Racism*, https://londonagainstracism.wordpress.com/people/john-sorrell/; Richard Bundy, interviewed by Geoff Brown 23 January 2018.

117   "Aug 13" video, Spectacle Archive, http://www.spectacle.co.uk/spectacleblog/active-archive/lost-video-13-aug-on-battle-of-lewisham-1977-found-in-spectacle-archive/ accessed 14 July 2020.

118   *Socialist Worker* 20 August 1977, p8.

119   "Riot shields - protective or aggressive?" *New Scientist*, 22 September 1977, p739. Shields were borrowed from the army to be used at the Ladywood by-election the following week and again at the Notting Hill Carnival a fortnight later.

120 Phillips, 2020. Henry Blaxland, part of the legal support team, went to Lewisham police station to check Danny was okay. The duty officer told him: 'Mr Phillips is looking after himself fine.' He observed cops taking refuge in the police station chased by black youths.

121 John Dennis, in Roger Huddle & Red Saunders, *Reminiscences of RAR* (Redwords, 2016), p.54.

122 *Socialist Worker* 20 August 1977, p.8.

123 One example of how magistrates behaved was the fine imposed on Mark Dodgson for shouting 'scabs' on the Grunwick picket line, *Socialist Worker* 11 March 1978.

124 Paul Holborow, speaking in 'Confronting the Nazis: The Battle of Lewisham 1977', Marxism festival 2017, swpTVuk, https://www.youtube.com/watch?v=fi14XozEzW0.

125 Widgery, 1986, p.49.

126 Dave Glanz, private email, 31 July 1977.

127 Joseph Pearce, *Race with the Devil: My Journey from Racial Hatred to Rational Love* (Saint Benedict Press, 2013), p.59.

128 David McNee quoted in '214 seized, 110 hurt in clashes at Front march', *Sunday Times* 14 August 1977

129 *Daily Mail* 15 August 1977.

130 *Daily Mail* 15 August 1977,

131 'Lewisham and the Law', *Daily Telegraph* 15 August 1977.

132 *Morning Star* 17 August 1977.

133 *Guardian* 16 August 1977.

134 *Times* 15 August 1977.

135 There were three Special Branch reports. The first, a short report of the Metropolitan Police Special Branch debrief meeting, 23 August 1977, says that there were eighteen Special Branch on duty and also reports on the success of the police operation, https://www.ucpi.org.uk/wp-content/uploads/2021/04/MPS-0733369.pdf. The two subsequent reports are more frank on the failings of the police.

136 John Deason, interviewed by Geoff Brown 23 December 2023.

137 McAllister, 2018.

138 *Socialist Worker* 10 September 1977.

139 Lindsay Mackie, 'Left accused of attacking police', *Guardian* 15 August 1977.

140 *Guardian* 15 August 1977.

141 Duncan Hallas, 'Letters to the Editor', *Guardian* 17 August 1977.

142 See previous footnote.

143 John Bloomfield, *Morning Star* 20 August 1977.

144 *Morning Star* 12 August 1977.

145   *Morning Star* 15 August 1977.

146   Labour Party Annual Report 1977, p.314.

147   Dave Cook, 'They shall not pass', *Morning Star* 27 August 1977.

148   Mick Woods, 'Mick Woods remembers Lewisham '77', https://lewisham77.blogspot.com/2007/.

149   *Socialist Worker* 10 September 1977.

150   John Larkham, letter, *Socialist Worker*, 27 August 1977,

151   Phillips, 2020. Danny also recalled a senior police officer coming up with a team of SPG: 'He started to harass me and then I was arrested. In court, not one member of his team would give evidence against me'.

152   Buckwell, n.d., p.28.

153   Paul Holborow, 'The Anti Nazi League and its lessons for today', *International Socialism* 163, July 2019.

154   *Women's Voice* June 1978.

155   Daniel Rachel, *Walls Come Tumbling Down: The Music and Politics of Rock Against Racism, 2 Tone and Red Wedge* (Picador, 2016), p.111.

156   Rachel, p.96.

157   Fitzpatrick, 2016, p.77.

Launching the Anti Nazi League

1   *Socialist Worker* 20 August 1977.

2   The battle of Cable Street did not stop Mosley from marching in Bermondsey a year after Cable Street, October 1937, when 5,000 BUF supporters marched from Millbank to Bermondsey.

3   *Spearhead* 10th anniversary issue, May 1977.

4   Besides Webster's announcement, Tom Pendry, MP for Hyde, Greater Manchester, told the press the NF were planning to march in his constituency 10 September, *Guardian* 15 August 1977.

5   Jack Robertson, interviewed by Geoff Brown 5 November 2019.

6   For details of the violence see *Blood on the Streets: A Report on Racial Attacks in East London* (Bethnal Green and Stepney Trades Council, 1978)

7   Daniel Rachel, *Walls Come Tumbling Down: The Music and Politics of Rock Against Racism, 2 Tone and Red Wedge* (Picador, 2016), p.208.

8   *Countering Fascism: Towards an Alternative Approach* (Birmingham Counter-Fascism Group, 1978), personal archive.

9   Jenny Bourne, 2018, 'CARF: the life and times of-a frontline magazine', *Race & Class* vol.59, no.3; *Leveller*, November 1976, notes 'more than 200 anti racist/anti fascist committees' while *Searchlight*, July 1978, estimates a hundred local committees. See this book's accompanying website (in construction) for a list of anti-racist and anti-fascist groups. There were also those opposed to working in these committees, for example, the Revolutionary Communist Group, *The Anti Nazi League and the*

Struggle against Racism (RCG, 1978).

10   North Staffordshire Campaign Against Racism and Fascism (Nor SCARF) continues to be active, https://www.facebook.com/NorSCARF/?locale=en_GB.

11   Circular letter from LARAFC, 21 March 1978. LARAFC had a lifespan similar to the ANL, 1977–1981. Its substantial archive is in the Modern Records Centre, Warwick. See Doug Lowe, 'The Respectable Revolutionaries: Leamington Anti-Racist Anti-Fascist Committee 1977–1981', http://www.whatnextjournal.org.uk/Pages/Latest/LARAFC.html. LARAFC encouraged people to join the ANL, distributing membership cards and the Founding Statement. Its own activities included a well-attended march the day before the Victoria Park Carnival plus a coach to the Carnival. Leamington was where Robert Relf had put up his notorious 'For sale - to an English family only' sign and a racist had murdered Mrs Mohan Dev Gautam eighteen months earlier.

12   *North West Anti Fascist News* October 1974, p.4, reported the anti-fascist opposition to recent NF meetings in Bolton and Blackburn 'tended to be very disorganised. Manchester AFC discussed this and suggested in future that those coming to support should accept the organisation and discipline of the local group'.

13   ARAFCC included Women against Racism and Fascism (WARF), set up after Wood Green, which was prominent on the Grunwick mass pickets, 'Women against Racism and Fascism', CARF 2 August September 1977, p.10. Struggling to coordinate their activities, ARAFCC's attempt to found a national organisation at a national conference in June 1978 failed. 'After the emergence of the ANL, the London Co-ordinating Committee running CARF decided against competing with the new anti-fascist leadership and so disbanded in September 1978', see Simon Murdoch, 'From the Archive: Fascism is not our only scourge', https://hopenothate.org.uk/2020/08/30/from-the-archive-carf/#_ftn2. There was a regional coordination established by a number of AFCs in southern England, Andy Bell, *Searchlight* Interview 17 September 2015, *Searchlight* Oral Histories Collection.

14   Interim Report of the Right to Work Campaign March of Unemployed Workers, Manchester–London, 27 February–20 March 1976. See also Duncan Hallas, 'On the United Front Tactic: Some Preliminary Notes', *International Socialism* 85, January 1976.

15   See Chapter 3 'Fighting racism and fascism'. Deansgate is an area in the centre of Manchester.

16   Anna Paczuska, interviewed by Geoff Brown 26 February 2023.

17   'Dockers against Racism', *Socialist Worker* 24 August 1974, 'Dockers against Racism', *Socialist Worker* 19 June 1976. Roger Cox stood as a Socialist Worker candidate in a Brent Council by-election in November 1976. After being the SWP Central Committee suggested this was a mistake, the campaign was given an anti-NF focus. The Saturday before the poll a band on a lorry was organised. It drove down 'the high street of Harlesden. It turned into a "riot", older black women came out and they were dancing behind it… A mini carnival for about an hour'. Cox got 3.8 percent of the vote. Roger Cox interviewed by Geoff Brown December 2021; Roger Cox,

2019, 'Marxist politics at work during the long boom and its breakdown', *International Socialism* 161, https://isj.org.uk/marxist-politics-at-work/.

18   *Socialist Worker* 9 July 1977, p.13 https://www.marxists.org/history/etol/newspape/sw-gb/1977/535-09-jul-1977.pdf#page=12.90&gsr=0. See Chapter 4 'Grunwick and Lewisham'.

19   Martin Walker, *The National Front* (Fontana, 1977), p.232.

20   This had to include defending campaigners when facing arrest and prosecution, both when confronting the fascist demonstrations and in local activities. George Pogmore and Paul Lannen, members of York SWP, were fined a total of £500 for 'conduct likely to cause a breach of the peace' after clashes with NF members when handing out leaflets, *Socialist Worker* 22 April 1978. York Trades Council, affiliated to the ANL, set up a defence fund.

21   Hugo Young, 'Mrs Thatcher and the fascist figleaf', *Sunday Times* 5 February 1978.

22   Jim Nichol, private email 30 June 2020.

23   Jim Nichol, private email 20 August 2019.

24   On NVDA, the Peace Pledge Union 'Racism: Towards a non-violent approach' conference, Bradford, March 1978, came up with peace keeping proposals such as 'a Peace Bus that could be in an area a week before, say, a National Front march. The team would work in the area, distributing leaflets, talking with people. They could take as their symbol the orange, a fruit that retains a certain integrity whether as a whole or in segments. It can be shared as a pretext for wandering around talking with people as we distribute the individual segments, six to the left, two to the bystanders/reporters, two to the police, two to the NF': Brenda Thompson, 'Responses to Racism', *Peace News* 24 March 1978. See also Howard Clark, 'No to the politics of hate', *Peace News* 21 October 1978.

25   Geoff Brown remembers Colin Barnett asking him whether the SWP could control its 'wild boys' in a meeting with him early 1978.

26   Jim Nichol, interviewed by Geoff Brown 19 July 2019. The urgent appeal was made in 'The Urgent Challenge of Fascism' leaflet. See Chapter 1 'Rivers of Blood', note 10.

27   The argument continued. See 'Questions for Anti Nazi League', letter, *Socialist Worker* 28 January 1978. The ANL campaign conference in July 1978 passed a motion proposed by the SWP opposing all immigration controls. The conference also decided that this did not require opposition to all immigration controls as a condition of membership. See Chapter 9 'Counting down to the election'.

28   Nichol, private email 30 August 2019. There was an Anti Nazi League in the 1930s based in Hollywood. Nichol had no knowledge of this. See Hollywood Anti-Nazi League Organized, https://todayinclh.com/?event=hollywood-anti-nazi-league-organized.

29   Nichol, August 2019.

30   Director of Shelter (1974–1976), author of a pamphlet on the Ugandan Asian Crisis, previously Director of the Community and Race Relations Unit, British Council of Churches.

31   Nichol, 19 July 2019; David Renton, *Never Again: Rock Against*

Racism and the Anti-Nazi League 1976–1982 (Routledge, 2019), p.89.

32   Jim Nichol, private email 30 June 2020.

33   Nichol, 30 August 2019 and 30 June 2020. See also David Widgery, *Beating Time* (Chatto & Windus, 1986), pp.49–50.

34   Geoff Brown & Christian Hogsbjerg, *Apartheid is Not a Game* (Redwords, 2020), p.55.

35   Paul Holborow interviewed by Geoff Brown 16 December 2021. Holborow recalls that Tony Cliff was impressed by Holborow's ability to 'hide the dagger in the smile', one of the 'Thirty-Six Stratagems', a sixth-century Chinese essay. Cliff was a founding member of what became the International Socialists, generally recognised as its leading member.

36   Kevin Corr, interviewed by Geoff Brown January 2021. Holborow is the SWP organiser referred to in Liz Fekete, 'Dockers Against Racism: An interview with Micky Fenn', *Race & Class*, vol.58, no.1, pp.55–60, libcom.org/article/dockers-against-racism-interview-micky-fenn.

37   Paul Holborow, SWP member since 1969, had been 'active in East London since 1974, involved in the successful defence of the Lea Bridge Road mosque, the opposition to the NF paper sales in Barking and Stratford shopping precincts, the big anti-racist marches in Ilford and Hoxton and the anti-racist protest strike at Ford's Dagenham', Widgery, 1986, p.50.

38   Nichol, 30 August 2019.

39   Peter Hain, *Outside In* (Biteback Publishing, 2012), pp.118–120. Hain had been re-elected president of the Young Liberals at their Easter 1976 conference with an overwhelming majority (222 votes, his nearest rival receiving 61). At the time the left of the Young Liberals identified themselves as 'libertarian socialists', see *Guardian* 19 April 1976.

40   In his chapter 'Anti-racism and the socialist left, 1968–79', Satnam Virdee confuses the ANL 1977–1979 with the relaunched ANL, 1980–81, in Evan Smith & Matthew Worley, eds., *Against the Grain: The British Far Left from 1956* (Manchester University Press, 2014), p.221. See Chapter 10 'Taking down the beast', p.13.

41   Hain, pp.118–9. For 'Stop the Seventy Tour', see Brown & Hogsbjerg, 2020.

42   Ernie Roberts, *Workers' Control* (Allen & Unwin, 1973).

43   Roberts, 1973, p.89; Ernie Roberts, *Strike Back* (Self-published, 1994), pp.39–40; John Deason, interviewed by Geoff Brown 23 December 2023. Roberts gave the opening report for the afternoon session of the 'Britain's Colonies and the Colour Bar' conference convened by *Labour Monthly* 26 October 1958 with delegates from ninety-three TU, Co-op and Labour organisations. See *Labour Monthly* December 1958, p.529 & 563. He was on the platform of the Movement for Colonial Freedom (MCF) public meeting on immigration and race relations in November 1962 in Ipswich. Speakers included Dingle Foot and Johnny James, British Guiana.

44   Hain, p.118.

45   Paul Holborow interviewed in Rachel, 2016, p.121.

46   Paul Holborow, interviewed by Geoff Brown 11 May 2020.

47   Robertson, 2019.

48   The statement was printed with the names of sponsors. As the number of sponsors increased it was reprinted, at least twice, until the page could accommodate no more.

49   Walker, p.233.

50   Terry Verity, 'NF Gold Medallist Speaks Out', CARF Oct/Nov 1977 p.3, personal archive.

51   *Guardian* 17 August 1977; *Times* 18 August 1977.

52   Mike and Heather Luft, interviewed by Geoff Brown 23 November 2018.

53   Manchester Trades Council letter to TUC re Campaign against Racialism, 8 October 1978, personal archive.

54   Public order in Greater Manchester, Note of a meeting held on 5 September 1977, HO 4/8/26, personal archive.

55   The police operation cost £250,000, £1.4m at 2025 prices, 'Council faces dilemma over Front', Guardian 9 January 1978.

56   Ramila Patel, interviewed by Geoff Brown 15 September 2020.

57   Alan Gibbons, interviewed by Geoff Brown 8 May 2018. See also *New Manchester Review* 42, October 1977.

58   *New Manchester Review* 43, October/November 1977. Anderton's capacity to operate outside of accepted norms also included 'The Siege of Collyhurst', when, without informing the police authority or residents, a paramilitary anti-terrorist exercise was held in the Collyhurst area of Manchester which effectively sealed the area off for the duration of the exercise. Despite the public concern that was expressed, Anderton refused to discuss the operation: the *Guardian* 2 November 1977; *Morning Star* 3 November 1977; See also *State Research Bulletin* no.13, https://www.thesparrowsnest.org.uk/collections/public_archive/11623.pdf accessed 30 April 2025.

59   Bernard Levin, 'We call it free speech but it has to be paid for', *Times* 12 October 1977. The NF's ability to get close cooperation with the police did not last. 'The NF and the Police', *Review of Security and the State 1978* (Julian Friedman Books, 1978) pp.126–7.

60   'Anderton must go say unions', *New Manchester Review* 51 February 1978; 'Nazis out of Longsight and Levenshulme' leaflet, personal archive. Manchester Trades Council took a very different line circulating a set of eight questions for the Chief Constable calling on him to be accountable to the MPs and the ten district councils of Greater Manchester.

61   'Hate Mob Runs Riot', *Daily Mirror* 16 August 1977. Reed Herbert, the NF candidate, beat the Liberals into fourth place with 5.7 percent.

62   This group should not be confused with the BNP of the 1960s or with the BNP founded in 1982.

63   Richard Dunn, private email 1 June 2020.

64   An application was made by Neil Kinnock to the Rowntree Trust for the secretary's salary to be paid up to the general election. 'This caused one of the most difficult debates in the Rowntree Trust, not a charity, only accepting applications from non charities'. Lord Chitnis, trust director, crossbench peer, former national organiser of the Liberal Party, *Guardian*

19 September 1979. See also 'League against crude taunts', *Guardian* 29 March 1978.

65 *Guardian* 11 November 1977.

66 As previous footnote.

67 Interview with Neil Kinnock, 10 November 1977, House of Commons, http://bufvc.ac.uk/tvandradio/lbc/index.php/segment/0017000275008.

68 See Chapter 6. 'All power to the imagination! Carnival against the Nazis'.

69 Jon Flaig, private email 24 April 2023.

70 *Socialist Worker* 19 November 1978. See ANL election leaflet, 'What's behind the Front?: for the Information of the electors, Bye-election, Bournemouth East, November 1977', Working Class Movement Library.

71 *Bournemouth Evening Echo* 10 November 1977.

72 *Bournemouth Evening Echo* 11 November 1977.

73 Paul Holborow, interviewed by Geoff Brown 4 April 2024.

74 *Bournemouth Evening Echo* 15 November 1977.

75 ANL election leaflet, 'What's behind the Front?'.

76 Holborow, 11 May 2020. The NF sent the ANL leaflet to the DPP: *Bournemouth Evening Echo* 22 November 1977. 18,000 leaflets were distributed, 300 posters put up, 2 public meetings held, *Socialist Worker* 3 December 1977.

77 The Fire Brigades Union (FBU) were the only national union to strike against the government's pay policy.

78 Holborow, 4 April 2024.

79 Paul Holborow in Roger Huddle & Red Saunders, eds., *Reminiscences of RAR* (Redwords, 2021), p.141.

80 *Guardian* 18 November 1977.

81 *Evening Standard* 9 January 1978.

82 The *Lancashire Evening Telegraph* published a photo of Read standing next to the slogan 'I am a Nazi', which he'd had painted on to the gable end of his house.

83 *Socialist Worker* 28 January 1978.

84 ANL conference declaration, July 1979, personal archive.

85 Greg Dyke 1 September 2021.

86 Sabby Sagall, interviewed by Geoff Brown 17 April 2020.

87 ANL Sponsors Newsletter No. 3, circa October 1978; Letter to sponsors after 4 sponsors leave the ANL, 21 November 1978, both personal archive.

88 Anti Nazi League Founding Statement with final list of sponsors, personal archive.

89 Albie Sachs, the South African lawyer and anti-apartheid activist, and Nicholas Horsley, chairman of Northern Food were among those whose names were not on the statement as there wasn't sufficient space left to include them.

90 See Chapter 7.1, Into the workplace.

91 Karlin was the star of the successful TV comedy *The Rag Trade*, playing Paddy, a militant shop steward in a small clothing factory always ready to shout 'Everybody out' whenever there was a dispute with management.

92 *Coventry Evening Telegraph* 20 May 1978.

93 Chris Lymn, private email 11 July 2022.

94 George Melly, letter to Miriam Karlin, 20 January 1978. There were limits. The ANL was a united front, a labour movement initiative. Tory MPs were not asked. If Conservative MPs applied, their application form was ignored.

95 They were not the only people unsure of the name ANL. Stuart Hall wrote that 'Anti Fascist League' would be more accurate. However, the word Nazi was avoided and neither 'Doctors against the National Front' and 'Architects against the National Front' succeeded in taking off as groups.

96 Letter from Harry Secombe to Karlin and Sagall, 21 November 1977.

97 Letter from Esther Rantzen to Karlin and Sagall, 9 December 1977.

98 Letter from Mike Brearly to Sagall, 14 April 1978.

99 Rachel, 2016, p.119.

100 Nigel Harris, interviewed by Geoff Brown 30 August 2022.

101 James Cameron, 'Back to Front', *Guardian* 12 Dec 1977.

102 David Edgar, *Destiny* (Eyre Methuen, 1976).

103 *Daily Mail* 31 January 1978; *Daily Mail* 12 August 1978.

104 ANL newsletter, March 1978, personal archive.

105 David Edgar, 'Is this our destiny?' *Socialist Worker* 28 January 1978.

106 'Labour TV onslaught on National Front', *Times* 8 December 1977.

107 *Daily Mirror* 12 December 1977.

108 'Cloughie's verdict on the Front… SCUM!', *Daily Mirror* 13 December 1977. The article quotes Martin Webster talking about Clough: 'a great football manager. But what he says about politics has as much little significance as what my milk or coalman thinks'.

109 *Observer* 29 January 1978.

110 The exceptions left because of the use of the word 'fuck' a number of times in a poem. See Chapter 7.3, 'Into Schools', SKAN: School Students against the Nazis.

111 Sabby Sagall, interviewed by Geoff Brown 17 April 2020. See Chapter 7.5, 'Preparing for an October general election'.

112 Letter from Greville Janner to Sagall, 21 November 1977.

113 Letter from Henri Tajfel to Sagall, 24 November 1977. See Chapter 8, 'Winning support in the Jewish community'.

114 Dave Renton, 2002, 'Anti-fascism in the North West, 1976–1982', *North West Labour History Journal* no.27. Brown remembers being summoned by Barnett to his office at short notice when Barnett thought the ANL had failed to carry out something already agreed.

115   The North West TUC sponsored the Northern Carnival against the Nazis. Barnett led the march, walking the full distance from the rally outside Strangeways prison to the concert in Alexandra Park. See Chapter 7.

116   Ludmer shared the platform with NS Noor, IWA (GB) president, and Holborow at a meeting in Leamington. *Socialist Worker* 4 February 1978.

117   Colin McGregor, Bristol SWP, 'No fumbling with the ANL', *SWP Pre-conference Bulletin* no.3, 1978, personal archive.

118   'The National Front and the Jews/ briefing document', 1978, Anti Nazi League, personal archive.

119   Verrall was author of the Holocaust denial pamphlet *Did Six Million Die?* published in 1974 under the pseudonym Richard Harwood.

120   'Documentation on the politics of the National Front', 1978, Anti Nazi League, personal archive.

121   This is not a unique event. Moments when the situation needs a solution and when the initiative is launched it catches on with enormous speed include Punk taking off 1976–7, the Stop the War campaign in 2001 and, on a grander scale, the revolutions of 1848.

122   *Socialist Worker* 26 November 1977, p.14. See Chapter 7.

123   Anti Nazi League newsletter, March 1978, personal archive.

124   Anti Nazi League/ALARM Public Meeting: Wednesday 5 April 8pm, Lambeth Town Hall, Acre Lane, SW2, 'No Nazis in Brixton!'. Speakers: Peter Hain, Frank Osi Tutu (secretary, Western District SO UPW), Dick North (National Executive, NUT).

125   Helen Blair, interviewed by Geoff Brown September 2020.

126   Anti Nazi League leaflet, personal archive, which read 'The Anti-Nazi League would like to thank the organizers of the 7th Annual Thames Film Festival for their co-operation in making this meeting possible'.

127   Neil McAllister, interviewed by Geoff Brown 12 February 2018.

128   *Socialist Worker* 22 April 78; Julian Goss, interviewed by Geoff Brown 20 December 2023. Goss remembers the numbers volunteering for the committee as twenty-one with three or four SWP members on the committee: 'I don't think we lost a single argument in the committee meetings'. Not all such disagreements were easily solved. There were cases where they ran for months before a stable working arrangement was reached: John Jennings, chairman of ALCARAF, letter to Ernie Roberts, 30 March 1978, personal archive. It was the continuing success of the ANL that led to ALCARAF and SCARF and their leading figures Mike Power and John Jennings agreeing to settle a dispute. Another dispute between SE London ANL and SCARF centered on whether to call a demonstration after Foster, a black youth, was shot. A meeting organised by the boy's father, a local activist, and the SE London ANL agreed to call a demonstration while the SCARF secretary opposed it in a letter to the ANL national steering committee. The dispute between the two organisations was finally resolved by each organisation affiliating to the other: SE London Anti-Nazi League, Bishopsgate Institute file LHM/93, personal archive.

129   *Acton Gazette* 2 February 1978; *Socialist Worker* 4 February 1978; 'No Nazis here!', Billy Taylor, AUEW convenor London Transport Acton

works, *Engineers Charter*, February 1978. See Special Branch report listing attendees at an Anti-Nazi League meeting, https://www.ucpi.org.uk/wp-content/uploads/2021/04/UCPI0000011794.pdf.

130 Swansea ANL inaugural meeting with eighty people was sponsored by the local Trades Council, NUPE hospital branch, FBU West Glamorgan, civil servants union at DVLA, Swansea Uni student union: *Socialist Worker* 15 April 1978.

131 'How to Stop the National Front', *Socialist Worker* 4 March 1978 and 18 March 1978.

132 NUM archive file 463/1. Many invitations were sent by those who had heard Scargill speak at an ANL meeting.

133 Lancashire NUM and South Wales NUM were also quick to affiliate as were the shop steward committees in the Fords Body Plant Dagenham, East Works Longbridge, Rolls Royce Hillington, Rolls Royce East Kilbride, Chrysler Linwood. Also the Bury AUEW District committee and the Co-op Political committee: ANL newsletter, March 1978, personal archive.

134 'Front men face pits snub', *Daily Mirror* 9 May 1978. See also Chapter 7, 'Miners Against the Nazis'.

135 'There were school pupils, engineers, print workers, council workers, dock workers, mums, teachers, and other people black and white from all walks of life.' *Ipswich Evening Star* 'Extra'.

136 *Leicester Mercury* 17 February 1978. The picket of the NF paper sellers had run for twenty weeks, *Leicester Mercury* 23 February 1978. Four thousand signatures were collected on a petition calling for the council to withdraw the NF licence to sell papers on the street. Not every proposal to support the ANL succeeded. Ian Birchall remembers in early 1978 encountering 'considerable hostility', getting only a handful of votes as he tried to move affiliation to the ANL at the CP controlled Greater London Association of Trades Councils: Ian Birchall, private email 11 December 2023.

137 'Celebration Drink-In at the King's Arms, Colindale, N.W. London', *Socialist Worker* 28 January 1978.

138 Joan Rudder, interviewed by Geoff Brown 12 October 2021.

139 'In little more than four months a network of 250 local ANL branches appeared with approximately 45,000 dues paying members. On the strength of mostly small contributions the League raised £600,000 between 1977 and 1980. Despite its highly decentralised structure, the ANL's first national conference in July 1978 attracted over 800 delegates: Anthony M. Messina, 1987, 'Postwar protest movements in Britain: A challenge to parties', *Review of Politics*, vol.49, no.3, p.417.

140 The London office supplied leaflets in packs of 1,000 for 'general purposes, trade unionists, schoolkids, women, gay people' together with badges – Anti Nazi League, Rock Against Racism, Women Against Nazis, Gays Against Nazis, Schoolkids, NF = No Fun", Leeds ANL News No 1, June 1978, personal archive. The ANL produced '10 million leaflets with many different colours and templates and we had up to forty different leaflets', Paul Holborow interviewed in Rachel, 2016, p.119.

141 Holborow, 4 April 2024.

142 'Silence is the NF's best friend', *New Manchester Review* 48, January 1978.

143 'Asian youths lead Anti Nazi Demo', *Socialist Worker* 18 February 1978.

144 'Stop the Nazis in Bolton' leaflet, personal archive.

145 Letter to the ANL office, n.d (received March–April 1978), personal archive.

146 *Socialist Worker* 14 January 1978; *Socialist Worker* 28 January 1978.

147 *Temporary Hoarding* 6; *Socialist Worker* 24 February 1978; *Times* 20 February 1978. The following week two YNF leafleted a Stockport school. They were acquitted when charged under the Race Relations Act. 'Race charge against NF men fails', *Daily Telegraph* 1 March 1979.

148 *Socialist Worker* 22 April 78.

149 The NF also announced they would march through Notting Hill on the opening day of the Notting Hill Carnival in August. A letter to *Socialist Worker* argued the NF should be allowed to march through Notting Hill on carnival day, saying that with such generosity 'we could wipe out the nazis in this country and give us a few Saturday mornings in bed for a change', *Socialist Worker* 11 March 1978.

150 Philip Kleinman, 'The Press', *Jewish Chronicle* 10 March 1978.

151 *Evening Sentinel* 3 October 1978.

152 'Instructions to everybody taking part In Anti Nazi League activities', personal archive.

153 'Election meetings: "No time for NF case" – High Court', *National Front News* May 1978.

154 *Socialist Worker* 4 March 78; Ben Ross, 'Anti Nazi League: What it is and how to use it', *SWP Pre-conference Bulletin* no.2, April 1978, personal archive. Ross notes the confusion and unhappiness of some SWP members about how the demonstration at Ilford turned out and the difficulty in maintaining the united front when some SWP members wanted to find a way to stop the NF meeting.

155 *Jewish Chronicle* 10 March 1978.

156 CP/CENT/EC Central /Executive Committee minutes, Labour History Archive and Study Centre (LHASC).

157 *Morning Star* 10 January 1978; *Morning Star* 22 February 1978.

158 Supplement to CP Political Committee Weekly Letter No.11, 6 April 1978, LHASC.

159 'Carnival of Unity', *Morning Star* 20 April 1978.

160 Helen Blair, interviewed by Geoff Brown September 2020; Dave Sherry, interviewed by Geoff Brown October 2020.

161 *Socialist Worker* 13 May 78; Bob Cooney, *Proud Journey: A Spanish Civil War Memoir* (Manifesto Press, 2015). A leading local Communist Party member, John Peck, was on the platform at the Nottingham launch in April long with Nigel Harris (SWP & ANL), Arthur Palmer (NUM), and Malcolm Goldsmith (industrial advisor to the Bishop of Southwark). It could be argued that one reason for the CP affiliating to the ANL was its exclusion

from the Joint Campaign against Racism (JCAR), sometimes described as 'an alternative to the ANL for moderates', see Stan Taylor, *The National Front in English Politics* (Macmillan, 1982), p.139. JCAR was launched in December 1977, only allowing parties represented in parliament to affiliate.

162   The request was for the committee's support for the forthcoming ANL Carnival. The committee agreed to back the Carnival, circulate details and donate £5, 'Amendment to minutes, Manchester AUEW District Committee, 4 April 1978', WCML, personal archive. For details about the Carnival, see Chapter 6, 'All power to the imagination!'.

163   *North Wales Weekly News* 2 March 1978.

164   *Kent and Sussex Courier* 28 April 1978; 'MP to foster Anti-Nazi branch', *Coventry Evening Telegraph* 21 April 1978.

165   Andy Strouthous, 'Students vote against the Nazis', *Socialist Worker* 15 April 1978.

166   *Socialist Worker* 8 April 1978.

167   'League against crude taunts', *Guardian* 29 March 1978.

168   Anti Nazi League newsletter, March 1978, personal archive.

169   In his review of Widgery's *Beating Time*, having correctly dismissed the idea that the ANL was a popular front, Ian Birchall writes 'Nor was the ANL a united front in the classic sense'. Accepting that 'The Labour MPs, like Neil Kinnock and Gwyneth Dunwoody (yes really! Remember?) helped the ANL's credibility', he goes on: 'but it was Joe Strummer and Elvis Costello who pulled the crowds'. The key point he misses, however, is that there is no such a thing as 'a united front in the classic sense'. Every united front has its own characteristics. As Birchall puts it 'The history of it was in many ways a unique historical experience, one which, in Widgery's words, "genuinely brought culture and politics into each other's arms and set them dancing"'.

170   It is wrong to suggest, as Gilroy does, that 'The process in which anti-fascist and anti-racist activism became a movement rather than an aggregate of uneven and disparate local groups significantly had its origins outside the realm of politics', Paul Gilroy, *There Ain't No Black in the Union Jack* (Routledge, 1987), p.155.

171   *Coventry Evening Telegraph* 29 April 1978. There were still disagreements. In a letter to Ernie Roberts putting questions about the ANL's democracy, ALCARAF's secretary said he felt that with seventy-three local organisations affiliated, ALCARAF should be *the* anti-racist and anti-fascist organisation in the Lewisham area.

172   The large number of Manchester Polytechnic (now Manchester Metropolitan University) students who went to the Carnival on 30 April made a big contribution.

173   Bulletin of Watford Anti Racist Committee, June–July 1978, personal archive.

174   Colin McGregor, 'No fumbling with the ANL', Bristol SWP, *SWP Pre-conference Bulletin* 3, May 1978, personal archive.

All power to the imagination

1   'Artists salute Fine Tubes Strikers', *Socialist Worker* 18 March 1972; 'Shrewsbury Rally: Big crowd digs deep', *Socialist Worker* 22 December 1973. Nichol, private email 18 October 2021; Nichol, private communication, 4 April 2024.

2   Red Saunders, 'The original idea for a carnival came from Jim Nichol... a member of the Socialist Workers Party', Daniel Rachel, *Walls Come Tumbling Down: The Music and Politics of Rock Against Racism, 2 Tone and Red Wedge* (Picador, 2016), p.129.

3   Jim Nichol, private email 30 August 2019.

4   The name was taken from a remark made by Hugh Gaitskell, leader of the Labour Party, then in opposition, at a May Day rally in Glasgow, 1962. Faced by several hundred CND supporters, he said 'Let them ask Mr. Khrushchev to ban his bomb... We know that when it comes to the ballot, when it comes to the elections, these people are not worth a tinker's curse. They are peanuts – they don't count'; 'Mr Gaitskell in Angry Scenes', *Times* 7 May 1962.

5   Red Saunders, interviewed by Geoff Brown 23 September 2021.

6   Bill McDonnell, 'Jesters to the revolution: A history of Cartoon Archetypical Slogan Theatre (CAST), 1965–85.' *Theatre Notebook* vol.64, no.2.

7   Catherine Itzin, *Stages in the Revolution: Political Theatre Since 1968* (Eyre Methuen, 1980), p.12.

8   https://www.unfinishedhistories.com/history/companies/cast/

9   Roland Muldoon quoted in Itzin, p.15.

10   Saunders, 23 September 2021. Lyubov Popova was a leading Constructivist painter and designer. Sergei Eisenstein's films include *Strike* (1925), *Battleship Potemkin* (1925) and *October* (1928).

11   Itzin, p.17; David Edgar, *The Second Time as Farce* (Lawrence & Wishart, 1988), p.228. By 1978 there were over a hundred 'alternative' theatre companies, Itzin, p.xiv.

12   Roland Muldoon, 'Unfinished Histories: Recording the history of Alternative Theatre', https://www.unfinishedhistories.com/interviews/interviewees-l-q/roland-muldoon/roland-muldoon-topics-list/

13   Red Saunders & Roger Huddle, interview with Ian Goodyer 3 June 2000. 'We were influenced by Jefferson Airplane using projectors to put images on slides into their show', Red Saunders, interviewed by Geoff Brown 28 January 2025.

14   Roger Huddle & Red Saunders, eds., *Reminiscences of RAR* (Redwords, 2021), p.11. This may have been the Rank and File Conference Organising Committee conference on racialism in Birmingham, June 1975, 'Racialism: How - and why - it must be fought', *Socialist Worker* 21 June 1975; 'Conference against racism', *Rank and File Teacher*, June–July 1975.

15   The Right to Work Campaign was launched October 1975. Saunders & Huddle brought out a record in support of the campaign. Saunders & Huddle, 3 June 2000.

16   Saunders & Huddle, 3 June 2000.

17   John Street, *Politics and Popular Culture* (Polity Press, 1997), pp.74–75.

18   Ken Olende, 2016, 'All power to the imagination', https://web.archive.org/web/20170506042854/http://uaf.org.uk/2016/10/40-years-since-the-birth-of-rock-against-racism-rebel-music-that-broke-down-fear/. David Bowie Interview with Cameron Crowe, *Playboy* September 1976, https://www.playboy.com/read/playboy-interview-david-bowie.

19   Red Saunders in Huddle & Saunders, 2021, p.211.

20   Jack Robertson interviewed by Geoff Brown 5 November 2019.

21   Huddle & Saunders, pp.210–215. See brief quotes from some letters, *Socialist Worker* 2 October 1977.

22   Chris Ayton interviewed by Geoff Brown 26 August 2021.

23   Huddle & Saunders, 2021, p.84.

24   Huddle & Saunders, 2021, p.211.

25   Huddle & Saunders, 2021, p.213.

26   Mike Dempsey, *David King: King of Kings*, Graphic Journey blog, 8 April 2009. King told Dempsey how he was amused when he heard that the police had questioned some members of the ANL, asking which advertising agency had been responsible for its print material. Saunders commented, 'There was always a tension. In Aberystwyth or wherever, they may only have had a Gestetner. No Letraset etc, no skills like King, so they just had to get on with it', interviewed by Geoff Brown 28 January 2025.

27   John Hall interviewed by Geoff Brown 3 January 2018. John Rees remembers that there were places like the tube in East London where you didn't wear your badges or you would be beaten up, interview with Ian Goodyer 2001.

28   The editor, Chris Harman, immediately agreed to the request for a page, Saunders & Huddle 3 June 2000.

29   *Socialist Worker* 2 October 1976. Huddle's recollection, Ian Goodyer interview.

30   Sarfraz Manzoor, 'The year rock found the power to unite', *Observer* 20 April 2008.

31   *Leveller* January 1977.

32   See Radical Bookshops, 1960s–Present, https://www.leftontheshelfbooks.co.uk/pdf/Radical-bookshops-Listing.pdf#page=34.10

33   Jill Catlow interviewed by Geoff Brown 16 June 2021. Amamus was founded in 1971. There was also an IS bookshop in Blackburn set up by Peter Fielding.

34   Cazz Blasé ed., 'Invisible women: The role of women in punk fanzine creation', in *Ripped, Torn and Cut: Pop, Politics and Punk Fanzines from 1976*, The Subcultures Network, (Manchester University Press, 2018); *Guttersnipe* issue no.2 https://stillunusual.tumblr.com/post/168832418961/guttersnipe-fanzine. The Guttersnipe collective created the 1980 BBC *Open Door* programme, https://www.youtube.com/watch?v=ddDvlzTHkjQ.

35   Kate Webb, RAR's first full-time worker, pointed out that 'at the root [of RAR] was the shared love of music', Huddle & Saunders, 2021, p.228. See Rachel p.33.

36   James Womack, ed, *Vladimir Mayakovsky: And Other Poems* (Fyfieldbooks, 2016).

37   *Wedge: A Revolutionary Magazine of Cultural Practice and Theory*, no.2

38   Films shown included *Blow for Blow*, a fictional account of women in France occupying their textile factory, and which toured from Glasgow to Southampton. This was followed by showing *Ireland: Behind the Wire*, the South African film *Last Grave at Dimbaza* and *Spain: Dreams and Nightmares*, *The Miners' Film*, Cinema Action, http://www.cinemaaction.co.uk/miners-film. Widgery recalls attempting 'discussion on the relationship between the "classical" Marx/Trotsky analysis of high art and the Mayakovsky/Brecht/May events school of art-as-action', David Widgery, 1978, 'Carnival against the Nazis', *Radical America*, vol.12, no.5; 'Quick history of the rise, fall and rise again of the Agit-prop Committee in the Socialist Workers over the last three years', *Wedge* magazine, issue 2.

39   John McGrath & Nadine Holdsworth, eds., *John Mcgrath: Plays For England* (University of Exeter Press, 2005), p.29. The 7:84 theatre group derived its name from a 1966 article in the *Economist* noting that just 7 percent of the British population owned 84 percent of the wealth.

40   Red Saunders interviewed by Ken Olende, *Unite Against Fascism*, 2016. https://web.archive.org/web/20170506042854/http://uaf.org.uk/2016/10/40-years-since-the-birth-of-rock-against-racism-rebel-music-that-broke-down-fear/

41   Saunders & Huddle, 3 June 2000.

42   The Princess Alice gig was on 12 November 1976.

43   Saunders, 2016.

44   Huddle & Saunders, 2021, p.4.

45   Huddle & Saunders, 2021, pp.157–8.

46   John Dennis, in Huddle & Saunders, 2021, p.54.

47   *Agitator* October 1977.

48   Red Saunders in Huddle & Saunders, 2021, p.213; *Rentamob* 1, SWP agit-prop bulletin, https://splitsandfusions.wordpress.com/2022/09/25/rentamob/.

49   The Sex Pistols's manager, Malcolm McLaren, was highly influenced by Dadaism and Situationism. See Greil Marcus, *Lipstick Traces: A Secret History of the Twentieth Century* (Faber, 2011); Rick Blackman, *Babylon's Burning* (Bookmarks, 2021), p.123.

50   Ayton, 26 August 2021. The fanzine *Sideburns* printed a diagram showing three chords on a guitar, telling readers 'Here's three chords. Now form a band'. David Gilchrist, 'Punk: 1976–1978', *Socialist Worker* 31 May 2016.

51   Saunders & Huddle, 3 June 2000. See also Don Letts, 'Where Punk met reggae, the punky reggae thing', https://www.youtube.com/watch?v=BLgikuZ9XbQ; Keith Gildart, *Images of England through Popular*

Music: Class, Youth and Rock'n'roll, 1955–1976 (Palgrave, 2013).

52   Blackman, 2021, p.123; 'Everybody thinks of course the fascists couldn't have won but if you think back it wasn't just Clapton, it was David Bowie doing Sieg Heils, Siouxsie Sioux wearing swastikas, Sid Vicious wearing swastikas, it wasn't necessarily racism and fascism, it was 'Oh, how can we shock the last generation?', shock tactics through the punks but I think this made them realise that you just can't do things like that, it did make people stop and think, instead of just going with what your parents have told you or what somebody tells you. I think it made kids think', John Hall interviewed by Geoff Brown 3 January 2018.

53   Neil McAllister, interviewed by Geoff Brown 12 February 2018.

54   *Temporary Hoarding,* interview with Johnny Rotten. See also the arguments about punk in *Challenge,* June/July 1977 and also Gildart, 2013, p.179, describing how the UEA Student Union checked out the Sex Pistols before they could play. The contract included an NUS requirement that the group would use no fascist insignia on stage and no fascist lyrics in their songs. The issue came from Siouxsie Sioux wearing a Nazi armband during the Grundy interview. 'The Sex Pistols were averse to fascist politics. The lyrics of their songs did not contain any racist rhetoric and there is no evidence that they made any racist comments during performances'.

55   Ayton interview, 26 August 2021.

56   David Widgery, *Beating Time* (Chatto & Windus, 1986), p.61.

57   The Clash, 'White Riot', https://genius.com/The-clash-white-riot-lyrics

58   Roger Huddle, 'Hard rain', *Socialist Review* July–August 1978.

59   The challenge might be ignored. Dave Peers remembers 'a complete division between those of us who were book readers and pamphleteers and those who were into the music', Dave Peers interviewed by Geoff Brown 27 March 2023. The problem was not a new one, Lenin had said, 'Unfortunately, it is still true to say of many of our comrades, "Scratch a communist and a Philistine appears"', Clara Zetkin, 1924, *Reminiscences of Lenin,* https://www.marxists.org/archive/zetkin/1924/reminiscences-of-lenin.htm

60   *Socialist Worker Agitprop Bulletin* February 1976; *Rentamob* no.1; *Rentamob* no.2 August 1977.

61   David Renton, *When We Touched the Sky: The Anti-Nazi League 1977–1981* (New Clarion Press, 2006), p.46.

62   A Brief History Of Tom, http://www.tomrobinson.co.uk/pages/biog.htm, 'Inspired by an early Sex Pistols gig, Tom left Cafe Society and formed the more overtly political Tom Robinson Band (TRB) in 1977, aged 26. His band had a hit with "2-4-6-8 Motorway", quickly followed into the Top 20 by a live EP despite a BBC ban on the controversial lead track "Glad to Be Gay". Swept along by a tide of music press excitement, TRB's debut album *Power in the Darkness* went gold. But the band fell from favour equally quickly and broke up – demoralised and squabbling – in 1979'.

63   Huddle & Saunders, 2021, p.55.

64   *Socialist Worker* 17 September 1977.

65   Huddle & Saunders, 2021, p.204.

66   John Baine (Attila the Stockbroker), *Arguments Yard: My Autobiography,* (Cherry Red Books, 2015), p.22.

67   Huddle & Saunders, 2021, p.216.

68   The *Leveller's* claim went too far. RAR was preceded by the Stars Campaign for Interracial Friendship set up to challenge the racism that surged in 1958 with the anti-black riots in Notting Hill. See Rick Blackman, *Forty Miles of Bad Road: The Stars Campaign for Interracial Friendship and the 1958 Notting Hill Riots* (Redwords, 2017).

69   Roger Huddle, in Huddle & Saunders, 2021, p.13.

70   Red Saunders, in Huddle & Saunders, 2021, pp.212–3.

71   Saunders & Huddle, 3 June 2000. A collection of fanzines by Jake gives details of punk on the ground, see https://www.flickr.com/photos/stillunusual/albums/72157657899141379/with/22271772135/. This includes issue #2 of *Guttersnipe*. My thanks to Eamonn Kelly for this.

72   'RAR is a campaign. A political campaign', *Agitator* October 1977. *Agitator* was the journal of the National Organisation of International Socialist Societies (NOISS). The organisation was known by its acronym.

73   'What is racism?', *Temporary Hoarding* no.1 May 1977.

74   Huddle & Saunders, 2021, p.111.

75   Huddle & Saunders, 2021, p.295. John Ellis, RAR treasurer, remembers 'Bands were not paid fees for performing but we did try to cover their expenses and then there was the PA, publicity, accommodation, travel and other expenses', Huddle and Saunders, 2021, p.67.

76   Leeds Library Heritage Blog, https://secretlibraryleeds.net/2019/10/25/rock-against-racism/. Leeds Polytechnic is now Leeds Beckett University.

77   Huddle & Saunders, 2021, p.147.

78   Huddle & Saunders, 2021, p.134.

79   Baine, 2015, p.22. *Temporary Hoarding* would eventually build up a circulation of 12,000 copies per issue, Blackman, 2021, p.125, though there were always difficulties collecting the money, Mel Norris interviewed by Geoff Brown 29 January 2021.

80   Huddle & Saunders, 2021, p.217. By *Temporary Hoarding* no.5, Spring 1978, RAR had moved to its own office in Clerkenwell Close.

81   Neil Spencer, in Huddle & Saunders, 2021, p.218.

82   Huddle & Saunders, 2021, p.173. Misty and others went on to set up People Unite, an educational and creative arts centre in Southall. See Chapter 9 'Counting down to the election'.

83   *Temporary Hoarding* no.4.

84   Mike Simons, interviewed by Geoff Brown 20 February 2020.

85   Steve Cedar, private email 21 December 2020.

86   Bernie Wilcox, *What Can a Poor Boy Do?* (Bowden Publishing, 2009), pp.106–7. Having reached No.2 in the charts with their anti-monarchist 'God Save the Queen' the week of the Silver Jubilee celebrations,

they had been banned from almost every venue in the country. Over the previous two weeks they had done half a dozen gigs from Durham to Cornwall keeping each location secret. There is a well-produced leaflet for a RAR gig in Newcastle, November 1977, personal archive.

87   Nichol, 30 August 2019.

88   Helen Blair was on the coach with Chrysler workers, Helen Blair, interviewed by Geoff Brown 28 September 2020. Glasgow was arguably the leading SWP district at the time with stronger factory branches than any other district.

89   Huddle & Saunders, 2021, p.82.

90   Huddle & Saunders, 2021, p.169.

91   Rachel, 2016, p.137.

92   *Socialist Worker* 11 March 1978; Widgery, 1986, pp.80–1; *Guardian* 2 May 1978.

93   Communist Party Political Committee weekly letter, 'Our attitude to the Anti-Nazi League and broad campaign committees', Supplement 6 April 1978.

94   *Socialist Worker* 1 April 1978; *Socialist Worker* 8 April 1978.

95   *Sounds*, 'It can't happen here or can it?', 25 March 1978; Vivien Goldman, in Huddle & Saunders, 2021, p.102.

96   *Socialist Worker* 15 April 1978. With 29,000 workers, Dagenham may have been the largest workplace in Britain.

97   Counter Information Services, 1979, Ford, Anti Report No 20; *Socialist Worker* 22 April 1978. Gordon Davie, interviewed by Geoff Brown 26 August 2021.

98   *Socialist Worker* 22 April 1978.

99   *Socialist Worker* 29 April 1978.

100 Geoff Brown 'Workers' Organisation at Gardners: Its rise and fall, 1972–1982', (unpublished, 1986).

101 *Socialist Worker* 15 April 78. See Chapter 7.

102 *Socialist Worker* 22 April 1978; *Socialist Worker* 13 May 1978.

103 *Socialist Worker* 6 May 1978.

104 Nineteen of Manchester's coaches were organised by students. There were also half a dozen minibuses. Together with people going by car and train, around 2,500 people came from Greater Manchester. There were also coaches from Liverpool, Leeds, Sheffield, Middlesbrough, Aberystwyth, Norwich, Oxford. Blackman, 2021, p.142.

105 SKAN no.3, June–July 1978.

106 Comment on 'The Clash at Rock Against Racism Victoria Park London 1978.mov', https://www.youtube.com/watch?v=4xRaVbW-iBM.

107 Rehad Desai, 2004, *Born into Struggle*, https://www.youtube.com/watch?v=dJn-_7yYGI8.

108 *Time Out* 18 August 1978.

109 *Leeds ANL Bulletin* no.1, June 1978,

110   Widgery, 1986, p.84.

111   Colin Poole, interviewed by Geoff Brown 9 November 2022.

112   https://kmflett.wordpress.com/2018/04/30/30th-april-1979-rocking-against-racism-in-victoria-park-hackney/

113   The heads were made by Peter Fluck and Roger Law, later famous for their puppets on the *Spitting Image* satirical television puppet show, 1984–1996. *Socialist Worker* 29 April 1978 told readers, 'the idea was dreamed up by the stodgy old members of Lambeth NALGO branch'. Spectacular in their originality and size, the three heads attracted much media coverage.

114   Widgery, 1986, p .83. Not everyone got there. Balwinder Rana spent much of the night before with friends in Southall, decorating a lorry for a local Asian band to play on. By the time they set off it was so late that they got stuck in the huge traffic jam caused by the march and never managed to join it.

115   The speakers were Ian Mikardo, Paul Holborow, Peter Hain, Ernie Roberts, Miriam Karlin, Tom Robinson, Vishnu Sharma, Audrey Wise.

116   Thames TV, *Our People: Anti Nazi League, RAR, SKAN*, broadcast 22 February 1979, https://www.youtube.com/watch?v=tvmUVE05XRQ .

117   As the previous note.

118   David Rosenberg, 'Anti-Nazi League: The carnival is not over', *Rebel Notes* 30 April 2018, https://rebellion602.wordpress.com/?s=The+carnival+is+not+over

119   Pia Feig, interviewed by Geoff Brown 29 January 2020.

120   Pip Smith, 'Carnival Day – the Gay Way', *Gay News* no.143 May 1978.

121   *Guardian* 2 May 1978.

122   Rachel, 2016, p.138.

123   Huddle & Saunders, 2021, p.82.

124   Huddle & Saunders, 2021, p.158.

125   Kevin Corr, interviewed by Geoff Brown 4 January 2021.

126   *Observer* 30 April 1978.

127   Gurinder Chadha, film director. Her films include *Bend It Like Beckham* (2002) and *Blinded by the Light* (2019).

128   Huddle & Saunders, 2021, pp.48–9. Huddle adds that it is important to note the emptiness of the park at the start to counter those 'who always say that the crowd only came for the music', Huddle & Saunders, 2021, p.16.

129   Smith, 1978; https://rebellion602.wordpress.com/?s=The+carnival+is+not+over

130   Dav Gilchrist, in Huddle & Saunders, 2021.

131   Andy Strouthous private email 28 October 2020. £12,000 in 1978 is equivalent to approx. £65,000 February 2025.

132   Steel Pulse wrote the song after reading newspaper reports about a planned visit to Birmingham by David Duke, the Ku Klux Klan's Grand Wizard, due to address a meeting in Wolverhampton on 6 March 1978, a meeting banned by the local council at the urging of the newly formed anti-racist committee.

133 The Clash at Rock Against Racism Victoria Park, London 1978, https://www.youtube.com/watch?v=4xRaVbW-iBM.

134 *Time Out* 5 May 1978.

135 Sarfraz Manzoor, 'The year rock found the power to unite', *Observer* 20 April 2008.

136 Buzz Rodwell, private email 19 February 2022.

137 Huddle & Saunders, 2021, p.167.

138 Rachel, 2016, pp.145–6.

139 John Lockwood, one of the organisers of the Lewisham demonstration, also active in ALCARAF, was jailed for three months and lost his teaching job, 'Confronting the Nazis: The Battle of Lewisham in 1977', Marxism festival, July 2017, SWP TV, https://www.youtube.com/watch?v=fi14XozEzW0.

140 Prav Parmar, interviewed by Geoff Brown 27 February 2018.

141 *New Musical Express* 6 May 1978.

142 Rachel, 2016, p.148.

143 Sharon Spike, 'Straight at the head of the NF', *Northern Hoarding*.

144 Rachel, 2016, p.143.

145 Communist Party Political Committee Weekly Letter, 3 May 1978, CP/CENT/PC/14/23, LHASC. It is worth noting how this assessment contrasts with the experience of People's Jubilee organised by the Communist Party as a counter event to Queen Elizabeth's Silver Jubilee celebrations in the summer of 1977. There was significant opposition to these celebrations. Despite the BBC and commercial radio stations refusing to play it, the Sex Pistols' punk anthem 'God Save the Queen' reached number 1 in the *New Musical Express* chart on the week of the Jubilee and 40,000 copies of the 'Stuff the Jubilee' badge designed by Sherryl Janowitz sold in three months. Despite this opposition, the People's Jubilee failed to capture this mood. Eleven thousand people came, the event was overwhelmingly white, almost three quarters were CP members, a quarter of those attending were pensioners, Ben Harker, *The Chronology of Revolution* (University of Toronto Press, 2021), p.187. Similarly, the 5,000 strong anti-racist march across London's East End to a free festival in Victoria Park, 16 October 1977, also failed to inspire. Organised by Hackney Trades Council and Hackney Committee Against Racialism it included 'Turkish, West Indian, Greek, Cypriot and Indian musicians and dancers and also a Soul and Rock Band and a Reggae band', 'Campaigns & Reports, Hackney', *CARF* No 3, p17; Special Branch memorandum, Commander 'Operations', Special Demonstration Squad 1977, 1 3 March 1978, p14, https://www.ucpi.org.uk/wp-content/uploads/2022/05/MPS_0728981.pdf

146 *Socialist Challenge* 4 May 1978

147 Raphael Samuel, 'David Widgery: 1947–1993', *History Workshop Journal*, vol.35, no.1

148 Andy Strouthous, interviewed by Geoff Brown 1 July 2020; Alex Callinicos, 'When the music stops', *Socialist Review* no.3, June 1978, https://www.marxists.org/history/etol/newspape/socrev/1978/sr003/sr3.pdf. See also Communist Party Political Committee weekly letter, 6 April

1978, CP/CENT/PC/14/22, LHASC; and SWP Central Committee, 'Crisis in the Communist Party', *SWP Pre-Conference Bulletin* Issue 2, May 1978, p.8.

149 *The Asian* June 1978.

150 As Gramsci argued 'Permanent passion is a condition of orgasm and of spasm, which means operational incapacity. It excludes parties and excludes every plan of action worked out in advance'. Antonio Gramsci, *Selections from the Prison Notebooks* (Lawrence & Wishart, 1971), pp.138–9.

A mass movement: May 1978 to September 1978

1 Cliff contrasted the ANL with CND and the Vietnam Solidarity Campaign, both in their class composition – the ANL was more working class – but also in the speed with which they took off, *Socialist Worker* 13 May 1978.

2 *Socialist Worker* 13 May 1978.

3 Office for National Statistics , 24.6 million employees in 1978, https://www.ons.gov.uk/economy/nationalaccounts/uksectoraccounts/compendium/economicreview/april2019/longtermtrendsinukemploymen t1861to2018#employees-and-self-employed-workers. Union membership rose by 2 million during the 1970s to just below 13 million in 1979. Union density increased from 47 percent density to 54 percent of the employed workforce, Department of Employment Statistics Division (1892-1974); Certification Office (1974-2017).

4 'Closed shop' agreements with employers requiring all shop floor workers to be union members as a condition of employment. This meant that NF members could take part in union mass meetings. John Murphy, interviewed by Geoff Brown 26 February 2021, gives an example of this.

5 'Nationalsozialistische Betriebszellen Organisation'.

6 Set up in 1929, the NSBO had only 4,000 members in March 1931 when party members were told to join, boosting membership to 40,000 by the end of the year. This can be compared to trade union membership of over four million. See Gossweiler, 1986, 'Arbeiterklasse und Faschismus' (In German), p.15.

7 Fascists Defy Law, Eviction Sequel, *Daily Telegraph* 10 November 1933.

8 Philip Coupland, 2002, '"Left-Wing Fascism" in Theory and Practice: The Case of the British Union of Fascists', *Twentieth Century British History*, vol.13, no.1; Oswald Mosley, 1933, *10 Points of Fascist Policy: Fascism Explained*. The first sentence starts 'Fascism is a creed of patriotism and revolution'.

9 The estimate of 100,000 comes from the United Press report, see 'Mob in London pelts Mosley with tomatoes: 11 hurt in riot of 100,000 jamming Hyde Park to boo young fascist chief', *New York Herald Tribune* 10 September 1934. Both the Labour Party and the TUC opposed the rally which was largely organised by the Communist Party.

10 TUC, *Organising against fascism in the workplace*, (TUC, 2008), p.3, https://www.tuc.org.uk/sites/default/files/extras/tuc_fascism.pdf

11 TUC, 2008, p.3. *NF News* May 1978 reported David Matson trying to

raise £150 to challenge Bradford Trades Council's refusal to accept him as a National Union of Sheet Metal Workers' delegate.

12   The NF passed a motion at its 1972 conference to organise a foothold in the unions. Tyndall explained this in 'National Front and Trade Unions', *Spearhead* May 1974. The national meeting was in May 1974, the NFTUA founded in June.

13   *Spearhead* May 1974, quoted in S*earchlight* April 1975; The aim was put even more ambitiously in *Spearhead* July 1974: 'an alternative mechanism whereby whatever amount of support we achieve among the electorate may be transplanted into a proportional amount of actual power'. Quote from ASTMS 'Stop Racism at Work' leaflet, personal archive.

14   *Searchlight* February 1979.

15   *Hackney Peoples Press* June 1978.

16   Mark Dolan, interviewed by Geoff Brown 17 January 2022.

17   CARF reported that in a ballot for four positions on the union branch committee, five of the nine candidates were NF members or supporters, *CARF* June 1978

18   The total sum was equivalent to £7,000 in February 2025.

19   Mark Dolan, interviewed by Geoff Brown December 2021.

20   Quoted in *Hackney People's Press* June 1978. See also 'Postal workers fund Front', *Searchlight* June 1979. There was an ANL meeting in Blackpool during the UPW annual conference 24 May 1978. *Islington Gutter Press* reported that while there were a number of NF candidates for Islington Council working at the NDO, 'it seems that many of them did not even realise that they had been nominated by the NF', quoted in *Hackney Peoples Press* June 1978

21   TUC, 2008, p.3; 'Prison Warders join Front say MPs', *Jewish Gazette* 19 November 1976; Jamie Bennett et al., *Understanding Prison Staff* (Willan, 2008), p.51. 'The head of the Prison Service, Martin Narey, has admitted his organisation is "institutionally racist" and there are "pockets of blatant and malicious racism" among his officers', *Independent* 21 August 2000. As delegate to TUC congress, Mike McGrath remembers overhearing racist remarks made by Prison Officers Association (POA) delegates sitting near to him. The POA was the recognised union of prison staff.

22   National Front propaganda in prisons, National Archives, HO 413/5.

23   Lobb also claimed 300 card holders in Newham as a whole, two-thirds members of trade unions. Christopher Hitchens, 'White socialism', *New Statesman* 31 May 1974.

24   Murphy, 26 February 2021.

25   As previous endnote.

26   For more about the NF presence in the Longbridge factory and the struggle to get rid of it, see Murphy, 26 February 2021.

27   Frank Henderson, *Life on the Track: Memoirs of a Socialist Worker* (Bookmarks, 2009), pp.71–3.

28   *Guardian* 28 January 1978; *Socialist Worker* 3 February 1978.

29   Murphy, 26 February 2021.

30 John Hall interviewed by Geoff Brown 3 January 2018.

31 *World in Action*, 'The Nazi Party', 3 July 1978; *Morning Star* 6 July 1978. There were also a number of NF members at the Rover Solihull factory. These are 'branched' (disciplined) by the local union, leading to the breakup of their organisation, *Searchlight* February 1979.

32 *Socialist Worker* 6 May 1978 argued that 'every workplace should have a branch of the Anti Nazi League'. When at the national SWP meeting following the carnival, Geoff Brown, Manchester ANL organiser, claimed the sky was now the limit after 2,500 had gone to the carnival from Greater Manchester. Cliff brought him back to earth asking how many ANL branches did Manchester have, Daniel Rachel, *Walls Come Tumbling Down: The Music and Politics of Rock Against Racism, 2 Tone and Red Wedge* (Picador, 2016), p.149.

33 John Webster, 'Workers at Fords fight NF Nazis', letter to *Morning Star* 26 May 1978.

34 The committee had sent coaches to the mass picket at Grunwick and to Lewisham.

35 John Murphy 26 February 2021.

36 *Socialist Worker* 13 May 78.

37 Geoff Brown in 'Anti-fascism in the northwest', David Renton, 2002, *North West Labour History Journal*, p.22.

38 *Socialist Worker* 13 May 1978.

39 *Socialist Worker* 24 December 1977.

40 Neil McAllister, interviewed by Geoff Brown 12 February 2018,

41 Morrison's short-lived BNP should not be confused with either the earlier BNP, led by John Bean in the 1960s, see Chapter 1 'Rivers of Blood', or the BNP founded by John Tyndall in 1982.

42 *Redder Tape* Winter 1977.

43 Dave Field, 'Flushing out the Front', *Socialist Review* May 1978.

44 Steve Forey, interviewed by Geoff Brown 13 December 2021. See also, 'Steve and Dave on the railways', *Socialist Worker* 23 September 1978. NUR North London District Council had already organised against the NF, issuing a leaflet called 'Be On Guard' highlighting the dangers of National Front infiltration of the union, *Railway Worker*, 1976.

45 Circular letter from British Rail Chief Personnel Officer, Euston Station, 24 July 1978, British Railways Board Personnel Registry, The National Front, National Archives AN 174 1807. This management file also reports on apparently unsuccessful attempts to distribute NF materials to 'Senior Railmen' through the internal mail.

46 *Locomotive Journal* October 1977.

47 *Socialist Worker* 1 April 1978; ANL national newsletter March 1978.

48 *Socialist Worker* 1 April 78; Philip Bagwell, *The Railwaymen: The History of the National Union of Railwaymen* (HarperCollins, 1982), vol.2, p.278.

49 'Members face expulsion and the sack, Rail Union Ban the Front', *Daily Mirror* 1 April 1978; Unions act to tackle the Front, *Morning Star* 1

November 1978. National Front, activity of National Front Railwaymen's Association during election campaigns, National Archives AN 174/1807. See also National Archives AN 171/148. This includes 'correspondence from senior management expressing concern over the use of staff notice boards and union channels to distribute National Front material, and samples of the material found'.

50   *Socialist Worker* 27 May 1978.

51   *Socialist Worker* 14 October 1978.

52   Bagwell, 1982.

53   See article by John Smith who moved the conference motion, 'Declaration of War against the National Front', *ASLEF Locomotive Journal* July 1978.

54   TSSA organised the white-collar employees on the railways.

55   John Rose, *Solidarity Forever: 100 years of Kings Cross ASLEF*, (Kings Cross ASLEF, 1986), p.49; *Socialist Challenge* 15 June 1978, announced 'Rail against the Nazis, founding meeting, Mon 19 June, at The Roebuck, Tottenham Court Road. Speakers include Mike Caffoor, Anti Nazi League, and John Robson, chairperson of Wood Green ASLEF, 8pm, railway workers welcome'.

56   Steve Forey, interviewed by Geoff Brown 13 December 2021.

57   *Rail against the Nazis*, Bulletin No 1.

58   Dave Welsh, https://londonagainstracism.files.wordpress.com/2013/07/dave-welsh1.pdf

59   David Renton, *When We Touched the Sky*, (New Clarion Press, 2006), p.109.

60   Forey, 13 December 2021.

61   Paul Salveson, interviewed by Geoff Brown 22 November 2021.

62   Forey 13 December 2021.

63   West London Hospital Worker Oct/Nov 1975.

64   *Days of Hope*, 1975, directed by Ken Loach, produced by Tony Garnett.

65   Anne Robertson, interviewed by Geoff Brown 19 November 2021.

66   Mike McGrath, interviewed by Geoff Brown 11 November 2021, and private email 9 January 2022.

67   Harry McShane was one of the speakers. McShane was a remarkable figure on the left in Glasgow. He had been a member of the wartime Clyde Workers' Committee in 1915-1916, a close ally of John MacLean and a founder member of the British Communist Party in 1920. He left the CP in 1954 and later become close to the International Socialists

68   Mike Healy, interviewed by Beoff Brown 2 December 2021.

69   *Redder Tape* June 1978; 'They said no Anti Nazi badges, so everyone wore one...' *Socialist Challenge* 25 May 1978.

70   'Industrial relations – Political activities (The wearing of badges & display of notices on official premises)', National Archives, BN 121. More support came as a £500 donation by the CPSA to make good the ANL

office after it was firebombed. 'Campaign against Nazis to be stepped up', *Morning Star* 10 July 1978.

71   'Council Workers against the Nazis campaign against BM member in Cardiff Central Library', *Socialist Worker* 18 November 1978. There were sixteen civilian workers at Harrogate Police Station, all members of NALGO opposed to both the ANL and the NF, 'NALGO support for ANL criticised', *Searchlight* December 1979.

72   *Morning Star* 13 June 1978. The same commitment came from NUPE members in the Northwest where Colin Barnett was NUPE regional secretary.

73   Letter from G. Bennett to Scargill, ANL file, NUM archive, Barnsley; *Searchlight* February 1979; *Worksop Guardian* 9 December 1978.

74   *Socialist Worker* 18 March 1978.

75   *Collier* June/July 1978.

76   Ian Mitchell, interviewed by Geoff Brown 13 December 2021.

77   'Now for Miners against Nazis', *Socialist Worker* 17 June 1978,

78   Mitchell, 13 December 2021.

79   Nobby Lawton remembers going to the ANL carnivals in coaches organised by Notts NUM, Facebook post, 6 August 2024.

80   *Morning Star* 26 February. See also *Collier* March/April 1979.

81   'Equity not to join 'Anti-Nazis'', *Daily Telegraph* 10 November 1978.

82   'Trade Unions taking action against the Nazis of the National Front and against racists' Leicester Anti Racist Committee, Trade Union notebook.

83   'ANL and the labour and trade union movement', Report back from ANL Working Council, Birmingham 26 November 1978, *Merseyside Anti Nazi League Bulletin* No.2, December 1978.

84   John McClintock, 'Colour Bar Bus Strike', *Labour Worker* September 1964. McLintock did not cross the picket line.

85   Geoff Brown, 'Winning the right to wear the Sikh turban working on Manchester buses', (unpublished, 2024). See also 'Sikh bus drivers win turban fight', *Yorkshire Post* 26 October 1974; 'Turban bus-strike on again today?', *Yorkshire Post* 28 October 1974.

86   *Times* 22 January 1975; *Socialist Worker* 25 January 1975.

87   *Succeed* July 1976.

88   'Non-stop buses against the Nazis', *Socialist Worker* 2 September 1978.

89   'Coventry: Black bus driver attacked – then arrested', *Big Flame* August 1978.

90   Greater Manchester ANL newsletter May 1978, p.2. Supportive drivers were very helpful when it came to criss-crossing Warwickshire trying to get to the protest against the NF march on 20 August 1980. See Chapter 10 'Taking down the beast'. It was an ANL supporter from Birchfield garage who drove the bus from Manchester to the 'Nazis out of football 'demonstration in Hattersley 8 October 1978 aiming to 'disrupt the game" where the NF's 'Lillywhites' team were playing.

91   *Socialist Worker* 8 April 1978.

92   *The Platform: The Paper of the London Transport Rank & File Organisation*, Summer 1978. Prouse's motion was not carried but the NF member was ordered not to voice his opinions at work.

93   Hitler, September 1934 speech to the National Socialist Women's Organization, Max Doramus, *The Complete Hitler: A Digital Desktop Reference to His Speeches & Proclamations, 1932–1945* (Bolchazy-Carducci Publishers, 1990), p.532.

94   *Spearhead* January 1977. It was 'a reflection on the abilities of the men in the Conservative Party that their present leader is a woman', *Sunday Telegraph* magazine, 23 October 1977. The NF echoed the Nazis. Joseph Goebbels, the Nazi 's lead propagandist, 1934, 'The highest calling of women is always that of wife and mother'. There were women fascists. By one estimate, a quarter of the NF's membership were women. One of the most powerful examples of fascist propaganda is the film *Triumph of the Will*, 1935, was directed, produced, edited and co-written by Leni Riefenstahl, https://www.youtube.com/watch?v=p7hJVaTW45M. The NF argued that women were at particular risk of rape and mugging by black men. See the election leaflet in Brixton referred to by Anna Keene, interviewed by *Socialist Challenge* 6 July 1978.

95   Resisting the police on New Cross Road included WARF supporters throwing bricks, private conversation, July 2020, name withheld.

96   See *Camerawork* no.8, 1977, 'Lewisham: What are you taking pictures for?' p.13, for Peter Marlow's photo of New Cross Road shows three women who may have been members of the WARF contingent, https://archive.leftove.rs/documents/GQN/15.

97   Haringey TUC and London Socialist Historians Group, 2002, *The Battle of Wood Green*, p.10 notes that 'Photos of the demo do indeed suggest that the counter-demonstration was male dominated and this may have reflected the general profile of the left 45 years ago'. It could also be that the photos taken focused disproportionately on moments of 'male on male' confrontation.

98   Sarah Boston, *Women Workers and the Trade Unions* (Lawrence & Wishart, 1987), pp.329–30. While the 50,000+ demonstration against the anti-abortion Corrie Bill, 28 October 1979, had the support of the TUC, it was organised with little active involvement of the TUC. See *Socialist Worker* 'Defending women's right to choose', 6 November 2004. Women were 56.8 percent of union members in 2021, TUC Equality Audit 2022: https://socialistworker.co.uk/features/defending-women-s-right-to-choose. Two of the eleven members of the ANL steering committee were women: Miriam Karlin and Audrey Wise MP.

99   *Temporary Hoarding* no.6, Summer 1978; *Spare Rib* no.73, August 1978. The first song was about a man pursuing girls at a convent school. Having been challenged, the chorus of their second song was 'Tits, tits, tits'.

100   Daniel Rachel, *Walls Come Tumbling Down: The Music and Politics of Rock Against Racism, 2 Tone and Red Wedge* (Picador, 2016), p.84.

101   *Drastic Measures*, 'Rock against Sexism'. The challenge to the sexism and racism of the songs at an ANL fundraiser in Manchester, according to the gig organiser, was limited to people heckling and throwing empty

pint glasses. The organiser complained that this showed how, 'their ignorance displayed no sense of humour or irony to an act which essentially depends on humour and irony for its success', Letter from Manchester Environmental Health Dept Workers against Fascism and Racism to Geoff Brown, Manchester ANL organiser, 4 July 1979.

102   The Women and Fascism Study Group, Centre for Contemporary Cultural Studies, refers to WARF as 'having only a tenuous existence', *Red Rag* vol.14, 1979. Florence Binard, 2017, 'The British Women's Liberation Movement in the 1970s: Redefining the Personal and the Political', *Revue Française de Civilisation Britannique: French Journal of British Studies*, vol.30, no.1, https://journals.openedition.org/rfcb/1688.

103   'Women against fascism', *CARF* No 4 April 1978.

104   Binard, 2017.

105   Women Against the Nazis, 'Without Women we'll get nowhere', n.d.; Interview with Anna Keane, *Socialist Challenge* 6 July 1978.

106   As endnote above.

107   WAN leaflet, *Women's Voice*, May 1978. £3 for a thousand copies.

108   *Women's Voice* September 1978.

109   *Women's Voice* August 1978.

110   *Women's Voice*, 'Clean away racist filth', August 1978; Hackney Shoreditch paint out 24 June 1978, *Hackney People' Press* July 1978. This paint-out was followed up by eight paint outs a few weeks later, September 10th. One of these was in Kentish Town, 'Painting out the Nazis', *Women's Voice* October 1978, p.9.

111   Gay Activist Alliance, GAA, leaflet.

112   John D'Emilio, *Sexual Politics, Sexual Communities: The Making of a Homosexual Minority in the United States 1940–1970* (University of Chicago Press, 1983); Mike Davis & Jon Wiener, *Set the Night on Fire: L.A. in the Sixties* (Verso, 2020). The GLF was set up in London in October 1970,

113   Lisa Power, *No Bath but Plenty of Bubbles: An Oral History of the Gay Liberation Front, 1970–1973*, (Cassell, 1995), p.13.

114   Colin Wilson, *Socialists and Gay Liberation* (Socialist Worker, 1995), p.21. Though John Lindsay remembers GLF meetings in 1973 and 1974, unpublished letter to *International Socialism Journal*, http://vectors.usc.edu/thoughtmesh/publish/51.php. Nigel Young raises the question whether it is possible to explore the personal within a revolutionary organisation, Nigel Young, 'Crossroads: Which way now?', *Gay Left* no.15.

115   *Gay News* was Britain's best known gay publication with a fortnightly circulation of up to 18,000.

116   The Gay Activist Alliance (GAA).

117   Gay Rights at work, NALGO Gay Group/NALGO Action 1979.

118   See Diagnostic and Statistical Manual of Mental Disorders (DSM-II), 1968, http://queerbeyondlondon.com/leeds/302-0-glad-to-be-gay/

119   John Lindsey, 'Coming Out', *Socialist Worker* 26 August 1978.

120   In practice, 'licentious dancing' meant two women or two men dancing together.

121   List in GAA Anti-fascist Handbook. See also Gays against Fascism leaflet; see also the report in *Gay News* of attack in the Fenton, *Gay News* no.144, June 1–14 1978.

122   *Gay News* no.117, May 1977; Young, *Crossroads.*

123   Lindsay, http://vectors.usc.edu/thoughtmesh/publish/51.php

124   *Top of the Pops*, 2 March 1978. He also had a large RAR badge on his guitar.

125   *Gay News* no.143, May 1978.

126   Pip Smith, *Gay News* no.143, May 1978.

127   Eddie Prevost, interviewed by Geoff Brown 18 December 2020.

128   'Politics and sex', Lionel Starling, Islington District, for the SWP Gay Group, *Socialist Workers Party Bulletin*, October 1977.

129   Iain Ferguson interviewed by Geoff Brown 19 October 2020.

130   *Gay News* no.152, October 1978.

131   *Gay News* no.152, October 1978.

132   *Temporary Hoarding,* 1978, quoted in David Wilkinson, 'Ever Fallen in Love (With Someone You Shouldn't have?): Punk, Politics and Same-Sex Passion', in: *Punk is Dead: Modernity Killed Every Night*, Richard Cabut & Andrew Gallix eds, (Zero Books, 2017), p.70

133   Paul Furness, in Huddle & Saunders, p.86.

134   Bob Cant, 'Normal channels', in Bob Cant & Susan Hemmings, eds., *Radical Records: Thirty Years of Lesbian and Gay History, 1957–1987* (Taylor & Francis, 2010), pp.127–130.

135   *Teachers against Racism*, 1972, vol.1, no.1, February 1972 & no.2, June 1972. Teachers Against Racism (TAR), https://g.co/arts/rg1LfeCwAKXNDPws6 https://g.co/arts/378s2CHxkhmCPha7A

136   See above.

137   See above.

138   See Chapter 3 'Fighting racism and fascism'..

139   Hackney School Kids Against the Nazis, 1978, https://www.youtube.com/watch?v=16bRQaAx9h4

140   See above.

141   Greg Dyke, interviewed by Geoff Brown 1 September 2021.

142   Kevin Corr, interviewed by Geoff Brown 4 January 2021.

143   *Socialist Worker* 25 March 1978. Speakers included Dick North of the NUT executive, Steven Anden of the Institute of Race Relations, Arthur Latham MP, Peter Watts, head of Shoreditch School, and Farokh Gandhi of *Race Today*.

144   'Politics in the classroom', *Guardian* 31 Aug 1974.

145   'Tulse Hill, Fascists in schools', *Rank and File Teacher* September 1974.

146   National Front man resigns teaching job, *Times* 8 July 1975. Edmonds described himself as 'a victim of a campaign by other teachers', 'Anarchy at Tulse Hill', *Spearhead* no.85 July 1975.

147 Shaun Doherty, private conversation 25 September 2020.

148 'Fighting Racialism in School', discussion document, Holloway School, February 1978.

149 'Head bans race words in anti-Front drive', *Daily Telegraph* 3 February 1978; 'School turns the table on racism', *Socialist Worker* February 1978. The *Islington Gazette* put the story on its front page with the headline 'Head canes racist poison'. See also Shaun Doherty, in Roger Huddle & Red Saunders, eds., *Reminiscences of RAR* (Redwords, 2021), pp.63–4.

150 For more on the NUT tradition of class collaboration, see Duncan Hallas, *Indomitable Revolutionary* (Bookmarks, 2023), p.50.

151 'Anti-Nazis in drive to recruit teachers', *Birmingham Post* 22 February 1978.

152 See previous endnote.

153 *Searchlight* 33 March 1978.

154 *Socialist Worker* 6 May 1978; '"Political" teacher punished', *Sunday Telegraph* 23 April 1978.

155 *Socialist Worker* 4 February 1978.

156 Nick Grant, in Huddle & Saunders, 2021, p.106.

157 'Barking Teachers counter Young NF', *Searchlight* 33 March 1978.

158 Motion proposed by A. Stevens, NUT, Daneford School, 'That, in view of the Increasing local support for the National Front and other extreme right-wing political groups, the Daneford School branch of the N.U.T. agrees to sponsor and make a (voluntary) financial contribution towards the Anti Nazi league,' Bishopsgate archive, 18 October 1974.

159 Retired teacher, interviewed by Geoff Brown August 2021. Anonymity requested.

160 Both School Students Against the Nazis and School Kids Against the Nazis were used. When referring to themselves, it was almost always 'school students'.

161 'Schools Target!', Sue Roalman, *East End Advertiser* 28 October 1977. The article reports on a number of counter initiatives, Schools Campaign Against Racism (SCAR), with students from NELP involved. Activity was also planned by the East London Teachers Association secretary Bernie Regan, working with the National Union of School Students (NUSS) and Tower Hamlets Movement Against Racism and Fascism (THMARF). THMARF's annual meeting had a speaker from the Hackney CRC looking to the increased scope of the new 1976 Race Relations Act and the strengthened role it gave to the Commission for Racial Equality.

162 *Guardian* 24 October 1977. Pearce started editing the local *Bulldog* in Barking, which then became the YNF paper. See *Times* 9 March 1978.

163 *Daily Mirror* 7 November 1977.

164 Film demo flops, *Sunday Times* 22 January 1978. The ILEA staff inspector for secondary schools warned all headteachers to watch the film before showing it to pupils, *Socialist Worker* 11 March 1978.

165 *Daily Telegraph* 20 January 1978.

166   'How to Spot a Red Teacher', CP/CENT/SUBJ/04/15, LHASC.

167   'How to combat Red Teachers', 1978, National Front. *Searchlight* pointed out that the pamphlet left out Tyndall's view that 'In every school curriculum there should be a number of hours in the week set aside for activities which bring the young child into contact with rudimentary military procedures... Drill, marksmanship and field craft should be a central part of cadet activities... There should be a much greater emphasis on physical fitness and the object should be to produce a hard, tough youth, capable of great endurance and with a combative spirit', 'Education In The Classroom', *Spearhead,* October 1976.

168   It was a year before the ILEA had him summoned to court. *Socialist Challenge* 22 June 1978.

169   David Kersey, interviewed by Geoff Brown 12 February 2022.

170   'Education for national survival', 1976, National Front.

171   *Derbyshire Times* 17 February 1978.

172   *Sunday Mail* 26 February 1978. The Board of Deputies reported NF leafleting outside schools in Ipswich, Yarmouth, Ilkeston, Sunderland, Brighton and Worthing, *Jewish Chronicle* 26 May 1978.

173   'The Race Gauntlet of Fear', *Daily Mirror* 4 February 1978.

174   *Sunday Times* 13 November 1977

175   *Times* 25 November 1977. Williams rejected the request, *Times* 29 December 1977.

176   *Sunday Times* 27 November 1977.

177   *Daily Mail* 1 December 1977.

178   *Searchlight* 33 March 1978; 'Nazis at the school gates', *Labour Weekly* 20 January 1978.

179   S*earchlight no.*31 January 1978.

180   The Jehovah's Witnesses are a Christian evangelist movement. They were persecuted by the Nazis who sent an estimated 10,000 Jehovah's Witnesses to concentration camps.

181   Weyman Bennett interview with Steve Cunningham & Mike Lavalette, 10 January 2016 in Steve Cunningham & Michael Lavalette, *Schools Out!* (Bookmarks, 2016), p.151.

182   For soulboys, see BBC, 'British Style Genius, Street Style, Soulboys', https://www.bbc.co.uk/britishstylegenius/content/22248.shtml

183   Cunningham & Lavalette, pp.151–2.

184   Griffin was leader of the British National Party 1999–2014, taking over from John Tyndall. Under his leadership it had at one point more than fifty members elected onto local councils, one member of the London Assembly and two members of the European parliament, Griffin and Andrew Brons.

185   *Socialist Worker* 11 March 1978. According to the headteacher, who told the local press his main concern was road safety, 'A large group of pupils had gathered round those distributing the leaflets. Some fifth formers took exception to this and saw them off'. 'Students scuffle with racists', *Ipswich Star* 22 February 1978; *Morning Star* 13 April 1978; 'NF attacked at

school – claim', *Ipswich Star* 13 April 1978. After the first leafleting, the NF claimed on local radio that they left 'because they were cold and the leaflets were torn out of their hands because the kids were eager to read them'.

186 David Kersey 12 February 2022.

187 *Time Out* 24 November 1977; *Searchlight* no.31 January 1978.

188 *Peace News* 27 January 1978. The schools were Clissold Park and Highbury Grove.

189 See excerpt of interview with Randall, http://media.bufvc.ac.uk/lbc/B005/IRN_1978_00008_01_BU-B005-00394_1500.mp3

190 *SKAN* 2 April 1978.

191 *Socialist Worker* 8 April 1978; *SKAN* 2, April 1978.

192 *Peace News* 5 May 1978; *Women's Voice* no.18, June 1978.

193 Polly Wilson, in Huddle & Saunders, 2016, p.259.

194 People's names are frequently redacted by the Undercover Police Inquiry to keep the names of individuals confidential.

195 Undercover Police Inquiry, https://www.ucpi.org.uk/UCPI/0000013063/4, 4(e).

196 Roger Prouse, a local bus worker, spoke at the rally. Five days later he opened a parcel which exploded nearly killing him. See 'Bus workers against the Nazis' below.

197 *SKAN* 2 April 1978.

198 Reading School Students, *Socialist Worker* 26 Nov 1977; 'Reading school students drive out the Nazis', *Socialist Worker* 26 November 1977.

199 Jim Fagan, interviewed by Geoff Brown 15 February 2022. The leaflet called on readers to 'Become a supporter, Get leaflets, badges and stickers, Organise RAR gigs, Form SKAN groups in your school, Write, draw, report for SKAN – tell us if the Nazis have tried to leaflet your school and how you stopped them'.

200 Tyneside SKAN meetings were all followed by a new wave and reggae disco. There were many similar examples. See https://www.huckmag.com/perspectives/activism-2/the-british-school-kids-who-took-on-the-nazis-in-the-70s/

201 Roger Green, Thames Valley SWP organiser, based in Reading, who now moved to London to work as ANL organiser responsible for SKAN.

202 At least 220 letters were received.

203 Corrina Fisher, Diane Griffiths, Angela Peacock, Karolyn Shawcross, Sharon Stubbs, letter to the ANL 4 April 1978.

204 Julia Stockton, letter to ANL April 1978.

205 J Flowers, letter to the ANL 19 April 1978.

206 Ruth Jampel letter to ANL, n.d., (April 1978); 'School Students fight racism', Angela Phillips, *Young Observer* 19 March 1978.

207 Roger Green, in Huddle & Saunders, 2016, p.113.

208 *Socialist Challenge* 6 July 1978. *Socialist Challenge* 15 June reports: 'Oldham SKAN, After the suspension of two school students for wearing ANL badges, Oldham School Kids Against the Nazis are planning a series

of modest activities. Eight schools in the area are involved, with at least 60 school students taking part in the activity. Planned so far are a Rock Against Racism social, a meeting at which Tariq Ali will speak, and a mass petitioning of schools to demand the right to wear ANL badges'.

209   'We started with leafleting the school and sold 150 ANL badges... We sell about 200 copies of SKAN and about fifteen copies of Socialist Worker. There are seventy fully paid up members of SKAN', *Socialist Worker* 15 July 1978,

210   Rehad Desai, interviewed by Geoff Brown 28 February 2022.

211   As endnote 53. SKAN was not the only group to organise outside school gates, see the 'How to spot a fascist at your school gate' leaflet produced by Leicester and District Trades Council.

212   Brian Capaloff, interview 28 February 2022. The Thames TV documentary covered the Victoria Park Carnival as well as the footage showing 'Hackney School Kids against the Nazis'.

213   *Socialist Worker* 27 May 1978

214   *New Musical Express* 3 June 1978. The article was not only sympathetic, it also included SKAN's postal address, the ANL office.

215   Helen Blair, interview 28 September 2020.

216   Leeds ANL (Memo no.1 18 May 1978) reported its first SKAN meeting 'is on Sunday, 28th May at 2.30 p.m. in the Polytechnic Common Room. Speaker: Colin Burgon (teacher at Foxwood School); leaflets are available. A SKAN gig is also being organised'.

217   'Anti-Nazis in Bust-Up', *Daily Mirror* 20 November 1978. Keith Waterhouse, 'The Pot and the kettle', *Daily Mirror* 30 November 1978.

218   'Stars quit anti-Nazis over violent language', *Sunday Times* 19 November 1978.

219   'Anti-Nazi language rumpus', *Guardian* 20 November 1978. The article adds that SKAN, now in its fifth issue, had a circulation of 25,000.

220   Letter from ANL to Arthur Scargill, 21 November 1978, NUM archive.

221   Joan Rudder, interviewed by Geoff Brown 12 October 2021.

222   'My word! They don't like SKAN', *Socialist Worker* 25 November 1978.

223   Letter from Arthur Scargill to Brian Clough 21 November 1978, NUM archive.

224   Letter from Brian Clough to Arthur Scargill 28 November 1978, NUM archive.

225   *SKAN* 1, p.5.

226   *SKAN* 1, p.4. Besides the young people who had been involved with the NF who joined SKAN, there were also some who went the other way. See Nick Grant, in Huddle & Saunders, 2016, p.107.

227   See 'SWP dominated by old people aged 24', *Socialist Worker* 23 December 1978, pp.8–9. Roger Green was initially the youth organiser of the SWP, succeeded by Mike Pearse, SWP Internal Bulletin, August 1979.

228   Scotty, Glasgow punk and Right to Work marcher, 'SWP Rebel

weekend', *Socialist Worker* 26 August 1978

229 Colin Burgon, uncle of Richard Burgon, MP Leeds East.

230 Nigel Flanagan, interviewed by Geoff Brown 25 October 2021.

231 David Robins, *We Hate Humans* (Penguin, 1984).

232 Paul Rees, *The Three Degrees: The Men Who Changed British Football Forever* (Constable, 2014), p.131. See www.theguardian.com/football/2014/jul/25/west-brom-three-degrees-book-extract

233 As previous endnote.

234 Rees, p.30.

235 Rees, p.130. The commentator Gerald Sinstadt describes 'this almost laissez-faire attitude to the abuse of black players. It was sort of accepted', Rees, p.155.

236 Rees, pp.27–8.

237 BBC *Panorama*, 'F-Troop, Treatment and the Halfway Line', 14 November 1977. https://www.youtube.com/watch?v=ighcTmfAfr4.

238 Ashton was MP for Bassetlaw, near Sheffield. He had been a Sheffield City Councillor.

239 'Storm over Labour call, Crush the Front!' *Daily Mirror* 8 December 1977.

240 Robins, p.113.

241 'MP wins soccer bosses' help: Clough fights the Front and Jackie Charlton puts the boot in too', *Daily Mirror* 12 December 1977.

242 Wayne Minter, in Daniel Rachel, *Walls Come Tumbling Down: The Music and Politics of Rock Against Racism, 2 Tone and Red Wedge* (Picador, 2016), p.120.

243 Anonymous, private email 23 May 2022.

244 *Bulldog* n.d.

245 Garth Crooks, black player for Stoke City in 1978 and active member of the Professional Footballers' Association (PFA), a TUC affiliated union.

246 Mel Norris, interviewed by Geoff Brown 29 January 2021.

247 Richard Buckwell, n.d., 'Spurs Against the Nazis', updated 1 April 2025.

248 *Socialist Worker* 29 April 1978.

249 By early 1978 this included Dave Bowen, manager, Northampton; Pat Crerand, manager (Northampton till early 1977); Bill Dodgin, manager, Brentford; Terry Venables, manager, Crystal Palace; also, Dave Underwood, chairman Barnet Football Club and Dave Watson, footballer, Manchester City. *Socialist Worker* 4 March 78 reported that when Tommy Docherty had been approached to sponsor the ANL, he refused because Paddy Crerand was a member. Crerand wasn't but on hearing what Docherty said, decided to sponsor the ANL.

250 *Socialist Worker* 29 April 1978; 'Anti-Nazis move on to the terraces', *Acton Gazette and Post* 27 April 1978; 'Stand up against the mindless fans', *Acton Gazette* 1 June 1978.

251 These include West Bromwich Albion, Swansea, Oxford, Arsenal,

Manchester United, Manchester City, Everton, Norwich, Barnsley, Sheffield, Leyton Orient, West Ham, Partick Thistle and Oldham. See Chris Newrat, 'Anti-Nazis cross the great divide', *Morning Star* 12 May 1979. Newrat says that 'To date some 25 clubs have been leafleted and local groups complete with badges now number 20'; see also 'Sky Blues Against the Nazis', *Socialist Challenge* 12 October 1978.

252   Paul Thomas, 1995, 'Kicking Racism Out of Football: A Supporters View', *Race & Class* vol.36, no.4.

253   Steve Cedar, interviewed by Geoff Brown 10 August 2020.

254   Sheila Amrouche, 'Confronting the Nazis: The Battle of Lewisham in 1977', SWP TV, www.youtube.com/watch?v=fi14XozEzW0&t=2712s.

255   Clyde Best, one of the first black players in the First Division, played for West Ham 1968–76.

256   Cass Pennant, *Cass* (John Blake, 2002). Pennant's autobiography has been turned into a film *Cass*.

257   Mel Norris, interviewed by Geoff Brown 29 January 2021; *Socialist Worker* 18 November 1978.

258   'Orient ban anti-Nazi movement', *Guardian* 13 February 1979. *Socialist Challenge* 15 February 1979 had a report on setting up OAN.

259   ANL Newsletter no.1, February 1979. Longsight & Levenshulme Group Against Racism and Fascism Newsletter December 1978 reported that the NF 'organised some West Ham fans into Hammers Against the Marxists. Osvaldo ('Ossie') Ardiles and Ricardo Villa were Argentinian footballers who started playing for Tottenham in 1978.

260   'Bristol: 40 years ago, the far right in Bristol was faced down with music, pickets and ballots' thebristolcable.org/2020/01/40-years-ago-the-far-right-in-bristol-was-faced-down-with-music-pickets-and-ballots/; www.facebook.com/tom.archer.566148

261   'Carnival!', *Morning Star* 19 May 1978.

262   Buckwell, n.d. and private email 23 May 2022.

263   *NF News* June 1978 reported 9 percent in parts of Hertfordshire, 10 percent in Tyneside, Dudley 12 percent. Yorkshire was notably weak with the best results 7 percent in Halifax and 6 percent in Rotherham.

264   In Bradford, the NF 'polled 2,000 fewer votes, despite fielding more candidates. Their share of the vote fell from 12.3 to 5.1 per cent'. Bradford Anti-Fascist Committee and Bradford SWP members' letter to *Socialist Worker* 11 June 1977.

265   'Manchester has bought 60,000 leaflets; Leeds has ordered 35,000; another 20,000 to Liverpool: 25,000 to Wolverhampton; 40,000 to Birmingham; 20,000 to Glasgow; 15,000 to Bristol', 'Rocking the Front line against intolerance', *Guardian* 25 April 1978.

266   *Socialist Worker* 6 May 1978.

267   Two NF candidates and one BNP. The much smaller BNP dissolved itself into the NF early 1978.

268   The Board of Deputies distributed half a million copies of its leaflet, 'The National Front is a four-letter word – evil', 'National Front fielding over

900 candidates', *Jewish Chronicle* 28 April 1978.

269   Colin Sparks, 'Reading the Entrails', *Socialist Review* June 1978, p.7. The disappointing result also produced a threatened split inside the NF, 'Nazis condemn Tyndall', *Socialist Worker* 2 September 1978, p.4.

270   Poll warning on Front contenders in marginals, *Times* 31 August 1978.

271   *Socialist Worker* 6 May 1978.

272   *Socialist Worker* 24 June 1978. See also Chanie Rosenberg, 1988, 'Labour and the fight against fascism', *International Socialism* series 2, no.39.

273   See website endnote, 'Irlam Cadishead Anti Nazi League'.

274   See website endnote 'Greater Manchester ANL groups and affiliated organisations'.

275   Margaret Smith, interviewed by Geoff Brown 4 May 2018.

276   See website endnote 'Peter Cockcroft: Anti fascist memories, Manchester, Liverpool and Blackburn in the early 1970s'.

277   *Socialist Worker* 6 May 1978.

278   'Leicester, Anti-Racist Groups in Leicester, 1979', https://www.nednewitt.com/?page_id=98.

279   Jim Barlow, i interviewed by Geoff Brown 6 November 2020; *Socialist Worker* 27 August 1977; *Times* 26 August 1977.

280   David Renton, *When We Touched the Sky: The Anti-Nazi League 1977–1981* (New Clarion Press, 2006), p.110.

281   Colin Barker, in Daniel Rachel, *Walls Come Tumbling Down: The Music and Politics of Rock Against Racism, 2 Tone and Red Wedge* (Picador, 2016), p.119.

282   Lorna Chessum, *From Immigrants to Ethnic Minority: Making Black Community in Britain* (Routledge, 2000), p.222.

283   Unattributed report on Anti Nazi League Campaign Conference, 8 July 1978, ANL sling file, Working Class Movement Library, Salford.

284   At the time of writing, February 2025, £3,000 spent in May 1978 is equivalent to £16,000 today, https://www.ons.gov.uk/economy/inflationandpriceindices/timeseries/cdko/mm23

285   Anti Nazi League East Kent branch constitution, 3 July 1978. Original in Mick Murray, Communist Party organiser, ANL folder,1978–1979 Greater Manchester County Record Office.

286   Phil Ramsell, interviewed by Geoff Brown 16 February 2021. Wayne Minter makes the point that there is often no written record. What has survived is at best an incomplete record of what people did. Wayne Minter, full-time RAR organiser 1978–81, in Huddle & Saunders, 2016, p.181. See also Mike Davis & Jon Wiener, *Set the Night on Fire: L.A. in the Sixties* (Verso, 2020), p.7, an outstanding history of the movements from 'below' in Los Angeles that reshaped the city's political landscape. Also, much of what happened in CND went unrecorded and there is too little written about CND as a movement. See John Charlton, *Don't You Hear the H-bomb's Thunder? Youth and Politics on Tyneside in the Late 'Fifties and Early 'Sixties* (The

Merlin Press, 2009).

287 Student unions, which often mobilised the largest numbers for demonstrations and day to day activities, found their delegates accepted only as visitors when their affiliation fees had not been paid. See Tony Greenstein, *The Fight against Fascism in Brighton & the South Coast* (Brighton History Workshop, 2011), pp.35–7.

288 In Manchester Robert Lizar, Steve Cohen (IMG) and Rhys Vaughan and others gave representation and advice (including acting as 'MacKenzie men') for free or submitted bills that were never chased.

289 *Hackney People's Press* July 1978.

290 Chris Lymn, private email 26 July 2021.

291 Chris Lymn, private email 11 July 2022. He also writes, 'The only time it was tested was when a lad visited me and proposed fire bombing the NF HQ. His problem was that Alan Ross, a local anarchist, had tipped me off that he was a plant.'

292 Richard Dunn, interviewed by Geoff Brown 16 December 2019.

293 This included Geoff Brown and Bernie Wilcox, ANL and RAR organisers in Manchester, who made the initial proposal for a carnival in Manchester, Geoff Brown, in Huddle & Saunders, 2016, p.35; Bernie Wilcox, in Huddle & Saunders, 2016, pp.252–3

294 The details were already in *Temporary Hoarding* no.1, 'Guidelines for RAR gig organisers'. Hackney and Leicester had already put on an open air anti racist festival.

295 The strength of the ANL's labour movement support in Manchester, particularly the role played by Colin Barnett as secretary of the North West TUC, made the task of securing Alexandra Park, Moss Side, easier than elsewhere.

296 Coventry Anti Nazi League Newsletter, personal archive.

297 Staffordshire Moorlands District Council refused permission for a Rock Against Racism concert in a local town hall, October 1978. Worcester City Council stopped an ANL Rock Against Racism concert being held on the race course and in Malvern Winter Gardens because of alleged fears of NF disruption, August 1978. Ealing Council banned outdoor carnivals after the Southall carnival. *CARF*, no.8 n.d, p.3.

298 'A Festival for Racial Equality', Free Trade Hall, Manchester, 28 May 1978.

299 See book's website note for details of the cast.

300 Keith Rusby, in Huddle & Saunders, 2016, p.207.

301 'Rock Against Racism: The day Manchester and its bands stood proud against the far right', www.manchestereveningnews.co.uk/news/greater-manchester-news/rock-against-racism-day-manchester-14877439.

302 There were also carnivals in Bradford, Harwich, Nottingham and Southall. The Bristol carnival was in Ashton Court, 5–6 August. The publicity announced 'Misty and Aswad invited. Steve Hillage will play'. See Ian Goodyer, *Crisis Music: The Cultural Politics of Rock Against Racism* (Manchester University Press, 2009), p.27 citing *Temporary Hoarding* no.6.

Battles

1   The number killed remains disputed: 'Estimates for the total number of civilian and military deaths range from 500,000 to over 3 million'. https://www.nationalarchives.gov.uk/education/resources/the-independence-of-bangladesh-in-1971/ .
2   Shabna Begum, *From Sylhet to Spitalfields: Bengali Squatters in 1970s East London* (Lawrence Wishart, 2023), pp.10–11.
3   *Race Today* March 1976, p.52, 'the acronym 'Bhag' means 'tiger' in Bengali and 'share' in Urdu and Hindi', Shabna Begum, *From Sylhet to Spitalfields: Bengali Squatters in 1970s East London* (Lawrence & Wishart, 2023), p.81; 'Bengali Squat in the East End', *Race Today* vol.6, no.9, September 1974, pp.244–5. Mala Sen, member of the *Race Today* collective, a Bengali speaker, played a key role.
4   Sarah Glynn, *Class, Ethnicity and Religion in the Bengali East End: A Political History* (Manchester University Press, 2014), p.122
5   Kenneth Leech, *Brick Lane 1978: The Events and Their Significance*, (Stepney Books, 1994), p.14.
6   'The East End of London, Paki bashing in 1970', *Race Today* December 1973; 'Paki bashing a sport in Rochdale', *Manchester Evening News* 6 January 1971.
7   'Inquiry by Pakistanis on stabbing', *Times* 8 April 1970.
8   Begum, 2023, p.67.
9   Bethnal Green and Stepney Trades Council, 1978, *Blood on the streets: A report on racial attacks in East London* (BG&STC, 1978), p.22; David Widgery, *Some Lives* (Sinclair-Stevenson, 1991), pp.203–4.
10   Rafique Ullah, 'First Day at School', Oral histories of the Bengali East End, https://www.ideastore.co.uk/local-history/collections-and-digital-resources/oral-history/oral-histories-of-the-bengali-east-end
11   Bethnal Green and Stepney Trades Council, 1978, p.25.
12   Bethnal Green and Stepney Trades Council, 1978, pp.70–82.
13   Take home pay was around £30 a week, less than half average male wages. https://api.parliament.uk/historic-hansard/written-answers/1976/oct/28/wages See also Ullah, Oral histories.
14   Bethnal Green and Stepney Trades Council, 1978, p.26.
15   John Parker & Keith Dugmore, *Colour and the Allocation of GLC Housing*, Greater London Council, 21 November 1976, pp.69–71.
16   Newham Monitoring Project/Campaign against Racism and Fascism, 1991, *Newham: The Forging of a Black Community*, pp.5–6.
17   Bethnal Green and Stepney Trades Council, 1978, p.23.
18   Avtar Jouhl, Birmingham Indian Workers' Association, quoted in Shirin Hirsch, *In the Shadow of Enoch Powell* (Manchester University Press, 2018), p.60.
19   Newham Monitoring Project, 1991, p.23.
20   Bethnal Green and Stepney Trades Council, 1978, pp.54–5. See Chapter 3, 'Fighting racism and fascism', p.11. Leech says the meeting was organised by the Anti-Racist Committee of Asians in East London (ARCAEL).
21   David Widgery, *Beating Time* (Chatto & Windus, 1986), p.30.
22   *Guardian* 14 June 1976.
23   A. K. Azad Konor, *The Battle of Brick Lane* (Grosvenor House Publishing, 2019), p.13.

24   Ullah, Oral histories; Widgery, 1986, p.32; Ed Blanche, 'Frustration, anger grow among U.K. non-whites', *International Herald Tribune* 27-8 May 1978.
25   Leech, 1994, p.7.
26   Steve Cedar remembers getting comrades and a group of thirty students together after the SWP was asked by the CP organisers to help with security which also included members of a Tower Hamlets women's liberation group. Steve Cedar, private email 18 April 2022,
27   Anna Paczuska, interviewed by Geoff Brown 26 February 2023.
28   Paczuska, 26 February 2023.
29   Anna Paczuska, 'Shoreditch in the Front line', *Rank and File Teacher* May 1977.
30   Paczuska, May 1977; Bethnal Green and Stepney Trades Council, 1978, p.51.
31   'Two tokens in one: The only black and the only woman reporter', Juliet Alexander interviewed by Geoffery Sheridan, https://hackneyhistory.wordpress.com/tag/juliet-alexander/; 'Pickets Counter Fascist Meeting', *Hackney People's Press* June 1977, https://hackneyhistory.wordpress.com/2020/01/25/hackney-peoples-press-1977/ .
32   *SWP Internal Bulletin* no.7, May 1978, p.21. *Militant* reported 5–600 on the NF march, 6,000 on the labour movement demonstration.
33   'From grief to anger, after the murder of Altab Ali', *The Asian* June 1978.
34   Ullah, Oral histories.
35   See previous endnote. Few BYM members had a phone at home. Most of the phoning was done using public phone boxes.
36   Bethnal Green and Stepney Trades Council, 1978, p.56. '[T]he march was organised by the Action Committee against Racist Attacks and by the Anti Nazi League', *Socialist Worker* 20 May 1978. There was a large Newham ANL public meeting in Stratford Town with Jonathan Dimbleby, Johnny Speight, Dennis Skinner, Tariq Ali and Paul Holborow speaking, three days before the carnival, a week before the local election, *Socialist Worker* 27 April 1978.
37   *The Asian* June 1978.
38   *Socialist Worker* 20 May 1978; Bethnal Green and Stepney Trades Council, 1978, p.56; 'From grief to anger', June 1978.
39   Bethnal Green and Stepney Trades Council, 1978, p.56; Ullah, Oral histories.
40   'Despite riot, London Bengalis declare: We don't want ghetto housing', *Morning Star* 13 June 1978; *Socialist Worker* 10 June 1978. See also 'Housing Bengalis together', Letters to the editor, *Times* 12 June 1978 and 'Bengali 'Ghettoes' ruled out', *Daily Telegraph* 14 June 1978. Tassaduq Ahmed argued 'By rejecting outright and with one voice the proposed 'ghetto' solution to the housing and racial problems with which the Asian community is faced in East London, the 20,000 Bengalis have struck a blow for multiracialism and multiculturalism community life in Tower Hamlets', *The Asian* August 1978.
41   Leech, 1994, p.9. *Socialist Worker* 17 June 1978.
42   *Times* 12 June 1978. This was not the only organised attack by fascists in the area. A group of NF members, the 'Hoxton heavies', invaded a meeting of Christians against the Nazis in St Olave's church, Manor House, leaving when forty ANL supporters arrived, *Socialist Worker* 24 June 1978.

43   The ANL called it an 'All-London Anti Nazi League demonstration'. See 'Nazi Terror in Brick Lane, Never Again!', *Socialist Worker* 17 June 1978, p.1.
44   Leech,1994, p.10. Paul Holborow and Peter Hain also spoke.
45   'Brick Lane: The people take to the streets', *Socialist Worker* 24 June 1978. Aloke Biswas moved to Kolkata in the 1980s, working there with the Christian community, who titled him Reverend Aloke Biswas as a mark of their respect. He died in 2021, https://banglamirrornews.com/2021/10/04/veteran-anti-racist-activist-aloke-biswas-no-more/.
46   Konor, 2019.
47   'Murder and Arson', *Socialist Worker* 1 July 1978, p.1. The arson referred to in the headline was the firebombing of the ANL office three days before Ishaque Ali was murdered.
48   Bethnal Green and Stepney Trades Council, 1978, p.57. The march was led by Patrick Kodikara, chair of Hackney Community Relations Council, newly elected as a Labour councillor, *Socialist Challenge* 6 July 1978.
49   Bethnal Green and Stepney Trades Council, 1978, p.81. *Socialist Worker* 15 July 1978.
50   The NF had sold their paper on Brick Lane since 1976 or earlier. They were challenged by *Socialist Worker* sellers. The police, determined to ensure the NF could continue to sell, designated the side of Brick Lane north of Bethnal Green Road, exclusively for the National Front, then saying it would be allocated on a 'first-come first-served' basis and then changing their mind again back to their original decision.
51   Pat Arrowsmith, 'East End sit-down', *Peace News* 28 July 1978.
52   '12 arrested in East End Protest', *Times* 17 July 1978; The *Times* reported 'An advance guard, selling Socialist Worker newspapers, occupied the site early in the morning', Bethnal Green and Stepney Trades Council, 1978, p.58; Leech, 1994, p.10/18; *Time Out* 21 July 1978. See 'The Nazi Party', *World in Action*, 3 July 1978. Leamington AFC, Coventry CARF and the ANL organised a coach from Leamington and Coventry.
53   Widgery, 1986, p.32.
54   Reverend Kenneth Leech, quoted in David Widgery, 1986, p.32.
55   'Asians mob foreman at Ford plant', *Daily Mail* 19 July 1978. 'Anti-racism strike shuts Bangladeshi East End shops', *Daily Telegraph* 18 July 1978: 'In the late afternoon nearly a thousand young Bangladeshis took to the streets, with shouts of "We want action". [They] had held a day-long meeting in the Naz cinema, Brick Lane... Elder members of the community were excluded from the meeting... The only visitors allowed to participate in the rally was a handful of white members of the Anti-Nazi League and the Socialist Workers Party. Evidence of the sharp difference of attitudes between the generations was given by Mr Golam Mustafa, secretary of the trust that runs the Brick Lane Mosque. "We are warning all the political people, the Socialist Workers Party, the Anti-Nazi League, the Communist Party, and the Marxists to leave us alone". Mustafa was also scathing about the representatives of the three immigrant organisations, who last week advised Asians to set up "self-defence groups" and get far more involved in the work of the Anti Nazi League. The feelings of the younger Asians were articulated by Mr Shams Uddin, president of the newly formed Bangladesh Youth Association, who said that the Socialist Workers Party was most welcome. The idea of self-defence groups also appealed to him. "The police

have been searching us to see if we have been carrying anything'".
56 'Asians hold protest strike as Mr Rees discusses racialism', *Times* 18 July 1978.
57 '3,000 blocked the main road for nearly two hours until the three marchers were released', Bethnal Green and Stepney Trades Council, 1978, pp.58–9.
58 Widgery, 1986, p.34; 'Asians in sit-down protest over arrests', *Guardian* 18 July 1978.
59 'An 80-minute protest heralds a new era of East End struggle', *Guardian* 24 July 1978: Thames TV, *Our People*, first shown 1979, https://www.youtube.com/watch?v=Eyuw50IYk4A.
60 Konor, 2019, p.xi.
61 Martin Luther King Jr., 'Our Struggle,' Liberation, April 1956, in Carson Clayborne, ed, 1997, *The Papers of Martin Luther King Jr.*, vol. 3, (Berkeley: University of California Press, 1997), p.238.
62 Aloke Biswas, 'We'll organise the harvest of Brick Lane', *Socialist Worker* 29 July 1978. The argument was taken further in 'Ford Worker bulletin on the contribution Asian workers make', *Socialist Worker* 29 July 1978. See also Rahim Ali, 'Rahim in the sweatshops', *Socialist Worker* 23 September 1978. Not everybody supported the strike. *Race Today* interviewed six garment workers, none supporting the strike. Describing the Rally against Racist Violence as a 'circus', it called for independent black organisation 'Bengali Workers on strike, Charting the Asian Self Defence Movement', *Race Today* September-October 1978.
63 Konor, 2019, p.46; *Socialist Worker* 29 July 1978.
64 *Socialist Worker* 29 July 1978; *Socialist Worker* 5 August 1978.
65 Steve Cedar, interviewed by Geoff Brown 10 August 2020.
66 As previous endnote.
67 As previous endnote.
68 Joint Statement issued by Sibghat Kadri, President, The Standing Conference of Pakistani Organisations in UK, July 1978; Bethnal Green and Stepney Trades Council, 1978, p.95.
69 Bethnal Green and Stepney Trades Council, 1978, p.59.
70 As previous endnote.
71 'Southall calls for community self-defence not vigilante groups', *The Asian* August 1978. The two largest IWAs both called themselves IWA(GB). Prem Singh was general secretary of the pro-Moscow. IWA (GB). It supported the Communist Party of India (Marxist), or CPI(M). Avtar Jouhl was the general secretary of the pro-Beijing IWA (GB) supporting the Communist Party of India (Marxist Leninist), or CPI(ML).
72 *Socialist Worker* 5 August 1978.
73 As previous endnote.
74 Bethnal Green and Stepney Trades Council, 1978, p.60. See also Tower Hamlets Movement against Racism and Fascism, Broadsheet, September 1978; 'Brick Lane', *Peace News* 20 August 1978.
75 Bethnal Green and Stepney Trades Council, 1978, p.63. It was a joint statement issued, 'after a meeting in East London with the representatives of trade councils, community relations councils, anti-racist organisations of the local and Asian communities', *The Asian* August 1978.
76 Bethnal Green and Stepney Trades Council, 1978, p.60; *Socialist Worker* 26 August 1978.
77 Leech, 1994, p.10.

78   Bethnal Green and Stepney Trades Council, 1978, p.61.
79   Anti Racialist Carnival in London, circular letter, IWA (GB) (Marxist), 1 September 1978,
80   *Guardian* 31 August 1978.
81   The Greater Manchester train cost £2,000.
82   *Tribune* 7 July 1978. Patrick Kodikara was a Labour councillor and chair of Hackney and Tower Hamlets Defence Committee. Benn was Secretary of State for Energy, the only cabinet member to speak from an ANL platform.
83   'Anti-racialism trudge proves good natured', *Times* 25 September 1978
84   *Socialist Challenge* 5 October 1978.
85   Widgery, 1986, p.93.
86   'NF is moving headquarters to East End: EXCLUSIVE', *Observer* 17 September 1978. The *Guardian* had reported the move was to Tottenham, 'Front to move HQ', *Guardian* 24 August 1978
87   'Front will not march into sensitive street', *Times* 23 September 1978.
88   Paul Holborow, interviewed by Geoff Brown July 2008; Ian Birchall, *Tony Cliff: A Marxist for His Time* (Bookmarks, 2011), p.432.
89   *Times* 21 September 1978; The *Financial Times* 22 September 1922, quoted 'local members of the Anti Nazi League saying that they should not be dancing in Brixton but fighting in Shoreditch'.
90   'Front will not march into sensitive street', *Times* 23 September 1978.
91   'Police tactics ensure that National Front march is peaceful', *Times* 25 September 1978; '5,000 police keep Front and its opponents at bay', *Guardian* 25 September 1978. The Metropolitan Police had a force of 20,000. Some of the 5,000 were on duty at the carnival in Brixton. The *Daily Mail*, 25 September, reported 8,000 police on duty and 3,000 NF marcher. The *Times* quoted the police who counted 1,600 NF marchers.
92   Neil McAllister, interviewed by Geoff Brown 12 February 2018.
93   *Socialist Challenge* 28 September 1978.
94   'The ANL's plan to deal with the NF threat on 24 September', *Socialist Challenge* 21 September 1978.
95   *Morning Star* 25 September 1978, p.1.
96   Letter to the *Morning Star* 5 October 1978.
97   Tony Cliff, 'Still United', *Socialist Worker* 30 September 1978, p.7. Spitalfields ANL was founded a week after the Carnival, 'ANL organised in Spitalfields', *Socialist Challenge* 5 October 1978.
98   Paul Holborow, ANL secretary, letter to *Socialist Worker* 7 October 1978.
99   The ANL also worked hard to get headlines in its first couple of months, invading the former Waffen SS officer Hubert Meyer's press conference and calling out Judge McKinnon in the Kingsley Read trial. See Chapter 5 'Launching the Anti Nazi League'.
100 'Rightist and fascist developments',1969, p.2, Communist Party archive, LHASC.
101 Gavin Schaffer, *The Vision of a Nation, Making Multiculturalism on British Television, 1960–80* (Palgrave, 2014), p.67.
102 P. Harland, 'Reporting race: Some problems', in *Race and the Press* (Runnymede Trust, 1971), p.21; David Edgar, 'The National Front: The case for no television platform', (unpublished, n.d.), CP/CENT/PC/14/19-25, LHASC.

103   'An ideology red: White and blue in tooth and claw', David Edgar's *Destiny* (1978), Part 1 of 3, http://www.britishtelevisiondrama.org.uk/?p=7040. This gives a detailed description of the programme.
104   'British campaign to stop immigration', *Open Door*, February 1976.
105   *Leveller* January 1978.
106   Royal Television Society lecture, Yorkshire Centre, 17 May 1978.
107   See Chapter 5 'Launching the Anti Nazi League'.
108   'It ain't half racist, Mum', https://www.youtube.com/watch?v=m4oZtBfN87A, transcript: https://www.bcu.ac.uk/media/research/sir-lenny-henry-centre-for-media-diversity/representology-journal/articles/it-aint-half-racist-mum-transcript
109   Paul Rees, *The Three Degrees: The Men Who Changed British Football Forever* (Constable, 2014), p.155.
110   Graham Murdock & Peter Golding, 'The structure, ownership and control of the press', in G. Boyce, J. Curran & P. Wingate eds., *Newspaper History: From the 17th Century to the Present Day* (Constable, 1978), p.132.
111   Letter to Sigfrid Meyer and August Vogt in New York, 9 April 1870, *Marx Engels Collected Works*, vol.43, pp.474–5, https://www.marxists.org/archive/marx/works/1870/letters/70_04_09.htm
112   Shirin Hirsch, *In the Shadow of Enoch Powell* (Manchester University Press, 2018), p.8. Thousands of local readers responded, the great majority supporting Powell.
113   Bethnal Green and Stepney Trades Council, *Blood on the Streets: A Report on Racial Attacks in East London,* (BG&STC, 1978), p.51.
114   See Chapter 4, 'Grunwick and Lewisham'. There is also an excellent article by Tom Picton reviewing the press coverage of Lewisham in *Camerawork* 8, https://www.fourcornersarchive.org/archive/view/0000009
115   Sheila McGregor, private conversation 30 September 2020. One measure of the impact of the press coverage of Lewisham is how it seems to have contributed to the perception that the NF were 'the injured party' such that the local Lewisham Tories subsequently insisted on the NF's right to appear on joint platforms. See 'Tories demand that Front candidates get a hearing', *Times* 23 December 1977.
116   *Manchester Evening News*, Extra edition, 15 July 1978. Forty years on, the MEN made up its omission with an excellent online article, 'Rock Against Racism: The day Manchester and its bands stood proud against the far right', Aminah Khan, Chris Osuh, *Manchester Evening News* 10 July 2018, https://www.manchestereveningnews.co.uk/news/greater-manchester-news/rock-against-racism-day-manchester-14877439.
117   *Talkabout* 4 October 1979, 'Young people from schools and clubs all over the country pit their skills in a subject of their own choice against the knowledge and experience of an expert or two. They also choose the music and suggest guests to support their arguments. If you or your school or club have strong views on any subject that needs a good airing, contact: Talkabout', https://genome.ch.bbc.co.uk/schedules/service_bbc_radio_one/1979-10-04
118   On 'Rock Against Communism', see Chapter 10 'Taking down the beast'.
119   *Leveller* November 1979, 'Nazi Rock, part 2'.
120   Roger Huddle & Red Saunders, eds., *Reminiscences of RAR*

(Redwords, 2021), p.88; *News of the World* 25 April 1976; *News of the World* 11 December 1977.

121   'Clough fights the Front: And Jackie Charlton does too', *Daily Mirror* 12 December 1977.

122   *Harpers Queen* February 1977; David Moller, 'The ugly truth behind the National Front', *Reader's Digest* November 1977. *The Reader's Digest* article was reproduced as a leaflet. Other examples of mainstream media attacks on the National Front: Christopher Hitchens, 'Don't be taken for a sinister ride', *Daily Express* 6 May 1977; 'Front man wrote "war crimes leaflet"', *Evening Standard* 21 September 1977; 'The National Front: A suitable case for prayer', *Catholic Herald* 19 August 1977; 'Preachers of prejudice', *Slough Evening Mail* 18 August 1977.

123   NUJ Code of Conduct; NUJ Guidelines on race and journalists; NUJ Guidelines on reporting racist organisations; NUJ-NGA Agreement. See website endnote for details.

124   Denis MacShane, *Black and Front: Journalists and Race Reporting*, (NUJ Race Relations Sub Committee, 1978), p.16. The Press Council threw out the complaint, backing 'the right of journalists to be critical of the National Front and other racist politicians'.

125   Maurice Ludmer contrasted the anti-NF position of the *Bradford Telegraph and Argus* with the space given to Kingsley Read by the *Lancashire Evening Post*, *Searchlight* June 1976. See also interview with David Edgar who worked for the *Bradford Telegraph and Argus*, *Searchlight* Interview with David Edgar, 5 December 2015, *Searchlight* Oral Histories Collection, *Searchlight* archive.

126   See Thames Television, *Our People*, first broadcast 22 February 1979, https://www.youtube.com/watch?v=tvmUVE05XRQ

127   'No free press for fascists', *Red Weekly* 27 March 1975.

128   'Journalists to boycott the National Front', *Times* 16 June 1976.

129   CARM (Campaign Against Racism in the Media), 1976, 'Black and White: Racist reporting and how to fight it', personal archive.

130   Balwinder Rana, private email 21 July 2022. See CARM, 1976, p.35.

131   *Socialist Worker* 30 April 1977.

132   MacShane, 1978, p.7. Faced with this threat, the NUJ members dropped their action.

133   Lorna Chessum, *From Immigrants to Ethnic Minority: Making Black Community in Britain* (Routledge, 2000), p.221.

134   MacShane, 1978, p.7.

135   *Socialist Challenge* 2 March 1978, https://www.marxists.org/history/etol/newspape/socialist-challenge/sc-n35-mar-2-1978.pdf; *Socialist Worker* 4 March 1978.

136   *Socialist Worker* 12 August 1978; *Time Out* 8 September 1978.

137   Paul Holborow quoted in the *Evening Sentinel* 3 October 1978.

138   *Socialist Worker* 29 April 1978.

139   Edgar, 'The National Front'. See 'No Plugs for Nazis', *Searchlight* November 1978. Edgar's article, 'Why the Front is beyond the pale', *Sunday Times* 1 October 1978, is a shortened version.

140 As the previous endnote, pp.5–6. In his pamphlet, Denis MacShane, NUJ president, quoted Justice Oliver Wendell Holmes in a 1919 Supreme court decision: 'The most stringent protection of free speech would not protect a man falsely shouting fire in a theatre and causing panic.' The US constitution, 1st amendment, includes the right to free speech and freedom of the press.

141 As the previous endnote p.9.

142 BBC *Tonight*, 19 December 1977.

143 'The Nazi Party', *World in Action*, 3 July 1978, https://www.dailymotion.com/video/x31fh5b. Other TV broadcasts attacking the NF included, BBC2 *Inside Story*, 'Behind the Front', 15 February 1978; *Destiny* broadcast 31 January 1978, the day after Thatcher's 'swamped' speech.

144 Bookmarks, a left-wing bookshop, was based in Finsbury Park, north London. It is now in Bloomsbury Street, central London. Letter from Ray Fitzwalter, ed, *World in Action*, Granada TV, to Sabby Sagall, 18 July 1978. Film showings included in Leamington, Coventry, and at the Miners Against the Nazis conference in February 1979 in Sheffield.

145 Thames Television's *Our People* broadcast February 1979 gives a good picture of the ANL, RAR and SKAN in the East End and the April 1978 carnival https://www.youtube.com/watch?v=tvmUVE05XRQ https://docs.google.com/document/d/1QXD1IoLEk4wKcPikoIOjOp3dZ-LjRtRbhfCE9hoFW78/edit

146 *Spearhead* September 1976, quoted by the Board of Deputies leaflet, 'A four letter word that describes the National Front', https://photos.google.com/album/AF1QipO3yLCuyDSeV1ZOK17rBjCnoT6s4EJC68Yf-BLq

147 Doug Beesley, interviewed by Geoff Brown 23 November 2021.

148 *Leicester Mercury* 30 April 1977.

149 *Leicester Mercury* 29 April 1977, quoted in Nigel Copsey, *Anti-Fascism in Britain* (Palgrave MacMillan, 2000), p.144.

150 *Women's Voice* August 1978.

151 'Anti fascists march on Evening Argus', *Brighton Evening Argus* August 1978,

152 *Liverpool Daily Post* 5 February 1979; Merseyside Anti Nazi League Bulletin Issue Special Issue n.d.

153 Brian Parkin, 'BBC Leeds gets a shock as anti-racists occupy', *Socialist Worker* 3 July 1976.

154 *Birmingham Post* 2 October 1974, cited by Muhammad Anwar, 'Asian participation in the October 1974 general election', *Journal of Ethnic and Migration Studies* vol.4, no.3, September 1975. It could be argued that taking this stand won more votes from ethnic minorities than it lost from white communities.

155 Denis MacShane, 'Printers and Media Workers against the Nazis', *Morning Star* 23 June 1978.

156 Peter Bain & John Gennard, *A History of the Society of Graphical and Allied Trades* (Routledge, 1995), pp.441–5.

157 ANL national circular, July 1978, personal archive.

158   As previous endnote. Early in 1978, a motion at the annual conference of the ACTT, the union of the technical staff working in ITV, to pull the plugs on the NF had been narrowly lost. David Edgar, Manchester Against Racism conference, 18 March 1978.

159   The same argument was put to the Independent Broadcasting Authority (IBA), in charge of ITV, *Time Out* 22 September 1978.

160   'Blacking the Front', Mirror Comment, *Daily Mirror* 13 September 1978; 'No plug worth the pulling', *Guardian* 15 September 1978.

161   'Peter Hain and the forces of darkness', *Sunday Times* 17 September 1978.

162   'Noddy language like this is really best ignored', *Times* 15 September 1978; 'Let them speak if only for five minutes', Bernard Levin, *Times* 20 September 1978.

163   'Pots And Kettles', *Daily Telegraph* 13 September 1978; 'Campaign to gag Front "Danger to rule of law"', *Daily Telegraph* 13 September 1978.

164   James Cameron, 'Double vision', *Guardian* 25 September 1978,

165   David Edgar, 'Why the Front is beyond the pale', *Sunday Times* 1 October 1978; Letters to the editor, *Times*, 21 September 1978.

166   The nine pickets were in Birmingham, Manchester, Glasgow, Leeds, Norwich, Cardiff, Newcastle, Bristol and Southampton. They were also supported by the Campaign Against Racism in the Media.

167   See Draft letter to Frank Allaun MP, replying to a letter from Frank Allaun to Merlyn Rees, concerning NF's Party Political Broadcast(s), 3 April 1979, National Archives, H0 328/292.

168   See *Patterns for Prejudice*, vol.11, no.2, March-April 1977 for a more detailed analysis. Also, see the Anti Nazi League briefing document, 'The National Front and the Jews', 1978, personal archive.

169   Geoffrey Alderman, 'Anglo-Jewry, The Unspoken Fears', *Forum on the Jewish people, Zionism, and Israel* vol.3, no.7, Spring 1980, pp.53–60.

170   *Socialist Challenge* 2 November 1978.

171   *Jewish Chronicle* 16 June 1978. The John F. Kennedy memorial overlooking the Thames at Runnymede was daubed with the star of David and the word 'Jew.' The Eleventh Hour Brigade claimed responsibility.

172   Maurice Ludmer had helped with the information.

173   Martin Savitt, chairman of the Jewish defence and group relations committee, *Jewish Chronicle* 14 April 1978. One of Cardiff ANL's two Jewish members was Savitt's nephew, *Socialist Worker* 11 November 1978.

174   Geoffrey Alderman, 'Anti-semitism in Britain', letter to *The Times*, 30 September 1978. In the letter, Alderman thanked Dennis Signy, *Hendon Times* editor, for 'courageously refusing to bow to such pressure from the Board' [not to publicise antisemitic attacks].

175   Stan Taylor, *The National Front in English Politics* (Macmillan, 1982), p.32.

176   Jacob Gewirtz, 'The Anti-Nazi League: The case for the Board', *Jewish Chronicle* 20 October 1978.

177   People reading the leaflets would often not have known this as they

were published by the Woburn Press, Woburn House. This was the office of the Board of Deputies. The Board used extracts from mainstream press articles, for example in the *Daily Mirror* and the *News of the World*), for some of its leaflets.

178 *Jewish Chronicle* 23 December 1977. The two were Martin Bobker, of the Community Relations Council, and Aubrey Lewis, of the Jewish Socialist Group. Bobker became treasurer of Greater Manchester ANL.

179 'Miriam Karlin urges support for ANL', *Jewish Chronicle* 8 December 1978. See Chapter 5 'Launching the Anti Nazi League.

180 *Jewish Chronicle* 18 November 1977. J. Garnel considered Hain's anti-Zionism reason enough for the Board of Deputies to publicly refuse the invitation to join in with the refusal to join the ANL, *Jewish Chronicle* 17 March 1978.

181 'Anti-Nazi League answers Rep Council', *Jewish Gazette* 7 April 1978.

182 *Jewish Chronicle* 21 April 1978. The Defence Committee was established 1938 to fight the fascist threat in Britain. It worked closely with AJEX.

183 *Jewish Chronicle* 3 March 1978.

184 'Anti-Nazi League's role challenged', *Jewish Chronicle* 14 April 1978.

185 *Jewish Chronicle* 17 March 1978.

186 Derek Livingston, president, Glasgow Jewish Students' Society, David Raff, political affairs officer University College London Jewish Society, *Jewish Chronicle* 14 April 1978.

187 *Jewish Chronicle* 14 April 1978.

188 *Jewish Chronicle* 21 April 1978.

189 David Rosenberg, 'The carnival is not over', https://rebellion602.wordpress.com/2018/04/30/the-carnival-is-not-over/#comments

190 *Jewish Chronicle* 14 April 1978; *Jewish Chronicle* 5 May 1978. For 43 Group, see Chapter 3 'Fighting racism and fascism'.

191 *Jewish Chronicle* 19 May 1978.

192 Anti Nazi League, 1978, 'The National Front and the Jews', briefing document, personal archive. It was written by Nigel Harris. The detail here comes from the *Jewish Chronicle* 20 June 1978, with a comment from Martin Savitt that the Jewish community 'should not allow itself to be used by the ANL'.

193 Anti Nazi League, 1978 briefing document.

194 *Jewish Chronicle* 5 May 1978. See the letter to the *Jewish Chronicle* from Dennis Signy, editor of the *Hendon Times*, 27 October 1978.

195 *Jewish Chronicle* 26 May 1978.

196 *Jewish Chronicle* 7 July 1978.

197 *Jewish Chronicle* 11 August 1978.

198 *Jewish Chronicle* 25 August 1978. This was the main reason given by the Federation of Conservative Students for leaving the ANL. See Chapter 9 'Counting down to the elction'.

199 *Jewish Chronicle* 15 September 1978.

200 *Jewish Chronicle* 22 September 1978.

201 *Jewish Chronicle* 6 October 1978.

202 *Jewish Chronicle* 13 October 1978.

203 *Jewish Chronicle* 20 October 1978.

204 *Jewish Chronicle* 27 October 1978. See also 'Jewish split on NF', *Guardian* 3 November 1978.

205 'A Foolish Quarrel', *Searchlight* November 1978.

206 *Jewish Chronicle* 24 November 1978.

207 *Jewish Chronicle* 2 December 1978.

208 'Students' radical line', *Jewish Chronicle* 29 December 1978. Jewish students were also active with the ANL when David Irving, the Holocaust revisionist, was invited to speak to students at Imperial College members of the Jewish Society and the ANL barracked him and 150 demonstrators chased him out of the building, *Jewish Chronicle* 24 February 1978. Gewirtz met opposition in the Cardiff University Jewish Society, 'Dr Gewirz is Mr Hyde', Terry James, Cardiff ANL organiser, letter to *Socialist Worker* 11 November 1978.

209 *Jewish Chronicle* 24 November 1978.

210 *Jewish Chronicle* 29 December 1978.

211 *Jewish Chronicle* 26 January 1979.

212 'Frank talks with the Anti-Nazi League', *Jewish Chronicle* 26 January 1979.

213 'Call to Anti-Nazis', *Jewish Chronicle* 2 March 1979.

214 'Call to Anti-Nazis', *Jewish Chronicle* 2 March 1979.

215 'Ajex warns of Front progress', *Jewish Chronicle* 20 April 1979.

Counting down to the election

1   The conference was held 'to review the progress of the League so far, to discuss the activity leading up to the General Election, and to exchange local experience', ANL national circular announcing Emergency Campaign Conference, n.d. [end May/early June 1978].

2   Communist Party Political Committee weekly newsletter to members, 22 June 1978.

3   Unattributed report on Anti Nazi League Campaign Conference, 8 July 1978. See website endnote for link to text.

4   'Carnival to beat new nazis', *Morning Star* 4 July 1978.

5   See letter from John Jennings, secretary of ALCARAF, to Ernie Roberts, 30 March 1978. Ernie Roberts archive, Working Class Movement Library.

6   *Socialist Worker* 15 July 1978.

7   *Socialist Worker* 6 May 1978.

8   'By-passing issues in the Anti-Nazi League', Patrick Wintour, *New Statesman* July 1978. Kronstadt refers to the military suppression by the Bolshevik led Red Army units of an uprising by sailors controlling a

fortress on the island of Kronstadt, vital to the defence of Petrograd. The uprising took place in March 1921 at a moment of great economic crisis. If the uprising had been successful, it would have made Petrograd vulnerable to attack by the British, giving the counter-revolution a possibly decisive boost. The decision by the Bolsheviks to use force to defeat the uprising has divided the left ever since,

9   See Chapter 1 'Rivers of blood'.

10   Evan Smith, *British Communism and the Politics of Race* (Haymarket, 2018), p.127.

11   LARAFC report of Anti Nazi League conference Saturday, 8 July 1978, London; Unattributed report on Anti Nazi League Campaign Conference, 8 July 1978; *Morning Star* 10 July 1978; S*ocialist Worker* 15 July 1978; Kate Alexander private email 24 January 2025. The vote was presented as an amendment to the conference declaration.

12   The Tory MP Robert Adley asked in parliament if the police had been consulted 'concerning the plans of the Anti-Nazi League to establish vigilante groups in areas with a high proportion of immigrants'. The government minister, Shirley Summerskill, responded: 'To the knowledge of the police, no such vigilante groups have been formed. The Anti-Nazi League has not directly advocated their formation', Anti-Nazi League - *Hansard*, 3 August 1978.

13   The day after the firebombing of the Albany, a note was pushed through the door with the words 'Got you', Colin Fancy, in Roger Huddle & Red Saunders, eds., *Reminiscences of RAR* (Redwords, 2021), p.73; *Socialist Worker* 8 July 1978. An internal NF letter from a group of members, leaked to CARF, complained to Tyndall and Webster that 'Our name is only kept in the newspapers by gangs of bully boys who rampage through the East End of London beating up Asians', *Socialist Worker* 8 July 1978.

14   'Stop this Nazi violence...', leaflet for public meeting, Goldsmiths College Students Union 22 June 1978; Draft letter from SE London ANL to ALCARAF (n.d.); '"Race attack" march rapped by anti-fascist group leader', *South London Press* 27 June 1978; Statement made to 'South London Press' on 28th June 1978, South East London Anti Nazi League archive, Bishopsgate Institute.

15   'Anti-Nazi League urged to disassociate SE London branch', South East London Anti Nazi League archive, Bishopsgate Institute.

16   Peter Hain, letter to Eddie Longworth, FCS, 20 August 1978.

17   'Tory Students to Leave Anti-Nazi League', *Daily Telegraph* 8 September 1978. The *Times* reported that 'the league and its associated bodies 'are exploiting the issue of race for party political purposes'', 'Tory students cut link with anti-Nazi group', *Times* 8 September 1978.

18   'No to national League', *Huddersfield Daily Examiner* 1 August 1978.

19   Prices had been consistently rising at an annual rate of over 8 percent.

20   Shop floor resistance was further weakened by the crisis in the Communist Party, the largest grouping of trade union activists within the trade union movement. Since the early 1960s, its industrial strategy had focused on 'Broad Left' alliances with left officials, most importantly Jack

Jones, general secretary of the transport workers union (T&GWU) and Hugh Scanlon, president of the engineering union (AUEW). Now with Jones and Scanlon policing the 5 percent pay limit and telling workers to cross picket lines, the CP's shop floor influence was greatly reduced.

21   The Labour Party conference in October rejected the government's 5 percent pay rise guidelines by 4,017,000 to 1,924,000, John Shepherd, *Crisis? What Crisis? The Callaghan Government and the British "Winter of Discontent"* (Manchester University Press, 2016), p.47. Callaghan ignored this vote. 'In April 1978, an independent shop steward movement, the 'Ford Combine', had been formed by various Ford workers in left-wing groups to counteract existing shop stewards. The Ford management had endeavoured to bring twenty-three convenors onto the NJNC [National Joint Negotiating Committee] to incorporate shop-floor representatives into national wage negotiations'. Tara Martin, '"End of an era?" Class politics, memory and Britain's winter of discontent', PhD thesis, University of Manchester, 2008, pp.92–96, quoted in Shepherd, 2026, p.51. In larger workplaces, the acceptance of 'participation' schemes by senior union reps involving them in management decision making meant that union convenors and senior stewards were spending more time talking to managers than to their members.

22   The vote to return took place on 21 November 1978.

23   Documents reveal the Labour government was prepared to crush discontent, *Socialist Worker* 13 January 2009.

24   *Sun* 3 May 1979.

25   'La Grande Peur', *Socialist Review* editorial, February 1979.

26   Andy Beckett, *When the Lights Went Out: Britain in the Seventies* (Faber, 2009), p.484-494. Essential goods included hospital supplies, food, and animal feed.

27   Rehad Desai, interviewed by Geoff Brown 28 February 2022; Steve Cunningham & Michael Lavalette, *Schools Out!* (Bookmarks, 2016), p.173–4.

28   Voting Intention 1974–1979, https://pollingreport.uk/articles/voting-intention-1974-1979.

29   Examples include an NF member intervening violently trying to disrupt a strike vote at a meeting of local government manual workers in London in January 1979 and organising a banner opposing action at a mass meeting at Longbridge.

30   *Morning Star* 21 October 1978. *Searchlight* reported the collapse of the 'last stronghold of the National Party', *Searchlight* October 1978.

31   '28 arrested in Armistice Day scuffles', *Daily Telegraph* 13 November 1978.

32   'NF falls back on theory of a Jewish plot', *Guardian* 24 October 1978. One of the pamphlet launches was in a pub in Stockport, *Guardian* 22 January 1979. *Spearhead* had always been antisemitic, '*Spearhead* has been the party's "intellectual" showpiece with its long, tedious articles about world conspiracy...direct[ing] the attention of the party's "elite"...towards the anti-Semitism of classic Nazi ideology', *Searchlight* May 1979.

33   Tyndall told the conference the NF would make flying pickets by

striking workers illegal, 'When we take over the reins of government, as one day we shall, the moment that mobsters try by physical intimidation to prevent British workers doing their jobs, those mobsters will find themselves in police cells so quickly they won't know what hit them', *Guardian* 22 January 1979.

34   *Guardian* 22 January 1979.

35   Having made substantial gains every year since 1975, the Tories now had twice as many councillors as Labour.

36   *Searchlight* January 1979; *Socialist Worker* 9 December 1978. The town hall protesters went on to set up a Hillingdon ANL branch. Such reversals could go the opposite way. In the 1979 local elections in Yarmouth the Conservatives lost control. The new council reversed the decision to allow the NF to hold its annual conference in the town.

37   *Searchlight* 42 December 1978.

38   *Morning Star* 22 January 1979.

39   *Morning Star* 13 October 1978.

40   *Socialist Challenge* 2 November 1978.

41   *Socialist Challenge* 1 February 1979; *Guardian* 29 January 1979; *Searchlight* March 1979.

42   Miriam Karlin, *Some Sort of a Life* (Oberon, 2007), p.171, p.179; *Searchlight* April 1979.

43   *Morning Star* 30 December 1978.

44   *Labour Weekly* 5 May 1978; *Searchlight* no.41, November 1978; *Searchlight* no.43, January 1979; *Searchlight* no.42, December 1978; *Socialist Worker* 25 November 1978; *Socialist Worker* 13 January 1979; *Searchlight* January 1979; *Searchlight* April 1979; *Searchlight* May 1979.

45   'Build in the back streets', *Socialist Worker* 25 November 1978.

46   *Socialist Worker* 21 October 1978.

47   *Socialist Worker* 20 January 1979; *Hackney People's Press* February 1979.

48   Greater Manchester ANL had a general meeting planned for 13 September with a speaker from Brick Lane, Paddy Crerand & Holborow, leaflet for 'Anti-Nazi League Greater Manchester, General Meeting, 13 September 1978'.

49   *Socialist Worker* 2 December 1978.

50   *Searchlight* May 1979.

51   *Socialist Worker* 11 November 1978; *Women's Voice* December 1978, 'A seventy strong picket gave out 2,000 leaflets outside a shop where a violent racist was working in Kentish Town, North London'. A number of NF members were shop owners. ANL members picketed a jewellers' in Canterbury, owned by an NF member. Jon Flaig, interviewed by Geoff Brown 24 April 2023. Such picketing could require persistence. It wasn't till early 1979 that Arthur Calland, owner of North Wales record shops, Eclipse Records, announced he was leaving the BM following intensive picketing of his shops by the ANL.

52   *Socialist Worker* 11 November 1978.

53 As previous endnote.

54 Brack was NF candidate for Sheffield Brightside in May 1979.

55 'Closely Observed Trains', dir. Jiří Menzel (Czechoslovakia, 1966); *World in Action*, 'The Nazi Party', 3 July 1978.

56 *Socialist Worker* 2 September 1978; *Socialist Worker* 14 October 1978; *Socialist Worker* 21 October 1978. Community Relations Councils were set up as a link between ethnic minorities and the state. They varied according to the politics of their leadership, usually focused on gaining recognition as 'community leaders', on occasion accessing state funding.

57 *Morning Star* 16 October 1978.

58 Coventry Anti Nazi League Newsletter; *Socialist Worker* 2 September 1978. Bolton refused permission for a carnival because 'there was no suitable venue available', *Searchlight* March 1979.

59 *Socialist Worker* 25 November 1978; A year later, the *Preston Worker*, Journal of Preston Trades Council No 1, Autumn 1979, reported the Tory council banned the proposed ANL festival on Avenham Park on the grounds of 'the violence might arise'.

60 Bridget Parsons, interviewed by Geoff Brown 20 October 2020; *Socialist Worker* 7 April 1979; *Socialist Worker* 5 May 1979; Paul Foot, 'Racialism, Witch hunting in Birmingham', *New Statesman* 3 August 1980. See also 'Teacher victimised', *Rank & File Teacher* October 1979; leaflet: 'Fight Racism, Picket Pollyannas, Sat. 28th April' [1979].

61 Leaflet: South Bank Polytechnic Anti-Racist Week of Action, 12–16 February 1979.

62 *Socialist Worker* 2 December 1978. Other examples of authorities clamping down on ANL activity include expulsion of David Evans from North Trafford College by the principal for leafleting in the college canteen *Searchlight* January 1979, Alistair Graham, CPSA deputy general secretary, banned the ANL stall from CPSA annual conference arguing it would be divisive, Mike Healy interviewed by Geoff Brown October 2022; *Socialist Worker* 24 March 1979.

63 *Socialist Worker* 9 December 1978.

64 'Anti-Nazis Launch Workplace Drive', *Morning Star* 4 December 1978.

65 *Socialist Worker* 9 December 1978.

66 Dave Cook, 'Imposing a line spells disaster', *Morning Star* 13 October 1978.

67 Peter Hain, Letter to Eddie Longworth, FCS, 20 August 1978.

68 *Searchlight* April 1979.

69 CARF report on plans for the national ARAFCC conference 3-4 June 1978, CARF no 6, June 1978 p15; *Socialist Challenge* 8 June 1978.

70 *Searchlight* no.37, July 1978. *Big Flame*, 1980, 'The past against our future: Fighting racism and fascism, p35–37, https://bigflameuk.files.wordpress.com/2009/09/past-sec4.pdf. Having supported the conference, *Socialist Challenge* 30 November 1978 emphasised its political faults: 'when some of the women denounced the men present for their sexism, whilst

some [black people] denounced the women and gays for their racism, and some trade unionists denounced the "middle-class" present for their petty-bourgeois deviations.' Some commentators pointed to the organisers' failure to include workshops which, they argue, would have resolved the conflicts. Letter to *Socialist Challenge* 22 June 1978 p.14; ARAFC circular: Final Mailing from the Organising Committee, Ernie Roberts archive, Working Class Movement library.

71   CARF no.7, reprinted in *Socialist Challenge* 14 December 1978.

72   Relf was jailed for 'abusive and insulting' leaflets and 'incitement to racial hatred', *Guardian* 13 March 1979.

73   *Observer* 11 March; *Socialist Worker* 17 March 1979; *Searchlight* April 1979.

74   *Socialist Challenge* 15 March 1979.

75   'The winter of 79 – it's ours!', *Socialist Worker* 17 March 1979; 'Martin Webster's Fiasco', *Searchlight* April 1979.

76   As previous endnote. A week later, Saturday 17 March, twenty-six NF supporters held an all-night torch-lit vigil outside the prison. At midday the next day, 200 NF supporters were hemmed in by police and confronted by 200 ANL supporters, *Searchlight* April 1979.

77   David Widgery, *Beating Time* (Chatto & Windus, 1986), p.101.

78   *Socialist Worker* 20 January 1979. Manchester's regular RAR sessions were at Kelly's, Amber St. Merseyside's RAR night was every Thursday.

79   John Dennis, in Huddle & Saunders, 2021, p.56.

80   As previous endnote.

81   Widgery, 1986, p.104. Ross Turner and Golt recruited local bands Badstone and The Distractions alongside Top Sound, President (Amin) joining X-O-Dus.

82   Aswad, Angelic Upstarts, John Cooper Clarke, Dambala, The Ruts, Leyton Buzzards all performed, *'Voices of the Voteless', Socialist Challenge* 19 April 1979.

83   *New Musical Express* 28 April 1979

84   Jackie Kemp, 'We never ad it so good' – the 1979 election campaign, (Substack, 23 September 2023), *https://jackie125.substack.com/p/we-never-ad-it-so-good-the-1979-election*.

85   It is important to recognise how Thatcher proceeded cautiously. There is a tendency to see her at this point as already operating with the confidence she developed in later years.

86   *Observer* 1 April 1979.

87   Labour and Conservatives were each allocated five party political broadcasts, the Liberals three.

88   'Elections - NF instruct the faithful', *Searchlight* February 1979, quoting from the National Front Election Handbook. A further quote shows the clear intention to take complete control of who it admitted to its election meetings 'a Class 1 campaign certainly demands one major public meeting. The meeting should be described as a National Front meeting (not a public

meeting). The words, "Right of admission reserved" should be added to any notice of the meeting and a small nominal admission charge should be made'.

89 The CP stood thirty-seven candidates. Socialist Unity (IMG and Big Flame) stood twelve.

90 There were no NF candidates in Salford and south Manchester.

91 Greater Manchester ANL pre-election circular, 24 April 79.

92 *Leicester Mercury* 29 April 1979. Quoted in David Renton, *Never Again: Rock Against Racism and the Anti-Nazi League 1976–1982* (Routledge, 2019), p.152.

93 *Guardian* 1 May 1979.

94 *Guardian* 2 May 1979; *Socialist Challenge* 10 May 1979; *Socialist Worker* 5 May 1979. *Scotsman* 2 May 1979 reported that the meeting 'lasted only 40 minutes… only 15 people, almost all teenagers, attended', '1000 protest at Glasgow NF meeting', *Scotsman,* 2 May 1979.

95 *Guardian* 30 April 1979; *Sunday Telegraph* 29 April 1979; *Socialist Worker* 5 May 1979.

96 *Socialist Challenge* 1 May 1979.

97 Jon Flaig, interviewed by Geoff Brown 26 April 2023.

98 Alan Brown, interviewed by Geoff Brown 3 March 2023.

99 *Merseyside Anti-Nazi League bulletin* no.4, June 1979, pp.3–4.

100 *Socialist Worker* 5 May 1979.

101 *Guardian* 27 April 1979.

102 *Socialist Challenge* 1 May 1979. Alderson stood as a Liberal Party candidate in the 1983 general election.

103 *CARF* 9.

104 The three Leicester constituencies and nearby Blaby.

105 'All police leave cancelled in Leicester', *Observer* 1 April 1979; Lorna Chessum, *From Immigrants to Ethnic Minority: Making Black Community in Britain* (Routledge, 2000), p.218.

106 There were also undercover police 'with long hair and wearing scruffy jeans'. Colin Thomas, *Facing up to the Fascists: Confronting the National Front in Bristol* (Bristol Radical Pamphleteer, 2019), p.24.

107 'Anti Nazi League warns about NF Leicester march', *Tribune* 13 April 1979.

108 'No Nazis in Leicester', leaflet for 21 April 1979 counter-demonstration. This was backed by the ANL, the Trades Council, the Leicester Inter-Racial Solidarity Campaign (IRSC) and the Indian Workers Association.

109 *Socialist Challenge* 26 April 1979.

110 *Socialist Worker* reported 5,000 trying to stop the NF, *Socialist Challenge* 4,000, Steve Cedar remembers 3,000 to 4,000. There was no point at which it was possible to make a single count. Chessum, p.222, describes how some UPW members put 'Out of Order' notices on a dozen public phone boxes for ANL stewards to use.

111   *Sunday Telegraph* 22 April 1979. *Socialist Worker* reported 350 NF marchers, *Sunday Telegraph* 1,000, *Socialist Challenge* 500.

112   *Daily Telegraph* 23 April 1979.

113   Leicester April 21st Defence Committee, 1979, 'Support the Leicester 87!', p.10. Steve Cedar remembers thinking he was being chased by a police officer expecting to be arrested only for the policeman to run past him and grab a photographer's camera in order to smash it, Steve Cedar, interviewed by Geoff Brown 10 August 2020.

114   Leaflet 'Demonstration, Leicester JULY 21st, Leicester April 21st Defence Committee'.

115   *Socialist Challenge* 26 April 1979.

116   Merseyside Anti-Nazi League Bulletin no.4, June 1979. The NF smashed up an ANL coach travelling home at a motorway service station, Leicester April 21st Defence Committee, 1979, 'Support the Leicester 87!', p.8.

117   Michael Barker, 'Leicester's Fight against Racism', *Thoughts of a Leicester Socialist*, 24 November 2019, https://thoughtsofaleicestersocialist.wordpress.com/2019/11/24/leicesters-fight-against-racism-1959-1979/.

118   Cedar, 10 August 2020.

119   Satnam Kane was forced to 'confess' in the Southall police station to stealing £50 which was later found not to have been stolen, Campaign against Racism and Fascism/Southall Rights, *The Birth of a Black Community*, (Institute of Race Relations, 1981), p.57.

120   Beatrice Howard quoted in Francis Wheen & Elaine Potter, 'Southall, The not-so-thin blue line', *New Statesman* 4 May 1979.

121   On the day only five members of the public were admitted.

122   Despite its name, the IWA Southall was dominated by local business interests.

123   National Council of Civil Liberties, *Southall, 23 April 1979: Report of the unofficial committee of enquiry*, (NCCL, 1980), p.7. SWP members put the proposal to call for workers to strike, Southall SWP, *Southall: The Fight for Our Future* (Socialist Workers Party, 1979).

124   Balwinder Rana, personal email 12 June 2024.

125   David Renton, *When We Touched the Sky: The Anti-Nazi League 1977–1981* (New Clarion Press, 2006), p.141.

126   *CARF* 9, May 1979, Working Class Movement Library.

127   Francis Wheen, 'The not-so-thin blue line', *New Statesman* 4 May 1979. Gosse had okayed this when he met the SYM at their centre a few days earlier; NCCL, 1980, p.31.

128   *Socialist Challenge* 26 April 1979.

129   The first aid centre as well as doctors, nurses and lawyers had been forced by the police to abandon their original location at 45 High Street.

130   Joan Rudder, interviewed by Geoff Brown 12 October 2021

131   *Socialist Challenge* 26 April 1979.

132 Southall SWP, 1979.

133 Balwinder Rana, interviewed by Geoff Brown 4 March 2025; Balraj Purewal, *Southall Youth Movement 1976–1984* (The Asian Health Agency, 2023), pp.168–9.

134 *Evening Standard* 24 April 1979.

135 In English law, the intention of doing 'grievous bodily harm' is sufficient for the crime to be defined as murder, David Renton, 2014, 'The Killing of Blair Peach', *London Review of Books*, vol.36, no.10 https://www.lrb.co.uk/the-paper/v36/n10/david-renton/the-killing-of-blair-peach 2014. 342 was the largest number charged on a single day since the CND mass shutdowns in the early 1960s, Campaign against Racism and Fascism/Southall Rights, p.60.

136 There were also 200 picketing Southall police station early Tuesday morning and later that day 500 came to a press conference attended by fifty journalists, at which Sharma, Rana, Holborow and Tariq Ali spoke, *Socialist Challenge* 26 April 1979.

137 A decision upheld by the High Court, *Guardian* 25 April 1979. The NF election handbook as quoted by *Searchlight* makes it clear that the publicity should not use the phrase 'public meeting'.

138 Twenty-nine candidates got over 2.5 percent, twenty in the London area, five in the West Midlands, three In Leicester and one in Cardiff.

139 See website endnote for details of the NF general election results.

140 'Mrs Thatcher Touches a Nerve and British Racial Tension Is Suddenly a Political Issue', *New York Times* 22 February 1978; Conservative lead in opinion polls, January–June 1978; See website endnote for details of the Conservative lead in opinion polls, January–June 1978,

141 See website endnote for details of polls on main election issues and voting intentions. The *Economist* saw her campaign as focused on the issues where Callaghan was most vulnerable: taxation, inflation, unemployment, trade unions and strikes, 'A right-winger without theory?', *Economist* 21 April 1979.

142 See Kemp, 2023.

143 *Daily Mirror* 18 April 1979; see also http://ukpollingreport.co.uk/voting-intention-1974-1979. This is often seen as the end of the tacit agreement between Labour and the Conservatives not to openly compete on immigration at the polls which had held during the 1960s and most of the 1970s. Messina, A. M., 1985, 'Race and party competition in Britain: Policy formation in the post-consensus period', *Parliamentary Affairs* vol.38, no.4, pp.423–43; *Guardian* 6 April 1979; *Socialist Challenge* 19 April 1979. See 'How World in Action blotted its record', *Socialist Worker* 11 February 1978. This reports how the decision to show the Granada TV *World in Action* programme, which clashed completely with its record of radical reporting, in effect giving Thatcher a free party political broadcast, was made at the last minute after Granada's lawyers had vetoed the programme originally scheduled.

144 Hugo Young, 'Mrs Thatcher and the fascist figleaf', *Sunday Times* 5 February 1978.

145 The far right has benefitted in recent years from centre parties'

adoption of far-right anti-immigrant policies. It is hard to see how this did not also apply in this case.

146   Ian Goodyer, 'The year rock found the power to unite', interview with Sarfraz Manzoor, *Observer* 20 April 2008.

147   Paul Gilroy, *There Ain't No Black in the Union Jack* (Routledge, 1987), p.153. 'This definition of British neo-fascism exclusively in terms of the fascisms of the past against which the British had enjoyed their finest hours in battle, recurs again and again in the politics of anti-racism during the 1970s. Jones's words betray the central tension in the politics of the anti-racist struggle, namely the tendency to conceive of neo-fascism and racism as distinct and unrelated problems and to make the popular memory of the Second World War the dominant source of images with which to mobilize against the dangers of contemporary racism'.

148   There were ANL supporters who saw themselves as patriotic, and the Second World War as a war for democracy though it is hard to find examples of this that were connected with the working-class movement. The only ANL example I have found is in the Merseyside Anti Nazi League Bulletin no 2, December 1978, 'voice of the ANL on Merseyside'. This is the poster of an SS officer with an NF puppet of a string in front dancing on the grave of Tommy Atkins, 1922–1940, killed by the Nazis. See https://photos.google.com/search/dancing%20on%20your%20grave/photo/AF1QipMsFUniAA6egW Bi5gG1KzzV_LjOoKgOeT8Af4W6 It was also published as a leaflet by AF & R Publications, Birmingham, the *Searchlight* publishers. Tommy Atkins was the name used by Kipling in a poem lamenting how badly rank and file soldiers were treated in the British army, https://www.kiplingsociety.co.uk/poem/poems_tommy.htm

Howard Clark also refers to the cartoon in the article 'The carnival is over', *Peace News* 19 May 1978. Clark, at the time of writing one of the press officers for the York and District Anti Fascist Alliance, was on the march to Victoria Park and saw a group of military veterans going in the opposite directions. '[He] heard the call go up 'You fought them before, fight them again' – as if German conscripts were all fascists'. Further in the article he writes 'Stigmatise the NF as Nazi, intone Never Again, and we think we're putting up some sort of barrier against Britain turning fascist. But continually harking back to World War II (They're dancing on your grave, Tommy Boy – Searchlight) strengthens the very nationalism fascism needs – as if World War II was about fascism rather than European power-politics; as if internationalism and anti-militarism didn't go by the board when socialists went along with conscription or joined up'. There is also this report in *Searchlight* December 1979: 'Labour Party leader Coun. Eric Haldane... told the Barnstable Borough Gazette: "when Labour take over the council, one of the first things we shall do is ban them [the NF] from using council rooms... The Tories will soon be standing at the war memorial as a tribute to our soldiers who died fighting the very things the National Front stand for. It is an insult to the war dead"'.

149   See Chapter 8. There are a number of attacks on the NF from non-labour movement sources. The *Readers Digest* article, published as a leaflet, 1977 concludes: 'Lord Hailsham, a former Conservative MP and Lord Chancellor, recently spoke for the majority of tolerant Britons when he described the National Front as "A thoroughly detectable organisation.

Their policies could not be carried out without dictatorship and bloodshed. Perhaps the nastiest of all their characteristics is that they proclaim their odious and divisive policies under the shadow of massed Union Jacks, the very symbols of national unity and pride'. See also *Harpers Queen*, February 1977. For further examples see the Book's website endnotes.

150 Francis Wheen & Elaine Potter, 'Southall, The not-so-thin blue line', *New Statesman* 4 May 1979. The police knew that the claim was false as the Special Branch gathered details of those demonstrating collecting over a hundred names. See the much-redacted list, https://www.ucpi.org.uk/wp-content/uploads/2020/11/MPS-0733404.pdf.

151 'The police role', *Daily Mail* 24 April 1979.

152 *Searchlight* July 1979.

153 'Record of a telephone conversation between the prime minister and the home secretary at 15.40 on Wednesday 25 April 1979', National Archives PREM 16/2084. This may have been an example of what Callaghan saw as undermining Labour's election campaign, 'Jim Accuses the Southall wreckers', Manchester Evening News, 24 April 1979.

154 *Socialist Challenge* 1 May 1979: *Socialist Worker* 5 May 1979. See the Special Demonstration Squad report listing some of those who marched, https://www.ucpi.org.uk/wp-content/uploads/2021/04/UCPI0000021270.pdf. Greater Manchester ANL sent a coach to the demonstration.

155 ANL factsheet 'Who killed Blair Peach?', personal archive.

156 Southall SWP, 1979, p.4.

157 ANL factsheet, 'Who killed Blair Peach?; Louis Kushnick, 1999, '"Over Policed and Under Protected": Stephen Lawrence, Institutional and Police Practices' *Sociological Research Online* vol.4, no.1. Kushnick quotes Institute of Race Relations, 1979, 'Police Against Black People: Evidence Submitted to the Royal Commission on Criminal Procedure': 'All this evidence suggests that arrest and police powers are now being used to keep the black community in its place: physically, by penalising [black people] found out of their "ghettoes", and psychologically, by penalising those who attempt to demand their rights or protect another's'.

158 *Socialist Worker* 12 May 1979.

159 *Socialist Worker* 12 May 1979.

160 Equivalent to £25,000 in 2025.

161 Norwich ANL bulletin no 11, n.d., personal archive.

162 Derek and Judith Merrill, in Huddle & Saunders, 2021, p.176.

163 'After the Royal Court Theatre benefit: Facing the audience of the future', *Socialist Challenge* 26 July 1979; *Socialist Worker* 21 July 1979.

164 Southall Defence Committee bulletin, September 1979, personal archive.

165 *Searchlight* January 1980, p.11.

166 Southall Defence Committee 1979.

167 *Socialist Worker* 15 December 1979; *Socialist Challenge* 6 December 1979.

168 *Socialist Worker* 12 January 1980; *Socialist Challenge* 13 December

1979; *Socialist Challenge* 24 January 1980.

169   Richard North reviewed 'Southall on Trial' in *Listener* 27 September 1979, 'it doesn't pay to be black: which was pretty much what Open Door's edition from Southall was saying. It was more a show for news editors and leader writers to comment on than TV critics: in the sense that it ought to be the starting point of an examination of our police force – from within, but equally from without. Respectable, middle-aged black Englishmen and women must be listened to when they speak: no counter-attack about long-haired, over-educated, layabout subversives can be levelled at them. And when they say they cannot believe that such a thing could happen in London as happened on that April day, they cry out for close, shocked, attention', *Socialist Worker* 26 January 1980.

170   *Temporary Hoarding* 11 Jan/Feb 1980; *Socialist Challenge* 2 Aug 1979.

171   Leicester April 21st Defence Committee 'Support the Leicester 87!'; 'April 21 demo passes off quietly', *Leicester Mercury* 23 July 1979.

172   The legal definition of murder is one person killing another with the intention to cause either death or serious injury unlawfully, Hyam v. Director of Public Prosecutions, https://www.casebriefs.com/blog/law/criminal-law/criminal-law-keyed-to-lafave/homicide-using-mental-state-and-other-factors-to-classify-crimes/hyam-v-director-of-public-prosecutions/. Assisted by 31 officers, Cass carried out the investigation. A redacted and anonymised version of his report was made public in April 2010. McIntosh, 2016, p.113.

173   An identity parade was held mid-July, twelve weeks after Peach was murdered, *Socialist Worker* 21 July 1979.

174   The *Evening News* headline read: 'Man wasn't killed by a police truncheon', the *Evening Standard* headline 'Truncheon didn't kill riot victim'. The *Sun* attacked Socialist Worker for calling Blair Peach's death murder, 'Trots accuse the police of murder', *Sun* Friday 27 April 1979, p.2.

175   *Socialist Worker* 12 May 1979.

176   The coroner decided to make it two months, *Socialist Worker* 16 June 1979. The *Socialist Worker* report continued 'On Wednesday night, after the ANL released the pathologist's report, Sir David McNee spoke at a dinner in the Dorchester promising to crack down on football violence'. For a chronology see *Camerawork* no.17, 'Blair Peach - No cover up', p.6. https://www.fourcornersarchive.org/asset/3027/0000018_Camerawork_Magazine_Issue17_1980_full_reduced.pdf; Inquest, 'Report into death of Blair Peach released after nearly three decades of secrecy',

https://www.inquest.org.uk/blair-peach-death-report-released-30-years-secrecy, Metropolitan Police, 'Investigation into the death of Blair Peach', 27 April 2010.

177   Southall SWP, 1979, p.4.

178   8,000 signed the book of condolences, Jim Nichol, interviewed by Geoff Brown 19 February 2023.

Taking down the beast

1   https://media-studies.com/reception-theory-politics-poster/. The image was created from a group of twenty Young Conservatives in Hendon.

2   Callaghan was careful not to raise immigration though he was ready to talk about Labour's 1977 Green Paper on citizenship and immigration, which was only slightly less racist than the Tory proposals. It proposed to create a new category of citizenship: British Overseas Citizenship. British Overseas Citizens would be UK nationals but they would not be UK citizens so they would not have an automatic right to settle in Britain. James Fawcett, 1981, 'Nationality and citizenship', *The Round Table*, vol.71, np.28, p.9.

3   There was also a crisis of the revolutionary left in Europe and the US and the post-colonial regimes in Africa and Asia were hit hard by the end of the long boom. See Chris Harman, *The Fire Last Time: 1968 and After* (Bookmarks, 1995).

4   *Sun* 24 July 1979.

5   Attack on 'enemy within', *Times*, 20 July 1984.

6   https://www.margaretthatcher.org/document/110795. The plan was drawn up by the Tory MP, Nicholas Ridley. Initially secret, it was made public in the *Economist* 27 May 1978.

7   Conservative General Election Manifesto 1979, https://www.margaretthatcher.org/document/110858

8   A Chronology of Labour Law 1979–2023, https://www.ier.org.uk/a-chronology-of-labour-law-1979-2023/.

9   Thatcher also aimed to privatise all nationalised industries. In 1979, nationalised industries produced 10 percent of GDP. Over the next ten years more than forty state-owned businesses employing 600,000 workers were privatised. There was no mention of privatisation in the 1979 Conservative manifesto.

10   The Overthrow of Democracy in Chile: A Timeline, https://www.zinnedproject.org/materials/chile-coup-timeline/

11   By 1988, fifteen years after the coup, 48 percent of Chileans were living below the poverty line, https://www.macrotrends.net/countries/CHL/chile/poverty-rate

12   The employer was forced to accept worksharing in place of 500 redundancies.

13   *BBC News*, 18 February 1981; *Socialist Worker* 21 February 1981. https://www.ipsos.com/en-uk/voting-intentions-great-britain-1976-1987

14   There was also much work done looking unsuccessfully for an alternative economic strategy that the left could support.

15   Cliff initiated the discussion on the downturn, Tony Cliff, 'The balance of class forces in recent years', *International Socialism* series 2, no.6, Autumn 1979. Steve Jefferys, the party's national industrial organiser, countered with evidence of continuing rank and file strength, Steve Jefferys, 'Striking into the 80s, Modern British trade unionism, its limits and potential', *International Socialism* series 2, no.5, Summer 1979.

16   Peter Alexander, *Racism, Resistance and Revolution* (Bookmarks,

1987), p.45. Emphasis in the original.

17   ITN TV Interview 5 April 1982; Martin Barker, *The New Racism: Conservatives and the Ideology of the Tribe* (Junction Books, 1981).

18   Nationality Bill, *Times* 4 June 1981. Overseas British arriving would be required to wait five years before being able to apply for British citizenship. The application would cost £150 and include taking a language test. British Nationality Act 1981, https://www.legislation.gov.uk/ukpga/1981/61/section/1/enacted. Thatcher's racist agenda had already had an impact before the election. As Callaghan's government became more unpopular, Tories took control of a number of councils. One was Ealing where, as soon as it took control in May 1978, the new Tory majority tried to stop the Southall Carnival Against Racism in a local park. The council's attempt failed, Derek & Judith Merrell, in Roger Huddle & Red Saunders, eds., *Reminiscences of RAR* (Redwords, 2021), p.174; Campaign Against Racism and Fascism/Southall Rights, *Southall: The Birth of a Black Community* (Institute of Race Relations, 1981), p.43.

19   This included '9 million leaflets and three quarters of a million badges, and... [raising] the £150,000 necessary to finance the whole operation', Anti Nazi League Conference Declaration, 14 July 1979, personal archive.

20   See previous endnote.

21   'Southall calls for community self-defence not vigilante groups', *Asian* August 1978; Leaflet, 'The fight against the Nazis is a fight for our own survival', September 1978, personal archive.

22   Nine of the fifteen were members of the Labour Party.

23   Anti Nazi League shows unity in attack on 'institutionalised racism'', *Tribune* 20 July 1979.

24   *Socialist Challenge* 19 July 1979; S*ocialist Worker* 21 July 1979; Future activities of the ANL, Merseyside Anti Nazi League Bulletin, September /October 1979, personal archive. See also Sasha Josephides, 'Towards a History of the Indian Workers' Association', (University of Warwick, 1991), https://warwick.ac.uk/fac/soc/crer/research/publications/research_papers/rp_no.18.pdf

25   SWP Central Committee, 'ANL: A Balance Sheet', *SWP Internal Bulletin* no.2, May 1979, personal archive.

26   Special Branch report providing an assessment of the North-West London District of the SWP, the Engineers Charter Group and the Anti-Nazi League, Special Branch report, 11 July 1980, UCPI0000014118.

27   ANL national organiser's report to 1981 ANL conference, 28 March 1981,personal archive.

28   Leaflet, 'Trade Union Day School Racism in the Workplace', Saturday October 6th 1979, Leamington Spa, personal archive.

29   There was a march past the building on a Monday night in December 1979. The NF was prohibited from using Excalibur House for political activity in April 1980.

30   Report to 1981 ANL conference: 'This was a period of decline in activity and organisation, which affected almost every aspect of the League's work. This decline reflected the fortunes of the Nazis, particularly

the National Front, who became demoralised and divided following their electoral demise. Nevertheless, even in this period, there were a number of important mobilisations, particularly those connected with the Blair Peach cover-up and Southall Defence, the Campaign Against Racist Laws, and counter-demonstrations against the NF', Under Cover Police Inquiry, www.ucpi.org.uk, UCPI0000026579.

31   *Socialist Challenge* 19 July 1979; https://historyjournal.org.uk/2022/10/19/surprising-lessons-from-the-1980s-inspiration-from-anti-deportation-campaign-activism/.

32   Meeting convened by Prem Singh, General Secretary of IWA (GB) (Marxist), Avtar Jouhl, President of IWA (GB) (ML) and Vishnu Sharma, IWA Southall. The latter two were at the ANL steering committee meeting which agreed the ANL would participate in 'setting out a broad coordinating committee to fight the proposed new immigration regulations and nationality act', *Socialist Challenge* 27 September 1979. See also note on website of CARL materials in the Modern Records Centre, University of Warwick.

33   For a full list see website, Campaign Against Racist Laws sponsors, CARL archive , Modern Records Centre, University of Warwick; Prem Singh and Avtar Jouhl were joint chairs, Dave Cook was secretary and Jerry Fitzpatrick treasurer. Special Branch report on the 1981 National Conference of the Anti-Nazi League, https://www.ucpi.org.uk/wp-content/uploads/2020/11/UCPI0000016579.pdf, p.15. Alexander took over from Fitzpatrick as ANL organising secretary and CARL treasurer in summer 1980.

34   *Socialist Challenge* 29 November 1979; *Socialist Worker* 1 December 1979.

35   Abdul Azad was initially arrested and held for ten days accused of murdering his mother. This charge was dropped after he was made to sign a statement that he was an illegal immigrant. He was held for three months before being bailed. Leaflets, 'The Case of Abdul Azad', 'Why did the police harass the Ahmeds, Victory in Oldham, Abdul Azad stays'; 'Abdul Azad stays, OK!', *Socialist Challenge* 2 August 1979.

36   *Socialist Worker* 26 July 1980.

37   Nasira Begum's campaign succeeded, *Manchester Evening News* 30 July 1980. See also the campaign to keep Shukar Mohammed in Britain, organised by the Oldham Campaign Against Racist Laws, 'Manchester fights racism', *Socialist Challenge* 21 February 1980.

38   Our Migration Story, 'Families divided: the campaign for Anwar Ditta and her children', https://www.ourmigrationstory.org.uk/oms/families-divided-the-campaign-for-anwar-ditta-and-her-children ; *World in Action*: 'These Children Are Mine', broadcast 16 March 1981.

39   *Leveller* February/March 1981; *Socialist Worker* 21 February 1981. *Socialist Worker* reported 'Balwinder Rana, Secretary of Southall ANL, told Socialist Worker, "After the picket we marched to the Sarwar's house to show our solidarity. We are now joining the Asian Youth Movement in sleeping in at the house"'.

40   *Socialist Worker* 21 February 1981. In Rochdale, ANL members joined a picket of the Rochdale Indian Association when they invited

Timothy Raison, Minister of State for Immigration, to speak. *Rochdale Alternative Press* February 1981. At a conference of the European Association of Police Federations, October 1980, the British delegation refused to support a resolution opposing racist legislation, opposing racist actions by the police and strongly opposing all racist organisations, *Socialist Worker* 11 April 1981.

41   *Socialist Challenge* 15 Jan 1981; The CARL conference in January 1981 included all the Asian Workers Associations, the Standing Conference of Pakistani Organisations, the West Indian Standing Conference, the United Filipino Association and the Indian Youth Federation. It was opened by Anne Dummett, Joint Council for the Welfare of Immigrants. *Socialist Worker* 17 January 1981. See Ken Olende, 'The state of racism in Britain', *Socialist Worker* 16 October 2012.

42   '10,000 join nationality Bill march', *Times* 6 April 1981; *Socialist Worker* 21 March 1981. When Southall Indian Youth Association invited Roy Hattersley, Shadow Home Secretary, to speak about the Nationality Bill, he refused. Interview with Hardip Duhra, president Southall Indian Youth Association, *Socialist Worker* 21 March 1981. Hattersley was a supporter of immigration controls. At the same time, he was clear in his criticism of Powell: 'When he talks of re-immigration he is talking of the departure from Britain of families which were born here, educated here and have known no other home. There can be no question of their going home. They are home already.' Roy Hattersley Accuses Powell, *Searchlight* May 1981.

43   See IWA (GB) leaflet 'Another Racist Law On The Way', personal archive; Alien Culture, https://www.alienkulture.org/.

44   *Daily Mirror* 6 April 1981; 'New start Rock against Racism New style', *Leveller* 17 April 1981; '10,000 in demo – organised by Campaign Against Racist Laws – on migrants bill', *Daily Mirror* 6 April 1981; *Socialist Challenge* 9 April 1981; *Searchlight* November 1979. '10,000 in Demo on Migrants Bill', *Daily Mirror* 6 April 1981; 'After the GLC, a Greek lesson', *Times* 21 July 1983. The GLC gave money to CARL.

45   'Special Branch report on a picket organised by the Anti-Nazi League in support of the Blair Peach Memorial', *Undercover Policing Enquiry*, 17 Oct 1979, www.ucpi.org.uk/publications/special-branch-report-on-a-picket-organised-by-the-anti-nazi-league-in-support-of-the-blair-peach-memorial/

46   *Socialist Worker* 6 October 1979. Azeem Khan, 21, secretary Blackburn ANL, was interviewed by the *Lancashire Evening Telegraph*. The picket had the support of Hyndburn Trades Council.

47   *Lancashire Evening Telegraph* 10 October 1979.

48   'Hackney Against Racism. Fight back now!' Hackney Campaign against Racism, Bulletin no.1, Modern Records Centre, University of Warwick, (accessed 22 June 2022).

49   'Wanted For Murder', *Socialist Worker* 22 March 1980; 'Peach marchers chant officers' names', *Guardian* 28 April 1980; *Temporary Hoarding* no.12, n.d. The day before, Saturday 26 April, 1,000 ANL supporters and trade unionists marched through Glasgow to hand in a wreath to Strathclyde police in memory of Blair Peach. The same day, 26

April, RAR organised a Southall Anniversary Benefit at the University of London showing the *Open Door* programme 'Southall on Trial' and film of the SPG at Grunwick, 'All proceeds to the Blair Peach Memorial Fund'.

50   *Guardian* 28 April 1980.

51   *Socialist Worker* 22 March 1980. Commander Cass's eighty-seven-page report, based on 2,400 pages of statement, was completed on 12 July 1979. It was finally made public in 2009, https://www.met.police.uk/foi-ai/af/accessing-information/met/investigation-into-the-death-of-blair-peach/; https://en.wikipedia.org/wiki/Death_of_Blair_Peach#Cass_investigation.

52   'The Bristol confrontation: Racial but not racist', *Guardian* 5 April 1980; John Rose 'Bristol: A black and white revolt', *Socialist Worker* 12 April 1980; Roger Ball, *Violent Urban Disturbance in England 1980–81* (University of the West of England, 2012), p.25–27, https://uwe-repository.worktribe.com/output/943122.

53   See Colin Thomas, '40 years ago, the far right in Bristol was faced down…', *Bristol Cable*, 8 January 2020.

 https://thebristolcable.org/2020/01/40-years-ago-the-far-right-in-bristol-was-faced-down-with-music-pickets-and-ballots/. See also 'St Paul's youth on ANL demo in Bristol', *Socialist Worker* 3 May 1980.

54   ANL circular, 'Blair Peach: Inquest Re-Opens', 24 September 1979.

55   ANL circular, 'Blair Peach Inquest', 28 May 1980; 'Disband the SPG', *Socialist Worker* 1 December 1979; *Socialist Worker,* 31 May 1980. There were two riders to the jury's verdict: 1. That the SPG should be kept more under the control of its officers; 2. That the SPG should not have access to unauthorised weapons. See also 'DPP admits many guilty police go free', *Guardian* 7 February 1981, 'Asked for the first time about his decision not to prosecute any officer for the death of the Anti-Nazi League demonstrator Blair Peach, he said: "After very thorough investigation, and it was indeed one of the best investigations I've ever seen into any complaint against the police, there just was not sufficient evidence to prosecute any individual police officer. It wasn't a question of 49 per cent or 51 per cent. It was never near sufficient evidence against any individual"'.

56   'The NF in a climax of filth', *Labour Weekly* 2 November 1979; *Searchlight* November 1979. *Labour Weekly* estimated no more than 200 at the conference.

57   Lez Scott, interviewed by Geoff Brown September 2016.

58   Martin Ford interviewed by Terry James, *Socialist Worker* 10 May 1980. He had joined the NF as a sixteen-year-old schoolboy in Cardiff.

59   NF Internal Wrangle, *Searchlight* June 1979; *Guardian* 14 July 1979.

60   *New Society* 26 March 1981; *Searchlight* August 1979. At the end of the month, the leading body, the directorate, voted not to pursue complaints against Webster but to investigate Fountaine's behaviour.

61   'Sticking the knives into the Front', *Labour Weekly* 30 November 1979; *Searchlight* January 1980. There had always been criticisms of Tyndall's leadership. When Kingsley Read attacked John Tyndall for having 'the autocratic style of the Fuehrer', Tyndall responded that he believed in democracy, 'but perhaps I see democracy in a different way… At the moment every little minority's will is being allowed to frustrate the will of

the majority', 'What John Tyndall means by "democracy"', *Observer* 4 July 1976.

62 *Socialist Worker* 19 January 1980. Tyndall was found guilty of breaching the injunction not to use the NF HQ as a 'social centre', fined £250 with £4,000 costs awarded against him.

63 *Searchlight* November 1979. *Searchlight* January 1981 estimated 3,000–4,000.

64 *Times* 21 January 1980.

65 Maurice Ludmer, 'Tyndall out in NF split', *Socialist Worker* 26 January 1980.

66 'NF chairman resigns after failing to win more power', *Times* 21 January 1980; *Searchlight* January 1980; Former National Front leader starts new group, *Times* 27 June 1980; 'Why the National Front keeps splitting its sides', *Searchlight* January 1981. This article details the breakup of the NF. Tyndall did not accept the NF's rules regarding its leadership. The Yarmouth conference threw out Tyndall's proposal for a clear 'Fuehrer' [leader] principle, *Searchlight* November 1979. Tyndall's problem with the young recruits to the NF was not with their violence but with their lack of discipline. When challenged that his organisation attracted thugs, and asked him how he could condone their behaviour, he replied 'We only have members who will defend us against the Reds who try to disrupt us. It is purely in self-defence'. Tyndall now began to refer openly to Webster being gay, adding 'the issue of homosexuality is not the only reason why I have left', *Searchlight* February 1980.

67 Colin Sparks, 'NF and the local elections: Reading the entrails', *Socialist Review* June 1978; *Guardian* 30 May 1979. After the US was finally defeated in Vietnam in 1975, the city of Paris took more Vietnamese refugees than the whole of Britain, *Socialist Worker* 28 July 1979. Becky Taylor, "Our Most Foreign Refugees': Refugees from Vietnam in Britain', in Becky Taylor et al, *When Boat People were Resettled, 1975–1983* (Palgrave, 2021), pp.109–143. In Merseyside, the NF's anti-Vietnamese activities were boosted by the local *Birkenhead News*. Its report of a meeting on the Woodchurch estate now suffering unemployment, empty properties and vandalism, was headed 'Help Our Forgotten City Not Boat People'. See Merseyside Anti Nazi League Bulletin no.6 Nov/Dec 1979.

68 See the book's website for details of the share of the NF vote in local elections 1976–80.

69 Ray Hill & Andy Bell, *The Other Face of Terror, Inside Europe's Neo-Nazi Network* (Grafton Books, 1988), p.36; Thames TV, *TV Eye*, 'The British Movement', first shown 4 December 1980, https://www.youtube.com/watch?v=D2AYk4aBbIo. A letter from a mother to the *Rochdale Alternative Paper* April 1981 described how the BM had tried to recruit her two sons at school, sold papers openly, planned to celebrate Hitler's birthday, had 'manoeuvres on the moors', weekend camps in the Lake District and wanted drummers for their local band.

70 Letter from Glennis, York ANL, 30 September 1980 on BM support in York and prospect of BM march in Dewsbury; see interview with Martin Ford, former NF member in South Wales, explaining that the BM are arguably a bigger threat than the NF, though joint membership was not

uncommon, *Socialist Worker* 10 May 1980.

71   *Searchlight* February 1980.

72   Red Saunders always issued strict instructions never to let anyone take control of the stage. If the stage was invaded, then the PA had to be defended.

73   'Nazi Rock, Spittin' hate at the future of rock n' roll', *Leveller* October 1979,
 https://www.thesparrowsnest.org.uk/collections/public_archive/12014.pdf .

74   John Hall interviewed by Geoff Brown, 3 January 2018.

75   *Leveller* 20 Feb–5 March 1981. The story comes from the court reports. See also the BBC report on Nicky Crane, a leading figure in the attack 'Nicky Crane: The secret double life of a gay neo-Nazi', https://www.bbc.co.uk/news/magazine-25142557. There will have been similar attacks which never led to court proceedings.

76   'Our plans for the 1980s', National Front Members Bulletin July 1980, quoted in *Searchlight* September 1980. This strategy was not for some long-standing NF members, such as Mr Philip Baker, local chairperson and organiser of the Reading NF branch, 'Quite frankly', he said, 'I don't think I could devote any more time and effort to a body which stands no chance of being elected to power as a British government. I have resigned because I don't fancy another 10 or 15 years struggle to get back to where we were. For some time I have had misgivings about the future there – have been three splits and there are now effectively four National Fronts', *Searchlight* October 1980. On the question of fascist strategy see also Reed Herbert's view, 'The 'patriotic pincer strategy' explained, NF offshoot [BDP] allies with BM', *Searchlight* December 1980.

77   Benjamin Bowling, *Violent Racism: Victimization, Policing and Social Context* (Oxford University Press, 1999), p.59

78   Merseyside Anti-Racist, Anti-Fascist Bulletin No1 April 1980.

79   Merseyside Anti-Racist, Anti-Fascist Bulletin No1 April 1980; 'Gravesend – A model for racial harmony?' Gravesend Anti Nazi League.

80   Conrad Martin, 'Oldham against the Nazis', letter to *Socialist Worker* 3 May 1980.

81   Conrad, 1980. The police made thirty-five arrests leading to 200 picketing the police station, *Socialist Challenge* 17 Apr 1980.

82   The factory was in Calne, Wiltshire. *Searchlight* no.58 April 1980; Andrew Milner, 'The Nazis: Down but not out', *Socialist Review*, July–September 1980. LARAFC press release, 12 March 1980, 'In recent weeks large areas of Leamington and the surrounding district have been flooded with racist propaganda in the form of a newspaper called "Choice"'.

83   The NF told the press that Lewisham was chosen because the council had refused them a room for an election meeting for a council seat by-election. Knowing the council would be unsuccessful in trying to get the march banned, Webster was confident that he would have sufficient police protection. *Guardian* 21 April 1980. The press reported between 500 and 1,000 anti-fascists and 4,000 police. Of the sixty-seven arrests, two thirds

were anti-fascists, *Daily Telegraph* 21 April 1980; Diary comment, *Tribune* 25 April 1980; *Searchlight* April 1980; Tony Greenstein, *The Fight against Fascism in Brighton & the South Coast* (Brighton History Workshop, 2011), p.45; *Observer* 27 April 1980; *Sunday Times* 27 April 1980; *Socialist Challenge* 1 May 1980. MACE Archive, 'National Front, Corby', ATV Today, 28 April 1980.

84   Anti Nazi League steering committee statement, 'The Way Forward', September 1980. The statement listed thirteen public demonstrations, Southwark, Lewisham. Corby, Central London. Brighton. Halifax, Tonbridge Wells, Preston. Glasgow, Blackpool, Nottingham, Nuneaton and Hoxton. There were also the British Movement marches in Dewsbury and Welling.

85   *Searchlight* July 1980, Anti Nazi League, Report to 1981 conference, https://www.ucpi.org.uk/wp-content/uploads/2020/11/UCPI0000016579.pdf. See also 'Open letter to the anti-racist anti-fascist movement', *Searchlight* August 1980.

86   Newham Monitoring Project/Campaign against Racism and Fascism, *Newham: The forging of a black community* (Newham Monitoring Project, 1991), p.40, gives the figure of 2,500 on the march, on p.41, Unmesh Desai remembers it as 'the most angry and militant march that I had been on'. An earlier criticism of a poor mobilisation, the counter-demonstration to the NF march against the Vietnamese 'boat-people', 23 June 1979, 'Don't fob us off about the Front', *Socialist Worker* 21 July 1979.

87   Kate Alexander private email, February 2023. *Socialist Worker* issues in October and November 1980 give a picture of what was happening. They included many campaigns against cuts, the Right to Work Campaign, march from South Wales to the TUC in Brighton, the national campaign against nuclear cruise missiles and the 'blanket' protests for political status by Irish republican prisoners in Long Kesh.

88   Peter Alexander and Kate Alexander are the same person.

89   The emergency meeting was attended by Sandwell CARF, Birmingham ANL, Birmingham CARF, Wolverhampton ARC and the IWA (GB) General Secretary, Avtar Jouhl. The joint agreement to mobilise as many as possible did not include an agreement on tactics on the day with 'SCARF looking to avoid directly opposing NF'. See letter from Jerry Fitzpatrick to Clive [Gilson, LARAFC?], n.d. [first week of August 1980].

90   ANL circular, 23 July 1980.

91   *Socialist Worker* 2 August 1980; *Socialist Worker* 9 August 1980.

92   'Blame the Tories, not the blacks', *Socialist Worker* 16 August 1980.

93   The pressure was also stepped up with NF marches in Halifax and Tunbridge Wells the weekend before 17th.

94   *Searchlight* October 1980; *Times* 18 August 1980; *Daily Telegraph* 19 August 1980. Report Of The Chief Constable Of The West Midlands Police For The Year 1980, https://www.ojp.gov/pdffiles1/Digitization/77897NCJRS.pdf. The police made eight arrests including Paul Holborow. ANL supporters protested against the arrests outside the police station with a delegation including Les Huckfield, the local MP, meeting the police. Holborow was subsequently acquitted. The Nuneaton Committee Against Racism and Fascism organised an anti-racist march in the town the

following month. *Searchlight* (October 1980) reported a number of leading Labour councillors in Nuneaton knew the day before that the NF would march in Nuneaton though when Nuneaton CARF wrote to the council about this, they received only denials. Nuneaton CARF gave the figures 700 anti-fascists opposing 250 NF supporters. *Searchlight* September 1980 reported the absence of skinheads on the Nuneaton demonstration.

95 'The most violent incident happened when two coaches of National Front supporters... were leaving... just outside the town centre heavy steel missiles broke four windows, showering occupants with glass and causing some cuts', *Times* 18 August 1980.

96 'Like many other similar organisations, Croydon CARF activities died down after 1979 as many members concentrated on fighting the Tories' policies', *Searchlight,* May 1981. 'The Way Forward', Anti Nazi League Steering Committee statement, personal archive.

97 Webster organised marches in Preston and Hoxton, outnumbering anti-fascists on both occasions. Four hundred NF members marched in Preston in September. The ANL mobilised 300, *Socialist Challenge* 18 September 1980; *Guardian* 15 September 1980 reported, 750–800 NF, 350–400 counter demonstrators, a street sit-down to try to stop the march, twenty-three arrests. The 5 October NF demonstration in Hoxton had 500 marching, 'At short notice, the ANL managed to get 200 to oppose them', *Socialist Worker* 11 October 1980. The BM got 300 mainly young, supporters of the British Movement to march in Welling, South-East London, 19 October 1980, outnumbered by the ANL and Bexley CARF, 'How to stop Hitler Youth', Pete Alexander, *Socialist Worker* 25 October 1980. See also Special Branch report, https://www.ucpi.org.uk/publications/special-branch-report-on-a-counter-demonstration-organised-by-the-bexley-campaign-against-racism-and-fascism-and-the-anti-nazi-league/. 'Protected by over 2,300 police from 400 counter-demonstrators, the BM supporters sang 'There's only one Adolf Hitler' and 'We've Gotta Get Rid of the Reds' and shouted 'Sieg Heil'. The counter-demonstrators were kept penned in a side street by the police', *Searchlight* December 1980.

98 It could be added that there was an urgent need to rebuild the finances. Already in December 1979 a national circular launched an urgent financial appeal promoting a Christmas Raffle pointing out that the ANL 'funded the bulk of the expenses of the CARL demo, and we now face £10,000 debt for the legal representation at the Blair Peach inquest'.

99 The Leamington conference was on 18 October. It was called in July. ANL national circular, 23 July 1980, personal archive.

100 'We must Rebuild the Movement', *Searchlight* December 1980. The conference was promoted for three weeks in a row by *Socialist Worker*. The invitation made it clear that the conference was intended for local activists.

101 Having acted as national organiser from 1 September 1980. As a well-known figure in the public eye, Holborow remained national secretary, Kate Alexander, interviewed by Geoff Brown February 2023 and April 2024.

102 The BM had sixty supporters in Dewsbury. They were bussed in from all over the North of England, protected from 200 counter-demonstrators by about 800 police, *Searchlight* December 1980.

103 The revolutionary left – the SWP, organised around *Rebel,* and the

IMG, organised round *Revolution* – took over the NUSS from the Young Communist League at its 1979 conference. In a meeting full of heckling, with little defence by the previous leadership, Erika Laredo remembers being impressed by the dedication and organisational skills of the SWP activists. Hardy Desai was elected president, Steve Marsh national organiser and Laredo northern officer. While the national leadership could intervene in schools and lead walkouts again and again, it was unable to establish local branches, Steve Cunningham & Michael Lavalette, *Schools Out!* (Bookmarks, 2016), pp.159–60.

104 'Anti-Nazi activity to increase', *Times* 11 November 1980; 'Drive to counter activities of new extremists', *Guardian* 10 November 1980.

105 *Guardian* 10 November 1980. Hackney, Leamington and Glasgow, had their own relaunches. 'Racist attacks led to Hackney ANL being reactivated', Special Branch report https://www.ucpi.org.uk/wp-content/uploads/2021/04/UCPI0000016370.pdf, Leamington ARAFC relaunch meeting, 'West of Scotland ANL, 'Stop the New Nazis', Peter Alexander, Organising Secretary ANL, Charin Atwal, IWA, TUC Club, Glasgow, Monday 16 March', *Socialist Worker* 1 March 1980.

106 'Rebuilding the Anti Nazi League, CARF interviews Peter Hain, ANL Press Officer', *Searchlight* February 1981. The NF found it harder to kick its way into the headlines. When it succeeded, it found the media coverage more hostile, 'The Press Council throws out NF complaint, NF riot report complaint rejected', *Guardian* 10 August 1981.

107 Paul Ginsborg, *A History of Contemporary Italy* (Penguin, 1990), p.423.

108 'The Way Forward', Anti Nazi League steering committee statement, September 1980. Other violence in the summer of 1980 included 'the machine gunning of synagogue schools and war memorials and raids on Jewish and immigrant quarters'. The Henri Curiel Association reported there had been 159 fascist and racist attacks in France since 1977, 'French Anti Nazi League needed to counter bombings', *Socialist Challenge* 9 October 1980.

109 Amato was assassinated by the Nuclei Armati Rivoluzionari in June 1980. The parents of two British students killed by the Bologna bomb were among the audience.

110 Information, Association of Jewish Refugees in Britain, vol.36, no.2 February 1981, https://ajr.org.uk/wp-content/uploads/2018/02/1981_february.pdf. Heinemann spoke at four ANL meetings in Portsmouth, Birmingham Sheffield, Edinburgh, December 11–17, *Socialist Worker* 13 December 1980.

111 *Socialist Worker* 13 December 1980.

112 'International Rally against Nazism', *Searchlight* February 1981, Grene's speech did not only upset some people in the audience. When the European Association of Police Federations held a conference in Belfast, the British Police Federation chair protested that the French police had sent a speaker to the ANL rally, *Socialist Worker* 11 April 1981. Already in the summer of 1978, the ANL had an international impact with ANL materials displayed in the Anne Frank Museum exhibition. Penny Foskett, letter, *Socialist Worker* 2 September 1978.

113   Elizabeth Dekeyser, *Islam, Exclusivity, and the State in France* (Massachusetts Institute of Technology, 2019), p.135; 'Open letter to Morning Star" *Socialist Worker* 3 January 1981.

114   'French CP marches against immigrants', *Socialist Worker* 17 January 1981. Marius Apostolate, head of the CGT immigrant organisation, also tried to oppose the bulldozing. Daniel Gordon, 2012, Immigrants and Intellectuals, p.206. I am grateful to Ian Birchall for this reference.

115   Kate Alexander, private email 28 January 2024; Hill & Bell, 1988, pp.121–2. See note on early 1981 ANL pamphlet, 'British Movement, Nazis off our streets'. See also the point made in 'The Anti Nazi League', *SWP Internal Bulletin*, early January 1981, personal archive, 'Many young people identify with the Nazis for cultural reasons (i.e. football, music, violence) rather than because they are attracted to racist ideas and these kids will welcome anti-racist arguments'.

116   'I used to go to the Tootal Road youth club in the early '70s. They were all skinheads and suede heads but they were skinheads and suede heads who were into Ska music. I went to a convention in Little Hulton precinct, meeting up with lots of skinheads and suede heads and that was where there was a split among the skinheads there because a lot of them were into nasty racist stuff. And there were others who weren't, were into Ska. Thank god for that.' Colette Crosdale, interviewed by Geoff Brown, 23 May 2018.

117   Sham 69, Borstal Breakout, Live At The Roundhouse 1978 https://www.youtube.com/watch?v=lo7vhBeLg5w

118   Sharon Spike, Skins, *Temporary Hoarding*, no.6, Summer 1978.

119   'Putting the boot on the left foot OR: Skins Against The Nazis', Gary Bushell, *Sounds* 30 September 1978.

120   *Times* 11 October 1980.

121   Jay Williams, interviewed by Geoff Brown 6 March 2023.

122   *Socialist Worker* 7 March 1981. For a detailed interview with Steve see 'In and out of the British Movement', *Socialist Worker* 28 February 1981. Jay Williams remembers Steve's speech as 'a wonderful moment'. The conference endorsed a three-page statement that 'outlined the problems and suggested responses' and agreed to a co-ordinating committee including the Indian Youth Association, the National Union of School Students, the Labour Party Young Socialists, and the Student Christian Movement. 'Report on Youth against the Nazis conference', *Leveller* 6 March 1981. Support from students remained strong. The NUS Easter conference voted solid support for anti-racist motions including backing ANL and CARL, *Leveller* 20 March 1981.

123   'Giz a Job: An oral history of the 1981 People's March for Jobs', https://vimeo.com/913634001.

124   'Anti-Nazi Youth League Conference', *Searchlight* April 1981. Sheffield ANL bulletin, March–April 1981, *Socialist Worker* 21 March 1981; See website for details of ANL leafleting of twenty-two football matches, Saturday 21 March 1981. Linton Kwesi Johnson recited his poem 'All we doin' is defendin'' at the concert which was sponsored by the TGWU, *Socialist Worker* 23 May 1981, *Socialist Worker* 6 June 1981. ANL circular March 1981, 'A small committee comprising the sponsoring organisations

was set up to coordinate activities'

125 'Fascism is not inevitable', *Socialist Worker* 1 November 1980.

126 ANL Newsletter no.1, January 1981. Compare this to Eric Lanzetti's description of the work of the CPUSA in Lower East side Manhattan, mainly Jewish working-class quarter where the party had a greater density of membership than anywhere else and through the YCL set up forty or fifty Youth Clubs consisting of neighbourhood kids who, on the Lower East Side, were often pretty tough. 'The rules of these clubs,' Lanzetti says, sounding like the Father Flanagan of the Left, 'were no stealing, no mugging. You could drink beer but not whiskey, you could neck but not fuck, you could fight but no guns or knives, you could play cards but no gambling. In short: we were the first social workers on the Lower East Side. And it was terrific, how these kids responded. And then, of course,' he laughs, 'every now and then, one of them wandered down to CP headquarters, just to see what it was all about, all this Commie stuff that the YCL worker at the club seemed so hot on.' Vivian Gornick, *The Romance of American Communism* (Verso, 2020), p.121.

127 *Sounds* 8 April 1978.

128 Paul Furness, interviewed by Geoff Brown 10 November 2022; 'Pogo on a Nazi', *Searchlight* 44 February 1979.

129 'No Fun with the Front', Mark Ellen, *New Musical Express* 25 August, 1979, https://standupandspit.wordpress.com/2015/04/26/fight-dem-back-nazi-punk/

130 'Oi and Garry Bushell', letter, *Socialist Worker* 8 August 1981.

131 Merseyside Anti Nazi League Bulletin Issue no.6 Nov/Dec 1979, personal archive.

132 *Socialist Challenge* 5 July 1979. The article includes references to recent attacks on RAR gig in Ealing and a YCL gig in Ealing Tech; Benjamin Zephaniah, 'Call It What Yu Like', *City Psalms*, quoted in David Renton, *When We Touched the Sky: The Anti-Nazi League 1977–1981* (New Clarion Press, 2006), p.163.

133 There was an unsuccessful attempt to relaunch RAR nationally in 1981, John Dennis, in Huddle & Saunders, 2021, pp.59–61; 'RAR returns', *Leveller* 3 April 1981; Kate Webb writes that 'she left RAR in 1981 as the central collective was tearing itself apart over differences about the way we should proceed (an argument, as I recall, between becoming more corporate and professional, or returning to the grass roots and staying outside the mainstream – and inflamed as these things often are by personal animosities). See https://history-is-made-at-night.blogspot.com/2011/07/rock-against-racism-documents-1979_18.html.

134 '150 black and white skins together with punks, soulies, mods and rockers', *Socialist Worker* 7 February 1981.

135 'Sheffield RAR report', *Temporary Hoarding* August 1981; 'New start Rock against Racism New style', *Leveller* 17 April 1981. Also ANL circular, week beginning Monday 23 April1981, 'RAR is getting going again and is producing a "How to Organise a Gig leaflet". Someone from RAR will be working in the ANL office and will be able to provide help for Youth Against the Nazis groups who want to put on gigs/discos'; 'The return of the Anti

Nazi League, Peter Hain interview', *New Musical Express* 7 March 1981.

136   *Daily Mail* 27 October 1980; *Bulldog* no.20, n.d.

137   *Searchlight* November 1980.

138   *Socialist Worker* 6 December 1980.

139   *Socialist Worker* 21 February 1981; Paul Thomas, 'Kicking Racism Out of Football - A Supporter's View,' *Race & Class*, 1995,vol.36, no.4, pp.95–100.

140   'Call to probe Front soccer menace', *Daily Mail* 28 October 1980; 'Anti-Nazi activity to increase', *Times* 11 November 1980; 'Reds against the Nazis', Manchester Anti-Nazi League Newsletter, no.1, May 1981. The article reports 'the response from the leaflets has been quite incredible, with replies from Barrow and Durham in the north to London in the south. It looks like Reds against the Nazis will have to be organised on a national scale!'.

141   See website for details of planned ANL leafletting, 21 March 1981.

142   'Turf the Nazis off the terraces', *Socialist Worker* 28 March 1981.

143   Special Branch report, 8 April 1981, www.ucpi.org.uk/wp-content/uploads/2022/05/UCPI0000016599.pdf; *Socialist Worker* 18 April 1981. See website for leaflet copied from Special Branch report. The leaflet is worth reading as an example of how an anti-fascist leaflet can be written for football fan reader

144   Kate Alexander, interviewed by Geoff Brown 21 February 2023.

145   *Socialist Worker* 7 March 198; 'Hackey ANL to organise benefit in aid to the New Cross Massacre Action Committee', *Socialist Worker* 18 July 1981.

146   Kate Alexander, private email 22 February 2023.

147   'Home Office begins race attacks inquiry', *Times* 20 February 1981. Leading ANL members such as Peter Hain and Miriam Karlin were targeted with bricks through windows, threatening phone calls and excrement through letterboxes. An ANL delegation, including Hain, visited Scotland Yard to discuss the police response. *Guardian* 7 March 1981. Whitelaw told the Cabinet they 'should be under no illusions about the fact that the British Movement, a neo-fascist group, had replaced the National Front as the main promoter of racial harassment'. The Home Office file, 'Possible Organised Racist Attacks against Ethnic Minorities', National Archives, HO 325/411, contains materials sent to the Home Office and details of delegations visiting Whitelaw.

148   'Tories against the Nazis?' editorial, *Socialist Worker* 14 February 1981.

149   *Searchlight* March 1981; *Socialist Worker* 14 March 1981.

150   'Glasgow's streets closed to Nazis', *Socialist Worker* 15 March 1980. After 100 Loyalist NF supporters tried unsuccessfully to march, they took their revenge with arson attacks on the CP's social club and bookshop. *Socialist Worker,* 9 February 1980. See also 'A message to the people of Glasgow, the National Front is a Nazi front'. Anti NF Leaflet produced by Glasgow Trades Council, circa Saturday 15 March 1980. This does not mention the ANL.

151   For studies of the moves to an increasingly militarised form of public

order policing, see Gerry Northam, *Shooting in the Dark: Riot Police in Britain* (Faber, 1988), and Morag Livingstone & Matt Foot, *Charged: How the Police Try to Suppress Protest* (Verso, 2022).

152   *Irish Times* 20 March 1981.

153   Joanna Rollo, 'Police Bans: thin end of the wedge' *Socialist Worker* 11 April 1981. A ban had been imposed a year earlier in Glasgow after Webster announced a march. Faced with the prospect of a massive opposition by the local labour movement, the Chief Constable imposed a blanket ban on all marches for a month, 'Glasgow's streets closed to Nazis', *Socialist Worker* 15 March 1980.

154   *Socialist Worker* 4 April 1981; https://www.birminghammail.co.uk/news/local-news/from-the-archives-unlikely-killer-embarked-on-campaign-154645.

155   ANL National Conference Report, *Searchlight* May 1981. There was a march against police harassment of skinheads in Sheffield in late June 1981, 'Sheffield skinhead demonstration against police harassment, Under the skin', *Yorkshire Post* 6 July 1981.

156   Bill Dunn, ANL Steering Committee, ANL National Conference Report, *Searchlight* May 1981; Special Branch report of the Anti Nazi League national conference, 28 March 1981, https://www.ucpi.org.uk/publications/special-branch-report-on-the-1981-national-conference-of-the-anti-nazi-league/.

157   Five were hospitalised, one had 120 stitches, *Socialist Challenge* 29 November 1979; *Searchlight* January 1980.

158   Johnny Clark, 'Where the resistance failed to suffice', *Socialist Worker* 18 April 1981. The article argues that the racism in West Ham is the result of despair. In the housing crisis, Labour is seen as the 'council' on the 'other side', the political establishment, opening the way for the fascists.

159   Special Branch Report on the death of Markland Chambers, Swindon, 10 April 1981, National Archives, HO 325/411, Possible Organised Racist Attacks against Ethnic Minorities; Swindon Anti-Nazi League leaflet 'Racist Murder In Eldene', April 1981; *Socialist Challenge* 16 April 1981

160   *SWP Internal Bulletin* no.6, 1981.

161   £8,000 was raised to pay the fines, many times what was needed. *Evening Post, Gravesham and Dartford*, 23 April 1981, 24 April 1981; *Guardian* 24 April 1981: Balwinder Rana, interviewed by Geoff Brown 17 February 2025.

162   *Socialist Worker* 2 May 1981; *Socialist Challenge* 7 May 1981. The same day 150 occupied a Newham school playground in Newham forcing the NF to abandon an election rally. The NF were not confronted everywhere. 'In Watford, Saturday 2 May over 400 people, black and white...marched peacefully, but not quietly, through Watford to register our disgust with the NF (who had been in Watford the previous week)', *Leveller* 15 May 1981.

163   'Poll blow for Nazis', Peter Alexander, ANL national organiser, *Socialist Worker* 18 May 1981. 200,000 ANL leaflets were distributed. Compared to 1979, in Newham although their total vote was down, their share of the poll was up from 4.7 percent to 6.3 percent. In Birmingham

they averaged 1.9 percent, slightly higher than in 1979.

164   John Carr, interviewed by Geoff Brown 7 March 2023.

165   Phil Allsop, Huddle & Saunders, 2021, p.23.

166   Carr, 7 March 2023.

167   Martin Luther King, 14 March 1968, Grosse Pointe High School, Michigan. King was assassinated three weeks later, https://www.gphistorical.org/mlk/mlkspeech/#:~:text=And%20I%20must%20say%20tonight,last%20twelve%20or%20fifteen%20years

168   Mike Phillips, 'Who is really on the rampage? Police overreaction is causing a siege mentality in black people', *New Statesman* 27 June 1980. Phillips's article details examples of police operating in Moss Side and elsewhere like an occupying army.

169   'Race Today Collective: Policing in Manchester', *Race Today*, May 1980.

170   Tyrone interview, *Socialist Review* May–June 1981.

171   This was not the only example of collective resistance to police racism. There were seventy pickets outside Southall police station protesting the police decision to prosecute Satvinder Singh for wasting police time when he complained to them that fascists had carved 'YNF' on his stomach, *Socialist Worker* 6 June 1981.

172   Campaign against Racism and Fascism/Southall Rights, 1981, p.63.

173   *Socialist Worker* 11 July 1981.

174   *Socialist Worker* 11 July 1981; 'Night the 'skins' came crawling', *South China Morning Post* 12 July 1981.

175   Ilene Melish, *Guardian,* 31 July 1981, quoted in Harman, 'The summer of 1981', *International Socialism* series 2, no.14, Autumn 1981.

176   Harman, 'The summer of 1981'. Also, Godfrey Hodgson, 'A witches' brew of urban woes', *Boston Globe* 19 July 1981. See 'Merseyside police view of the NF: Police racism in Merseyside… National Front is a 'normal democratic party' Merseyside Anti Nazi League Bulletin, Special Issue, Liverpool Trades Council march against Racism, 14 July 1979.

177   Mary Beaken, 'Report on Manchester riots', *Socialist Worker* 18 July 1981.

178   There were serious disturbances in Handsworth, Birmingham (10–12 July), Bedford, Bristol, Edinburgh, Gloucester, Halifax, Chapeltown and Harehills, Leeds (11–13 July), Leicester, Southampton, Wolverhampton.

179   Bradley Graham, 'Extremists Exploit Hard Times in Britain: Britain's Woes Profitable for Extremists', *Washington Post* 26 July 1981. For blaming the left, see Peter Shipley, *Extremism and the Left* (Conservative Central Office, 1981).

180   The funding was often called 'riot money'. See Gus John, '"A violent eruption of protest": Reflections on the 1981 Moss Side "riots" (part one)', *Mule*, 15 August 2011.

181   Yuri Prasad, 'Race, Class and Identity', *Socialist Review* June 2019.

182   Steve Marsh, *Socialist Worker* 25 July 1981. See also *Red Rebel*, August 1981, 'Rioting and Organising, Where now?' 'Leeds Carnival:

Thousands support the ANL... whilst the Front march sees 80 thugs arrested', *Searchlight* September 1981; Carnival Against Racism 1981, 11 November 2018, Danny Friar https://leedsmasmedia.wordpress.com/2018/11/11/carnival-against-racism-leeds-west-indian-carnival-1981/, *Socialist Worker* 11 July 1981.

183   Neville Staple quoted by Lynval Golding, Daniel Rachel, *Walls Come Tumbling Down: The Music and Politics of Rock Against Racism, 2 Tone and Red Wedge* (Picador, 2016), p.324.

184   Holborow had to deal with those who tried to occupy the stage.

185   Jerry Dammers in Huddle & Saunders, 2021, p.50.

186   Rachel, 2016, p.324 & 325.

187   Roger Huddle, in Huddle & Saunders, 2021, p.15; *Socialist Worker* 11 July 1981. See the superb short film about RAR, its impact in Leeds and the Leeds carnival, https://www.youtube.com/watch?v=DR01x9waNqI

188   Rachel, 2016, p.227.

189   https://louderthanwar.com/from-the-sex-pistols-to-janet-jackson-journalist-paul-wellings-top-10-favourite-gigs-since-the-punk-days/; See also 'Carnival against Racism, 4 July 1981, Leeds: Marchers keep the peace', *Yorkshire Post 6* July 1981. Webster was also in Leeds trying without success to disrupt the carnival. Outnumbered by ANL supporters, the NF held a 'red, white and blue slug' of a march, as Jerry Dammers saw them, Rachel, 2016, p.321. The NF were moved into and out of the city in two hours by the police who arrested eighty of them. However, 'the police radios 'got scrambled and this made it possible for us to charge on to the 500 fascists battling towards the station. Leeds United were playing at home that day and Webster got beaten up by Leeds fans... when he was in the hospital, care was taken to make sure that he was treated by a black nurse and a Jewish doctor', Sally Kincaid, interviewed by Geoff Brown 20 January 2020.

Why did the ANL succeed

1   Chris Harman, 1981, 'The summer of 1981: A post-riot analysis', *International Socialism* series 2, no.14. The speaker was at the Labour Co-ordinating Committee 'Trade Unions and Socialism' conference, 18 July 1981.

2   The chief constable was Kenneth Oxford. See 'Oxford Out' poster, https://www.liverpoolmuseums.org.uk/artifact/oxford-out. An ANL coach came from London to join the march. *Socialist Challenge* 20 August 1981 reported 15,000 on the march, *Socialist Worker* 22 August 1981, 10,000, *Sunday Times* 16 August 1981 3,000. Balwinder Rana spoke for the ANL, pointing to the grand buildings on the Liverpool skyline whose origins lay in the wealth produced by the slave trade.

3   John Grayson, 'Training the Community', in Mayo, Marjorie & Jane Thompson, eds., *Adult Learning: Critical Intelligence and Social Change* (National Institute of Adult Continuing Education, 1995), p.220.

4   'Heseltine hit by egg', *Guardian* 27 February 1982; Balwinder Rana, private email 21 October 2023.

5   They marched for a mile and a half from the Old Bailey to Scotland Yard, *Searchlight* April 1982. Pearce was convicted for committing 'an

offence to publish or distribute written material that is threatening, abusive or insulting with intent to stir up racial hatred', Section 5 of the Public Order Act 1936.

6   'Racism kills! 25 people have been killed in racist attacks since January', *Socialist Worker* 25 July 1981; Hounslow Community Relations Council report, 31 July 1981, National Archives, HO 325/411, Possible Organised Racist Attacks against Ethnic Minorities.

7   *Guardian* 10 July 1981.

8   Brons kept his job as a lecturer on condition that he was not active politically in the college. ANL national circular 'Brons must go' campaign, June 1981.

9   See 'This Nazi works in our library', *Kred* March 1989, p.5. https://media.www.kent.ac.uk/se/17908/Kredno90_reduced.pdf and brief political biography of Whiting https://patria-uk.com/who-we-are/.

10   Name withheld, interviewed by Geoff Brown January 2018.

11   Tony Greenstein, 'The fight against fascism in Brighton & the South Coast', *Brighton History Workshop*, 2011, pp.55ff. When Kingsley Read died in 1985, Phil Webster wrote: 'In recent years his views have remained the same. By all accounts, he was waiting to make a political comeback', *Socialist Worker* 5 October 1985.

12   Paul Holborow in Roger Huddle & Red Saunders, *Reminiscences of RAR* (Rewords, 2021), p.143. The memorial took place 4 December 1992 at the LSE.

13   Selwyn Brown in Huddle & Saunders, 2021, p.37.

14   Hassan Mahamdallie in Huddle & Saunders, 2021, p.167.

15   Jerry Fitzpatrick in Huddle & Saunders, 2021, p.83.

16   Ian Birchall, 'Only rock and roll?' *International Socialism* series 2 no.33, Autumn 1986. Quote from David Widgery, *Beating Time* (Chatto & Windus, 1986), p.84.

17   Red Saunders, interviewed by Geoff Brown January 2025.

18   'TUC, 'United against Racialism'', *Searchlight* September 1979. There is some indication that this was followed through at a local level. See 'New London-based anti-racist bulletin planned by GLATC', *Searchlight* January 1980.

19   Marian Peacock, interviewed by Geoff Brown 13 January 2020.

20   The ANL steering committee met at short notice in September 1981 to discuss 'The start of the football season [and] the beginning of a new campaign by the National Front and the British Movement'. Peter Alexander letter to Steering Committee members, 16 September 1981. Anti-racist campaigning continued. See Paul Thomas, 1995, 'Kicking racism out of football: A supporter's view', *Race & Class*, vol.36, no.4.

21   Rick Blackman, *Babylon's Burning* (Bookmarks, 2021), p.163.

22   Widgery, 1986, p.111.

23   Pete Jackson, Facebook, 23 April 2019.

24   SWP Central Committee, 1981, 'Fighting the Fascists YES: Squadism NO!', private archive.

25   See Chapter 5, 'Launching the Anti Nazi League'.

26   Huddle & Saunders, 2021, p.135.

27   Nina Hammill in Huddle & Saunders, 2021, p.130.

28   Daniel Rachel, *Walls Come Tumbling Down: The Music and Politics of Rock Against Racism, 2 Tone and Red Wedge* (Picador, 2016), p.222.

29   Red Saunders in Huddle & Saunders, 2021, p.210; Jerry Fitzpatrick in Huddle & Saunders, 2021, p.82.

30   Reference to Mike Barton and Joan Rudder.

31   Jerry Fitzpatrick in Huddle & Saunders, 2021, p.83.

32   *Morning Star* 4 July 1978.

33   Jerry Fitzpatrick in Huddle & Saunders, 2021, p.83.

34   Red Saunders, interviewed by Geoff Brown 28 January 2025.

35   Felix Morrow, *Revolution and Counter-Revolution in Spain* (Pathfinder, 1974); Alex Callinicos, *The New Age of Catastrophe* (Polity, 2023), pp.169–171.

36   *Socialist Worker* 6 May 1978.

37   Examples include Bob Cooney who fought in Spain, see Chapter 5 'Launching the Anti Nazi League', and Edward Redcliffe, active in the Austrian Communist Party in the 1930s and member of Huddersfield ANL. Martin Bobker, Greater Manchester ANL treasurer, fought the Blackshirts as a member of the Young Communist League. Mike Luft, Greater Manchester ANL chair, fought Mosley in the early 1960s.

38   Hal Draper, 1966, 'The two souls of socialism', *New Politics* vol.5, no.1; Duncan Hallas, 1976, 'On the united front tactic: Some preliminary notes', *International Socialism* 85. One example of CP involvement was Mick Murray, the Manchester CP organiser, putting together a detailed programme of activity for the Northern Carnival, leafleting factories, estates and schools and organising a float for the march. Murray worked closely with the Manchester ANL organiser. He was concerned that the SWP shouldn't exploit the sponsors as the Workers Revolutionary Party had a reputation for doing.

39   'Trotskyist bid to take over the Anti Nazi League', *Sunday Express* 30 April 1978.

40   Interviewed in *Evening Sentinel* 3 October 1978; Hain and Holborow, Letters to the editor, *Times* 21 September 1978.

41   Jim Nichol, interviewed by Geoff Brown 19 July 2019.

42   Ralph Darlington & Dave Lyddon, *Glorious Summer* (Bookmarks, 2001), pp.229–231; Chris Harman, *The Fire Last Time: 1968 and After* (Bookmarks, 1988).

43   'No fumbling with the ANL', Colin McGregor, SWP Pre conference Bulletin 3, 1978

44   First witness statement of the Rt Hon. Lord Peter Hain of Neath, 3 March 2020, https://www.ucpi.org.uk/wp-content/uploads/2021/04/UCPI0000034091.pdf.

45   Keith Waterhouse, 'Rock around the plot', *Daily Mirror* 25 September

1978; *Sunday Express* 30 April 1978. See also Paul Morley's mainly negative comments on the ANL and RAR in *New Musical Express* 22 July 1978, after Northern Carnival against the Nazis.

46   'Open letter from John Shiers on Gays and Fascism', *Gay Left* no.6, Summer 1978, pp.30–31. This lengthy piece is helpful in understanding the arguments that were raised on the floor of the national anti-racist, anti-fascist conference that was held in June 1978 in London.

47   Martin Walker, *The National Front* (Fontana, 1977), p.232. See Chapter 5 'Launching the Anti Nazi League'.

48   London Gay Activist Alliance, 1978, *An Anti-Fascist Handbook*, p.79. See Chapter 9 'Counting down to the election'. There were 350 people attending the conference including 100 delegates from ARAF committee.

49   It is worth recalling that Marx pointed out how 'the development of socialist sectarianism and that of the real labour movement always stand in indirect proportion to each other', *Marx Engels Collected Works 44*: p.252, quoted in Alex Callinicos, 'Marx's politics', *International Socialism* series 2, no.158, Spring 2018.

50   Trotsky argued this in the debate in the Communist International on the united front, 'The question of the united front', February 1922, https://www.marxists.org/archive/trotsky/1922/02/uf.htm; Joseph Choonara, 'Trotskyism under the Spotlight', *Socialist Review* June 2018, https://socialistworker.co.uk/socialist-review-archive/trotskyism-under-spotlight/. With different language the same argument can be found in the black civil rights movement in the early 1960s with efforts to pull the Student Non-violent Coordinating Committee (SNCC) into less confrontational work, and, before it, the National Association for the Advancement of Coloured People (NAACP), away from its focus on combating racist violence, towards less confrontational educational work. Megan Ming Francis, 2015, 'Do Foundations Co-opt Civil Rights Organisations?' *HistPhil* 17 August, https://histphil.org/2015/ 08/17/do-foundations-co-opt-civil-rights-organizations cited in Nadia Sayed, 'More than a moment: What did Black Lives Matter achieve?' *International Socialism* 175, Summer 2022

51   Tony Cliff & Donny Gluckstein, *The Labour Party: A Marxist history* (Bookmarks, 1996), p.335. See also Blackman, 2021, p.235.

52   *Sounds* 25 March 1978. This edition had its front cover and an eight-page article on the fight against racism with a centre page spread promoting the carnival.

53   'SWP alleged to influence Anti-Nazi League', *Times* 16 September 1978.

54   Pre-conference issue 1, Socialist Workers Party Bulletin, April 1978, no2.

55   See Chapter 3 'Fighting racism and fascism'.

56   Kate Alexander, private email 25 April 2024.

57   Lucy Whitman in Huddle & Saunders, 2021, p.238.

58   Gavin Weightman, 'Flogging anti-racism', *New Society* 11 May 1978.

59   Ian Birchall, *Tony Cliff: A Marxist for His Time* (Bookmarks, 2011), p.423.

60 SWP Central Committee, 1981, 'Fighting the Fascists YES; Squadism NO!'. After a period of discussion, around thirty members who could not accept the rejection of squadism were expelled from the SWP. Some others who shared their views left of their own accord.

61 Ian Birchall, 'Only rock and roll?', *International Socialism* series 2, no.33. This is Birchall's review of David Widgery's *Beating Time*, the first written history of RAR,

https://www.marxists.org/history/etol/writers/birchall/1986/xx/beatingtime.html

62 First Witness Statement of Lord Peter Hain, UCPI, 3 March 2020, https://www.ucpi.org.uk/publications/first-witness-statement-of-lord-peter-hain/.

63 Owen Jones argues: 'the SWP has long punched above its weight', 'British politics urgently needs a new force – a movement on the Left to counter capitalism's crisis', *Independent* 20 January 2013.

https://www.independent.co.uk/voices/comment/british-politics-urgently-needs-a-new-force-a-movement-on-the-left-to-counter-capitalism-s-crisis-8459099.html

64 Julian Goss, interviewed by Geoff Brown 20 December 2023. There was an ANL counter demo to the NF march against Bloody Sunday commemoration, Cardiff, 'Fascists on the run: Keep the pressure on!', *Socialist Worker* 24 January 1981.

65 Jerry Dammers in Huddle & Saunders, 2021, p.48.

66 Julian Goss, 20 December 2023. There is also the BNP's return to Brick Lane and the push to get rid of them. Dave Gilchrist remembers being there 'when we drove the Nazis off that patch at the top of Brick Lane for the final time', Huddle & Saunders, 2021, p.92. See https://socialistworker.co.uk/features/london-s-radical-east-end/

67 'John McDonnell: Revive Anti-Nazi League to oppose far right', *Guardian* 7 August 2018.

68 'We need to unite against the rising threat of racism and fascism in the UK', *Guardian* 15 August 2018. The letter was signed by Peter Hain, Paul Holborow, Red Saunders, Roger Huddle, Jerry Dammers, Carol Grimes, Tom Robinson and Mykaell Riley.

69 Charge, Oxy and the Morons and local bands played, René of Oxy and the Morons, 'Bands against repression', *Socialist Challenge* 5 July 1979; Rachel, 2016, pp.156–7: John Dennis in Huddle & Saunders, 2021, pp.58–9. David Widgery (ed), 1980, *The Book of the Year*, pp.144–6. 'Rock the block' followed a year later with a free gig in West Belfast supporting Irish republican prisoners. The date, 9 August 1980, was the ninth anniversary of the introduction of internment without trial in Northern Ireland. The prisoners were in the Armagh women's prison and the Long Kesh H blocks, demanding to be recognised as political prisoners and consequently refusing to wear prison clothing, going naked, wrapped only in blankets. Their protest was often described as being 'on the blanket'.

70 "Rock gegen Rechts' 16–17 June 1979, Frankfurt', *Temporary Hoarding* August 1981. Fifty thousand came to the concert. The march to the concert was organised by the DGB, the German trade union federation.

71   Rock Against Racism USA, *Leveller* August 1979. See also *Overthrow* April 1979, Youth International Party Information Service (Yippie!) vol.1, no.1, p.9, https://archive.org/details/overthrow-vol-1-no-1-april-1979.compressed/page/9/mode/2up. Two years later, CND had a 'Northern Carnival Against Missiles' following the same route across Manchester to the same park as the Northern Carnival against the Nazis three years earlier. There was a 'No Nukes Music' group organising a concert tour in support of CND. There was also a concert in aid of the 'Scrap SUS Campaign', 25 May 1979. Rock Against Bush was a project mobilizing punk and alternative musicians against the 2004 US Presidential re-election campaign of George W. Bush, Lars J. Kristiansen, 2016, '"Rock Against Bush:" Punk, Politics, and the 2004 U.S. Presidential Election', *International Communication Research Journal* vol.51, issue 1. A 'Rock Against Genocide' concert in Oslo was advertised in September 2024. A 'Rock Against Trump' compilation album vol.2 is being prepared at the time of writing, March 2025.

72   KEERFA Movement Founding Declaration with list of supporters/sponsors, 2009, (translated into English) https://antiracismfascism-org.translate.goog/index.php/keerfa/%CE%B9%CE%B4%CF%81%CF%85%CF%84%CE%B9%CE%BA%CE%AE/64-2013-10-30-21-16-22?_x_tr_sl=el&_x_tr_tl=en&_x_tr_hl=en&_x_tr_pto=wapp

73   *Socialist Worker* 14 October 2020; Petros Constantinou, 2021, 'How we smashed Golden Dawn', *International Socialism* 169. Smaller examples can be included showing the possibility of starting at a local level. French comrades spoke at the SWP's Marxism 2022 festival on how they used a united front approach to organise against RN in a Paris working-class suburb. Steve Cedar played a leading role in the united front campaign to get rid of five fascist councillor on the council of Vic, a small town in Catalonia. See Steve Cedar, interviewed by Geoff Brown 10 August 2020.

74   Joseph Lorieu, Karl Criton & Serge Dumont, 1985, *Le Système Le Pen* (Editions EPO), p.94, quoted in Jacques Fournier, 'The parliamentary road…to capitalism: The Socialist Party and the left in France 1981–86', *International Socialism* 33, 1986.

75   Peter Fish & Jim Wolfreys, *The Politics of Racism in France* (MacMillan, 1998), p.97.

76   Jonathan Marcus, *The National Front and French Politics: The Resistible Rise of Jean-Marie Le Pen* (MacMillan, 1995), p.52.

77   Fysh & Wolfreys, 1998, pp.43–49.

78   Fysh & Wolfreys, 1998, p.164.

79   Fysh & Wolfreys, 1998, p.166.

80   Fysh & Wolfreys, 1998, p.184

81   I am grateful to Mark Thomas for assistance in the section covering France.

82   Callinicos, 2023; Antonio Gramsci, *Selections from the Prison Notebooks*, pp.275–6.

83   Callinicos, 2023. The title of Callinicos's book refers to Eric Hobsbawm, *Age of Extremes: The Short Twentieth Century, 1914–1991*, pp.21–222. The first part of the book is titled 'The Age of Catastrophe, 1914–1945'.

84   Alvin Tillery, 'From civil rights to racial justice: Understanding African-American social justice movements', Foreign Press Center, US Department of State, 23 April 2021,

https://2021-2025.state.gov/briefings-foreign-press-centers/from-civil-rights-to-racial-justice-understanding-african-american-social-justice-movements/

85   Larry Buchanan, Quoctrung Bui & Jugal K. Patel, 'Black Lives Matter may be the largest movement in U.S. history', *New York Times* July 3, 2020.

86   See also the report in the *Guardian* recording protests in at least 260 cities and towns in Britian, Aamna Mohdin, Glenn Swann, & Caroline Bannock, 'How George Floyd's death sparked a wave of UK anti-racism protests', *Guardian* 29 July 2020.

87   Unite Against Fascism, https://www.facebook.com/UAFpage/?locale=en_GB Stand Up to Racism, https://standuptoracism.org.uk/. The British National Party, founded by Tyndall in 1982, led by Nick Griffin, had over fifty councillors after the 2008 local elections, Electoral performance of the British National Party in the UK, SN/SG/5064, 15 May 2009, https://researchbriefings.files.parliament.uk/documents/SN05064/SN05064.pdf#page=4.99. By May 2012, they had two councillors. After May 2018 they had none. Griffin was elected to the European parliament in 2009 with 8 percent of the vote, Andrew Brons was elected with 9.8 percent. Both lost their seats in the 2014 election, Griffin's vote down to 1.9 percent, Brons getting 1.6 percent. Street-based initiatives such as the English Defence League and the Football Lads Alliance have consistently failed to establish themselves.

88   Lenin, Works, vol.14, pt.1, p.11, quoted by Trotsky, 1970, *The Third International After Lenin*, p.179.

89   Karl Marx, 'Critique of the Gotha Programme' (Progress Publishers, 1970), https://www.marxists.org/archive/marx/works/1875/gotha/ch01.htm

Abbreviations/Acronyms

Action Against Racism	AAR
All Lambeth Action Against Racism	ALARM
All Lewisham Campaign Against Racism and Fascism	ALCARAF
All London Anti-Racist Anti-Fascist Coordinating Committee	ALARAFCC
All London Teachers Against Racism and Fascism	ALTARF
Alternatively für Deutschland	AfD
Amalgamated Engineering Union	AEU
Amalgamated Union of Engineering Workers	AUEW
Anti Nazi League	ANL
Anti-Racist Anti-Fascist Coordinating Committee	ARAFCC
Anti-Racist Committee of Asians in East London	ARCAEL
Asian Youth Organisation	AYO
Associated Society of Locomotive Engineers and Firemen	ASLEF
Association of Broadcasting and Allied Staffs	ABS
Association of Cinematograph, Television and Allied Technicians	ACTT
Association of Jewish Ex-Servicemen and Women	AJEX
Bangladesh Youth Front	BYF
Bengali Housing Action Group	BHAG
Bethnal Green and Stepney Trades Council	BG&STC
Black Unity and Freedom Party	BUFP
British Movement	BM
British National Party	BNP
British Union of Fascists	BUF
Campaign Against Racial Discrimination	CARD
Campaign Against Racism and Fascism	CARF
Campaign Against Racism in the Media	CARM
Campaign Against Racist Laws	CARL
Campaign for Homosexual Equality	CHE
Campaign for Nuclear Disarmament	CND
Cartoon Archetypical Slogan Theatre	CAST
Christians Against Racism And Fascism	CARAF
Civil Servants against the Nazis	CSAN
Communist Party	CP
Communist Party of India (Marxist Leninist)	CPI(ML)
Communist Party of India (Marxist)	CPI(M)
Confederation of British Industry	CBI
Confederation of Shipbuilding and Engineering Unions	CSEU
Constituency Labour Party	CLP
Council Workers against the Nazis	CWAN
Deutschnationale Volkspartei, German National People's Party	DNVP
European Economic Community	EEC
Fascist Union of British Workers	FUBW
Fire Brigades Union	FBU
Football Association	FA
Front National	FN
Gay Activists Alliance	GAA
Gay Liberation Front	GLF

Greater London Council	GLC
Independent Broadcasting Authority	IBA
Independent Labour Party	ILP
Indian Workers Association	IWA
Inner London Education Authority	ILEA
Institute of Race Relations	IRR
Inter-Racial Solidarity Campaign	IRSC
International African Service Bureau	IASB
International Marxist Group	IMG
International Socialists	IS
Joint Campaign Against Racism	JCAR
Joint Council for the Welfare of Immigrants	JCWI
Kommunistische Partei Deutschlands, Communist Party of Germany	KPD
Labour History Archive and Study Centre	LHASC
Leamington Anti-Racist Anti-Fascist Committee	LARAFC
Leicester Council for Community Relations	LCCR
Leicester Inter-Racial Solidarity Campaign	IRSC
Movement for Colonial Freedom	MCF
National Association For Freedom	NAFF
National Council for Civil Liberties	NCCL
National Front	NF
National front Railwaymen Association	NFRA
National Graphical Association	NGA
National Organisation of International Socialist Societies	NOISS
National Socialist Movement	NSM
National Socialist Workplace Cell Organisation	NSBO
National Society of Operative Printers and Assistants	NATSOPA
National Unemployed Workers Movement	NUWM
National Union of Hosiery and Knitwear Workers	NUHKW
National Union of Journalists	NUJ
National Union of Mineworkers	NUM
National Union of School Students	NUSS
National Union of Students	NUS
National Union of Teachers	NUT
Nationaldemokratische Partei Deutschlands	NPD
Nationalsozialistische Deutsche Arbeiterpartei National Socialist German Workers Party	NSDAP
Nonviolent Direct Action	NVDA
North East London Polytechnic	NELP
North Manchester Campaign Against Racism	NORMANCAR
North Staffordshire Campaign Against Racism and Fascism	NorSCARF
Organisation of Arab Petroleum Exporting Countries	OAPEC
Paddington Campaign against Racism	PCAR
Prison Officers Association	POA
Professional Footballers Association	PFA
Racial Awareness Action Society	RAAS
Rassemblement National	RN
Right to Work Campaign	RtWC

Rock against Racism	RAR
Sandwell Campaign Against Racism and Fascism	SCARF
School Kids Against the Nazis	SKAN
Schools Campaign against Racism	SCAR
Scottish Immigrant Labour Council	SILC
Social Democratic Party	SDP
Socialist Workers Party	SWP
Society of Graphical and Allied Trades	SOGAT
Sosialistikó Ergatikó Kómma	SEK
Southall Youth Movement	SYM
Southwark Campaign against Racism and Fascism	SCARF
Special Patrol Group	SPG
Special Demonstration Squad	SDS
Student Campaign against the Nazis	SCAN
Sturmabteilung	SA
Teachers Against Racism	TAR
Tom Robinson Band	TRB
Trade Union Anti-Immigration Movement	TRUAIM
Trades Union Congress	TUC
Transport and General Workers Union	TGWU
Transport and Salaried Staff Association	TSSA
Undercover Policing Inquiry	UCPI
Union of Jewish Students	UJS
Union of Post Office Workers	UPW
Vegetarians against the Nazis	VAN
Women against the Nazis	WAN
Women against Racism and Fascism	WARF
Young Communist League	YCL
Young National Front	YNF
Κίνηση Ενωμένοι Ενάντια στο Ρατσισμό και τη Φασιστική Απειλή, "United Against Racism and the threat of Fascism"	KEERFA

Select bibliography

Interviews and private conversations and emails with Geoff Brown

Mohammed Ajeeb, Dusty Rhodes, Lala Younas, meeting 20 June 2023
Chris Ayton, interview 26 August 2021
Colin Barker, recollections 12 April 2017
Jim Barlow, interview 6 November 2020
Mike Barton, interview 25 May 2020
Doug Beesley, interview 23 November 2021
Helen Blair, interview 28 Sept 2020
Alan Brown, interview 3 March 2023
Jean Boyle, conversation 29 May 2018
Jan Brooker, conversation 30 May 2022
Brian Capaloff, interview 28 February 2022
John Carr, interview 7 March 2023
Jill Catlow, interview 16 June 2021
Steve Cedar, interview 10 August 2020
Lin Clark, interviews 11 August 2021 and 9 September 2021
Peter Cockcroft, emails, 23 December 2019 - 22 January 2020
Kevin Corr, interview 4 January 2021
Roger Cox, interview 1 December 2021
Colette Crosdale, interview 27 May 2018
Michael Crowley, interview 23 September 2021
George Davies, email 11 March 2020
John Deason, interview 23 December 2023
Rehad Desai, interview 28 February 2022
Shaun Doherty, private conversation 25 September 2020
Mark Dolan, interview 17 January 2022
Jan Erik Dubbelman, interview 26 September 2022
Richard Dunn, email 26 February 2020
Greg Dyke, interview 1 September 2021
Pia Feig, interview 29 January 2020
Iain Ferguson, interview Glasgow, 19 October 2020
Jon Flaig, interview 26 April 2023
Nigel Flanagan, interview 25 October 2021
Steve Forey, interview 13 December 2021
George Fuller, interview 19 January 2021
Pete Fysh, interview 31 December 2021
Alan Gibbons, interview 8 May 2018
Alan Gibson, conversation 27 January 2022
David Glanz, interview 18 August 2022
Julian Goss, interview 20 December 2023
Kath Grant, conversation 21 June 2023
Roger Green, interview 1 April 2022
Peter Hain, interview 19 September 2023
Nigel Harris, interview 30 August 2022

Mike Healy, interview 2 December 2021
Paul Holborow, interview 11 May 2020
Sue Johnston and Nick Maloney, interview 26 July 2023
Malcolm Jones, conversation 29 May 2022
Pat Jones, conversation 5 November 2019
Eamonn Kelly, conversation 16 June 2022
David Kersey, interview 12 February 2022
Sally Kincaid, interview 20 January 2020
Bob Light, emails December 2020 - January 2021
Mike and Heather Luft, interviews, 23 November 2018, and 15 November 2021
Chris Lymn, emails 26 July, 2 August, 11 August 2021
Phil Marfleet, interviews 4 December 2019 and 4 March 2023
John Maffia, interview 8 April 2020
Steven Marsh, interview 2 December 2022
Neil McAllister, interview 12 February 2018
Mike McGrath, interview 11 November 2021
Ian Mitchell, interview 13 December 2021
John Murphy, interview 26 February 2021
Jim Nichol, interview 19 July 2019, emails August 2019, 30 June 2020
Mel Norris, interview 29 January 2021
Anna Paczuska, interview 26 February 2023
Brian Parkin, interview 21 August 2022
Pravin Parmar, interview 27 February 2018
Ramila Patel, interview 15 September 2020
Bridget Parsons, interview 20 October 2020
Marian Peacock, interview 13 January 2020
Sheila Peacock, interview 28 September 2021
Dave Peers, interview 27 March 2023
Danny Phillips, interview 2 June 2020
Dick Pitt, interview 7 March 2022
Malcolm Pittock, interview 2 October 2015
Eddie Prevost, interview 18 December 2020
Phil Ramsell, interview 16 February 2021
Balwinder Rana, interview 8 January 2020
Jane Rana, interview 3 March 2023
Dusty Rhodes, conversation 26 June 2021
Anne Robertson, interview 19 November 2021
Jack Robertson, interview 5 November 2019
Joan Rudder, interview 12 October 2021
Sabby Sagall, interview 17 April 2020
Paul Salveson, interview 22 November 2021
Red Saunders, interviews 23 September 2021, 28 January 2025
Dave Sherry, interviews 7 and 16 October 2020, 29 December 2021
David Shonfield, conversation 18 August 2022
Mike Simons, interview 20 February 2020.
Maggie Smith, interview 19 July 2021

Margaret Smith, interview 4 May 2018
Andy Strouthous, interview 1 July 2020, emails 14 July and 8 September 2020
Adrian Sugar, interview 14 October 2021
Colin Thomas, conversation 28 October 2022
Rafique Ullah, interview 4 May 2022
Phil Webster, conversation 13 June 2021
Aidan White, interview 27 April 2020
Jay Williams, interview 6 March 2023

Published works

Action against Racism, *Racism in the Workplace: Report of Conference, Blackburn, 18 June 1977*
Adi, Hakim, *African and Caribbean People in Britain: A History* (Allen Lane, 2022)
Alderman, Geoffrey, 'Anglo-Jewry: The unspoken fears', *Forum on the Jewish people, Zionism, and Israel* vol.3, no.7, 1980, p53–60
Alexander, Peter, *Racism, Resistance and Revolution* (Bookmarks, 1987)
Allen, Peter, '*Socialist Worker*: Paper with a purpose', *Media, Culture and Society*, vol.7, no.2, 1985
Allen, Theodore, *The Invention of the White Race: The Origin of Racial Oppression* (Verso, 2021)
Allen, William, *The Nazi Seizure of Power* (Eyre and Spottiswoode, 1966)
Amin-Smith, Maya, 'Grunwick changed me', *BBC Radio 4*, 2016, https://www.bbc.co.uk/programmes/b07npvfh
Andrews, Geoff, 2004, *Endgames and New Times: The Final Years of British Communism 1964–1991* (Lawrence & Wishart)
Anti Nazi League, 1978, *Documentation on the Politics of the National Front*
Anti Nazi League, 1978, *The National Front and the Jews: Briefing document*
Anti Nazi League, 1978, *Women Against the Nazis*
Anti Nazi League, 1979, *Who Killed Blair Peach?*
Attila the Stockbroker (John Baine), *Arguments Yard: My Autobiography* (Cherry Red Books, 2015)
Avon NUT, *After the Fire: Education in St. Pauls, Bristol* (National Union of Teachers, 1981)
Azad Konor, A. K., *The Battle of Brick Lane* (Grosvenor House Publishing, 2019)
Back, Les, 'Memory, city life and walking', in Bates, Charlotte & Alex Rhys-Taylor, ed., *Walking Through Social Research* (Routledge, 2017)
Bagwell, Philip, *The Railwaymen: The History of the National Union of Railwaymen* (HarperCollins, 1982)
Bain, Peter & John Gennard, *A History of the Society of Graphical and Allied Trades* (Routledge, 1995)
Ball, Roger, *Violent Urban Disturbance in England 1980–81* (University of the West of England, 2012), https://uwe-repository.worktribe.com/out-

put/943122.
Ballard, Roger, 'Up against the Front', *New Society*, 6 May 1976
Barker, Colin, Gareth Dale & Neil Davidson, *Revolutionary Rehearsals in a Neoliberal Age* (Haymarket, 2021)
Beckett, Andy, *When the Lights Went Out: Britain in the Seventies* (Faber, 2009)
Beckman, Morris, *The 43 Group* (Centerprise, 2000)
Beetham, David, *Marxists in Face of Fascism* (Manchester Uni Press, 1983)
Beetham, David, *Transport and Turbans: A Comparative Study in Local Politics* (Oxford Uni Press, 1970)
Begum, Shabna, *From Sylhet to Spitalfields: Bengali Squatters in 1970s East London* (Lawrence & Wishart, 2023)
Bentley, Stuart, 'Merrick and the British Campaign to Stop Immigration: Populist racism and political influence', *Race & Class* vol.36, no.3, 1995.
Bethnal Green and Stepney Trades Council, *Blood on the Streets: A report on racial attacks in East London* (BG&STC, 1978)
Bevins, Vincent, *If We Burn: The Mass Protest Decade and the Missing Revolution* (Wildfire, 2023)
Big Flame, *The Past against Our Future: Fighting Racism and Fascism*, (Big Flame, 1980)
Billig, Michael, *Psychology, Racism & Fascism* (A. F. & R. Publications, 1979)
Binard, Florence, 'The British women's liberation movement in the 1970s: Redefining the personal and the political', *Revue Française de Civilisation Britannique – French Journal of British Studies*, vol.30, no.1, 2017.
Birchall, Ian, 'Only rock and roll?', *International Socialism* series 2, no.33, 1986.
Birchall, Ian, *The Smallest Mass Party in the World: Socialist Workers Party, 1951–1979* (Socialists Unlimited, 1981)
Birchall, Ian, *Tony Cliff: A Marxist for His Time* (Bookmarks, 2011)
Birchall, Sean, *Beating the Fascists: The Untold Story of Anti-Fascist Action* (Freedom Press, 2010)
Birmingham Counter-Fascism Group, 1978, *Countering Fascism: Towards an Alternative Approach*
Biswas, Alok in John Eade ed., *Tales of Three Generations of Bengalis in the UK* (Nirmul Committee, 2006)
Blackman, Rick, *Babylon's Burning* (Bookmarks, 2021)
Blackman, Rick, *Forty Miles of Bad Road: The Stars Campaign for Interracial Friendship and the 1958 Notting Hill Riots* (Redwords, 2017)
Blake, Nick, *The Police, the Law and the People* (Haldane Society of Socialist Lawyers, 1980)
Bland, Benjamin, 'Publish and be damned? Race, crisis, and the press in England during the long, hot summer of 1976', *Immigrants & Minoritie*s vol.37, no.3, 2019.
Blasé, Cazz, 'Invisible women: The role of women in punk fanzine creation', in *Ripped, Torn and Cut: Pop, Politics and Punk Fanzines from 1976*: The subcultures network ed. (Manchester Uni Press, 2018)

Bolsover, Phil, *No Colour Bar for Britain* (Communist Party of Great Britain, 1955)
Bonham, Mark, *Inside the National Front: Sheffield's Nazis Uncovered* (Sheffield Anti-Nazi League, 1978)
Boston, Sarah, *Women Workers and the Trade Unions* (Lawrence & Wishart, 1987)
Bourne, Jenny, 'CARF: The life and times of a frontline magazine', *Race & Class* vol.59, no.3, 2018
Bourne, Jenny, 'Lewisham '77: Success or failure?' *Institute of Race Relations*, 2007, https://irr.org.uk/article/lewisham-77-success-or-failure/
Bradford Trades Council, *No to fascists!* (BTUC, 1976)
Branson, Noreen, *History of the Communist Party of Great Britain: 1927–1941* (Lawrence & Wishart, 1985)
Bristol Trades Union Council, *Slumbering Volcano? Report of an Enquiry into the Origins of the Eruption in St Paul's, Bristol, on 2nd April 1980* (Bristol TUC, 1980)
Brittan, Philip, 'Fighting fascism in Britain: The role of the Anti-Nazi League', *Social Alternatives*, vol.6, no.4, 1987.
Brown, Geoff & Christian Hogsbjerg, *Apartheid is Not a Game* (Redwords, 2020)
Brown, Geoff, 'John Tocher and the limits of commitment', *North West Labour History Journal* vol.42, 2017
Bunsee, Bennie, 'Women in struggle: The Mansfield Hosiery strike', *Spare Rib* vol.21, 1974
Bunyan, Tony, 'The police against the people', *Race & Class*, vol.23, no.2–3, 1981
Caffoor, Mike, *The Fight against Racialism* (Pluto Press, 1971)
Callinicos, Alex, 'Marxism and the crisis in social history', in *Essays on Historical Materialism* John Rees ed. (Bookmarks, 1998)
Callinicos, Alex, 'Race and class', *International Socialism* 55, 1992
Callinicos, Alex, *The New Age of Catastrophe* (Polity, 2023)
Camerawork 17, 'January/February 1980' (Half Moon Photography Workshop)
Camerawork 8, 'Lewisham: What are you taking pictures for?' (Half Moon Photography Workshop)
Campaign against Racism and Fascism/Southall Rights, 1981, *The Birth of a Black Community*
Campaign against Racism in the Media, 1976, *In Black and White: Racist Reporting and How to Fight it*
Campbell, Greig, ed., *So We Marched! An Oral History of the 1981 People's March for Jobs* (Vauxhall Community Law & Information Centre, 2024)
Cant, Bob, 'Normal channels', in Bob Cant & Susan Hemmings, eds. *Radical Records: Thirty Years of Lesbian and Gay History 1957–1987* (Taylor & Francis, 2010)
Carter, Alex, 'The dog that didn't bark?' in Copsey, Nigel & Matthew Worley eds., *Tomorrow Belongs to Us: The British Far Right since 1967* (Routledge, 2017)

Carter, Trevor, *Shattering Illusions: West Indians in British Politics* (Lawrence & Wishart, 1986)
Chessum Lorna, *From Immigrants to Ethnic Minority: Making Black Community in Britain* (Routledge, 2000)
Choonara, Joseph, 'Trotskyism under the Spotlight', *Socialist Review* June 2018
Clark, Howard, 'Non-violent resistance and social defence', in Chester, Gail & Andrew Rigby eds., *Articles of Peace: Celebrating Fifty Years of Peace News* (Prism Press, 1986)
Cliff, Tony & Donny Gluckstein, *The Labour Party: A Marxist history* (Bookmarks, 1996)
Cliff, Tony, *A World to Win* (Bookmarks, 2000)
Cliff, Tony, *The Crisis, Social Contract or Socialism* (Pluto Press, 1975)
Clutterbuck, Richard, *Britain in Agony: The Growth of Political Violence* (Faber & Faber, 1978)
Coard, Bernard, *How the West Indian Child is Made Educationally Sub-Normal in the British School System* (New Beacon, 1971)
Cockerell, Michael, 'Inside the National Front', *Listener* 28 December 1972
Colin Roach Centre, *Anti Nazi League: A Critical Examination, 1977–81/2 & 1992–95* (Resistance, 1995)
Communist Party, *The British Road to Socialism*, (Farleigh Press Ltd., 1977)
Communist Party, *Racism: How to Combat It* (Communist Party National Race Relations Cttee, 1978)
Conservative Party, General Election Manifesto 1979
Constantine, Learie, *The Colour Bar* (Stanley Paul, 1954)
Constantinou, Petros, 'How we smashed Golden Dawn', *International Socialism* 169, 2021
Cook, Dave, *A Knife at the Throat of Us All: Racism and the National Front* (Communist Party of Great Britain, 1978)
Cooney, Bob, *Proud Journey: A Spanish Civil War Memoir* (Manifesto Press, 2015)
Copsey, Nigel & David Renton, eds., *British Fascism, the Labour Movement and the State* (Palgrave, 2005)
Copsey, Nigel & Matthew Worley, 'The far right, punk and British youth culture', *JOMEC Journal* 9, 2016.
Copsey, Nigel, *Anti-Fascism in Britain* (Palgrave MacMillan, 2000)
Copsey, Nigel, *Anti-Fascism in Britain* (Routledge, 2016)
Counter Information Services, 1979, *Ford: Anti Report No 20*
Coupland, Philip, '"Left-wing fascism" in theory and practice: The case of the British Union of Fascists', *Twentieth Century British History*, vol.13, no.1, 2002
Cox, Judy & Colm Bryce, *We Fought the Law: Political Protests and Police Violence in Britain 1968–2021* (Bookmarks, 2022)
Cox, Oliver, *Caste, Class and Race* (Monthly Review Press, 2000)
Cross, Colin, *Fascism in Britain* (Barrie & Rockcliffe, 1961)
Crossman, Richard, *The Diaries of a Cabinet Minister, vol.1* (Cape, 1975)
Croucher, Richard, *Engineers at War 1939–1945* (Merlin, 1982)

Crowley, Michael, *Comrades Come Rally: Manchester Communists in the 1930s and 1940s* (Bookmarks, 2022)
Cunningham, Steve & Michael Lavalette, *Schools Out!* (Bookmarks, 2016)
Darlington, Ralph & Dave Lyddon, *Glorious Summer* (Bookmarks, 2001)
Davis, Mike & Jon Wiener, *Set the Night on Fire: L.A. in the Sixties* (Verso, 2020)
Deason, John, 'One year of the Right to Work campaign', *International Socialism* 93, 1976
D'Emilio, John, *Sexual Politics, Sexual Communities: The Making of a Homosexual Minority in the United States 1940–1970* (Chicago Uni Press, 1983)
Dempsey, Mike, 'David King: King of Kings', *Graphic Journey*, 2009, https://mikedempsey.typepad.com/graphic_journey_blog/2009/04/king-of-kings.html
Dresser, Madge, *Black and White on the Buses: The Colour Bar Dispute in Bristol* (Bookmarks, 2013)
Dummett, Michael, *Southall 23 April 1979: Report of the Unofficial Committee of Enquiry* (National Council of Civil Liberties, 1980)
Dyke, Greg, 'Race: Can Labour make up the ground it lost by dodging the issue?' *Tribune* 3 September 1976
Eatwell, Roger, *Western Democracies and the New Extreme Right Challenge* (Routledge, 2004)
Edgar, David, 'The National Front: The case for no television platform', typescript, Communist Party archive, LHASC, n.d.
Edgar, David, 'Racism, fascism and the politics of the National Front', *Race & Class*, vol.19, no. 2, 1977
Edgar, David, *Support the Wolverhampton Anti-racists: Drop All the Charges!* (Wolverhampton Anti-Racist Committee, 1978)
Edgar, David, *The Second Time as Farce* (Lawrence & Wishart, 1988)
Elizabeth Dekeyser, *Islam, Exclusivity, and the State in France* (Massachusetts Institute of Technology, 2019)
Esteves, Olivier & Stéphane Porion, eds., *The Lives and Afterlives of Enoch Powell: The Undying Political Animal* (Routledge, 2019)
Fanon, Frantz, *The Wretched of the Earth* (Penguin, 1967)
Farrar, Max, 'Social movements and the struggle over 'race", in: Todd, Malcolm J. & Gary Taylor, *Democracy and Participation: Popular Protest and New Social Movements* (Merlin Press, 2004)
Fielding, Nigel, *The National Front* (Routledge, 1981)
Fielding, Peter & Laurie Flynn, *He's the Nazi from Lancashire: The Truth about Kingsley Read and His National Party* (Socialist Worker, 1976).
Fighting Talk, 'Brief encounters: A history of anti-fascism in Oxford', *Libcom.org*, 2019, https://libcom.org/library/brief-encounters-history-anti-fascism-oxford
Flett, Keith, 'The Battle of Wood Green 23rd April 1977', *KMFlett's Blog*, 2017, https://kmflett.wordpress.com/2017/08/13/the-battle-of-wood-green-23rd-april-1977/
Paul Foad of the Au Pairs, interviewed by Alex Bradley, July 2023,

Foot, John, *Blood and Power: The Rise and Fall of Italian Fascism* (Bloomsbury, 2022)
Foot, Paul, *Immigration and Race in British Politics* (Penguin, 1965)
Foot, Paul, *The Rise of Enoch Powell* (Penguin, 1969)
Foot, Paul, *Workers Against Racism* (International Socialists, 1973),
Frith, Simon & John Street, 'Rock Against Racism and Red Wedge: From music to politics, from politics to music', in Garafola, Reebee, ed., *Rockin' the Boat: Mass Music and Mass Movements,* (South End Press, 1992).
Fryer, Peter, *Staying Power: The History of Black People in Britain* (Pluto Press, 1984)
Gable, Gerry & Maurice Ludmer, *A Well-oiled Nazi Machine: An Analysis of the Growth of the Extreme Right in Britain* (A F & R Publications, 1974)
Gale, Jack, *The Anti-Nazi League and Fascism* (News Line, 1978)
Gilbert, Tony & Jim Thakoordin, *Eradicate Racism: A Murderous Crime* (Liberation, 1985)
Gilbert, Tony, *Danger: Racialists at Work* (Liberation, 1974)
Gilbert, Tony, *Only One Died* (Kay Beauchamp, 1975)
Gildart, Keith, *Images of England Through Popular Music: Class, Youth and Rock'n'Roll, 1955–1976* (Palgrave, 2013)
Gilroy, Paul, *There Ain't No Black in the Union Jack* (Routledge, 1987)
Ginsborg, Paul, *A History of Contemporary Italy* (Penguin, 1990)
Gluckstein, Donny, *The Nazis, Capitalism and the Working Class* (Bookmarks, 1999)
Glynn, Sarah, *Class, Ethnicity and Religion in the Bengali East End: A Political History* (Manchester Uni Press, 2014)
Goodyer, Ian, *Crisis Music: The Cultural Politics of Rock Against Racism* (Manchester Uni Press, 2009)
Gopal, Priyamvada, *Insurgent Empire: Anticolonial Resistance and British Dissent* (Verso, 2019)
Gossweiler, Arbeiterklasse und Faschismus, 1986, https://www.globale-leipzig.de/wp-content/uploads/2022/11/Arbeiterklasse-und-Faschismus.pdf
Gramsci, Antonio, *Selections from the Prison Notebooks* (Lawrence & Wishart, 1971)
Grant, Ted, *The Menace of Fascism: What It Is and How to Fight It* (Revolutionary Communist Party, 1948)
Gravesend Anti Nazi League, *Blair Peach: Anti-Racist Socialist Murdered, 23 April 1979* Gravesend Anti Nazi League, *Gravesend: A Model for Racial Harmony?*, 1981
Greenstein, Tony, *The Fight Against Fascism in Brighton & the South Coast* (Brighton History Workshop, 2011)
Griffin, Roger, *The Nature of Fascism* (Routledge, 1993)
Guerin, Daniel, *Fascism and Big Business* (Monad Press, 1973)
Hain, Peter, *Outside in* (Biteback Publishing, 2012)
Hallas, Duncan, 'On the united front tactic: Some preliminary notes', *International Socialism* 85, 1976
Hallas, Duncan, *Indomitable Revolutionary* (Bookmarks, 2023)

Hancox, Alfie, 'The Anti-Nazi League, "Another White Organisation"? British Black Radicals agaisnt Racial Fascism', *Historical Materialism*, vol. 31, no.3, 2023

Hann, Dave & Steve Tilzey, *No Retreat* (Milo Books, 2003)

Hann, Dave, *Physical Resistance: A Hundred Years of Anti-Fascism* (Zero Books, 2013)

Haringey TUC & London Socialist Historians Group, 2002, *The Battle of Wood Green*

Harker, Ben, *Class Act: The Cultural and Political Life of Ewan MacColl* (Pluto, 2007).

Harman, Chris, 'The summer of 1981: A post-riot analysis', *International Socialism* series 2, no.14, 1981

Harvey, David, *A Short History of Neoliberalism* (Oxford Uni Press, 2005)

Haslam, Dave, *Manchester, England: The Story of the Pop Cult City* (Fourth Estate, 2010)

Heineman, Benjamin, *The Politics of the Powerless* (Oxford Uni Press, 1972)

Henderson, Frank, *Life on the Track: Memoirs of a Socialist Worker* (Bookmarks, 2009)

Herbert, Michael, *Never Counted Out! The Story of Len Johnson: Manchester's Black Boxing Hero and Communist* (Dropped Aitches Press, 1992)

Hick, John, *The New Nazism of the National Front and National Party: A Warning to Christians* (AFFOR, 1977)

Hill, Christopher, 'Political discourse in early 17th century England', in *A Nation of Change and Novelty* (Routledge, 1990)

Hill, Ray with Andy Bell, *The Other Face of Terror: Inside Europe's Neo-Nazi Network* (Grafton Books, 1988)

Hippe, Oskar, *And Red Is the Colour of Our Flag* (Index, 1991)

Hirsch, Shirin & Geoff Brown, 'Breaking the 'colour bar': Len Johnson, Manchester and anti-racism', *Race & Class* vol.64, no.3, 2023

Hirsch, Shirin, 'Young people against racism in 1980s London schools', *UCL Special Collections*, 2023, https://blogs.ucl.ac.uk/special-collections/2023/01/09/young-people-against-racism-in-1980s-london-schools/

Hirsch, Shirin, *In the Shadow of Enoch Powell* (Manchester Uni Press, 2018)

Hobsbawm, Eric, *Age of Extremes: The Short Twentieth Century, 1914–1991* (Michael Joseph, 1994)

Hobsbawm, Eric & Terence Ranger, eds., *The Invention of Tradition* (Cambridge Uni Press, 1983)

Holborow, Paul, 'The Anti Nazi League and its lessons for today', *International Socialism* 163, 2019

Home Office, 2024, *The Historical Roots of the Windrush Scandal: Independent Research Report*

Howard, N. & I. Taylor, 'How the National Front organised in Rotherham', *Leveller* 1, 1976

Howe, Darcus, *From Bobby to Babylon: Blacks and the British Police* (Bookmarks, 2020)

Huddle, Roger & Red Saunders, eds., *Reminiscences of RAR* (Redwords, 2021)
Huddle, Roger, 'Hard rain', *Socialist Review* 4, 1978
Humphries, Barbara, *The Origins and Development of the Labour Movement in West London 1918–1970* (Reading Uni, 2018), http://centaur.reading.ac.uk/85254/12/22827343_Humphries_thesis_updated.pdf
International Marxist Group, *Fascism: How to Smash It* (IMG, 1974)
International Socialists, *National Front: The New Nazis* (IS, 1974)
International Socialists/Chingari, 1974, *The Black Worker in Britain*
Itzin, Catherine, *Stages in the Revolution: Political Theatre Since 1968* (Eyre Methuen, 1980)
Jacobs, Joe, *Out of the Ghetto: My Youth in the East End, Communism and Fascism, 1913–39* (Janet Simon, 1978)
Jones, Terry, *British Movement: Nazis on Our Street* (Anti Nazi League, c1981)
Josephides, Sasha, *Towards a History of the Indian Workers' Association*, 1991, https://warwick.ac.uk/fac/soc/crer/research/publications/research_papers/rp_no.18.pdf
Jouhl, Avtar Singh, 'LIfe-long fighter against racism', *International Socialism* 164, 2019
Kaes, Anton, Martin Jay & Edward Dimendberg, eds., *The Weimar Republic Sourcebook* (Uni of California Press, 1994)
Karlin, Miriam, *Some Sort of a Life* (Oberon, 2007)
Kershaw, Ian, *Hitler: 1889–1936: Hubris* (Penguin, 1998)
Kinnock, Neil interviewed by LBC, 'The Anti-Nazi League formed', London Broadcasting Company, 10 November 1977
Klemperer, Victor, *I Shall Bear Witness* (Weidenfeld & Nicolson, 1998)
Kureishi, Hanif, *My Beautiful Laundrette and The Rainbow Sign* (Faber, 1986)
Kushner, Tony & Nadia Valman, *Remembering Cable Street: Fascism and Anti-fascism in British Society* (Vallentine Mitchell, 1999)
Kushnick, Louis, '"Over policed and under protected": Stephen Lawrence, institutional and police practices', *Sociological Research Online*, vol.4, no.1, 1999, <http://www.socresonline.org.uk/4/1/kushnick.html>
Kyriakides, Christopher, *The Anti-Racist State: An Investigation into the Relationship Between Representations of 'Racism', Anti-Racist Typification and the State: A 'Scottish' Case Study* (Glasgow Uni, 2005).
Labour Party, 1979, *Labour Manifesto*
Labour Party, n.d. [c1976], *Labour against Racism*
Leech, Kenneth, *Brick Lane 1978: The Events and Their Significance* (Stepney Books, 1994)
Leeds Libraries, 'Rock Against Racism (1977)', The Secret Library, 2019, https://secretlibraryleeds.net/2019/10/25/rock-against-racism/ (Accessed 13 May 2025)
Leicester April 21st Defence Committee, *Support the Leicester 87!* (Anti Nazi League, 1979)
Lindop, Fred, 'Racism and the working class: Strikes in support of Enoch

Powell in 1968', *Labour History Review* vol.66, no.1, 2001

Linehan, Thomas, *British fascism, 1918–1939: Parties, Ideology and Culture* (Manchester Uni Press, 2021)

Livingstone, Morag & Matt Foot, *Charged: How the Police Try to Suppress Protest* (Verso, 2022)

London Gay Activist Alliance, *An Anti-Fascist Handbook* (LGAA, 1978)

Macklin, Graham, *Failed Führers: A History of Britain's Extreme Right* (Routledge, 2020)

MacShane, Denis, *Black and Front: Journalists and Race Reporting,* (NUJ Race Relations Sub Committee, 1978)

Mahamdallie, Hassan, 'A history of Muslim workers in Britain', *International Socialism* 113, 2007

Manningham Defence Committee, 1976, *Carnival Sit-down Against the National Front*

Marcus, Greil, *Lipstick Traces: A Secret History of the Twentieth Century* (Faber, 2011)

Marsh, Kevin & Robert Griffiths, *Granite and Honey: The Story of Phil Piratin, Communist MP* (Manifesto Press, 2012)

Martin Barker, *The New Racism: Conservatives and the Ideology of the Tribe* (Junction Books, 1981)

Martin López, Tara, *The Winter of Discontent: Myth, Memory, and History* (Liverpool Uni Press, 2014)

Mason, Lisa, *The Development of the Monday Club and its Contribution to the Conservative Party and the Modern British Right, 1961 to 1990* (Wolverhampton Uni, 2004)

Mason, Paul, *How to Stop Fascism* (Allen Lane, 2021)

Mayakovsky, Vladimir, ed. James Womack, *Vladimir Mayakovsky: And Other Poems*, (Fyfieldbooks, 2026)

McCarthy, Liam, 'The National Front and the BNP in Leicester and Leicestershire', (University of Leicester, 2021).

McDonnell, Bill, 'Jesters to the revolution: A history of Cartoon Archetypical Slogan Theatre (CAST), 1965–85', *Theatre Notebook* vol.64, no.2, 2010

McGrath, John, ed. Nadine Holdsworth, *John Mcgrath: Plays for England* (Exeter Uni Press, 2005)

McIntosh, Sam, *Open Justice and Investigations into Deaths at the Hands of the Police, or in Police or Prison Custody* (City University, London, 2016), https://openaccess.city.ac.uk/id/eprint/15340/1/McIntosh,%20Sam.pdf.

Messina, A. M., 'Race and party competition in Britain: Policy formation in the post-consensus period', *Parliamentary Affairs* vol.38, no.4, 1985

Messina, Anthony, *Race and Party Competition in Britain* (Clarendon Press, 1989)

Miles, Robert & Annie Phizacklea, 'The T.U.C. and Black Workers 1974–76', *British Journal of Industrial Relations* vol.16, no.2, 1978

Moore, Robert, *Racism and Black Resistance in Britain* (Pluto Press, 1975)

Morgan, Kevin et al, *Communists and British Society 1920–1991: People of a Special Mold* (Rivers Oram Press, 2005)

Mosley, Oswald, interviewed by David Frost with live audience on Rediffusion 15 November 1967
https://youtu.be/oWqIExUfp4Q?si=NMB3NCaRRou01zef
Murphy, Dylan Lee, *The Communist Party of Great Britain and its Struggle Against fascism 1933–1939* (Huddersfield, 1999), https://eprints.hud.ac.uk/id/eprint/4855/1/323773.pdf#page=3.06
National Front, 1978, *How to Combat Red Teachers*
National Front, *Education for National Survival* (National Front Policy Department, 1976)
National Front, *Taking the Lid off the Anti Nazi League* (National Front News Research Department, 1978)
National Union of Students, *The Myth of Red Lion Square* (NUS, 1974)
Newham Monitoring Project/Campaign against Racism and Fascism, *Newham: The Forging of a Black Community* (Newham Monitoring Project, 1991)
Newsinger, John, 'In the middle of the road: Fenner Brockway, the Independent Labour Party and the class struggle', *International Socialism* series 2, no.179, 2023
Newsinger, John, *The Blood Never Dried: A People's History of the British Empire* (Bookmarks, 2013)
Nicholson, Brian, *Racialism, Fascism and the Trade Unions* (TGWU, Region 1, Docks Group, 1974)
Northam, Gerry, *Shooting in the Dark: Riot Police in Britain* (Faber, 1988)
Nugent, N., 'The anti-immigration groups', *New Community* 5, 1976
Orwell, George, *Collected Essays, Journalism and Letters, vol.1, 1920–1940* (Penguin, 1970)
Parsons, Tony, *Stories We Could Tell* (HarperCollins, 2005)
Paxton, Robert O, *The Anatomy of Fascism* (Penguin, 2005)
Pearce, Joseph, *Race with the Devil: My Journey from Racial Hatred to Rational Love* (Saint Benedict Press, 2013)
Peukert, Detlev, *Inside Nazi Germany* (Penguin, 1989)
Peukert, Detlev, *The Weimar Republic* (Penguin, 1991)
Phillips, Trevor & Mike Phillips, *Windrush: The Irresistible Rise of Multi-Racial Britain* (HarperCollins, 1998)
Piratin, Phil, *Our Flag Stays Red* (Lawrence & Wishart, 1978)
Polsgrove, Carol, *Ending British Rule in Africa: Writers in a Common Cause* (Manchester Uni Press, 2009)
Power, Lisa, *No Bath but Plenty of Bubbles: An Oral History of the Gay Liberation Front, 1970–1973* (Cassell, 1995)
Power, Mike, *The Fascist Threat: A Young Communist Review of Fascist and Authoritarian Trends* (YCL, 1974)
Power, Mike, *The Struggle Against Fascism and War in Britain, 1931–1939* (History Group of the Communist Party, 1977)
Purewal, Balraj, *Southall Youth Movement 1976–1984* (The Asian Health Agency, 2023)
Rachel, Daniel, *Walls Come Tumbling Down: The Music and Politics of Rock Against Racism, 2 Tone and Red Wedge* (Picador, 2016)

Ramamurthy, Anandi, 'The politics of Britain's Asian Youth Movements', *Race & Class* vol.48, no.2, 2006

Ramamuthy, Anandi, *Black Star: Britain's Asian Youth Movements* (Pluto, 2013)

Ramelson, Bert, *The Social Contract: Cure-all or Con-trick?* (Communist Party of Great Britain, 1974)

Rana, Balwinder, '"Fifty pints of lager, please!": Half a century of British Asian struggles', *International Socialism* 172, 2021

Randall, Kevin interview with LBC, 'Kevin Randall on teachers' National Front opposition' http://bufvc.ac.uk/tvandradio/lbc/index.php/segment/0000800394008

Ranson, David, *The Blair Peach Case: Licence to Kill* (Friends of the Blair Peach Committee, 1980)

Red Action, *We are Red Action* (Red Action, n.d.)

Rees, Paul, *The Three Degrees: The Men Who Changed British Football Forever* (Constable, 2014)

Reilly, Jimmy, *Anger on the Road* (Bookmarks, 1979)

Renn, Margaret, *Paul Foot: A Life in Politics* (Verso, 2024)

Renton, David, 'Anti-fascism in the North West 1976–1982', *North West Labour History Journal* 27, 2002

Renton, David, 'Guarding the barricades: Working-class anti-fascism 1974–1979', in Copsey, Nigel & David Renton eds., *Fascism, the Labour Movement and the State* (Palgrave, 2005)

Renton, David, 'Politics that breaks down people's fear: The Anti-Nazi League in retrospect', *Overland* 212, 2012

Renton, David, 'The killing of Blair Peach', *London Review of Books,* vol.36, no.10, 2014, https://www.lrb.co.uk/the-paper/v36/n10/david-renton/the-killing-of-blair-peach

Renton, David, 'Was fascism an ideology? British fascism reconsidered', *Race & Class* vol.41, no.3, 2000

Renton, David, *Fascism: Theory and Practice* (Pluto, 1999)

Renton, David, *Never Again: Rock Against Racism and the Anti-Nazi League 1976–1982* (Routledge, 2019)

Renton, David, *When We Touched the Sky: The Anti-Nazi League 1977–1981* (New Clarion Press, 2006)

Revolutionary Communist Group, 1979, *The Anti-Nazi League and the Struggle Against Racism*

Richard Buckwell, 'Spurs against the Nazis', n.d., https://antifascistarchive.net/wp-content/uploads/2012/09/spurs-against-the-nazis.pdf

Richards, Frank, *Under a National Flag: Fascism, Racism and the Labour Movement* (Revolutionary Communist Tendency, 1978)

Right to Work Campaign, *Interim Report of the March of Unemployed Workers, Manchester–London, 27 February–20 March 1976*

Rippingdale, James, 'Lewisham, London 1977: Notes on fighting fascism', *AlJazeera*, 24 Nov 2018 www.aljazeera.com/features/2018/11/24/lewisham-london-1977-notes-on-fighting-fascism

Roberts, Ernie, *Strike Back* (Self-published, 1994)

Roberts, Ernie, *Workers' Control* (Allen & Unwin, 1973)
Roberts, Robert, *The Classic Slum* (Penguin, 1971)
Robins, David, We Hate Humans (Penguin, 1984)
Robinson, Geoff, *Never Again: The lessons of 1976* (Bradford Trades Union Council)
Robinson, Lucy, *Gay Men and the Left in Post-war Britain: How the Personal Got Political* (Manchester Uni Press, 2011)
Rogaly, Joe, *Grunwick* (Penguin Books, 1977)
Roots Oral History Project, *Rude Awakening: African/Caribbean Settlers in Manchester: An Account* (Ahmed Iqbal Ullah Race Relations Resource Centre, Manchester Central Library, 1992)
Rose, John, 'The Southall Asian Youth Movement', *International Socialism* 91, 1976
Rose, John, *Solidarity Forever: 100 years of Kings Cross ASLEF* (Kings Cross ASLEF, 1986)
Rose, Sonya O., 'Race, empire and British wartime national identity 1939–45', *Historical Research*, vol.74, no.184, 2001
Rosenberg, Chanie, 'Labour and the fight against fascism', *International Socialism* series 2, no.39, 1988
Rosenberg, David, 'Anti-Nazi League: The carnival is not over', *Rebel Notes*, 30 April 2018, https://rebellion602.wordpress.com/?s=The+carnival+is+not+over
Rosenhaft, Eve, *Beating the Fascists?: The German Communists and Political Violence, 1929–1933* (Cambridge Uni Press, 1983)
Rudge, John, *Rebel Rebel: The Youth Publications of the SWP from the 1950s to the 1980s* (Ian Birchall's blog, 2015), https://grimanddim.org/tony-cliff-biography/rebel-rebel/
Ryback, Timothy, *Takeover: Hitler's Final Rise to Power* (Headline, 2024)
Said, Edward, *Culture and Imperialism* (Vintage, 1994)
Samuel, Raphael, 'David Widgery 1947–1993', *History Workshop Journal*, vol.35, no.1
Saunders, Red, interviewed by Ken Olende, 2016 https://web.archive.org/web/20170506042854/http://uaf.org.uk/2016/10/40-years-since-the-birth-of-rock-against-racism-rebel-music-that-broke-down-fear/
Sayed, Nadia, 'More than a moment: What did Black Lives Matter achieve?' *International Socialism* 175, 2022
Red Saunders and Roger Huddle, interviewed by Ian Goodyer, 3 June 2000,
Schorske, Carl, *Fin-de-siecle Vienna: Politics and Culture* (Knopf, 1980)
Schwarz, Bill, *The White Man's World* (Oxford Uni Press, 2011)
Searle, Chris ed., *One for Blair* (Young World, 1989)
Sedgwick, Peter, 'The problem of fascism', *International Socialism* series 1, no.42, 1970
Serdiville, Rosie, *The Battle of Stockton: How a Small Town Saw off Fascists in 1933* (The Historical Association, 2018)
Shaffer, Ryan, *Music, Youth and International Links in Post-War British Fascism: The Transformation of Extremism* (Springer, 2017)

Sheffield Anti Nazi League, 1978, *Inside the National Front: Sheffield's Nazis Uncovered*
Shelton, Syd, *Rock Against Racism 1976–1981* (Autograph ABP, 2015)
Shepherd, John, *Crisis? What crisis? The Callaghan Government and the British 'Winter of Discontent'* (Manchester Uni Press, 2016)
Sherwood, Marika, *Claudia Jones: A Life in Exile* (Lawrence & Wishart, 1999)
Shiers, John, 'Fighting fascism: An open letter', *Gay Left* 6, Summer 1978
Shipley, Peter, *Extremism and the left* (Conservative Central Office, 1981)
Sillett, Paul, 'By any means necessary: Physical resistance: A hundred years of anti-fascism, *International Socialism* series 2, no.143, 2014
Sim, Joe, '"We are not animals..." Prisons, protest, and politics in England and Wales 1969–1990', *Social Justice* vol.18, no.3, 1991
Sivanandan, Ambalavaner, 'From resistance to rebellion: Asian and Afro-Caribbean struggles in Britain', *Race & Class* vol.23, no.2–3, 1981
Smith, Evan, '"By whatever means necessary": The origins of the "no platform" policy', *New Historical Express*, 2015, https://hatfulofhistory.wordpress.com/2015/11/03/by-whatever-means-necessary-the-origins-of-the-no-platform-policy/
Smith, Evan, 'A bulwark diminished? The Communist Party, the SWP and anti-fascism in the 1970s', *Socialist History* vol.35, 2009
Smith, Evan, 'Class before Race: British communism and the place of empire in postwar race relations', *Science & Society* vol.72, no. 4, 2008
Smith, Evan, *British Communism and the Politics of Race* (Haymarket, 2018)
Smith, Evan, *No Platform: A History of Anti-Fascism, Universities and the Limits of Free Speech* (Routledge, 2020)
Socialist Worker, 'How we stopped the Nazis in the 1970s', 22 October 2005
Socialist Worker, 'Remembering Rock Against Racism: How music helped to fight the Nazis', 6 December 2016
Socialist Workers Party, *The Fight against Fascism and for Socialism* (SWP, 1978)
Sonabend, Daniel, *We Fight Fascists: The 43 Group and Their Forgotten Battle for Post-War Britain* (Verso, 2019)
Southall SWP, *Southall: The Fight for Our Future* (SWP, 1979)
Sparks, Colin, 'Fascism and the working class part 1: The German experience', *International Socialism* series 2, no.2, 1978
Sparks, Colin, 'Fascism and the working class part 2: National Front today', *International Socialism* series 2, no.3, 1978
Sparks, Colin, 'Fascism in Britain', *International Socialism* series 1, no.71, 1974
Sparks, Colin, *Fascism and the National Front* (SWP, 1977)
Sparks, Colin, *Never Again! The Hows and Whys of Stopping Fascism* (Bookmarks, 1980)
Spike, Sharon, 'Straight at the head of the NF', *Northern Hoarding*
Spriano, Paolo, *The Occupation of the Factories* (Pluto Press, 1975)
Street, John, *Politics and Popular Culture* (Polity Press, 1997)

Taylor, Becky, '"Our most foreign refugees": Refugees from Vietnam in Britain', in Becky Taylor et al, *When Boat People were Resettled 1975–1983* (Palgrave, 2021)

Taylor, Richard & Colin Pritchard, *The Protest Makers: The British Nuclear Disarmament Movement of 1958–1965, Twenty Years On* (Pergamon, 1980)

Taylor, Richard, *Against the Bomb: The British Peace Movement 1958–1965* (Oxford Uni Press, 1988)

Taylor, Stan, 'The far right fragments', *New Society* 26 March 1981

Taylor, Stan, *The National Front in English Politics* (Macmillan, 1982)

Teachers Against the Nazis, 1978, 'Nazis begin with this...and end with this: Urgent information for teachers'

Thackara, John, 'The mass media and racism', in Garder, Carl ed., *Media, Politics and Culture: A Socialist View* (MacMillan, 1979)

Thomas, Colin, *Facing up to the Fascists: Confronting the National Front in Bristol* (Bristol Radical Pamphleteer, 2019)

Thomas, Mark L., 'Fascism in Europe today', *International Socialism* 162, 2019

Thomas, Paul, 'Kicking Racism Out of Football: A supporter's view', *Race & Class* vol.36, no.4, 1995

Thomas, Robert, *Sir Bob* (Senior Publications, 1984)

Thurlow, Richard, 'The failure of British fascism 1930 to 1940 in Andrew Thorpe ed., *The Failure of Political Extremism in Interwar Britain* (Exeter Uni Press, 1989)

Thurlow, Richard, *Fascism in Modern Britain* (Sutton, 2000)

Trades Union Congress, *Equality for Women within Trade Unions* (TUC, 1989)

Trades Union Congress, *Organising Against Fascism in the Workplace* (TUC, 2008)

Trotsky, Leon, *History of the Russian Revolution* (Pluto, 1977)

Trotsky, Leon, *The Struggle against Fascism in Germany* (Pathfinder, 1971)

Turnbull, Eileen, *A Very British Conspiracy* (Verso, 2022)

Tyndall, John, *Beyond Capitalism and Socialism: Industrial Policy for the Modern Age* (National Front, 1975)

Tyndall, John, *Six Principles of British Nationalism* (Albion Press, 1966)

Utley, T. E., *Enoch Powell: The Man and His Thinking* (William Kimber, 1968)

Virdee, Satnam, 'Anti-racism and the socialist left 1968–79', in Evan Smith & Matthew Worley eds., *Against the Grain: The British Far Left from 1956* (Manchester Uni Press, 2014).

Virdee, Satnam, *Racism, Class and the Racialized Outsider* (Palgrave, 2016)

Walker, Martin, 'The National Front', in H. M. Drucker ed., *Multi-Party Britain* (Macmillan, 1979).

Walker, Martin, *The National Front* (Fontana, 1977)

Ward, Paul, Graham Hellawell & Sally Lloyd, 'Witness Seminar: Anti-Fascism in 1970s Huddersfield', *Contemporary British History*, vol.20, no.1, 2006, https://doi.org/10.1080/13619460500444981

Webber, G., 'Patterns of membership and support for the British Union of Fascists', *Journal of Contemporary History* vol.19, no.4, 1984

Weightman, Gavin, 'Flogging anti-racism', *New Society* 11 May 1978

Widgery, David ed., *The Book of the Year* (Ink Links, 1980)

Widgery, David, 'Quick history of the rise, fall and rise again of the Agit-prop Committee in the Socialist Workers Party over the last three years, *Wedge* magazine, issue 2, 1978.

Widgery, David, *Beating Time* (Chatto & Windus, 1986)

Widgery, David, Carnival against the Nazis, *Radical America*, vol.12, no.5, 1978

Widgery, David, *Some Lives* (Sinclair-Stevenson, 1991)

Widgery, David, *The Left in Britain 1956–68* (Penguin, 1976)

Wilcox, Bernie, *What Can a Poor Boy Do?* (Bowden Publishing, 2009)

Wild, Rosalind Eleanor, *Black Was the Colour of Our Fight: Black Power in Britain, 1955–1976* (Sheffield Uni Press, 2008)

Wilde, Florian, 'Divided they fell: The German left and the rise of Hitler', *International Socialism* 137, 2013

Wilkinson, Bruce, *Hidden Culture, Forgotten History: A Northern Poetic Underground and its Countercultural Impact* (Penniless Press Publications, 2017)

Williams, Gwyn, *Proletarian Order* (Pluto Press, 1975)

Wills, Clair, *Lovers and Strangers: An Immigrant History of Post-war Britain* (Allen Lane, 2017)

Wilson, Colin, *Socialists and Gay Liberation* (Socialist Worker, 1995)

Wolfreys, Jim, '"The centre cannot hold": Fascism, the left and the crisis of French politics', *International Socialism* series 2, no.95, 2002

Women and Fascism Study Group, Centre for Contemporary Cultural Studies, 'Patriarchy and Patriotism', *Red Rag* 13, 1978

Women and Fascism Study Group, Centre for Contemporary Cultural Studies, 'Women and the National Front', *Red Rag* 14, 1979

Woodruff, William, *The Road to Nab End* (Eland, 2000)

Wrench, John, 'Unequal comrades: Trade unions, equal opportunity and racism', (University of Warwick, 1986)

Zinn, Howard, *People's History of the United States* (HarperCollins, 2009)

Zinn, Howard, *You Can't Be Neutral on a Moving Train* (Beacon Press, 2002)

TV, Film and video

Adrian Cousins, *Eddie Prevost: 1968 The Year the World Caught Fire*, 31 May 2008, https://www.youtube.com/watch?v=aNHXMw8SVDU

AP Archive, *News Item*, 17 November 2016, https://www.youtube.com/watch?v=r76zd5p5r-M

AP Archive, *SYND 18 6 78, Anti Nazi League Meeting in E. London*, 24 July 2015, www.youtube.com/watch?v=uxCxyXBPFJ4

AP Archive, *SYND 24 4 76 National Front March in Bradford*, 24 July 2015, https://www.youtube.com/watch?v=k4Br6V9cAGE

AP Newsroom, *SYND 30 4 78, Anti Nazi League March Against National*

Front Party, 13 March 2010, www.aparchive.com/metadata/UK-ANTI-NA-ZI-MARCH/3a77a65fe80b96426d7035127d33270d

AP Newsroom, *SYND 9 1 78, Demonstrations in East London Against Judge*, 28 January 2010, www.aparchive.com/metadata/UK-DEMO/0ca97e951dd402b8c90a087c5c665767

Bagheera, *Blacks' Britannica*, 23 December 2016, https://youtu.be/lsKeRFpyKNw

BBC 1, Tonight, 16 October 1978 'including an enquiry into the origins and aims of the Anti Nazi League'. Presented by Sally Hardcastle https://genome.ch.bbc.co.uk/schedules/service_bbc_one_london/1978-10-16, see 'SWP not helped by Anti-Nazi campaign, *Jewish Chronicle* 27 October 1978

Brian Knight, *World in Action: These Children Are Mine*, 11 May 2021, www.youtube.com/watch?v=g-T4lcI8ork

DailyMotion, *World in Action – The Nazi Party (3rd July 1978)*, 8 December 2015, https://player.bfi.org.uk/free/film/watch-the-national-party-1976-online

Desai, Rehad dir., *Born into Struggle*, Uhuru Digital, 2004, https://www.youtube.com/watch?v=dJn-_7yYGI8

digitalworks51, *Young Rebels: The Story of the Southall Youth Movement*, 13 August 2014, https://www.youtube.com/watch?v=OGWX233kHPg

Edgar, David, *Destiny*, 1976 (Eyre Methuen)

Faro, Muniro, 'The struggle of black workers', Workers Film Association, 1982,

Football Fans Against Fascism, *Micky Fenn (1938-1996) Docker, Trade Unionist, Anti-Fascist*, 2 August 2018, https://www.youtube.com/watch?v=51CEnTXaTng

Hardy, Noel dir., *Somebody's Daughter*, ILEA Television, 1978, https://www.imdb.com/title/tt0887236/

Heaven, Simon dir., *A Safe Place to Be* (Spitalfields), Compass Films, 1980, https://player.bfi.org.uk/free/film/watch-a-safe-place-to-be-1980-online#:~:text=This%20episode%20of%20Home%20from,the%20Bangladeshi%20community%20living%20there.

IMDb, 'The National Front', *This Week*, ITV, 5 September 1974, https://www.imdb.com/title/tt2214327/?ref_=ttrel_rel_tt

Jeremiah Quinn, *Oluwale*, 14 October 2023, https://youtu.be/wJHc5KvoATM?si=I88Oz3cVgp-6AobZ

leedsmuseums, *Rock Against Racism*, 15 August 2017, https://www.youtube.com/watch?v=DR01x9waNqI

mrchristianjohnson, *The Clash at Rock against Racism Victoria Park*, 18 June 2010, https://www.youtube.com/watch?v=4xRaVbW-iBM

National Portrait Gallery, *Navir Singh – Southall 79*, 13 December 2021 https://www.youtube.com/watch?app=desktop&v=F1n4l4zesSA&feature=youtu.be

Newsreel Collective dir., *Divide and Rule – Never!*, 1978, https://player.bfi.org.uk/free/film/watch-divide-and-rule-never-1978-online

Nothern Carnival, *The Day It Became Cool To Be Anti Racist - Manchester's Carnival Against The Nazis*, July 1978, https://www.youtube.com/

watch?v=_OZBjPCcdps
Richard Marks (AntiFascistArchive), *Archive in Focus: Syd Shelton, Rock Against Racism*, 7 September 2013, https://www.youtube.com/watch?v=kQs8gfiUnCE&t=30s
Southall Campaign Committee, 'Southall on Trial', BBC *Open Door* 22 September 1979
SWP TV, *Confronting the Nazis: The Battle of Lewisham 1977*, 2017, https://www.youtube.com/watch?v=fi14XozEzW0
ThamesTv, *Racism | East London | Asian Community | Our People | 1978*, 18 September 2016, https://youtu.be/Eyuw50IYk4A
ThamesTv, *Anti Nazi League| Rock against Racism | Protest | Demonstration | Thames Television |1978*, 17 September 2016, www.youtube.com/watch?v=tvmUVE05XRQ
ThamesTv, *Racism in Britain | The danger of the right | British Movement | British far-right |This Week | 1980*, 4 May 2021, https://www.youtube.com/watch?v=D2AYk4aBbIo
Woodford, Sue dir., 'The National Party', *World in Action*, 22 November 1976, https://player.bfi.org.uk/free/film/watch-the-national-party-1976-online

Photos
Camerawork no.8, Lewisham: What are you taking pictures for? Half Moon Photography Workshop, , 1977, https://archive.leftove.rs/documents/GQN/1. See also Paul Trevor interviewed by Carla Mitchell, 11 May 2017, Oral History Recording, https://www.fourcornersarchive.org/archive/view/0003826
Whitmore, Greg, 'Flares and fury: The Battle of Lewisham 1977 – in pictures, *Guardian* 12 August 2017, https://www.theguardian.com/uk-news/gallery/2017/aug/12/flares-and-fury-the-battle-of-lewisham-1977?fbclid=IwAR1tbxNvv-px060g7LztYbhqYeHLkX80NNE5eZCRw5Bw-5eghoZqvSastZw

Archives
The following libraries and archives hold Anti Nazi League and other relevant material.
Ahmed Iqbal Ullah Race Relation Resource Centre (AIU), Manchester Central Library
Archives +. Manchester Central Library
Bishopsgate Institute, Bishopsgate, London
Bradford Collections, West Yorkshire Archive Service
British Library, King's Cross, London
Labour History Archive and Study Centre (LHASC) People's History Museum, Manchester
Leeds Discovery Centre
Modern Records Centre, University of Warwick. This includes the National Union of Mineworkers archive
National Archives (NA), Kew, London
Working Class Movement Library (WCML), Salford

Index

43 Group, 57, 262
7:84, 154

Accrington, 41
Action Against Racism (AAR), 56, 71, 75, 132
Afgan, Sher, 194
Ahmed, Tassaduq, 116
Albany Empire, 272
Albert against the Nazis, 230
Alderman, Geoffrey, 265
Alexander, Juliet, 239
Alexander, Peter/Kate, 303, 310-2, 315-6, 319-20, 326, 342
Alhadidi, Ribhi, 72
Ali, Altab, 239-40, 246
Ali, Ishaque, 241, 244
Ali, Tariq, 143, 174, 277, 285, 342
Ali, Tosir, 236
All Leeds Campaign Against Racism, 271
All Lewisham Campaign Against Racism and Fascism (ALCARAF), 79, 91
All London Anti-Racist Anti-Fascist Coordinating Committee (ARAFCC), 92, 112, 279, 341,380 (note 70), 381 (note 89), 385 (note 13)
All London Teachers Against Racism and Fascism (ALTARF), 203
Allen, Dave, 218
Allen, Jim, 189, 190
Allende, Salvador, 42
Amalgamated Union of Engineering Workers (AUEW), 54, 59, 118, 138, 142, 185, 186
Amrouche, Sheila, 86, 226
Anderson, Viv, 225
Anderton Must Go campaign, 122, 388 (note 60)
Anderton, James, 121-2, 137, 198, 324, 388 (note 58)
Archer, Tom, 228
Arnold Labour Club, 139
Arsenal, 224, 254
Ashton, Joe, 124, 128, 130, 134, 137, 223, 340
Asian Youth Organisation (AYO), 73, 75, 122, 137
Association of Broadcasting and Allied Staffs (ABS), 258
Association of Jewish Ex-Servicemen and Women (AJEX), 259, 260, 265, 269
Aswad, 159, 327
August 13th Ad Hoc Organising Committee, 93
Auschwitz, 128
Ayton, Chris, 149, 156
Azad Konor, A. K., 243
Azai, Ben, 263

Bain, Peter, 165
Baine, John (Attila the Stockbroker), 158, 161
Balham, 78
Balwinder, Rana, 55, 253; in Gravesend, 74; in Southall, 285, 329
Bangladesh Welfare Association, 237, 239
Bangladesh Youth Front (BYF), 237, 241, 243
Barker, Colin, 129, 132, 183, 209, 212
Barking, 166, 206
Barlow, Jim, 230
Barnett, Colin, 121, 131, 137, 386 (note 25)

Barrett, Terry, 15
Barton, Mike, 136, 140
Bass, Alfie, 128
Bath, 229
Batson, Brendan, 222
Battle of Manchester, 113
Beale, Tania, 262
Beard, Gerald, 48
Bedfordshire, 190
Beesley, Doug, 227, 256
Beevers, Pete, 192
Bengali Housing Action Group (BHAG), 235, 240
Benn, Tony, 132, 246, 301, 314, 375 (note 193)
Bennett, Weyman, 211
Bethnal Green, 206
Bidwell, Syd, 107
Birchall, Ian, 332, 334 (note 8), (note 10), 362 (note 1), 367 (note 76), 392 (note 136)
Birmingham Action Committee Against Racism in Clubs, 278
Birmingham Trades Council, 138
Birmingham, 7, 15, 16, 53, 55, 73, 87, 123, 163, 177, 180, 181, 204, 257, 311, 320, 365 (note 49), 377 (note 18)
Bishop of Southwark, 96-7
Biswas, Aloke, 191, 240-1, 243
Blackburn, 39-42, 44-5, 56, 59, 70-1, 74-5, 152, 188, 305, 373 (note 154)
Black Echoes, 149
Black Solidarity Day Strike against Racism, 241-2, 244-5
Black Unity and Freedom Party, 59
Blair, Helen, 217
Board of Deputies of British Jews, 96, 131, 244, 259-61, 264-7, 278
Bobker, Martin, 132, 260
Bolton, 41, 73-5, 122, 137-8, 173, 291
Booth, Albert, 190
Bournemouth, 125
Bow, 236
Bowie, David, 151
Bowdler, John, 204
Bracknell Against Nazis, 247
Bradford, 41, 53, 67, 69, 70, 77, 228, 278, 282, 291, 305, 325, 371 (notes 123, 130, 132, 136)
Bradford Telegraph and Argus, 252,
Bragg, Billy, 172
Brearley, Mike, 129
Brent council, 283, 385 (note 17)
Brent Trades Council, 81
Brentford Football Club, 226-7
Brentford Supporters Against the Nazis, 226
Brick Lane, 75, 175, 187, 217, 235-270
Brighton, 135, 148, 195, 229, 331
Brighton and Hove Anti-fascist Committee, 257
Brighton Evening Argus, 257
Bristol, 49, 134, 142, 168, 206, 208, 228, 233, 254, 307, 339, 351, 353 (notes 3, 5)
Bristol Rovers, 226
British Council of Churches, 264
British Leyland, 177
British Movement (BM), 40, 112, 166, 190, 308-9, 311, 315-6, 321-2

Index **485**

British National Party (BNP), 15, 33, 123, 185
British Union of Fascists (BUF), 30-2, 57, 62, 106, 121, 178, 358 (note 24)
Brockwell Park, see Carnival
Brons, Andrew, 330
Brown, Geoff, 168, 418 (note 293)
Buckton, Ray, 186
Buckwell, Richard, 108, 225, 228, 379 (note 51)
Bulldog, 103, 209-12, 318, 330
Bundy, Richard, 101
Burgess, Ken, 254
Burgon, Colin, 222
Bus workers, 48, 53, 193-4, 230
Bus Workers against the Nazis, 193
Byrne, Colin, 173

Cable Street, 31, 55-6, 99, 106, 109, 365 (note 55), 366 (note 57), 384 (note 2)
Callaghan, James, 65-6, 198, 273-4, 281, 293, 338, 370 (note 110)
Camden 277
Camden Journal, 253-4
Camerawork 256
Cameron, James, 129, 258
Campaign Against Racism and Fascism (CARF), 93, 271
Campaign Against Racism in the Media (CARM), 250, 253
Campaign Against Racist Laws (CARL), 303-5
Campaign Against Racist Slogans, 238
Campaign for Nuclear Disarmament (CND), 320, 395 (note 4)
Canaries Against the Nazis, 227
Capeloff, Brian, 216
Cardiff, 135, 190, 233, 316, 322, 345
CARF (newspaper), 93, 231, 384 (note 9)
Carleton Greene, Hugh, 249
Carnival Procession Against the Nazis, 233
Carnival, Brockwell Park, 246, 248, 316
Carnival, Victoria Park, 165-175
Carron, Bill, 54
Carthy, Martin, 233
Cartoon Archetypical Slogan Theatre (CAST), 146-7, 153, 278
Castle, Barbara, 56
Catlow, Jill, 152
Cedar, Steve, 154, 226, 244, 284
Chadha, Gurinder, 170-1
Chaggar, Gurdip Singh, 72-3, 78, 92, 126, 237
Challinor, Ray, 50
Chamberlain, Bob, 104
Chand, Gokal, 96
Chapel Market, 276
Chapeltown, 53
Charles, Wilf, 49
Charlton, Jack, 128, 130, 224, 251
Chelmsford, 217
Chelsea, 224, 318-9
Chelsea Town Hall, 189
Cheltenham, 184, 321
Chesterton, A.K., 32-4
Chichester cathedral, 45
Chile, 42, 153, 300
Choudhri, Dinesh, 72
Christian Aid, 96
Christians Against Racism and Fascism, 79
Churchill, Winston, 36, 55, 263, 354 (note 13)

Cimarons, 155, 162
Civil servants, 135, 189-190
Civil Servants against the Nazis (CSAN), 190
Clapham, Mike, 192
Clapton, Eric, 148-9, 151, 397 (note 52)
Clash, 156, 166, 171
Cliff, Tony, 117, 177, 247-8, 297, 339, 387 (note 35)
Clough, Brian, 128, 130, 218-9, 224, 228, 390 (note 108)
Coard, Bernard, 202
Cohen, Manny, 142
Cole, Stan, 142
Communist Party of Great Britain (CP) 15, 57-8, 78, 90, 92, 106-8, 118, 135, 141-2, 147, 166, 180, 211, 229, 238, 271-2, 301, 335, 338, 402 (note145)
Communist Party of India, 53
Community Relations Council, 74-5 88, 112, 116, 230, 278, 289, 374 (notes 176, 181)
Concert for Bangladesh, 145
Confederation of Shipbuilding and Engineering Unions (CSEU) 230
Conservative Party, 32-3, 41, 44, 63, 273
Constantine, Learie, 48
Constructivism, 153-4
Conway Hall, 63 -4, 251, 317, 369 (note 99)
Cook, Dave, 107, 228, 279
Cooney, Bob, 142
Cooper Clark, John, 233
Copleston High School, 211
Corby Against Nazis, 247
Corr, Kevin, 170
Cosmopolitan, 257
Costello, Elvis, 247
Council workers, 190, 230, 282
Council Workers Against the Nazis (CWAN) 190
Cousins, Jane, 129
Coventry, 64, 118, 148, 194, 197, 233, 278, 322-3, 364 (note 32)
Cox, Roger, 82, 385 (note 17)
Crawley, 198, 282
Crerand, Pat, 129, 319
Crewe, 215
Cricklewood, 82
Crisis (band), 215
Critchley, Julian, 255
Crooks, Garth, 225
Crowley, Michael, 96-7, 99
Cullis, Cathy, 85
Cunliffe, Lawrence, 137
Cunningham, Laurie, 223
Curran, Charles, 249

Dagenham, 167, 227
Daily Herald, 55
Daneford School, 206
Dash, Jack, 107, 354 (note 8)
Dassu, Mohammed Ali, 75
Davies, George, 56
Davies, John, 361 (note 91)
Davies, Julie, 89
De Freitas, Michael, 50
Deason, John, 105
Dennis, John, 102, 155, 336
Deptford, 66, 94-5, 104, 185, 204, 239, 261, 272, 319

Derbyshire Times, 210
Desai, Jayaben, 81, 83, 135
Desai, Rehad, 73, 216
'Destiny', 130
Dewsbury, 138, 313
Digbeth Hall, 138, 163
Director of Public Prosecutions, 85, 210, 305,
Dobie, Keith, 102
Dockers, 14-15, 61-2, 79, 83, 154
Dockers Against Racism, 79, 113, 368 (note 85)
Dockers Against the Nazis, 61
Dodgin, Bill, 226
Doherty, Shaun, 204
Dolan, Mark, 179
Drabble, Margaret, 128
Drastic Measures, 195, 408 (note 101)
Dromey, Jack, 81
Duckett's Common, 88
Duncan, John, 225
Dunn, Bill, 141, 271, 273, 337
Dunne, Julian, 254
Durham, 57,
Durham cathedral, 192
Dyke, Greg, 75-6

Eagle, Peggy, 197
Ealing, 163
Ealing Council, 233, 278, 284-6, 291, 293, 418, (note 297)
Ealing NUT, 205
East Ender (Bristol), 228
East Ender (London), 87, 252, 254
Eccles Journal 256
Economist, 52, 65
Edgar, David, 130, 254-6, 258
Edgbaston, 53
Edinburgh, 200, 210, 233
Edmonds, Richard, 44, 86, 204
Edmondson, John, 168
Edwards, Beresford 55
Eisenstein, Sergei, 147, 150
Electrical Trades Union, 96
Equity, 192
Evening of Music and Comedy, 233
Excalibur House, 247, 277
Exodus, 233

Fabulous Poodles, 195
Fascist Union of British Workers (FUBW), 178
Federation of Bangladeshi Organisations, 244
Federation of Conservative Students, 273
Feig, Pia, 56, 169
Fenn, Micky, 368 (note 85)
Ferguson, Iain, 200
Finchley School Kids against Nazis, 168, 216
Fire Brigades Union (FBU), 135, 167
Fisher, Samuel, 266-9
Fitzgerald, Patrik, 171
Fitzpatrick, Jerry, 90-2, 108, 165, 331, 336-7
Flame, 85,
Flanagan, Nigel, 220-2
Flannery, Martin, 124, 342
Fokriuddin, Ahmed, 244
Folk Against Racism, 233
Foot, Paul, 58, 65, 87, 143
Ford Dagenham, 183, 272
Ford Halewood, 274

Ford Langley, 286
Ford Workers Against the Nazis, 167
Forey, Steve, 188
Foster, Christopher, 85
Foster, David, 273
Fountaine, Andrew, 38, 307
France, 26, 153, 337, 348-50
Friend, Richard, 267
Fuller, Simon, 205
Furness, Paul, 150, 158, 161, 317

Gandhi, Kamlesh, 143
Gardner, 167
Garnett, Tony, 255
Gately, Kevin, 64-5
Gay Liberation Front, 157, 197, 271
Gay News, 198-201
Gay News Defence Committee, 198
Gays Against Fascism, 198-9
Gays Against the Nazis, 172, 201
GEC Elliot, 196
Generation X, 155, 162
Gewirtz, Jacob, 264-5
Gibbons, Alan, 71, 98
Gilbert, Clive, 25
Gilbert, Tony, 65, 368 (note 95)
Gilchrist, Dave, 171
Gill, Harpal Singh, 72
Gill, Ken, 297
Gilroy, Paul, 292, 394 (note 170), 441 (note 147)
Glanz, David, 95, 102
Glasgow, 142, 217, 277, 320
Glasgow Trades Council, 193
Golders Green, 262, 278
Goldman, Vivian, 158, 167
Goodyer, Ian, 292
Gordon, Kim, 377 (note 21)
Gormley, Joe, 42
Granada Reports, 129, 231
Grans and Kids Against Nazis, 247
Grant, Alec, 193
Grant, Nick, 205
Gravesend, 74-5
Greaves, Bob, 129
Gregory, Ruth, 161
Griffin, Nick, 211
Grimes, Carol, 154-5, 159
Grunwald, Henry, 260
Grunwick strike, 81-4, 184
Grunwick Strike Committee, 143
Guardian, 44, 90, 104-6, 129, 130, 143, 203-4, 218, 258
Guterman, Henry, 263
Guttersnipe, 152

Habershon, Roy, 64
Habonim, 262
Hackney, 74, 274 (note 176)
Hackney Campaign against Racism, 166
Hackney and Tower Hamlets Defence Committee, 241-2, 247
Hackney Downs School, 217
Hackney Gazette, 239, 253
Hackney Town Hall, 155, 162, 277
Hailsham (Quintin Hogg), 104, 251
Hain, Peter, 117-8, 124, 136, 139-40, 142, 258, 260, 273, 279, 302, 313, 314, 340, 345, 387

(note 39)
Hall, John, 150, 183, 309
Hallas, Duncan, 106, 325
Halliday, Dave, 182
Hammill, Steve, 192
Hammill, Nina, 336
Harding, Suzy, 97
Haringey Councillors Against Racism, 88
Harpers & Queen, 251
Harraway, Sid, 272
Harris, Nigel, 129
Hattersley, Roy, 17, 257
Heath, Edward/Ted, 14, 43, 178, 184, 291, 357 (note 1)
Helm, David, 106, 285, 290
Hemel Hempstead, 123
Henderson, Frank, 181-2
Henry, Owen, 49
High Wycombe, 194, 215, 219, 232
Hillingdon, 205, 276
Hillock synagogue, 259
Holborn Trades Council 48
Holborow, Paul, 116-9, 124-6, 136-7, 139, 143, 191, 219, 231, 245, 247-8, 258, 261, 264, 267, 271, 277, 285, 321, 337, 339, 387 (note 37)
Hospitals, 135, 186, 189, 230, 273, 277, 293
Hounslow Anti Nazi League, 226
Hounslow Festival against Racism, 278
Hounslow Town Hall, 40
Howe, Darcus, 237, 331
Hoxton, 239, 277,
Huddersfield, 23, 38, 168, 291
Huddersfield Trades Council, 79, 84
Huddle, Roger, 146-9, 151, 154, 159, 165
Hull, 275
Humm, Bob, 161
Hunjan, Jaswant, 74
Hunt Saboteurs Association, 231-2
Hyde, 121-2, 137

Ilford, 139- 141, 168, 261, 393 (note 154)
Imperial Typewriters, 46, 51-3, 58, 177, 179
Imperialism, 24, 181-2, 367 (note 81)
Indian Workers' Associations (IWAs), 53, 72-3, 194, 237, 245-6, 283, 285, 287, 303, 305, 311, 322, 364 (note 32), 422 (note 71), 436 (note 122), 443 (note 32)
Inner London Education Authority (ILEA), 203, 209, 220, 411 (note 164)
Inter-Racial Solidarity Campaign (IRSC), 58, 79, 283-4
International Marxist Group (IMG), 59, 65,
International Socialists (IS), 59, 68, 74-5, 85 105, 147, 343, 354 (note 10), 366 (note 69), 387 (note 35)
Irlam, 229
IS Agit-prop Committee, 153, 397 (note 38)
Islington, 45, 180, 212, 253, 276
Islington 18 Defence Committee, 85, 159, 377 (note 17)
Islington Gazette, 254, 411 (note 149)
Islington Gutter Press, 404 (note 20)

Jackson, Glenda, 128
Jackson, Pete, 334
Jackson, Tom, 105
Janner, Greville, 131

Jarvis, William, 55
Jefferys, Steve, 121, 441 (note 15)
Jenkins, Roy, 45, 56, 70, 202, 365 (note 49)
Jewish Chronicle, 140, 261, 263, 265-6
Jewish Socialist Group, 171, 260
John, Gus, 202, 455 (note 180)
Johnson, Len, 48, 363 (note 12)
Johnson, Linton Kwesi, 109, 316, 451 (note 124)
Joint Committee Against Racialism (JCAR), 264
Jones, Anthony, 183
Jones, Jack, 43, 52, 66, 368 (note 94 and note 95)
Jones, Mick, 166
Jones, Ron, 193
Jordan, Colin, 308
Joseph, Keith, 82
Jouhl, Avtar, 53, 302, 311, 422 (note 71)

Karlin, Miriam, 127-8, 197, 260, 264, 390 (note 91), 408 (note 98), 453 (note 147)
Kartoon Klowns, 147
Keane, Anna, 196
Kennedy, Graham, 248
Kent Workers Against Racism, 253
Kersey, David, 211
Keys, Bill, 245-6, 278
King, David, 110, 124-5, 150, 396 (note 26)
King, Ken, 183
King, Martin Luther, 13, 243, 371 (note 128)
King's Cross, 187-8
Kingston Campaign Against Racism and Fascism, 79
Kinnock, Neil, 124, 125, 267, 388 (note 64)
Kleinman, Philip , 140
Kodikara, Patrick, 246, 248, 421 (note 48), 422 (note 82)
Kornilov, Lavr, 60

Labour left, 56
Labour Party, 16-7, **54-6**, 57-8, 66, 72, 75-77, 87, 92, 99, 117, 119, 127,130, 139, 142, 183, 193, 203, 232, 237, 255, 272, 301, 310, 338, 340, 342, 346, 365 (note 43), 431 (note 21), 442 (note 22)
Labour Party Young Socialists, 179
Ladywell Fields, 93, 96
Lancashire Evening Telegraph, 70-1
Lane, David, 245
Lansbury, George, 55-6
Latham, Arthur, 232, 246
Lauder, Charles, 253
Lazenby, Peter, 261
League of Coloured Peoples, 48
Leamington, 167, 311
Leamington Anti Racist Anti Fascist Committee (LARAFC), 112, 143, 256, 303, 312, 385 (note 11)
Leeds, 53, 112, 127, 161, 195, 198-99, 220-22, 231, 253, 257, 259-61, 271 , 273, 305, 308, 317, 319-20, 325, 326, 329, 331, 456 (note 189)
Leeds Supporters Against the Nazis, 226
Leeds Trades Council, 139
Leeds WARF, 197
Leicester, 38-44, 51, 58, 70, 79, 128, 230, 254, 256, 260, **283-4**, 292, 294-5, 307, 376 (note 199)
Leicester Trades Council, 136
Leicester Mercury, 52, 256, 260, 282
Lemon, Denis, 198-9

Lenin, Vladimir, 153, 351,
Leveller, 399 (note 68)
Levenshulme, 122
Levin, Bernard, 122, 258
Lewis, Aubrey, 260
Lewis, Jerry, 260
Lewisham, 21, 85-6, **91-109**, 111-3, 119-20, 195, 200, 302, 332, 380 (note 68), 394 (note 171)
Lewisham 21 Defence Committee, 85, 97
Lewisham council, 94
Lewisham Trades Council, 91
Leyton Orient, 226, 227
Liberal Party, 119, 168, 304, 361 (note 88)
Liberation, 63, 368 (notes 92, 94), 369 (note 98)
Light, Bob, 10, 78, 154
Limousine, 155
Lindsay, John, 199
Lissitzky, El, 153
Liverpool, 32, 41, 163, 257, 280, 316-7, 322, 325, 329, 400 (note 104), 416 (note 265), 455 (note 176), 456 (note 2)
Lobb, Michael, 62, 180
London Gay Activist Alliance, 79
Longbridge, **180-183**, 392 (note 133), 404 (note 26), 431 (note 29)
Loughton, 259
Ludmer, Maurice, 79, 124, 132, 266, 308, 425 (note 125)
Ludovic Kennedy, 255
Luxemburg, Rosa, 25
Lyddon, Dave, 10, 195
Lymn, Chris, 128
Lyon, Alex, 70

MacColl, Ewan, 136, 233
Madeleine (pseudonym), 97
Mahamdallie, Hassan, 172
Maitles, Henry, 217
Makin, Andy, 169
Makonnen, Ras, 48, 367 (note 81)
Malawi, 70
Manchester, 40-1, 45, 48-9, 55, 59, 121, 127, 129, 132, 136, 153, 163, 168, 180, 189, 190, 193, 194, 198, 229-30, 232-3, 251, 263, 277, 280-2, 310, 319, 358 (note 24), 366 (note 73), 394 (note 162, note 172), 400 (note 104), 405 (note 32), 417 (note 288), 458 (note 38)
Manchester AUEW district committee, 142
Manchester Evening News, 251
Manchester Polytechnic, 144, 183-4
Manchester Royal Infirmary, 48
Manchester Trades Council, 121, 388 (note 60)
Mankowitz, Gered, 166
Manley, Norman, 48
Manningham, 67-9
Manningham Defence Committee, 68-9
Mansfield Hosiery Mills, 50-1, 53,
Mapam, 262
Marley, Bob, 98, 145-6
Martyn, John, 233
Matumbi, 155
Mayakovsky, Vladimir, 146, 153,
McAllister, Neil, 135
McGahey, Mick, 141
McGregor, Colin, 184
McGregor, Sheila, 87, 251
McKechnie, Andy, 199

McKinnon, Neil, 126-7
McLennan, Gordon, 141
McLintock, John, 193
McNee, David, 94-5, 104-5, 139, 290-1, 293-4
Meerut, 57
Megahy, Tom, 138
Mehmood, Fazal, 68
Mehmood, Tariq, 69
Mellish, Bob, 70
Melly, George, 128
Melody Maker, 149, 159
Merrick, Jim, 40-1, 67, 249
Merrill, Derek, 162
Merton, 193
Meyer, Hubert, 126
Mikardo, Ian, 169, 401 (note 115)
Militant Entertainment, 280
Military Revolutionary Committee, 60
Milligan, Spike, 219
Millwall, 223, 227, 319
Miners Against the Nazis, 191-2
Minter, Wayne, 108, 155, 417 (note 286)
Misty in Roots, 162, 166, 287, 237, 399 (note 82)
Mitchell, Ian, 191
Mitchell, Warren, 128, 260
Mokgatle, Barney, 152
Moody, Harold, 48
Moonman, Eric, 265
Morning Star, 57, 78, 106-7, 141, 271, 337
Morrison, Eddie, 185, 317,
Mosley, Oswald, 30-2, 35, 57, 121, 239
Moss Side, 233, 325
Murray, Len, 82, 245

Nassa, Aminur, 244
National Association for Freedom (NAFF), 82
National Association for Multi-Racial Education, 206
National Front (NF), 7, 32, 34, 38, 44, 53, 56, 62, 70, 86, 87, 99, 105, 119, 122, 169, 179-80, 191, 194, 197, 203, 206, 210, 220, 222, 239, 247, 308, 309
National Front Constitutional Movement, 307
National Front News/NF News, 87, 228, 259
National Front Railwaymen Association (NFRA), 186
National Front Students Association, 67
National Front Trade Union Association (NFTUA), 179
National Graphical Association (NGA), 252
National Party, 45, 66, 71, 78, 239. 358 (note 29), 368 (note 87), 373 (notes 153, 155), 374 (note 181), 431 (note 30)
National Socialist Workplace Cell Organisation (NSBO), 178
National Unemployed Workers Movement (NUWM), 57
National Union of Journalists (NUJ), 252-4, 257, 281, 425 (note 132)
National Union of Public Employees (NUPE), 121, 186, 189, 190, 277, 294
National Union of Railwaymen (NUR), 186, 188, 405 (note 44)
National Union of School Students (NUSS), 212, 313, 411 (note 161), 451 (note 122)
National Union of Students (NUS), 62, 64, 142, 264

National Union of Teachers (NUT), 143, 204, 210
Nerva, Lawrie, 265
New Cross, 85-6, 91, 319-20
New Musical Express (NME), 149, 158, 173, 217, 219, 402 (note 145), 414 (note 214)
New National Front, 308
Newcastle Chronicle, 163
Newham, 61, 62, 78, 113,180, 236, 244, 248, 276, 367 (note 84), 404 (note 23), 420 (note 36) 447 (note 86), 454 (notes 162, 163)
Newham Recorder, 62, 203, 256
Newport, 229
Nichol, Jim, 10, 34, 65, 114, 145, 165, 192, 335, 339, 369 (note 102
Niemoeller, Martin, 134
No Platform, 62-3, 368, (note 90)
Noor, Naranjan Singh, 245
Norman, Roger, 252
Norris, Mel, 225
North London Divisional Post Office (NDO), 179
North London Polytechnic, 127
North London WARF, 196
North Manchester Campaign Against Racism (NORMANCAR), 232
North Staffordshire Campaign Against Racism and Fascism (NorSCARF), 112
Northwest Hackney ANL, 231
North West Committee Against Racialism, 233
North West Spanner, 153
Norwich, 227
Notting Hill Carnival, 53, 85, 156, 365 (note 41), 382, (note 119), 393 (note 149)
Nottingham, 42, 139, 168, 277, 393 (note 161), 418 (note 302), 448 (note 84)
Nottingham Forest, 128, 224, 227

Okon, Uduaci, 184
Oldham, 41, 216, 273, 304, 309, 413 (note 208), 415 (note 251), 443 (notes 35, 37)
Open Door, 67, 249, 250, 295, 396,(note 34), 440 (note 169)
Operation PNH, 85
Orbach, Maurice, 260
Orient Against the Nazis, 227
Oxford, 229, 277, 321, 400 (note 104), 415 (note 251)

Paczuska, Anna, 238
Paddington, 313
Page, Andie, 215
Pakistan, 41, 88, 116, 244, 361 (note 87)
Pan-African 48
Parker, Ted, 378 (note 30)
Parkinson, Michael, 218
Parks, Rosa, 243
Parmar, Prav, 173
Parry, Steve, 62
Parsons, Tony, 100
Partington, 163
Patel, Abdullah, 50
Patel, Ramila, 73, 122, 168
Peach, Blair, **288-291**, 293, **294**, 296, 299, 305-6, 437 (not 135), 440 (note 174), 443 (note30), 444 (notes 45, 49), 445 (note 55)
Peacock, Marian, 168, 333
Pearse, Mike, 219

Peel, John, 158, 162
Pennant, Cass, 227, 417 (note 256)
People Unite, 287
Perryman, Steve, 225
Phillips, Danny, 108
Pimlico Comprehensive School, 205
Pinner, Hayim, 267
Pinochet, Augusto, 82, 300
Piratin, Phil 107, 277
Plaid Cymru 135
Poale Zion, 265
Pontefract, 135, 191
Poole, Colin, 168
Popova, Liubov, 147
popular front, 57, 61, 78, 92, 337, 394 (note 169)
Potter, David, 205
Povey, Megan, 68
Powell, Enoch, 7, 14, 17-8, 21, 23, 39, 41, 43-4, 69, 85-6, 353 (notes 3 and 4), 354 (note 17), 355 (notes 23, 24), 356 (note 37), 357 (note 1), 361 (notes 88, 92)
Power, Mike, 92, 96, 379 (note 65)
Poynter, Julia, 97
Prentice, Reg, 375 (note 198)
Preston, 39, 50, 83, 135, 185, 228-9, 449 (note 97)
Prestwich, 259, 358 (note 24)
Prevost, Eddie, 199
Price, Bill, 142
Prince Charles, 85
Printers and Media Workers Against the Nazis, 257
Prouse, Roger, 194, 413 (note 196)
Pursey, Jimmy, 166, 171

Race Relations Act 1965, 17, 65, 167, 251, 411 (note 161)
Race Today, 235, 237
Racial Awareness Action Society (RAAS), 50
Raeburn, Anna, 108
Rail Against the Nazis, 187-8, 278, 406 (note 55)
Ramelson, Bert, 92
Randall, Kevin, 212
Rank and File Teacher, 204
Ray, Ghosh, 237
Reader's Digest, 251
Reading Schools Against Nazis, 215
Red Lion Square, 64, 114, 139
Red Rebel, 220
Red Scar Mill, 50
Redder Tape, 189
Reed Herbert, Anthony, 44
Rees, Merlyn, 94, 242, 285, 293, 296
Relf, Robert, 66, 73, 167, 280
Rhodes, Bernie, 166
Rhodesia, 37, 82, 360 (note 59)
Right to Work Campaign (RtWC), 71, 113, 118-9, 148, 159, 163, 165, 185, 316, 342, 372 (note 150), 373(note 150), 380 (note 70)
Robert Montefiore school, 242
Roberts, Bill, 178
Roberts, Ernie, 47, 51, 71, 117, 119, 124, 267
Robertson, Anne, 189
Robertson, Jack, 10, 111, 149
Robinson, Tom, 158, 161, 165-6, 169, 171, 199, 200, 201, 215, 216, 398 (note 62)
Rochdale, 39, 41, 282, 304, 443, (note 40), 446

(note 69)
Rochdale Human Rights Campaign, 230
Rock Against Communism, 251
Rock Against Racism (RAR), see Chapter 6, 145-176, 182, 194-5, 201, 212, 214-6, 218-9, 229-30, 273, 278, 280-1, 294, 311, 316-8, 331-2, 336-8, 341-6, 397 (note 35), 399 (note 68), 418 (note 293), (note 294), 434 (note 78), 444 (note 49), 452 (notes 132, 133 and 135), 456 (note 187), 459-60 (note 45)
Rock Against Sexism, 195, 196, 201, 333, 343, 408 (note 101)
Rodchenko, Alexander, 146-7, 153-4
Rodwell, Buzz, 172
Rolnick, Len, 262
Rose, John, 186
Rosenberg, Chanie, 380 (note 68)
Rosenberg, David, 171
Rotherham, 66-7, 78, 136, 291, 320, 370 (note 114), 416 (note 263)
Rotten, Johnny, 155-6
Royal College of Art, 102, 155
Rudder, Joan, 136, 217, 219, 287
Rugby (game), 33, 36, 323, 345
Rugby (town), 142

Sagall, Sabby, 10, 127
Saltman, Ashley, 185
Salveson, Paul, 188
Samuel, Raphael, 174
Sapper, Alan, 257
Saunders, Red, 10, 146, 151, 159, 169, 220, 272, 281, 336, 346, 395, (note 2), 447 (note 72)
Savitt, Martin, 96, 131, 260, 263, 265, 269, 428 (note 192)
Sawh, Roy, 50
Scanlon, Hugh, 43, 66, 370 (note 110)
Scargill, Arthur, 135
Scarman, Leslie, 65
Scarsdale Road Against Racism, 231
School students, 54, 73, 135, 162, 194, 205, 208-217, 219, 322
School Students Against the Nazis 133, 136, 168, 202, 208, 214-5, 217-219, 230, 275
Schools Kids Against the Nazis (SKAN), 133, 204, 268
School students, 54, 73, 135, 162, 194, 205, 208-217, 219, 322
Scottish Immigrant Labour Council (SILC), 142, 277
Searchlight, 45, 789, 279, 438 (note 148)
Searle, Chris, 77
Seeger, Peggy, 136
Seifert, Michael, 116
Sex Pistols, 155
Seymour, David, 158
Sham 69, 166, 171, 247, 309, 315, 317
Sharma, Vishnu, 141, 285-6, 302-3
Sheffield, 57, 78, 123, 186, 209, 211-2, 218, 277, 280, 291, 305, 315, **316**, 318, 320, 326, 342, 426 (note 144), 454 (note 155)
Sheffield Wednesday, 128, 223-4
Shelton, Syd, 161, 166
Sheridan, Joe, 55
Shoreditch, 197, 247-8, 423 (note 89)
Shoreditch Comprehensive School, 113, 238
Short, Renée, 56

Silverwood NUM, 191
Sims, Stuart, 128
Singh, Atvar, 47
Singh, Raghbir, 49
Skateboarders Against Nazis, 247
Slipman, Sue, 105
Smith, Marcus, 138
Smith, Margaret, 230
Smith, Pip, 169, 199
Social Contract, 43-4, 65-6, 83, 92, 185, 196, 273-5, 291, 301, 333, 343
Socialist Worker, 64, 70, 108, 111, 150-1, 344
Socialist Worker Youth Movement, 220
Socialist Workers Party (SWP), 8, 85-6, 88, 104-5, 339, 343, 345, 354 (note 10), 381 (note 95), 395 (note 2), 421 (note 55)
Society of Graphical and Allied Trades (SOGAT), 55
Sorrell, John, 101
SOS Racisme, 349-50
Sounds, 149
South East London Mercury, 252
South East London Trade Unionists Against the Nazis, 185
South Hackney and Shoreditch Anti Nazi League, 197
South Oxhey, 144
Southall, 15, **72-3**, 75, 78, 107, 162-3, 233, 237, 244-5, 282, **284-292**, 292-5, 302-6, 310, 315, 322, 334, 373 (note 159), 418 (note 297), 440 (note 169), 442 (note 18), 443 (note 39), 455 (note 171)
Southall Carnival Against Racism, 233
Southampton, 127
Southwark Campaign Against Racism and Fascism (SCARF), 91, 273, 391 (note 128)
Soweto, 54, 73, 152, 216
Special Demonstration Squad (SDS), 214, 362 (note 96), 439 (note 154)
Special Patrol Group (SPG), 64, 101, 140, 248, 297, 305, 306
Specials, 309, 323, 327
Spike, Sharon, 173, 315
Spinners, 75
Spinoza, George, 204
Spitalfields, 235-6, 237, 240-1, 423 (note 97)
Spurley Hey High School, 210
Spurs Against the Nazis, 167, 225, 277, 319
Squadism, 344, 460 (note 60)
Standing Conference of Pakistani Organisations, 244
Star Centre College of Further Education, 184
Steel Pulse, 171, 216, 331, 401 (note 132)
Stiff Little Fingers, 247
Stockport, 41, 122, 184, 189, 216, 393 (note 147), 431 (note 32)
Stockton, 57
Stockton, Julia, 216
Stoker, Bob, 84
Stop the Seventy Tour campaign, 116-7
Strangeways, 180, 310
Stratford Express, 256
Strouthous, Andy, 10, 93, 171, 199
Strummer, Joe, 166, 394 (note 169)
Sun, 70, 219, 300, 440 (note 174)
Sunday Mail, 210
Sunday Times, 124, 150, 218, 258, 292, 305

Sunderland Against Nazis, 247
Swann, Michael, 250,
Swansea, 135, 229, 391 (note 130)

Tailor and Garment Workers Union (NUTGW), 239, 243
Tajfel, Henri, 131
Tameside Trades Council, 122
Tana, Dan, 226
Tate & Lyle, 62
Tatlin, Vladimir, 153
Teachers Against Racism, 201
Teachers Against the Nazis, 204, 289
Telford, 152
Temporary Hoarding, 158-63, 195, 201, 315, 343
Thatcher, Margaret, 167, 275, 281, 291-2, **299-301**, 308, 325, 329
Thomas, Bob, 48
Thompson, E. P., 129
Thurrock, 66
Tilbe, Douglas, 116
Time Out, 168
Tizard, Bill, 189
Toothpaste, Lucy, 195, 343
Tooting, 78, 190
Top of the Pops, 158, 199
Tottenham, 168, 194, 224-5, 227, 247
Tottenham Weekly Herald, 253
Tower Hamlets, 77, 235-7, 239, 241-2, 244, 246-7
Tower Hamlets Movement against Racism and Fascism, 166, 210, 240
Toxteth, 325, 329
Trade Union Anti-Immigration Movement (TRUAIM), 178
Transport and General Workers Union (TGWU), 43, 50-2, 185, 194
Transport and Salaried Staff Association (TSSA), 187
Tribune, 56
Trotsky, Leon, 29, 59-61, 65, 114
Tyndall, John, 34-5, 40, 44-5, 62, 67, 100, 120, 125, 132, 164, 169, 171, 179, 206-8, 247, 251, 257, 275-6, 282-4, 307-8, 376-7 (note 1), 403 (note 12), 411 (note 167), 416 (note 269), 435 (note 3), 449 (notes 61 and 66)

Ullah, Rafique, 236
Ulster Workers Council, 179
Undercover Policing Inquiry, 97
Union of Jewish Students (UJS), 267
Union of Post Office Workers (UPW), 117, 180
united front, 8, 60-1, 63, 92, 113-5, 118-9, 131, 133, 139, 143-4, 166, 248, 269, 272, 277, 284, 304, 335-8, 341-2, 344, 347, 350, 373 (note 154), 394 (note 169), 458 (note 38), 459 (note 50), 461 (note 73)
Unity Theatre, 146
Uxbridge, 41

Vaughan, Frankie, 131, 260
Vegetarians against the Nazis (VAN), 232
Verity, Terry, 120
Verrall, Richard, 359 (note 48), 391 (note 119)
Victoria Park, see Carnival
Vietnam Solidarity Campaign (VSC), 147, 403 (note 1)
Virdee, Satnam, 84
Virk, Joginder, Valrinder, Mohinder and Sukhrinder, 244

Wainwright, Richard, 273
Wakefield, 192
Wales, 142, 167, 301, 310, 322, 392 (note 133)
Walker, Martin, 113
Waltham Forest, 89
Walthamstow, 33
Wandsworth, 75
Warriors, 74
Warwick University, 64
Watford, 96, 144, 186
Watson, Dave, 129
Weaver, Reg, 51
Webster, Martin, 22, 34, 36, 120, 132, 167, 206, 207, 223, 254, 307, 370 (note 112), 377 (note 18)
Webb, Kate, 162, 341, 397 (note 35)
Welsh, Dave, 187
Wembley Arena, 233
West Bromwich, 41, 222, 282, 292, 294, 311-2, 315, 370 (note 112), 372 (note 147)
West Ham Trades Council, 78
West London Hospital Worker, 189
Whitechapel, 235
Whitehouse, Mary, 198
Widgery, David, 102, 153, 157, 159, 161, 242, 331-2, 336, 394 (note 169), 397 (note 38)
Wilcox, Bernie, 10, 399 (note 86), 418 (note 293)
Williams, Billy, 135
Williams, Jay, 315
Williams, Shirley, 210
Wilson, Harold (Deptford), 95
Harold Wilson (Labour PM), 16
Wilson, Poly, 214
Wilson, Tony, 129
Wise, Audrey, 124, 169, 273, 408 (note 98)
Witts, Dick, 163
Wolverhampton Anti-Racist Committee, 56
Wolverhampton Express and Star, 250
Women against Racism and Fascism, 79, 91, 195, 199, 385 (note 13)
Women Against the Nazis (WAN),
Women's Voice, 134, 197, 384 (note 154), 409 (note 110)
Wood Green, 88, 91, 112, 159, 195, 199, 253, 378, 406 (note 55), 408 (note 97)
Woods, Mick, 107
World In Action, 183, 241, 255, 278, 291, 304, 374 (note 182)

X-Ray Spex, 166, 216

Yorkshire Campaign to Stop Immigration, 67
Young Communist League (YCL), 92, 248
Young Mapam, 265
Young National Front, 35, 138, 204, 209, 334
Young, Hugo, 258

Zephaniah, Benjamin, 53-4, 317